EXPLORE BRITAIN
1001 places to visit

EXPLORE BRITAIN
1001 places to visit

George Philip

Maps and map index edited by R. W. Lidbetter, with research by H. Snape, and prepared by the cartographic staff of George Philip Cartographic Services Ltd under the direction of Alan Poynter MA, Director of Cartography.

Printed in Italy

Filmset in England by Tameside Filmsetting Limited, Ashton-under-Lyne, Lancashire

First published 1982 under the title *On Route*

British Library Cataloguing in Publication Data
Explore Britain – 1001 places to visit
   1. Great Britain—Description and travel—1971–
   —Guide-books
   I. On route
   914.1′04858   DA650
   ISBN 0-540-05505-0

Contents

Contents continued on next page

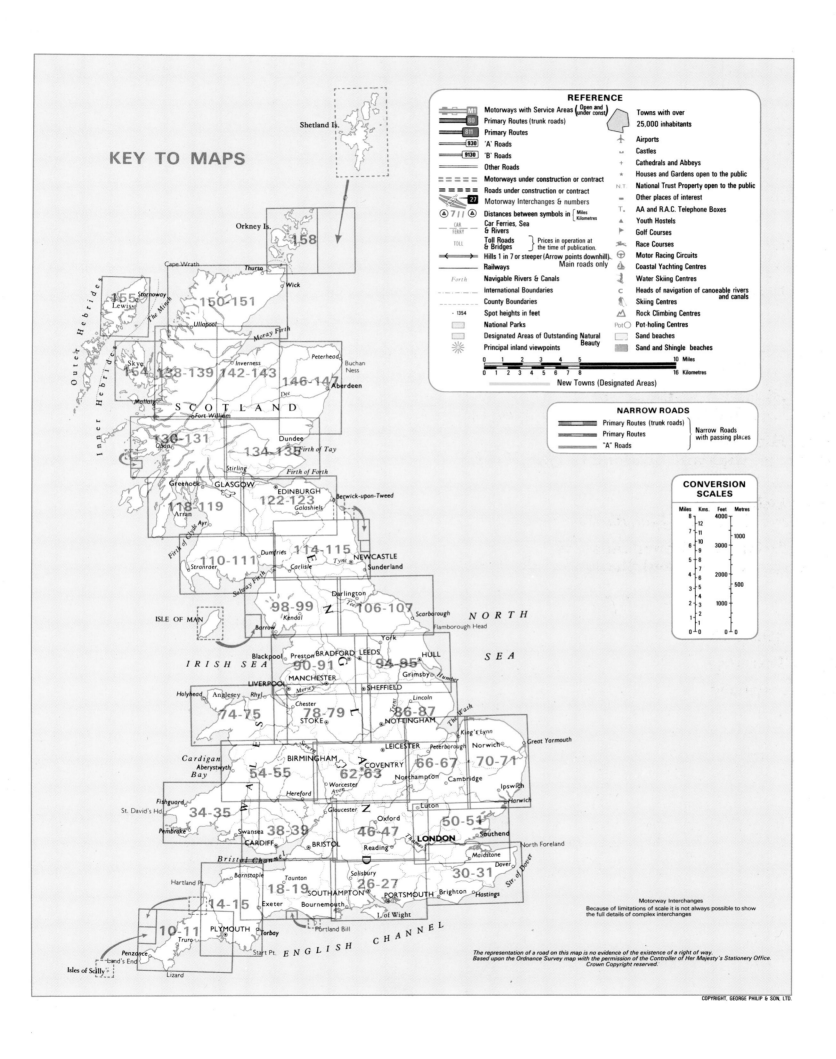

KEY TO MAPS

REFERENCE

M1	Motorways with Service Areas (Open and under const)
30	Primary Routes (trunk roads)
811	Primary Routes
930	'A' Roads
9130	'B' Roads
	Other Roads
=====	Motorways under construction or contract
	Roads under construction or contract
27	Motorway Interchanges & numbers
7 11	Distances between symbols in [Miles / Kilometres]
CAR FERRY	Car Ferries, Sea & Rivers
TOLL	Toll Roads & Bridges } Prices in operation at the time of publication.
	Hills 1 in 7 or steeper (Arrow points downhill). Main roads only
	Railways
Forth	Navigable Rivers & Canals
	International Boundaries
	County Boundaries
· 1354	Spot heights in feet
	National Parks
	Designated Areas of Outstanding Natural Beauty
✳	Principal inland viewpoints

	Towns with over 25,000 inhabitants
✈	Airports
⚲	Castles
+	Cathedrals and Abbeys
★	Houses and Gardens open to the public
N.T.	National Trust Property open to the public
▬	Other places of interest
T.	AA and R.A.C. Telephone Boxes
▲	Youth Hostels
►	Golf Courses
⚞	Race Courses
⊕	Motor Racing Circuits
⚓	Coastal Yachting Centres
⚑	Water Skiing Centres
C	Heads of navigation of canoeable rivers and canals
⚡	Skiing Centres
△	Rock Climbing Centres
Pot○	Pot-holing Centres
	Sand beaches
	Sand and Shingle beaches

New Towns (Designated Areas)

Miles: 0 1 2 3 4 5 ... 10 Miles
Kilometres: 0 1 2 3 4 5 6 7 8 ... 16 Kilometres

NARROW ROADS

Primary Routes (trunk roads)	
Primary Routes	} Narrow Roads with passing places
"A" Roads	

CONVERSION SCALES

Miles	Kms.	Feet	Metres
8	12	4000	
7	11		1000
6	10	3000	
5	9, 8		
4	7, 6	2000	500
3	5		
2	4, 3	1000	
1	2		
0	0	0	0

Motorway Interchanges
Because of limitations of scale it is not always possible to show the full details of complex interchanges

The representation of a road on this map is no evidence of the existence of a right of way.
Based upon the Ordnance Survey map with the permission of the Controller of Her Majesty's Stationery Office.
Crown Copyright reserved.

Shetland Is.

Orkney Is. 158

Cape Wrath / Thurso / Wick

150-151

Stornoway / Lewis 155

Ullapool

Outer Hebrides / The Minch

Moray Firth

Skye / Inverness / Peterhead / Buchan Ness

154 / 138-139 / 142-143 / 146-147

Mallaig / Dee / Aberdeen

Inner Hebrides

SCOTLAND / Fort William

Oban 130-131 / 134-135 / Firth of Tay

Stirling / Firth of Forth

Greenock / GLASGOW / EDINBURGH / Berwick-upon-Tweed

118-119 / 122-123 / Galashiels

Arran / Ayr

Firth of Clyde

110-111 / Dumfries / 114-115 / NEWCASTLE

Stranraer / Carlisle / Tyne / Sunderland

Solway Firth

Darlington

ISLE OF MAN / 98-99 / Tees / 106-107 / Scarborough

Kendal / Flamborough Head

Barrow / York

NORTH SEA

Blackpool / Preston / BRADFORD LEEDS / HULL

IRISH SEA / 90-91 / 94-95 / Grimsby / Humber

LIVERPOOL / MANCHESTER / Mersey

Holyhead / Anglesey / Rhyl / SHEFFIELD / Lincoln

Chester / Trent / The Wash

74-75 / 78-79 / 86-87 / King's Lynn

STOKE / NOTTINGHAM

Cardigan Bay / Aberystwyth / LEICESTER / Peterborough / Norwich / Great Yarmouth

WALES / BIRMINGHAM / 66-67 / 70-71

54-55 / 62-63 / COVENTRY / Ipswich

Hereford / Worcester / Northampton / Cambridge / Harwich

Avon

Fishguard / Gloucester / Luton / 50-51

St. David's Hd. / 34-35 / Oxford

Pembroke / Swansea / 38-39 / 46-47 / LONDON / Southend

CARDIFF / BRISTOL / Reading / North Foreland

Bristol Channel / Thames / Maidstone / Dover

Salisbury / 30-31 / Str. of Dover

Hartland Pt. / Barnstaple / Taunton / 26-27 / PORTSMOUTH / Brighton / Hastings

18-19 / SOUTHAMPTON

14-15 / Exeter / Bournemouth / I. of Wight

10-11 / PLYMOUTH / Torbay / Portland Bill

Penzance / Truro / Start Pt. / ENGLISH CHANNEL

Isles of Scilly / Land's End / Lizard

Illustration Acknowledgments

HALF TITLE Tintern Abbey *(J. Allan Cash)*; TITLE Old Harry rocks, near Swanage, Dorset *(Feature-Pix)*.

Aerofilms p 24, p 25, p 68 (top), p 85 (top right), p 102 (left), p 104 (left), p 113 (top), p 126 (right), p 127 (below), p 128 (below left), p 129 (right above and below), p 152, p 153 (right), p 160 (centre); *J. Allan Cash* p 13 (right above and below), p 16 (top, below), p 20, p 21 (right), p 22 (centre above), p 23 (below centre and right), p 28, p 37, p 41 (above), p 43 (above), pp 44–5 (top centre and right, right centre), p 48 (top), p 52, p 56, p 58–9 (top centre and right, below centre and right), p 61 (below right), p 64 (top), p 73 (right), p 77 (top), p 80 (top), p 82 (bottom left), p 103 (top), p 108 (right), p 109, p 121 (top), p 124, p 128 (top), p 133, p 137 (bottom), p 140–1 (below, top right), p 144 (top right), p 157 (bottom right), p 159; *Heather Angel* p 42 (top right); *J. and C. Bord* p 12–13 (centre left, below left), p 16 (bottom), p 21 (bottom), p 33 (top), p 44 (centre, bottom), p 53, p 57 (top), p 58 (bottom left), p 68 (bottom), p 72 (top, bottom left), p 76 (left), p 80 (bottom), p 84 (top), p 89 (bottom), p 100, p 113 (bottom), p 126 (left above and below), p 127 (above), p 144 (bottom right), p 147 (bottom); *British Tourist Authority* p 82 (centre), p 105 (centre right); *G. L. Carlisle* p 128 (below right, all three); *Bruce Coleman* p 23 (above right), p 42 (above left, below left), p 43 (below right); *Clive Coote* p 85 (centre left); *Country Life* p 72–3 (below centre); *J. Forde Johnston* p 60–1 (below centre); *Fay Godwin* p 48 (below), p 92 (below), p 157 (below left); *Gwyn Headley* p 104 (above), p 105 (above left); *Eric Hosking* p 129 (below left); *A. F. Kersting* p 40 (above); *Colin Molyneux* p 105 (below); *Derek Pratt* p 44 (above left), p 45 (centre left, bottom), p 84 (below), p 85 (above left, bottom left and right); *The National Trust* p 21 (centre left), p 29, p 32, p 40 (below), p 49, p 57 (below), p 64 (left), p 68 (centre), p 69, p 81, p 92 (above), p 105 (above right), p 117; *The National Trust for Scotland* p 120, p 121 (below), p 140 (above), p 144 (above left), p 146–7 (above centre, centre left, below left); *Scottish Development Department* p 112, p 125 (above), p 136 (below left), p 153 (left); *Scottish Tourist Board* p 125 (below), p 132, p 144 (below left), p 156, p 157 (above), p 160 (above, bottom); *Sefton Photo Library* p 96 (right), p 97; *Spectrum* p 96 (left); *Derek Widdicombe* p 17, p 22 (below), p 33 (below), p 36, p 41 (below), p 42–3 (below centre), p 60 (left above and below), p 61 (above), p 76 (right), p 77 (below), p 82–3 (centre above, right and below, right above and below), p 88, p 89 (above), p 93, p 101, p 102–3 (centre above, centre, centre below, right centre and below), p 108 (below left), p 116 (above), p 136–7 (centre above) – of these p 17, p 33, p 36, p 41, p 42–3, p 60 (below), p 61, p 76, p 77, p 101, p 116, p 136–7 are by Noel Habgood.

Introduction

This book is primarily a guidebook to rural Britain – what to see and, of vital importance, how to get there. The map and gazetteer sections have been designed to be read together – every place keyed onto the maps appears in the following gazetteer section in alphabetical order while each gazetteer entry also contains a reference to the map section. For example, the reference H8 at the end of an entry indicates that the site concerned is located on the accompanying map page in the square formed by the grid references H and 8. Bold type in the text indicates locations marked on the map pages and cross references to major entries.

Opening times have been included where relevant but readers are advised to check these before visiting the property concerned.

♿ Facilities provided for the disabled vary widely. This symbol indicates that there is access for the disabled to the property concerned. It may mean that all the property can be viewed but in many cases only part of a house or collection can be seen, generally because there are no lifts to the first floor. In some instances the symbol has been used when only the gardens of a house are accessible to the disabled, or where there is access to the site but not to the buildings as such. However, the symbol may also mean that there are full facilities for the disabled available, such as wheelchairs and toilets. Readers are strongly advised to check on the position at any particular site before visiting it.

Useful Addresses

Cumbria Tourist Board
Ashleigh
Holly Road
Windermere
Cumbria

Tel: Windermere (096 62) 4444

East Anglia Tourist Board
Tottesfield Hall
Hadleigh
Suffolk   IP7 5DN

Tel: Hadleigh (0473) 822922

East Midlands Tourist Board
Exchequergate
Lincoln   LN2 1PZ

Tel: Lincoln (0522) 31521

Heart of England Tourist Board
2–4 Trinity Street
Worcester   WR1 2PW

Tel: Worcester (0905) 613132

London Visitor and Convention Bureau
National Tourist Information
Victoria Station
London   SW1

Tel: 01-730-3488

Northumbria Tourist Board
9 Osborne Terrace
Jesmond
Newcastle upon Tyne   NE2 1NT

Tel: Newcastle upon Tyne (0632) 817744

North West Tourist Board
The Last Drop Village
Bromley Cross
Bolton
Lancs   BL7 9PZ

Tel: Bolton (0204) 591511

South East England Tourist Board
Cheviot House
4–6 Monson Road
Tunbridge Wells
Kent   TN1 1NH

Tel: Tunbridge Wells (0892) 40766

Southern Tourist Board
The Old Town Hall
Leigh Road
Eastleigh
Hampshire   SO5 4DE

Tel: Eastleigh (0703) 616027

Thames & Chilterns Tourist Board
8 The Market Place
Abingdon
Oxfordshire   OX14 3UD

Tel: Abingdon (0235) 22711

West Country Tourist Board
Trinity Court
37 Southernhay East
Exeter
Devon   EX1 1QS

Tel: Exeter (0392) 76351

Yorkshire & Humberside Tourist Board
312 Tadcaster Road
York   YO2 2HF

Tel: York (0904) 707961

Isle of Man Tourist Board
13 Victoria Street
Douglas
Isle of Man

Tel: Douglas (0624) 4323

Isle of Wight Tourist Board
21 High Street
Newport
Isle of Wight   PO30 1JS

Tel: Newport (0983) 524343

Scottish Tourist Board
23 Ravelston Terrace
Edinburgh   EH4 3EU

Tel: 031-332-2433

Wales Tourist Board
Brunel House
2 Fitzalan Road
Cardiff   CF2 1UY

Tel: Cardiff (0222) 499909

Wales Tourist Board
North Wales Regional Office
77 Conway Road
Colwyn Bay
Clwyd   LL29 7LN

Tel: Colwyn Bay (0492) 31731

Wales Tourist Board
Mid Wales Regional Office
Canolfan
Owain Glyndwr Institute
Machynlleth
Powys   SY20 8EE

Tel: Machynlleth (0654) 2653

Wales Tourist Board
South Wales Regional Office
Tycroso
Gloucester Place
Swansea   SA1 1TY

Tel: Swansea (0792) 465204

Abbreviations

Cadw   Welsh Historic Monuments
EH   English Heritage
FC   Forestry Commission
NCC   Nature Conservancy Council
NT   The National Trust
NTS   The National Trust for Scotland
RSPB   Royal Society for the Protection of Birds
SDD   Scottish Development Department
SWT   Scottish Wildlife Trust
YNT   Yorkshire Naturalists' Trust

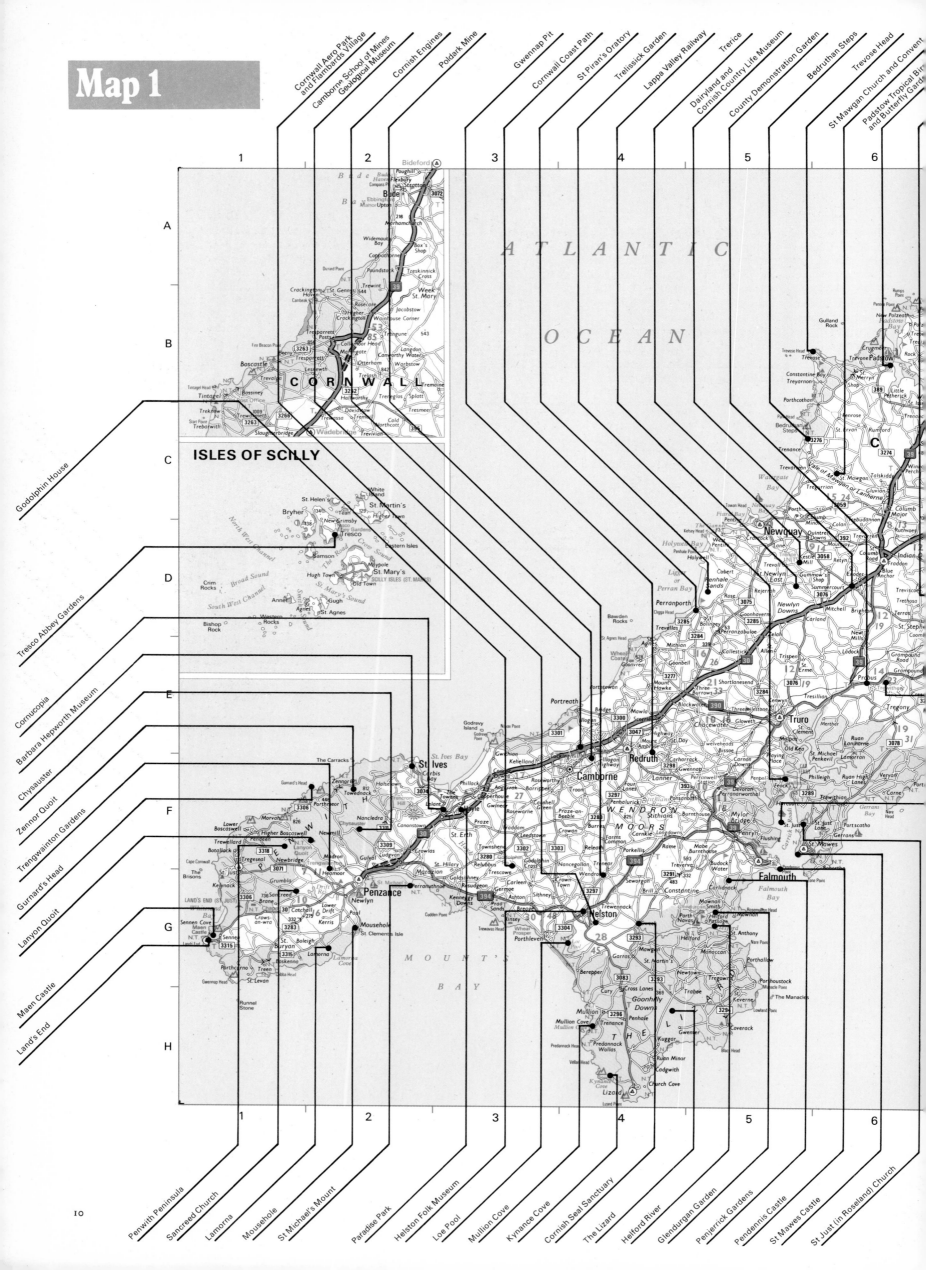

Map 1

Cornwall Aero Park and Flambards Village
Camborne School of Mines Geological Museum
Cornish Engines
Poldark Mine
Gwennap Pit
Cornwall Coast Path
St Piran's Oratory
Trelissick Garden
Lappa Valley Railway
Trerice
Dairyland and Cornish Country Life Museum
County Demonstration Garden
Bedruthan Steps
Trevose Head
St Mawgan Church and Convent
Padstow Tropical Bird and Butterfly Garden

Godolphin House
Tresco Abbey Gardens
Cornucopia
Barbara Hepworth Museum
Chysauster
Zennor Quoit
Trengwainton Gardens
Gurnard's Head
Lanyon Quoit
Maen Castle
Land's End

ISLES OF SCILLY

ATLANTIC OCEAN

CORNWALL

Penwith Peninsula
Sancreed Church
Lamorna
Mousehole
St Michael's Mount
Paradise Park
Helston Folk Museum
Loe Pool
Mullion Cove
Kynance Cove
Cornish Seal Sanctuary
The Lizard
Helford River
Glendurgan Garden
Penjerrick Gardens
Pendennis Castle
St Mawes Castle
St Just (in Roseland) Church

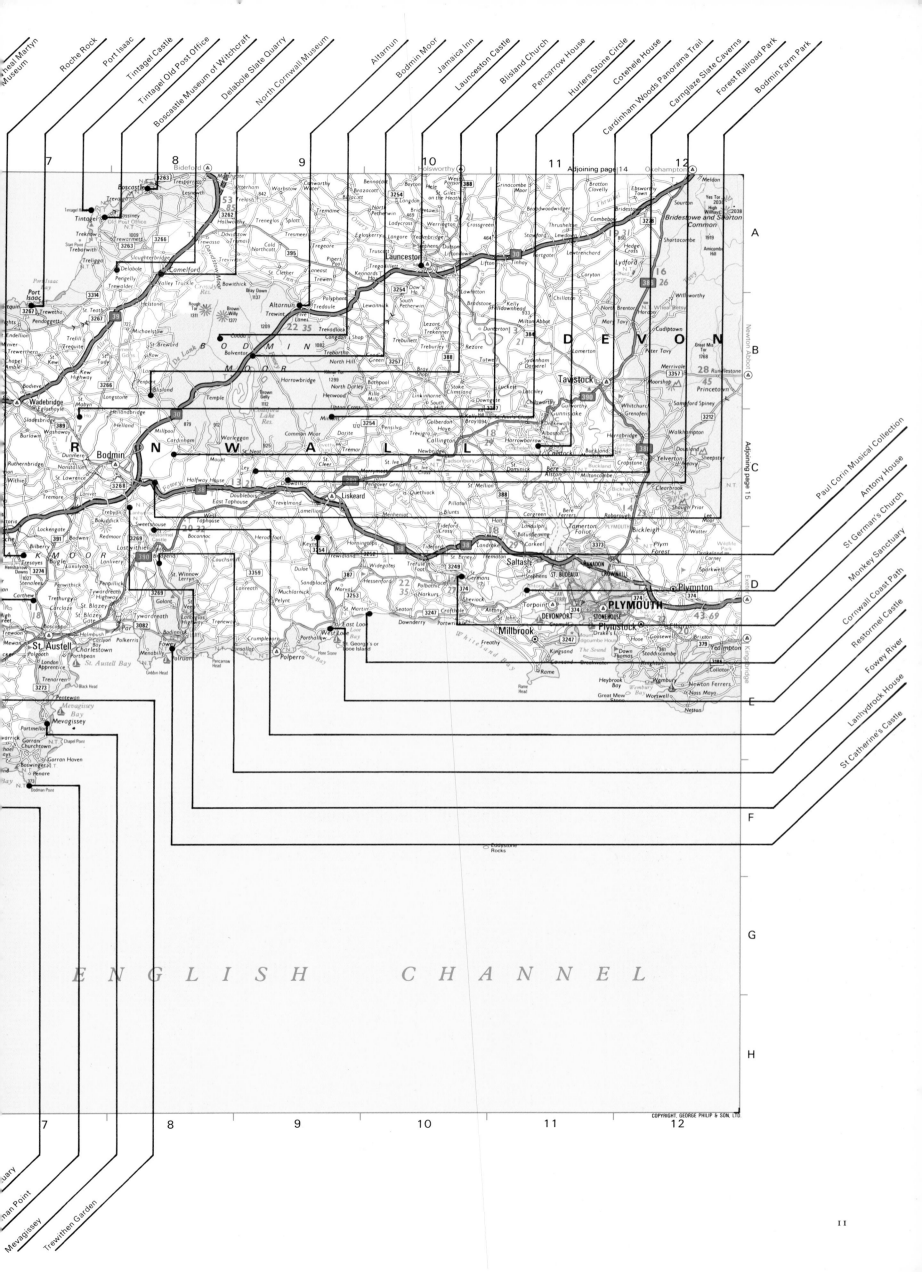

West Country

Altarnun Charming linear village on north-east edge of Bodmin Moor centred on one of the finest churches (early 16th-century) in the West Country, popularly known as the Cathedral of the Moor, with a lofty tower, Norman font, 16th-century bench ends and noble rood screen. (B9)

Antony House (NT) Beautifully proportioned and still lived in Queen Anne mansion built 1711–21 with many contemporary items of furniture and beautiful panelled rooms. The park slopes down to the river Lynher. (D11)

Barbara Hepworth Museum, Barnoon Hill, St Ives Photographs, letters, sculpture and other relics in the cottage Dame Barbara used as a studio for 26 years. ⓑ (F2)

Bedruthan Steps (NT) Reached by a dramatic staircase cut in the cliff, these huge granite rocks are said to have formed stepping stones across the sands for a Cornish giant. (C5)

Blisland Church Remarkable Norman and medieval building with richly decorated altar and screen, irregular wagon roofs and old brasses. It stands in a picturesque village centred on a green, the scene of a lively sheep fair in September. (B8)

Bodmin Farm Park, Fletchers Bridge Designed for children, working farm with friendly farm animals, pets' corner and pony and donkey rides. Collection of old farm tools. Access from A38. (C8)

Bodmin Moor One of the wildest areas in the West Country, this 800 ft (244 m) high plateau covers 144 sq miles (372 sq km), a mixture of boggy moorland, granite tors and remote river valleys. The highest point is Brown Willy, 1,377 ft (420 m), the tallest hill in Cornwall (B8). On the north edge is the second highest peak, the rugged granite outcrop of Rough Tor, 1,311 ft (400 m), crowned by a memorial to the Wessex regiment, and with the remains of Bronze Age hut circles on its flanks (B8). On the western edge of the moor are the spectacular Hanter Gantick valley and the nearby Hannan valley. Of the numerous prehistoric remains the most impressive is probably the *Stripple Stones*, a stone circle on Hawkstor near Temple, just north of the A30, the only road that crosses the moor. (B8/9)

Boscastle Museum of Witchcraft, The Witches House One of the largest museums of its kind in Europe, with grisly exhibits, ointments and potions and a witches' altar. Boscastle harbour. (A8)

Camborne School of Mines Geological Museum, Pool Fascinating geological collection of minerals and ores. ⓑ (E4)

Cardinham Woods Panorama Trail Starting at picnic site west of village, strenuous walk of 2 miles (3.2 km) with fine views of Glynn valley. (C8)

Carnglaze Slate Caverns, St Neot Disused quarry with huge underground chambers and lake where the temperature never rises above 52°F (11°C). 1 mile (1.6 km) south on unclassified road through Loveney valley. (C9)

Chysauster (EH) Iron Age 'village' of 8 oval-shaped houses built in pairs with thick stone walls, paved rooms and small courtyards. Access by path of ½ mile (0.8 km) from nearest road. (F2)

Cornish Engines, East Pool (NT) Old stone engine house and stack on the site of the deserted East Pool mine containing impressive relics of the tin mining industry, a 30 in (762 mm) beam winding engine and a 90 in (2,286 mm) beam pumping engine used for clearing water from depths of 2,000 ft (609 m) or more and for winding men and tin ore. The engines exemplify the use of high pressure steam patented by the Cornish engineer Richard Trevithick in 1802. On either side of A3047. (E4)

Cornish Seal Sanctuary, Gweek Five large pools on the wooded Helford river for the care of sick and injured seals washed up on the beaches around Cornwall. Signposted in village. ⓑ (G4)

Cornucopia, Lelant Miniature village built to scale which portrays some of Cornwall's more important buildings. The landscaped grounds contain museum, art gallery, water gardens, and displays devoted to tin mining, smuggling, shipwreck, landscaped model railways. Also an exhibition on Camelot and the legend of King Arthur and his Knights of the Round Table. ⓑ (F3)

Cornwall Aero Park and Flambards Victorian Village, Helston Flambards is a life-size Victorian village with cobbled streets, carriages, shops and fashions. The Aero Park contains large collection of historic aircraft, motor vehicles, Battle of Britain gallery, helicopters, Concorde flight deck and SR2 simulator. Also a life-size street in which visitors experience a recreation of 'Britain in the Blitz'. ½ mile (0.8 km) off A3083, adjoining Culdrose Air Station. ⓑ (G4)

Cornwall Coast Path A waymarked route right round the Cornish coast from Morwenstow (Map 2, D1) to the Tamar near Plymouth which often follows old coastguards' paths along the clifftops. It encompasses a wide range of seashore life and passes by fortifications, harbours, stone circles and lighthouses. The north coast route is 135 miles (216 km) long, bleak and inhospitable at the start then characterised by long stretches of sand before becoming rugged again near St Ives Bay; many points of access include Padstow (B6), Perranporth (D5), Portreath (E4) and St Ives (F2). The south coast section, 133 miles (213 km) long, is difficult walking because the continuity of the shoreline is broken by drowned river valleys; access points include **Mousehole** (G2), **Lizard** (H4), **St Mawes** (F6) and **Looe** (D9). Neither route should be undertaken in rough, windy or foggy weather. Part of the South West Peninsula Coast Path.

Cotehele House (NT) Wonderfully preserved medieval house in a remote setting on the west bank of the Tamar river, with fine terraced gardens sloping down to woodlands lining the river. Most of the rooms are hung with 17th-century tapestries and contain a rare collection of Jacobean and Stuart furniture. The house is part of the Cotehele Estate. This includes *Cotehele Quay*, with a Maritime Museum and *Shamrock*, the last Tamar sailing barge, and *Cotehele Mill*, with a working water-wheel, blacksmith's and carpenter's shops. Gardens contain a medieval stewpond and dovecote. ⓑ (C11)

County Demonstration Garden, Probus Display areas showing different methods of gardening including children's gardens, plots suitable for retired and disabled people. Frequent demonstrations. Arboretum, wild flower collection. East of village on A390. ⓑ (E6)

Dairyland and Cornish Country Life Museum, Summercourt Working farm where visitors can watch automated milking of cows. Also collection of old agricultural machinery and exhibits including farm kitchen and blacksmith's shop. ⓑ (D6)

Delabole Slate Quarry Huge quarry 500 ft (152 m) deep worked continuously for over 400 years. Public viewing platform. Access from Pengelly. ⓑ (A8)

Dodman Point (NT) Headland ending in an Iron Age cliff castle and topped by a granite cross erected 1896 as a mark for fishermen. A frequent scene of shipwreck, with notorious offshore currents. (F7)

Fal Estuary Formed by 5 tributaries flowing into a 4-mile (6.5 km) long drowned valley known as Carrick Roads. On the west bank is Falmouth, largest town in Cornwall. One of the prettiest places overlooking the water is Flushing, an elegant village of Queen Anne houses reached by ferry, another creek-side St Just, ringed by subtropical gardens. (F5/6)

Forest Railroad Park, Dobwalls Extensive miniature passenger-carrying railway (2 miles, 3.2 km) modelled on the age of steam in the United States together with railroad exhibition, model railway and picnic areas. (C9)

Fowey River Long and lovely river, richly wooded along much of its course, which rises on Bodmin Moor and ends at the resort of the same name. Most scenic is the stretch between Lostwithiel (D8) and Doublebois (C9). South of resort of Fowey is Readymoney Cove, a sandy beach good for swimming. (D8)

Glendurgan Garden (NT) One of the most beautiful gardens in Cornwall, with exotic trees and shrubs, walled and water areas, laurel maze and a wooded valley running down to the peaceful NT village of Durgan on the north bank of Helford river. Access from road to Helford Passage. ⓑ (G5)

Godolphin House The centre of a working farm, long and low mainly 15th-century house, with unique 17th-century front resting on massive columns of local granite. Good furniture, tapestries and pictures, including John Wootton's painting of the Godolphin Arab racehorse, one of 3 main ancestors of British bloodstock. ½ mile (0.8 km) north-west of Godolphin Cross. (F3)

Gurnard's Head A wild grand headland on a bold and rugged coast with fine views west to the Isles of Scilly. On the isthmus are the remains of a once great cliff castle. Access by footpath from B3306. (F2)

Gwennap Pit, Redruth The Methodist 'cathedral', a terraced circular pit seating 20,000 people where Wesley first preached in 1762. Religious services are still held there in summer. 1 mile (1.6 km) south-east off A393. (F4)

Helford River Beautiful tree-lined river forming a lush valley at its most idyllic in its secluded branches, like Frenchman's Creek, made famous by the novel of that name by Daphne du Maurier. Near the river mouth is charming Helford village, linked by ferry with Helford Passage on the opposite shore. The best way to explore the river is by boat, perhaps one hired from Helford village. (G5)

Helston Folk Museum, Old Butter Market Exhibits dealing with life in the Lizard Peninsula including great cider press, grist mill and old implements of all kinds. (G4)

Hurlers Stone Circle, Minions Standing stones which according to legend are men turned to stone for playing the old Cornish game of hurling on Sunday. Access by path ¼ mile (0.4 km) west. (C9)

Jamaica Inn, Bolventor In lonely spot on Bodmin Moor, once the Bolventor Temperance Hotel and now a popular drinking place. Daphne du Maurier used it as a basis for one of her novels. (B9)

Kynance Cove (NT) Famous bay on west coast of Lizard Peninsula flanked by cliffs streaked with serpentine rock of many colours. A steep path leads down to firm sands and a series of caves visible only at low tide. Offshore are Asparagus Island, Gull Rock and the Lion Rock. (H4)

Lamorna Quiet village in wooded valley bisected by a trout stream running down to a rocky cove enclosing a sandy beach. (G2)

Land's End Rugged and undulating headland, the westernmost point in England, below which (accessible at low tide) is a large cavern called Land's End Hole. Visible on a clear day are the Isles of Scilly, 28 miles (45 km) away. South is jagged island of the Armed Knight, a bird sanctuary on nearby Enys Dodnan and most impressive of all the rock pillars of Pordenack Point just to the south. 2 miles (3.2 km) west is the Longship's lighthouse. (G1)

Lanhydrock House (NT) Grand Jacobean house including imposing long gallery with magnificent plaster ceiling. The extensive kitchen and Victorian servants' quarters also make interesting viewing. The formal gardens (laid out in 1857) and the park reach down to the **Fowey River**. Access from B3268. ⓑ (C8)

Lanyon Quoit

Lanyon Quoit, Morvah (NT) Much visited megalithic burial chamber once covered by a mound. The 18 ft (5.4 m)

Kynance Cove

wide capstone rests on 3 uprights 5 ft (1.5 m) high. 2 miles (3.2 km) south-east near Madron road. (F2)

Lappa Valley Railway, Newlyn East Narrow-gauge railway running through wooded valley at end of which passengers may explore the site of an old silver-lead mine and adjoining pleasure park. Round trip of 2 miles (3.2 km). (D5)

Launceston Castle (EH) Dominant 13th-century fortress with one keep inside another and well-preserved north gateway. The grounds are laid out as a public park. (A10)

The Lizard Rugged peninsula composed of serpentine with treeless central plateau ablaze with heather from spring to autumn. On the plateau is the satellite tracking station of Goonhilly Downs. Lizard Point with its lighthouse is the southernmost place in England and one of the most dangerous for shipping. The coast is fringed with tall cliffs and caverns with beaches at only a few places, such as (from west to east) Polurrian, Mullion, Housel, Kennack and Porthoustock. (H4)

Loe Pool (NT) Largest freshwater lake in Cornwall, 2 miles (3.2 km) long, behind great bank of shingle thrown up by the sea known locally as Loe Bar. Set back from the wooded banks are car parks linked by an extensive network of footpaths. Maritime flora, waders and seabirds, marsh and woodland habitats. (G4)

Maen Castle (NT) Iron Age hill fort typical of the cliff castles or defended headlands found along the Cornish coast. (G1)

Mevagissey Picturesque fishing village with inner and outer harbours and a folk museum on East Quay featuring local crafts and pastimes. (E7)

Monkey Sanctuary, East Looe Open zoo where rare Amazon woolly monkeys are allowed to roam free together with prairie marmots, donkeys and rabbits. 3 miles (4.8 km) east at Murrayton. (D10)

Mousehole Quaint fishing village of winding streets, colour washed cottages

and attractive small harbour flanked by piers. The name is pronounced Mowsle. (G2)

Mullion Cove Above the picture-postcard harbour (NT) are rocks piled on rocks like the ruins of a vast cathedral. Caves and a sandy beach are visible at low tide. (H4)

North Cornwall Museum, The Cleave, Camelford Exhibits illustrating rural life from 50 to 100 years ago, with sections on agriculture, slate and granite quarrying, cobbling and dairying. 🔗 (A8)

Padstow Tropical Bird and Butterfly Gardens, Fentonluna Lane In a restful garden setting, colourful and unusual birds and around 6000 beautiful butterflies. (B6)

Paradise Park, Hayle Known worldwide for its rare and beautiful birds. Free-flying parrots, penguins, cranes, flamingoes, toucans. Paradise Farm with rare breeds, Cornwall's Wildlife Conservation Sanctuary, and miniature steam railway. Just off the B3302. 🔗 (F3)

Paul Corin Musical Collection, St Keyne Fine collection of instruments from the golden age of automatic music, including theatre, fair, street and dance organs. 🔗 (D9)

Pencarrow House Georgian mansion housing English, French and Oriental furniture and china and fine collection of 18th-century paintings, including works by Reynolds, Devis, Scott, Wilson, Neefs, Raeburn and Northcote. Large formal gardens and woodlands with noted conifer collection. Access from A389 and B3266. 🔗 (C7)

Pendennis Castle (EH) Coastal fort built 1544-6 by Henry VIII to guard the entrance to Falmouth harbour, enclosed by an outer ring of walls and moats added in 1590. The building houses an exhibition of Tudor coastal defences. Access by scenic one-way road. 🔗 (F5)

Penjerrick Gardens, Budock Fine subtropical gardens covering 6 acres (2.4 hectares) which include display of rhododendrons, magnolias and camellias. Also woodland walk. Access off B3291. (G5)

Penwith Peninsula Noted for its ever-changing light and terminating in Land's End, this granite peninsula has some of the most dramatic scenery in the West Country. Bisected by the A30, it has only 2 towns (Penzance and St Ives) and few villages. Much of the north coast can only be reached on foot from the beautiful B3306. On the central uplands, which rise to 826 ft (252 m), are numerous prehistoric remains. (F/G1/2)

Poldark Mine, Wendron Old Cornish tin mine together with large collection of bygones and industrial and domestic antiques, including a 40 ft (12 m) high beam engine. Access from B3297. (G4)

Port Isaac Still active fishing village of character with narrow streets and alleys and colour-washed houses piled one on top of the other within a narrow combe. At low tide the sands are firm enough to drive on. (B7)

Restormel Castle (EH) Medieval fortress of slate and granite on a conical hill overlooking the Fowey valley. Notable round keep and rectangular 13th-century chapel. Access off A390. (D8)

Roche Rock The tallest of a cluster of crags topped by a ruined chapel which formed part of a hermitage when built in 1409. Access by path from Bugle road. (D7)

St Catherine's Castle, Fowey (EH) One of two ruined forts at the mouth of the river which had a chain strung between them in the 15th century to slice off the masts of French ships raiding the port. (E8)

St Just in Roseland

St German's Church Mainly Norman church of monastic origin with a fine doorway and a window by Burne Jones, interesting more for its architecture than for its contents. (D10)

St Just (in Roseland) Church Granite church of 13th-15th century famous for the beautiful churchyard and interesting tombstones surrounding it. (F5)

St Mawes Castle (EH) One of the best preserved Tudor castles in Britain, built 1542 on a distinctive clover-leaf plan to guard the entrance to Falmouth harbour. This was the age of cannon and gunpowder and the castle has angled bastions to give the widest possible field of fire. 🔗 (F5)

St Mawgan Church and Convent In a quiet and pretty village, a church with the best collection of brasses in Cornwall, all commemorating the Arundell family. Their Tudor mansion above the church (not open) has been a convent since 1794. (C6)

St Michael's Mount

St Michael's Mount (NT) Granite island in Mount's Bay topped by a spectacular castle dating from the 14th century. Reached at high tide by a ferry and at low tide by a causeway from Marazion. (G2)

St Piran's Oratory, Perranporth Tucked away among the dunes to the north-east, a walk of over 1 mile (1.6 km), the ruins of a 7th-century church said to be one of the oldest places of worship in England. It marks the burial place of St Piran, an early Irish missionary later adopted as the patron saint of Cornwall. (D5)

Sancreed Church Small 15th-century church of Cornish granite in which the Tudor rood screen bears some curious figures. There is a fine 11th-century cross in the churchyard. (G1)

Tintagel Castle (EH) On a headland almost cut off by the sea, ruined castle linked by legend with King Arthur but in fact dating from the 12th century. Access from B3263. (A7)

Tintagel Old Post Office (NT) Fascinating small 14th-century stone house used in the 19th century as a sorting office; now restored as such. 🔗 (A7)

Trelissick Garden (NT) Extensive park, farmland and woods. Large garden planted with exotic trees and shrubs particularly noted for its hydrangeas. Beautiful views over Fal estuary; woodland walks beside the river. On both sides of B3289. 🔗 (F5)

Trengwainton Gardens (NT) Large shrub garden with fine collection of magnolias and rhododendrons and walled area with many tender plants. Magnificent views over Mount's Bay. 🔗 (F2)

Trerice (NT) Elizabethan manor house set in formal gardens with notable plaster ceilings and fireplaces, great hall window, oak and walnut furniture and fine tapestries. 🔗 (D5)

Tresco Abbey Gardens, Isles of Scilly Botanical garden with unique collection of subtropical flora together with lake garden and island walks. (D2)

Trevose Head Prominent headland reached by a toll road commanding a great sweep of coast from Hartland Point almost to Land's End. The views from the coastguard lookout and the lighthouse are superb. (B5)

Trewithen Garden Internationally famous garden with outstanding collection of rare camellias, rhododendrons and magnolias in a landscaped 18th-century setting. 🔗 (E6)

Wheal Martyn Museum, Carthew Open-air museum of the Cornish china clay industry from 1745 to present day which includes granite settling tanks, water wheels and pumps, kiln, wagons and rolling stock. Interesting indoor displays and slide shows. Spectacular pit-viewing area, and nature trail, also recently opened. Access from A391. 🔗 (D7)

Zennor Quoit On windswept moor, double-chambered tomb dating from 3000 BC covered by a great stone slab 18 ft (5.4 m) by 10 ft (3 m). The rectangular main chamber is totally enclosed. The stones were originally covered by a mound of earth. Access by path ½ mile (0.8 km) south-east. (F2)

Map 2

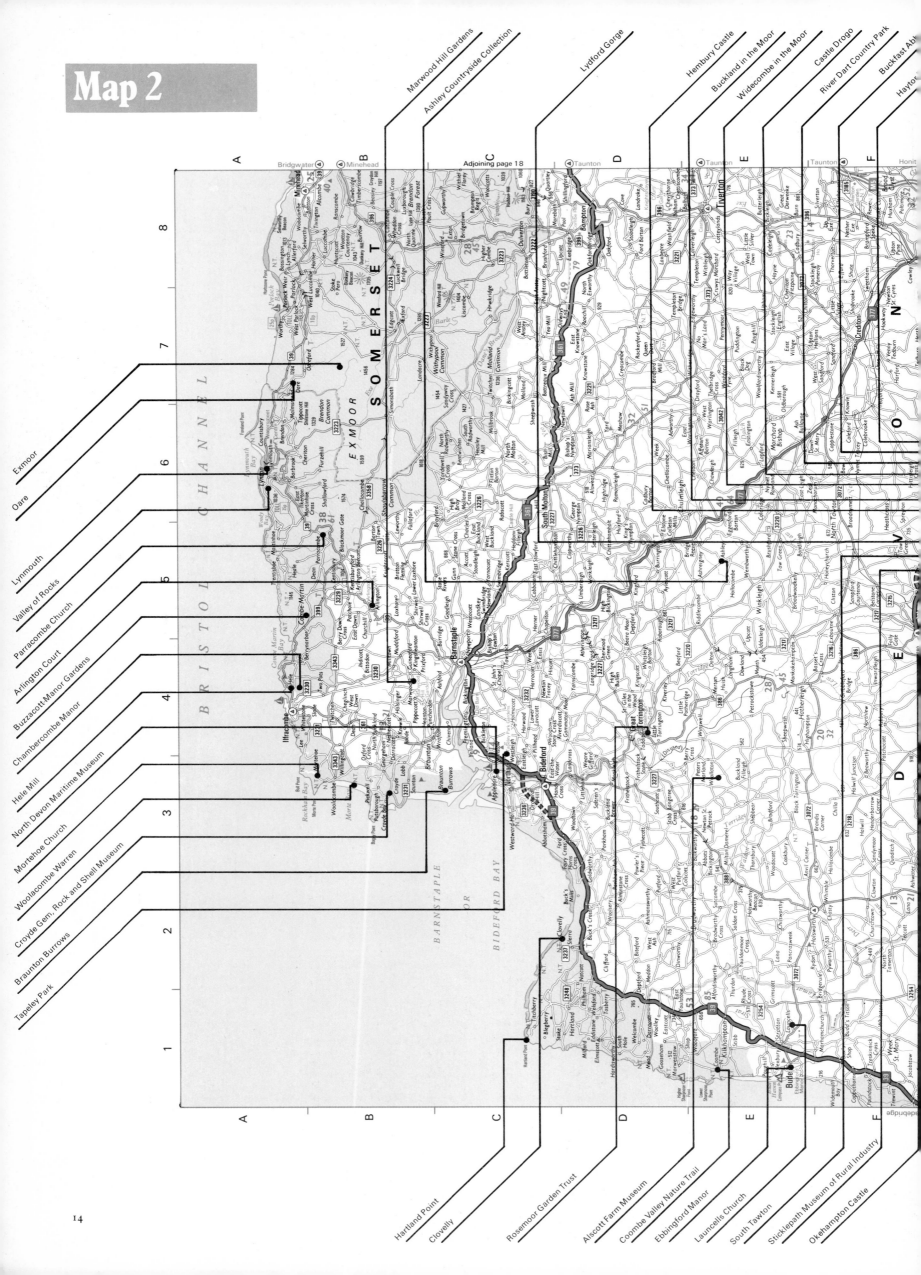

Marwood Hill Gardens
Ashley Countryside Collection
Lydford Gorge
Hembury Castle
Buckland in the Moor
Widecombe in the Moor
Castle Drogo
River Dart Country Park
Buckfast Abbey
Haytor

Exmoor
Oare
Lynmouth
Valley of Rocks
Parracombe Church
Arlington Court
Buzzacott Manor Gardens
Chambercombe Manor
Hele Mill
North Devon Maritime Museum
Mortehoe Church
Woolacombe Warren
Croyde Gem, Rock and Shell Museum
Braunton Burrows
Tapeley Park

Hartland Point
Clovelly
Rosemoor Garden Trust
Alscott Farm Museum
Coombe Valley Nature Trail
Ebbingford Manor
Launcells Church
South Tawton
Sticklepath Museum of Rural Industry
Okehampton Castle

Adjoining page 18

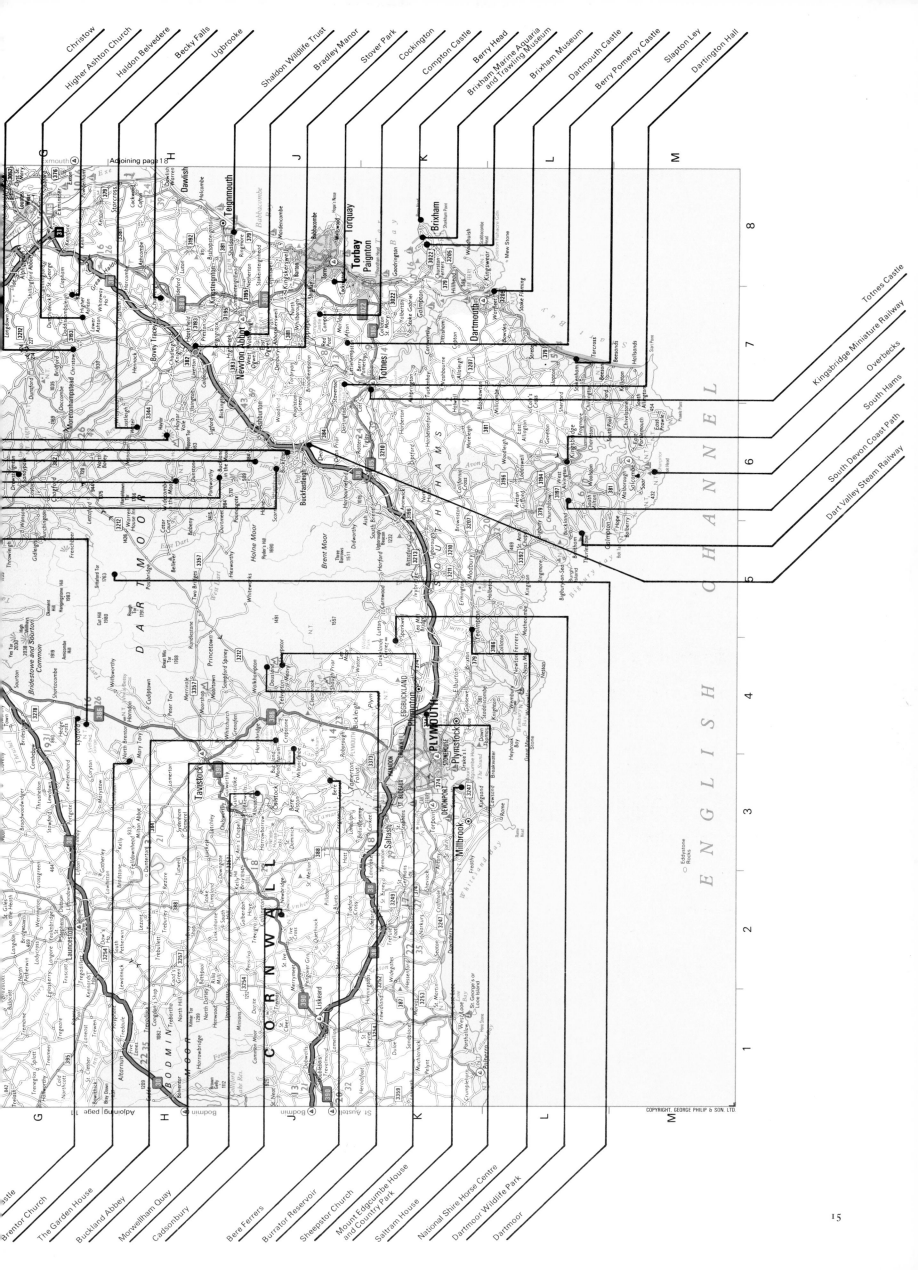

Christow
Higher Ashton Church
Haldon Belvedere
Becky Falls
Ugbrooke
Shaldon Wildlife Trust
Bradley Manor
Stover Park
Cockington
Compton Castle
Berry Head
Brixham Marine Aquaria and Trawling Museum
Brixham Museum
Dartmouth Castle
Berry Pomeroy Castle
Slapton Ley
Dartington Hall

Totnes Castle
Kingsbridge Miniature Railway
Overbecks
South Hams
South Devon Coast Path
Dart Valley Steam Railway

Brentor Church
The Garden House
Buckland Abbey
Morwellham Quay
Cadsonbury
Bere Ferrers
Burrator Reservoir
Sheepstor Church
Mount Edgcumbe House and Country Park
Saltram House
National Shire Horse Centre
Dartmoor Wildlife Park
Dartmoor

COPYRIGHT, GEORGE PHILIP & SON, LTD.

15

West Country

Alscott Farm Museum, Shebbear
Vintage agricultural, dairy and domestic implements, and photographs of rural life in north Devon. 2½ miles (4 km) north-east off Langtree road. 🚗 (E3)

Arlington Court (NT) Sumptuously appointed Regency house containing fascinating collections of small objets d'art, model ships, pewter, costumes, furniture and fixtures of the last century. Victorian formal garden set in steep wooded parkland, with wildfowl refuge, nature trail of 2 miles (3.2 km) and lakeside walks. Stable block with large collection of horse-drawn vehicles. Carriage rides. Access from A39. 🚗 (B5)

Ashley Countryside Collection
Unique collection of 48 breeds of rare and not so rare British sheep. Fleeces exhibition and over 1,000 items of ox, horse and open fireplace era, including wheelwrights', coopers', blacksmiths' and country craftsmen's workshops and tools. Access from B3220 and A377. 🚗 (E5)

Becky Falls, Manaton Dartmoor beauty spot where the Becka brook falls 70 ft (21 m) over a series of boulders in a wooded gorge. 1 mile (1.6 km) south-east on B3344. (H6)

Bere Ferrers Peaceful riverside village in beautiful setting on a tongue of land near the confluence of the Tamar and the Tavy. The outstanding feature of the 14th-century church is the glass in the east window. (J3)

Berry Head, Brixham South horn of Torbay, flat limestone headland 200 ft (60 m) high still with traces of fortifications put up during Napoleonic wars. Now country park of 100 acres (40 hectares) offering magnificent coastal views. The **South Devon Coast Path** runs right round the headland. (K8)

Berry Pomeroy Castle Strikingly ruined castle built by the Pomeroys who came over with William the Conqueror. They held it until 1548 when they sold it to the Seymours, who built the great Elizabethan house in the courtyard of which only the shell remains. (K7)

Bradley Manor, Newton Abbot (NT) Small roughcast 15th-century manor house built round a great hall with fine collar beam roof and screens passage. Also of interest is the Perpendicular chapel and the buttery. Access from A381. (J7)

Braunton Burrows Nature reserve of 2,000 acres (809 hectares) on largest area of sand dunes in England, with rare flora and fauna. The area to the north is used for military training. Access from A361 and B3231. (C3)

Brentor Church Small and simple 13th-century church isolated on top of a volcanic cone, with truly magnificent views. 1 mile (1.6 km) south-west of North Brentor off Tavistock road. (H3)

Brixham Marine Aquaria and Trawling Museum Specimens of fish caught offshore including sharks, sting rays and octopus with displays illustrating methods of trawling. On the harbour. 🚗 (K8)

Brixham Museum, Bolton Cross
Maritime exhibits detailing history of fishing from the port; also natural history section. Incorporates national coastguard museum. Town centre. (K8)

Buckfast Abbey Imposing Gothic-style Benedictine monastery on an ancient site. Cruciform church built by the monks 1906-38 with 15-bell tower 158 ft

(48 m) high, beautiful mosaics and splendid metalwork. The monks are noted for their Gregorian chants. 🚗 (J6)

Buckland Abbey (NT) Elizabethan house adapted from a monastery and bought by Sir Francis Drake in 1581. A

Ancient cross at Buckland Abbey

major part occupies the nave, the crossing and the chancel of the ancient church. The house is now a naval and Devon folk museum. In the grounds is a medieval tithe barn 180 ft (55 m) long. (J4)

Buckland in the Moor On the southern edge of Dartmoor, a delightful village in a wooded setting centred on the little 13th- to 15th-century granite church of St Peter, with an external stair turret on its sturdy west tower and inside a fine screen and Norman font. (H6)

Burrator Reservoir Created 1891-8, beautiful man-made lake of 150 acres (60 hectares), the largest in Devon, and a popular picnic spot for the people of Plymouth, whose main supply of water it is. There is an attractive drive round the reservoir. (J4)

Buzzacott Manor Gardens, Combe Martin 4 acre (1.6 hectare) garden set in 20 acres (8 hectares) of meadow and woodland, with fountains, streams and lake, many large specimen trees, bamboo grove and palm walk. Access from A399. (A5)

Cadsonbury (NT) Unexcavated univallate hill fort, possibly of Iron Age date. Access by footpath from Newbridge-Crift road. (J2)

Castle Drogo (NT) Granite castle on a hilltop built 1910-31 by Sir Edwin Lutyens for Julius Drewe, founder of the Home and Colonial grocery chain. The building is a masterpiece of design, with varying levels and an unexpected vista at every turn. Terraced gardens with wide views, woodland walks. Access off A382. 🚗 (G6)

Brentor Church

Chambercombe Manor, Ilfracombe
Charming 14th-century farmhouse with interesting historical associations built round cobbled courtyard with private chapel and fine period furniture, armour and porcelain. Garden with lake and waterfowl. 1 mile (1.6 km) south-east off A399. (A4)

Christow Pretty village in the upper Teign valley with a happy mix of old and new buildings and a handsome 15th-century church with carved roof bosses in the nave and a delicately painted screen. (G7)

Clovelly Occupying a steep and narrow combe, one of the most picturesque villages in Devon, with stepped and cobbled streets lined with neat colour-washed cottages and uncluttered by traffic. The main street drops sharply from 400 ft (122 m) to the tiny harbour. Popularised in Charles Kingsley's *Westward Ho!*, it is one of the sights of Britain and very crowded in season. (C2)

Houses by the quay, Clovelly

Cockington Thatched village popular with tourists nestling in sheltered valley on western edge of Torquay complete with forge, pond, old watermill and charming mainly 15th-century church with Tudor pulpit, restored 14th-century rood screen and carved bench ends below the tower. The village was built in 1800 for workers on the estate of Cockington Court, an Elizabethan house with pleasant grounds for a stroll. (J8)

Compton Castle (NT) Fortified manor house of great historical interest built by the Gilbert family at three periods – 1320, 1440 and 1520 – and still their home. The medieval layout includes buttery, watch tower, solar, chapel and restored great hall. Access off A3022. 🚗 (J7)

Coombe Valley Nature Trail Waymarked walk of 1½ miles (2.4 km) through a wooded sheltered valley which starts in the charming village (NT), complete with watermill. (E1)

Croyde Gem, Rock and Shell Museum Working museum where semiprecious stones from all parts of the world are displayed after being fashioned by skilled craftsmen. 🚗 (B3)

Dartington Hall Private centre of Dartington Hall Trust's enterprises in agriculture, industry and the arts. 14th-century hall may be seen when not in use. Attractive modern gardens. Displays of Trust's work, and shops at nearby Cider Press Centre. (J7)

Dartmoor National park covering 365 sq miles (945 sq km) of magnificent countryside, a mixture of granite tors and sweeping moorland, sparkling streams and wooded valleys. About 180 sq miles (466 sq km) is open moor, the habitat of wild ponies and the source of over a dozen fast-running streams. Some parts, mostly in the north-west, are military firing ranges. Many lovely old villages and historic towns. The two highest points are Yes Tor (2,030 ft, 618 m) and High Willhays (2,038 ft, 621 m) with superb views from the summits of both (G4). These two tors are in the military firing area and a red flag on Yes Tor warns of danger from artillery practice.

Walk from Meldon or Okehampton. See also **Burrator Reservoir, Haytor**.

Dartmoor Wildlife Park, Sparkwell 25 acre (10 hectare) park on the edge of Dartmoor with a wide variety of animals and birds, including tigers, bears, wolves and deer. Walk through enclosure of 3 acres (1.2 hectares). (K4)

Dartmouth Castle (EH) 15th-century castle designed for defence (and used as such as recently as the last war) housing armour from the Civil War period. Inside the walls is the 16th-century church of St Petroc. Access from B3205. (L7)

Dart Valley Steam Railway, Buckfastleigh Closed by British Rail in 1962 and reopened by enthusiasts in 1969, steam railway operating the 7 miles (11 km) to Totnes and return along an exceptionally pretty stretch of the Dart. Passengers can stop off at Staverton Bridge, a 7-arched bridge across the river built in the 15th century. The return journey takes about 80 minutes. (J6)

Ebbingford Manor, Bude Typical Cornish manor house dating from 12th century containing interesting exhibition about the house and the families associated with it. Walled garden. Towpath walks along nearby Bude canal. (E1)

Exmoor Rolling plateau of heather and grass moors interspersed with dense woodlands covering 265 sq miles (686 sq km) and ending on the north in steep and rugged coast cut by coombes and river valleys. Haunt of wild ponies and red deer. Highest point is Dunkery Beacon, 1,705 ft (519 m) high (B8). Many picnic sites and paths for walkers. (B6/7/8)

The Garden House, Buckland Monachorum Trees, lawns and terraced gardens in an attractive landscape with many rare plants and unusual varieties of flowering shrubs. (J4)

Haldon Belvedere, Dunchideock Otherwise known as Lawrence Castle, tower at altitude of 821 ft (250 m) on summit of Haldon Hills built in 1770 as a memorial to General Stringer Lawrence, commander of British forces in India 1747–67. A spiral staircase climbs 70 ft (21 m) to the top. 1 mile (1.6 km) south on Trusham road. (G7)

Hartland Point Westernmost point of Devon, windswept and savage headland 'a sailor's grave by day or night'. Reached by a toll road, the point itself is fenced off but the lighthouse on a lower promontory is accessible. The tremendous grey cliffs, stepped in parallel ridges, take the full force of the Atlantic breakers. (C1)

Haytor Spectacular crags 1,490 ft (454 m) high pock-marked by quarries from which came the stone to build London's British Museum and National Gallery. From the car park it is a deceptively long walk to the base of the tor, itself popular with novice rock climbers. (H6)

Hele Mill Working watermill of 1525 with 18 ft (5.4 m) overshot wheel and quaint machinery. (A4)

Hembury Castle Otherwise known as Danes' Camp, Iron Age hill fort covering 7 acres (2.8 hectares) surrounded by 374 acres (151 hectares) of beautiful NT woodland on west flank of Dart valley. The main entrance was on the west but the best view of the earthwork is from the north end. 1 mile (1.6 km) below the fort, Broadhembury is one of the finest thatched villages in the West Country, shaded by mature trees and with a fine 14th- to 15th-century church. (J6)

Higher Ashton Church Church notable for its beautiful woodwork, arch braced roof and pews and deeply carved rood screen with fine figure paintings, all of the 15th century. (G7)

Kingsbridge Miniature Railway A 7¼ in (184 mm) gauge passenger carrying miniature railway giving a return ride of ½ mile (0.8 km). Starts at The Quay. (L6)

Launcells Church 15th-century church of interest for its beautiful interior with ancient roof, fine bench ends, box pews, reredos and Norman font. (E1)

Lydford Castle (EH) Ruined Norman castle with square keep on a high mound surrounded on 3 sides by the river Lyd. (G4)

Lydford Gorge (NT) Famous beauty spot where river Lyd has cut a deep ravine 1½ miles (2.4 km) long to emerge in a wooded valley. A delightful if strenuous riverside walk to the White Lady waterfall which drops 90 ft (27 m). (G4)

Lynmouth Hemmed in by steep cliffs, picturesque harbour resort where the rivers East and West Lyn meet, now fully recovered from the devastating floods of 1952. East of town is Foreland Point, at 900 ft (274 m) the tallest cliffs in England. (A6)

Marwood Hill Gardens Small estate with lake, unusual bog garden, large collection of rare trees and shrubs, wall plants, Australian plant collection. (B4)

Mortehoe Church In charming village, small cruciform 13th- to 16th-century building with good 13th-century bench ends and striking 20th-century mosaic of angels. A path near the church leads to the dramatic slate cliffs of Morte Point. (B3)

Morwellham Quay Fascinating amalgam of Victorian village, copper mine, riverside tramway, ancient river port and industrial archaeological trails, all in unspoilt wooded country. Access off A390. (H3)

Mount Edgcumbe House and Country Park On a fine stretch of coast overlooking Plymouth Sound, 850 acres (340 hectares) of beautiful parkland and formal gardens. The handsome Tudor house was rebuilt after being bombed in the last war. Access from B3247, or by ferry from Plymouth. (K3)

National Shire Horse Centre, Yealmpton 60 acre (24 hectare) cattle and sheep farm worked entirely by Shire horses. 18th-century farm buildings, parades of horses and foals, cart rides, pets, displays of horse-drawn machinery, harness and brasses. Also Craft Centre and workshops with saddler, potter, blacksmith, wheelwright and glassengraver. Children's assault course with large Western fort and death slides. 1 mile (1.6 km) east off A379. (K4)

North Devon Maritime Museum, Odun Road, Appledore In an ancient and pretty fishing village, models in authentic settings, photographs and paintings illustrating shipbuilding and the history of seafaring. (C3)

Oare Hamlet in deep valley rich in *Lorna Doone* associations, particularly the church of St Mary the Virgin where Jan Ridd married the heroine. One of the memorials is to R.D. Blackmore, the author of the book, whose father was rector of Oare 1809–42. 1 mile (1.6 km) west is the valley of Badgworthy Water, otherwise known as Doone Valley. (A7)

Okehampton Castle (EH) Melancholy ruin of 12th-century castle dismantled in the 16th century. The hall, kitchen and other parts of the building are identified by plaques. (F5)

Overbecks Museum and Garden (NT) House containing the Overbecks Museum, with good collections of butterflies and shells and a section devoted to local shipbuilding with models, shipwrights' tools and photographs. Beautiful 6 acre (2.4 hectare) terraced garden with rare plants and shrubs and wide views over Salcombe estuary. *Formerly known as Sharpitor*. (M6)

Parracombe Church Church with unspoiled Georgian interior of box pews, screen with tympanum and mural tablets. (B5)

River Dart Country Park, Ashburton Alongside river Dart, 90 acres (36 hectares) of gardens, meadow and woodland, with fishing in the river, lakes for swimming and boating, nature and forest trails and picnic areas. Access 1½ miles (2.4 km) north-west on Two Bridges Road. (J6)

Rosemoor Garden Trust Medium-size gardens, with ornamental trees and shrubs, roses, scree and alpine plants, dwarf conifers and young arboretum. Access from B3220. (D4)

Saltram House (NT) George II mansion, still with its original contents, set in a landscaped park. Outstanding interior plasterwork and decorations (two rooms designed by Robert Adam), with fine period furniture, china and pictures. Interesting garden with orangery, rare trees and shrubs and 18th-century summer house. Access from A38. (K4)

Shaldon Wildlife Trust Variety of small mammals and exotic birds including marmosets, coatis, margay, agouti, macaws, owls and newly-arrived lemurs. Situated on the Ness. Access from A379 or from Shaldon bridge. (J8)

Sheepstor Church Focal point of sleepy village in hollow at foot of **Burrator Reservoir**. The church is dedicated to the Brooke family who were rajahs of Sarawak 1841–1945. Three of them are buried in the churchyard. (J4)

Slapton Ley Large freshwater lake shut off from the sea by Slapton Sands, a bank of shingle 2½ miles (4 km) long used as a training ground by troops taking part in the Normandy landings. The lake is the habitat of wildfowl and rare marsh birds. Access from A379. (L7)

South Devon Coast Path Waymarked route 93 miles (150 km) long from Plymouth Sound (at Turnchapel) to Lyme Regis (Map 3, G7) passing through a geologically complex shoreline which includes estuaries, sandy flats and impressive chalk and sandstone headlands. It forms part of the waymarked South West Peninsula Coast Path. Many access points include Wembury (L4), Newton Ferrers (L4), Noss Mayo (L4), Thurlestone (L5), Brixham (K8).

Widecombe in the Moor

South Hams Low-lying peninsula, deeply cut by rivers, famous for its gentle landscapes and varied coastline. An area of character, it is dotted with small farms ('hams' means enclosed pastures) producing most of Devon's clotted cream.

The 'capital' is the market town of Kingsbridge at the head of a long estuary with branching creeks, known throughout the West Country for its July fair. Popular beaches are sandy Bigbury and Thurlestone (L5) and pebbly Slapton Sands (L7). (L5/6/7)

South Tawton Charming old hill village built around a sloping square and adjoining 15th-century granite church, with a light and airy interior. (F5)

Sticklepath Museum of Rural Industry In an old mill, water-powered tilt hammers and other machinery shown working. (F5)

Stover Park Part of former country estate, this country park covering 114 acres (46 hectares) is largely woodland. Lake. Access from A382 south of Drumbridges roundabout (junction with A38). (H7)

Tapeley Park Terraced garden of great variety laid out in Italian style includes many rare plants. Woodland walks and lily pond. Walled kitchen garden. Beautiful views. Conducted tours of house (furniture, porcelain, plasterwork) when numbers permit. Access from Westleigh–Barnstaple road. (C3)

Totnes Castle (EH) Ruins of a motte and bailey fortress built by the Normans consisting of earthworks, shell keep and some outer walls. (K7)

Ugbrooke, Chudleigh Great castle-style house rebuilt in the 18th century by Robert Adam with corner towers and battlements. In the elegantly furnished interior is a fine collection of paintings, restoration portraits and one of the best collections of embroidery and needlework. Separate from the house is the Italianate chapel. Sweeping parkland with two lakes laid out by 'Capability' Brown. (H7)

Valley of Rocks, Lynton Natural amphitheatre formed from the old bed of the river Lyn overlooked by eroded sandstone pillars like Castle Rock, 800 ft (243 m) high with steps cut in the side to make climbing it easier. Access from coast road. (A6)

Widecombe in the Moor Beautiful village set in a wooded hollow against a background of bleak moors made famous by the popular song *Widecombe Fair*, an event still held on the second Tuesday in September. The church has a fine pinnacled tower 120 ft (36 m) high, mysteriously struck by a 'bolt of fire' during a storm in 1638, a happening explained inside. (H6)

Woolacombe Warren (NT) Rising downland and sandhills overlooking 2 miles (3.2 km) of golden sands, one of the best surf beaches in the West Country, though bathing is only safe in the flagged areas. (B3)

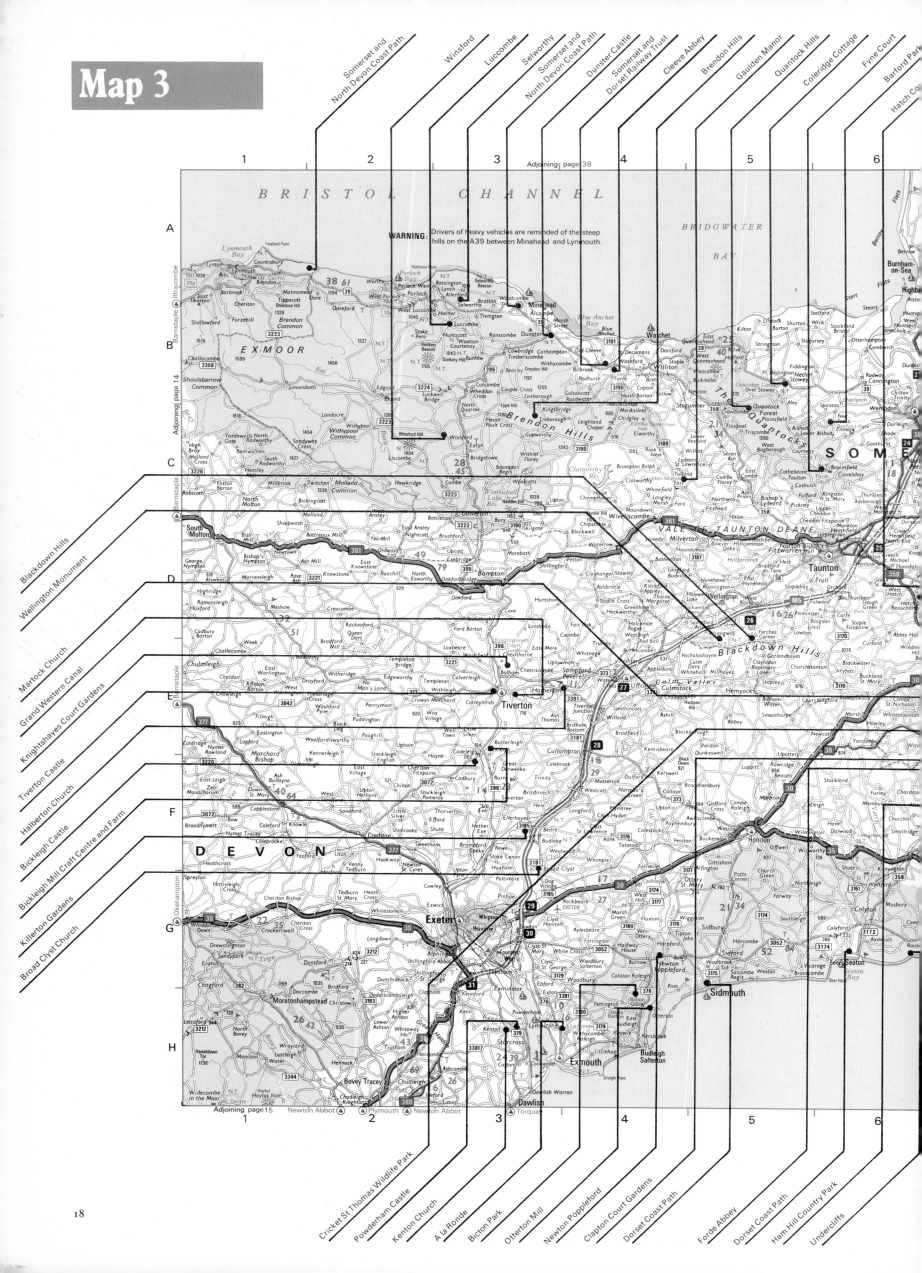

Map 3

BRISTOL CHANNEL

BRIDGWATER BAY

WARNING: Drivers of heavy vehicles are reminded of the steep hills on the A39 between Minehead and Lynmouth.

EXMOOR

Brendon Hills

The Quantocks

VALE OF TAUNTON DEANE

Blackdown Hills

Culm Valley

DEVON

SOMERSET

Somerset and North Devon Coast Path
Winsford
Luccombe
Selworthy
Somerset and North Devon Coast Path
Dunster Castle
Somerset and Dorset Railway Trust
Cleeve Abbey
Brendon Hills
Gaulden Manor
Quantock Hills
Coleridge Cottage
Fyne Court
Barford Park
Hatch Court

Blackdown Hills
Wellington Monument
Martock Church
Grand Western Canal
Knightshayes Court Gardens
Tiverton Castle
Halberton Church
Bickleigh Castle
Bickleigh Mill Craft Centre and Farm
Killerton Gardens
Broad Clyst Church

Adjoining page 14
Barnstaple / Ilfracombe
Barnstaple
Barnstaple
Okehampton
Adjoining page 15

Cricket St Thomas Wildlife Park
Powderham Castle
Kenton Church
A la Ronde
Bicton Park
Otterton Mill
Newton Poppleford
Clapton Court Gardens
Dorset Coast Path
Forde Abbey
Dorset Coast Path
Ham Hill Country Park
Undercliffs

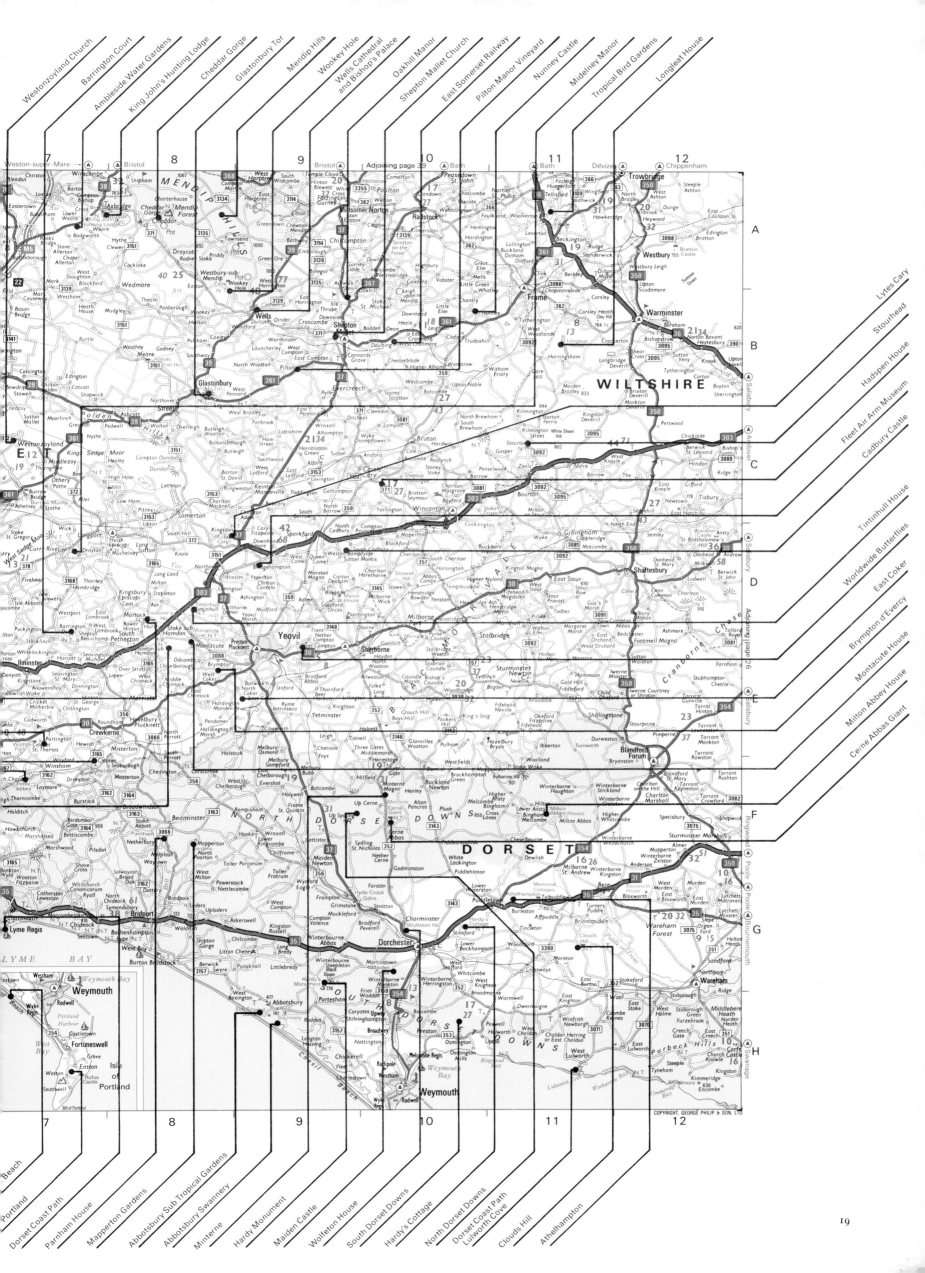

Gazetteer 3

West Country

Abbotsbury Sub Tropical Gardens 20 acres (8 hectares) of grounds where palms, camellias and other subtropical varieties grow in profusion. Collection of fine trees and flowering shrubs; old-fashioned shrub roses. ♿ (H9)

Abbotsbury Swannery Historic breeding ground of some 500 mute swans at edge of long saltwater lagoon and the habitat of many other species of birds. ♿ The beautiful village is also famous for its great 15th-century tithe barn. (H9)

A la Ronde Curious 16-sided house designed 1795 by the Misses Parminter. 45-foot (14-m) octagon. Shell gallery. Oddly shaped windows and many original furnishings. ♿ (H4)

Ambleside Water Gardens, Lower Weare Well-planned gardens around 2 ornamental lakes with over 250 species of birds together with rabbits, gerbils, monkeys and guinea pigs. (A7)

Athelhampton Fine medieval house with 15th-century great hall, Tudor great chamber and interesting furniture. Landscaped gardens of 10 acres (4 hectares) in 6 walled enclosures, with pavilions, terraces, pools and fountains. ♿ (G11)

Barford Park Charming red-brick Georgian mansion in miniature with large Victorian pleasure ground reclaimed from the wild. (C6)

Barrington Court (NT) Beautiful 16th-century mansion built of local stone to an E-shaped plan with Gothic and Renaissance features. Late 17th-century stable block. Extensive gardens laid out in the 1920s to a scheme by Gertrude Jekyll. ♿ (D7)

Bickleigh Castle Ancestral home of the heirs of the earls of Devon, with great hall, armoury and guardroom. Gatehouse, farmhouse and 11th-century chapel. Collection of weapons and armour. Moated garden. Exhibition of artefacts from Tudor ship, *Mary Rose*, a 'stable' of Victorian rocking-horses which children may ride, and large collection of World War II spy and escape gadgets. ♿ (F3)

Bickleigh Mill Craft Centre and Farm One of most comprehensive craft centres in West Country, adjoining heritage farm with rare breeds of animals and poultry worked as it would have been at the turn of the century. (F3)

Bicton Park 55 acres (22 hectares) of gardens and pinetum, with Le Nôtre-designed Italian Garden laid out in 1735 incorporating terraces, pools and orangery. Large theme halls, countryside museum, adventure playground and assault course, putting green and narrow-gauge woodland railway. Picnic areas. Access from A376. ♿ (H4)

Blackdown Hills East-west range of hills crowned by the **Wellington Monument** (NT). Highest point of the range, a mixture of cultivated land, heath and woods, is Buckland Hill (922 ft, 280 m), giving wide views over the Vale of Taunton to Exmoor and the **Quantocks**. (E5)

Brendon Hills Forming part of Exmoor National Park, chain of hills running east-west traversed by the Elworthy–Wheddon Cross road and rising in west to 1,390 ft (423 m) Lype Hill. (C3)

Broad Clyst Church Handsome church in pretty village with some splendid monuments inside, the most lavish being to Sir John Acland. (F3)

Brympton d'Evercy Imposing mansion with late 17th-century south front and Tudor west front, with state rooms, extensive gardens, vineyard, priest house museum, Zanussi Domestic Appliance Collection, I Zingari cricket club collection and 14th-century parish church alongside. (E8)

Cadbury Castle Dominating the village of South Cadbury, one of the finest natural forts in Britain, a flat-topped hill with immense fortifications dating from Neolithic times and linked by legend with King Arthur. (D9)

Cerne Abbas Giant (NT) Pagan fertility figure, 180 ft (54 m) high, cut in the chalk downs, possibly dating from AD 191 and until recently the centre of midsummer rites. Access by path $\frac{1}{2}$ mile (0.8 km) north of village. (F10)

Cheddar Gorge Impressive cleft with sheer escarpments in places 480 ft (146 m) high honeycombed with cave systems revealing vaulted chambers, clear pools and fascinating stalagmite and stalactite formations. At the head of the gorge is a 1 mile (1.6 km) trail through Black Rock nature reserve. (A8)

Chesil Beach Remarkable stretch of shingle 18 miles (29 km) long and 600 ft (182 m) wide in which the pebbles are graded by the action of the tide, small on the west and large on the east. (H7)

Clapton Court Gardens Beautiful gardens of 10 acres (4 hectares) with rare trees and shrubs in formal and woodland settings. Access from B3165. ♿ (F7)

Cleeve Abbey (EH) Remains of Cistercian abbey founded 1198 which include 16th-century gatehouse, well-preserved dormitory and 15th-century refectory, with fine timber roof. (B4)

Clouds Hill (NT) Cottage home of T.E. Lawrence (Lawrence of Arabia) when he rejoined the RAF in 1925. It contains his furniture and other relics. (G11)

Coleridge Cottage (NT) House where the poet lived for three years from 1797 to 1800 writing *The Ancient Mariner* and other works. Access from A39. (B5)

Cricket St Thomas Wildlife Park An estate of 1,000 acres (404 hectares) where animals and birds live in relative freedom. Heavy horse centre and country life museum. Access from A30. ♿ (E7)

Dorset Coast Path Easternmost section of the waymarked South West Peninsula Coast Path centred on Weymouth. It runs for 72 miles (116 km) from Poole Harbour (Map 4 G2) in the east to Lyme Regis (G7) in the west and crosses limestone cliffs and grassy downlands, the pebble formation of **Chesil Beach** and the sand dunes behind Poole Harbour. The easternmost section of the **South Devon Coast Path** (see Gazetteer 2), from Exmouth to Lyme Regis, joins it. Between Lulworth (H11) and Kimmeridge (H12) the path runs through a military firing range – check access. Many joining points such as Sidmouth (G5) and Seaton (G6) for the SDCP, Abbotsbury (H9) and Lulworth (H11) for the DCP.

Dunster Castle (NT) Romantically towered and castellated building dating from 13th century and remodelled by Anthony Salvin in 19th. Fine 17th-century staircase and plaster ceilings. Deer park and subtropical shrubs. ♿ (B3)

East Coker Harmonious village of amber-coloured stone with manor house and 17th-century almshouses. The American-born poet, T.S. Eliot, who commemorated this his adopted home in the *Four Quartets*, is buried in the churchyard. (E9)

East Somerset Railway, Cranmore Railway Station Founded by artist David Shepherd, a collection of steam locomotives and rolling stock in restored station. Art gallery. Steam hauled passenger services. ♿ (B10)

Fleet Air Arm Museum, Yeovilton Europe's largest collection of historic military aircraft under one roof with Concorde prototype and captured Argentinian aircraft, fascinating ship and aircraft scale models and other memorabilia associated with the Royal Naval Air Service and the Fleet Air Arm. Access from A303, A37 and B3151. ♿ (D9)

Forde Abbey Magnificent 12th-century Cistercian monastery converted to a private house in mid 17th century. Fine informal gardens and lakes. Contents include famous tapestry copies of Raphael cartoons woven at Mortlake during the reign of Charles I. ♿ (F7)

Fyne Court, Broomfield (NT) Headquarters of Somerset Trust for Nature Conservation and visitor centre for the **Quantocks**. ♿ (C6)

Gaulden Manor Charming and historic grange going back to 12th century or earlier incorporating great hall with magnificent plaster ceiling and containing fine antique furniture. Bog and herb gardens. ♿ (C4)

Glastonbury Tor (NT) Conical hill crowned by a ruined 15th-century church tower. Joseph of Arimathea is said to have buried the chalice used at the Last Supper on the slopes of the hill. Superb views from the top over Glastonbury, Wells and Bristol Channel. Access from A361. (B8)

Grand Western Canal, Tiverton Starting at Tiverton Basin (signposted), 11 miles (17.6 km) of restored canal and towpath extending east to Somerset border. Boat hire. (E3)

Hadspen House Beautiful gardens of 6 acres (2.4 hectares) with trees planted for bark and foliage, shrubs, hostas, roses and tender wall plants. Access from A371. (C9/10)

Halberton Church Handsome, mainly 14th-century sandstone building with richly carved 15th-century rood screen and striking pulpit. (E4)

Ham Hill Country Park, Stoke sub Hamdon Grassland and famous quarry site of 153 acres (62 hectares) established on an elongated hill 426 ft (130 m) high ringed by the earthworks of an Iron Age fort. Access from A3088. (E8)

Hardy's Cottage (NT) Modest thatched cottage where Thomas Hardy was born (1840) and wrote *Under the Greenwood Tree* (1872) and *Far from the Madding Crowd* (1874). ♿ (G10)

Hardy Monument (NT) Tower 74 ft (22.5 m) high erected by public subscription in 1846 to the memory of Nelson's flag captain Vice-Admiral Hardy. (G9)

Hatch Court Elegant Palladian-style Georgian house containing small Canadian military museum. China room. Deer park with fine views. (D6)

Isle of Portland Rocky peninsula $4\frac{1}{2}$ miles (7.2 km) long and $1\frac{3}{4}$ miles (2.8 km) wide, famous for its building stone, connected to the mainland by the shingle bar of **Chesil Beach**. A royal manor since the 11th century, the island has the largest harbour in Britain (2,107 acres, 852 hectares) as well as several castles, of which all but Portland Castle (EH) are ruined. It ends on the south in the rock mass of Portland Bill, with an ancient lighthouse and dangerous currents offshore. (H7)

Kenton Church Fine late 14th-century church of red sandstone with carved capitals, stately rood screen, medieval pulpit and imposing monuments. (H3)

Killerton Gardens (NT) Hillside gardens of 15 acres (6 hectares) which sweep down to open lawns, with vantage points giving views of the Clyst and Culm valleys. The house, the family home of the Aclands since the 17th century, was rebuilt in 1778 and now houses the Paulise de Bush Collection of Costumes shown in period settings. Access from B3185. ♿ (F3)

King John's Hunting Lodge, Axbridge (NT) Early Tudor merchant's house, restored in 1971, with a museum of local history and archaeology. (A7)

Knightshayes Court Gardens (NT) One of the finest gardens in the West Country, with specimen trees, formal terraces and rare shrubs, interesting at any time of year. House is a rare survival of the work of William Burges and contains Sir John Amory's collection of Old Masters. ♿ (E3)

Longleat House Splendid country house, seat of the Marquess of Bath, built 1559–80, with fine library and state rooms, valuable furniture and pictures and many other treasures, including first folio Shakespeare and letters of Elizabeth I. In the grounds landscaped by 'Capability' Brown is Europe's first safari park. Access from A362. (B11)

Luccombe (NT) Picturesque village reached by steep and narrow roads. A stream flowing through the village has its source on 1,705 ft (520 m) Dunkery Beacon, to the south, from which there are fine views. (B3)

Luccombe

Lulworth Cove Remarkable circular bay about 1,500 ft (457 m) in diameter almost landlocked by chalk cliffs and fringed by pebble and sand beaches. (H11)

Lytes Cary (NT) Fascinating medieval manor incorporating great 15th-century hall with arch braced roof, original fireplace, carved timber cornice and triple light windows. Adjoining it is the great parlour with early 17th-century panelling and above that the 'great chamber' with a plaster ceiling of 1533. ♿ (D8)

Maiden Castle (EH) Largest and most elaborate prehistoric hill fort in Britain covering 100 acres (40 hectares) of flat hilltop, with traces of several lines of defence. On the eastern edge are the remains of a 4th-century Roman temple. Access off A354. (G10)

Mapperton Gardens Terraced and hillside gardens, formal borders, specimen shrubs and trees, orangery and 18th-century stone fishponds and summerhouse. (F8)

Martock Church Perpendicular building with 13th-century chancel and great clerestory nave with magnificent tie beam roof, one of the finest of its kind. In the clerestory are 17th-century paintings of the Apostles. (D8)

Mendip Hills Bleak limestone chain 25 miles (40 km) long and 5 miles (8 km) wide running north-west to south-east and rising to 1,067 ft (325 m) on Black Down, in north-west. The steep south slopes are honeycombed with caves, the most spectacular of which are at **Cheddar Gorge** and Wookey Hole. (A8)

Midelney Manor Plain stone 16th- to 18th-century manor house, originally the island manor of abbots of Muchelney and the property of the Trevilian family since the Dissolution. Gardens, heronry and 17th-century falcons' mews. ♿ (D7)

Milton Abbey House Now a school, elegant 18th-century Gothic-style house with ceilings and decorations by James Wyatt. Built round a courtyard and incorporating 15th-century abbot's hall with original hammer beam roof and carved screen. The finest part of the abbey church (now the school chapel) is the vaulted ceiling. ♿ (F11)

Minterne Beautiful rhododendron gardens established in a valley landscaped in the 18th century with streams, and small lakes. (F10)

Montacute House (NT) This masterpiece of Elizabethan architecture is a beautiful H-plan house of 3 storeys with forecourt pavilions and balustrades, shaped gables and sculptured figures. Much of the original plasterwork has survived and there is a fine carved screen

North Dorset Downs Chalk uplands ('the Chalks') running east to west for some 25 miles (40 km) and throwing out on the way a string of hills mostly over 800 ft (244 m), all crowned by earthworks, tumuli and other prehistoric remains. (F9)

Nunney Castle (EH) Remains of fortified house of 1373 consisting of three walls with a tower at each corner surrounded by a particularly deep moat. (B10)

Oakhill Manor Charming small furnished mansion set in 8 acres (3.2 hectares) of delightful gardens. Miniature railway. Important museum of models relating to transport. Access from A37. ♿ (B9)

Otterton Mill Restored watermill on river Otter with exhibition gallery and craftsmen turning out pottery, furniture, glass and lace. ♿ (H4)

Parnham House Fine Tudor mansion with later additions. Grounds include formal terraces with water channels and cascades, delightful riverside walks and picnic areas shaded by magnificent trees. Well-preserved interior. Also notable as the home of furniture designer, John Makepeace. His furniture workshops, housed in the stables, can be viewed. ♿ (F8)

The east front of Montacute

Powderham Castle 14th-century seat of Courtenays, Earls of Devon, set in its own deer park on west bank of Exe estuary with a splendidly decorated and furnished interior and pretty chapel. ♿ (H3)

Quantock Hills Ridge of hills some 12 miles (19 km) long by 3 miles (4.8 km) wide and 1,260 ft (384 m) at its highest point where woods alternate with heather and bracken. Fine seaward views. Wild red deer hunted in spring and autumn. A footpath runs the length of the ridge. (See also **Fyne Court**.) (B/C5)

Selworthy (NT) Pretty village of colour-washed cottages in a superb setting on the side of a wooded hill. Green and fine 15th-century church with plastered walls, wagon roofs, medieval glass and carved bench ends. A pleasant walk of ¾ mile (1.2 km) leads to Selworthy Beacon, 1,013 ft (308 m) high. (B3)

Shepton Mallet Church Notable for its triple windowed tower, intricate panelled nave roof, late 12th-century arcades and Perpendicular stone pulpit. (B9)

Somerset and Dorset Railway Trust, Washford An indoor and outdoor museum of locomotives, wagons and other railwayana, including a working reconstruction of a typical mechanical signal box. (B4)

Tiverton Castle Historic fortress of Henry I built 1106 with imposing medieval gatehouse. Joan of Arc gallery, Chapel of St Francis, Clock Museum. (E3)

Tropical Bird Gardens, Rode Over 180 different species of exotic birds in 17 acres (6.8 hectares) of beautiful grounds with woodlands, flower gardens and ornamental lakes. ♿ (A11)

Undercliffs, Lyme Regis Lunar-like coastal strip 8 miles (12.8 km) long covering 800 acres (323 hectares) where a massive landslip occurred in 1839. Traversed by nature trail from Lyme Regis to Seaton revealing large variety of wildlife. Access off A3052. (G7)

Wellington Monument (NT) Erected 1818, 175 ft (53 m) obelisk commemorating military achievements of Iron Duke standing 900 ft (274 m) up on **Blackdown Hills**. A winding staircase of 235 steps leads to the top from which the views are breathtaking. (D5)

Wells Cathedral and Bishop's Palace 13th-century church famous for its west front with 297 surviving medieval statues, many life size, its mechanical medieval clock and curious inverted arches in the nave. Beyond the cloisters is the walled and moated 13th-century bishop's palace. A popular sight are the

Wells Cathedral, the West front

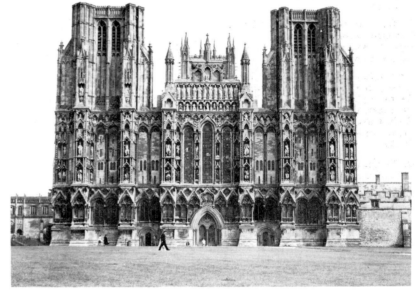

in the great hall. Exhibition of 16th- and early 17th-century portraits from the National Portrait Gallery in the long gallery. ♿ (E8)

Newton Poppleford Pretty linear village founded in 13th century with 17th- and 18th-century cob and thatched cottages and market place. (G4)

Maiden Castle

Pilton Manor Vineyard Vineyard of 15 acres (6 hectares) established 1189 by monks of Glastonbury and recently replanted with Riesling-Sylvaner and other modern hybrids. Harvesting and wine-making machinery, wine tastings. On A361, on estate of manor. ♿ The village is also notable for its 12th-century church and great 14th-century tithe barn. (B9)

Somerset and North Devon Coast Path 82 mile (131 km) section of the South West Peninsula Coast Path which starts at Minehead (B3) and continues over the heights of Exmoor, with rapid changes of scene between Lynmouth (A1) and Ilfracombe (Map 2 A4), to end beyond rugged Hartland Point (Map 2 D1) at the Cornish boundary. (A1/2/3)

South Dorset Downs Great ridge of chalk cloaked in springy turf and heather extending west for nearly 35 miles (56 km) in a narrow band between the Frome valley and the coast from the Purbeck hills to Lyme Regis and beyond. The inner hills are crowned by some of the most formidable earthworks in Britain, the greatest being **Maiden Castle** south-west of Dorchester. This is the country described so well in the novels of Thomas Hardy. (H7 to 12)

Stourhead (NT) 18th-century Palladian house containing furniture by the younger Chippendale and fine pictures. Best known for its magnificent landscaped gardens, with notable trees and shrubs and lakes surrounded by temples and grottoes. Access from B3092. ♿ (C11)

Tintinhull House (NT) Modern formal garden with mixed shrub and herbaceous borders and pool garden laid out in grounds of 17th-century house with 18th-century facade. ♿ (D8)

swans which ring a bell by the gatehouse when hungry. (B9)

Westonzoyland Church 14th- and 15th-century building noted for its fine tower and the tie beam roof of the nave. A plan in the porch shows the way to the site of the battle of Sedgemoor, fought in July 1685. (C7)

Winsford Picturesque village built around a green with a rambling old inn and handsome parish church. The oldest of the village's seven bridges is a pack-horse bridge. (C3)

Wolfeton House Outstanding medieval and Elizabethan manor house with large mullioned windows and magnificent wood and stone work, fireplaces and ceilings. 17th-century furniture and pictures, chapel and cider house. (G10)

Wookey Hole Interesting if commercialised cave system occupied from Palaeolithic to Roman times. (A9)

Worldwide Butterflies Ltd and Lullingstone Silk Farm, Compton House In grounds of 16th-century manor house, butterfly breeding centre with specimen tropical jungle and palm house. Adjoining silk farm which produced the material for robes at the last two coronations and the Princess of Wales's wedding dress. (E9)

Coastal Footpaths

On 20 January 1978 John Merrill set off from St Paul's Cathedral to walk round the British coastline – a distance of 7,000 miles (11,200 km). This mileage is likely to greatly exceed what most people achieve in a lifetime, but Merrill's ten-month journey admirably demonstrated the 'on-foot' potential of Britain's coastline.

The scenery of the British shoreline is very varied, ranging from sand-dunes to rocky indentations, mudflats and cliffs. For those who love views and the sight and sound of the sea, coastal walking is an unbeatable experience. As in the case of the countryside generally, however, the very best sections of the coast are usually only accessible to people who are prepared to walk away from the towns and well-known beauty spots (although this may only entail going a few hundred yards from the nearest car park).

Along much of the coast walkers can follow legally defined rights of way, many of which date from a time when coastguards patrolled the shores in search of smugglers. All such footpaths are indicated by red dots or dashes on Ordnance Survey maps (1 : 50,000 series). In addition, several miles of footpaths have been officially designated by the Countryside Commission as long-distance trails, waymarked by the Commission's distinctive acorn symbol at various points along the way. The three officially recognised coastal footpaths: the Cleveland Way, the Pembrokeshire Coast Path and the South West Peninsula Coast Path will shortly be joined by a fourth, the North Norfolk Coast Path.

The Cleveland Way is the coastal section of a 100 mile (160 km) horseshoe path that skirts the North York Moors National Park, following high cliffs designated as Heritage Coast (outstanding stretches of undeveloped coastline), taking the walker over Boulby, one of the highest cliffs (666 ft, 200 m) along the English coastline. The path also includes such attractions as the fishing village of Staithes (where Captain Cook was apprenticed to a local grocer), red-roofed Runswick Bay and Robin Hood's Bay (named not after the bow and arrow hero but derived from the Celtic work 'raphen', meaning cliff). Further south the Cleveland Way coincides with Cleveland Street, once marched upon by Roman legions, as well as the old railway line that used to carry ironstone and alum to Middlesbrough.

The ragged outline and craggy cliffs of the Pembrokeshire Coast Path resemble the coastline of Cornwall, but this beautiful stretch of South Wales remains far less known and visited. Even during the peak holiday season it feels remote, a wild seascape where you can wander for hours on end without meeting a soul. The Path follows the ups, downs, ins and outs of the shoreline for 167 miles (267 km) within the boundaries of the National Park, from St Dogmaels in the north to Amroth in the south, taking in the enormous sweep of St Brides Bay. Apart from its scenic beauty the Pembrokeshire coastline is renowned for its beautiful wild flowers and hordes of seabirds, including cormorants, shags, choughs, guillemots and razorbills. The area is also a favourite haunt of geologists who come to examine rocks that date back 2,000 million years; even the untrained eye will appreciate the elemental forces that have twisted and folded the land masses, and the erosive power of the sea that has created caves, arches, stacks and other text-book features. There is evidence of Early Man, too, in the flint chippings left by Stone Age people some 10,000 years ago, and in the Iron Age forts built on several promontories.

The South West Peninsula Coast Path, following the coasts of Cornwall, Devon, Somerset and Dorset, is the longest of all the officially designated long-distance footpaths. It stretches for 515 miles (824 km) from Minehead in Somerset, around the country's westernmost extremity, and back along the southern shoreline to Poole Harbour in Dorset. At the beginning of its journey the Path passes through the Exmoor National Park and then continues along the North Devon Area of Outstand-

ing Natural Beauty (AONB), passing cliff scenery, woods, beaches and some delightful villages, such as Bossington, Porlock Weir and Clovelly. At Marshland Mouth (north of Morwenstow) the path becomes Cornish and the scenery gradually more rugged but after rounding Land's End and the Lizard the landscapes are more subdued, shaped by drowned valleys (rias), such as those of the Fal and Tamar. Several sections along the south qualify as Heritage Coast and many miles are owned by the National Trust. The Cornish section is also famous for its memorials to a mining past, with hag-tooth ruins of engine houses that pumped the tin mines and china clay workings.

South Devon takes over where Cornwall leaves off and tends to be a busier section of the route

because of the presence of large towns (Torbay, Plymouth, Salcombe, Exmouth, Seaton and Lyme Regis). Many non-urban stretches, however, fall within an AONB, the most delightful sections lying between Bolt Tail and Bolt Head (both on National Trust land), Salcombe and Prawle Point, Sidmouth and Branscombe. The landslip nature reserve between Seaton and Lyme Regis has some tricky walking but is thrilling for its geological and botanical specimens. Finally to Dorset, the shortest (72 mile, 115 km) stretch of the South West Path but one that offers some splendid cliff walking. For the first time in its journey the path takes a significant turn inland at Abbotsbury (with its 14th-century swannery and nature reserve) and parallels Chesil Beach for some 16 miles (25 km)

along the length of water known as the Fleet. The most beautiful miles lie between Charmouth and West Bay and Lulworth Cove (check on the army range firing times before making plans) and Swanage.

The North Norfolk Coast Path is destined to become an officially designated route, linking up with the ancient Peddar's Way at Hunstanton and continuing east, then south, for 87 miles (140 km) until reaching Cromer. Many sections of the route are already open and the rewards are immense; the north Norfolk coastline, despite its proximity to London and the south, is still one of the wildest, least developed stretches in Great Britain, a world of salt marshes, sand dunes, spits of land and varied and plentiful bird life.

The Pembrokeshire Coast Path offers splendid coastal walking, much of it through wild and sparsely-populated country where peaceful sandy bays (above left) alternate with rocky and craggy sections (above right). In contrast the Cleveland Way is never very far from civilization. Robin Hood's Bay (below left) is a huddle of houses round a tiny harbour but Scarborough, near the southern end of the route, is a busy seaside town with all the usual attractions (below centre). The South West Peninsula Coast Path is the longest long-distance path in Great Britain; although there are several towns and villages en route, there are also many wild and beautiful sections as this stretch in north Devon, near Lynmouth, clearly shows (below right).

Hill Figures

Britain's chalk downlands have provided a wonderful opportunity for those with a taste for large-scale visual effects. Chalk is usually only thinly covered with soil and the white rock surface can be relatively easily exposed. Hill figures cut by the turf artist include lions, crowns and military emblems but Britain's seventeen white horses are undoubtedly the most dazzling and memorable of these bizarre works of art. Most of these white horses (with the exception of Uffington) are not of great antiquity and date from the late eighteenth and early nineteenth century, the product of a time when the art of landscape creation was at its full flowering. Of the seventeen horses to be seen today, eleven are in the chalk country of southern England. Several, all dating from the nineteenth century, can be seen on the Marlborough Downs alone, including the Cherhill horse at Calne dating from 1780, the Pewsey horse (1812), the Alton Barnes horse, the Granham Hill horse, the Broad Town horse (1863) and the Hackpen Hill horse (1838). There is a standing horse at Westbury dating from the 18th century and at Upton in Dorset there's a figure of George III on horseback. Horse figures are rare in the north of England but include one of the few figures cut into a rock other than chalk – the horse of white quartz near the village of Stichen in Aberdeenshire. The best known northern horse is that on Roulston Scar above the village of Kilburn in north Yorkshire. This was dug out in 1857 and covered in white stone by the village schoolmaster, Thomas Hodgson.

The oldest surviving white horse is thought to be the White Horse of Uffington, possibly of Iron Age origin. As with some other ancient hill figures, the horse is close to a hill fort. The stylized outline of the horse, similar to representations on Celtic metal work, also supports this theory. Indeed the figure is strikingly unlike the conventional beast and has a curious arched neck and long drooping tail.

Two other surviving hill figures seem to be of considerable antiquity – the Cerne Abbas Giant and the Long Man of Wilmington. The Long Man, 240 ft (73 m) high and holding a thin staff in each hand, may be Celtic. The Giant, like the Uffington White Horse, is associated with an Iron Age enclosure and may date back to the second century AD.

Unfortunately the figures themselves are unlikely to yield evidence about their origins as they incorporate no dateable materials. In view of the speed with which any exposed chalk figure will become recolonised by vegetation, it is remarkable that any ancient examples have survived.

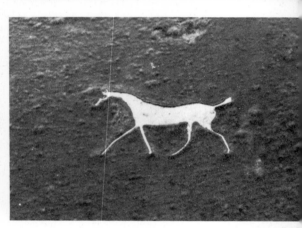

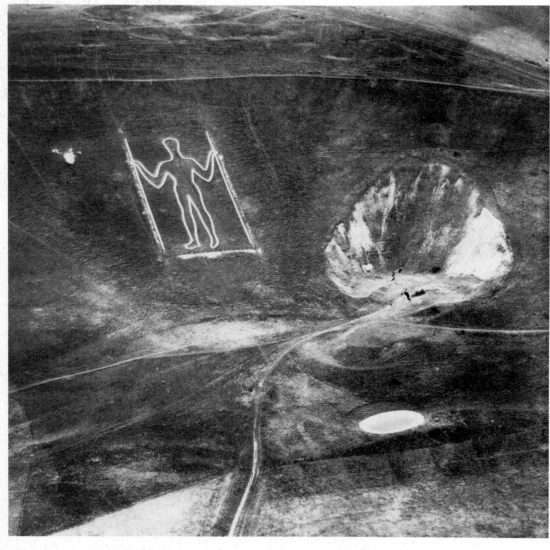

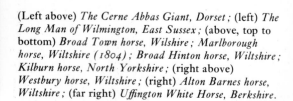

(Left above) *The Cerne Abbas Giant, Dorset*; (left) *The Long Man of Wilmington, East Sussex*; (above, top to bottom) *Broad Town horse, Wilshire*; *Marlborough horse, Wiltshire (1804)*; *Broad Hinton horse, Wiltshire*; *Kilburn horse, North Yorkshire*; (right above) *Westbury horse, Wiltshire*; (right) *Alton Barnes horse, Wiltshire*; (far right) *Uffington White Horse, Berkshire*.

Map 4

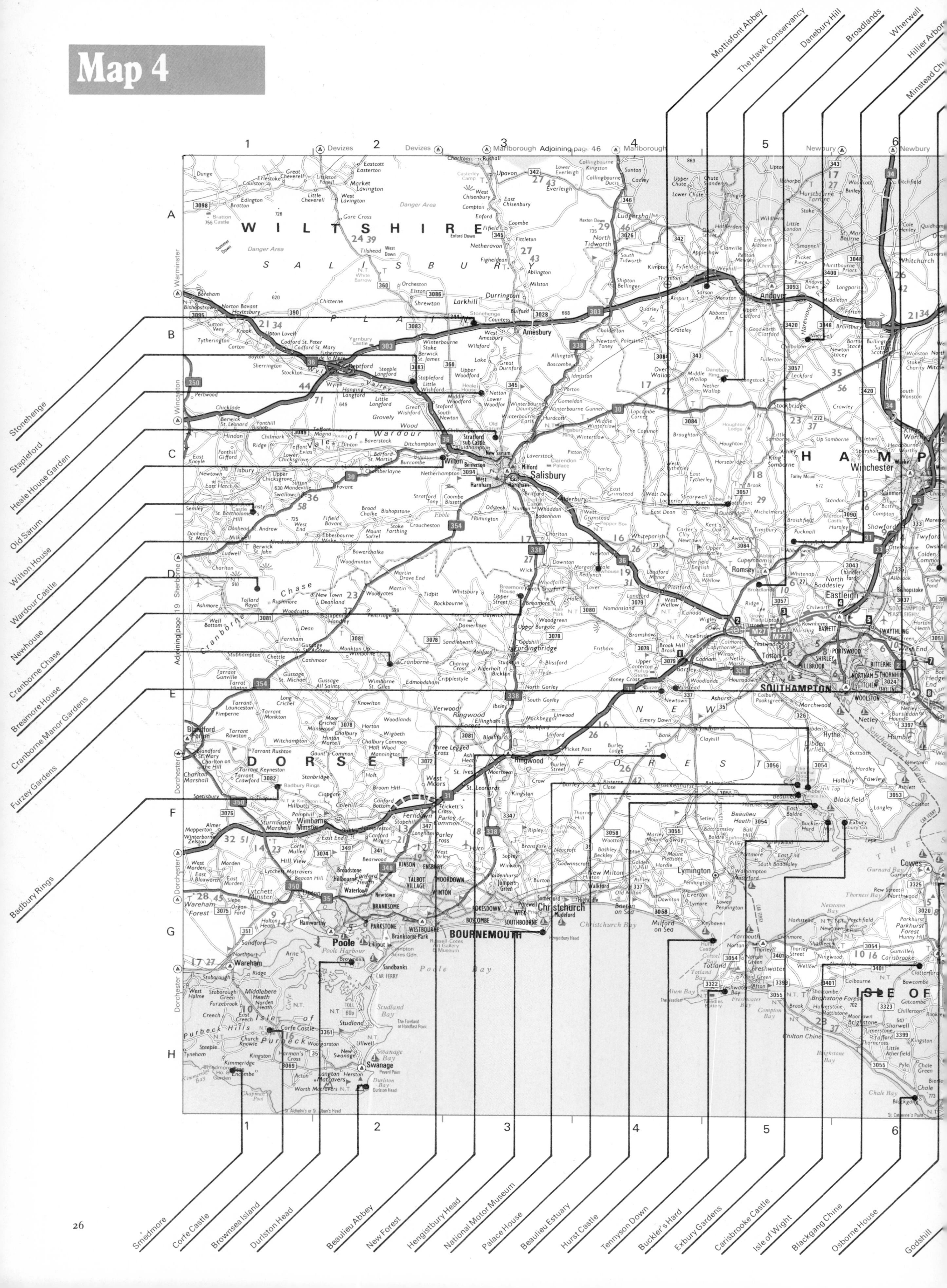

WILTSHIRE

SALISBURY PLAIN

DORSET

HAMPSHIRE

NEW FOREST

ISLE OF WIGHT

Salisbury
Amesbury
Andover
Winchester
Romsey
Eastleigh
SOUTHAMPTON
BOURNEMOUTH
Poole
Wareham
Swanage
Christchurch
Ringwood
Fordingbridge
Blandford Forum
Wimborne Minster
Lymington

Top labels:
Mottisfont Abbey · The Hawk Conservancy · Danebury Hill · Broadlands · Wherwell · Hillier Arbor... · Minstead Ch...

Left-side labels:
Stonehenge · Stapleford · Heale House Garden · Old Sarum · Wilton House · Wardour Castle · Newhouse · Cranborne Chase · Breamore House · Cranborne Manor Gardens · Furzey Gardens · Badbury Rings

Bottom labels:
Smedmore · Corfe Castle · Brownsea Island · Durlston Head · Beaulieu Abbey · New Forest · Hengistbury Head · National Motor Museum · Palace House · Beaulieu Estuary · Hurst Castle · Tennyson Down · Buckler's Hard · Exbury Gardens · Carisbrooke Castle · Isle of Wight · Blackgang Chine · Osborne House · Godshill

27

Southern England

Amberley Charming old village with partly Norman church and 14th-century castle (not open). Open-air *Chalk Pits Museum* (36 acres, 14 hectares), ¾ mile (1.2 km) south on B2139; tools, crafts, machines and buildings of past regional industries. ⅃ (E11)

Arundel Park As well as visiting Arundel Castle, you can explore its hilly, well-timbered park (1,100 acres, 450 hectares). Main feature is beautiful Swanbourne Lake, reached by side road north from Arundel Bridge (½ mile, .8 km). (E11)

Avington Park This urbane 17th-century mansion, red brick with classical portico, looks like a house out of a novel by Jane Austen (who lived not far away at Chawton). State rooms include ballroom with splendid painted ceiling. 42-acre (17-hectare) park. Turn north from A31. See **Jane Austen's House.** ⅃ (C7)

Badbury Rings Iron Age hill-fort with triple line of earthworks. Magnificent view from tree-crowned summit. 5 miles (8 km) north-west of Wimborne Minster on B3082. (F1)

Basing House Ruins of Tudor fortified mansion, stormed by Cromwell in Civil War (1645). The imposing gatehouse and tall dovecote with 500 nests survived intact. ½ mile (.8 km) south-west of Basing, entrance in Old Basing. ⅃ (A8)

Beaulieu Abbey The remains of this great Cistercian Abbey (1204) include lancet-windowed refectory (now the parish church), cloisters, dormitory. (F5)

Beaulieu Estuary Yachtsmen love this sheltered waterway, on whose wooded shores you can visit **Buckler's Hard** and **Exbury Gardens.** The quiet surrounding countryside, rich in bird life, can be explored by minor roads leading to attractive little spots like Lepe on the Solent coast. (F5)

Bignor Roman Villa Exceptionally fine mosaic pavements, museum of finds. ¼ mile (.4 km) east of Bignor, access from road to Bury. ⅃ (E11)

Black Down (NT) Wooded hill (919 ft, 280 m), highest point in Sussex, 1¼ miles (2 km) south-east of Haslemere. Access from Tennyson's Lane (south from B2131); car park, footpaths. (C10)

Bohunt Manor Gardens Medium-sized garden with fine trees, herbaceous borders, lakeside walk, waterfowl. Access from A3, ½ mile (.8 km) south of Liphook. ⅃ (C9)

Bosham Characterful old waterside village, a favourite with yachtsmen and artists. The church, partly Saxon, is depicted on the Bayeux Tapestry. (F9)

Boxgrove Priory Beautiful 12th/13th-century church of former Benedictine priory (now the parish church), with mingling of Norman and Early English features. Chancel vault painted in 16th century. (E10)

Breamore House Elizabethan manor, gabled and mullioned, with important art collection, countryside museum, carriage museum. In the park stands Breamore's Saxon church (c. AD 1000). Side road west from A338, 3 miles (4.8 km) north of Fordingbridge. (D3)

Broadlands Classical 18th-century mansion overlooking river Test. Former home of the Victorian Prime Minister Lord Palmerston and of Admiral of the Fleet the Earl Mountbatten of Burma, whose career is depicted in a special exhibition. Rich interiors, fine art collection. ½ mile (.8 km) south of Romsey, access from A31 (Romsey bypass). ⅃ (D5)

Brownsea Island (NT) Wooded island of enchantment in Poole Harbour, one of the last haunts of the red squirrel. Its 500 acres (200 hectares) include Nature Reserve with lagoon, lakes, heronry. Sandy beaches. Castle (not open). Ferries from Poole and Sandbanks. (G2)

Buckler's Hard Secluded waterside hamlet, once busy with the construction of wooden warships. *Maritime Museum,* with models of ships built here for Nelson's victorious fleet. (F5)

Chichester Harbour Sea inlet with wide waterways, highly popular with yachtsmen and waterfowl. Landlubbers can capture its flavour at salty little places like Dell Quay, West Itchenor, **Bosham,** Chidham, West Thorney. (F9)

Cissbury Ring (NT) Largest hill-fort on South Downs (Iron Age, c. 300 BC), with ramparts enclosing 60 acres (24 hectares). Minor road east from Findon (1¼ miles, 2 km) to small car park at foot of hill. A 2½-mile (4-km) Downland walk leads north to the well-known viewpoint of *Chanctonbury Ring* (Roman site). (E12)

Clandon Park (NT) Unusual Baroque Palladian house, built 1731–5 by Leoni, with sumptuous Baroque interior. Contains famous Gubbay collection of Chinese porcelain birds. Access off A427. ⅃ (A11)

Compton Church 11th-century village church famed for unique two-storey chancel, with a chapel above the sanctuary. Saxon tower. (A11)

Corfe Castle

Corfe Castle (NT) This dramatic ruin of a hilltop Norman fortress dominates the picturesque stone-tiled village bearing its name. Blown up by the Roundheads who captured it in 1643. (H1)

Cranborne Chase Region of hills and dense woodlands, rich in prehistoric antiquities. Good walks. (D1)

Cranborne Manor Gardens Originally laid out in 17th century. Yew hedges, lawns, herb and knot gardens, old-fashioned roses. On B3078, entrance near Cranborne church. (E2)

Danebury Hill Crowned by massive Iron Age stronghold, with triple ramparts enclosing 13 acres (5 hectares). 4 miles (6.4 km) north-west of Stockbridge, access by minor road north from A30. (B5)

Denmans Garden, Fontwell Walled garden, beautiful at all seasons. Access by Denmans Lane (south from A27). ⅃ (E10)

Devil's Punchbowl (NT) Great semi-circular depression in the Hindhead hills; spectacular views from A3 as it ascends to the rim. (C10)

Durlston Head Prominent headland 1 mile (1.6 km) south of Swanage, reached by Lighthouse Road. The 'sights' include the Stone Globe of the world and the Lighthouse (open). Panoramic cliff walk west to St Aldhelm's Head (4½ miles, 7.2 km). (H2)

Exbury Gardens Woodland gardens (250 acres, 100 hectares) noted for magnificent trees and displays of flowering shrubs. Entrance opposite Exbury church. (F6)

Fishbourne Roman Palace Remains of largest Roman residence yet discovered in Britain, with many mosaic floors, restored Roman garden, museum, audio-visual theatre. 1½ miles (2.4 km) west of Chichester, signposted road north from A27. (F9)

Furzey Gardens, Minstead Fine collection of trees, flowering shrubs, lilies, heathers, etc. Water garden. 8 acres (3 hectares). Craft gallery. Access by lane at side of village hall. (E4)

Goodwood This great house (1616–1800), domed and colonnaded, forms three sides of Wyatt's proposed octagon. Beautiful rooms with important art collection. 40-acre (16-hectare) 'home park', with cedars and cork trees. 3½ miles (5.6 km) north-east of Chichester. ⅃ (E10)

Hatchlands (NT) Red-brick Georgian house with elegant rooms noted for the earliest known interior decorations by Robert Adam (1759). Pleasant garden. Minor road east from East Clandon (¼ mile, .4 km). ⅃ (A12)

The Hawk Conservancy The birds of prey on view include eagles, hawks, falcons (which give flying demonstrations), vultures, owls, kites. 3 miles (4.8 km) west of Andover, side road from A303. (B5)

Heale House Garden, Middle Woodford The Avon flows through this 8-acre (3-hectare) garden, enhancing the beauty of its lawns, roses and herbaceous borders. Authentic Japanese tea house on wooden bridge over the river; Japanese water garden. 4 miles (6.4 km) north of Salisbury by Avon valley road. ⅃ (B3)

Hengistbury Head Defended by the prehistoric but still formidable Double Dykes, this promontory offers Bronze Age barrows, sea views and a varied bird life. 1½ miles (2.4 km) south-east of Southbourne by minor road (cars) or coastal path. (G3)

Highdown Hill (NT) Favourite viewpoint (266 ft, 81 m), site of Iron Age fort. 'Miller's Tomb' near summit, burial-place (1793) of eccentric local mill-owner. Ascent by footpath from A259. *Highdown Garden* on southern slopes, noted chalk garden in old quarry; entrance on A259. (F12)

Hillier Arboretum 160 acres (64.8 hectares) planted with wide-ranging collection of trees, shrubs and flowers. 2 miles (3.2 km) west of Ampfield, side road west from A31. ⅃ (D5)

Hog's Back Narrow ridge rising to 500 ft (150 m) and providing A31 (Guildford-Farnham) with far-reaching views on either side. Several car parks. (A10)

Hurst Castle (EH) One of Henry VIII's coastal fortresses (enlarged in 19th century), commanding Solent from extremity of narrow shingle promontory. Reached by 1½-mile (2.4-km) walk out to sea from south-east outskirts of Milford or by ferry from Keyhaven. (G5)

Jane Austen's House, Chawton Simple brick house where Jane Austen lived 1809–17 and wrote *Mansfield Park, Emma* and *Persuasion.* Many personal relics. ⅃ (B8)

Leith Hill (NT) Highest point of North Downs (965 ft, 294 m), surmounted by tower. Easy ascent from nearby car park on the minor road which branches south from A25 near Wotton. *Leith Hill Rhododendron Wood* (NT), ½ mile (.8 km) farther south on same road. (B12)

Loseley House Many-gabled grey-stone Elizabethan house (1562), with fine panelling, ceilings, furniture, tapestries. Minor road west from A3100, 1 mile (1.6 km) south of Guildford. ⅃ (A11)

Marwell Zoological Park Nearly 1,000 animals of 130 species, including big cats, primates and hoofed animals. 7 miles (11.2 km) from Winchester on the Winchester to Bishop's Waltham road. ⅃ (D6)

Mid-Hants Railway, New Alresford Steam trains operate on the preserved 'Watercress Line' (10 miles, 16 km) between Alresford and Alton Station, passing through famous watercress-growing areas of Hampshire. Various steam locomotives on show at Ropley. (C7)

Minstead Church Unusual brick church with several rarities: 2-decker pulpit (17th-century), minstrel gallery, 2 pew rooms. Burial place of Sir Arthur Conan Doyle. (E4)

Mottisfont Abbey (NT) Imposing house converted from monastery in Tudor times; further alterations in 18th century. Drawing room with *trompe l'oeil* decorations by Rex Whistler. Riverside grounds (29 acres, 12 hectares) with rose garden. Entrance in Mottisfont village. (C5)

National Motor Museum, Beaulieu Outstanding collection of over 200 vehicles, dating from 1895 onwards. Includes four Land Speed Record holders. (F5)

New Forest Declared a royal hunting ground by William the Conqueror in 1079, the Forest now comprises about 105 square miles (272 sq km) of woodland and open heath, a wonderful domain for walkers, riders and nature lovers. Rich in animal life, including the famous New Forest ponies, deer, foxes, badgers, reptiles and birds. Note especially the two *Ornamental Drives* (cars admitted) which leave A35 2½ miles (4 km) south-west of Lyndhurst and give access to waymarked walks through fine Forest scenery. The Bolderwood Drive (north from A35) passes near the celebrated 300-year-old Knightwood Oak and leads to the Bolderwood and Mark Ash Walks. From the Rhinefield Drive (south from A35), colourful with flowering shrubs in May–June, you can follow the Blackwater, Brock Hill and Tall Trees Walks. (Details of Drives and Walks from Forestry Commission, Queen's House, Southampton Road, Lyndhurst.) The *Rufus Stone* (side road north from A31, 1¾ miles (2.8 km) south-west of Cadnam) marks the supposed spot where William II (Rufus) was killed by an arrow in 1100. (E/F4/5)

Newhouse Rare example of country house built in form of a Y, with Jacobean central section and Georgian wings. Family portraits, Nelson relics. 2 miles (3.2 km) east of Redlynch. (D4)

Oates Memorial Museum and Gilbert White Museum, Selborne The Wakes – home of Gilbert White, author of *The Natural History of Selborne* – is now a museum of mementoes to the village naturalist (1720–93). Also exhibits on 19th-century explorers: Frank Oates in Africa and Lawrence Oates in Antarctica. (C9)

Old Sarum (EH) Massive ramparts ring the site of an Ancient British and Roman camp, which became a Norman hill-town (11th century) complete with castle and cathedral. In 13th century the bishopric was moved to a new site (the present Salisbury) and Old Sarum was left to decay. Foundations of castle and cathedral clearly outlined. 2 miles (3.2 km) north of Salisbury, access from A345. (C3)

Palace House, Beaulieu Originally the Great Gatehouse of Beaulieu Abbey, extended and transformed into stately riverside residence in the 1870s. 14th-century vaulted ceilings, costume tableaux, family portraits. (F5)

Parham Characteristic E-shaped Elizabethan house, which welcomed Elizabeth herself in 1591. Fine furniture, portraits, tapestries, needlework. Apartments shown include panelled Great Hall and Long Gallery. Walled flower gardens; 350-acre (140-hectare) park with church, lake, deer. Access from A283. (E12)

Petworth

Petworth House and Park (NT) Late 17th-century Renaissance mansion with 320 ft (97 m) facade surveying magnificent 738-acre (298-hectare) deer park, landscaped by 'Capability' Brown. Important art collection (many Van Dycks and Turners); Grinling Gibbons carvings. *Note:* visitors to Park only (open daily) use car park on A283, 1½ miles (2.4 km) north of Petworth. (D11)

Pilgrims' Way Popular with present-day walkers is the footpath section east of Compton (B11), which crosses Losely Park and ascends to the hilltop ruin of 14th-century St Catherine's Chapel, once a halting place for Canterbury-bound pilgrims. The Way climbs again to St Martin's Chapel (now restored as Chilworth parish church) and follows the hills to Ranmore Common (A12) and beyond. See also **North Downs Way**, Gazetteer 5.

Polesden Lacey (NT) Regency-Edwardian house commanding superb views of wooded hills. Richly decorated rooms with Greville collection of paintings, furniture, tapestries, porcelain. Extensive lawns and gardens. Signposted road south from Great Bookham (1½ miles, 2.4 km). (A12)

Portchester Castle (EH) One of Britain's most remarkable historical monuments: a 12th-century castle and fine Norman church built within the well-preserved walls of the original Roman fortress. Side road south from A27. (F7)

Queen Elizabeth Country Park Comprises 1,400 acres (566 hectares) of forest and open downland on either side of A3, 4 miles (6.4 km) south of Petersfield. Waymarked trails, picnic areas, riding, grass-skiing, Butser ancient farm, etc. Fine views from Butser Hill. (D9)

Shipley Windmill Beautiful white smock mill, restored as memorial to author Hilaire Belloc (1870–1953), who lived nearby. At south end of village. (D12)

Slindon Park Wood (NT) The woodland track (1 mile, 1.6 km) passes through stands of mature beeches, many of impressive height. Entrance on A29, ¼ mile (.4 km) south of junction with A27. (E11)

Smedmore 17th/18th-century manor house with collections of marquetry furniture and antique dolls. Walled gardens. 1 mile (1.6 km) south-east of Kimmeridge. (H1)

South Downs Range of chalk hills stretching from Hampshire–Sussex borderland to Beachy Head. Highest point: Butser Hill (888 ft, 270 m) in **Queen Elizabeth Country Park**. The *South Downs Way*, walking route along the entire range, is accessible from the roads crossing the Downs. From A24 ½ mile (.8 km) south of Washington, for example, the Way leads west to Amberley and east to Chanctonbury Ring (783 ft, 235 m), whose clump of trees, planted 1760, is a familiar landmark (see **Cissbury Ring**). See also **South Downs Way**, Gazetteer 5. (E9-12)

Stane Street Walkers can follow the track of this Roman road (which ran from Chichester to London) for 4 miles (6.4 km) over the South Downs, from Slindon Woods, off unclassified road 1 mile (1.6 km) north of Eartham, to the northern escarpment of the range; widespread views. Steep descent to Bignor and its Roman villa. (E11)

Stapleford Perhaps the prettiest of the Wylye Valley villages: a picture-book cluster of thatched cottages, with Norman church. (B2)

Stonehenge (EH) One of Europe's most renowned prehistoric monuments: a circular assembly of huge monoliths and trilithons (c. 1800 BC). Original purpose still wrapped in mystery. Access from A360, near junction with A303. (B3)

Uppark (NT) Classical 1690 house, high on the slopes of the South Downs. Noted for the preservation of much of its 18th-century interior decoration and furnishings (even curtains and wallpaper) in their original state. 1½ miles (2.4 km) south of South Harting on B2146. (D9)

The Vyne (NT) Handsome red-brick Tudor house overlooking lake; chapel (1510), Long Gallery with linenfold panelling. Remodelled in mid 17th century, when it became the first country house in England with a classical portico; 18th-century rococo rooms, Palladian staircase. Garden with spacious lawns. 4 miles (6.4 km) north of Basingstoke. (A8)

Wardour Castle There are two Wardour Castles. The 14th-century Old Castle (EH), picturesque ruin near the lake, suffered much in Civil War. The New Castle (1768) is a Palladian mansion with fine rooms and remarkable double-flight staircase (now Cranborne Chase School). Access to both by signposted turnings south from Tisbury–Semley road. (C1)

Watts Gallery, Compton Paintings by G.F. Watts (1817–1904) who lived at Compton. The Gallery was designed by Christopher Turnor; the striking nearby *Memorial Chapel*, with bell tower and elaborate symbolic decorations, by the artist's second wife, Mary. (A11)

Weald and Downland Open Air Museum, Singleton 40-acre (16-hectare) site on which various rural buildings have been re-erected: medieval farmhouses, market hall, blacksmith's forge, working water-mill, etc. Also comprises country park. Access from A286. (E10)

West Dean Gardens Wide range of trees and shrubs, pergola, walled garden, greenhouses. Picnic area. On A286, 6 miles (9.6 km) north of Chichester. (E10)

Wherwell Village in Test Valley with delightful array of thatched and timbered cottages. (B5)

Wilton House Inigo Jones masterpiece in setting of lawns and cedars. Outstanding collection of paintings and furniture. The 17th-century state rooms include the famous 'Double Cube' hung with Van Dycks. Palladian bridge in park. (C3)

Winkworth Arboretum (NT) Hillside (99 acres, 40 hectares) planted with rare trees and shrubs; fine colour displays in spring and autumn. 3 miles (4.8 km) south-east of Godalming on B2130. (B11)

Isle of Wight

The chief beauty of the 'Garden Isle' lies in the rolling hills and grand cliff scenery of its southern half (see **Tennyson Down**). The northern coastline also has great appeal, notably in the vicinity of the former royal estate of **Osborne** and around the peaceful inlet of Newtown Harbour (NT), the island's main port before it silted up. (G/H5/6/7)

Arreton Manor Mellow 17th-century house with panelled rooms, period furniture, Folk Museum, 'Echoes of Childhood' collection, National Wireless Museum. ¾ mile (1.2 km) north-west of Arreton on A3056. (G7)

Blackgang Chine Chines (cliff ravines) are a speciality of the Isle of Wight. This one will keep the family occupied for hours. A colourful theme park built on 400 ft (130 m) high cliffs, its attractions include adventure parks, fantasy worlds, model villages, maze, museum (with 70 ft (21 m) skeleton of whale stranded on beach, 1842), life-size dinosaur models etc. Access from A3055 1 mile (1.6 km) south of Chale. (H6)

Brading Roman Villa Well-preserved mosaic pavements, hypocaust, museum. 1 mile (1.6 km) south-west of Brading, access by signposted road west from A3055. (G7)

Carisbrooke Castle (EH) Norman fortress where Charles I was imprisoned, 1647–8. Impressive gatehouse. 16th-century waterwheel in wellhouse, still worked by donkey. The Governor's Lodgings now house the *Isle of Wight County Museum*; collection includes personal relics of Charles I. (G6)

Godshill Godshill's Perpendicular church and the neighbouring thatched cottages feature on many a picture-postcard. You can also see them in miniature (1/10 scale), along with the village inn and other local landmarks, in the delightful *Model Village* in the Old Vicarage garden. (H7)

Isle of Wight Steam Railway, Haven Street Steam services operating from Haven Street Station on 1¾ mile (2.8 km) line. Vintage locomotives and rolling stock on view. (G7)

Osborne House (EH) Italianate seaside residence built (1845) for Queen Victoria and Prince Consort. Their private apartments, including room where Victoria died in 1901, remain virtually unchanged. Ornate Durbar Room. Swiss Cottage where the royal children played at housekeeping. Access from A3021. (G6)

Tennyson Down (NT) Green hill ascended by track west from Freshwater Bay and crowned by memorial to the poet Tennyson, who lived at nearby Farringford House (now hotel). Cliff walk west, with view of the sea-washed chalk pinnacles of The Needles, to Alum Bay, famous for its coloured sands (bottled for souvenirs). Chair lift to beach. The walk can be continued north to Totland Bay. Total distance of about 5 miles (8 km). (G5)

Map 5

South-East England

Alfriston Includes 15th-century Star Inn, once a hostel for mendicant friars, and the Ship Inn with fine timber framing. Part of a medieval Market Cross may be seen in the main street. The 14th-century *Clergy House* (NT) is notable, being timber-framed and thatched and considered unique in England. It was restored in 1896 and was the first property to be acquired by the National Trust. (H4)

Appledore A port in 13th century before the Rother changed its course. In 892, 250 Danish ships harboured here as a threat to King Alfred. 14th-century St Peter and St Paul Church was built after the former one was burnt by the French in 1380. The tower doorway carries the arms of Archbishop Warham above it. Attractive houses, 16th century onwards, line turf-bordered main street. (E8)

Bateman's (NT) Rudyard Kipling's home 1902–36 with his rooms and study exactly as they were. A mill in the gardens has been recently restored to full working order and grinds flour for sale. Also on view is the oldest working water-driven turbine in the world, installed by Kipling to generate electricity for domestic use. (F5)

Battle Abbey (EH) Approached through gatehouse which dominates the Market Square. It was founded by William the Conqueror to commemorate his victory in 1066 and occupies the spot where Harold erected his Royal standard and later fell. The famous 'Roll of Battle Abbey' was probably compiled in the 14th century. (F6)

Bedgebury National Pinetum Belongs to the Forestry Commission. Has largest collection of conifers in Europe, including Californian redwoods. Also magnificent rhododendrons and small lake. Access from B2079. (E6)

Betchworth Village on the River Mole, with an ancient church, St Michael's, dating from the reign of Edward the Confessor. Font (1951) by Eric Kennington. The cottages in the little square outside are 17th century, the vicarage 1715 and the 'Old House' is Queen Anne period. (C1)

Biddenden Once a part of the Flemish weaving industry. Note the beautiful 16th-century Old Cloth Hall, seven gabled, tile hung and timbered. Almost every building is designated an 'ancient monument'. (D7)

Bodiam Castle (NT) A well-preserved 14th-century fortress, with towers mirrored in the wide moat. An audio-visual presentation about life in a medieval castle may be enjoyed during the summer season. (E6)

Borde Hill Gardens Large garden and woodland of great botanical interest and beauty. Has rare trees and shrubs, extensive views and woodland walks. Also camellias, magnolias, rhododendrons, azaleas in season. Picnic area. (F2)

Boughton Monchelsea Place Elizabethan and Regency manor with fine furniture and tapestries. 18th-century deer park. Magnificent views of the Kentish Weald. Records preserved since 1570. Collection of dresses, carriages and agricultural implements. (C6)

Bramber A pleasant village on the River Adur, once a busy port. *Bramber Castle* (NT), a Norman stronghold formerly owned by the Dukes of Norfolk, is now a ruin. Good views of South Downs. *House of Pipes* (won BTA commendation), with 35,000 exhibits, gives an insight into social history relating to smoking habits over 1,500 years. Set in 19th-century shopping arcade. (G1)

Brenchley Noted for its Tudor houses. Near Brenchley Manor, 16th century, is an old oak tree mentioned in the Domesday Book. An avenue of 350-year-old yew trees leads to 13th-century sandstone church. (D5)

Bridge Cottage, High Street, Uckfield 600-year-old, timber-framed, aisled 'Wealden' hall, recently restored as a Heritage Centre. (F3)

Brockham Famous for its associations with W. G. Grace who played cricket on its classic triangular village green. Church in 13th-century style was built 1846 and has good German stained glass. (C1)

Chartwell (NT) Former home of Sir Winston Churchill, kept as it was during Churchill's lifetime. House remodelled by Philip Tilden. Terraced gardens descend towards the lake with the famous black swans. Garden studio contains many of his paintings. (C3)

Chiddingstone Castle A 'Gothick' castle built 18th to 19th century. Contains pictures, furnishings and royal Stuart, Jacobite and Egyptian collections as well as oriental art treasures, including largest collection of Japanese lacquer on show outside Japan. (D4)

Chilham Castle Present house dates back to 1616, and is possibly by Inigo Jones. Octagonal Norman keep survives from former castle. Park landscaped by 'Capability' Brown. Jousting, falconry displays. (C9)

Deal Castle (EH) Situated at Deal where Julius Caesar is believed to have landed in 55 BC. The castle was built by Henry VIII for coastal defence. Has excellent vaulted chambers and galleries. On display are relics of Deal's history and Iron Age implements. (C12)

De Tillens A 15th-century Wealden Hall House with kingpost roof. Largest collection of medals in the UK and fine display of furniture, china, porcelain and guns. Access off A25. (C3)

Dover Castle (EH) Norman castle with keep (1181–7), containing 242 ft (74 m) deep well. Keep also contains armoury and Norman chapel. Underground passages and casemates may be viewed. The nearby 'Pharos' is possibly the oldest standing building in England c. AD 50. (D12)

Drusilla's, near Alfriston Zoo specialising in endangered species and rare breeds of farm animals. There is also a

Bodiam Castle

collection of tropical moths and butterflies. Railway. (H4)

Eastry Focussed around the 13th-century church of St Mary the Virgin with its 66 ft (20 m) Norman tower. On a column in the nave is carved a circle believed to be a primitive calendar. Legend has it that Eastry was the site of the palace of the kings of ancient Kent. (C11)

Emmetts Garden, Ide Hill, Sevenoaks (NT) The garden covers 4 acres (1.6 hectares) and is set on a hillside, being one of the highest gardens in Kent with fine collections of rare trees and shrubs. (C4)

Faversham Maison Dieu, Ospringe (EH) A timber-framed 15th-century house containing a unique collection of Roman pottery and a museum of local history. (B8)

Godstone On the Roman road from London to Brighton. Has timber-framed cottages and an Elizabethan inn, the White Hart, where the Tsar of Russia is said to have stopped off on his way to a prize fight in 1815. The village green with cricket pitch is surrounded with trees. There are no less than seven ponds in this village. (C2)

Grange Museum and Art Gallery, Rottingdean Originally a Georgian house, later remodelled by Lutyens. Houses an art gallery, library and museum with Kipling exhibits and part of the National Toy Museum. Holds temporary exhibitions throughout the year. In centre of village, by green. (H3)

Great Dixter A 15th-century manor house converted and enlarged by Lutyens who added a timber-framed hall house. It is surrounded by an 'English' garden. (F7)

Herstmonceux Castle and Royal Greenwich Observatory A red-brick castle dating from 15th century. Restored 1930s, it now houses the Royal Greenwich Observatory (not open to the public). Astronomical and historical exhibition and castle grounds may be visited. (G5)

Hever Castle This 13th-century moated castle with drawbridge was one of the places where Henry VIII pressed his suit on Anne Boleyn, whose home it was. Has extensive grounds, including fine Italian garden, lake, fountains and topiary work. (D4)

Horsham Museum, The Causeway A 16th-century timbered black-and-white house. Contains local history exhibition of costume, jewellery, toys and bicycles. Also crafts and industries of Sussex, with forge, wheelwright's and saddler's shops. (E1)

Howletts Zoo Park, Bekesbourne John Aspinall's famous collection of wild animals. There is a breeding group of gorillas as well as tigers, deer and antelope. Also snow leopards, tapirs and wild boar. (C10)

Hythe Seaside town at the edge of **Romney Marsh** with a history that goes back 700 years to the founding of the Cinque Ports. *Romney, Hythe and Dymchurch Light Railway* and the **Royal Military Canal** start here. (E10)

Ightham A show village with excellently restored Tudor houses. The church is 14th to 15th century and the St George and Dragon Inn and Tower House with overhanging gables are 16th century. (B5)

Lamb House, West Street, Rye (NT) An early Georgian town house which was Henry James' home 1898–1916. The walled garden, the staircase hall, the morning room, dining room and study on the ground floor may be viewed. (F8)

Leigh One of fourteen villages by this name in Britain. It has the perfect triangular village green, with local church at the apex and lined with timbered and tiled cottages displaying climbing roses. Plough Inn serves real ale from the cask and is mainly 14th century. (C1)

Lingfield Famous for its racecourse. A Wealden village with 15th-century Perpendicular church called the 'Westminster Abbey of Surrey' by some. The village gaol, the Cage, was last used in 1882 to imprison a poacher. Period houses and cottages. (D3)

Lewes Castle and Museum of Sussex Archaeology, Barbican House, High Street, Lewes Contains an important collection of prehistoric, Roman, Saxon and medieval relics and antiquities of Sussex. The Norman castle has a shell keep and 14th-century barbican. (G3)

Marlipins Museum, High Street, Shoreham-by-Sea This museum is housed in an interesting 12th-century building and specialises in maritime and local history. Collection of old maps, photographs and prints. A Sussex Archaeological Society property. (H1)

Michelham Priory, Forge and Wheelwrights Museum, Upper Dicker An Augustinian priory founded in 1229 with Tudor addition and 14th-century gatehouse, enclosed by large moat. Period furniture, tapestries, ironwork, musical instruments and watermill. Also Wheelwrights Museum. (G4)

Museum of Local History, Anne of Cleves House, Southover High Street, Lewes The house dates from 1599. The museum has extensive collections of domestic bygones, exhibition on Wealden ironworking industry and gallery on history of Lewes. (G3)

Newtimber Place A moated 17th-century house with Etruscan-style decoration. Garden. Near Pycombe. Access off A23. (G2)

North Downs Way 141 miles (226 km) long, linking Farnham, Surrey (Map 4 B10) in the west with Dover, Kent (D11) in the east. It crosses both the Surrey hills and the Kent downs and offers considerable variety with woods, often of beech, an attractive feature. From Farnham it follows a west-east route south of A31 and then north of A25 (after Guildford), through Otford (B4) and Wrotham (B5), north-east to the M2 Medway bridge, south-east to Detling (B7), Wye (D9) and Dover (D11). At Boughton Lees (C9) a second branch goes through Chilham to Canterbury. Attractive viewpoints are Box Hill (NT) (C1), Bluebell Hill (B6) and Colley Hill, near Merstham (C2). It includes the historic **Pilgrims' Way** (see Gazetteer 4); medieval pilgrimages were made from Winchester, the nation's former political capital, to the tomb of the martyr, Saint Thomas à

Beckett in Canterbury Cathedral. The North Downs Way was used by traders as far back as 2,000 years ago and although five rivers cut through the Downs, it is mainly a dry and uncomplicated route. Being so close to London, this walk is well served by public transport with British Rail stations at either end. Waymarked with acorn symbol. (B9 to D12)

Nymans Garden (NT) One of the great gardens of the Sussex Weald, with 30 acres (12 hectares) of many rare trees, shrubs and plants from all over the world. Beautiful spring, summer and autumn walks. & (E2)

(The) Old Mill, Outwood England's oldest working mill, built 1665. 39 ft (12 m) high, with spring sails each measuring 59 ft (18 m), it was restored in 1952. Small museum. & (D2)

Penshurst Place Developed from a medieval manor house with unique chestnut-beamed great hall, c. 1340, 64 ft (19.5 m) long and the oldest of its kind in England. Notable collection of early portraits, tapestries, furniture; toy museum; Tudor gardens, venture playground. & (D4)

Pevensey Castle (EH) A Norman castle with keep c. 1080, 13th-century gatehouse and inner bailey. It is set in the south-east angle of an enclosure of 10 acres (4 hectares), surrounded by a Roman wall with towers. This was one of the Saxon Shore fortresses. & (H5)

Polegate Windmill and Milling Museum This red-brick tower windmill has a white domed cap, 1817. Fully working until World War II. Restored 1967. Internal machinery intact. Adjoining milling museum with interesting exhibition. West of A22. (H5)

Post Mill Lies 1 mile (1.6 km) north of Nutley village off Nutley to Crowborough Road. This is the oldest working open-trestle post windmill in Sussex (c. 1670). Was derelict from 1908 until restored between 1968–74. Machinery intact. (E3)

Quebec House (NT) Lies at the east end of the village of Westerham on the north side of A25. General Wolfe spent his boyhood in this 17th-century gabled red-brick house. Interesting collection of relics of Wolfe, his family, and of Montcalm the opposing French general who also fell at Quebec in Canada. On display are portraits, prints, maps, letters and arms. (C3)

Richborough Castle (EH) Believed to be the site of a Roman landing in AD 43. In 3rd century it was important part of the Saxon Shore. The south-west and north walls of the fort still extant and in places 25 ft (8 m) high. Within the walls are remains from Roman and Saxon times. (B12)

Romney Marsh Comprises Walland, Guldeford and Denge Marshes as well as Romney Marsh proper. The **Royal Military Canal** and sea make it practically an island. The name Romney is derived from the Anglo-Saxon 'Rumnea' – meaning marsh water. It is believed that the land has been reclaimed over generations and it is not known when reclamation was begun. Some of the reclamation was carried out during the Roman occupation, as discovered in the last century when a Roman pottery works was found near Dymchurch. The Marsh is one of the most deserted parts of England and extends from Hythe to the Sussex border. It is approximately 18 miles (29 km) long and 12 miles (19.2 km) across at the widest point. (E/F8/9)

Royal Military Canal (part NT) 23 miles (37 km) long, curving round **Romney Marsh** from the Rother near Rye to link with Hythe. It was built in 1804–6 as a defence against Napoleon. Partly tree-lined and a delightful place for a stroll. (F8 to E10)

Scotney Castle

Scotney Castle Garden (NT) Picturesque landscaped garden disposed around the ruins of a moated castle (occasionally used for exhibitions). The garden was created by the Hussey family in the 1840s. Access from A21. & (D6)

Sedlescombe A beautiful one-street village which broadens into the village green with pump and fountain. It is flanked with 16th- and 17th-century houses. The west tower of the original 14th/15th-century church remains but the rest is Victorian. (F6)

Sheffield Park Garden (NT) A garden of 100 acres (40.5 hectares) with five lakes, originally laid out by 'Capability' Brown. Has many mature trees, rare shrubs and water lilies. Particularly good autumn colours. Access from A275. & (F3)

Sissinghurst Castle Garden (NT) Created by the author Vita Sackville West, with her husband Sir Harold Nicolson. Spring garden and herb garden, Tudor buildings and tower. Famous for its roses in June and July and for the White Garden, where all the flowers are white and all leaves, silver. & (D7)

South Downs Way Route extends 80 miles (128 km) from Eastbourne in East Sussex (H5) to Buriton near the Hampshire border (Map 4 D8) and there are plans to extend it to Winchester. From east to west the route runs through **Alfriston** (H4), Southease (H3), Ditchling Beacon (G2), Devil's Dyke (G2), Chanctonbury Ring, near Findon (Map 4 E12), Houghton (Map 4 E11), Graffham Down (Map 4 D10), Linch Down (Map 4 D9). It also includes the cliff walk from Beachy Head (H5) to Cuckmere Haven, east of Seaford. This dry chalk track goes back as far as historical memory and probably was used by travellers to the ancient religious centre of **Stonehenge** (see Gazetteer 4) on Salisbury Plain. Chanctonbury Ring marks the site of an Iron Age fort and the ruins of a Roman Temple. Across the Weald, once dense forest, can be seen the North Downs and to the south, the coastline. Rudyard Kipling described these downs as 'whale backed' and the finest views are enjoyed at the former Beacon sites of Ditchling and Firle (G4) and at Devil's Dyke. The Way is well signposted in the more open eastern section by stone plinths and in the western section, which tends to be more wooded, by signs made of oak. The Way can be walked in a series of day trips from London. It is well serviced by bus and train and has railway stations at both ends – Eastbourne and Petersfield. See also **South Downs**, Gazetteer 4. (Map 4 D8 to Map 5 H5)

Spring Hill Wildfowl Park Lies 1¼ miles (2 km) south-west of the village of Forest Row. About 1,000 birds, including flamingoes, cranes, peacocks and swans, are to be seen in this 12 acre (5 hectare) Ashdown forest garden designed around a 15th-century house. & (E3)

The South Downs from Berwick

Standen (NT) A large family house of the 1890s, designed by Philip Webb, friend of William Morris – the only one of Webb's major houses to remain intact. William Morris textiles and wallpapers, period furniture, paintings and pottery. Hillside garden. & (D3)

Steyning Church Founded in 8th century by St Cuthman. Notable for the late Norman arches in the nave c. 1150. The aisles are c. 1050. Near to Purbeck marble font was found the pre-Christian 'Steyning Stone'. (G1)

Swanton Mill, Lower Mersham A 17th-century weather-boarded mill. Winner of a European Architectural Award and in full working order. Grinds wholemeal flour which is for sale. Has a milling museum. Garden with 3 acre (1.2 hectare) nature reserve, lake and trees. (D9)

Tenterden Church In the town where William Caxton the printer was born c. 1422. The 15th-century Perpendicular church tower is considered the finest example of its kind in Kent. (E7)

Union Mill, Stone Street, Cranbrook 75 ft (22 m) high and the tallest mill in southern England. It is a white smock mill built 1814 with fantail added 1840 and converted to steam 1863. (D6)

Wadhurst An old iron industry village of weather-boarded and tile-hung houses. The church dates in part from the 12th century. It has iron tomb slabs dated 1614–1790. (E5)

Wakehurst Place Gardens (NT) Created by Gerald W.E. Loder, later Lord Wakehurst, whose name lives on in the *loderi* group of rhododendrons. Now administered by the Royal Botanical Gardens, Kew. 460 acres (186 hectares) with lakes and ponds linked by picturesque water courses, flowering shrubs, exotic plants and rare trees. (E2)

Watermill Museum, Haxted A working watermill built c. 1600. Milling museum has working models and exhibits from Kent and Sussex watermills, picture gallery and slides shown with taped commentaries on the history of watermills and the Wealden iron industry. & (D3)

Woods Mill 1 mile (1.6 km) south of Henfield on A2037. Wildlife and countryside exhibition with audio-visual presentation in 18th-century watermill. Headquarters of the Sussex Trust for Nature Conservation. Self-guided nature trails in 15 acre (6 hectare) grounds. (G1)

Map 6

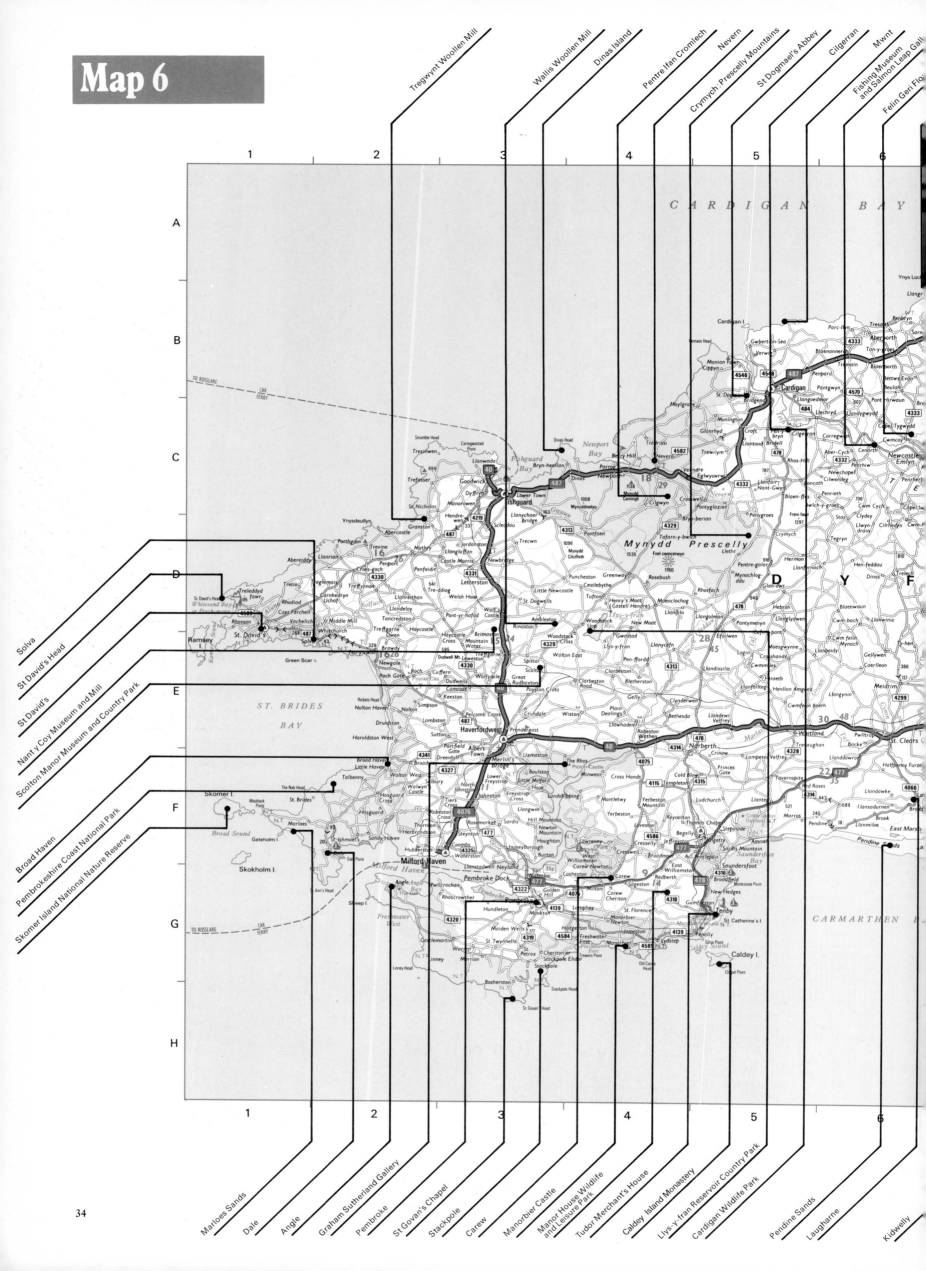

Tregwynt Woollen Mill

Wallis Woollen Mill

Dinas Island

Pentre Ifan Cromlech

Nevern

Crymych: Prescelly Mountains

St Dogmael's Abbey

Cilgerran

Mwnt

Fishing Museum and Salmon Leap Gallery

Felin Geri Flour

Solva

St David's Head

St David's

Nant y Coy Museum and Mill

Scolton Manor Museum and Country Park

Broad Haven

Pembrokeshire Coast National Park

Skomer Island National Nature Reserve

Marloes Sands

Dale

Angle

Graham Sutherland Gallery

Pembroke

St Govan's Chapel

Stackpole

Carew

Manorbier Castle

Manor House Wildlife and Leisure Park

Tudor Merchant's House

Caldey Island Monastery

Llys-y-fran Reservoir Country Park

Cardigan Wildlife Park

Pendine Sands

Laugharne

Kidwelly

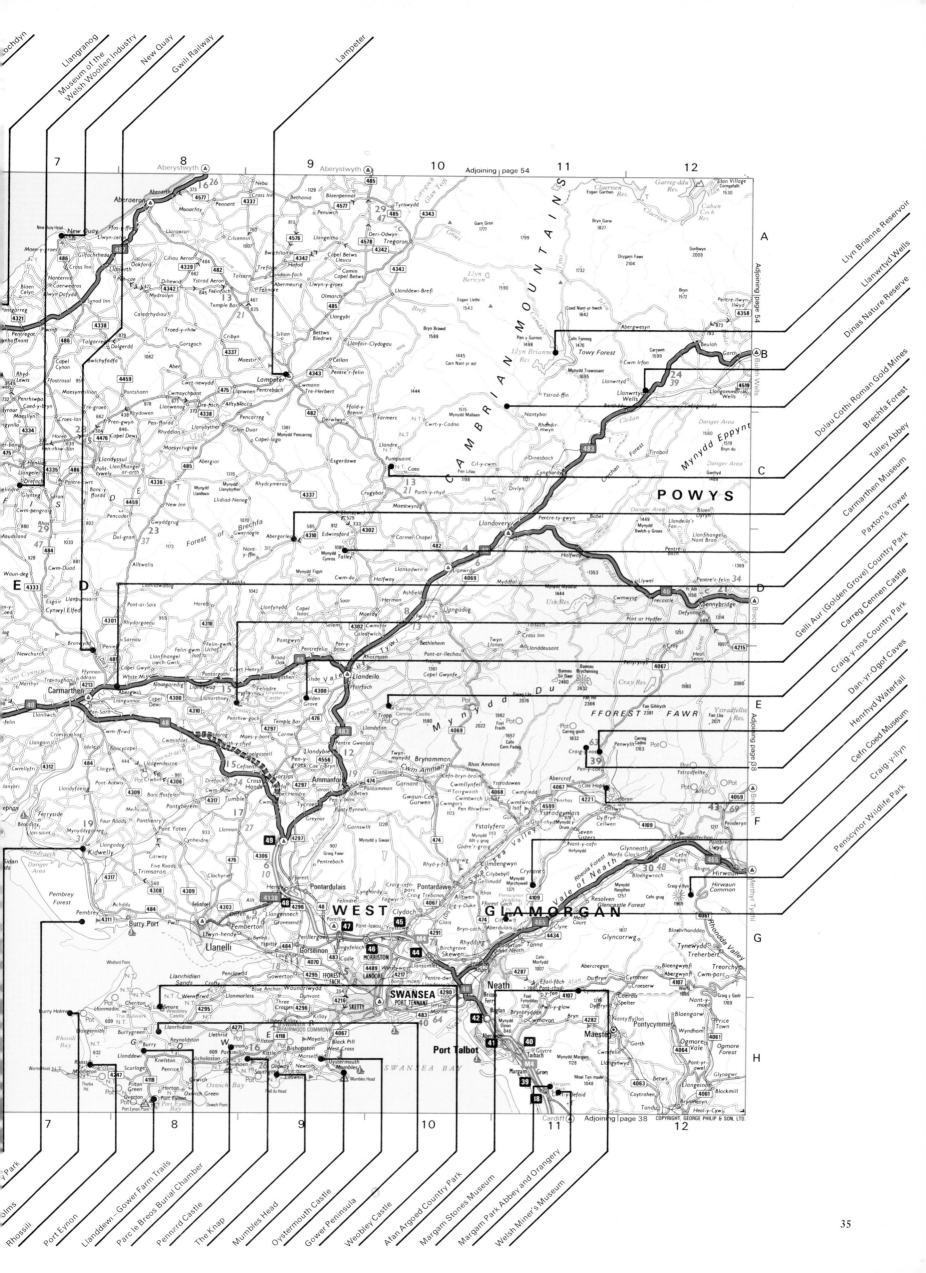

35

Gazetteer 6

South-West Wales

Afan Argoed Country Park Located in the lovely Afan Valley off A4107, near Cynonville. Waymarked, easy walks of 1–5 miles (1.6–8 km) from the countryside centre into surrounding forest. Fine views, picnic areas, nature trails, cycle hire centre. Park also contains **Welsh Miner's Museum.** ♿ (G11)

Angle Pretty fishing and lifeboat village with colonial-style Globe Inn. Good, sandy beach $\frac{1}{2}$ mile (0.8 km) west at West Angle Bay. (G2)

Brechfa Forest The starting point of a waymarked forest walk through the lovely Cothi Valley ($1\frac{3}{4}$ miles, 2.8 km) is on the east side of Abergorlech village where there is a picnic area beside a stream. (D9)

Broad Haven Extensive sandy beach and safe bathing has been attracting visitors here since the 19th century. National Park Information Centre in the car park provides a lot of details on the spectacular coastline. Car park is also starting point for guided walks. (F2)

Burry Holms Limestone island with remains of Iron Age earthwork fort. Access to the island when the causeway is dry. (H7)

Caldey Island Monastery Benedictines founded the first monastery in the 12th century, parts of which remain, returning early this century to build the present priory. In 1929, the Cistercians took over. They sell clotted cream and perfume to visitors but allow only men into the monastery. Ancient chapel has a stone with an inscription in Ogham, 8th-century script. Caldy measures $1\frac{1}{2}$ miles (2.4 km) by 1 mile (1.6 km) and lies $2\frac{1}{2}$ miles (4 km) offshore from Tenby. In summer there's a regular boat service from Tenby Harbour. (G5)

Cardigan Wildlife Park Specialises in Welsh and European breeds, past and present. Set in 50 acres (20 hectares) of natural habitats. Nature trails, local crafts, coracles, fishing. Entrance south of River Teifi on edge of Cilgerran village, with 1 mile (1.6 km) drive along old railway track. ♿ (C5)

Carew Hamlet with 2 buildings of interest. The castle dates from the 13th century and has an 11th-century cross at its entrance; Carew French Mill is the last tidal mill in Wales. There is a picnic site beside the mill pond. (G4)

Carmarthen Museum, Abergwili Well laid out local and prehistoric, Roman and medieval displays; also folk material, military history, costumes and ceramics. Housed in former Bishop's Palace. ♿ (E7)

Carreg Cennen Castle (WO) 13th-century ruin spectacularly sited with a precipitous drop on one side to the valley floor and overlooking the Black Mountains. (E10)

Cefn Coed Museum Mining machinery, including steam-winding engine, boilers, simulated underground mining gallery with exhibitions. Picnic area and nearby forest walks. On A4109 south of Crynant. ♿ (G11)

Cilgerran Village renowned for picturesque ruins of 13th-century castle (WO) above the River Teifi, which have inspired many artists, including Turner. ♿ Coracle races are held every August and beached coracles (their design hardly altered in 2,000 years) may often be seen on a former slate quay by the river, below the castle. (C5)

Craig-y-llyn Waymarked $2\frac{1}{2}$ mile (3.2 km) walk along a ridge affording panoramic views of the wooded Rhondda, Aberdare and Neath Valleys. Starts at Mynydd Beili-glas on A4061. (G12)

Craig-y-nos Country Park Series of walks in a small but pretty part of the upper Tawe Valley, in 40 acres (16 hectares) of woodland, within the Brecon Beacons National Park. Information centre. Demonstrations of country skills (sheep-shearing, horse-shoeing) and guided walks in summer. Picnic sites. (E11)

Crymych: Prescelly Mountains Energetic types will enjoy hiking on the gentle slopes of these mountains. Walk west on Bronze Age road; 6 miles (9.6 km) all at 1,000 ft (305 m). Numerous relics from Bronze and Stone Ages visible on route. (D5)

Dale Sheltered sea-shore yachting village with many sandy beaches surrounding it; said to be the sunniest place in Wales. A 6 mile (9.6 km) walk around the peninsula along the *Pembrokeshire Coast Path* starts from the Griffin Inn, passes Mill Bay (where Henry Tudor landed in 1485 to claim the English crown), an Iron Age promontory fort at Great Castle Head, and St Anne's lighthouse (open). See **Pembrokeshire Coast National Park.** (F2)

Dan-yr-Ogof Caves, Abercraf Western Europe's largest showcaves, with breathtaking, floodlit formations. Geological trail and Dinosaur Park, museum. (F11)

Dinas Island A circuit of this headland, which is divided from the mainland by a steep valley, can be made. It is about 3 miles (4.8 km) right round the 'island'; shorter walks of just over 1 mile (1.6 km) start from Pwllgwaelod (near Brynhenllan) on the west, or Cwm-yr-Eglwys on the east, to Dinas Point. The walk follows the cliff path, in parts quite steep, climbing to nearly 500 ft (152 m) at Dinas Head. Guidebook available from West Wales Naturalist's Trust, 20A High Street, Haverfordwest. (C3)

Dinas Nature Reserve (RSPB) Public nature trail of 2 miles (3.2 km) from car park by St Paulinus' Church $2\frac{1}{2}$ miles (4 km) north Rhandirmwyn, through oakwoods and river gorge. Many flowers and birds, including buzzard, raven, redstart, pied flycatcher. About 11 miles (18 km) north of Llandovery. (C11)

Dolau Cothi Roman Gold Mines (NT) Gold mining began almost as soon as the Romans had conquered Wales *c*. AD 80. The mines are clearly signposted off the A482 at Pumpsaint. Picnic site. 2 marked trails of $\frac{1}{2}$ mile (0.8 km) to 2 miles (3.2 km) start at Ogofau Lodge on the Cwrt-y-Cadno road and follow remains of Roman opencast workings and aqueduct system. (C10)

Felin Geri Flour Mill, Cwmcoy Built in 1604, this is one of the last remaining water-powered mills grinding wholemeal flour on a regular commercial basis. Rare water-powered saw mill, bakery shop and small museum. (C6)

Fishing Museum and Salmon Leap Gallery, Cenarth Ideally located adjacent to the foaming Cenarth Falls, this rod and line museum has over 300 exhibits, including 19th-century tackle and poaching equipment confiscated by local bailiffs. Coracles may still be seen on this stretch of the River Teifi. (C6)

Gelli Aur (Golden Grove) Country Park Gelli Aur mansion is a residential agricultural college and the public can enjoy the fine 99 acre (40 hectare) landscaped grounds during college vacations. Views, nature trails, arboretum. Access from the village of Golden Grove, lying between B4300 and A476, $3\frac{1}{2}$ miles (5.6 km) south-west of Llandeilo. Entrance is from a link road between A476 and B4300. (E9)

Gower Peninsula The first area in Britain designated 'An Area of Outstanding Natural Beauty', it stretches for some 14 miles (22.4 km) from The Mumbles to Worms Head in the west. Considering the Gower's proximity to Swansea and that it is a leisure paradise for the industrial towns of South Wales, it has remained very unspoilt. Many of the sandy bays on the south coast can only be reached on foot and are rarely crowded. Salt marshes are the more typical landscape in the north, while inland tiny hamlets nestle in wooded valleys. Ruined castles and ancient remains abound. Much of the south coast is managed by the National Trust, notably Thurba Head and a number of beauty spots including the 180 acres (73 hectares) of cliff scenery at Paviland Cliffs (west of Port Eynon) and the nature reserve at Whiteford Burrows in the north-west. (H7/8/9)

Graham Sutherland Gallery, Picton Castle Adapted building in courtyard near castle contains largest collection of Sutherland works available to the public. Extensive gardens, pleasant walks. There are also special exhibitions during summer months. ♿ (F3)

Gwili Railway, Bronwydd Arms First standard gauge steam passenger line in south Wales with $1\frac{3}{4}$ miles (3 km) operating from Bronwydd Arms to Llwyfan Cerrig picnic site. Road access at Bronwydd Arms only. (E7)

Henrhyd Waterfall (NT) An easy, $\frac{1}{2}$ mile (0.8 km) walk from Coelbren to the 90 ft (27.4 m) high falls on the Nabt Llech, on the southern edge of the Brecon Beacons National Park, 2 miles (3.2 km) east of Abercraf, between A4067 and B4109. (F11)

Kidwelly Castle

Kidwelly One of the oldest boroughs in Wales dominated by the extremely well-preserved 12th-century castle (WO) which commands superb views over the river estuary. (F7)

The Knap, Bishopston Valley Steep-sided ravine leading to remote and lovely Pwll-du Bay. An energetic walk of 6 miles (9.6 km) from Bishopston, returning via Hunts Farm, passes through cliff and woodland scenery. (H9)

Lampeter Market town with *St David's College*, founded 1822. Neo-Gothic buildings (1827) resemble Oxford colleges; library contains rare manuscripts. (B9)

Laugharne Pleasant little town with ruined castle, a few elegant Georgian houses, a church dating from the 13th century where poet Dylan Thomas is buried, and the boathouse where he lived on and off until his death in 1953 (usually open). (F6)

Llanddewi – Gower Farm Trails A walk in West Gower with three cut-off points at different distances (2–6 miles, 3.2–9.6 km) that examines the working of farms. Leaflet 'Gower Farm Trails' from Swansea Tourist Information Centre, Guildhall Kiosk. Walk starts from Llanddewi. (H8)

Llangranog Tiny, colourful village with miles of family, clifftop walks; north to the 540 ft (164 m) headlands of Ynys Lochdyn (NT) with two sandy coves and prehistoric earthworks, or south to the sandy beaches of Penbryn. (A6)

Llanwrtyd Wells Once 80,000 people a year visited this town in search of health, now holidaymakers come for the scenery and pony-trekking, but at Rock Park Pump Room, spa waters, said to alleviate gout, can still be taken. (B12)

Llyn Brianne Reservoir Located at the southern edge of the vast Towy Forest. Various easy-going walks start from the car park, reached by the Rhandirmwyn road from Llandovery. (B11)

Llys-y-fran Reservoir Country Park 308 acres (124.5 hectares) of pleasant countryside on the southern flank of the Prescelly Mountains. Main recreation is fishing (permits from warden's office at the cafeteria, signposted within park). Also picnic facilities, impressive views. A $7\frac{1}{2}$ mile (12 km) footpath circles the reservoir. Signposted off B4329. (E3)

Manorbier Castle Well-preserved remains of a moated Norman castle standing on the north slope of a valley about $\frac{1}{2}$ mile (0.8 km) from the shore, birthplace of historian Giraldus Cambrensis in 1146. (G4)

Manor House Wildlife and Leisure Park Apes, monkeys, otters, deer and birds in 12 acres (4.8 hectares) of wooded grounds. Children's amusements. Floral gardens. 1 mile (1.6 km) from St Florence, on B4318 to Tenby. (G4)

Margam Park Abbey and Orangery Within 850 acres (344 hectares) of fine park and woodland are the splendid 18th-century orangery, Tudor-Gothic Margam Castle, remains of an old Cistercian Abbey; also a herd of fallow deer, picnic areas, waymarked walks and a landscaped lake. ♿ (H11)

Margam Stones Museum Adjacent to Margam churchyard. Small collection of Early Christian and pre-Norman carved stones and crosses. Just outside country park; signposted. ♿ (H11)

Marloes Sands Nature trail (1 mile, 1.6 km), from car park 1 mile (1.6 km) west of village, exploring sandstone cliffs, Iron Age fort, Marloes Mere and giving splendid coastal views. Reached by a minor road leaving the B4327 north of Dale. (F1)

Mumbles Head Spectacular, easy cliff-top walk of 3 miles (4.8 km) to Langland and Caswell Bays. From Mumbles Head car park. (H9)

Museum of the Welsh Woollen Industry and Drefach-Felindre Trail, Llandyssul A branch of the National Museum of Wales, occupying site of the former Cambrian Mills. Textile machinery, dating back to the 18th century, a working mill, and an exhibition of photographs, trace the development of the woollen industry from the Middle Ages to modern times. Trail shows early stages in development of industry. ♿ (C7)

Mwnt (NT) A delightful sandy cove with car-parking at the top of the cliffs and a steep path down to the beach. At the foot of a hill rising 250 ft (76 m) to the north, from which Mwnt takes its name, is a white-washed church, one of the oldest in Wales. (B5)

Nant y Coy Museum and Mill, Treffgarne Collection of farmhouse furnishings, Victoriana. Nature walk in private grounds now a wildlife conservation area noted for Treffgarne Rocks, prominent for miles around. (E3)

Nevern Pretty village in secluded valley with Norman Church of St Brynach. Magolocunus Stone (Latin and Ogham inscription); Cross Stone (Viking pattern) and 10th-century cross in churchyard. (C4)

New Quay Delightful village with steep, winding streets, once a flourishing fishing port, now a popular holiday centre. Safe bathing. Bird colonies. (A7)

Oystermouth Castle Fine view of Swansea Bay from this castle which dates from about 1280. (H9)

Parc le Breos Burial Chamber (WO) One of the best preserved passage tombs in Wales, in 70 ft (21 m) cairn. ½ mile (0.8 km) north-west of Parkmill. (H8)

Paxton's Tower (NT) Triangular, triple-towered monument to Lord Nelson, built 1811. (E8)

Pembrey Country Park 520 acres (210 hectares) of pleasant parkland with unrestricted public access to beach, grassland and woodland. Guided walks; natural history exhibition. Several waymarked trails from visitor centre at woodland car park. Also, an adventure playground and miniature railway. Park signposted from A484 in Pembrey. (G7)

Pembroke Ancient borough was built around the great fortress of Pembroke Castle, once the hub of a complex, 14 mile (22.4 km) wide medieval defence system. Centuries-old fair takes place every October. (G3)

Pembrokeshire Coast National Park No part of this park, which covers 225 sq miles (583 sq km) is more than 10 miles (16 km) from the sea. It comprises the coastline from Amroth (F5) in the south to Cemaes (B5) in the north – a dramatic coast along which the sea has carved the predominantly limestone and old red sandstone cliffs into a jagged, indented shore. Other features include the deepwater harbour at Milford Haven, the Prescelly Mountains with their prehistoric remains, and an abundance of

Near Strumble Head, Pembrokeshire

castles. *The Pembrokeshire Coast Path* lies entirely within the national park. It was the first designated long-distance footpath in Wales, running 167 miles (269 km) from Amroth to St Dogmael's (B5). It traverses a coastline of tremendous variety with an abundance of wild flowers and wildlife all around. The line of the path is as near to the cliff edge as is practicable but over some stretches the path is forced back from the cliff as at Linney Head (G2), an MoD training area. There are only three towns of any size on the route – Tenby (G5), Pembroke (G3) and Fishguard (C3) – but the Milford Haven oil refineries (F2/3) should be avoided. Some of the finest views are on the stretch round St David's Head (D1). The coast and the offshore islands have some of the largest and most diverse seabird populations in Britain. Nature reserves (as on Skomer and Skokholm islands) and field centres (Dale Fort and Orielton, near Pembroke) have been established to enhance the public's appreciation of the area's natural beauty. (B5 to F5)

Pendine Sands 6 miles (9.6 km) of hard sands used in the 1920s by Sir Malcolm Campbell and J.G. Parry-Thomas for attempts on the world land speed record. Amy Johnson began her epic transatlantic flight here in 1933. All but the most western mile is now under military control but open unless MoD signs say otherwise. (F6)

Pennard Castle Extensive, crumbling ruins, standing high on a windswept crag, reached by a footpath ½ mile (0.8 km) south of Parkmill. (H9)

Penscynor Wildlife Park, Cilfrew 15 acres (6 hectares) on the slopes of a wooded hillside. Large bird collection (including cockatoos, flamingoes), and many animals, especially monkeys and chimpanzees. ⬧ (G11)

Pentre Ifan Cromlech (WO) Majestic, 5,000-year-old barrow, said to be the finest of its kind in Britain, is situated 3 miles (4.8 km) south-east of Newport off a minor road. (D4)

Port Eynon Attractive village and noted surfing centre, combining magnificent coastal views with interesting bird and plant life in seashore and cliff habitat. 2¾ mile (4.4 km) trail to Port Eynon Point along limestone cliffs starts from car park at end of A4118. (H8)

Rhossili A tiny village, but ideal centre from which to explore the superb coastal scenery. 3 mile (4.8 km) Gower coast nature trail starts from the car park, traverses cliffs with limestone flora. North is Rhossili Bay where sands are backed by a 3 mile (4.8 km) coastal hill walk to **Burry Holms**. West is islet of Worms Head, accessible at low tide. South is 4 mile (6.4 km) walk along 200 ft (61 m) high cliffs to spectacular Culver Hole south of **Port Eynon**. Much of coast is NT. (H7)

St David's Cathedral

St David's Despite a village atmosphere, this is a city by virtue of its 12th-century cathedral containing the shrine of St David and fascinating carvings. Across a brook are the ruins of the 14th-century Bishop's Palace (WO). (D1)

St David's Head (NT) Carn Llidi hill fort stands some 600 ft (182 m) above sea level with superb views on one of the National Trust's coastal stretches in the area. At the very end of St David's Head is a small Iron Age promontory fort with ramparts and several stone huts. Seals often seen in the bay. (D1)

St Dogmael's Abbey (St Mary the Virgin) (WO) Ruins of abbey founded *c.* 1115 for monks of the austere French order of Tiron. Fine carvings. (B5)

St Govan's Chapel, St Govan's Head Tiny, stone-built 13th-century chapel set in a cleft in the cliffs just above high-tide mark. Only reached by footpath from above. Off B4319, via Bosherston. *No access when Castlemartin firing range is in use.* (H3)

Scolton Manor Museum and Country Park Late Georgian mansion housing display of history of area. Set in 40 acres (16 hectares) of parkland with many fine trees. Arboretum, nature trail, butterfly centre, picnic sites. Countryside centre with natural history displays. Entrance east of Spittal, on B4329 Haverfordwest to Cardigan. ⬧ (E3)

Skomer Island National Nature Reserve Covering some 700 acres (283 hectares) and noted for excellent seabird colonies. Two routes around the island;

no permit required. It lies 1 mile (1.6 km) from the mainland and boat trips can be arranged from Martin's Haven, just east of Wooltack Point. Small landing charge. (F1)

Solva Tiny, pretty, hillside village, convenient starting point for rambles along St David's Peninsula and visits to National Trust properties in area. Row of disused, 19th-century limekilns may be seen on the hill on the east side of a fiord-like creek near the road bridge. (E2)

Stackpole 8 miles (12.8 km) of National Trust coast, and a good centre for walking with paths giving access to cliffs, woods, bays, lakes. Wide variety of flora and fauna. (G3)

Talley Abbey (WO) Ruins of abbey founded late 12th century for French order. Lovely setting at head of the Talley Lakes. (D9)

Tregwynt Woollen Mill, St Nicholas This probably developed from an early fulling mill in the 18th century and has worked continuously ever since. Pretty location. ⬧ (C2)

Tudor Merchant's House, Tenby (NT) Good example of merchant's house of late 15th century. Early wall paintings. (G5)

Wallis Woollen Mill, Ambleston Working mill, established 1812, with a flannel press dating back to 1795. Audio-visual presentation. (D3)

Welsh Miner's Museum, Cynonville Located in **Afan Argoed Country Park**. Exhibits of local history, industry and wildlife. Visitors can wander through a recreated coal mine. ⬧ (G11)

Weobley Castle (WO) Well-fortified manor house in attractive setting, built 13th to 14th centuries, restored and modified in Tudor times. ⬧ (H8)

Ynys Lochdyn National Trust 'island' reached by a cliff path from Llangranog. Many seabirds and seals. (A6)

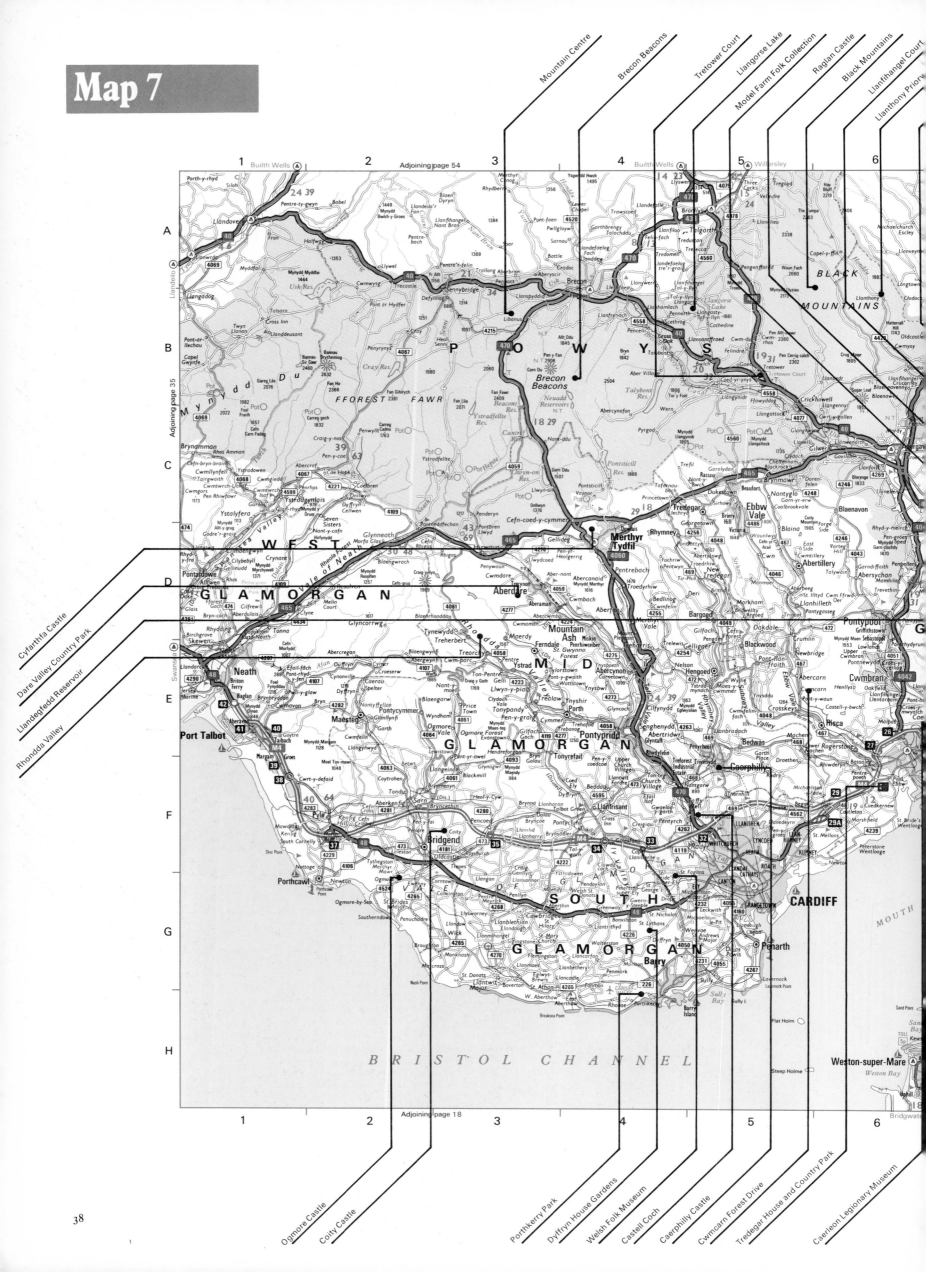

Map 7

Mountain Centre
Brecon Beacons
Tretower Court
Llangorse Lake
Model Farm Folk Collection
Raglan Castle
Black Mountains
Llanfihangel Court
Llanthony Priory

Cyfarthfa Castle
Dare Valley Country Park
Llandegfedd Reservoir
Rhondda Valley

Ogmore Castle
Coity Castle
Porthkerry Park
Dyffryn House Gardens
Welsh Folk Museum
Castell Coch
Caerphilly Castle
Cwmcarn Forest Drive
Tredegar House and Country Park
Caerleon Legionary Museum

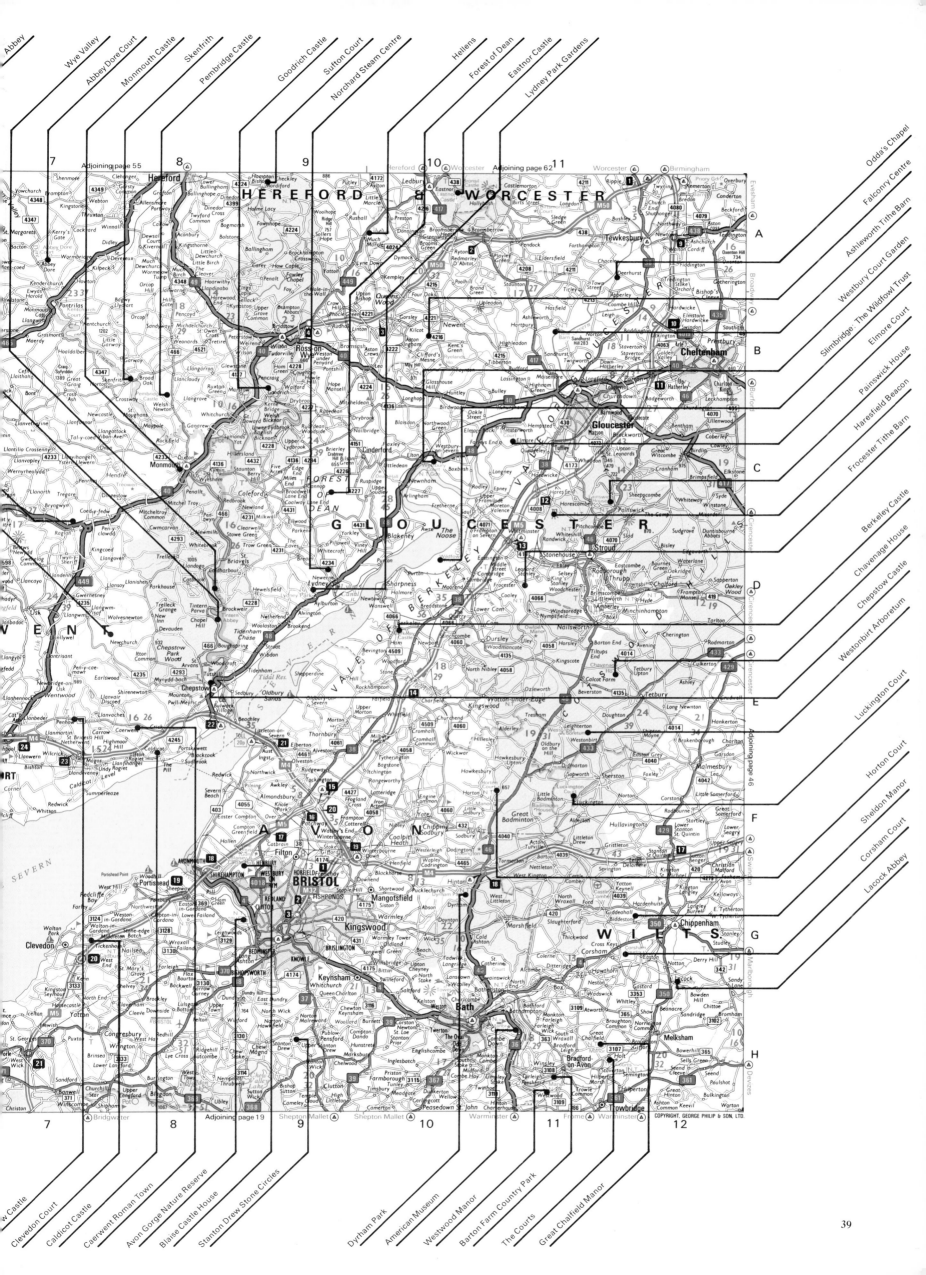

South Wales and Severn Estuary

Abbey Dore Court Recently reclaimed 4 acre (1.5 hectare) garden bordered by river Dore. Many herbaceous plants and shrubs, fern border, circular herb garden area, walled garden with unusual plants, orchard and vines. ⌂ (A7)

American Museum, Claverton Manor First museum of its kind established outside the US. Reconstructed interiors of American homes from late 17th to 19th century. Sections tell the story of the American Indian and the opening of the West. ⌂ (H11)

Ashleworth Tithe Barn (NT) On west bank of river Severn, stone built 15th-century barn, 120 ft (37 m) long, with two projecting porch bays and interesting roof timbering. (B11)

Avon Gorge Nature Reserve (NT) 159 acres (64 hectares) of woods giving shelter to unusual flowers and fungi. Iron Age hill fort. No marked route, visitors may wander at will. Access from A369. (G8/9)

Barton Farm Country Park, Bradford-on-Avon 36 acre (4 hectare) park surrounded by an outstanding group of medieval and later buildings which include a 14th-century tithe barn and 8th-century Saxon church. Flanked on one side by the Kennet and Avon canal and on the other by the river Avon. Access south of river bridge. ⌂ (H11)

Berkeley Castle Great medieval fortress overlooking Severn estuary, home of the Berkeley family since 1153, still entered by a bridge over the moat with the keep looming high above. Scene in 1327 of the brutal murder of Edward II, buried in a martyr's grave in Gloucester cathedral. (D10)

Black Mountains Mountain mass within **Brecon Beacons** National Park bounded by rivers Usk and **Wye** with narrow ridges separating the valleys. Pen-y-Gadair Fawr 2,624 ft (779 m), near Mynydd Llysiau (B5) and Waun Fach (B5) 2,660 ft (800 m) are the highest points. Fine ridge walks and one road from Llanthony (B6) to Hay (Map 10, H8) give magnificent views. The best known valley is the Honddu (A6), the best known touring centre Abergavenny (C6). (A/C6)

Blaise Castle House Mansion containing interesting museum of West Country life 1750–1900 set in extensive woodlands and gardens landscaped by Humphry Repton and decorated with buildings designed by John Nash. Access off A4018. ⌂ (F9)

Brecon Beacons Designated a national park in 1957, this mountain range was named from its use for signal fires and stretches 40 miles (64 km) from Hay-on-Wye (Map 10, H8) and Abergavenny (C6) to Llandeilo near Carmarthen (Map 6, E9). Highest of the old red sandstone peaks at its centre is Pen-y-Fan (B3), 2,906 ft (886 m). Popular walking and pony trekking area. Park information centres at Glamorgan St, Brecon (B4), Monk St, Abergavenny (C6), 8 Broad St, Llandovery (Map 6, D11) and Libanus (B3).

Caerleon Legionary Museum (Cadw) On the site of the Roman station of Isca, built AD 75 to house 2nd Augustan Legion and covering 50 acres (20 hectares). Excavations have revealed riverside quay, magnificent amphitheatre and much else. The museum has good displays of weapons, sculpture and inscriptions. ⌂ (E6)

Caerphilly Castle

Caerphilly Castle (Cadw) Imposing shell of one of largest castles in Europe, in Britain second only in size to Windsor. It was built 1271 and has an intricate system of water defences. Cromwell's cannon are supposed to have blasted the famous 'leaning tower' 9 ft (2.7 m) out of true. ⌂ (F5)

Caerwent Roman Town (Cadw) Impressive remains of Venta Silurum, market town of the Silures tribe founded by the Romans in AD 75. It continued to be occupied until AD 350. It had a basilica, forum, temples, heated baths, houses and shops all laid out on a grid pattern. Not all of it has been excavated. ⌂ (E8)

Caldicot Castle Norman castle with 13th-century round keep on a mound and a 14th-century gatehouse on the south flanked by towers, forming the centrepiece of a country park of 49 acres (20 hectares). Museum collection includes period rooms, local history and craft exhibits. (E8)

Castell Coch (Cadw) Enchanting castle, a mixture of Victorian Gothic fantasy and medieval romance, with distinctive round towers and conical turrets and set on a wooded hillside. Originally built by Earl Gilbert de Clare in the 13th century, it was recreated in the 19th century by the 3rd Marquess of Bute. Inside, the extravagant decoration includes fantastic murals depicting Aesop's Fables, and a spectacular blue and gold rib-vaulted ceiling, adorned with painted birds and carved butterflies. Access from A470. (F5)

Chavenage House Cotswold manor house on an E plan with two projecting wings and a central porch. The most impressive rooms are the great hall, with its original screen, fireplace and old stained glass, and the two bedrooms lined with tapestries where Cromwell and one of his generals slept. ⌂ (E12)

Chepstow Castle (Cadw) Perched on a cliff above the Wye, the earliest Norman stone castle in Wales, with a great gatehouse, soaring towers and massive defences spanning many periods. A curtain wall divides the middle and lower baileys. (E8)

Clevedon Court (NT) Charming 14th-century manor house, once part fortified, incorporating 12th-century tower and 13th-century hall and housing a collection of Nailsea glass and Eltonware. Terraced gardens with rare shrubs. (G7)

Coity Castle (Cadw) One of the castles built to defend the fertile Vale of Glamorgan. The oldest surviving parts, the square keep and polygonal curtain wall, date from the 12th century. The gatehouses, living quarters and round tower were added later. ⌂ (F3)

Corsham Court Fascinating Elizabethan mansion containing notable paintings set in park landscaped by 'Capability' Brown. Part of the house is used by the Bath Academy of Art. ⌂ (G12)

The Courts, Holt (NT) Garden of 7 acres (3 hectares) with topiary, lily pond

and arboretum of interest to both professional and amateur. Access from A3053. ⌂ (H11)

Cwmcarn Forest Drive Waymarked route of 7 miles (11 km) laid out by the Forestry Commission through mixed coniferous woodland east from Cwmcarn with fine views over the Bristol Channel. From A467 south of Abercarn. (E5)

Cyfarthfa Castle, Merthyr Tydfil Mock Gothic castellated house built for William Crawshay II, famous Merthyr ironmaster, in 1824. Set in beautiful parkland, the house overlooks a lake which supplied water to the ironworks nearby. The building now houses the town museum and art gallery. Access from A470. (D4)

Dare Valley Country Park 477 acres (193 hectares) of reclaimed industrial land surrounded by mountains, with lakes and moorland walks. Visitor centre. Access off B4277 west of Aberdare. (D3)

Dyffryn House Gardens, St Nicholas Magnificent landscaped botanic gardens created by Reginald Cory, a well-known horticulturist. ⌂ (G4)

Dyrham Park (NT) Mansion built 1691–1702, still with most of its original furnishings and interior decor. Fine paintings. Parkland of 263 acres (106 hectares) with herd of fallow deer. Concealed drive on A46. ⌂ (G10)

Dyrham Park

Eastnor Castle Massive stone building with corner towers and cast iron roof built by Smirke 1812–15 for the 1st Lord Somers. Some elaborate plasterwork, collection of armour, 17th-century tapestries and frescoes brought from Carlton House Terrace in London. ⌂ (A10)

Elmore Court Elizabethan house still with much of its original Renaissance furniture and tapestries. (C11)

Falconry Centre, Newent Large collection of birds of prey, with breeding aviaries, hawk walk or weathering ground where trained birds may be seen and flying ground where – except when it rains – they exercise. Access 1 mile (1.6 km) south-west on Clifford's Mesne road. ⌂ (B10)

Forest of Dean Royal forest of beech and oak isolated by rivers **Wye** and Severn. Covers 200 sq miles (518 sq km) which includes a national forest park of 57 sq miles (147 sq km). This is one of the oldest coal mining areas in Britain, still with several privately-owned pits. Many interesting walks and drives. 'Capital' of the forest is the small town of Coleford. (C9)

Frocester Tithe Barn Well-preserved 13th-century tithe barn, 184 ft (56 m) long, 30 ft (9 m) wide and 36 ft (11 m) high to roof ridge, the walls being 12 ft (3.5 m) high to the eaves. Inside are 13 bays divided by raised base crucks (uprights) which support the great weight of the stone tiled roof. The barn stands in the grounds of Frocester Court, originally the court house of a monastic estate. (D11)

Goodrich Castle (EH) Ruined fortress, dating mainly from the 13th century, built to guard a crossing of the Wye. (B9)

Great Chalfield Manor (NT) Restored 15th-century manor house with great hall, screen and contemporary mural portrait of the builder, mainly of specialist architectural interest. (H11)

Haresfield Beacon (NT) 713 ft (217 m) high hill giving views over the Severn, the likely site of a promontory fort. It forms part of a 348 acre (140 hectare) NT property on the northern edge of the Cotswolds. (C11)

Hellens, Much Marcle Charming Jacobean manor house remodelled in the 17th century where the Black Prince and Bloody Mary stayed. Many original furnishings and collection of 19th-century carriages. (A10)

Horton Court (NT) Cotswold manor house with 12th-century Norman hall. There is a medieval ambulatory or covered walk separate from the house. ⌂ (F11)

Lacock Abbey (NT) Augustinian abbey founded 1232 and converted to country house in 1539 with medieval cloisters, sacristy and chapter house. At entrance gates Fox Talbot museum of early photography commemorates pioneer work done by William Henry Fox Talbot 1800–77. The village, also NT, is considered one of the most picturesque in England. ⌂ (G12)

Llandegfedd Reservoir Vast expanse of water popular for sailing and fishing. Near car park on south shore is *Llandegfedd Farm Park* with a rare breed collection and displays of farm implements. Access from A4042. (D6)

Llanfihangel Court Fine Elizabethan manor house remodelled in the 17th century with a beautifully furnished interior and magnificent gardens. Concealed drive on east side of A465. (B6)

Llangorse Lake In a beautiful setting, Wales's second largest natural lake which lends itself to every kind of water sport and is particularly popular with anglers. Boat hire. Traces of a prehistoric settlement have been found on the island in the lake. Access from B4560. (B5)

Llanthony Priory (Cadw) Majestic ruins of 12th-century Augustinian priory. Most of the monastic buildings are now occupied by a hotel but there are extensive remains of the church. ⟨⟩ (A6)

Luckington Court Magnificent group of buildings mainly of Queen Anne period (seen by appointment) set in formal gardens with fine collection of ornamental trees and shrubs. ⟨⟩ (F11)

Lydney Park Gardens Famous valley garden of 8 acres (3.2 hectares) with trees, lakes and many varieties of flowering shrubs, particularly rhododendrons and azaleas. Deer park with specimen trees, Roman temple site and museum. (D9)

Model Farm Folk Collection and Craft Centre, Wolvesnewton Agricultural and domestic life since the time of Queen Victoria including fascinating collection of farm wagons, carts and sleds. Craft centre. ⟨⟩ (D8)

Monmouth Castle (Cadw) Ruined fortress where Henry V – then known as Harry of Monmouth – was born 1387. The oldest part is the two-storey Great Tower dating from the 12th century. In Norman times the castle was the hub of a highly effective defence system, part of which was the fortified Monnow gate over the river, the only surviving example of its kind in Britain. ⟨⟩ (C8)

Lacock village

dating from 1056 commemorating Odda's brother Alfric. Nearby is the Saxon church of St Mary with a documented history from 804. ⟨⟩ (A11)

Ogmore Castle (Cadw) Ruined Norman castle with remains of rectangular three-storey keep and curtain wall against pleasant backdrop of tidal river and sand dunes. (G2)

France in the wake of William the Conqueror. (E7)

Porthkerry Park Seaside country park of 225 acres (91 hectares) in valley flanked by wooded hills and ending in pebble beach. Picnic and games areas adjoin car park and there are paths through the woods. Access ½ mile (0.8 km) west of Barry off B4266. (H4)

Raglan Castle (Cadw) Imposing and extensive angular ruins of border castle enlarged in the 15th and again in the 16th century. Most impressive are the Great or Yellow Tower, moated from the elaborate living quarters, and the Great Hall, the best preserved of the later buildings. ⟨⟩ (C7)

Rhondda Valley Rhondda Fawr (Great Rhondda) and, branching off it to the east at Porth, Rhondda Fach (Little Rhondda), typical of the industrialised valleys of South Wales, stand on what was once the most intensively mined coalfield in the world. They set the scene for a unique anthill culture with every close-knit community having its library, chapel and club and every other one its brass band or male voice choir. Now all the collieries are closed and many local people work elsewhere. In recent years there has been greater appreciation of the industrial heritage of the valleys and their often beautiful scenery and breathtaking views. (E3)

Sheldon Manor Charming Jacobean manor house with 13th-century porch and detached chapel of the 15th century. The interior is crammed with fascinating bric-à-brac. Terraced garden with many rare trees and shrubs. ⟨⟩ (G12)

Skenfrith Delightful old village on Welsh bank of river Monnow dominated by its castle (NT) which, with nearby Grosmont and the White Castle near Llantilio Crossenny, guarded the western frontier of England in the days of the Normans. The castle was rebuilt in 1232 on a rectangular plan enclosing a round keep with towers at the angles of the curtain walls. ⟨⟩ There are welcoming old inns in the village and the church contains an altar tomb and minstrels' gallery. (B8)

Slimbridge: The Wildfowl Trust Well-equipped breeding and research station for swans, geese and ducks of almost every known species. Rarer species are kept in pens but many birds live in open enclosures. With 2,500 birds of more than 180 species the Trust now has the largest collection of waterfowl in the world. ⟨⟩ (D10)

Stanton Drew Stone Circles Three stone circles in meadow probably erected 1800 BC. Near the churchyard is a trio of huge stones of equally mysterious purpose. (H9)

Sufton Court, Mordiford Small 18th-century Palladian mansion designed by James Wyatt set in grounds landscaped by Humphry Repton. Contains antique china, lace and embroideries. (A9)

Tintern Abbey (Cadw) Cistercian abbey founded 1131 in a beautiful setting in Wye Valley. Ruins covering 27 acres (11 hectares) include church of unusual

Tintern Abbey

length. The Anchor Inn was originally the abbey's watergate. ⟨⟩ (D8)

Tredegar House and Country Park Fine baroque mansion of 17th century with imposing north-east and north-west fronts, stable block and orangery, surrounded by park of 90 acres (36 hectares) with picnic sites, children's farm, visitor centre and exhibition and lake for fishing and boating. West of Newport off A48 near junction 28 of M4. (F6)

Tretower Court (Cadw) Fine example of fortified medieval manor house built around central courtyard. The original owners moved there from the now ruined castle nearby. ⟨⟩ (B5)

Usk Castle Small ruined castle overlooking the river, still with its 12th-century keep, round towers and curtain walls. Open by appointment. (D7)

Welsh Folk Museum Centuries' old buildings from all parts of Wales re-erected in a woodland setting of 100 acres (40 hectares) around the Elizabethan mansion of St Fagan's Castle. Many of the buildings are working exhibits. (F4)

Westbury Court Garden (NT) Unique 17th-century formal water garden, the earliest surviving example of its kind in England, with canals and yew hedges. ⟨⟩ (C10)

Westonbirt Arboretum One of the world's finest collections of trees started 1829 and covering 581 acres (232 hectares). Managed by Forestry Commission. Many rare specimens. Visitors' Centre. Access from A433. ⟨⟩ (E11)

Westwood Manor (NT) 15th-century stone manor house remodelled in the late 16th century, with fine plasterwork. Modern topiary garden. Access off B3109. (H11)

Wye Valley Famous salmon river rising on Plynlimon and flowing for 130 miles (209 km) in wide loops to its confluence with the Severn. Most beautiful are the wooded lower reaches from Monmouth to Chepstow. Famous beauty spots and viewpoints along the river are **Goodrich Castle** (B9), Symonds Yat (C9), just east of the village, and **Tintern Abbey** (D8), whose grounds are the starting point for waymarked forest walks. (E8 to A9)

Mountain Centre, Libanus Information on **Brecon Beacons** National Park, picnic area, lounge, starting point of waymarked walks, magnificent views. ¾ mile (1.2 km) from A470; signposted. (B3)

Norchard Steam Centre, New Mills Steam and diesel locomotives, rolling stock and equipment with station, railway buildings and track. 1 mile (1.6 km) north-west of Lydney on B4234. ⟨⟩ (D9)

Odda's Chapel, Deerhurst (EH) Attached to half-timbered house, chapel

Painswick House 18th-century Palladian mansion enlarged 1827 by Basevi who added a wing on each side, one of which is given over to a vast dining-room. Concealed drive off B4073. (C11)

Pembridge Castle Small 13th-century moated border castle with impressive gatehouse, chapel and delightful central courtyard. (B8)

Penhow Castle Oldest inhabited Norman border castle in Wales, once the home of the famous Seymour (St Maur) family, who came from Touraine in

Royal Forests

When the Normans produced the famous Domesday survey in the 11th century Britain was heavily wooded and forests dominated the lives of ordinary people, none more so than in those parts earmarked as royal hunting grounds where the game was the preserve of the king. Folk living in such areas were subject to harsh and complex forest laws, outside the common law. William I introduced the forest laws and later monarchs increased the number of royal forests until there was one or more in every English county – a valuable source of fresh meat for the court as it moved from place to place. Most important of the game were the deer, though boar provided better sport. Timber was royal property too and no one was allowed to cut the undergrowth and thickets giving food and shelter to the deer.

Forest dwellers' dogs had to have their claws cut and in the breeding season in mid-summer all movement through the forest was restricted. Fences had to be low enough for the deer to jump in and out of crops and commoners' rights to graze their own animals were strictly controlled. Any poachers caught were invariably hanged as an example to others but lesser culprits were penalised by way of dues and fines, a lucrative source of revenue for the Crown.

Royal forests were not so much uninterrupted woodland as open heath and scrub interspersed with glades. Some had hardly any woodland at all. Forest laws were administered by various officers, most of them unpaid. They included the warden of the forest, the foresters of fee, the regarders, the woodwards and the elected verderers, the only ancient office to survive. Chases such as Malvern Chase and Cranborne Chase were areas where the hunting rights had been given by royal grant to private individuals. To enclose part of a chase – where deer could be fattened or tree seedlings

protected – still required a licence from the king. As chases were deforested the number of deer dwindled and foxhunting developed instead.

Although many royal forests have dwindled in size since they were hunting grounds, notable areas do still remain today. Most famous of these is the New Forest in Hampshire, decreed a royal hunting ground by William the Conqueror in 1079 – for whom it was literally a 'new forest'. Now mostly in the care of the Forestry Commission, it covers 105 sq miles (272 sq km) and is a mecca for walkers, riders and naturalists, being criss-crossed by miles of good paths and full of wildlife of all kinds, including deer. Although much of the Forest is wooded (species include oak, ash, chestnut and beech), the trees are often broken up by streams, ponds and glades and there are also areas of heath and moorland and villages included within its borders. The region was an important source of oak for the Royal Navy; many boats were built there during the time of Nelson's command and launched from Buckler's Hard.

Even older is the Forest of Dean, where Canute hunted deer. But this royal forest was much more than a mere hunting ground. Long before the

Normans arrived it had its miners and woodcutters, the miners using primitive picks and shovels to extract haematite iron ore from the carboniferous limestone, the woodcutters and charcoal burners supplying the fuel for smelting the ore in forge and furnace.

In medieval times the timber of the Dean was in demand for mining, shipbuilding and house construction. Oak bark was called for on an increasing scale for tanning. But the greatest need was for coppice and branch wood for poles and staves which, added to the damage caused by the browsing of deer, boar and other animals, meant not only that a lot of timber went to waste but also that little regeneration took place.

Some mines still exist in the Dean, worked by 'free miners', the descendants of those granted special privileges by the early Plantagenet kings as a reward for services rendered in war. The mining rights originally applied only to iron ore but were later extended to cover coal and other minerals.

Towards the end of the 16th century the use of the forest as a royal hunting preserve began to decline while its importance as a source of timber for the Royal Navy grew. In the 17th century the Dean was still supplying most of the oak for shipbuilding with little thought being given to replanting the trees that were felled. From 1600 to 1650 the forest was exploited as never before, first with the introduction of blast furnaces consuming vast quantities of charcoal, then with the Stuart kings granting wholesale timber and mining concessions. In 1640 the process culminated in Charles I selling almost the whole of the Dean to Sir John Wintour

of Lydney, including its minerals and ironworks. Fellings increased and although one-sixth of the forest was fenced off to protect young trees local people petitioned the Crown to restore their grazing rights and the devastation continued. By 1670 there was not a single timber-size tree left.

In 1668 a reafforestation act authorised the Crown to fence off 11,000 acres (4,450 hectares) at any one time and to limit the deer in the forest to 800. New verderers were appointed and the forest divided into six walks, each under a keeper. But troubles with the miners and the commoners continued. In the late 18th century fellings were on a vast scale, reaching a peak during the Napoleonic Wars. Nelson visited the Dean in 1803 and was critical of its management, insisting that the oak plantations needed to be heavily thinned to promote wide spreading crowns suitable for ship timber. By that time forests covered no more than 5 per cent of Britain's land area and those in authority began to recognise the danger of a country being dependent on others for its timber. With the appointment of a new deputy surveyor in 1808 a steady programme of reafforestation took place in the Dean up to the 1850s, giving the forest the 'traditional' appearance it has today.

Covering 57 sq miles (147 sq km) the forest of Dean is one of the most fascinating regions in England. Isolated by the tidal rivers of the Severn and the Wye, it has preserved a pattern of land use quite different from its neighbours. A countryside of small farms interspersed with woodlands and commons, it is dotted with mines and quarries and its high ground commands fine views, as do its famous vantage points along the Wye. In 1924 the Dean was transferred to the Forestry Commission and in 1938 the Commissioners made it England's first national forest park. Pedestrian access is virtually unrestricted; there are some 30 miles (48 km) of waymarked paths, 12 nature trails and forest walks and one signposted scenic drive, with marked picnic places and viewpoints on the route. In common with several other former royal hunting grounds this forest, once the preserve of the privileged and wealthy, now forms a valuable area of accessible countryside visited by thousands every year.

The New Forest (below centre) is probably the most visited of surviving Royal Forests, its ponies (below left) being a particular feature. Although now largely a tourist attraction, it was formerly of major importance as a source of timber for shipbuilding. Today many trees still bear evidence of former pollarding for free wood by those with rights to the forest (above, far left). The *massive oak trees of Sherwood Forest were also in great demand for shipbuilding and a few of them can still be seen. Major Oak (below), measuring 9 m (30 ft) around the trunk, is still alive and growing. The Forest of Dean was important not only for its wood but also for its mineral resources. A few mines still exist but most have been abandoned and the tips are being recolonised by the* *forest (above centre). The Forest of Dean encompasses some particularly fine scenery within its borders and includes famous vantage points along the Wye, such as Symonds Yat (above).*

Bridges

Bridges are essentially romantic structures. No matter of what period, size or style each has presented somebody with a challenge, and because each challenge has differed from any other each bridge is an individual structure. Even the humblest bridge across a small stream represents a forward step by mankind, a leap to the opposite bank, with character and personality added through the materials used and the building methods of the time. Few bridges are ugly; many are beautiful, with graceful curves and rhythms, interesting textures, lights and shadows, changing colours and reflections.

Primitive bridges were stone slabs – single slabs for a clam, multiple ones for a clapper (as at Dartmoor's Postbridge and Tarr Steps on the edge of Exmoor). These bridges were used for centuries and survivals could be medieval, or 2,000 years old, or comparatively recent. The clapper bridges at Lower Slaughter, Bourton-on-the-Water and Eastleach Martin – all in Cotswold country – are 18th century. None of Britain's Roman bridges survives, but the massive stone abutments of a Roman timber bridge across the North Tyne can still be seen near Chollerford.

In medieval times fords were the commonest type of river crossing. The earliest important bridges were usually built at two places on a river – the lowest point where it could be crossed and a port established (as at London) and the lowest point fordable in all weathers (as at Wallingford). By the 13th century stone was beginning to replace timber for bridge-building, and the oldest surviving bridges look sturdy and solid, with strong piers whose pointed cutwaters were often extended upwards to make triangular refuges in the roadway for pedestrians. Ribbed arches, the earliest ones pointed, made a lighter structure and saved material.

Among the best medieval bridges are those at Durham, Bradford-on-Avon, Bakewell, East Farleigh (Kent), Swarkestone and Geddington (in the Midlands) and – one of the oldest – Sturminster Marshall (Dorset) where White Mill Bridge dates from 1175. This is one of several Dorset bridges with 'Transportation for Life' metal plates fixed to a parapet – notices dating from 1827–8 when an Act was passed to try to stop vandalism! Radcot Bridge, near Faringdon, Berkshire, is one of the oldest of Thames bridges (14th century), and retains on one parapet a raised stone which has a

recess that may have been a plague-bowl or font, or the socket of an old cross.

Monasteries, religious guilds, town corporations and private landowners were responsible for much early bridge-building, financed mainly from private bequests or church indulgences, with subsequent maintenance covered frequently by tolls. Wool merchants' fortunes probably endowed the splendid estuary bridges at Bideford and Barnstaple in Devon, Wadebridge in Cornwall, and Sir Hugh Clopton's fine stone span at Stratford-upon-Avon, now only half its original length, but whose fourteen arches are strong enough to carry today's very heavy volume of traffic. Two fortified bridges survive, at Monmouth, where a massive 13th-century tower dominates Monnow Bridge, and at Warkworth, Northumberland, whose fortification is smaller and more ruinous, but in a most delightful setting.

Three bridges retain the chapels with which they were formerly dedicated – Wakefield and Rotherham (Yorkshire) and, best of all, St Ives (Cambridgeshire). The corbelling of the medieval chapel on the bridge at Bradford-on-Avon (Wiltshire) was used to support a lock-up built in the 17th century. Lincolnshire has the unique Crowland Bridge, a three-way arch to nowhere, originally spanning streams, now dry land. Probably built in 1360 by the local abbey as a symbol of the Trinity, it is graced by a weather-worn statue that may represent a saint, or a Saxon king, or Our

Lord. Twizel Bridge, in the Border region of Northumberland, has the longest single-arch medieval span in Britain, its delicate shape anticipating the many plain stone arches which proliferated in the 16th and 17th centuries.

Until the Renaissance bridge-builders were mainly anonymous, local stonemasons who applied their craft in the materials they knew and using the techniques of the day. Although bridges continued to be built in the medieval manner – Berwick, Corbridge, Stirling, Ross-on-Wye – Palladian ideas introduced lighter piers and wider arches, and named architects enter the story. Landowners added classical bridges to their estates as at Blenheim, 1711 (Vanbrugh) and Wilton, 1737, designs that were copied at Stowe and Bath. Other examples are at Chatsworth, 1762, and Wallington, about the same time. Colonnades and balustrades, pierced spandrels and niched piers added grace and elegance to handsome stone bridges in the 18th century across the Thames, Severn, Tyne, Dee, Tay, and other major rivers. Indeed, most counties possess good examples of such classical bridges, the style persisting throughout much of the 19th century, although the Industrial Revolution had, in 1779, introduced the world's first iron bridge over the Severn in Shropshire. Britain's greatest bridge-builder, Telford, was using the new material by the end of the century, first in canal aqueducts (Chirk and Pontcysyllte), and subsequently in his

superb structures at Betws-y-coed and Craigellachie (across the Spey), but he learned his craft as a stonemason at Langholm (Dumfries) where Townhead Bridge across the Esk still reveals his mason's mark. His early Severn bridges at Mountford (1792) and Bewdley (1798) were of stone, and his near-contemporaries Rennie and Smeaton also used stone for some of their greatest work, Rennie's canal aqueducts at Lancaster and near Bath being massively magnificent.

The Union Chain Bridge across the Tweed at Horncliffe, a few miles west of Berwick, was Britain's first major suspension bridge (1820); the same principle is used in the huge new estuarine spans of steel and concrete across the Forth, Severn and Humber.

But of Britain's 200,000 road bridges it may be that the smallest are most appreciated. Stone-built, with low parapets or none at all, the hundreds of packhorse bridges were once the very hinges of commerce. Dating mainly from 1660–1760 they now enjoy a new lease of life on quiet lanes, bridleways and footpaths, particularly in country districts and in lonely places among northern and Welsh hills. Regularly used by farmers, walkers and climbers, they are universally loved. Too often we cross bridges without seeing them; most bridges merit a closer look and some reflection on the many people that have passed that way before.

(Below left) *Clapper bridge over the East Dart at Postbridge, Devon, an example of the most primitive form of bridge;* (top, left to right) *Monnow Bridge, Monmouth, Gwent, dominated by a thirteenth-century tower; the bridge at St Ives, Cambridgeshire, with its medieval chapel; a Palladian bridge in the park at Stowe, Buckinghamshire, an example of the ornamental bridges which formed an integral part of the design of* many landscape parks in the eighteenth century; (centre, left to right) *Packhorse bridge at Allerford, Somerset, on Exmoor; the world's first iron bridge over the Severn in Shropshire, recorded in the name of the town of Iron Bridge; the medieval bridge at Bradford-on-Avon, Wiltshire;* (below) *the Humber suspension bridge, opened in 1981, the largest single-span bridge in Britain.*

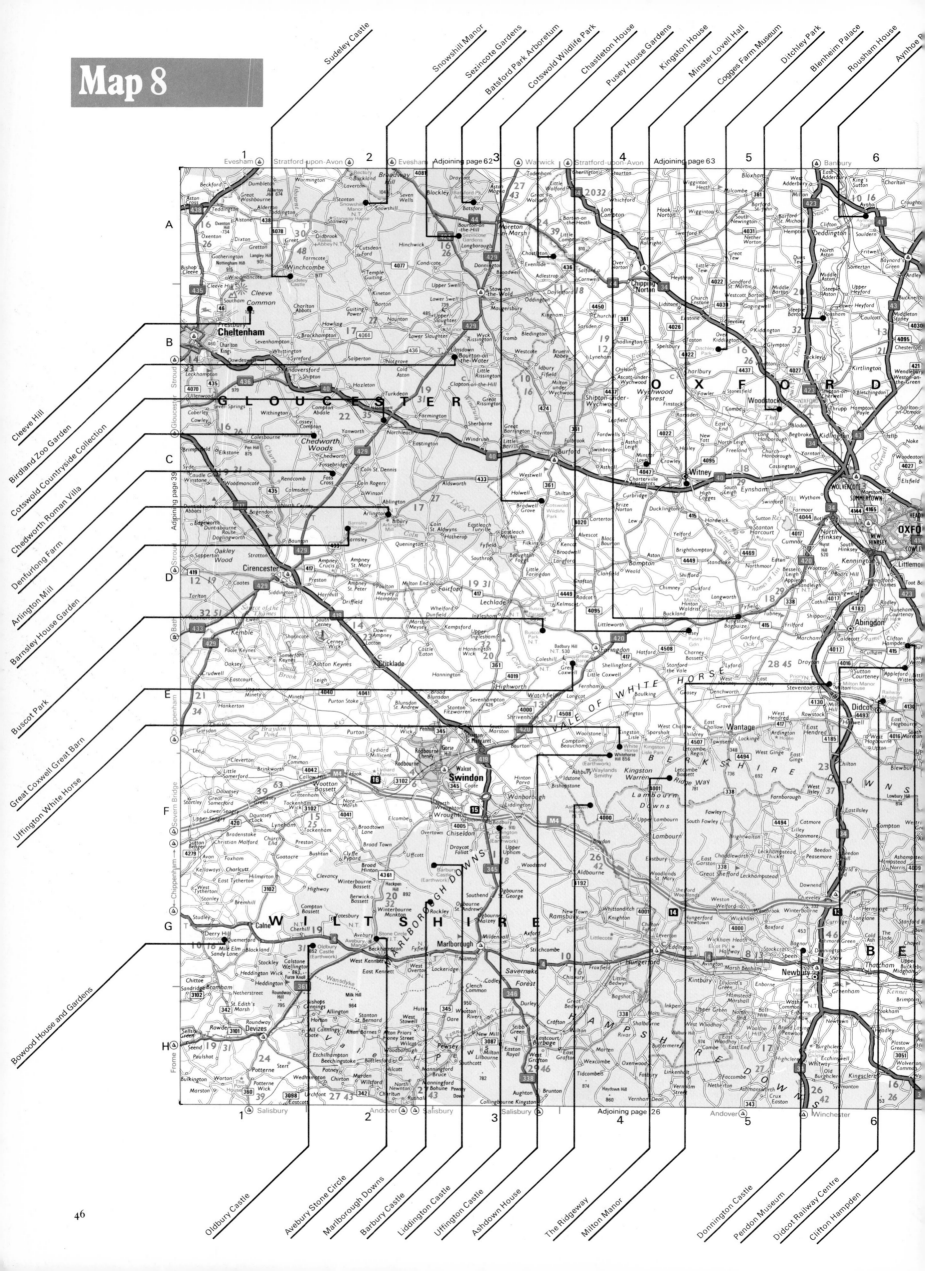

Map 8

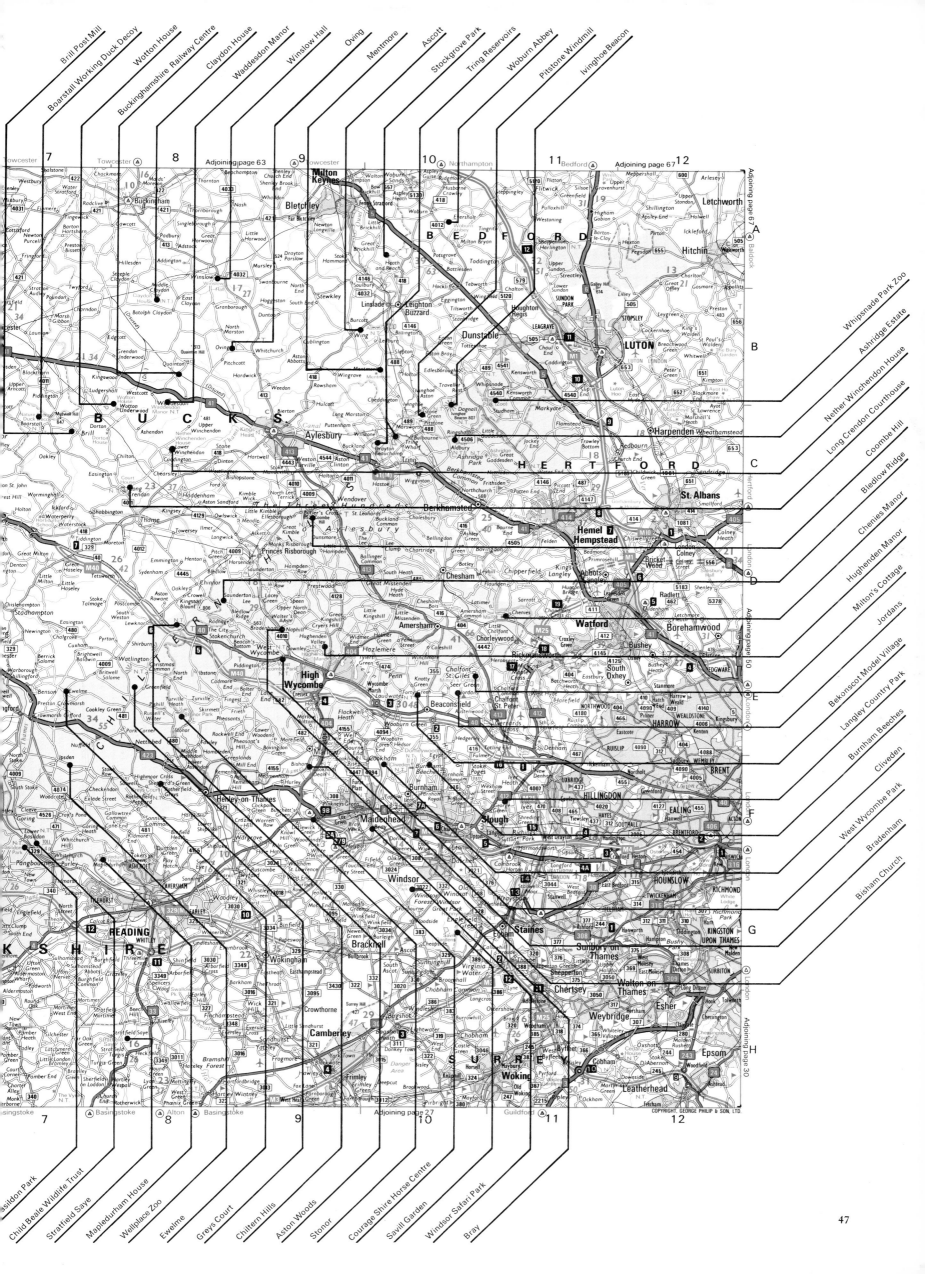

Thames and Chilterns

Arlington Mill, Bibury 17th-century corn mill, still with its original machinery, now housing country museum of farm implements, costumes and furniture. Trout in mill race. Nearby and equally famous is *Arlington Row* (NT), a

The village of Arlington is famous for this row of 17th-century weavers' cottages

terrace of 17th-century weavers' cottages (not open) with stone-tiled roofs. (C2)

Ascott (NT) Charming house containing the Anthony de Rothschild collection of French and Chippendale furniture, valuable pictures, rare porcelain and other treasures, so popular that entry is by timed ticket. Lovely gardens with unusual trees, topiary sundial, water lilies. Access from A418. (B9)

Ashdown House (NT) 17th-century house built for William 1st Earl Craven who devoted his life to Elizabeth of Bohemia, Charles I's ill-fated sister. The building rises through four storeys to a hipped roof crowned by a cupola. The massive staircase fills nearly a quarter of the interior and is hung with Craven family portraits. (F4)

Ashridge Estate (NT) Nearly 4,000 acres (1,618 hectares) of common, down, wood and farm land centred on the Bridgewater Monument, a landmark put up in 1832 in memory of the famous duke of Bridgewater, the 'father of inland navigation'. It marks the start of a 1½ miles (2.4 km) long nature trail. Access off B4506. (C10/11)

Aston Woods (NT) Famous beauty spot where woodlands flank the A40 and adjoining them (between A40 and M40), a nature reserve with a well-documented information centre and nature trail. 1 mile (1.6 km) south-east of Aston Rowant. (D8)

Avebury Stone Circle (NT) Largest megalithic monument in Europe, pre-dating Stonehenge, originally consisting of 2, possibly 3, stone circles. Later an outer stone circle, bank and ditch were built. *Alexander Keiller Museum* (EH); *museum of Wiltshire rural life* in Great Barn. (G2)

Aynhoe Park Fine 17th-century mansion, with alterations by Thomas Archer and Sir John Soane, part converted into flats. In centre of lovely village of honey coloured stone. (A6)

Barbury Castle Iron Age hill fort covering some 12 acres (5 hectares) on 879 ft (268 m) summit of **Marlborough Downs**. Encircled by two ditches and a rampart, it overlooks the ancient trackway known as the **Ridgeway**. The fort is at the centre of a country park 131 acres (53 hectares) in extent. (F2/3)

Barnsley House Garden Original 18th-century garden replanned in 1960 with 18th-century summerhouses, laburnum and lime walks, knot and herb gardens. (D2)

Basildon Park (NT) Classical late Georgian house of Bath stone built 1776 by John Carr of York in a beautiful setting overlooking the Thames valley, with an imposing central block flanked by two pavilions. Highlights of the interior are the unusual Octagon room, some fine plasterwork and important paintings and furniture. (F7)

Batsford Park Arboretum Over 900 named varieties of trees in 50 acres (20 hectares) of delightful Cotswold countryside, with bronze Oriental statuary and beautiful views. Access 1 mile (1.6 km) from intersection of A44 and A429 on Evesham road. (A3)

Avebury

Bekonscot Model Village, Warwick Road, Beaconsfield Laid out in a charmingly designed rock garden, model community complete with roads, shops, churches, hotels and miniature railway. Off B474, signposted from A40 and A355. (E10)

Birdland Zoo Garden, Bourton-on-the-Water Famous collection of over 600 exotic birds, some free flying, together with fine penguin pool, flamingoes on the lawns and tropical houses. (B3)

Bisham Church Thameside church famous for its splendid 16th-century monuments to the Hoby family, owners at one time of Bisham Abbey a short way upstream. (F9)

Bledlow Ridge Hogsback of the **Chilterns** 730 ft (222 m) high giving glorious views over the Vale of Aylesbury. The historic Icknield Way (part of the **Ridgeway**) runs below the ridge. (D9)

Blenheim Palace Vanbrugh's masterpiece, an enormous baroque palace covering 3 acres (1.2 hectares) and set in over 2,000 acres (809 hectares) of parkland landscaped by 'Capability' Brown, with terraced water gardens and a lake, and a plant and butterfly centre. Valuable furnishings and pictures. Home of the 11th Duke of Marlborough and birthplace of Sir Winston Churchill. Winston Churchill memorabilia. (B5)

Boarstall Working Duck Decoy (NT) An 18th-century duck decoy in working order in 13 acres (5 hectares) of natural woodland. (C7)

Bowood House and Gardens Laid out by 'Capability' Brown, 82 acres (33 hectares) of beautiful parkland with formal gardens, lake walks, temple, cascade and grotto. Arboretum and pinetum. Magnificent rhododendrons and azaleas in spring. (G1)

Bradenham (NT) Picturesque village in a wooded setting built around its manor and 15th-century St Botolph's church. The adjoining woods are a well-known beauty spot. (D9)

Bray Charming old village on a beautiful reach of the Thames. The imposing church is a reminder of the celebrated Vicar of Bray (Simon Alleyn), who changed his religion three times to keep the living. (F10)

Brill Post Mill Famous 17th-century windmill 600 ft (183 m) high, a vantage point for wide views over Oxfordshire and the Vale of Aylesbury. (C7)

Buckinghamshire Railway Centre, Quainton Housed in a disused station, largest collection of industrial and BR steam locomotives in Britain together with steam-hauled passenger trains and many items of railway equipment. Access from Westcott road 1 mile (1.6 km) south-west. (B8)

Burnham Beeches 375 acres (152 hectares) of woodland, mostly venerable pollarded beech trees, a magnificent sight in autumn. Rich in animal and plant life, it is intersected by well-defined footpaths. (F10)

Buscot Park (NT) 18th-century Adam-style house containing the Faringdon collection of fine furniture, porcelain and paintings, notably the Burne-Jones *Briar Rose* series. Charming water gardens in 55 acre (22 hectare) park. Access from A417. (D3)

Chastleton House Huge Jacobean mansion built by a wool merchant of Witney who supervised the building, as did his descendants the subsequent repair and renovation. As a result the house is little different from when it was built, with most of the original furniture still in place along with fine plasterwork and panelling. (A3)

Chedworth Roman Villa (NT) In a beautiful woodland setting, the remains of a Romano-British villa excavated 1864–6 with well-preserved mosaic pavements and bath house. A museum displays the smaller finds. (C2)

Chenies Manor Massive and imposing red-brick house built 1460 by the Cheyne family with a south wing added 1523 by the 1st earl of Bedford prior to entertaining Henry VIII. In the nearby church is an astonishing array of Bedford family tombs and monuments. (D11)

Child Beale Wildlife Trust Ornamental birds and water fowl in a lakeside setting, many of them free flying. Rare sheep. Picnic sites and Thameside walks. On east side of A329 facing **Basildon Park**. (F7)

Chiltern Hills Beautiful chalk downlands forming a ridge running diagonally north-east to south-west to the Thames at Goring (F7) from south Bedfordshire. With 1,500 miles (24,000 km) of waymarked footpaths they are a paradise for ramblers. See also **Bledlow Ridge**. (D8)

Claydon House (NT) Surviving wing of great house built 1752–80 by the 2nd earl Verney containing a celebrated rococo suite of rooms. The redoubtable Florence Nightingale often visited Claydon to stay with her sister Lady Verney and in her apartments are mementoes of her life and the Crimean War. Access by north drive only (from Middle Claydon). (B8)

Cleeve Hill Bleak moorland plateau, at 1,083 ft (330 m) one of the highest points in the Cotswolds, stretching for 2½ miles (4 km) above the 1,000 ft (305 m) contour south from Cleeve Hill. Near the summit are traces of several prehistoric sites. Access from A46. (B1)

Clifton Hampden Beautiful and much visited village of timber-framed houses set in a loop of the Thames. Across the river is the charming old black-and-white Barley Mow inn, immortalised in Jerome K. Jerome's *Three Men in a Boat*. (D6)

Cliveden (NT) Imposing 19th-century house now occupied by an American university (only two rooms shown). Extensive historic gardens with hanging woods overlooking a beautiful reach of the Thames: parterre of box hedges, rustic theatre, water garden, wooded walks and 18th-century temples. Concealed drive on B476. (F10)

Cogges Farm Museum Recreated Edwardian farm in Cotswold village, with 19 acres (7.6 hectares) of farmland, agricultural machinery, livestock and dairy. House contains a working kitchen, dining room and parlour, also in Edwardian style. (C5)

Coombe Hill (NT) Viewpoint 843 ft (257 m) up in the **Chilterns** overlooking the Vale of Aylesbury. Nature trail ¾ mile (1.2 km) long. Access on B4010. (C/D9)

Cotswold Countryside Collection, Northleach Housed in an 18th-century 'house of correction', exhibits illustrating rural life in the Cotswolds including wagons, agricultural machinery and tools. (C2)

Cotswold Wildlife Park Large collection of mammals, birds, reptiles and fish. 3 acre (1.2 hectare) walled garden enclosing bird aviaries, penguins, otters, monkeys and other small animals. Tropical bird house, pets' corner, butterfly house with 45 ft (13.7 m) flight cage. Access from A361. ♿ (C3)

Courage Shire Horse Centre A glimpse into the world of the heavy horse which once provided the motive power for farms and industry. On A4 ½ mile (0.8 km) west of junction with A423 (M). ♿ (F9)

Denfurlong Farm, Chedworth The workings of a dairy farm explained by illustrated displays on a self-conducted tour round fields and buildings (approx. 2 hours). Access off A429. (C2)

Didcot Railway Centre Working museum of the Great Western Railway with large collection of steam engines in the original engine shed; recreated station. (E6)

Ditchley Park Splendid mansion in extensive grounds, one of the great 18th-century houses of Oxfordshire, famous for its magnificent interior decoration by William Kent and Henry Flitcroft. Now an Anglo-American conference centre. (B5)

Donnington Castle (EH) Ruins of castle built 1358 and twice besieged by Cromwell's troops in the Civil War. There are extensive earthworks but only the imposing barbican of the Civil War period remains. Access from B4494. ♿ (G5)

Ewelme Charming village still with its original nucleus of 15th-century church, almshouses and school. The church is a storehouse of 15th-century art – carved font cover, screens, doors and roof, early brasses and superb altar tomb of Alice, duchess of Suffolk. (E7)

Great Coxwell Great Barn (NT) Tithe barn built 1250 by Cistercian monks, cruciform in plan and with handsome doorways and massive buttresses supporting its walls. ♿ (E4)

Greys Court (NT) Fascinating Tudor house with 18th-century improvements containing fine furniture and plasterwork and standing within the original medieval manor of Robert de Grey, one of the first knights of the Garter. ♿ (F8)

Hughenden Manor (NT) House Benjamin Disraeli bought in 1847 and lived in until his death in 1881. A typical example of a Victorian gentleman's residence, it contains many relics of the great statesman. Access from A4128. ♿ (E9)

Ivinghoe Beacon One of the highest viewpoints in the **Chilterns**, an 800 ft (244 m) hill named from its use for signal fires. It marks the start of the **Ridgeway** long-distance footpath. Access from B489. (C10)

Jordans Picturesque wooded village, famous as the location of the Mayflower Barn of the Society of Friends reputed to have been built from the timbers of the ship that took the Pilgrim Fathers to America. Nearby is the Friends' Meeting House, erected 1688, and the graves of William Penn, founder of Pennsylvania, his 2 wives and 10 of their 16 children. (E10)

Kingston House Finely furnished Charles II manor house with a beautiful garden noted for its collection of rare trees, flowering shrubs and bulbs. Access at junction of A415 and A420. ♿ (D5)

Langley Country Park Deer park, woodlands and shrub gardens of 136 acres (55 hectares) with views of Windsor Castle. Nature trail. Access from A412. (F11)

Liddington Castle Iron Age fort built to command the country north of the **Ridgeway** in a superb scenic and strategic location on a 910 ft (277 m) hill, one of the highest points on the **Marlborough Downs**. On a clear day the views take in most of the Thames valley. (F3)

Long Crendon Courthouse (NT) 14th-century building with an overhanging upper storey where manorial justice was meted out from the time of Henry V until early this century. Only large upper room is open. (C8)

Mapledurham House Late Elizabethan mansion with an impressive red-brick facade closed by wings on either side. Inside are the original moulded ceilings, great oak staircases, 16th, 17th and 18th-century pictures and a private chapel dating from 1789. Other buildings include a 15th-century watermill in full working order. Access only from north side of river or by launch from Caversham. (F8)

Marlborough Downs Hill range west, south-west and north-west of Marlborough rising to 964 ft (294 m) Milk Hill (H2). Many Iron Age hill forts, long barrows, tumuli and other ancient remains, the most important of which is **Avebury Stone Circle**. Also Sarsen Stones, left isolated by erosion of the surrounding rock. The White Horse on the downs near Marlborough was cut in 1804. (G2)

Mentmore A spectacular Victorian mansion, built by Sir Joseph Paxton, architect of the Crystal Palace. Superb gilt interiors, Rubens fireplace, and panoramic views of the Chilterns. 12 miles (19 km) north-east of Aylesbury. (B10)

Milton Manor In a charming village, small 17th-century manor designed by Inigo Jones with Georgian wings and chapel and library in Strawberry Hill Gothick. It contains a remarkable collection of 200 teapots from around the world. ♿ (E6)

Milton's Cottage, Chalfont St Giles 16th-century timber-framed house preserved as it was when the poet lived there in the plague year of 1665 (during which he completed *Paradise Lost*). It contains many Milton relics and a library of first and early editions. Access from B4442 Seer Green road. ♿ (E10)

Minster Lovell Hall (EH) Picturesque ruined and reputedly haunted 15th-century seat of the Lovell family in a romantic setting by the river Windrush. In the delightful old village the bridge over the river and the part timber-framed Swan Inn are both of the 15th century. (C4)

Nether Winchendon House In a pretty, unspoilt village, the house has been a family home for generations. It has a medieval interior with fine woodwork. The gardens slope down to the river Thame. (C8)

Oldbury Castle Iron Age fort on Cherhill Down 852 ft (260 m) high with a white horse cut in the northern flank. 6 tumuli surround it. (G2)

Oving Secluded old-world village of quiet cottages, old manor house, ancient timbered Black Boy inn and tiny 13th-century church. (B9)

Pendon Museum, Long Wittenham Accurate and detailed model trains set in landscapes featuring exquisitely modelled cottages, farms, fields and lanes to give glimpses of the English countryside as it was in the early 1930s. (E6)

Pitstone Windmill (NT) Post mill reconstructed from the timbers of the original mill of 1627, making it the earliest dated windmill in England. It continued working until 1902. Access from B488. (C10)

Pusey House Gardens Beautiful garden covering 15 acres (6 hectares) with many fine trees, walled and water gardens, herbaceous borders and a large collection of shrubs and roses. ♿ (D5)

The Ridgeway Long-distance footpath of 85 miles (136 km) either side of Goring mostly following the line of ancient trackways. Extending from **Ivinghoe Beacon** (C10) to Overton Hill (G2) near Avebury it runs for much of the way along the edge of the chalk escarpment of the Berkshire Downs and **Chilterns** and is strung with relics of the Bronze and Iron Ages, such as **Uffington Castle**. The path is divided into two nearly equal parts by the Thames at Goring (F7). The western part, from Overton Hill to Streatley, follows the true Ridgeway, a distinct upland track dating from neolithic times. The route of the prehistoric eastern section, later known as the Icknield Way, is in many places now a surfaced road and local footpaths have been used instead. The western half is open to horse riders as well as walkers. Signposted and waymarked throughout.

Rousham House Great Jacobean mansion built 1635 with rooms decorated by William Kent in 1738. The garden is Kent's only surviving landscape design, with classical temples, cascades, statues and vistas in 30 acres (12 hectares) of hanging woods above the Cherwell. Concealed drive off B4030. (B6)

Savill Garden, Englefield Green Woodland garden of 35 acres (14 hectares) created 1932 and now considered one of the finest of its kind. Wide variety of rhododendrons, camellias, magnolias and other shrubs and trees. A more formal area is devoted to roses and there is an interesting dry garden. ♿ (G10)

Sezincote Gardens Oriental water garden by Repton and Daniell surrounding a house in Indian style (open) with rounded arches and onion domes, the inspiration for Brighton Pavilion. (A3)

Snowshill Manor (NT) Cotswold manor house crammed with unique collection of toys, weavers' and spinners' tools, penny farthings, Japanese armour, model ships, musical instruments. ♿ (A2)

Stockgrove Park Country park of 74 acres (30 hectares) laid out in part of landscaped grounds of country house. It covers a small valley and includes woodland and an artificial lake. Access off road to Great Brickhill ¾ mile (1.2 km) north of Heath and Reach. ♿ (A10)

Stonor Medieval house overlaid by 18th-century red-brick front and centred on a great hall of *c.* 1190 containing material relating to the worship of Roman Catholicism in secret. Fine Italian paintings and sculptures. The Stonor family have lived in the house since the 12th century. (E8)

Pitstone Windmill

Stratfield Saye Long, low house, built 1630s, presented to the Duke of Wellington in 1817. Magnificent collection of pictures the duke brought back from Spain as spoils of war. The stable block houses the Wellington Exhibition. Gardens and 20 acre (8 hectare) wildfowl sanctuary. ♿ (H8)

Sudeley Castle One time medieval home of Katherine Parr incorporated in mock Gothic reconstruction of 1858. It contains fine pictures, tapestries, furniture, and toy collection. Falconry displays in summer. Access from A46. ♿ (A1)

Tring Reservoirs Adjoining reservoirs built 1802–39 to feed the Grand Union Canal where it cuts through the **Chilterns** nearly 400 ft (122 m) above sea level. Now national nature reserves and major birdwatching sites. Nature trail of 3 miles (5 km) starts at Startops End. Access from B488–B489. (C10)

Uffington Castle (NT) Dominating the **Ridgeway**, Iron Age hill fort 856 ft (261 m) high dating from 1st century BC surrounded by a strong bank and ditch. (F4)

Uffington White Horse (NT) Figure of a horse 360 ft (110 m) long cut in the chalk downland, possibly early Iron Age. Car park and picnic area nearby. Access from B4507. (E4)

Waddesdon Manor (NT) French Renaissance style house built for Baron Ferdinand de Rothschild 1874–89 containing superb collections of Italian and Dutch paintings, portraits by Reynolds and Gainsborough and magnificent 18th-century furniture, porcelain and carpets. In the 150 acre (60 hectare) grounds is an aviary with free-flying birds. ♿ (C8)

Wellplace Zoo, Ipsden Farm housing many varieties of birds, including rheas, flamingoes, penguins. Also mammals including monkeys and otters. ♿ (F7)

West Wycombe Park (NT) House rebuilt in Palladian style in the 18th century when double colonnades and porticoes were added and the grounds laid out with temples and an artificial lake. Access from A40. Nearby West Wycombe village is also NT. (E9)

Whipsnade Park Zoo Beautiful open zoo high in the **Chiltern Hills** in 500 acres (202 hectares) of parkland, with a collection of around 2,000 animals and birds, many of which roam freely. Children's zoo, Umfolozi railway. Access from B4540. ♿ (C10)

Windsor Safari Park Seven drive-through reserves where wild animals from all over the world roam in natural surroundings. Children's farmyard and boating lake, tropical house and Sea-world marine mammals complex. (G10)

Winslow Hall Delightful town house built 1698–1702 by Christopher Wren, architect of St Paul's Cathedral, one of the few he designed to survive without structural alteration. It is furnished for the most part with early 18th-century furniture and paintings. (B8)

Woburn Abbey Cistercian abbey founded 1145, damaged by fire in the 16th century and rebuilt as a Jacobean mansion. Home of the dukes of Bedford. Contains one of the most important private art collections in the world and perhaps the finest exhibition of model soldiers. In the beautiful landscaped 3,000 acre (1,214 hectare) deer park is the *Wild Animal Kingdom*, Britain's largest drive-through safari park. (A10)

Wotton House Built 1704 to a plan which served as a model for Buckingham House (later Buckingham Palace). The interior was remodelled by Sir John Soane in 1820. Gardens landscaped by 'Capability' Brown. (C8)

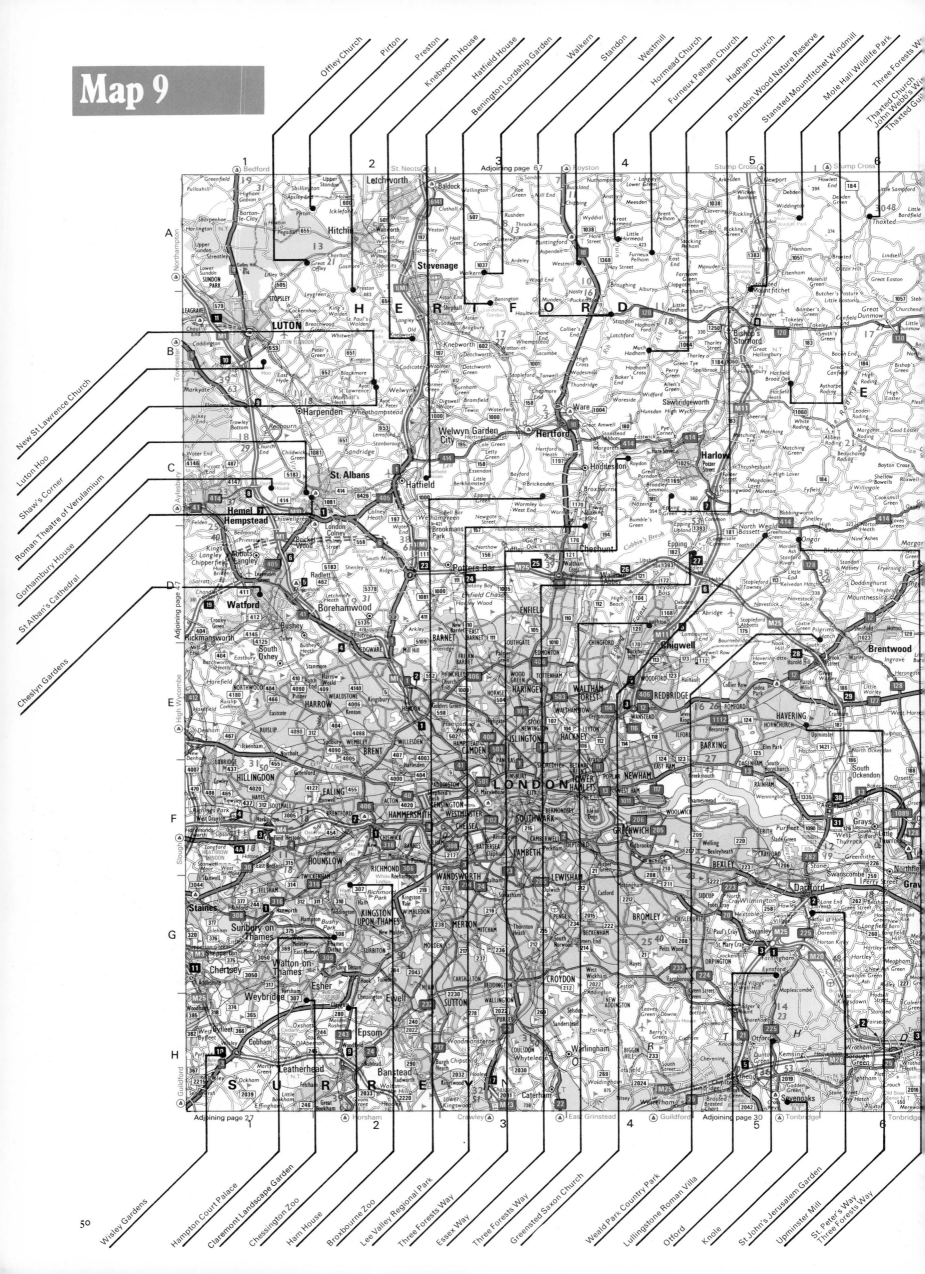

Map 9

Spains Hall
Finchingfield
Great Bardfield Church
Saling Hall
Paycocke's
Silver End
Stour Valley Railway Centre
Fingringhoe Wick
Nature Reserve
Bourne Mill
Hollytrees
Dedham
Essex Way
Beth Chatto Gardens

London and the Thames Estuary

Allington Castle Moated 13th-century castle, former home of the Tudor poet, Sir Thomas Wyatt. Restored by Lord Conway in early part of 20th century. Retains castellated curtain wall, gatehouse and great hall. Access from A229 north of Maidstone. ⓖ (H7)

Aylesford Friary This Carmelite friary was dissolved by Henry VIII but the Carmelites returned in 1949, the first repossession to take place in England. Much of the old fabric remains and some traces of 13th-century work are still visible. The Shrine Church (to St Simon Stock) was built by Sir Gilbert Scott on the site of the sanctuary of the priory church. (H7)

Benington Lordship Garden An old garden around the site of a Norman castle. Includes a moat, ruined keep, lakes, folly, water/rock garden, rose garden and magnificent herbaceous borders. (B3)

Beth Chatto Gardens, White Boar House, Elmstead Market Landscaped gardens of 4 acres (1.6 hectares). Include extensive water gardens, a shade garden and many aromatic drought-loving plants in the 'Mediterranean' garden. (B10)

Bourne Mill, Bourne Road, Colchester (NT) Dutch-gabled fishing lodge built 1591 from materials from St John's Abbey. Later converted into a mill. Machinery is in full working order. ⓖ (B10)

Broxbourne Zoo The zoo includes woodland and a drive-in picnic area. Animals include lions, tigers, leopards, pumas, bears, racoons, badgers and highland cattle. In Bell Lane, off the A10 bypass. ⓖ (C4)

Canterbury Cathedral Architecture spans five centuries. The oldest portions were built under the direction of the Norman Archbishop Lanfranc in 1070. The cathedral is the mother church of Christianity in England and the shrine of St Thomas à Beckett who was murdered here on 29 December 1170. The south porch is the main entrance and commemorates the victory of Agincourt in 1415. Note the magnificent stained glass. (H11)

Chart Gunpowder Mills, Westbrook Walk, Faversham The town was once the centre of the gunpowder industry. One of the former mills, dating from the late 18th century, has been fully restored. (H10)

Cheslyn Gardens, Nascot Wood Road, Watford One of the most attractive ornamental gardens in Hertfordshire. It includes an aviary and woodland as well as a good display of shrubs, bulbs and rare plants. ⓖ (D1)

Chessington Zoo Popular zoo and amusement park set in 65 acres (26 hectares) of countryside. Varied collection of animals, including gorillas and chimpanzees. Bird garden, children's zoo, circus. Access from A243. (H2)

Chilham Timber-framed Tudor and Jacobean houses covered with camellias, jasmine, roses and creeper surround a small square. In 'The Street', note the over-hanging houses, especially Robin's Croft (the old vicarage) where above the door is written 'The sparrow hath found a house and the swallow a nest for herself'. (H10)

Claremont Landscape Garden (NT) The earliest surviving English landscape garden, recently restored. Begun by Vanbrugh and Bridgeman (who designed the huge grass amphitheatre c. 1725), extended and naturalised by Kent (responsible for the lake with its island pavilion) and later altered by 'Capability' Brown, working for Clive of India after 1768. ⓖ (H1)

Cobham Has associations with Dickens, such as the half-timbered Leather Bottle Inn. *Cobham Hall* (open to the public during school holidays) includes decorations by Inigo Jones and the Adams. In the Repton-designed grounds is a Roman Villa. The chancel of St Mary Magdalene Church has a fine collection of 13th-and 14th-century brasses. (G7)

Dedham A dignified village in the heart of Constable country. The church, built 1492–1520, appears in many of his paintings. *Castle House*, the home of Sir Alfred Munnings, lies 1 mile (1.6 km) south-east. (A10)

Essex Way A 70 mile (112 km) route which begins at Epping Station and finishes at **Dedham** in Constable country. Non-motorists can take the train to Manningtree Station, 2 miles (3.2 km) from Dedham, or to Epping Station on the Central Line depending which end they wish to start. The route is mainly via country lanes and field paths. (D4 to A10)

Finchingfield Much photographed example of the perfect English village. From the west, the visitor will see bridge, green and pond with white-fronted and gabled houses lining the road climbing towards the Norman church. Patrick Brontë, father of the famous novelists, was curate here 1806–8. (A7)

Finchingfield

Fingringhoe Wick Nature Reserve 5 miles (8 km) south-east of Colchester on west bank of Colne Estuary. It is an Essex Naturalists' Trust reserve and an excellent place to observe a wide variety of birdlife from seven bird hides. Visitors are welcome to explore the public nature trail. (B10)

Fordwich In medieval times a port for incoming stores for Canterbury's two monasteries as well as for Caen stone for **Canterbury Cathedral**. The timber-framed *Town Hall* dates from c. 1540, has herringbone brickwork and is said to be the smallest in England. (H11)

Greensted Church

Furneux Pelham Church Large tower with fine Perpendicular work in flint. Has stained glass by Burne-Jones and William Morris and an interesting collection of old prints. (A4)

Gorhambury House Entry from A414 by **Roman Theatre of Verulamium**, St Albans. Palladian mansion built 1777–84 by Sir Robert Taylor. Chippendale furniture, historic portraits and 16th-century enamelled glass. (C1)

Great Bardfield Church (St Mary the Virgin) Built during the 14th century, with the tower, chancel, south aisle and south porch being the oldest parts. Note interesting tracery of the aisle windows. The windows of the north aisle have much original stained glass. Attractive village, full of old houses. (A7)

Greensted Saxon Church Church dates from c. 850 and is the nation's only example of a Saxon log-built church. The nave is of split oak tree trunks set upright on a sill. The brick choir dates from c. 1500. The body of St Edmund lay here in 1013 en route from London to Bury St Edmunds. 1 mile (1.6 km) west of Chipping Ongar. (D5)

Hadham Church, Much Hadham Unusually large for a village church. The Perpendicular fittings comprise a font, screen, pulpit and stained glass. The two headstops for the west door are by the sculptor Henry Moore, who lives locally. (B4)

Hadleigh Castle (EH) Familiar from Constable's paintings, it stands on a bluff overlooking the Leigh Marshes. Founded 1231 by Hubert de Burgh. Rebuilt 1359–70 as a residence for Edward III. Retains two original towers, single large bailey 200 ft (61 m) high. (E8)

Ham House (NT) There is a sign-posted pedestrian entrance on the right off Petersham Road, soon after it leaves Richmond. A Stuart house built 1610 and redecorated and furnished to the fashion of the time in 1670 for the Duke and Duchess of Lauderdale. Much of the original furniture is still to be seen in its place in the house. Also 17th-century garden. ⓖ (G2)

Hampton Court Palace (DoE) Begun 1514 by Cardinal Wolsey but in 1529 'acquired' by Henry VIII. From then on a favourite royal residence. Worth visiting for its picture gallery, the state apartments, the notable gatehouse and clock court. There were additions by Wren, including The Fountain Court c. 1689. The maze is of special interest. ⓖ (G2)

Hatfield House Erected 1607–11 by Robert Cecil, first Earl of Salisbury and Chief Minister to James I. State rooms display portraits by Van Dyck, Reynolds and Rubens, furniture, tapestries and historic armour, a valuable collection of manuscripts, state papers and relics of Elizabeth I. Also Tony Durose Vehicle Collection of vintage cars and National Collection of Model Soldiers. Attractive gardens. (C2)

Hollytrees, High Street, Colchester Particularly fine example of Georgian family house. Built 1718. Contains fine collection of costumes and antiquities. (A10)

Hormead Church, Little Hormead This famous little church is almost completely Norman. Note the 12th-century north door which retains its original ironwork. Inside it is very simply furnished. (A4)

John Webb's Windmill, Thaxted Built on the site of an earlier mill. Recently restored by the Windmill Trust. Machinery of upper floors intact. A museum occupies the lower floor. ⓖ (A6)

Knebworth House Home of the Lytton family since 1490, it contains many superb rooms and magnificent Jacobean Banqueting Hall. A fine collection of portraits, furniture, books and manuscripts, plus memorabilia of Bulwer-Lytton (1803–73), who wrote many of his novels here. Formal gardens, country park and children's adventure playground. (B2)

Knole (NT) Built in 1456 and added to in 1603 to become one of the largest houses in England. State portraits by Reynolds and Gainsborough, also tapestries, hangings and chairs upholstered in 17th-century silks and velvets. Magnificent deer path with ancient trees. Access from A225. 🔵 (H5)

Langdon Hills Includes two parks – Westley Heights, 135 acres (54.6 hectares), and One Tree Hill, 165 acres (66.8 hectares). Overlooks the Thames estuary and includes open grassland, deciduous woodlands, thorn scrub and sandy heaths. (E7)

Lea Valley Regional Park Covers 6,500 acres (2,630 hectares) from Stanstead Abbots (C4) to Newham in London (F4). It contains the remains of Rye House, 1 mile (1.6 km) north-east of Hoddesdon, where an abortive plot to assassinate Charles II was hatched. This large parkland is situated along the Essex/Herts boundary and includes landscaped open spaces, sailing, angling, picnic and camping facilities. At Broxbourne (C4) there is a riverside complex including leisure centre, picnic area and riverside terraces. (C4 to F4)

Lullingstone Roman Villa (EH) Opposite Eynsford church a narrow road spans the Darent by a stone bridge and passes under a railway viaduct $\frac{3}{4}$ mile (1.2 km) to the remains of this first-century villa with its fine mosaic, a tesselated pavement. The villa has been roofed in and further exhibits are in an adjoining gallery. 🔵 (G5)

Luton Hoo House built by Robert Adam was gutted by fire and refashioned 1903–7. Now houses Werner Collection of paintings, Fabergé jewellery and other art treasures. 1,500 acre (607 hectare) park by 'Capability' Brown. 🔵 (B1)

Marsh Farm Country Park At South Woodham Ferrers, a modern working farm with cattle, sheep and a commercial pig unit under cover, with inbuilt walkways for visitors. Displays, indoor picnic area, country park and nature reserve. 🔵 (D8)

Minster Abbey, Minster-in-Thanet Dating back to AD 725, it is one of the oldest inhabited houses in Kent. The west range is late 11th-century. Excavations have revealed the plan of the church outlined on the ground. The vaulted passage and chapel can also be seen. The abbey is now the home of Benedictine nuns. 🔵 (G12)

Mole Hall Wildlife Park, Widdington Has the only North American otters breeding in England. Also British otters, serval cats, snowy owls, wallabies, lemurs, guanacos and waterfowl. 🔵 (A5)

Naze Point Has 70 ft (21.3 m) cliffs which give magnificent views across the Naze to Harwich. Rich in fossils and an important landfall for migrant birds, especially in autumn. Tern, ringed plover and oystercatcher nest here. North of Walton-on-the-Naze. (B12)

New St Lawrence Church, Ayot St Lawrence Built by Sir Lionel Lyde in 1770 when he was prevented from demolishing completely the medieval church which 'spoiled his view'. Architect Nicholas Revett designed a classical temple with portico at the east end. Every April, in a charming ceremony, silkworms, mulberry bushes and raw silk are blessed here. (B2)

Offley Church, Great Offley From the outside it bears evidence of many fashions of architecture. Dates originally from 12th century. Inside is a beautiful 14th-century font, many monuments by Nollekens. In the chancel are unusual stucco moulding and busts of the Salusbury family. (A1)

Otford The panelling in the Bull Inn in the High Street may have come from the Archbishop's Palace. Broughton Manor has a medieval hall and 16th-century gable. The church by the green has a squat Norman tower and an 11th-century nave. (H5)

Parndon Wood Nature Reserve This reserve lies on the south boundary of Harlow. There are two nature trails with hides for observing the varied wildlife. Also a study centre. (C5)

Patrixbourne Genuine Flemish-gabled houses intermingle with 19th-century mock-Tudor and neo-Georgian. The flint and Caen stone church is Norman and the north doorway is interestingly carved. (H11)

doorway, c. 1160, has two statues which are possibly the oldest of their kind in England. In the choir, note wall paintings and choir stalls. Fine Early English vaulting in crypt. (G7)

Roman Theatre of Verulamium Verulamium Theatre, Museum and Hypocaust is near St Michael's Church in St Albans. Verulamium was the capital of Roman Britain – the city's name was later changed to St Albans – and covered 200 acres (81 hectares). The hypocaust (system for heating bath water) remains intact and the theatre, which is unique in Britain, has a stage rather than an amphitheatre. The museum has many relics of Roman times. (C2)

St Alban's Cathedral Originally the Abbey Church; designated a cathedral in 1877. Has undergone many additions and restorations. Said to be the second longest cathedral in England (550 ft, 168 m). Note the shrine of St Alban and 13th-century wall paintings. Reached by a passage from the High St. (C2)

Paycocke's, Coggeshall

Paycocke's, Coggeshall (NT) One of England's finest timber-framed buildings. Built by clothier, Thomas Paycocke, c. 1500. Rich panelling, wood carving, small garden. 🔵 (B8)

Pirton Has ruins of a Norman castle covering about 4 acres (1.6 hectares), built on the site of a much earlier building. Some beautiful old houses but what is remarkable is the sympathetic use of local materials in recent building. Much attention to layout and design has resulted in a development which is as aesthetically pleasing as many older villages. (A2)

Powell-Cotton Museum, Birchington In the grounds of Quex Park (1813), which William III used as a staging-post on his journeys to and from Holland. It is a museum of natural history and ethnography with big game exhibits from Africa and Asia. (G12)

Preston Once an estate of the Knights Templars. Lutyens built some houses here and there is an attractive group of cottages around the green. Simple church has fine Early English chancel. (A2)

Rayleigh Windmill This tower mill contains a local history museum, with mill implements and craft exhibitions. 🔵 (E8)

Reculver Towers and Roman Fort (EH) Reculver was the site of the Roman fort of Regulbium. The Norman church was erected within the castle in 669 and demolished in 1809. The west towers were preserved as a mariners' landmark. The plan of the Saxon church can be seen. (G12)

Rochester Cathedral Its origins date back to the 6th century. The present building is mainly Norman and was consecrated in 1130. The Norman west

St John's Jerusalem Garden (NT) The River Darent forms a moat round the garden. The main walls of the house once formed the church of a commandery of the Knights Hospitallers. Completely rebuilt inside with a section at the east end kept as a chapel, later a billiard room. This and the garden are open. Access from A225. 🔵 (G5)

St Peter's Way A 45 mile (72 km) walk from Chipping Ongar (D6) to the chapel at St Peter's-on-the-Wall at Bradwell (C10), via Blackmore (D6), Stock (D7), Hanningfield Reservoir (D7), Purleigh (D8), Steeple (D9), Tillingham (D10). Non-motorists can go by British Rail to Southminster or to Chipping Ongar on the Central Line, depending which end they wish to begin. Highlights of the route are the birds around Hanningfield Reservoir, the marshlands of the Essex coast and the wild flowers in spring. (D5 to C10)

Saling Hall Grounds of 12 acres (4.8 hectares) include a small park with unusual trees, water gardens and a walled garden built in 1698. (A7)

Shaw's Corner, Ayot St Lawrence (NT) The home of George Bernard Shaw for the last 44 years of his life is of great interest because of its contents which are kept exactly as they were during the writer's life. This includes even his distinctive hats. (B2)

Silver End A village of box-like houses in the International Modern style interspersed with rows of houses built to a neo-Georgian design. F.H. Crittall created a new village where his firm's products, metal house fittings, could be prominently displayed. Thatched church. (B8)

Spains Hall Lies 1 mile (1.6 km) north-west of Finchingfield on unclassified

road. Elizabethan manor with panelled rooms containing 18th- and 19th-century furniture and art collection, including fine tapestries. Flower and kitchen gardens with 17th-century Cedar of Lebanon. (A7)

Standon At the junction of two Roman roads. The High Street is wide with grass verges on the east side and has houses from 16th-century onward. Church has a detached tower. (B4)

Stansted Mountfitchet Windmill Best preserved tower mill in Essex, built 1787. Still retains most of the original machinery, including rare boulter and curved ladder to fit cap. (A5)

Stour Valley Railway Centre At Chappel Station between Colchester and Halstead off the A604. Steam locomotives, old coaches and signal equipment under restoration and in service. (A9)

Thaxted Church (St John the Baptist, St Mary and St Lawrence) Described as 'the finest parish church in England', this is a 14th/15th-century church and has a 180 ft (55 m) crocketed spire, buttresses and gargoyles and a frieze of small animals. Gustav Holst composed 'The Planets' when he was organist here. (A6)

Thaxted Guildhall, Town Street Built by the cutlers upon wooden pillars c. 1390 when Thaxted was important in the cutlery industry. Considerably renovated and now contains small museum with regular demonstrations. (A6)

Three Forests Way A 60 mile (96 km) circular walk, taking in Epping, Hatfield and Hainault Forests. Goes across fields and commons, along lanes with the occasional road. From Loughton the Way goes through Epping Forest to Roydon (C4), Sawbridgeworth (C5), Little Hallingbury (B5), through Hatfield Forest to Hatfield Broad Oak (B5), White Roding (B6), Fyfield (C5), Chipping Ongar (D5), Abridge (D5), through Hainault Forest to Loughton. Access from stations at Loughton, Ongar; also Central Line tube, Green Line and Eastern National buses. Booklet available. (E4 to B5)

Twyritt-Drake Museum of Carriages, Mill Street, Maidstone Provides a display of 17th- to 19th-century horse-drawn vehicles. The exhibition is in the 14th-century medieval barn which was the stables of the Archbishop's Palace. Just south of road bridge. (H7)

Upminster Mill, 4 Plough Rise, Cranham, Upminster Built 1803, this is a particularly fine example of a smock mill. The original machinery is still intact. Guided tours available. (E5)

Walkern The River Beane runs parallel with the High Street. A lane fords this and leads to the church – originally Norman but much altered in 15th and 19th centuries. (A3)

Weald Park Country Park 1 mile (1.6 km) north-west of Brentwood, covering 420 acres (170 hectares) of woodland. There are lakes and open parkland available to the public for informal recreation. Also fishing and riding by permission. Access from South Weald. (D6)

Westmill Rows of colour-washed cottages set back from the road behind beautifully tended lawns and lime trees. There is a small triangular green with a village pump in the middle and to the north more picturesque cottages. The house past the church, Westmill Bury, is a very fine example of 18th-century architecture (not open). (A4)

Wisley Gardens Show place of the Royal Horticultural Society with an outstanding collection of plants and trees. Massed rhododendrons and azaleas, pinetum, rock garden, model fruit and vegetable gardens. Off A3. 🔵 (H1)

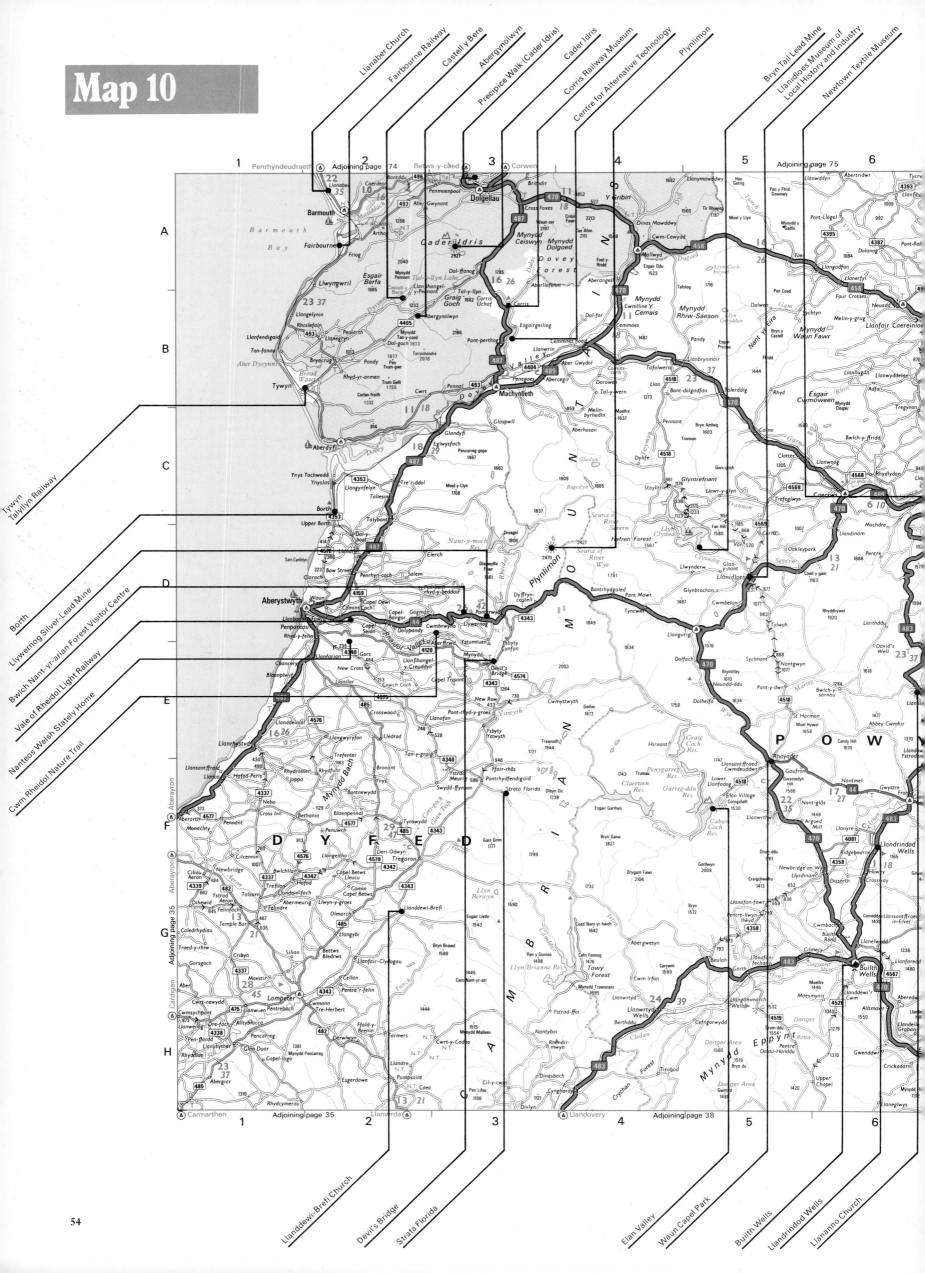

Map 10

Tywyn
Talyllyn Railway

Borth

Llywernog Silver-Lead Mine

Bwlch Nant-yr-arian Forest Visitor Centre

Vale of Rheidol Light Railway

Nanteos Welsh Stately Home

Cwm Rheidol Nature Trail

Llanaber Church

Fairbourne Railway

Castell y Bere

Abergynolwyn

Precipice Walk (Cader Idris)

Cader Idris

Corris Railway Museum

Centre for Alternative Technology

Plynlimon

Bryn Tail Lead Mine

Llanidloes Museum of
Local History and Industry

Newtown Textile Museum

Llanddewi-Brefi Church

Devil's Bridge

Strata Florida

Elan Valley

Waun Capel Park

Builth Wells

Llandrindod Wells

Llananno Church

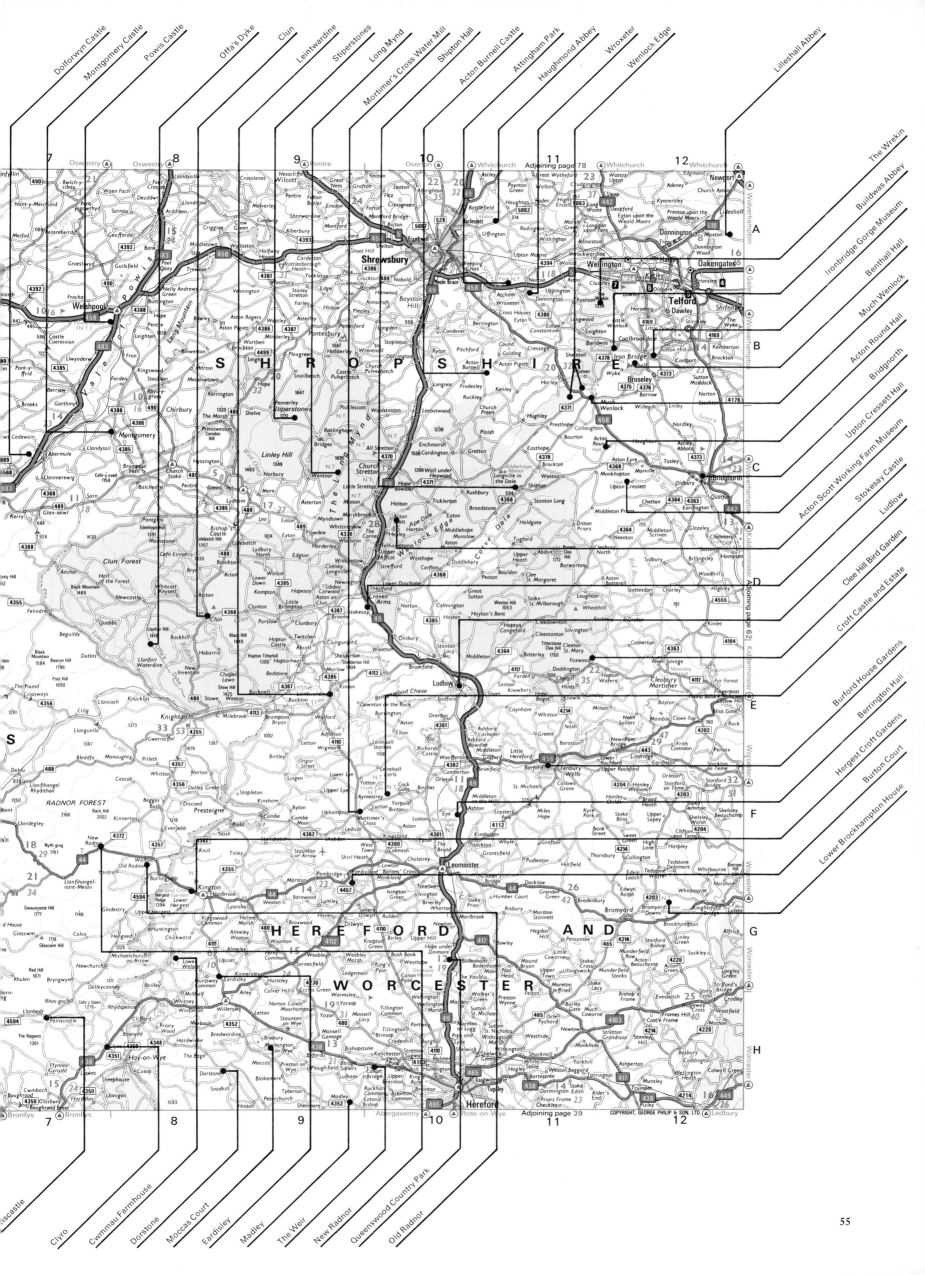

55

Central Wales and Welsh Borders

Abergynolwyn Situated on the Dysynni river, which flows from Lake Tal-y-llyn, 3 miles (4.8 km) to the north-east, this is a good base from which to explore the scenery around Cader Idris. Mountain terminus of **Talyllyn Railway**. The village museum, 14 Water St, has 200 or so relics of the time when this was a busy slate-mining town. (B2)

Acton Burnell Castle (EH) A 13th-century fortified manor house, now in ruins, standing in grounds of an 18th-century house. ⬧ (B10)

Acton Round Hall Mellow, red-brick, early 18th-century house with little-altered interior, many rooms with original panelling and fireplaces. (C11)

Acton Scott Working Farm Museum The working farm, covering some 22 acres (8.9 hectares), is aimed at demonstrating agricultural methods before the internal combustion engine. It is stocked with rare breeds of farm animals and work is mostly done by hand or horse. Visitors may actively participate in doing necessary farm jobs throughout the year. Demonstrations of traditional crafts at weekends. ⬧ (C10)

Attingham Park (NT) Impressive Palladian mansion set in landscaped park. Fine interior with octagonal study, circular boudoir and Nash's splendid picture-gallery and staircase, incorporated in 1805. ⬧ (A11)

Benthall Hall (NT) Stone house c. 1583 of moderate size with mullion windows, moulded brick chimneys and later alterations like a carved oak staircase, plaster ceilings, oak panelling. Small garden. ⬧ (B12)

Berrington Hall (NT) Impressive, porticoed, pink-sandstone house designed by Henry Holland, standing in a park designed by his father-in-law, 'Capability' Brown. Exquisite interior with fine chimney pieces and delicately painted friezes. Outbuildings include the Victorian laundry and original dairy. ⬧ (F10)

Borth Popular holiday resort with over 3 miles (4.8 km) of sand and a 2 mile (3.2 km) promenade. At low tide, evidence of a submerged forest can be seen. The Ynyslas Dunes lying to the north of Borth act as a wall protecting the Dovey estuary from the wilder excesses of the Cardigan Bay sea and have created a special environment – the home of some rare plants and animals. The Nature Conservancy Council's waymarked Ynyslas Nature Trail, part of a Nature Reserve of nearly 4,000 acres (1,619 hectares), reveals interesting flora, fauna; also waders and other wildfowl. (C2)

Bridgnorth Ancient market town by River Severn with 17th-century, half-timbered town hall; Bishop Percy's house, built 1580; the medieval North Gate, now a museum, and the Church of St Mary Magdalene, by Thomas Telford. Only a tower remains of the Norman castle, but it leans at 17°, an even steeper angle than that of the more famous tower of Pisa. (C12)

Bryn Tail Lead Mine (Cadw) Scenic 6½ mile (10.4 km) trail around the shores of Llyn Clywedog takes in the remains of the mine (1 mile, 1.6 km) on the eastern shore. Path from Clywedog Dam, 3½ miles (5.6 km) north-west of Llanidloes, off B4518. (D5)

Buildwas Abbey (EH) Imposing ruins of abbey founded 1135 in attractive

Buildwas Abbey

setting. Vaulted Chapter House dates from late 12th or early 13th century. (B11)

Builth Wells One of the great farming centres of mid-Wales, this small town rose to popularity in the 18th century when spas became popular. Only a mound is left of the 11th-century castle (along a path from the Lion Hotel). (G6)

Burford House Gardens Great range of plants, many rare and unusual, in 5 acre (2 hectare) gardens by River Teme. (F11)

Burton Court Mainly Georgian, moderate-sized house built in a free Tudor style with stone porch added by Clough Williams-Ellis, architect of **Portmeirion**, 1912 (see Gazetteer 14). 14th-century great hall. Costume and natural history exhibition. ⬧ (G9)

Bwlch Nant-yr-arian Forest Visitor Centre, Rheidol Forest Located in a col in the foothills of the **Plynlimon** Mountains, it is operated by the Forestry Commission. Exhibition interpreting the local landscape, picnic areas, two walks. On A44, 3 miles (4.8 km) west of Ponterwyd. ⬧ (D3)

Cader Idris Main summit of Cader Idris range of mountains is 2,927 ft (892 m) Pen-y-gader (A3). From here,

Cader Idris from the Fox's Path

panoramic views take in a vast area – on fine days it is possible to see the snow-capped top of Snaefell in the Isle of Man. Excellent views of Cader Idris and the Mawddach Estuary can be had from the steep, 3 mile (4.8 km) **Precipice Walk**, 2¾ miles (4.4 km) north of Dolgellau, off Llanfachreth road towards Ty'n-Groes. (A3)

Castell y Bere (Cadw) Lofty ruins of medieval mountain stronghold built by Llewelyn the Great to a typically Welsh design. Fine views. (B2)

Centre for Alternative Technology, Llwyn-gwern Working demonstration of equipment using solar, water and wind power, and organic gardening, showing the possibilities of living with renewable energy sources. Also crafts, steam engine. ⬧ (B3)

Clee Hill Bird Garden Over 400 birds (poultry, waterfowl) on show in attractive garden. At Hoptonbank off A4117, west of Cleobury Mortimer. (E11)

Clun A village that has been lived in since prehistoric times. In the *Town Hall's museum* (the original courthouse to Clun Castle) are flint and stone tools, the partly cremated remains of a Bronze Age inhabitant and exhibits of local history and geology. Houses dating from 17th century include the Hospital of the Holy and Undivided Trinity. (D8)

Clyro Set in lovely surroundings, this is a village of much charm, with its white and colourwashed stone buildings clustering round the 13th-century church. A mound beside the road leading to Hay-on-Wye marks the site of the Norman castle, and remains of a Roman fort have been uncovered in nearby fields. (H7)

Corris Railway Museum Housed in old railway building. Photographs of operation of Corris Narrow Gauge Railway; wagons on short length of track. In the village, 300 yards (275 m) from A487. ⬧ (B3)

Croft Castle and Estate (NT) The house retains its original walls and towers of the 14th to 15th centuries; later modifications include 18th-century Gothic staircase and ceilings. 1,400 acres

(566 hectares) of woods and common with fine trees. ⬧ (F10)

Cwmmau Farmhouse, Brilley (NT) Early 17th-century timber-framed and stone-tiled farmhouse. Small motte commanding wide views. (G8)

Cwm Rheidol Nature Trail The 2½ mile (4 km) trail – suitable for families in casual clothes – encircles a reservoir with birds, plants and trees of interest en route. Follow unclassified road off A44 through Dolypandy to car park at Cwm Rheidol power station. Leaflet available. Viewing terrace, floodlit at night, at power station. (D2)

Devil's Bridge Magnificent wooded gorge scenery with waterfalls, including 300 ft (91.5 m) Mynach Falls. Steep steps and winding paths lead from below the Hafod Arms Hotel. The three bridges spanning the gorge are built one above the other. The lowest was completed in c. 1087, the second in 1708 and both are now crossed by the modern steel bridge carrying the A4120. (E3)

Dolforwyn Castle (Cadw) The fragmentary remains of 13th-century fortress, 1 mile (1.6 km) west of Abermule. Access via track off minor road. (C7)

Dorstone Trim stone cottages circle the neat village green. St Faith's Church, rebuilt twice during the 19th century, retains evidence of earlier churches, while the Pandy Inn dates back 500 years. On Dorstone Hill, above the village, is *Arthur's Stone* (EH), an entrance to a collective burial chamber c. 3000 BC with one enormous capstone. (H8)

Eardisley Black-and-white half-timbered cottages line this quiet village's single street; Church of St Mary Magdalene has a Norman font in perfect condition. (G8)

Elan Valley Often described as the 'Lake District of Wales', this beautiful region has four large adjacent reservoirs built by damming the Claerwen river valleys in the first half of this century. Forest and moorland, fishing in lakes, superb walking along attractive paths. The Elan Reservoirs begin 3 miles (4.8 km) south of Rhayader, off B4518. (F5)

Fairbourne Railway Lavishly rebuilt narrow-gauge railway line which runs for over 2 miles (3.2 km) along the Cambrian coast from Fairbourne to Barmouth, with spectacular views over the Mawddach Estuary. 1st, 2nd and 3rd-class coaches, platform entertainment, Punch and Judy shows, Butterfly Safari Park. Journey takes 20 minutes each way. Steam and diesel. (A2)

Haughmond Abbey (EH) Extensive remains of house of Augustinian canons, founded c.1135. Chapter house has ornamental Norman entrance and the abbot's lodging is well preserved. (A11)

Hergest Croft Gardens Gardens with flowers, trees, shrubs and herbaceous borders; also a wooded valley filled with rhododendrons up to 33 ft (10 m) tall. ⬧ (G8)

Ironbridge Gorge Museum Britain's first industrial museum, covering 3 sq miles (7.8 sq km) along the Severn Gorge, from Coalbrookdale to Coalport and including four major sites associated with the age of coal, steam, railways and canals: *The Severn Warehouse*, the *Museum of Iron, Coalport China Museum* and *Blists Hill Open Air Museum*. There is much to see. At Blists Hill Open Air Museum, for example, a late 19th-century industrial community is being reconstructed and includes a stretch of canal, the Hay Inclined Plane linking canal and river, a toll-house, a saw mill, a candle factory, an original squatter's house, working foundry, Victorian pub and many other features. Next to the great Iron Bridge itself (built 1779 and now pedestrianised) is the original toll-

house, now a Tourist Information Centre, selling pamphlets on local nature and industrial heritage trails. ☒ (B12)

Leintwardine Weathered brick and stone houses, black-and-white cottages line this hillside village. At the junction of High St and Church St is a wall with the filled-in doorway of the local lock-up. Church of St Mary Magdalene provides evidence of the village's turbulent past, with its defensive 14th-century tower, 76 ft (23.2 m) to the top of its battlements, with 6 ft (2 m) thick walls. (E9)

Lilleshall Abbey (EH) Considerable remains of abbey established *c*. 1148 by Augustinian canons. 1½ miles (2.4 km) south-east of Lilleshall, off A518 on unclassified road. (A12)

Llanaber Church One of the best examples of Early English architecture in North Wales, the church (St Mary's) was completed in 1250 after 50 years work and has a large collection of early Christian monuments. (A2)

Llananno Church Small church with skilfully carved 16th-century rood loft and screen. On A483, 1 mile (1.6 km) north of junction with B4356 at Llanbister. (E6)

Llanddewi-Brefi Church Sited on a mound, this church (St David's) dominates the peaceful village. It is said to have risen miraculously beneath St David's feet when he rose to address a meeting in the 6th century. The churchyard has Celtic crosses and there are early Christian memorial stones in the church. (G2)

Llandrindod Wells Elegant streets are a legacy of the town's spa days. *The Museum*, Temple St, contains objects excavated from Roman camp at Castell Collen (north of the town), Paterson Doll Collection, Victorian spa gallery with period costume. (F6)

Llanidloes Museum of Local History and Industry On upper floor of half-timbered, early 17th-century market hall, one of the finest in Wales. (D5)

Llywernog Silver-Lead Mine, Ponterwyd (Mid Wales Mining Museum) Mid 19th-century water-powered metal mine restored to provide interpretative facilities for the region's bygone mining industry. Waymarked trail, California of Wales exhibition, underground tunnel, water-wheels, museum. (D3)

Long Mynd (NT) This elevated, heather-covered plateau provides magnificent views of the Shropshire and Cheshire plains and the Black Mountains and has many prehistoric remains. Church Stretton is a good centre for exploration. (C9)

Lower Brockhampton House (NT) Late 14th-century, half-timbered moated manor house with an unusual 15th-century gatehouse and ruined 12th-century chapel. ☒ (G12)

Ludlow Historic town with 15th-century church of St Lawrence, 16th-century Feathers Hotel, extensive town wall and

The Feathers Hotel, Ludlow

streets of timber-framed and Georgian brick houses. On a cliff above the River Teme is the ruined castle, dating from the 11th to 16th centuries. (E10)

Madley Historic village lying between River Wye and Black Mountains, supposed birthplace of St Dyfrig, who crowned King Arthur. Very fine, spacious church, virtually unaltered since 1320, with one of the largest medieval fonts in Britain. (H9)

Moccas Court Built 1775–81 to Adam designs. The setting of the house owes much to 'Capability' Brown, who planned the fine parkland. (H9)

Montgomery Castle (Cadw) Scanty ruins of castle dating from 1223 perched on a high rock overlooking the little border town. (C8)

Mortimer's Cross Water Mill, Lucton (EH) Undershot, 18th-century watermill which was working until 1940. ☒ (F10)

Much Wenlock Of note in this small town is the *Guildhall*, a striking, half-timbered building dating from 1577 with fine oak panelling and furnishings; the *Museum* (High St) has geological, social and local history exhibits and the abbey ruins of 13th century *Wenlock Priory* (EH) are open to the public. (B11)

Nanteos Welsh Stately Home Notable mansion with parts dating back to 1100, but extensively rebuilt 1739–57. Wagner is said to have composed some of *Parsifal* here. Carved oak staircase, period kitchen, music room. Currently undergoing extensive repair work, but visitors are still welcome. ☒ (D2)

New Radnor Founded 1064 to replace **Old Radnor** 3 miles (5 km) to the southeast as a border stronghold, this village was a borough until 1886. Of note is the Norman gridiron street pattern, easily seen from the mound which is all that remains of the Norman castle. Spectacular scenery all around. (F7)

Lower Brockhampton

The Feathers Hotel, Ludlow

Newtown Textile Museum, 5–7 Commercial St For years Newtown was an important centre of the woollen industry. Housed in a composite building which, in the days of the handloom weavers, was half-living accommodation, half-workshop, the museum tells the story of the town's industrial past, also illustrating 18th- and 19th-century social history. Displays of wool and processing; exhibitions of fabrics made in Newtown and elsewhere in Wales, past and present. (C6)

Offa's Dyke Built by Offa, King of Mercia, between AD 750–800, probably as a border marker, the Dyke once stood 20 ft (6 m) high in most parts. Only in a few places does it follow the England–Wales border as now fixed. Unique among designated long-distance footpaths in that it follows an archaeological feature rather than a geographical one, the route stretches from Prestatyn (Map 14 B10) at the north end to Chepstow (Map 7 E8) at the south. It passes through lovely border country, with scenery ranging from mountain ridges to tightly-knit woodlands. Easily accessible even by car; many sections suitable for walking in short distances. Entire length is signposted. (A–G8)

Old Radnor A small village which in pre-Conquest times was a seat of local government. The 14th-century church of St Stephen – one of the finest in Wales – has the oldest organ case (*c*. 1500) and font in Britain. (F8)

Painscastle Ruins of traditional Norman motte and bailey castle with extensive keep surrounded by deep double earthbanks. (H7)

Plynlimon As high, moorland hills rising to 2,000 ft (608 m) surround Plynlimon, its full height of 2,470 ft (752 m) is not easily evident. Only from the west at the level of 1,150 ft (350 m) Nant-y-Moch Reservoir can the mountain be fully appreciated. On a good day, views from the summit of Plynlimon take in most of Wales from Snowdonia to the Prescelly Mountains and the Brecon Beacons. To the south of the range is the scattered Rheidol Forest; to the east, the Hafren Forest (the second largest in Wales) where a series of walks (the Cascades Trail, Blaenhafren Falls Walk and Source of Severn Walk) start from the car park on the Old Hall road (minor road approached from turning left at Old Market Hall in Llanidloes and following Old Hall signs). (D3)

Powis Castle (NT) Medieval stronghold with late 16th-century plasterwork and panelling; contents include paintings, tapestries, early Georgian furniture, relics of Clive of India, early 18th-century terraced garden. 1 mile (1.6 km) south of Welshpool on A483. ☒ (B8)

Queenswood Country Park Half working forest, mainly oak and birch,

half arboretum of 170 acres (69 hectares) on Dinmore Hill. Over 400 species, woodland walks, viewpoint. On A49 between Hereford and Leominster. Car park beside cafe at summit of Dinmore Hill, just south of Hope under Dinmore on west side of A49. (G10)

Shipton Hall Elizabethan stone manor house in picturesque Corvedale setting, with Georgian stable block, stone walled garden, medieval dovecote and old parish church. (C11)

Stiperstones The rocky crags of the 1,700 ft (518 m) Stiperstones can be reached easily on foot from the car park and offer fine views of surrounding wooded valleys and farmlands where Roman lead mines once flourished. Approach from a minor road east of A488 at Ploxgreen. (C9)

Stokesay Castle, Craven Arms The oldest and best-preserved moated and fortified medieval manor house in England. Originally a farm, it was bought in 1280 by Lawrence of Ludlow, the richest wool merchant of his day, and fortified under licence from Edward I. The present family acquired Stokesay in 1869. Located 8 miles (12.8 km) north-west of Ludlow on minor road off A49. (D10)

Strata Florida (WO) Evocative ruins of church and cloister of a Norman Abbey founded for the Cistercians in 1164, standing in tranquil, remote setting. ☒ (F3)

Talyllyn Railway Running 7¼ miles (11.6 km) from **Tywyn** to Nant Gwernol, this narrow-gauge line has operated continuously since 1865. Narrow Gauge Railway Museum at Tywyn. Pleasant walks past waterfalls from Dolgoch, and forest walks at Nant Gwernol. (B2)

Tywyn Holiday resort with 3 mile (4.8 km) sand and shingle beach almost surrounded by the twin flanks of Cader Idris. Church has 7th-century Cadfan's Stone, the earliest known sample of written Welsh. (See **Talyllyn Railway**.) (B1)

Upton Cressett Hall Red-brick Tudor gatehouse and a larger, more irregular manor house with fine panelling, plasterwork and a 14th-century great hall. (C12)

Vale of Rheidol Light Railway Narrow gauge steam railway, 11¼ miles (18 km) from Aberystywyth to Devil's Bridge, runs through a beautiful gorge with lovely views. The only steam railway operated by British Rail and the only one originally built for tourists, 1902. (D/E1–3)

Waun Capel Park One of the loveliest public parks in Wales, on the banks of the Wye in the attractive market town of Rhayader. Sylvan riverside walk on the west bank. (F5)

The Weir, Swainshill (NT) Spring garden with good views of River Wye from cliff-garden walks. (H10)

Wenlock Edge Escarpment of ancient landscape forming a well-known landmark to south-west of **Much Wenlock**. Good viewpoints of Apedale and the Church Stretton Hills along its narrow, wooded crest. Of note is the vertical limestone rock of Major's Leap, with its legend of Civil War heroism, north of the B4371, 2½ miles (4 km) from Much Wenlock. (C/D10/11)

The Wrekin Isolated hill of 1,334 ft (406 m) commanding lovely views over the Vale of the Upper Severn. Important hill fort of Iron Age Britain, later used as a beacon hill. 2 miles (3.2 km) south of Wellington, off A5. (B11)

Wroxeter (EH) The small, present-day village developed a little distance from the actual site of the fourth largest city of Roman Britain in the 2nd century AD. Remains include earthworks, which were once city ramparts, stone foundations of the baths and a colonnade. (B11)

Medieval Castles

Medieval castles, which were built for about four hundred years (1066–1485), can be divided into two fundamental groups: those with keeps and those without. A keep is a great stone tower, as much as 100 ft (30 m) high, which is the main refuge in time of danger. It normally stands within, or half in and half out of, a walled bailey, so that the arrangement can be described as a keep-and-bailey castle. Castles with keeps of one sort or another remained in fashion for about two centuries, from 1066 until the reign of Edward I (1272–1307), by which time, however, other types of castle, without keeps, had come into use. The earliest keeps, those most closely identified with the Norman conquerors, were rectangular in plan – up to 100 ft (30 m) square – with walls 10–15 ft (3–4.5 m) thick. They were normally entered, for security reasons, at first-floor level, with the ground floor, accessible only from above, used for storage. There were normally three storeys above the ground floor, the first often a common hall, the second the main or lord's hall, and the third a more private family room. Rectangular keeps were built for about a century (1066–c. 1180), and there are many excellent surviving examples: The Tower of London, Rochester and Dover (Kent), Portchester (Hampshire), Corfe (Dorset), Hedingham (Essex), Norwich and Castle Rising (Norfolk), Ludlow (Shropshire), Richmond and Scarborough (North Yorkshire), Bamburgh (Northumberland), Newcastle (Tyne and Wear), and Carlisle, Appleby and Brougham (Cumbria), to mention only the larger types.

Although they looked very formidable, rectangular keeps had certain drawbacks and these eventually brought about a trend towards circular keeps around the year 1180. Because its angles can be attacked from two sides at once, a rectangular keep is vulnerable to undermining, a common method of attack in medieval warfare. In a circular keep, on the other hand, with no vulnerable corners, any attempt to undermine the wall had to be made directly from the front and this made the attempt that much more difficult. One of the first circular keeps to be built was Conisbrough in South Yorkshire (c. 1180), still standing almost to its original height, and this was followed by others at Pembroke (Dyfed), Caldicot and Sken-

rith (Gwent), Bronllys (Powys), Longtown (Hereford and Worcester), Chartley (Staffordshire), Bothwell (Strathclyde), Kildrummy (Grampian), Dirleton (Lothian), Doldabarn (Gwynedd) and Hawarden and Flint (Clwyd), the latter built by Edward I in 1277 and one of the last circular keeps to be constructed. In addition to rectangular and circular keeps, there were also a few of intermediate shape: polygonal (Chilham, Kent, and Orford, Suffolk), D-shaped (Ewloe, Clwyd, Castell y Bere, Gwynedd, and Helmsley, North Yorkshire), and quatrefoil (Clifford's Tower, York).

The last type of keep to be described is the shell keep. This consists of a circular or polygonal wall standing on a motte or mound. It is not a building with a roof in the same way as the keeps just described. It is simply a defensive wall around the open space at the top of the motte. There were certainly roofed buildings involved but they were built in lean-to fashion against the inside of the wall, leaving an open space or courtyard in the middle. The outstanding example of a shell keep is the Round Tower at Windsor Castle, although this was heightened and restored in the 19th century. There are other surviving examples at Tonbridge (Kent), Lewes and Arundel (West Sussex), Restormel and Launceston (Cornwall), Totnes (Devon), Cardiff (South Glamorgan), Berkeley (Gloucestershire), Warwick (Warwickshire), Tamworth (Staffordshire), Castle Acre (Norfolk), Durham (Co Durham), Berkhamsted (Hertfordshire), Carisbrooke (Isle of Wight) and Rothesay (Bute).

Castles with keeps of the various types just described were built for about two centuries, from 1066 until c. 1280. For the last eighty years or so of this period, however, they were accompanied by new types of castle in which the keep had no place. There had always been a few such castles, from the earliest days of the Conquest, but after about 1200 castles without keeps began to appear in much larger numbers. Defence was now concentrated on a high enclosing wall (called a curtain wall), reinforced with wall towers. These towers, circular in plan, projected forward boldly so that they could command the walls on either side. To the same end, the stretches of wall between the towers were made straight (rather than curved as

they had tended to be earlier), with the result that the castles became polygonal in plan. This was very quickly transformed into a rectangular plan with towers at the four angles projecting for three-quarters of their circumference. Two more such towers, side by side, protected the entrance, and this rapidly developed into the double-towered gatehouse, one of the outstanding features of 13th-century, and later, military architecture. Examples of castles without keeps include Framlingham (Suffolk), an early example with square towers, Beeston (Cheshire), Bolingbroke (Lincolnshire), Barnwell (Northamptonshire), Clifford (Hereford and Worcester), Cilgerran and Llanstephan (Dyfed), White Castle (Gwent) and Inverlochy (Highland).

A noticeable feature of 13th-century (and later) castle building was the use of water defences. The use of wet ditches was not in itself new, although the majority of castles probably had dry ditches, whatever period they belonged to. At a number of castles built during the 13th century, however, elaborate measures were taken to provide a surrounding body of protective water. The main technique, where local conditions permitted, was to dam a stream or river in order to build up an artificial lake around the castle. Such conditions

obtained outstandingly at three sites: Kenilworth (Warwickshire), Leeds (Kent), and Caerphilly (Mid Glamorgan). Kenilworth is now dry but both Leeds and Caerphilly are still surrounded by wide stretches of water with the castles rising like battleships above the surface. There are also surviving water defences at Bodiam and Herstmonceux (East Sussex), Whittington (Shropshire), White Castle (Gwent), and Beaumaris (Gwynedd), as well as indications at many other sites, now dry, that water once formed a part of their defence apparatus.

Some of the greatest medieval castles were built on the orders of Edward I, who was particularly active in North Wales. Many of his castles there were an elaboration of the rectangular plan, consisting of two curtain walls, one inside the other, each with its own towers and gatehouses, and are known as concentric castles. Most concentric castles are royal works: Rhuddlan (Clwyd), Harlech and Beaumaris (Gwynedd) and Aberystwyth (Dyfed). The Tower of London, as rebuilt by Edward, is also of the concentric type, as is Caerphilly, an outstanding baronial castle. Because of their situation, not all of Edward's castles were rectangular in plan. At two of his greatest works, *Continued overleaf*

(Above left) *Leeds Castle, Kent, an outstanding example of a castle protected by water defences;* (above) *Helmsley Castle, North Yorkshire, has a D-shaped keep intermediate in style between a rectangular and circular keep;* (below left) *Caerlaverock Castle, Dumfries and Galloway, has a formidable defensive exterior dating from the Edwardian period but an elegant Renaissance interior of 1634;* (below centre) *Cawdor Castle,*

Highland, one of the many hundreds of Scottish tower-houses; (below right) the rectangular keep of Castle Rising, Norfolk, is typical of the many built 1066 – c. 1180.

Continued from previous page

Conwy and Caernarfon, the plan is dictated by the situation, but both still outstandingly exemplify the curtain wall and regular tower principle. Other castles of the Edwardian period include Kidwelly and Carreg Cennen (Dyfed), and Caerlaverock and Tibbers (Dumfries and Galloway).

The two main developments of the late medieval period (*c.* 1300–1485), when defence was no longer an overriding consideration, were the courtyard castle and the tower house. The courtyard castle was a development of the rectangular Edwardian castle, with ranges of elaborate domestic buildings on all four sides of the courtyard. Internally it was a great mansion, but externally it still had much of its Edwardian predecessors' military appearance. The best known of these courtyard castles are Bodiam and Herstmonceux, but there are equally well-preserved examples at Bolton (North Yorkshire), Lumley (Co Durham) and Maxstoke (Warwickshire). There are also lesser remains at Kirby Muxloe (Leicestershire) and Farleigh Hungerford (Somerset).

In the same period (1300–1485) the tower principle re-appeared in the form of the tower-house. These were very common in the northern counties of England (as pele towers) and in Scotland and Ireland, and are manor houses rather than true castles. However, a few elaborate examples were built elsewhere in England and are worth noting here. Some were self-contained residences, capable of standing a siege, while others were simply additional accommodation in tower form. English towers of this period include Nunney (Somerset), Wardour (Wiltshire), Tattershall (Lincolnshire), Dudley (West Midlands), Ashby de la Zouch (Leicestershire), Knaresborough (North Yorkshire), and Warkworth (Northumberland). In Wales there is an outstanding example at Raglan Castle (Gwent), as well as early examples (both *c.* 1300) at Marten's Tower in Chepstow Castle and the Eagle Tower in Caernarfon Castle. Among the many hundreds of Scottish tower-houses the following are worthy of mention: Borthwick, Crichton and Elphinstone (Lothian), Hermitage (Borders), Cawdor (Highland), Threave (Dumfries and Galloway), Drum and Craigievar (Grampian), Craigmillar (Edinburgh), and Glamis, Claypotts and Coune (Tayside). In a limited sense the wheel had gone full circle, from the early Norman tower-keep back, if not to a keep then at least, in a small number of cases, to keep-like accommodation in tower form.

(Below) *Arundel Castle, Sussex, a shell-keep on a motte;*
(above) *Caernarfon Castle was one of nine new or
virtually new castles that Edward I built in north Wales
and was sited so that it could be supplied by sea. Its plan
exemplifies the curtain wall and regular tower principle;*
(above left) *the Lilburn Tower of Dunstanburgh Castle.
Built in the early fourteenth century, this was the first
entirely new castle of the post-Edwardian period;* (below
left) *Castle Bolton, North Yorkshire, is a courtyard
castle, one of the standard types of the post-Edwardian
period;* (right) *the keep at Chepstow Castle, Gwent,
began as an oblong, two-storey hall block and was
converted into a keep by the addition of a third, tall
storey in the second half of the thirteenth century.*

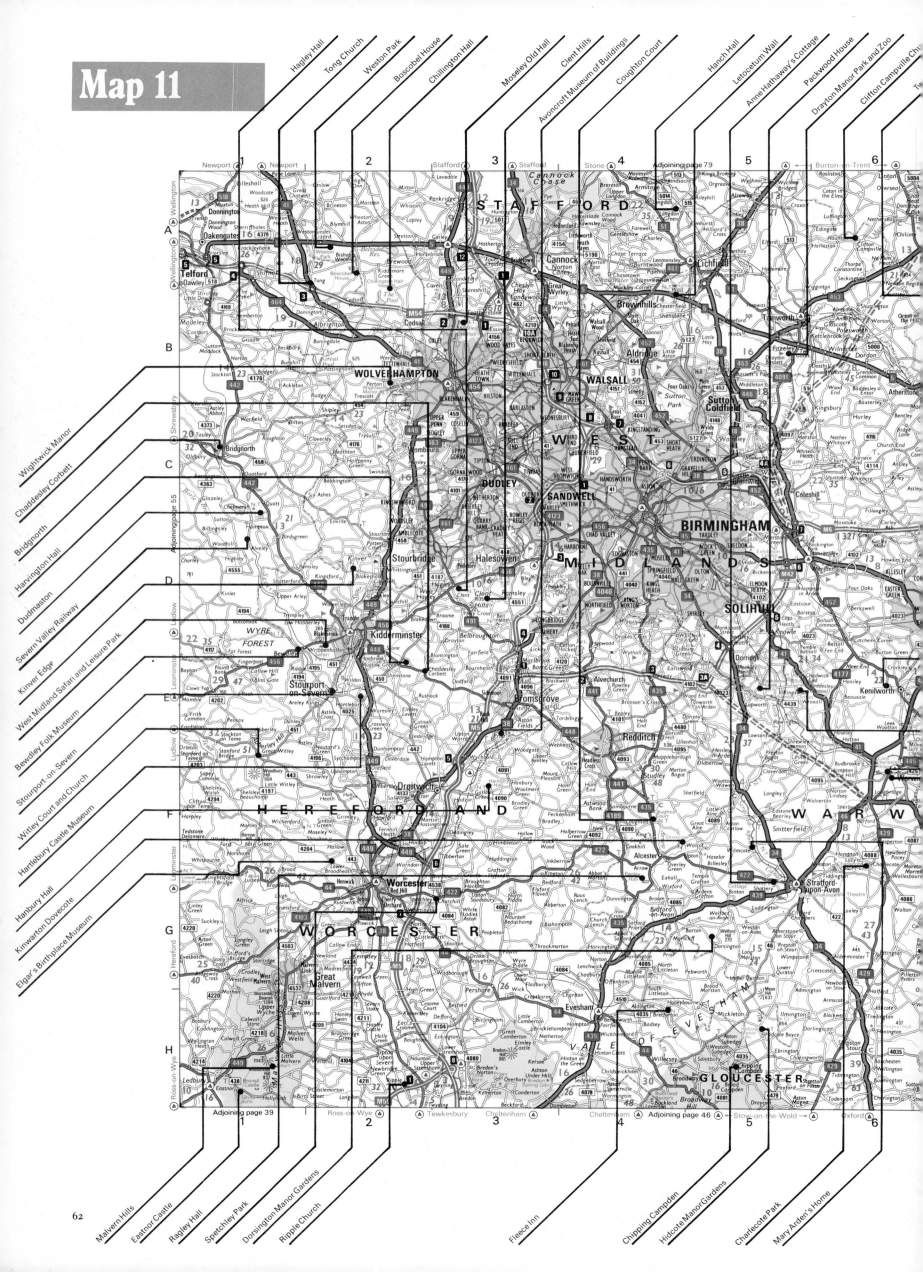

Map 11

Ashby-de-la-Zouch Castle
Arbury Hall
Battlefield of Bosworth
Donington-le-Heath Manor House
Charnwood Forest
Coombe Abbey
Beacon Hill
Bradgate Park and Swithland Woods
Kirby Muxloe Castle
Stanford Hall
Kenilworth Castle
Foxton Locks

Oakham Castle
Rutland County Museum
Rutland Water
Lyddington Bede House
Deene Park
Kirby Hall
Rockingham Castle
Rushton Triangular Lodge
Boughton House
Naseby Battle and Farm Museum
Lamport Hall
Coton Manor Gardens
Guilsborough Grange Wildlife Park
Castle Ashby

Farnborough Hall
Southam Zoo
Warwick Castle
Sulgrave Manor
Lord Leycester Hospital
Baddesley Clinton
Althorp
Stowe Gardens
Waterways Museum
Stoke Park Pavilions
Billing Aquadrome and Milling Museum
Chicheley Hall

COPYRIGHT, GEORGE PHILIP & SON, LTD.

South Midlands

Althorp The Spencer family home since 1506, altered by Henry Holland around 1790 and completely rearranged by Earl and Countess Spencer in 1976. Magnificent portraits by Van Dyck, Gainsborough, Reynolds and Rubens, superb 18th-century porcelain, rare French and English furniture. ♿ (F10)

Anne Hathaway's Cottage, Shottery Early home of Shakespeare's wife; originally a thatched farmhouse, its fabric essentially unaltered. On west edge of Stratford between A422 and A439. (G5)

Arbury Hall This splendid example of 18th-century 'Gothick' features in novels by George Eliot, who grew up on the estate owned by the Newdigates since 1586. Numerous portraits, chair covers worked by ladies of the family. ♿ (C7)

Ashby-de-la-Zouch Castle (EH) Extensive ruins mainly of 15th-century self-contained fortified manor house of much architectural and historic interest. ♿ (A7)

Avoncroft Museum of Buildings, Stoke Heath, Bromsgrove Fine, growing collection of re-erected buildings include working windmill, nail and chain-making workshops, timber-framed merchants' house, barns, granary, forge and 1946 prefab, all saved from demolition elsewhere. Off A38 between junctions 4 and 5 of M5. ♿ (E3)

Baddesley Clinton (NT) Medieval moated manor house, dating from 1300 and little altered since 1634. Elizabethan fireplaces, hiding places, panelled rooms, tapestries and heraldic glass give the house the perfect atmosphere. Stands in a remnant of the Forest of Arden. Just west of A41. (E6)

Battlefield of Bosworth (Leicestershire County Council) Site of the decisive battle of 1485 which brought Tudors to the throne. History imaginatively brought to life through films, models, exhibits and trails over battlefield in rolling rural countryside. Signposted from A447, A5, A444 and B585. ♿ (B7)

Beacon Hill, Woodhouse Eaves (Leicestershire County Council) 180 acres (72.8 hectares) of undulating heathland, bracken, woods and rhododendrons. Superb view from rock summit 818 ft (249.3 m). Remains of Bronze Age settlement. Access from B591. (A8)

Bewdley Folk Museum, Load Street Crafts and folk life of old Worcestershire displayed in former market stalls of 18th-century Shambles. Craft demonstrations. Brass foundry. ♿ (E1)

Billing Aquadrome and Milling Museum Swimming, boating and fishing in a country park. Restored corn mill with working machinery and wheel now a milling museum. Funfair. Entrance on minor road 1 mile (1.6 km) south of A45. (F11)

Boscobel House (EH) 16th-century house enlarged in 17th century with built-in hiding places used by Charles II after escaping from Battle of Worcester, 1651. A descendant of the oak tree in which he also hid stands in the park. ♿ (A2)

Boughton House Late 17th-century French style mansion with traces of Tudor and earlier monastic house. Magnificent furnishings include early Persian carpets, Mortlake tapestries and fine paintings. Celebrated armoury. Beautiful parkland with lakes. Entrance off A43 at Geddington. ♿ (D12)

Bradgate Park and Swithland Woods 850 acres (344 hectares) of natural parkland in heart of Charnwood Forest surrounding ruined birthplace of Lady Jane Grey. Interpretation centre in former chapel. 300 red and fallow deer. Entrance on B5327 in Newtown Linford village. ♿ (A8)

Bridgnorth Two delightful towns in one: Upper Town and Lower linked by Britain's steepest cliff tramway. Many interesting old buildings include leaning castle keep, and town hall spanning main street. (C1)

Broughton Castle Moated 14th-century manor transformed into Elizabethan mansion and barely touched since externally. Internally a delightful mixture of styles with many medieval and Tudor features. Good fireplaces, plaster ceilings. Entrance on B4035. ♿ (H7)

Castle Ashby Elizabethan mansion splendidly sited in rolling Northamptonshire countryside. Interior noted for paintings, including early 16th-century Flemish triptych in chapel, furnishings and 17th-century woodwork. ♿ (F12)

Chaddesley Corbett Attractive village with wealth of half-timbered buildings. Fine church dedicated to little known St Cassian. (E2)

Charlecote Park (NT) Shakespeare reputedly poached deer in 250 acre (100 hectare) park surrounding the house. Deer remain, and Jacob sheep; the house, built 1558, was altered and enlarged in 19th century. Gatehouse, however, is pure Tudor. Interesting paintings and furniture. Entrance on B4086. ♿ (F6)

Charlecote gatehouse, from the hall

Charnwood Forest Some of England's oldest rocks are contained in the Forest's 60 sq miles (155.4 sq km), bisected by the M1. It is forest in the old sense of wild country, and though much is now cultivated there are areas of open heathland and exposed rock (see entries for **Beacon Hill** and **Bradgate Park**) and richly varied wildlife. Many local roofs and churchyard headstones are of Swithland Slate from now disused quarries. The ruined priories of Grace Dieu and Ulverscroft are private, but the Cister-

cian Abbey of Mount St Bernard (founded 1835), near Whitwick (A8), may be visited. (A8/9)

Chicheley Hall Early 18th-century house by Francis Smith of Warwick. Unusual Dutch style Baroque exterior approached up double avenue of limes. The interior is little changed since the 18th century, but now contains seascapes, portraits and other memorabilia of the 1st Earl Beatty, grandfather of the present owner. ♿ (G12)

Chillington Hall Home of the Giffards for 800 years. Present Georgian house by Francis Smith and Sir John Soane. Contemporary furniture and fine plasterwork. Grounds laid out by 'Capability' Brown contain enormous lake and superb oak avenue. (B2)

Chipping Campden One of England's loveliest small towns, built out of wool trade profits and preserved by the trade's collapse. Many medieval and 17th-century houses. Notable Perpendicular 'wool' church. (H5)

Clent Hills An area of heathland, woods and farmland rising to 1,000 ft (304.8 m), largely under National Trust care, north and east of Clent village. They provide good, fairly easy walking. (D3)

Clifton Campville Church Fine 14th-century church with tall spire, good carvings, unusual monuments and ancient chest carved from solid tree-trunk in an unspoilt rural village. (A6)

Coombe Abbey Ruins of Cistercian abbey in almost 250 acres (100 hectares) of natural parkland. Formal gardens; angling and boating on large lake. ♿ (D7)

Coton Manor Gardens One of England's great gardens. Flamingoes, cranes and waterfowl roam in water gardens. Signposted from A50 at Creaton and A428. ♿ (E10)

Coughton Court (NT) Mainly Elizabethan house with impressive gatehouse of 1509 wherein wives of Gunpowder plotters awaited news from London. Jacobean relics belonging to Throckmortons, whose home it has been since 1409. (F4)

Deene Park Vast, battlemented house which has grown in variety of styles

under Brudenell ownership since 1514. Externally basically Gothic of 1810, but interior contains two 16th-century great halls. 7th Earl of Cardigan, who led the Charge of the Light Brigade, figures among family portraits. Extensive park, gardens and lake. (C12)

Donington-le-Heath Manor House (Leicestershire County Council) The oldest house in Leicestershire and one of the oldest in England. Built about 1280, it stands virtually unchanged apart from minor 16th and 17th-century alterations. Original roof trusses survive over great hall. Splendidly restored since being used as piggery in 1960. Entrance on minor road off B585. ♿ (A7)

Dorsington Manor Gardens Home of the Domestic Fowl Trust, a survival centre for domestic fowl from all over the world set in gardens of Dorsington Manor. Entrance from Welford–Barton road. ♿ (G5)

Drayton Manor Park and Zoo Pleasure area of 160 acres (64.8 hectares) once belonging to Sir Robert Peel now contains a zoo, lakes, amusement park and 'Lost World' with dinosaurs. Follow AA signs. ♿ (B5)

Dudmaston (NT) One of the most beautiful Shropshire estates, it has not changed hands, except by inheritance, since 1200. Late 17th-century house with fine furniture and collection of 17th-century Dutch flower paintings which used to belong to Francis Darby of Coalbrookdale. It also has a magnificent collection of modern art, with works by Matisse, Ben Nicholson, Barbara Hepworth and Henry Moore. Set in extensive lakeside gardens with walks through the Dingle. ♿ (C1)

Eastnor Castle Dramatic, lavish, Georgian Gothic castle by Robert Smirke for 1st Earl Somers. Extensive later internal changes include Pugin decorations and great hall 60 ft (18.3 m) high. Considerable Italian art work and furniture. ♿ (H1)

Elgar's Birthplace Museum, Crown East Lane, Lower Broadheath Small cottage containing personal belongings, manuscripts, letters etc. of the composer. Turn north for Broadheath at Crown East Church on A44 3 miles (4.8 km) west of Worcester. ♿ (F2)

Farnborough Hall (NT) Classical stone-built house with early 18th-century west front by William and Francis Smith of Warwick. Remainder was reconstructed about 1750, probably by Sanderson Miller. Exuberant internal plasterwork. Fine views from attractive terrace walk. Entrance ½ mile (.8 km) off A423. ♿ (G8)

Fleece Inn, Bretforton (NT) Medieval farmhouse which has been the village inn since 1848 and remains essentially unaltered. Family collection of furniture. In village centre on B4035. (H4)

The Market Hall, Chipping Campden

Foxton Locks (Leicestershire County Council) Spectacular flight of locks on Leicester section of the Grand Union Canal. Two staircases of five locks, each surmounting a 75 ft (23 m) change of level. Car park, picnic site and access on minor road between Foxton and Gumley off A6. (C10)

Guilsborough Grange Wildlife Park, West Haddon Road, Guilsborough Birds, pets and wildlife in country house and garden setting with fine views. On outskirts of Guilsborough off A50 and B4036. ♿ (E10)

Hagley Hall Palladian house of 1756 by Sanderson Miller for the Lyttelton family who have been in possession since 1564. Restored after fire in 1925. Fine rococo plasterwork, tapestries and furniture. Notable portraits, and marble busts by Rysbrack and Scheemakers. Temples and ornaments in park by Sanderson Miller and James Stuart. (D3)

Hanbury Hall (NT) Wren-style brick house of 1701, little altered. Notable ceiling paintings and staircase by Sir John Thornhill. The Watney collection of porcelain is displayed. Entrance on minor road 1 mile (1.6 km) north of B4090 and $1\frac{1}{2}$ miles (2.4 km) west of B4091. ♿ (F3)

Hanch Hall Handsome Queen Anne garden front, but medieval timbers and 17th-century panelling upstairs and later additions elsewhere suggest an old house much altered over centuries. Impressive early Victorian carved staircase. Entrance on B5014. ♿ (A4)

Hartlebury Castle Museum (Hereford and Worcester County Council) The County Museum in the north wing of the Bishop's Palace splendidly illustrates the arts, crafts and domestic life of the area over 400 years. ♿ (E2)

Harvington Hall This moated Tudor manor house built round an earlier house is famed for its wealth of priests' hiding holes. Several Elizabethan wall-paintings have been uncovered this century. Entrance off A450. ♿ (E2)

Hidcote Manor Garden (NT) One of Britain's finest 20th-century gardens, laid out by Major Lawrence Johnston, an American officer, around 17th-century Cotswold manor house. Signposted from Mickleton on A46. ♿ (H5)

Kenilworth Castle (EH) Impressive ruins of one of England's great fortresses, immortalised by Sir Walter Scott. 12th-century keep and much work built for John of Gaunt and Robert Dudley, Earl of Leicester, survive. (E6)

Kinver Edge (NT) 283 acres (114.5 hectares) of high heath and woodland with Iron Age fort above Holy Austin Rock, a medieval hermitage carved out of rock and reoccupied in 19th century. Another 19th-century rock dwelling lies below Nanny's Rock. Fine views. Access from Kinver. (D2)

Kinwarton Dovecote (NT) Circular 14th-century stone dovehouse. In field at end of lane south of B4089. Key at Glebe Farm, next door. (F5)

Kirby Hall (EH) Ruins of fine Elizabethan stone mansion with alterations by Inigo Jones 1638–40. House abandoned in late 18th century but still partly roofed. Good carvings. 17th-century garden. Near Deene village 2 miles (3.2 km) north of A43. ♿ (C12)

Kirby Muxloe Castle (EH) The great gatehouse and one of four angle-towers remain of moated, fortified, brick-built manor house started by the ambitious Lord Hastings in 1480 and left unfinished after his execution. Access from Oxcroft Avenue in village. ♿ (B8)

Lamport Hall The Isham family, who first settled here in 1560, commissioned John Webb to build the house in 1654 and Francis Smith of Warwick to enlarge it nearly a century later. Fine paintings, furniture and china. Wooded gardens and park include earliest English Alpine garden with prototype gnome. ♿ (E11)

Letocetum, Wall (EH/NT) Bath house and remains of a dwelling at junction of two important Roman roads. Finds from site in small museum. Just north of A5. (B4)

Lord Leycester Hospital, High Street, Warwick This wonderful collection of 15th-century half-timbered buildings has been a retired soldiers' home since 1571. Its guildhall, the military museum, great hall, and chapel over town's West Gate, especially impressive. (F6)

Lyddington Bede House (DoE) Mainly 15th-century residence of Bishops of Lincoln, with elaborate timber ceiling, in attractive limestone single-street village. Signposted from A6003 and A47. (B12)

Malvern Hills A 9 mile (14.5 km) long range of hills rising to the 1,394 ft (424.8 m) summit of Worcestershire Beacon. Cropped grass and bracken provides easy walking, though with steep gradients; marvellous views westward to Wales and eastward across the Midlands. Iron Age forts on Herefordshire Beacon (1,114 ft, 340 m) and Midsummer Hill (NT) (H1). The five Malvern towns mainly line terraces on the lower slopes. Great Malvern, the largest, has magnificent Priory church of Norman and Perpendicular architecture. Elgar is buried in Roman Catholic churchyard at Little Malvern (H1). (G/H1)

Mary Arden's Home, Wilmcote The home of Shakespeare's mother before her marriage is a mainly 16th-century farmhouse of close-timbered oak beams and local stone. The outbuildings make a perfect setting for a museum of farming and rural life. Off A34. (F5)

Moseley Old Hall (NT) Small manor house of Elizabethan origin, with later alterations, where Charles II took refuge after Battle of Worcester, 1651. His bed, and secret hiding places, on view. Small garden reconstructed in 17th-century style. In narrow lane between A449 and A460, $\frac{3}{4}$ mile (1.2 km) west of A460. Car park with concealed entrance opposite. ♿ (B3)

Naseby Battle and Farm Museum, Purlieu Farm, Naseby Miniature lay-out of battlefield with commentary. Relics from battlefield. Farm hand tools and machinery, vintage tractors, village history. At southern end of village off B4036. (D10)

Oakham Castle (Leicestershire County Council) Late Norman banqueting hall of 12th-century fortified manor house, containing remarkable collection of horseshoes left by Royalty and peers entering Oakham Lordship. Off Market Place. ♿ (A12)

Packwood House (NT) Elizabethan manor house, with later additions, in charming Arden setting. Noted for remarkable topiary garden of around 1650 representing the Sermon on the Mount. $1\frac{1}{4}$ miles (2 km) north of Lapworth off B4439. (E5)

Ragley Hall This very stately home of the Marquess of Hertford stands at the highest point of 'Capability' Brown's noble park. Built by Robert Hooke *c.* 1680, with additions by James Wyatt a century later, the house contains remarkable entrance hall by James Gibbs, 'the finest Baroque interior in England'. Much good rococo plasterwork. Recent restoration after period of dereliction includes modern mural by Graham Rust. Fine furniture, late Georgian silver and excellent portrait collection. Adventure wood, trails, picnic areas and lake in park. Entrance on A435. ♿ (G4)

Ripple Church Fine 15th-century misericords depict agricultural scenes. Attractive village grouped around green. Minor road off A38. (H2)

Rockingham Castle A mainly Elizabethan house within walls of Norman castle on pre-Norman defensive hilltop site. A Royal fortress from the 11th to 15th centuries, it has been occupied by Watson family since 1530. Paintings and furniture covering five centuries. Collection of Rockingham china. Gardens amongst fortifications. (C12)

Rushton Triangular Lodge (EH) Built by Sir Thomas Tresham for his warriner, it has three sides, each with three gables, three floors, trefoil windows and other features in threes or divisible by three to symbolise the Trinity. In grounds of Rushton Hall, but separate entrance on minor road from A6. (D11)

Rutland County Museum, Catmos Street, Oakham (Leicestershire County Council) Fascinating collection of Rutland bygones including Victorian shop, trade tools, farm wagons and agricultural implements. Town centre on A6003. ♿ (A12)

Rutland Water (Empingham Reservoir) Lake of 3,000 acres (1,214 hectares) with sailing, trout fishing and nature reserves. Four car parks with picnic areas, three off A606. ♿ (A/B12)

Severn Valley Railway Steam trains run through beautiful valley between Bridgnorth (C1) and Bewdley (D1) with intermediate stops. Summer only.

Southam Zoo 10 acres (4.5 hectares) of wildlife park with wild animals and exotic birds. Picnic area. ♿ (F7)

Spetchley Park Garden of 30 acres (12 hectares) containing many unusual trees, shrubs and plants. Red and fallow deer in park. Garden Centre. ♿ (G2)

Stanford Hall Dignified William and Mary house begun by William and Francis Smith of Warwick in 1697, continued by Francis alone in 1737, the ballroom remodelled by his son, another William, in 1745. Fine collections of pictures, antiques and family costumes. Motor cycle museum. Replica flying machine of 1898. Entrance on minor road South Kilworth to Stanford-on-Avon. ♿ (D9)

Stoke Park Pavilions Two wings and a colonnade survive, in a lovely, isolated garden, of England's first Palladian country house, built in 1630, almost certainly by Inigo Jones, and destroyed by fire in 1886. Access by signposted private road $\frac{1}{2}$ mile (.8 km) beyond Stoke Bruerne village, approached off A508 6 miles (9.6 km) south of Northampton. ♿ (G10)

Stourport-on-Severn England's only Georgian canal town, created on site of 'sandy, barren common' at western end of Brindley's Staffordshire and Worcestershire Canal. Dignified warehouses, canal inns and nautical flavour. (E2)

Stowe Gardens Bridgeman, William Kent and 'Capability' Brown all helped to make this one of England's great gardens. Vanbrugh and Kent were responsible for most of the surviving temples, grottoes and follies on this 250 acre (100 hectare) estate of the Dukes of Buckingham. (H10)

Sulgrave Manor Early English home of George Washington's ancestors. Small manor house of Tudor period with Queen Anne and 20th-century additions. Many Washington souvenirs. In Sulgrave village off B4525. (G9)

Tong Church Splendid early 15th-century church containing wonderful collection of monuments to Pembruge and Vernon families. Just off A41. (A2)

Twycross Zoo Spacious, well laid-out zoo famous for its primates. Pet's corner, children's playground. On A444. ♿ (B6)

Upton House (NT) This 17th-century house was extensively remodelled in 1927 to display a wonderful collection of works of art, including more than 250 paintings and notable 18th-century porcelain. ♿ (H7)

Warwick Castle One of the great fortresses of Europe, romantically placed above unspoilt market town, and one of few still habitable. Earliest parts of present buildings date from 14th century, with important additions in 15th and subsequent centuries. 'Capability' Brown laid out the grounds. ♿ (F6)

Waterways Museum, Stoke Bruerne Relics of all aspects of canal life in natural setting on canal side. In village street, off A508. (G11)

West Midland Safari and Leisure Park, Spring Grove, Bewdley Wild animals in 200 acre (81 hectare) park with 4 miles (6.4 km) of drives through animal reserves. On A456 between Bewdley and Kidderminster. ♿ (E2)

Weston Park Designed by Lady Wilbraham for herself in 1671, this is one of the finest examples of the post-Restoration period. Home of the Earls of Bradford for nearly 300 years, its interior has recently been restored to its Palladian splendour. Magnificent collection of paintings, tapestries, furniture, porcelain and silver. James Paine's Temple of Diana is a feature of the huge park landscaped by 'Capability' Brown. Also a Woodland Adventure Playground, aquarium, pottery, miniature railway, Museum of Country Bygones, butterfly farm, nature and architectural trails. ♿ (A2)

Wightwick Manor (NT) A treasure-house of Victoriana. Morris wallpaper, Kempe glass, Pre-Raphaelite pictures and contemporary furnishings in late-Victorian house. Fine plasterwork ceilings. Delightful garden. Just north of A454. (B2)

Witley Court and Church, Great Witley Magnificent baroque church of 1735 with ceiling paintings by Laguerre, massive Rysbrack monument and a riot of colours compensates for sad wreck of 18th-century mansion after 1937 fire. Concealed entrance to rough private drive at junction of A443 and A451. (F1)

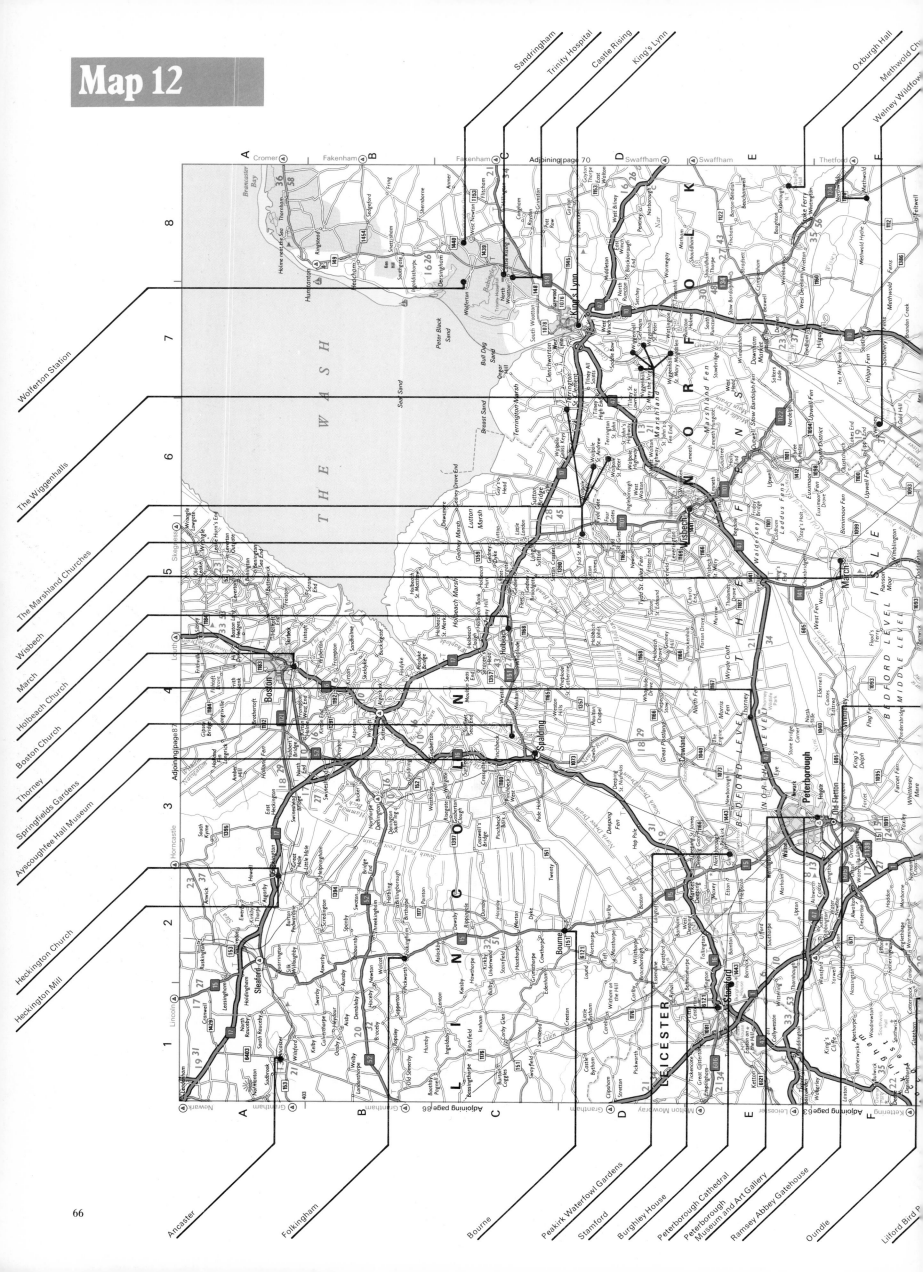

Map 12

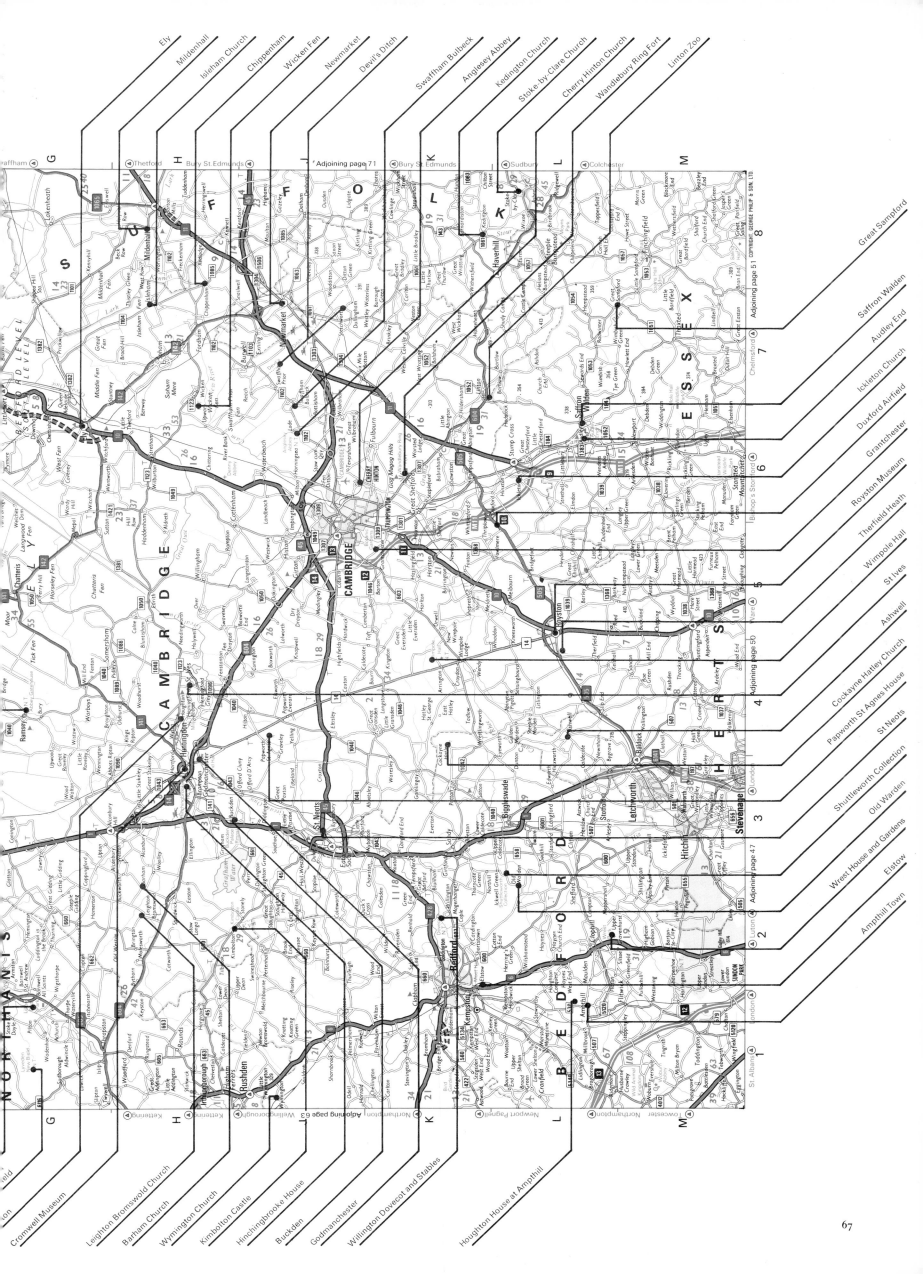

East Anglia

Ancaster Roman remains of the settlement of Cuasennae. Remnants of earthworks, town walls. Access from village on B6403. (A1)

Ampthill Town A very attractive town, well-restored with many fine houses in and around its centre. Avenue House, in Church Street, an 18th-century redbrick house, is probably the town's finest building. Note also the 18th-century White Hart Hotel in Dunstable Street and the Oxford Hospital Almshouses, erected by Wren and founded by John Cross of the university for old servants of Oxford colleges. (L1)

Anglesey Abbey (NT) A 17th-century house with a 13th-century Augustinian crypt contained within it. Fairhaven collection of paintings and furniture. The house is best known for its remarkable gardens, laid out since 1926 to a

Anglesey Abbey

grand and intricate geometric pattern. ⬧ (J6)

Ashwell Museum of village life from Stone Age, in a timber-framed Tudor tithe-office. Many fine village buildings. Early graffiti in 14th-century church, one referring to Black Death. Note the Guildhall in the High Street, a long building of the 16th century with closely-spaced timber uprights. (L4)

Audley End (EH) One of the most graciously-set stately homes, in extensive park. Only part of the original huge Jacobean house remains. Superb state rooms. Fine pictures. Miniature railway. ⬧ (L6)

Ayscoughfee Hall Museum, Spalding Natural history museum, with emphasis on bird displays, in a restored 15th-century house on banks of River Welland. (C3)

Barham Church (St Mary's) Norman church with font of 13th century. (H2)

Boston Church (St Botolph's) An enormous parish church whose 'Stump', a 272 ft (83 m) tower, dominates the surrounding area. It once housed a light to guide ships and was restored in the 1930s from money raised in Boston's American namesake. It can be seen from the far side of the Wash. The tower was completed in 1470. The church, with its fine interior, was begun in 1309. (A4)

Bourne Although the castle is now only a moated mound, this atmospheric market town is worth a visit. Note Tudor Red Hall, South Street, and Priory (town centre). (D2)

Buckden Remains of a splendid palace, once home of the Bishops of Lincoln,

with notable tower and gateway. Two ancient inns; 17th-century manor. (H3)

Burghley House A huge house built by one of Queen Elizabeth's newly rich councillors, William Cecil. Finished 1587, it is totally of its epoch. Luxurious interior including Verrio's painted Heaven Room. Furniture, tapestries, silver fireplaces. Rose garden. Horse trials held in the park in September. Access from B1443, Barnack road. (E1)

Castle Rising (EH) The huge earthworks of this massive Norman castle cover over 12 acres (4.8 hectares). The big Norman keep, similar to that at Norwich, can be explored on two floors. Dry moat. ⬧ (C8)

Cherry Hinton Church On the Fulbourn road on the outskirts of Cambridge, this is an Early English church with fine chancel. (K6)

Chippenham A 'model' village of the 18th-century with red-brick school and cottages. (H8)

Cockayne Hatley Church Set in rolling country with orchards, this medieval church has unusual Flemish carvings. (K4)

Castle Rising

Cromwell Museum, Huntingdon At the old Grammar School in the Market Place, where both the Protector and Pepys were pupils. Displays objects connected with the period and the man. (H3)

Devil's Ditch On Newmarket Heath. With the nearby Flean Dyke, a system of defences raised during the Dark Ages. Footpath along ditch from Reach (J6) to Stetchworth (J7) with access also from B1102, A1304 and B1061. (J7)

Duxford Airfield (Imperial War Museum) Over 70 aircraft on display at this preserved Battle of Britain fighter station, including Concord 01. Also tanks, military vehicles, special exhibitions. Access from A505, next to Junction 10, M11. ⬧ (K6)

Boston Church (the Stump)

Elstow Just outside Bedford, this village is associated with John Bunyan and much of this part of Bedfordshire figures in his *Pilgrim's Progress* (1676). The green, moot-hall (early 16th-century) and parish church all have Bunyan connections. (K2)

Ely One of Britain's most beautiful cathedrals dominates this small town, and indeed can be seen for miles – it's known as the Ship of the Fens. Originally Norman, it has a unique lantern over the main crossing. Much fine carving, a painted roof and an ornate Lady Chapel are just a few of Ely's other splendours. The many interesting houses in the town merit a slow and lingering ramble. (G6)

Folkingham Fine coaching inn in this village, once an important centre. Ruined House of Correction. 15th-century church has a splendid tower and screen. (B2)

Godmanchester An ancient Roman town that is joined to Huntingdon by an ancient bridge crossing the Ouse. Charming half-timbered houses, some with thatch. The parish church of St Mary is mainly 13th to 15th century with a tower added in 1623. There is a rare 13th-century mass dial on one of the buttresses of the chancel. Late 15th-century misericords in the stalls are finely carved with a variety of animals. (H3)

Grantchester Immortalised in the famous poem by Rupert Brooke (1887–1915). Brooke settled at the Old Vicarage on leaving King's College, Cambridge. Village can be reached on foot from Cambridge by walk along west bank of Cam, off A603. Tea garden. (K5)

Great Sampford 14th-century church with a 15th-century bowl font on a 14th-century stem. (L7)

Heckington Church Built in the 14th century by the rich abbots of Bardney, this is one of the finest Decorated cruciform churches in the country, with rich tracery and carving on the exterior. Note man playing bagpipes. (A2)

Heckington Mill Early 19th-century 8-sail windmill, still in working order. (A2)

Hinchingbrooke House 13th-century nunnery converted to a Tudor mansion in mid 16th century with later additions. Historic connections, most famous being with Cromwell and Samuel Pepys. Now a school. Access from A141. (H3)

Holbeach Church Market town with a pure unaltered church of 1380, except for odd turrets. It marks the transition from Decorated to Perpendicular.

There's a mystery brass showing a netted man. (C5)

Houghton A pretty village which will reward the walker with views of the river and old cottages. Timber watermill on the Ouse (NT). (H4)

Houghton House at Ampthill (EH) This startling ruin on the rise of a hill is the one-time home of Philip Sydney's sister, the Countess of Pembroke. May also be Bunyan's 'House Beautiful'. Thought to have been designed c. 1600 by John Thorpe and Inigo Jones. Fine views. 🔊 (L1)

Ickleton Church A Norman building containing Roman columns. Nearby, following the route of the A11, is the Icknield Way. (L6)

Isleham Church Stone and flint-faced, largely Decorated building. There are some good brasses and fine Jacobean communion rails. Also note misericords. (H7)

Kedington Church Fascinating church of many periods. There are 18th-century box pews, a Jacobean screen and three-decker Jacobean pulpit. Interior also includes a number of important monuments, most of which are to members of the Barnardiston family. (K8)

Kimbolton Castle The castle started as a medieval house, but was remodelled by Vanbrugh. 18th-century murals and a gatehouse by Robert Adam. Now a school. (H2)

King's Lynn A splendid town, worthy of exploration on foot. A long history of trading, based on the harbour, is reflected in fine houses of the merchant classes from the Tudor period and the 17th and 18th centuries. The *Guildhall* (1421) and Town Hall (1895) in Queen Street are both built in a striking chequer design in flint. Inside the Guildhall is a collection of regalia including 14th-century King John's Cup, a piece of medieval plate with inset precious stones. Close by is the 18th-century gaol. The church of St Margaret in the Saturday Market Place was founded c. 1100 and rebuilt in 13th century. It contains 14th-century screens, misericords, an early-Georgian pulpit, an organ by Snetzler (1754) and two elaborate brasses. *St George's Guildhall* in King Street dates from 1406 and is the largest surviving medieval guildhall in England. It was adapted as a theatre in the 1950s and is now owned by the National Trust. Other notable buildings include the 17th-century custom's house on the Ouse by Henry Bell). *Lynn Museum of Local History* 🔊 is in Market Street and the *Museum of Social History* is in King Street. Lynn Festival in July is an annual musical event. (C/D7)

Leighton Bromswold Church 17th-century nave and tower married to medieval transepts. Delightful 17th-century furnishings include twin pulpits. (H2)

Lilford Bird Park Picnic park with large collection of birds of prey. Children's farm; adventure playground. (G1)

Linton Zoo A wide-ranging collection of wildlife from snakes and tarantula spiders up to big cats and bears. Set in over 10 acres (4 hectares) of landscaped gardens. On the Hadstock road (B1052). 🔊 (K7)

Lyveden New Bield (NT) A symbolic unfinished work by a member of a persecuted Catholic family. This shell of a house symbolised the Passion to its 16th-century creator, Sir Thomas Tresham, later involved in the Gunpowder Plot (1605). Walk ½ mile (0.8 km) across two fields from nearest minor road. (G1)

Lyveden New Bield

March Market town famous for its great 15th-century church (St Wendreda's) with a particularly spectacular double hammer-beam roof. There are finely-carved angels with outspread wings on every conceivable vantage point. Also early brasses. (F5)

The Marshland Churches A grouping along the A17 south of the Wash of Early English and Perpendicular churches with many remarkable features. Examples include Walpole St Peter, Walpole St Andrew, Terrington St Clement (all D6) and Tydd St Mary (D5).

Methwold Church A 14th-century church with a fantastic, 120 ft (36 m) spire, a local landmark. (F8)

Mildenhall A pleasant walk around this small Suffolk town with market cross and Georgian buildings. The splendid big Perpendicular church is one of the finest for miles around, with many notable features. The roof is elaborately carved with biblical scenes, fantastic beasts and other designs and also with a host of angels. (H8)

Newmarket A racing town for 300 years, you can often see horses being exercised around this pleasant small centre. Open walks on heathland; access from A11 or B1304. Georgian buildings in town. (J7)

Old Warden Charming and picturesque village with thatched cottages, brick chimneys. The church of St Leonard is late 12th century, its tower a little older. It contains much good woodwork, several interesting monuments and some stained glass from Warden Abbey. (L2)

Oundle Pleasant town with many fine 17th- and 18th-century houses. Famous school. Note White Lion Inn. Pleasant river walks by the Nene. (G1)

Oxburgh Hall (NT) The huge and distinctive gatehouse – a rare, virtually untouched example of 15th-century architecture and brickwork – is the focal point of this moated mansion. Superb King's Room inside the gatehouse, and room nearby has wall hangings with sections worked by Mary, Queen of Scots and Bess of Hardwick. Wood carvings by Grinling Gibbons. Notable French parterre garden. 🔊 (E8)

Papworth St Agnes House Fascinating red-brick and stone house, built 1585 for a descendant of the author of *Morte d'Arthur*. Interesting plaster ceilings. Open by appointment. (J4)

Peakirk Waterfowl Gardens Wildfowl Trust where hundreds of waterfowl and flamingos may be seen in wooded grounds. Migrating species. 🔊 (E3)

Peterborough Cathedral The deeply recessed west front hides an almost pure

Romanesque building with many original features (started 1118). Note particularly painted wooden ceiling in the nave. (F3)

Peterborough Museum and Art Gallery, Priestgate Strong on local history, archaeology, natural history. In town centre. (E3)

Ramsey Abbey Gatehouse (NT) Remnant of Benedictine abbey but with much decoration still intact. (G4)

Royston Museum Local history with changing exhibitions. Also 20th-century ceramics and glassware. 🔊 (L5)

Saffron Walden Ancient British town with earth-works (maze) and a Norman castle, as well as interesting timber-framed medieval houses, some pargeted. Particularly fine large Perpendicular church. (L6)

St Ives Fine Elizabethan manor house with brick chimneys (not open). Medieval bridge over the Ouse, with a tiny, two-storey chapel (open). Pretty setting. (H4)

St Neots Pleasant walks along the Hen Brook with interesting 17th-century houses. Access from town centre. Also walk south along east bank of Ouse. (J3)

Sandringham Built for Edward VII when young, now the Queen's private country home. Large, well-maintained estate with woods and shrubberies, rose and water gardens. House, grounds, museum and country park are closed when the Queen or any member of the Royal Family is in residence. Access from A149. (C8)

Shuttleworth Collection, Old Warden Museum of old aeroplanes (special flying days); also cars, motorcycles and other transport. 🔊 (L3)

Springfields Gardens Seasonal displays of bulbs and roses at this pretty spot near Spalding. Off A151 on unclassified road to Wykeham. 🔊 (C3)

Stamford A fascinating stone-built town of great antiquity and beauty. The architecture is renowned and there are many Queen Anne houses and Georgian mansions. A town to explore slowly on foot. Fine churches, remnants of town wall, almshouses, coaching inns. (E1)

Stoke-by-Clare Church 14th-century Perpendicular church with 16th-century wall painting. Village is located in pleasant open country of the Stour valley. (L8)

Swaffham Bulbeck A green, a moated farm, and several small old houses make a walk around this village rewarding. (J7)

Therfield Heath Bronze Age barrows with some up to 13 ft (4 m) high. One

Neolithic example is almost 131 ft (40 m) long. Access from unclassified road to Therfield off A505. (L4)

Thorney The site of a monastery founded at the end of the 7th century. Much of it was removed at the Dissolution to provide building material for Corpus Christi College, Cambridge. The west front and the nave are incorporated in the parish church. Many buildings in the village, which includes some fine 17th-century houses, were built to the order of the Dukes of Bedford who owned land round about. (E4)

Trinity Hospital A group of 17th-century almshouses round a court with notable chapel, hall and tower. Inhabitants wear scarlet cloaks on Sundays. 🔊 (C8)

Wandlebury Ring Fort Circular Iron Age encampment on the Gogmagog Hills (access from A1307). Note also track of the Roman Via Devana which runs by camp (minor road parallel with A1307). (K6)

Welney Wildfowl Trust Home of many thousands of waterbirds, which can be viewed from hides, and observatory. Floodlit. Access from Welney village on A1101. 🔊 (F6)

Wicken Fen (NT) Ornithologists will find the Fen fascinating – rich plant, bird and insect life. Access from Wicken village on B1123. Car park. Display in Thorpe Building at access point to fen. (H6)

The Wiggenhalls Four villages in lonely country south of King's Lynn. One of the parish churches (St Peter) is ruined, but the other three all have fine 15th-century carved bench ends; those in Wiggenhall St Mary, an Early English and Perpendicular church, are particularly outstanding. Wiggenhall St Mary Magdalene has some interesting glass. (D7)

Willington Dovecot and Stables (NT) Two Tudor buildings are neighbours here – one a stable, the other a splendid stone dovecote of considerable size with stepped gables. Open by appointment only except on special weekends. (K2)

Wimpole Hall (NT) Original house 17th century, but many later additions and alterations, including Soane's Yellow Drawing Room and Gibbs's great library and chapel (decorated by James Thornhill). 'Capability' Brown extended the park c. 1767. 🔊 (K4)

Wisbech Remarkable for its harmonious architecture, with splendid large houses along the Nene. The most famous of these is *Peckover House* (NT), built in the 1720s and an important example of the domestic architecture of the period. When Wisbech was a port there was much trade with Holland and the Dutch influence on the Georgian architecture of Peckover and its neighbours is clear. There is fine plaster and wood interior decoration while the house opens out into magnificent mature gardens laid out in Victorian times. 🔊 The church of St Peter and St Paul has unusual twin nave and aisles and there is much sculptural detail on the 16th-century tower. *The Wisbech and Fenland Museum*, near the site of the castle, has natural history, ceramics, coin and pottery collections. 🔊 (E6)

Wolferton Station This one-time railway station on the Royal Estate has had its Royal waiting rooms preserved. Railway memorabilia. 🔊 (C8)

Wrest House and Gardens (EH) A house in French style with formal canal-side gardens, work by 'Capability' Brown and a banqueting house. Access from Silsoe. 🔊 (L2)

Wymington Church A 14th-century church containing good brasses and notable pews. (J1)

Map 13

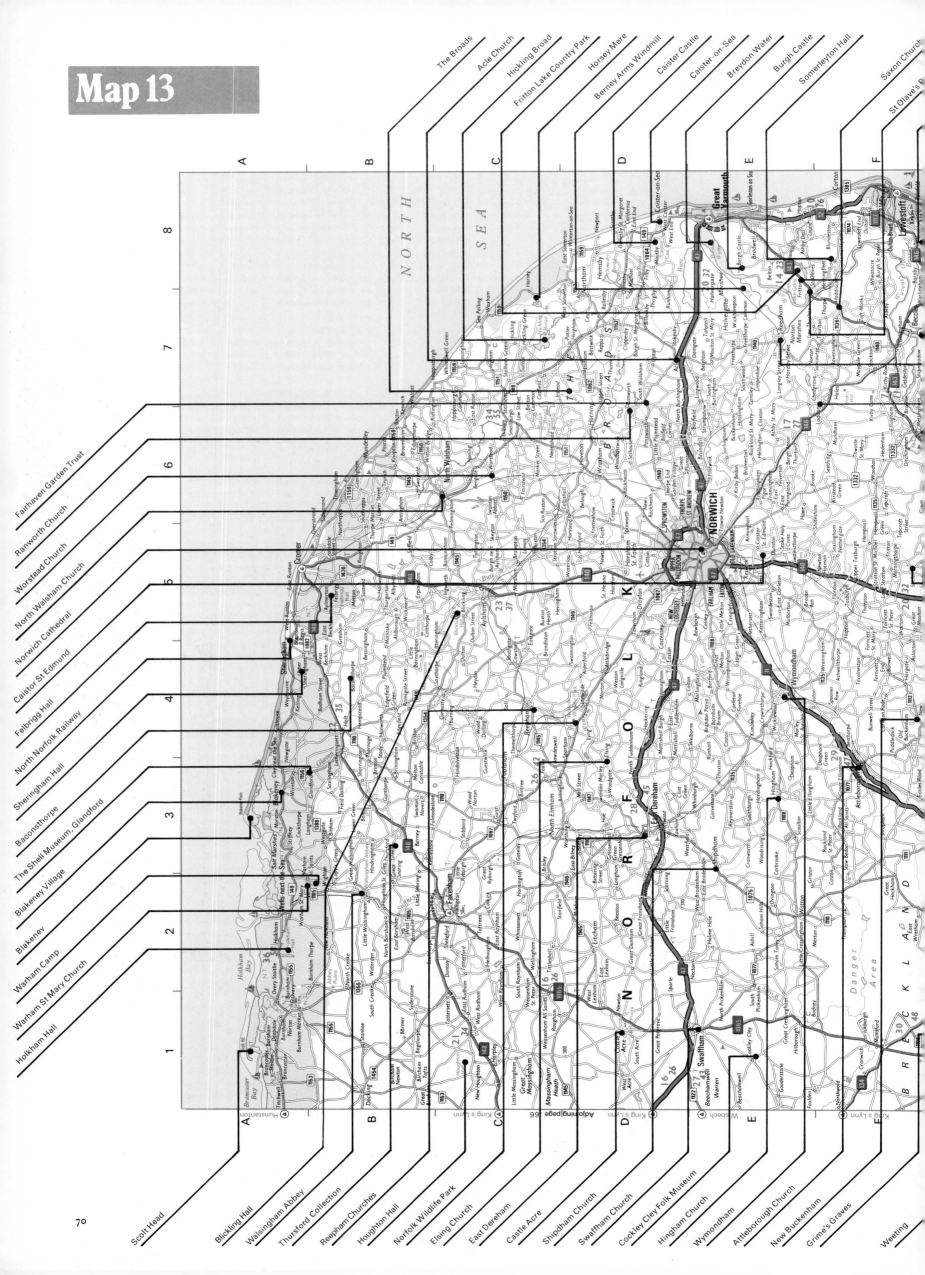

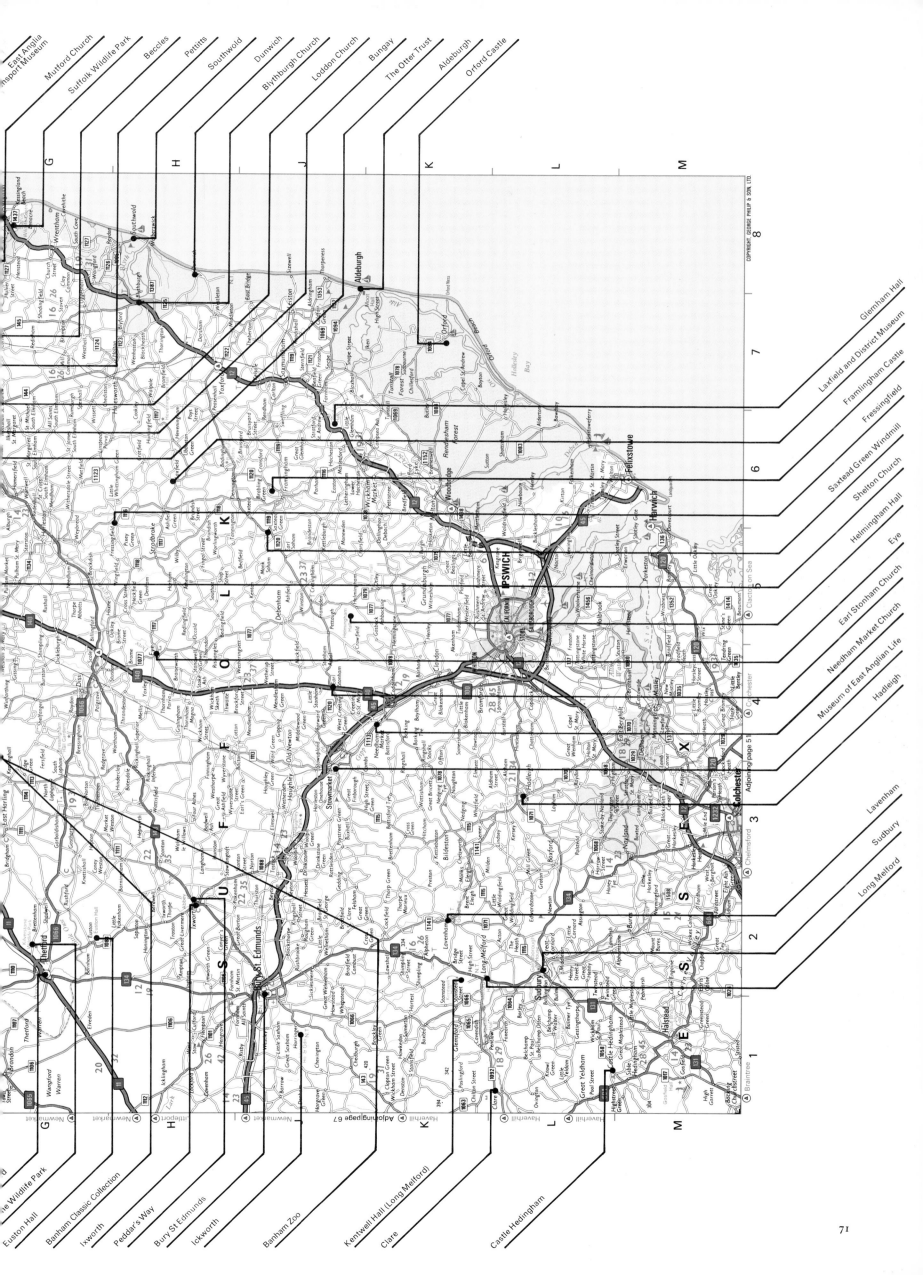

East Anglia

Acle Church Handsome, round-towered church of 14th century with lion font. The village is a good centre point for exploring the **Broads**. (D7)

Aldeburgh Seaside village with two well-known bird sanctuaries nearby. Fine two-storey Moot Hall with outside stair. Also many musical and literary connections. The Red House, home of Benjamin Britten, contains Britten-Pears Musical Library. Memorials in church to poet George Crabbe, and Britten. Snape Maltings Concert Hall nearby. (J8)

Attleborough Church Splendid late 15th-century rood screen and contemporary murals. Also notable West window; cast-iron lectern. (F3)

Baconsthorpe (DoE) Romantic remains of a semi-fortified manor house of 1486 with a gatehouse and towers, also a moat. ⌖ (B4)

Banham Classic Collection Adjoining **Banham Zoo**, a collection of antique cars, motorcycles, racing cars and children's pedal cars, displayed in imaginative setting. (G4)

Banham Zoo A very wide collection of primates, but also includes black panthers, camels, otters, sea-lions, penguins, wallabies, flamingoes and other species in over 20 acres (8 hectares) of grounds. (G4)

Beccles A pretty old town on the river with fine Georgian houses. Note old Town Hall and 18th-century St Peter's House (not open). French writer Chateaubriand stayed in the town. (F7)

Berney Arms Windmill (EH) This gaunt windmill stands in an isolated marshland setting, a survivor of the many once to be seen here. Access by rail (Berney Arms Station) or boat. (E7)

Blakeney (NT) Bird sanctuary on coast with nesting colonies of terns and other species (oyster catchers, redshank, plover). Wild open walks along sea on sand-dunes and shingle spit. Access limited when birds nesting. (A3)

Blakeney Village Charming steep main street. Church has a magnificent 15th-century west tower. 14th-century Guildhall. (A3)

Blickling Hall (NT) Very fine early 17th-century mansion in a park with many Jacobean features such as the plaster ceiling in the long gallery, fine staircase. Furniture, pictures, tapestries. Garden, largely Georgian in layout, with early 19th-century orangery. ⌖ (C5)

Blythburgh Church This commanding church of the 15th century is built on a knoll and looks particularly impressive

Bench-end, depicting slander, in Blythburgh Church

when floodlit. Good carving – note seven deadly sins as bench-ends. Roof angels were once used as target practice by iconoclasts. (H7)

Breydon Water The three main Broadland rivers, Waveney, Yare and Bure, flow into this saltwater estuary and there are many wading birds to be seen on the tidal flats. Fine sunsets over marshland in winter and walks along elevated dykes with wide views. Access from A47 (north shore) or from Burgh Castle (south shore). (E8)

The Broads There are about 30 of these famous stretches of shallow water, connected by rivers and 'cuts'. They are largely man-made and are thought to be the water-filled pits left by turf cutters long ago. Some are fresh water, some salt, but all are famous for the magnificent boating and fishing they provide, and for the multitude of birds, flowers, insects and plants that they support. Bird watching is particularly rewarding; rare species include bitterns and long-tailed tits. Many areas are now managed as nature reserves to protect this unique habitat and its flora and fauna (see **Hickling Broad, Horsey Mere**). The broads are gradually silting up and constant efforts have to be made to keep the waterways free and open. This triangular area east from an apex at Norwich also includes many pretty villages such as Martham (D8), Ludham (D7), Ranworth (D7) and Horning (D6). (C/D6–8)

Bungay Remains of 12th-century castle from which there are open views over Waveney valley. Octagonal market cross. Holy Trinity church is Norman with a round tower. Mainly Georgian houses. (F6)

Burgh Castle (EH) Huge flint Roman walls remain from the one-time fortress, part of an early shore defence system, with six bastions. Parish church of St Furzie has a Norman tower using Roman materials. Off A143 following Burgh village signs. (E8)

Bury St Edmunds Fascinating old town with buildings of many periods. By the cathedral is the church of St Mary with carved hammer-beam roof. Also extensive park with ecclesiastical ruins. Museums at *Angel Corner*, Angel Hill (NT), a Queen Anne house containing the Gersham-Parkington collection of clocks and watches; *Moyses Hall* in Cornhill (Norman building with local history, natural history and archaeology) ⌖; and the *Suffolk Regiment Museum* in Out Risbygate (historical exhibits including weapons, uniforms, medals, drums). See also the 18th-century Athenaeum in Angel Hill, the Guildhall with Norman ornaments on its porch (*c.* 1480), and the 18th-century Unitarian chapel (1711), with a double pulpit, in Churchgate Street. Rare early 19th-century theatre (NT) in Westgate Street and many other Georgian buildings (particularly Abbeygate Street). (J2)

Caister Castle Ruined moated castle, *c.* 1432, with 100 ft (30 m) tower with magnificent views. Home of Shakespeare's Falstaff and the Paston Letters. Motor Museum (a variety of vehicles in unusual arena setting) and Tree Walk. Off A1064. (D8)

Caister-on-Sea Seaside village with life-boat shed on fine sand beach. Roman remains (DoE) of town walls and small military settlement. (D8)

Caistor St Edmund This was Venta Icenorum, the town of Boadicea's Iceni tribe. 35 acres (14 hectares) with walls. At certain times in summer the town plan can be seen from the nearby hill (road to Stoke Holy Cross) outlined in crop patterns. (E5)

Castle Acre (EH) The 13th-century entrance to a castle (now ruined) spans the village street. Cluniac priory, mostly

ruins, but some buildings survive. 13th- to 14th-century parish church has misericords, early paintings. (D1)

Castle Hedingham Well-preserved Norman keep, one of the most impressive in England, joined to picturesque village by medieval bridge. Norman church with misericords. (L1)

Clare Interesting small town, fascinating mix of architectural periods from medieval to 19th century, with many spacious houses, some pargeted. Castle ruins, Perpendicular church. (L1)

Pargeting on a house at Clare

Cockley Cley Folk Museum Reconstruction of a village of the Iceni tribe. The Museum has exhibits covering life from pre-history. ⌖ (E1)

Dunwich Most of this once-large port is now beneath the sea. Ruins of friary and 12th-century chapel. Beach and cliff walks south from the village (NT land). (H8)

Earl Stonham Church A splendid Perpendicular building with two hammer-beam roofs, carved angels. Note the pulpit with its four hourglasses, carved bench ends and unusual font. (J4)

East Anglia Transport Museum, Carlton Colville Stress on East Anglian transport, such as old buses and trams, as well as a range of antique cars. Access from B1384 off A146. ⌖ (F8)

East Dereham Market town with interesting parish church in town centre containing tomb of William Cowper. *Bishop Bonner's Cottage*, off Church Street, is a museum showing local pargeting (coloured plaster work). (D3)

Elsing Church Wide, yet aisle-less Decorated 14th-century church with interesting stained glass and octagonal covered font. Brass, 1347, commemorates the founder. (D3)

Euston Hall 18th-century house with fine collection of 17th- and 18th-century pictures. Set in landscaped park by Evelyn, Kent and 'Capability' Brown. The church in the grounds was refashioned in the 17th century with carvings attributed to Grinling Gibbons. (G2)

Eye Once on an island, this ancient town has remains of a priory and a timber-framed, early 16th-century guildhall. Note flint and stone faced church tower. (H4)

Fairhaven Garden Trust Woodland and water gardens at South Walsham with rare shrubs and plants. Attractive walks through beech and rhododendron avenues beside private broad. Bird sanctuary. On main road through village. (D7)

Felbrigg Hall (NT) Very fine Jacobean house with carved stone facade. Notable plaster ceiling in west wing. Original 18th-century furniture and pictures.

Walled garden. Park renowned for fine trees. ⌖ (B5)

Framlingham Castle (EH) On the castle tower unlucky Mary Tudor watched for her army. Now ruined, but with towers, walls, moat and huge chimneys to see. ⌖ Fine Perpendicular church in village with monuments. (J6)

Fressingfield Interesting 14th-century church with good and notable organ; carving on wooden benches. (H5)

Fritton Lake Country Park Charming woodland lake with fishing and pleasure boats for hire. Unusual plants in gardens and pretty walks. Off A143. ⌖ (E8)

Glemham Hall Queen Anne house with handsome red-brick facade and good gardens. Lived-in house with fine furniture. Access off A12. ⌖ (J6)

Grimes Graves (EH) Fascinating pre-historic site with hundreds of mine shafts dug by Neolithic man to find flints. Antler picks were used to dig through chalk. One shaft with underground galleries open – take a flashlight. Follow B1108 from A1065. ⌖ (F1)

Hadleigh Splendid 15th-century Guildhall, Deanery Tower (same date, not open) and church noted for its furnishings, including 14th-century font, organ-case, misericords. This was once a wool town. (L3)

Helmingham Hall Handsome moated house (not open) and gardens. Herds of fallow and red deer, highland cattle and Soay sheep in park. ⌖ (J5)

Hickling Broad Largest of the **Broads**, 3 miles (5 km) in circumference, and a bird sanctuary. Path from Potter Heigham along south-west shore. (C7)

Hingham Church In the Decorated church (hammer-beam roof and medieval German glass) the connection with Abraham Lincoln is perpetuated with a bust to Robert Lincoln (a local resident and earliest known ancestor of the president). (E3)

Holkham Hall Imposing Palladian mansion with impressively grand state rooms. The inside is all sumptuous 18th-century grandeur and contains an extensive collection of tapestries, paintings, statuary and furnishings. Rooms are arranged in a long vista. (A2)

Horsey Mere (NT) Wild atmospheric part of the **Broads** with a drainage windmill on B1159. This is the most salt of all the Broads, with unusual plant and marine life and rare birds, including bitterns. Access restricted. (C7)

Houghton Hall Fine Palladian mansion built 1727–35 for Sir Robert Walpole, with interior decoration by William Kent. Magnificent furniture, paintings and china, and a splendid collection of model soldiers and militaria. 13 miles (21 km) east of King's Lynn. ⟁ (C1)

Ickworth (NT) Great house built c. 1794–1830 by a bishop to house his collections. A huge oval rotunda is centrepiece and is connected by two carved corridors to flanking wings. Sumptuous state rooms with late Regency and 18th-century furniture, magnificent silver, picture collection. Walks and picnics in the splendid park. Access from A143. ⟁ (J1)

Ixworth House contains largely complete 13th-century cloister within it. Adaptation of the monastic buildings, made at the time of the Dissolution c. 1540, and extensive additions c. 1690 are faced by Georgian facades. The ruins of the Priory church are in the gardens (H2)

Kilverstone Wildlife Park South American animals and birds. Deer park garden walks, picnicking. Miniature horses. ⟁ (G2)

Lavenham A pretty half-timbered town with a 16th-century *Guildhall* (NT), now a local museum. ⟁ Also *Little Hall*, 15th-century house containing museum of antiquities. Much carving and pargeting. Old inns. Splendid 15th-century 'wool' church. (K2)

Helmingham Hall

Laxfield and District Museum, The Guildhall, Laxfield Folk and local history in 16th-century building. (H6)

Loddon Church In this small and charming market town is a 15th-century church with notable font, monuments and brasses and a Jacobean pulpit. Note ancient almsboxes. (F6)

Long Melford Long-streeted village with many interesting buildings, a fine 15th-century church and a green. *Melford Hall* (NT) is an Elizabethan brick mansion with an original panelled banqueting hall, 18th-century drawing room, and Regency library. Fine 17th- and 18th-century furniture, Sèvres china and Chinese porcelain. Beatrix Potter display. ⟁ *Kentwell Hall* is a moated Tudor hall with a long lime avenue. The east wing and centre of the house were substantially remodelled by Thomas Hopper c. 1826 after fire. Ground floor largely renovated; most of house open to view. Moated formal walled garden and brick dovecote. ⟁ (K2)

Museum of East Anglian Life, Stowmarket Open-air museum of rural life in East Anglia including extensive collections of agricultural implements, carts and wagons. Craft demonstrations. Re-erected buildings. ⟁ (J3)

Mutford Church Norman church with round tower and wall painting of St Christopher. (G8)

Needham Market Church Fine 14th-century church with angel roof. (K4)

New Buckenham The charming market hall has a pillory. Remains of a Norman castle nearby. (F4)

Norfolk Wildlife Park Large collection of European mammals and birds exhibited in 40 acres (16 hectares) of enclosures and aviaries – all designed to be as natural as possible. (D4)

North Norfolk Railway This privately-owned steam railway winds along the coast through an Area of Outstanding Natural Beauty. Can be joined at Sheringham from where it meanders to Weybourne. ⟁ (A4)

North Walsham Church Striking ruined tower to west. Noble interior, in which can be found the fine monument to Paston (died 1608), founder of Paston School at which Nelson was a pupil. (C6)

Orford Castle

Norwich Cathedral Largely Norman work with a unique bishop's throne and tall spire. View from tower. Remarkable coloured bosses in unusual double-storeyed cloister. Visitor's exhibition. (D5)

Orford Castle (EH) has unusual many-sided keep. ⟁ Picturesque town with 13th-century inn. Ruined church with Norman work. Fine walks along shore. (K7)

The Otter Trust, Earsham 23 acre (9 hectare) site with more than 20 natural enclosures for breeding otters and 3 lakes for waterfowl. Riverside and woodland walks. (F6)

Peddar's Way, running from Ixworth (H2) to the Wash, is an ancient trackway of prehistoric origins. It crosses Breckland and can be reached from the A11 near Thetford. Look for the signs.

Pettitts, Reedham Gardens with many unusual fowl on show. Fascinating flower-craft and feather-craft workshops and taxidermy demonstrations. Tame animals, picnic area, children's amusements and Falabella miniature horse stud. (E7)

Ranworth Church St Helen's church has Norfolk's most complete screen of the early 15th century with rood loft and painted saints. (D7)

Reepham Churches Three medieval churches in one churchyard – though one is but a ruined tower. A 17th-century pulpit in Perpendicular St Michael's; a Norman font and medieval tombs in St Mary's. (C4)

St Olave's Priory (EH) Close to wide sweep of the Waveney is the ruin of an early Augustinian building with fine 13th-century brickwork. ⟁ (E7)

Saxon Churches Between Great Yarmouth and Beccles there are many ancient round-towered churches, usually of flint construction and often with Norman work, generally standing in prominent positions. Haddiscoe (F7) and Fritton (E7) are good examples.

Saxtead Green Windmill (EH) Although the present superstructure was built in 1854, this was originally an 18th-century post mill – the whole building revolves on its base. Machinery viewable. (J6)

Scolt Head (NT) A shingled dune, home to thousands of terns. Splendid open country but walks along beach are restricted when birds nesting. A long walk from Overy Staithe. (A1)

The Shell Museum, Glandford A comprehensive shell collection in quaint gabled house in charming village. (A3)

Shelton Church Fine stained glass in this red-brick Perpendicular church; also a carving of the Royal Arms. (F5)

Sheringham Hall Splendid large rhododendron woods and park surround the Hall, a Regency house with gardens by Humphry Repton. House not open. Access from A149. (A4)

Shipdham Church A 13th-century church with a double lantern and, inside, a wooden medieval lectern. (E3)

Somerleyton Hall An early Victorian mansion with elegant state rooms. Winter garden with statuary and 12 acre (4.8 hectare) grounds planted with rare shrubs and trees and including a maze. Miniature railway and garden trail. ⟁ (F8)

Southwold Pretty seaside town and fishing port of great charm. Good walks from town on surrounding open heathland. Large Perpendicular church with notable woodwork, one of most splendid churches of east Suffolk. (H8)

Sudbury Note Moot Hall, medieval houses. Three good Perpendicular churches. Home of the painter Gainsborough whose house on Gainsborough Street (*Gainsborough's House Museum*) contains an art gallery and museum illustrating aspects of his work. ⟁ (L2)

Suffolk Wildlife Park A wide variety of animals and birds from around the world in pretty park setting. Picnic areas. ⟁ (G8)

Swaffham Church Two hammer-beam roofs in this 15th-century church – one in the porch, and a splendid double one with angels over the nave. Look for the figure of a peddlar who founded the church. (E1)

Thetford Home town of Thomas Paine, a signatory of the US Declaration of Independence and author of *The Age of Reason*. His birthplace (1737) is preserved in town centre (cottage marked by tablet near White Hart Street). Many relics of a once-glorious past include ruins of medieval buildings and earthworks. *Ancient House Museum*, White Hart Street, has a collection of historical objects and wildlife exhibits relating to local and Breckland life. (G2)

Thursford Collection Steam engines of all kinds from the railway to the fairground, also agricultural. Large collection of fairground and mechanical organs; concerts on the Wurlitzer! ⟁ (B3)

Walsingham Abbey Centre for pilgrimages, this ruined priory received many important medieval visitors. It was dissolved by Henry VIII but Catholic pilgrimages were revived to the Slipper Chapel at Houghton St Giles in the late 19th century and the Anglican shrine at Walsingham was revived in 1931. Local *Shirehall Museum* (village centre) is a Georgian courthouse with original fittings and a display showing the Pilgrimage's history. ⟁ (B2)

Warham Camp A circular Iron Age fort bordered by the River Stiffkey. At Warham All Saints from B1149. (A2)

Warham St Mary Church Partly Norman but look for the 18th-century pulpit. (A2)

Weeting (EH) A ruined manor house of the 12th century with keep and moat. (G1)

Worstead Church Fine 14th-century high-towered church in this village, which has given its name to the wool trade. Hammer-beam roof, box pews, brasses and painted rood screen. (C6)

Wymondham Church, once part of a Norman abbey, has towers at both ends, hammer-beam roof and modern (1935) reredos. The home of Robert Kett who led a local peasants' revolt (1549), the town has handsome timbered houses and a market cross. (E4)

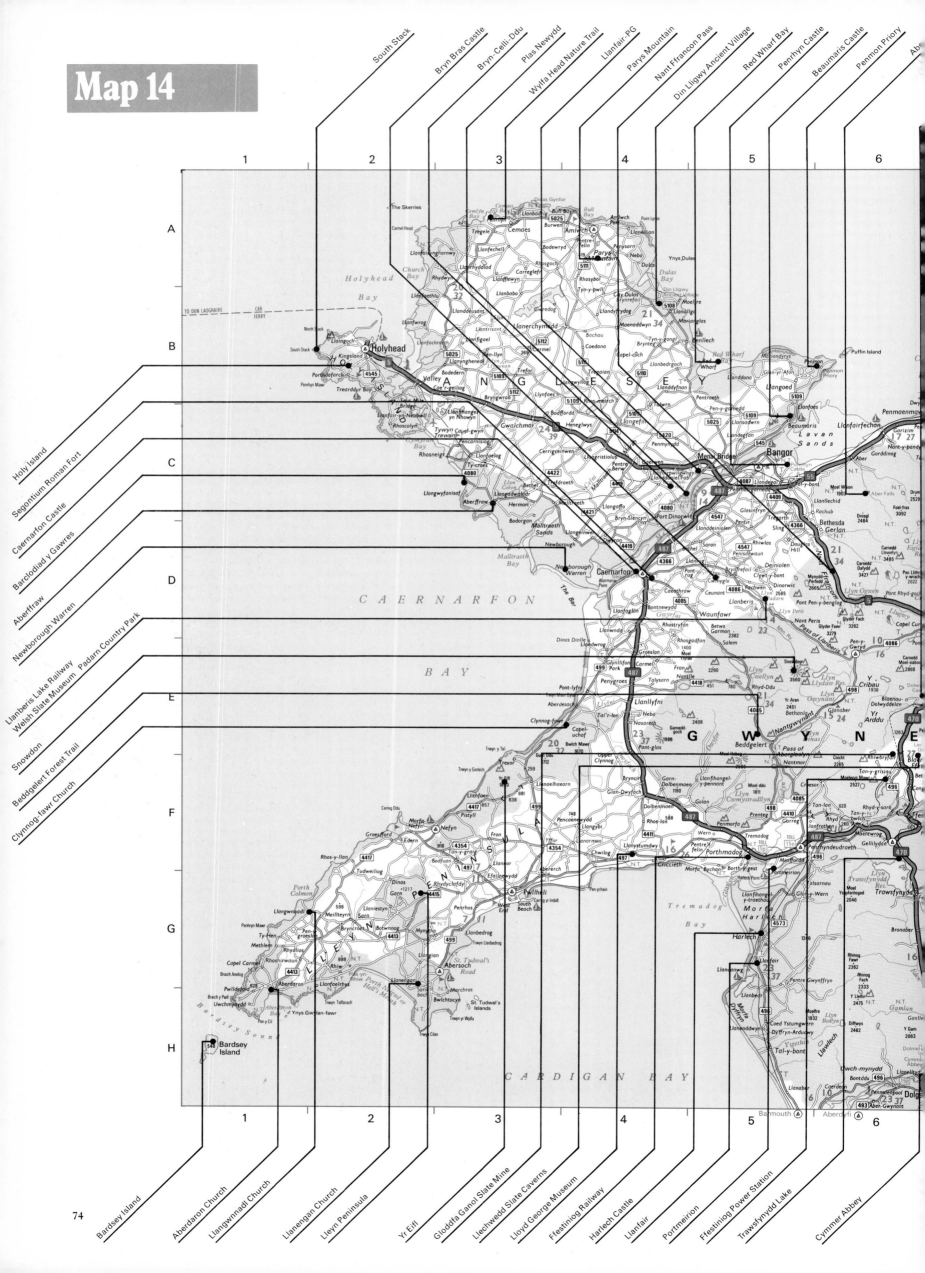

Map 14

South Stack
Bryn Bras Castle
Bryn-Celli-Ddu
Plas Newydd
Wylfa Head Nature Trail
Llanfair-PG
Parys Mountain
Nant Ffrancon Pass
Din Lligwy Ancient Village
Red Wharf Bay
Penrhyn Castle
Beaumaris Castle
Penmon Priory

Holy Island
Segontium Roman Fort
Caernarfon Castle
Barclodiad y Gawres
Aberffraw
Newborough Warren
Llanberis Lake Railway
Welsh Slate Museum / Padarn Country Park
Snowdon
Beddgelert Forest Trail
Clynnog-fawr Church

Bardsey Island
Aberdaron Church
Llangwnnadl Church
Llanengan Church
Lleyn Peninsula
Yr Eifl
Gloddfa Ganol Slate Mine
Llechwedd Slate Caverns
Lloyd George Museum
Ffestiniog Railway
Harlech Castle
Llanfair
Portmeirion
Ffestiniog Power Station
Trawsfynydd Lake
Cymmer Abbey

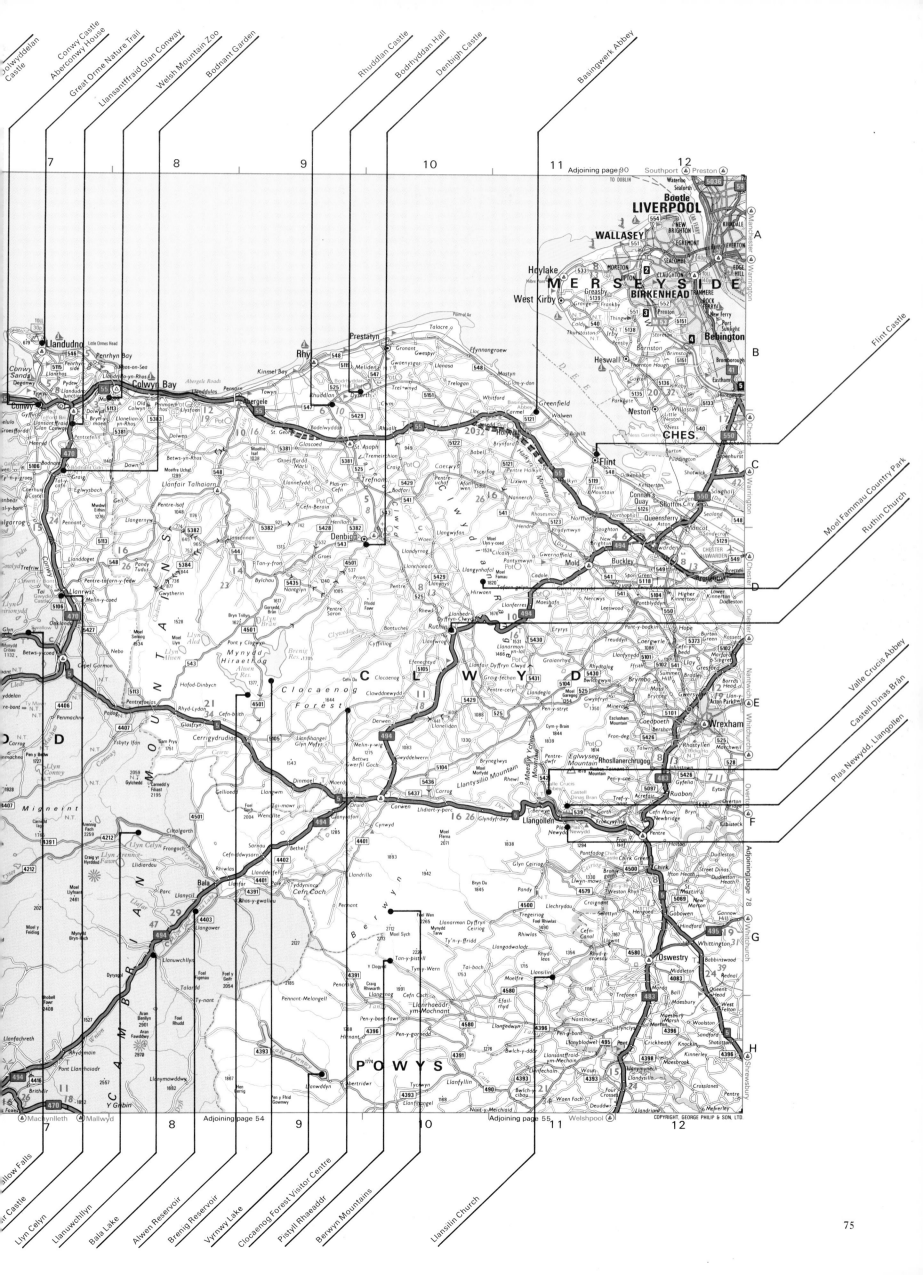

North Wales

Aberconwy House, High Street, Conwy (NT) Picturesque three-storey timber-framed medieval house with asymmetrical front and leaded casement windows. Contains exhibits depicting life in Conwy from Roman times to present day. (B7)

Aber Falls Spectacular waterfall which tumbles 120 ft (36 m) in a mare's tail and forms the centrepiece of the newly-created Coedydd Aber nature reserve. Reached by a scenic walk of 1¼ miles (2 km) through natural woodlands from Bontnewydd, south-east of Aber. (C6)

Aberdaron Church 12th-century church built at the point where medieval pilgrims embarked for offshore Bardsey Island. Inside are two naves linked by a five-bay arcade. (H1)

Aberffraw Pleasant riverside village near long and gently shelving beach. In the 7th century it was the seat of the princes of Gwynedd, founders of Wales, and remained so until 1282. The only visible reminder of those times is the little 12th-century church of St Gwyfan on an island in the bay accessible at low tide. (C3)

Alwen Reservoir Great forest-ringed lake over 3 miles (4.8 km) long which supplies water to Birkenhead. A nature trail of 4½ miles (7.2 km) encircles the reservoir starting at the car park at the base of the dam. The nearby Cronfa Alwen Visitor Centre houses an exhibition tracing the history of the project. Access from B4501 at Pont-yr-Alwen 2½ miles (4 km) north of Cerrigydrudion. (E8)

Bala Lake Largest natural lake in Wales with waters which vary suddenly from shallow to very deep and are the haunt of the gwyniad, an elusive member of the salmon family. Otherwise known as Llyn Tegid, the lake is a popular venue for sailing and canoeing. A narrow gauge railway runs for 3¾ miles (6 km) along the eastern shore between the outskirts of Bala and **Llanuwchllyn**. (G8)

Barclodiad y Gawres (Cadw) Neolithic burial chamber on headland decorated inside with primitive murals made by pocking or hammering. 1 mile (1.6 km) south of Llanfaelog on west side of A4080. (C3)

Bardsey Island Small island separated from the mainland by 2 miles (3.2 km) of tidal currents which acquired special sanctity as a place of pilgrimage after the death there of St Dubricus in AD 612. In medieval times three pilgrimages to Bardsey were the equal of one to Rome. The ruins on the island are of a 13th-century Augustinian monastery. Boats from Aberdaron. (H1)

Basingwerk Abbey (Cadw) Founded 1132 by monks from Savigny in France. The remains of the cloister and church are typical of the Cistercian style. (C11)

Beaumaris Castle (Cadw) Perfectly designed concentric castle, last in the chain of fortresses built by Edward I to subdue the Welsh. The only feasible site was on marshland, *beau marais* in medieval French, from which the place took its name. Building began in 1295 and took three years. Highlights of the interior are the great hall and chapel. 🕭 (C5)

Beddgelert Forest Trail A walk of ¾ mile (1.2 km) through majestic wooded scenery which starts at the campsite 1 mile (1.6 km) north-west of Beddgelert on A4085. (E5)

Berwyn Mountains Broad range of high moorland (much now forested) with a central spine rising to over 2,000 ft (609 m), the highest summits being Moel Sych (G10) 2,713 ft (827 m) and Cadair Berwyn (G10) 2,712 ft (827 m). (G9/10)

Bodnant Garden (NT) One of the finest gardens in Britain terraced up the side of the Conwy valley. Magnificent collection of rhododendrons, camellias, magnolias, shrubs and trees. Fine views of Snowdonia from terraces. Entrance ½ mile (0.8 km) from A470 on Eglwysbach road. 🕭 (C7)

Bodrhyddan Hall Dignified red-brick manor house of 17th century containing fine collection of paintings, furniture and armour. Extensive garden. 🕭 (B9)

Brenig Reservoir Opened in 1976, 919 acre (372 hectare) man-made lake on headwaters of river Dee 1,400 ft (426 m) up in the moorlands of Clwyd. A field studies and interpretative centre near the dam head are available to visitors. A waymarked walk starts at the information centre on the south-west. The north shore is part of a nature reserve. Access from B4501. (E9)

Bryn Bras Castle Architectural fantasy built in 1830 around an earlier structure. Highlights are the drawing room, Louis XV suite, galleried staircase and splendid ceilings. In the extensive gardens are lawns and woodland walks, waterfalls and pools. 🕭 (D5)

Bryn-Celli-Ddu (Cadw) Well preserved 5 sided Bronze Age burial

The entrance to Bryn-Celli-Ddu

chamber. A mound was built over the cairn after excavation but its outline is still visible. Access from A4080. (C4)

Caernarfon Castle (Cadw) Grandest of chain of castles built by Edward I to subdue the Welsh, with massive towers and unusually tall turrets. Arrow loops and spy holes guard the approach from almost every angle. Housed in one of the towers is the regimental museum of the Royal Welch Fusiliers. (D4)

Castell Dinas Brân, Llangollen (Cadw) Substantial remains of strategically sited 13th-century castle above Dee valley showing outline of rectangular courtyard, square keep and apsidal tower. (F11)

Clocaenog Forest Vast coniferous dome covering 30 sq miles (78 sq km), one of the largest man-made plantations in Wales. An exhibition presenting the forest in its ecological and historical setting is displayed in a cottage in a clearing above a small lake with picnic site nearby at Pont Petryal, 3 miles (4.8 km) north-east of Llanfihangel Glyn Myfyr on B5105. Waymarked walks up to 2¾ miles (4.4 km) long start near the lakeside. (E9)

Clynnog-fawr Church Imposing collegiate building housing the 7th-century shrine of St Bueno on the pilgrims' route to **Bardsey Island**. Rebuilding to a cruciform plan began in 1480. The wide nave has a carved and panelled oak roof and there are Tudor stalls with misericords in the chancel. A passage leads to St Bueno's chapel. (E4)

Conwy Castle (Cadw) Huge castle built by Edward I in 1283–9 on a spur at the confluence of the rivers Gyffin and Conwy, the plan following the contours of the rock on which it stands. Roughly rectangular, it has 8 round towers set in the curtain walls and a fortified barbican at each end. The interior is divided into inner and outer wards. (B7)

Cymmer Abbey (Cadw) In a peaceful riverside setting are remains of austere Cistercian abbey founded 1199 as an offshoot of Cwmhir in Powys. Access off A494 on east bank of Mawddach. The famous *Precipice Walk* (see **Cader Idris**, Gazetteer 10) encircling 1,069 ft (326 m) Foel Cynwch to the north passes through the site. (H6)

Denbigh Castle (Cadw) Ruined 13th-century castle on a hill behind town. Remains include an elaborate gatehouse. The building houses a museum featuring exhibits relating to the famous explorer Henry Morton Stanley, born in Denbigh in 1841. He emigrated to America and as news correspondent for the *New York Herald* led the expedition to Africa in search of Dr Livingstone. (D9)

Din Lligwy Ancient Village (Cadw) Well-preserved remains of Iron Age settlement with boundary wall enclosing two round and seven rectangular buildings. In a nearby field is a Stone Age burial chamber with small upright stones supporting a 28-tonne capstone. (B4)

Dolwyddelan Castle (Cadw) Ruined 12th-century fortress dominating the lovely Lledr valley. Traditional birthplace in 1173 of Llywelyn the Great. North of the castle lies Gwydir forest, 19,473 acres (7,880 hectares). (E6)

Ffestiniog Power Station Hydroelectric pumped storage scheme on west shore of Tan-y-grisiau reservoir linked to Stwlan reservoir 1,000 ft (304 m) above on west. Bus service to upper lake and permits for trout fishing from visitor centre. Access off B4414 ½ mile (0.8 m) south-west of Blaenau Ffestiniog. (F6)

Ffestiniog Railway Built in 1836 to carry slate from the huge quarries of Blaenau Ffestiniog through the beautiful Vale of Ffestiniog to Porthmadog harbour and reopened by enthusiasts in 1955. Steam engines, including the unique Double Fairlie type, haul both historic and modern corridor carriages. The northern terminus is at Blaenau Ffestiniog. The main station is at Porthmadog where there is a small railway museum. 🕭 (F5)

Flint Castle (Cadw) Built in the late 13th century, the unusually strong and massive round tower was placed outside one corner of the rectangular curtain wall and connected to the main building by a drawbridge. (C11)

Gloddfa Ganol Slate Mine, Blaenau Ffestiniog Slate mine with 42 miles (67 km) of tunnels, workshops, interpretative museum and narrow-gauge

railway centre. On west side of A470. (F6)

Great Orme Nature Trail, Llandudno Waymarked walk, 5 miles (8 km) long, on Great Orme Head (679 ft, 207 m) beginning at Happy Valley north-west of the pier. Moderate gradients. (B7)

Gwydir Castle Historic Tudor mansion added to and rebuilt over the years. Furnished from the Tudor and Victorian periods. Beautiful grounds with a number of peacocks. In the woods overlooking the castle is the small Gwydir Uchaf chapel notable for its four-bay painted ceiling. (D7)

Harlech Castle (Cadw) Famous clifftop fortress, many times the scene of heroic defence. The sea lapped the cliff when it was begun in 1283, an outer ward protecting the water gate. From the ramparts the views of Snowdon and across Tremadog Bay to the Lleyn are unforgettable. (G5)

Harlech Castle (Snowdon on left)

Holy Island Joined to Anglesey by a causeway and a bridge and rising to 715 ft (218 m) on Holyhead Mountain, topped by the remains of an ancient fortress and ending in the great headlands of North and **South Stack**. Most of the north shore of the island is taken up by Holyhead, the closest sea-port to Ireland. (B2)

Llanberis Lake Railway Narrow-gauge steam trains reveal magnificent scenery on old slate-carrying line along the east shore of Lake Padarn. Terminal station is in **Padarn Country Park** at the south end of the lake. Access off B4086 opposite terminus of Snowdon Mountain Railway. 🕭 (D5)

Llanengan Church 16th-century building on 6th-century foundations with a beautifully carved rood screen and holy vessels from the now ruined abbey on **Bardsey Island**. (G2)

Llanfair Village noted for its quarry where slate was worked from 1874 to 1906, honeycombing the hill with vast caverns lit by air vents high above. (G5)

Llanfair-PG The usual abbreviation for the famous village with a 58-letter place name, Llanfairpwllgwyngyllgogerychwyrndrobwllllantysyliogogogoch, where the longest platform ticket in the world can be bought at the station. Nearby is the *Marquis of Anglesey column* erected in 1816 in honour of Wellington's second-in-command at Waterloo. Inside 115 steps lead to the top. (C4)

Llangwnnadl Church Beautiful 16th-century church, wider than it is long, with three naves separated by three bay arcades. (G1)

Llansantffraid Glan Conway Village of interest for Felin Isaf watermill, its restored and operational machinery dating from 1730 and its stonework and roof structure largely unaltered. On A470 south-west. (B7)

Llansilin Church Fine church with twin naves and magnificent roof, carved stalls and pews and many 17th- and 18th-century monuments. (G11)

Llanuwchllyn Peaceful mountain-ringed village at south end of Lake **Bala**, the home of Urdd Gobiath Cymru, the Welsh League of Youth. Starting point for the ascent of the Arans, to south – 2,901 ft (884 m) Aran Benllyn and 2,970 ft (905 m) Aran Fawddwy, with a tiny corrie lake on the summit of each (both H8). A narrow road goes partway, to Nant-y-Barcud (off unclassified road at Talardd). (G8)

Llechwedd Slate Caverns, Blaenau Ffestiniog Two tours of biggest working slate mine in Wales made up of a network of tunnels, underground lake and unbelievably large caverns dating back to 1846. Surface attractions include slate heritage theatre and tramway exhibition. ⬚ (F6)

Lleyn Peninsula The 'Land's End' of North Wales, a remote region of small farms and unspoilt fishing villages linked by ultra-narrow roads where Welsh traditions are still strong. A backbone of mountains reaches 1,800 ft (548 m). There is excellent bathing all along the east and south shores. Pwllheli is the largest town on the peninsula, and Abersoch, an attractive village, is noted for its sailing facilities. Criccieth is also a popular resort, with the 13th-century ruins of *Criccieth Castle* (Cadw) perched above the bay. The high twin-towered gatehouse remains standing and there is an interesting exhibition on the castles of the Welsh princes. (F3)

Lloyd George Museum, Llanystumdwy Collection of relics from the statesman's turbulent political career and illustrated story of his life. Nearby, high above the river Dwyfor, is his burial place capped with a rough stone. ⬚ (F4)

Llyn Celyn Holding reservoir in the Tryweryn Valley built to control the flow of water in the river Dee. The lake is 150 ft (45 m) deep, 2½ miles (4 km) long and 1 mile (1.6 km) across at its widest point. A granite chapel on the north bank replaces the one that now lies beneath the waters. (F8)

Moel Fammau Country Park 2,375 acres (961 hectares) of open moorland around the Clwyd hills crowned by prehistoric forts on the line of Offa's Dyke Path. The park takes its name from the central 1,820 ft (554 m) peak topped by George III's Jubilee Tower. Access 6 miles (9.5 km) west of Mold off A494. (D11)

Nant Ffrancon Pass The Glencoe of Wales, remarkable for the great heights pressing in on either side. There was no vehicular road through the pass until Telford built the A5 in the early 19th century. Beside the road flows the Ogwen which on the south cascades down the falls of Benglog. (D6)

Newborough Warren Vast nature reserve covering 1,565 acres (633 hectares) and one of the largest expanses of sand dunes in Britain. Fronting it is the 4 mile (6.4 km) wide estuary of Llandwyn Bay exposing large sand banks at low tide where migrant birds gather in season. A road (running south from Newborough) through the 2,000 acre (809 hectare) Newborough Forest, on the west, leads to a car park and picnic sites by the sea. Overlooking the small harbour on Llanddwyn Island are cottages housing exhibits mounted by the Nature Conservancy Council. (D4)

Padarn Country Park 325 acres (130 hectares) of wood and slate quarry at south end of Llyn (Lake) Padarn, with museum, lake railway, trails, Quarry Hospital Visitor Centre and picnic sites. Access from B4086. ⬚ (D5)

Parys Mountain Spectacular example of industrial archaeology which began as series of small workings in 1760s and became by 1790 largest copper mine in Europe with a workforce of 1,500 men, women and children. The now deserted mountain is full of dangerous shafts and not recommended for families with children. The windmill crowning the summit was used to drain the workings. Access from B5111 2 miles (3.2 km) south of Amlwch. (A4)

Penmon Priory (Cadw) Ruined monastic settlement which includes prior's house, refectory and church founded in 6th century by St Seiriol but with 12th-century tower, nave and transepts. Nearby is massive dovecot with beehive dome built in the 16th century. Access by toll road. ⬚ (B6)

Penrhyn Castle (NT) Neo-Norman castle built 1827–40 for slate magnate Lord Penrhyn. Lovely grounds with fine views of Anglesey. Industrial railway museum, natural history exhibits and collection of dolls. Access from A55. ⬚ (C5)

Pistyll Rhaeaddr Highest waterfall in Wales which drops 240 ft (73 m) in two stages, first into a rock pool then in a series of leaps amid trees and rocky outcrops. At Tan-y-pistyll, 4 miles (6.4 km) north-west of Llanrhaeadr-ym-Mochnant. (G10)

Plas Newydd (NT) Georgian Gothick house of character set in 169 acres (68 hectares) of gardens, parks and woodlands bordering the Menai Strait. The main attractions of the splendidly furnished interior are Rex Whistler's largest wall painting and a military museum with relics of the 1st Marquess of Anglesey and the Battle of Waterloo. (C4)

Plas Newydd, Llangollen Black-and-white timbered house, the home for 50 years of the Ladies of Llangollen, 18th-century eccentrics who played host to all the notables of the day. As a result the house, now a museum, is crammed with mementoes of the famous. (F11)

Portmeirion Architectural fantasy of pastel-coloured buildings modelled on Portofino in Italy, the creation in 1926 of the late Sir Clough Williams-Ellis, half hidden in 175 acres (70 hectares) of subtropical gardens at the edge of Cardigan Bay. Visitors pay an entrance fee. (F5)

Portmeirion

Red Wharf Bay Vast estuary (Traeth Coch in Welsh) with nearly 3 miles (4.8 km) of sands and sea pools, famous for its cockle beds. Bathing is safe except on the ebbing tide. (B5)

Rhuddlan Castle (Cadw) Famous fortress reflected in the waters of the river Clwyd, built on a lozenge-shaped plan with massive round towers at the corners. (B9)

Ruthin Church (St Peters) Divided into two naves by a colonnade of five pointed arches supporting two coalescing roofs which date from the 16th century. Both are divided into square oak panels finely carved with heraldic designs presented to the townsfolk by Henry VII. Town centre. (D10)

Segontium Roman Fort, Caernarfon (Cadw and National Museum of Wales) Auxiliary fort founded AD 78 and occupied until the end of the fourth century. A museum on the site displays objects discovered during excavations. 1 mile (1.6 km) south-east on A4085. (D4)

Snowdon At 3,560 ft (1,085 m) the highest mountain in Wales and perhaps the biggest tourist attraction in the country. Easiest way to the summit is by the only rack and pinion railway in Britain, a 4½ mile (7.2 km) journey from Llanberis, but in season over 1,000 people get to the top by one means or another every day. Most popular of the five routes for walkers is the path beside the railway. Snowdon gives its name to a national park covering 840 square miles (2,175 sq km). (E5)

Crib Goch ridge leading to the summit of Snowdon

South Stack A headland honeycombed with great caverns and famous for its lighthouse. The clifftop is ablaze with wild flowers in summer. (B2)

Swallow Falls Popular beauty spot where river Llugwy flows into a chasm some 60 ft (18 m) wide. Jagged rocks break the flow of water into three large falls. (E7)

Trawsfynydd Lake 1,200 acre (485 hectare) man-made lake warmed by the outfall of a nuclear power station. A 2 mile (3.2 km) long nature trail starts near the power station on the north shore off the A470. (F6)

Valle Crucis Abbey (Cadw) Substantial ruins of church and conventual buildings of a Cistercian abbey – the Vale of the Cross – founded in 1201. (F11)

Vyrnwy Lake Beautiful man-made lake wooded to the water's edge covering 1,121 acres (453 hectares). A scenic drive of 11 miles (18 km) hugs the shoreline and there are many marked paths across the conifer plantations as well as the Craig Garth-Bwlch nature trail laid out by the RSPB starting at the visitor centre near the dam; it is 3 miles (4.8 km) long and involves two steep hills. (H9)

Welsh Mountain Zoo Wooded 37 acre (15 hectare) estate overlooking Colwyn Bay with collections of animals from many lands housed in large enclosures interspersed with gardens and trees. Displays of falconry in summer. ½ mile (0.8 km) west of Colwyn off B5113. Signposted. ⬚ (B8)

Welsh Slate Museum, Llanberis (Cadw) Former workshops of Dinorwig Quarry, one of the largest slate quarries in the world, now a branch of the National Museum of Wales. Exhibits include a water wheel, foundry, smithy and slate-sawing tables, quarry locomotive and wagons. Audio-visual display. Access off B4086. ⬚ (D5)

Wylfa Head Nature Trail Walk of 1 mile (1.6 km) in eight stages around seaward headland, the habitat of sea-birds and coastal flowers. Starts at power station. Access 1 mile (1.6 km) west of Cemaes Bay off A5025. (A3)

Yr Eifl Triple-peaked mountain anglicised as The Rivals with the easternmost summit (1,591 ft, 485 m) crowned by Tre'r Ceiri ('Town of the Giants'), an Iron Age hill fort occupied as late as Roman times. Outer walls still 12 ft (3.6 m) high in places enclose remains of some 150 roughly circular stone dwellings arranged in concentric bands. Access from B4417 1 mile (1.6 km) south-west of Llanaelhaern. (F3)

Map 15

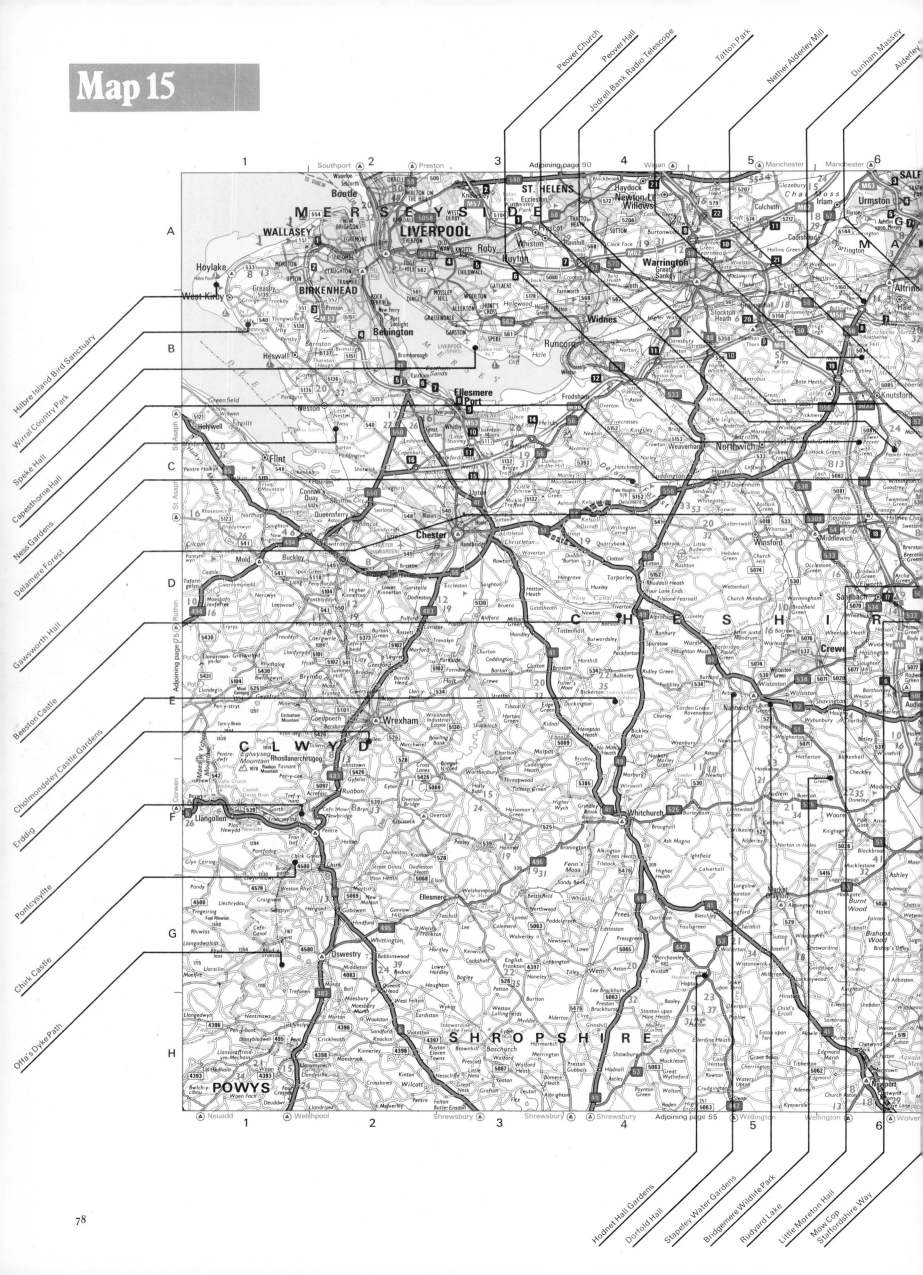

Peover Church
Peover Hall
Jodrell Bank Radio Telescope
Tatton Park
Nether Alderley Mill
Dunham Massey
Alderley

Hilbre Island Bird Sanctuary
Wirral Country Park
Speke Hall
Capesthorne Hall
Ness Gardens
Delamere Forest
Gawsworth Hall
Beeston Castle
Cholmondeley Castle Gardens
Erddig
Pontcysyllte
Chirk Castle
Offa's Dyke Path

Hodnet Hall Gardens
Dorfold Hall
Stapeley Water Gardens
Bridgemere Wildlife Park
Rudyard Lake
Little Moreton Hall
Mow Cop
Staffordshire Way

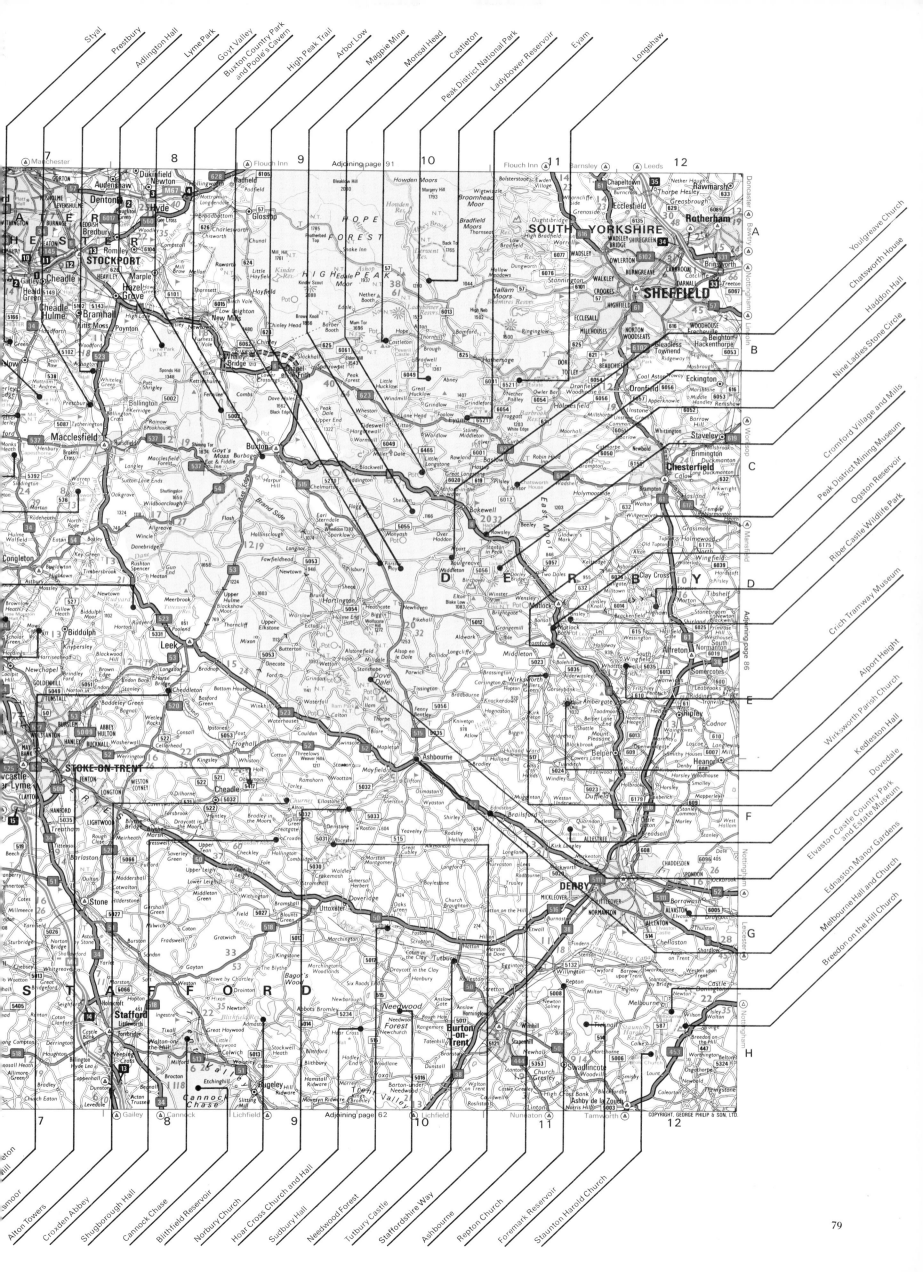

North Midlands

Adlington Hall Charming manor house built round flagged courtyard. Great hall, Elizabethan black-and-white half-timbering, wide brick entrance front with tall classical portico (1757). Completed 1505, the hall has mullioned, transomed windows, massive hammer-beam roof and late 17th-century organ on which Handel played. ☙ (B7)

Alderley Edge (NT) Magnificent views from wooded escarpment of 221 acres (89.4 hectares) astride B5087. Copper was mined on site from prehistoric times to 19th century. Highest point is site of beacon, used since medieval times to signal important events. (C7)

Alport Height (NT) Fine views from 1,032 ft (314.5 m) peak on 9 acres (3.6 hectares) of grassy hilltop. Alport Stone is a prominent gritstone monolith which has survived weathering. On minor road 2 miles (3.2 km) south-east Wirksworth. (E11)

Alton Towers Vast pleasure park with great variety of amusements surrounds many towered and turretted ruins (now being restored) of 19th-century Gothic mansion of Earls of Shrewsbury. 15th Earl converted virtual desert into superb gardens in delightful setting. Entrance just north of B5032. ☙ (F9)

Arbor Low (EH) Strange, atmospheric place where 40 recumbent stones lie in circle probably for form of worship as at Stonehenge, which is contemporary. Wide views over empty limestone uplands. 1 mile (1.6 km) east of Parsley Hay (A515). Access through very muddy farmyard. (D10)

Ashbourne Attractive small market town famous for gingerbread and Shrovetide football. Fine, large, medieval church with affecting monument to Penelope Boothby. Variety of good buildings. (F10)

Beeston Castle (EH) Ruins of 13th-century castle magnificently command Cheshire Plain from steep rock. (D4)

Blithfield Reservoir 800 acres (323 hectares) of landscaped lake, opened 1953 in park of Blithfield Hall. (H9)

Breedon on the Hill Church Hilltop church high above village. Formerly the chancel (13th-century) of an Augustinian priory, it contains some 30 fragments of late 8th-century Saxon sculpture arranged in friezes, in addition to 17th-century squire's pew and 18th-century box pews. Steep motor road at south end of village across green from A453. (H12)

Bridgemere Wildlife Park Pumas, tigers, British animals, waterfowl, birds of prey. Picnic area. Off A51. ☙ (F6)

Buxton Country Park and Poole's Cavern, Green Lane, Buxton Natural limestone cave – one of traditional 'Seven Wonders of the Peak' – in 120 acres (48.5 hectares) of natural woodland. Fine stalactites and stalagmites in cavern accessible to wheelchairs. Entrance in Green Lane, off A515. ☙ (C9)

Cannock Chase Remains of a Royal hunting forest in which deer, badgers and other wildlife still abound. Areas of ancient beech and oak remain, with modern Forestry Commission plantations, but much of the 16 sq miles (41.4 sq km) of high ground rising to 800 ft (243.8 m) is open country covered with bracken and heather, ideal for walking and especially beautiful in spring and autumn. German and Commonwealth cemeteries for dead of two World Wars. (H8/9; also Map 11 A3/4)

Capesthorne Hall Early 18th-century house by William Smith (brother of Francis Smith of Warwick) heavily disguised under turrets and gables of Blore's remodelling in 1837 and Salvin's reconstruction after 1861 fire. Davenport family supervised these changes and their family history is well displayed in portraits and other forms of art. ☙ (C7)

Castleton Attractive Peakland village dominated by ruins of Norman castle (DoE). Below it, *Peak Cavern*, one of Peakland's traditional Seven Wonders, has awe-inspiring entrance. Other caverns ½ mile (.8 km) west of village on A625: *Speedwell*, visited by boat, *Treak Cliff* and *Blue John*, at foot of spectacular Winnats Pass (a Site of Special Scientific Interest). Examples of Blue John ware are well displayed in *Cavendish House Museum*, Cross Street. St Edmund's Church has fine Norman chancel arch and interesting library, including a 1611 'Breeches' Bible. Spacious car park at west end of village on A625. *Mam Tor*, the 'Shivering Mountain', 1 mile (1.6 km) west on A625 has remains of Iron Age fort on 1,696 ft (517 m) summit, and wonderful views from Hope Valley. (B10)

Chatsworth House 'The Palace of the Peak' is one of England's great houses. The 4th Earl (later 1st Duke) of Devonshire built the present classical mansion (1678–1708) on the site of Bess of Hardwick's Tudor house in a majestic setting, employing William Talman, and later Thomas Archer, as architects. Sir Jeffry Wyatville added the north wing and made other alterations 1818–32 for the 6th Duke. 'Capability' Brown laid out the park, James Paine designed the handsome stable block and two graceful bridges over the Derwent, and Sir Joseph Paxton, head gardener and general factotum, enriched the gardens. Rich carvings, furnishings, paintings, books and other forms of art make this a treasure house. ☙ (C11)

Cheddleton Flint Mill Actually two mills astride Churnet converted *c.* 1763–1800 to grind flint for Potteries and now partly restored, with wheels intact. Restored Caldon Canal a stone's throw away. ☙ (E8)

Chirk Castle (NT) Built by Roger Mortimer *c.* 1300 and occupied by Sir Thomas Myddleton and his descendants since 1595. Impressive entrance front with three round towers. Interior mainly 17th, 18th and 19th centuries. Long gallery richly carved by Thomas Dugdale 1687. Fine pictures, furniture and historical relics. Park gates 1719–21 by local Davies brothers particularly noteworthy. ☙ (F1)

Chirk Castle gates

Cholmondeley Castle Gardens Pleasure gardens with rare breeds of farm animals and picnic areas in grounds of 19th-century castle (not open). ☙ (E4)

Crich Tramway Museum Over 50 trams from all over the world, many in working order. Tram rides of 1 mile (1.6 km) with spectacular views. Top of Crich village, just off B5035. ☙ (E12)

Cromford Village and Mills Almost intact, early Industrial Revolution village of rare interest. Here Sir Richard Arkwright built the first mechanised textile factory in the world, equipping it with the cotton-spinning machinery he had recently invented. Many of the old cottages were built for his workpeople. His mills (1771 and later) are being converted into a museum. On restored Cromford Canal horse-drawn narrow boat trips at weekends. Small steam museum. (E11)

Croxden Abbey (EH) Substantial ruins of Cistercian abbey founded 1176 in pleasant setting above River Dove. Signposted from Rocester on B5030. Minor road bisects ruins. (F9)

Delamere Forest (Forestry Commission) Good, easy walking in forest with woodland trails, picnic areas and Information Centre, and a trail for the handicapped. On B5152 with car park at Hatchmere. Signposted from A556 at Delamere village. ☙ (C4)

Dorfold Hall Jacobean house of about 1616 noted for contemporary panelling and Georgian plasterwork ceilings. It stands in a large park approached along an avenue of trees. (E5)

Dovedale (NT) Most beautiful and most visited of the Peak's limestone dales. Lovely, gentle walk through narrow gorge with remarkably varied scenery and strange natural rock formations for 2 miles (3.2 km) can be extended through Mill Dale, Wolfscote and Beresford Dales to Hartington (8 miles, 12.8 km) alongside clear trout stream. No motor road through dales except ½ mile (.8 km) from Milldale to Lode Mill. Car parks at Ilam and in Hartington. (E10)

Dunham Massey (NT) 18th-century rebuilding of Elizabethan house on Norman castle site, with 20th-century alterations and redecorations. Portraits of Grey family, Earls of Stamford, early 18th-century furniture and Huguenot silver. Elizabethan mill in working order, deer house (1740) and early Georgian stables. Deer park. Entrance off A56. ☙ (B6)

Ednaston Manor Gardens, Brailsford Formal and woodland garden with rare trees, shrubs, roses and alpines in grounds of handsome Lutyens house (not open). Entrance on east side of A52, 1 mile (1.6 km) north Brailsford village at Ednaston. ☙ (F10)

ton in the 1830s around slightly earlier house designed by James Wyatt. Working museum showing how estate was run in late 19th century. On B5010 between A6 and A6005. ☙ (G12)

Erddig (NT) Late 17th-century house with 18th-century additions, containing much of original furniture. Laundry, bakehouse, smithy and sawmill in working order in outbuildings. Formal 18th-century garden. Entrance off A483. ☙ (E2)

Eyam Plague village, where 257 villagers died 1665–6, but disease confined to parish through heroic leadership of rector and his ejected predecessor. Plague Cottage, where disease started, and Riley Graves (NT) – on hillside ½ mile (.8 km) east of village – among relics of the plague year. Attractive stone village (pronounced EEM) with fine Saxon cross in churchyard. (C10)

Foremark Reservoir Attractively landscaped lake in pleasantly undulating countryside. Angling and sailing on lake; good easy walking and nature reserve close by. Car parks on minor road Repton to Ticknall and A514. (H11)

Gawsworth Hall Lovely black-and-white timbered house, basically Elizabethan but much altered. Formerly home of Mary Fitton, to whom Shakespeare dedicated his first folio. Fitton tombs in fine 15th-century church in beautiful village of woods and lakes. (C7)

Rock outcrop overlooking Goyt Valley

Goyt Valley Narrow, beautiful valley running south from Taxal, closed to motorists on Sundays when minibus service operates. Good, fairly easy walking at all times. Sailing and fishing on Errwood Reservoir. Car parks with picnic areas approached from A5002 or A537. (B/C8)

Haddon Hall Perhaps the most complete example of a medieval manor house extant in England. Built piecemeal between the 12th and 17th centuries, its last addition was the long gallery constructed by John Manners just after 1600 before he became Earl of Rutland and made Belvoir Castle his main seat. Charming terraced garden is Jacobean and earlier. (D10)

Hawksmoor (NT) Semi-natural oak and birch woodland, Forestry Commission plantations and open moorland cover this 307 acre (124.2 hectare) undulating nature reserve. Relics of charcoal burners and colliery tramway in woods. Entrance north side of B5417. (F9)

High Peak Trail (Derbyshire County Council) Walkers, cyclists and horse-riders can follow the track of the former Cromford and High Peak Railway from the Cromford Canal to Parsley Hay, 17½ miles (28 km) of comfortable walking, but two 1 in 7 gradients. Car parks at each end and at intermediate points. Southern entrance is at Highpeak Junction (A6) alongside Cromford Canal 1½ miles (2.4 km) south of Cromford, but no car park there. Car parking at Cromford Wharf, on road to Lea and Holloway, off A6; at Black Rock picnic site off B5036 (between Cromford and Wirksworth); and at Middleton Top Engine House, on minor road from Middleton-by-Worksworth to Ashbourne (access to trail also from last two points). (E11 to D10)

Elvaston Castle Country Park and Estate Museum 200 acres (80.9 hectares) of park and gardens laid out by William Barron for 4th Earl of Harring-

Hilbre Island Bird Sanctuary This 'delight of the bird watcher, botanist, geologist and sun bather' is a mile (1.6 km) offshore, access limited by tides. Car park at Dee Lane, West Kirby. (A1)

Hoar Cross Church and Hall Elaborately beautiful church of 1876 by G.F. Bodley for Emily Meynell Ingram in memory of her husband. Their large Victorian mansion nearby has ornamental plasterwork, oak panelling, William Morris wallpaper. Beautiful gardens undergoing restoration. 🔊 (H9)

Hodnet Hall Gardens Superb series of landscaped gardens covering 60 acres (24.3 hectares); flowers, lawns, trees and trout lakes around Elizabethan-style hall (not open). 🔊 (G5)

Jodrell Bank Radio Telescope (Manchester University) Huge radio telescope and smaller one for public use, with exhibitions, models, planetarium and arboretum. On A535. (C6)

Kedleston Hall Robert Adam at his most elegant with this vast Georgian classical mansion, unaltered since 1760s, which makes good use of local alabaster and Blue John stone. Splendid park and lake with Adam bridge. Impressive Curzon monuments in lovely 12th-century church adjoining house. Entrance on minor road to Hulland signposted from Derby ring road. (F11)

Ladybower Reservoir Newest and largest of three artificial lakes constructed between 1901 and 1945 on upper Derwent. Unclassified road from just west of Ashopton continues beyond Derwent Reservoir (where the Ruhr dams raid was rehearsed and later filmed) to Howden Reservoir through superb highland scenery. Return by same road. (A10/B10)

Little Moreton Hall (NT) One of England's loveliest black-and-white timber-framed houses, standing on a small moated island. Begun in 1480, com-

vast deer park with long established red deer herd. Entrance on A6 concealed from south. 🔊 (B8)

Magpie Mine, Sheldon Partly restored surface remains of lead mine with two engine houses, smithy, cottage and reconstructed horse gin. ½ mile (.8 km) south of Sheldon on unclassified Bakewell–Monyash road, access by public footpath. (D10)

Melbourne Hall and Church Charming 17th-century house with early Georgian alterations, completed 1720, in superb French-style garden by Royal gardeners, London and Wise. Opposite this former home of Lords Melbourne and Palmerston is a magnificent Norman church begun by the Bishop of Carlisle in 1134. 🔊 (H12)

Monsal Head Striking viewpoint commanding lovely stretch of Derbyshire Wye. Disused railway viaduct, deplored by Ruskin, fits impressively into natural landscape. Alongside B6465. (C10)

Mow Cop (NT) Splendid views from 10 acres (4 hectares) of rough hilltop surrounding folly tower built about 1750 nearly 1,100 ft (335.3 m) above sea level. Primitive Methodists held their inaugural meeting here in 1807. (E7)

Needwood Forest The remains of a former royal hunting forest covering nearly 10,000 acres (4,047 hectares) of plateau rising to almost 500 ft (152.4 m), now mostly devoted to intensive dairy farming and stock raising, but with belts of woodland, especially on north escarpment, offering occasional fine views, as from Hanbury churchyard (G10). Attractive countryside, thinly populated, but with interesting churches at Abbots Bromley (H9), Hamstall Ridware and Mavesyn Ridware (H9) and Hanbury and good black-and-white timber-framed houses in most villages. (G/H9/10)

Ness Gardens Comprehensive collection of plants. Herb garden. 🔊 (C2)

(Map 14 B10) to the Bristol Channel near Chepstow following dyke erected by King Offa of Mercia (750–800), probably as a boundary between his kingdom and the Welsh. The most spectacular stretches are farther south, but an attractive stretch between Pentre, junction of A5 and A483 (F1), and Llanymynech, A483 (H1). See also entry on Gazetteer 10. (F/G/H1)

Ogston Reservoir Sailing, angling or simply enjoying lovely scenery are the attractions of this 200 acre (81 hectare) stretch of water in the Amber Valley. Car park on south side of B6014. (D12)

Peak District Mining Museum, The Pavilion, Matlock Bath Lead mining history of the area over 2,000 years vividly displayed. Exhibits include unique 1819 giant water pressure engine and children's climbing shafts. On A6. (D11)

Peak District National Park England's oldest national park, designated 1951, is an area rich in natural beauty, mainly in Derbyshire but stretching into adjoining counties. Its 542 sq miles (1,403.8 sq km) can be divided into two areas: the White Peak (or Low Peak) of near white limestone in the centre and south, and the Dark Peak (or High Peak) of darker gritstone to the north and on the east and west fringes.

Both areas are paradises for walkers, but of markedly contrasting types. The White Peak offers glorious, easy walking along the Dales or on the *Tissington Trail*, a 17 mile (27.2 km) stroll along a disused railway track between Ashbourne (F10) and Parsley Hay (D10). The Dark Peak, especially in the north, involves extremely hard walking on a lonely moorland plateau of peat bog at up to 2,000 ft (609.6 m) and liable to sudden weather changes.

Bakewell (D10), an attractive small town, is the headquarters of the National Park. There is an information centre there (Peak National Park Office, Aldern House, Baslow Road), and other centres at Edale (B9), on right side of road from Edale station to village, Castleton (B10), near Parish Church, or Hartington (D9), Old Signal Box, Tissington Trail.

The pagan custom (now Christianised) of decorating village wells with flowers and plants in the form of pictures – usually depicting a Biblical story – is maintained in many of the stone-built villages, especially on the porous limestone, where the springs and wells were vitally important. This rare form of folkart may be seen in one village or another in almost any week between May and September. This, together with the ubiquitous stone walls marching across the landscape and the astonishing scenic contrasts, will be the main impressions left on the tourist on a first visit to this lovely area.

Peover Church, Lower Peover Charming 13th-century timber-framed church with 16th-century stone tower and a wealth of fine woodwork inside. Up cobbled lane in village off B5081. (C6)

Peover Hall, Peover Superior Pronounced 'Peever'. For many generations the moated home of the Mainwarings. Rebuilt 1585, mainly in brick, with many subsequent alterations. Fine stables of 1654 with elaborate woodwork and ceilings. Off A50. (C6)

Pontcysyllte Britain's most spectacular aqueduct (by Telford and Jessop 1795–1805) carries the Ellesmere Canal 1,007 ft (306.9 m) across the Dee at a height of 121 ft (36.8 m). Towpath accessible from Trevor, off A539 south of Traf-y-nant, or Fron (A5). (F2)

Prestbury A most attractive, opulent large village of many old black-and-white houses and a splendid church. (C7)

Repton Church Saxon chancel with Royal mausoleum of Mercian kings in Saxon crypt below. Repton was the birthplace of Mercian Christianity. (G11)

Riber Castle Wildlife Park European birds and animals, including outstanding Lynx collection, rare farm breeds, nature centre and garden centre, car museum, model railways and children's playground around shell of eccentric millionaire's 1862 Gothic castle. 1 mile (1.6 km) up Alders Lane from A615. (D11)

Rudyard Lake Canal reservoir (constructed 1831) 2 miles (3.2 km) long in lovely, wild, hilly setting where Kipling's parents met. Access through Rudyard village off B5331. (E8)

Shugborough Hall (NT) Late 17th-century house enlarged c. 1750 and by Samuel Wyatt about 1800. Neo-Grecian monuments by James 'Athenian' Stuart in beautiful park, some commemorating Admiral Anson, the circumnavigator. Naval relics and fine pictures in house. County folk museum in stables. 🔊 (H8)

Speke Hall (NT) One of Britain's most richly half-timbered houses, dating mainly from 16th century and formerly moated. Elaborate plasterwork, panelling, Mortlake tapestries and interesting furniture. Fine gardens and woodland. 1½ miles (2.4 km) south of A561 on east side of Liverpool Airport. 🔊 (B3)

Staffordshire Way (Staffordshire County Council) First stage of long-distance footpath – ultimately spanning the county – running for 32 miles (51.2 km) between Mow Cop (E7) and Rocester (F9), giving easy walking through varied scenery and offering good views. Waymarked.

Stapeley Water Gardens Aquatic plants, fish, display pool. On A51. 🔊 (E5)

Staunton Harold Church (NT) Superb small church built 1653 during Commonwealth as deliberate act of defiance. Complete, untouched Jacobean interior in intentionally anachronistic Gothic exterior. Idyllic valley setting off B587. (H12)

Styal (NT) Complete Industrial Revolution complex of village, chapels, school, apprentice house and Quarry Bank Mill (now a working textile museum) in glorious parkland setting. Entrance on B5166. (B7)

Sudbury Hall (NT) Richly decorated Charles II house with Grinling Gibbons wood carvings, Laguerre ceilings and Bradbury and Pettifer plasterwork. Delightful Museum of Childhood in the servants' wing. 🔊 (G10)

Tatton Park (NT) Something to please everyone in this 2,000 acre (809.4 hectare) park, including 60 acre (24.3 hectare) gardens, sailing and wildfowl on Tatton Mere, tithe barn and deserted village site. Late Georgian mansion chiefly by Lewis Wyatt, who also designed much of the exquisite furniture and fittings executed by Gillow of Lancaster. Entrance on A5034. 🔊 (B6)

Tutbury Castle Ruins of John of Gaunt's medieval castle on splendid defensive site above River Dove. Nearby Priory Church has fine Norman nave. (G10)

Wirksworth Parish Church Impressive 13th-century cruciform church in charming close. Fine monuments and a 7th-century Saxon sarcophagus with Byzantine-style carvings, Derbyshire's earliest Christian relic. Rugged little town is receiving Civic Trust restoration. (E11)

Wirral Country Park Linear country park with 12 mile (19.2 km) footpath along disused railway from West Kirby (B1) to Hooton (B2). Visitor Centre at Thurstaston Station, off A540 (B1).

Youlgreave Church Fine, mainly Norman, church with magnificent Perpendicular tower and alabaster monuments in pleasing upland village at heart of good walking country. (D10)

Little Moreton Hall

pleted 1580, it remains virtually untouched. Elaborate glass and woodwork, with newly discovered painted panelling. 🔊 (E7)

Longshaw (NT) Nearly 1,100 acres (445.2 hectares) of woodland and moorland rising to 1,200 ft (365.8 km) above Derwent valley, with superb views, prehistoric remains and NT information centre. On south side of A625. Car park off B6055 (road between A625 and B6054), ½ mile (.8 km) south of junction with A625 gives access by short footpath to information centre. (B11)

Lyme Park (NT) An Elizabethan house enlarged and Georgianised by Leoni, with slightly later alterations and additions by Lewis Wyatt. Large gardens,

Nether Alderley Mill (NT) Attractive 16th-century corn mill restored to working order with occasional demonstrations. (C7)

Nine Ladies Stone Circle, Stanton Moor (EH) Bronze Age circle of nine upright stones with single 'King' stone 30 yds (27 m) to south on moorland plateau rising to 1,000 ft (305 m) and rich in prehistoric remains. Reached from minor road encircling moor. (D10)

Norbury Church Splendid late 14th-century church, with impressive chancel and much medieval glass, in lovely wooded setting with manor house adjoining. Approached from concealed drive on north side of B5033. (F9)

Offa's Dyke Path 80 miles (128 km) of generally easy walking from Prestatyn

The Pennine Way

'The wide, health-giving moorlands and high places of solitude, the features of natural beauty and the places of historical interest along the Pennine Way give this route a special character and attractiveness which should be available for all time as a natural heritage of the youth of the country and of all who feel the call of the hills and the lonely places.'

This was the unanimous conclusion of a conference held in 1938 attended by representatives of open-air organisations, but it was not until 1951 that the creation of the Pennine Way was officially approved. The Way was to be the first of the long-distance footpaths established under the National Parks and Access to the Countryside Act 1949, and it was finally completed in 1977 when the Scottish leg was formally incorporated.

The Pennine Way now stretches from Edale in the Peak District National Park along the length of the Pennines and over the Cheviot Hills to end at Kirk Yetholm in Scotland. It takes the necessarily dedicated walker almost half the length of England, a distance of more than 250 miles (400 km), traversing three National Parks on the way.

The Way is mainly a high-level route, over the Pennine plateau, and crosses great stretches of shaggy moorland which offer some of the roughest walking in the country, often miles from the nearest habitation. Even the named peaks are in many cases no more than a swell above the general level of the surrounding moorland, with none of the consistently rugged grandeur of the Lake District.

However, although much of the Way does wind across featureless peat moors, there are many distinctive landmarks along the route and significant changes in landscape connected with the underlying geology. Starting in Edale the walker is on land underlain with millstone grit, giving rise to the famous edges where the beds in the rock are laid bare. The grit covers limestone which breaks out further north in Yorkshire, in pot-holing country where streams often vanish suddenly into the permeable rocks, as at Hunt Pot. Between the two are the Yoredale Beds (a mixture of limestone, shale and sandstone), while the far north of the route is underlain by igneous rock, most noticeable in the basalt ridge of the whin sill on which the Romans built Hadrian's Wall to mark the northern

boundary of their Empire. Scenic highlights on or near the route include Malham Cove, the limestone cleft of Gordale Scar, the waterfalls of Hardrow Force and Cauldron Snout, the chasm of High Cup Nick and the brooding summit of Pen y Ghent. Other attractions include lonely moorland villages such as Thwaite, the highest pub in England and the section passing through Brontë country. There is also much to interest the botanist and naturalist. Although the moorland heights generally have a limited flora, this is more than compensated for by the profusion and variety to be found on the lower slopes and in the dales. The flora of the limestone districts of Craven in Yorkshire, and Upper Teesdale (now partly a National Nature Reserve) is particularly well known and includes many rare sub-alpine species. Bird life is also plentiful with buzzards, ravens, peregrine falcon and curlew to be seen.

The Pennine Way is a challenging route, not to be undertaken lightly and without the right equipment, but there are considerable rewards for those who feel drawn to wild and lonely places.

Malham Tarn (below) *lies on the moors above Malham Cove* (right) *a soaring amphitheatre of limestone. At one time a stream flowing from Malham Tarn poured over the lip of the Cove. Further north the Way passes through the lonely village of Thwaite* (below left) *and across the River Swale* (below right), *shown here in a view towards Kidson (1,636 ft, 500 m) from near Keld. Stonesdale Beck and Stonesdale Moor* (above) *are typical of the wild beauty of the North Yorkshire dales with more dramatic scenery at Cauldron Snout* (left), *where the Tees falls 1,000 ft (300 m) in a series of cascades, and in the view from High Cup Nick* (far right), *looking across the Eden Valley towards the hills of the Lake District.*

Canals

Navigable canals were being constructed in Britain from the 16th century onwards – later than in China, Italy and France – but the real development of the canal network dates from the 1750s. Between then and the middle of the next century, but particularly between 1765 and 1805, about 3,000 miles (4,800 km) of canals were added to the existing 1,000 miles (1,600 km) of navigable rivers. After 1850, mainly as a result of competition from the railways, very little was done to improve or extend the system, although Britain's largest canal, the Manchester Ship Canal, was opened in 1894, the first and only canal in Britain to be excavated by machinery, not by men with spades.

The British canals are of four types. First, there are those which were built to take sea-going ships. The earliest of these was the Exeter ship canal (Devon), running between Exeter and Topsham. Begun and finished during the reign of Elizabeth I, this was the first canal in this country to use the pound-lock, the only type in use today, rather than the flash lock which has only one gate. Then there are the canals which were linked to river navigation and took river barges, and a number of very narrow canals, with locks only about 7 ft (2 m) wide, used mainly for local traffic. The fourth group comprises what were known as tub-boat canals. These were found chiefly in the hilly parts of Shropshire and the West Country, and took boats about 20 ft (6 m) long and 5 ft (1.5 m) wide, not too big to be hauled out of the water and carried up and down inclined planes, which in hilly country was cheaper than building tunnels or flights of locks.

The main sections of canal, and their bigger branches, were usually built by public companies, but occasionally by individual entrepreneurs. The construction of many of the smaller branch canals, however, often to coalmines or factories, was undertaken privately by the people who owned and operated them.

The British canal system became fossilised during the second half of the 19th century. The railways creamed off the traffic and the canals became less and less profitable to run. Maintenance was neglected and all but a few became derelict. The situation on the Continent was different. In Belgium, the Netherlands, France and Germany, for instance, the old canals have been widened and deepened to make them suitable for modern sea-going ships and large barges and still form an important part of the transport network. Campaigns to do the same for Britain have not so far been successful.

Since 1945, however, the British Waterways Board, which has owned the canals since 1962, has realised that, although our narrow, shallow canals may not have much commercial use, they are popular for pleasure-boating. Despite a chronic shortage of funds a great deal has already been done in the way of repairing locks, banks and towpaths and dredging and clearing the waterways, so that holidaymakers can travel respectable distances by canal without finding their route blocked.

Tunnels, of which British, unlike Dutch or Belgian, canals have a considerable number, constitute a major maintenance problem. The repair of masonry is extremely and in some cases impossibly expensive, and for this reason some stretches of canal are likely to remain closed for a long time, perhaps for ever. It is one thing to modernise canals which run through flat country, as they do in the Netherlands, and quite another to make them bigger when they have to find their

way through deep cuttings and to burrow through hills, as is so often the case in Britain. What, one wonders, would the Dutch engineers have done, if they had been faced with the British landscape?

Thirty-seven British canals are still navigable, at least for part of their length (full details can be found in the *Inland Waterways Guide*, published annually). Some are still used to carry freight, others carry only pleasure boats nowadays. The fine pattern of canals in Yorkshire, linking Goole, Sheffield, Leeds, Selby and Castleford, is being continuously improved to attract commercial traffic and is an interesting mixture of the industrial and the scenic, with oil tankers and coal barges on some sections and rural peace on others. The Kennet and Avon (passing through Avon, Wiltshire and Berkshire) is countryside all the way, and so are the Llangollen (a branch of the Shropshire Union passing through Cheshire, Shropshire and Clwyd) and the Oxford (through Oxfordshire and Warwickshire), but the Grand Union, from the Thames at Brentford to Birmingham, is something quite out of the ordinary, 135 navigable miles (216 km), with 165 locks. It offers urban and industrial stretches on the outskirts of London and in the Birmingham area and a pleasant rural atmosphere for most of the rest of the way. The Grand Union also has Blisworth tunnel, 3,056 yards (2,800 m) long, and the National Waterways Museum at Stoke Bruerne (Northamptonshire), which is run by the British Waterways Board.

Britain's hilly countryside forced canal builders to use tunnels and aqueducts and to construct flights of locks. Telford, born 1757, was one of the most famous canal builders. His Pontcysyllte Aqueduct (below), carrying the Ellesmere Canal over the Dee, is the highest and largest canal aqueduct in the British Isles. His aqueduct at Chirk (above), also on the Ellesmere Canal, is flanked by the railway viaduct. The Blisworth Tunnel (above centre), on the Grand Union, is the longest tunnel still in full use. The Bingley Five-Rise Staircase on the Leeds and Liverpool (centre) was the earliest staircase in

The canals, like the railways, take you through 19th-century Britain, the roads through 20th-century developments. To travel along a canal is to escape into the past and to build up a picture of how people earned a living a century and more ago. You can see the waterside villages, with their wharves where coal, roadstone, lime, and other heavy and bulky goods were landed, and agricultural produce loaded for shipment away. There is usually a warehouse and a public house nearby. There are mills by the side of the Birmingham canal, a warehouse at Worksop (Nottinghamshire), on the Chesterfield canal, which originally belonged to Pickfords (an important firm operating on the canals before they concentrated on road transport), and a pottery, the Gladstone Pottery, at Longton, Stoke-on-Trent, on the Trent and Mersey.

In Britain, the canals look backwards. They are deliciously nostalgic.

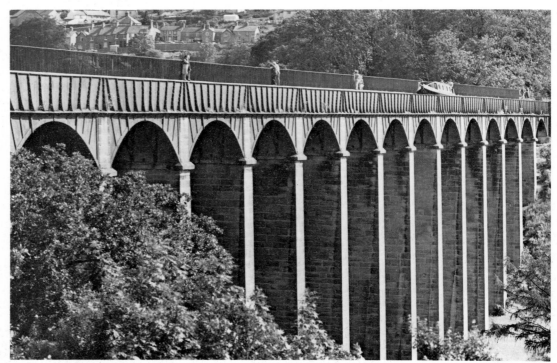

England with more than two chambers; (below centre) the Delph locks on the Dudley Canal at Brierley Hill. Thirty-seven British canals are still navigable and some, such as the Manchester Ship Canal (above right), are still used by ocean-going vessels. In contrast the rural peace of this stretch of the Oxford Canal (below right) typifies the many that are now only used by pleasure boats.

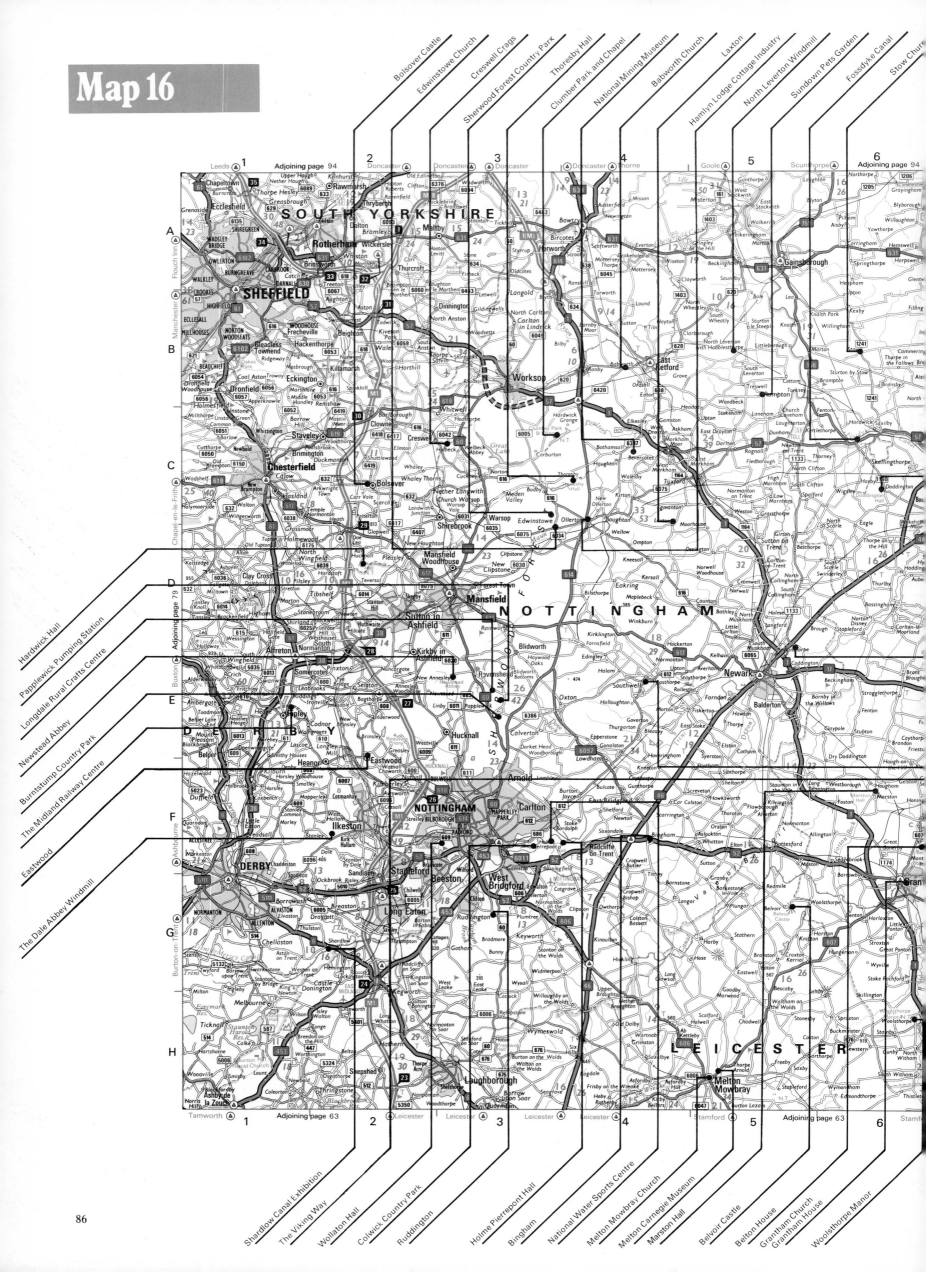

Map 16

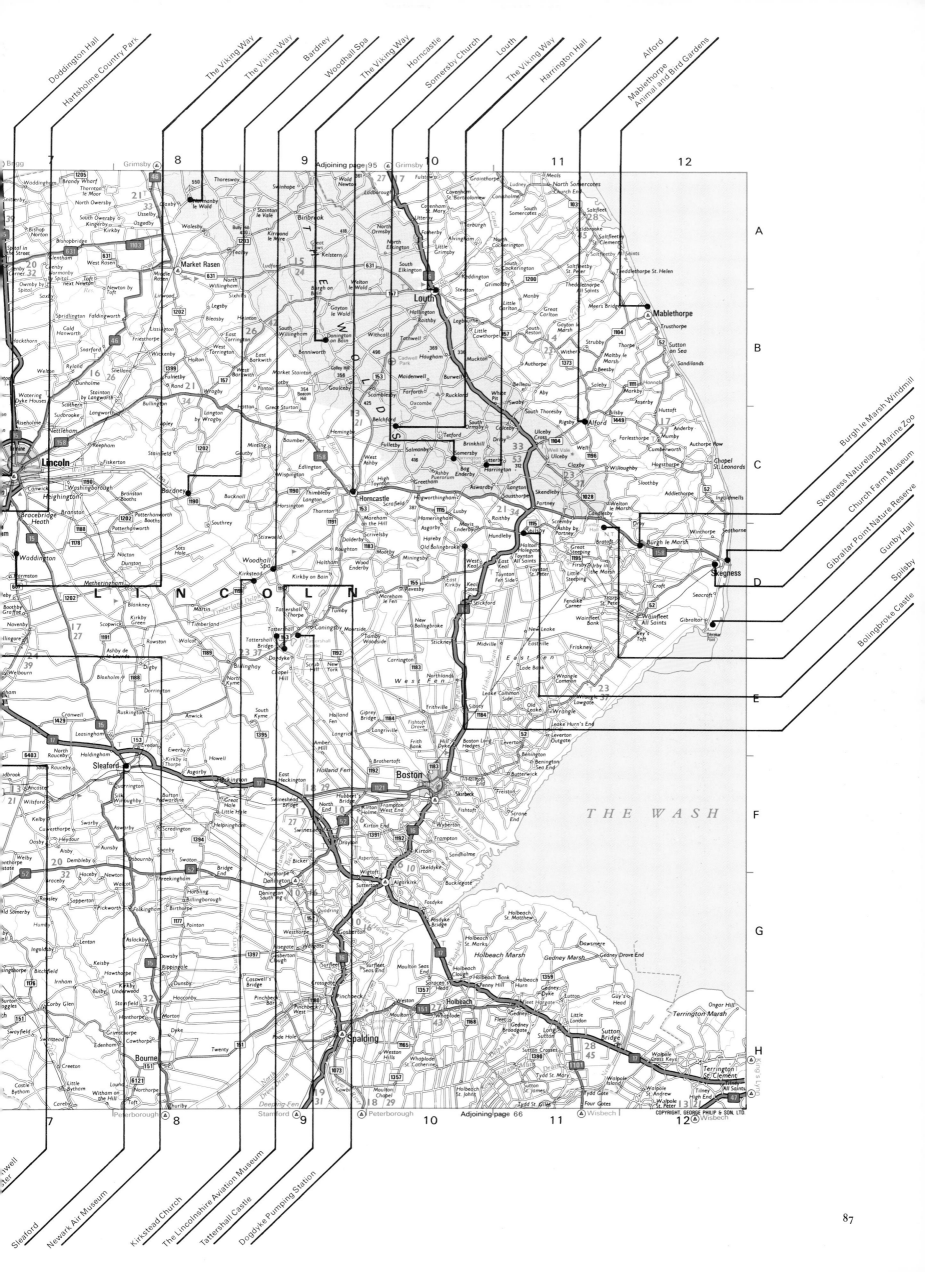

North Midlands

Alford A tiny town packed with places of interest, notably its restored tower mill, Friday crafts market (summer only), and *Manor House Folk Museum*, West Street. Also has three-day Alford festival during the late summer bank holiday. (C11)

Babworth Church (All Saints) Closely linked to the discovery of the New World: both William Brewster and William Bradford worshipped here before sailing in the *Mayflower*, and the font cover was made from a Devon cider vat whose wood also went into the making of the 'second' *Mayflower*, built in 1955. (B4)

Bardney *Bardney Museum* houses an exhibition devoted to the history of IX Squadron of the RAF, but is temporarily closed. There are also excavations in the village revealing the earlier presence of a Benedictine abbey, supposedly founded by Ethelred, King of Mercia, in the 7th century. (C8)

Belton House (NT) A 17th-century house of the Restoration period which contains a fine collection of family portraits, porcelain, tapestries, Grinling Gibbons carvings, Aubusson carpets. The house sits in a beautiful 75 acre (30 hectare) park which includes formal gardens near the house (roses, orangery), an 'adventure playground' for children, a riverside picnic area, miniature railway, and river rides. Just north of Grantham off the A607. (F6)

Belvoir Castle Seat of the Dukes of Rutland since the days of Henry VIII, it was originally built by Robert de Todeni, Standard Bearer to William the Conqueror, but was largely rebuilt in the medieval style by Wyatt, after a fire in 1816. Contents include notable art treasures, including works by Poussin, Holbein, Rubens and Reynolds, Gobelin and Mortlake tapestries, Chinese silks, furniture, fine porcelain and sculpture. Terraced gardens are built into the hillside below the castle. There is also a military museum devoted to the 17th/21st Lancers with an impressive medal collection and the bugle used in the 'Charge of the Light Brigade'. Magnificent views over the Vale of Belvoir. 7 miles (11 km) south-west of Grantham off the A607, beyond Denton. (G5)

Bingham The Butter Cross, capped by a steeple, was the centre for dairy trading in the town's earlier days as a thriving market centre. (F4)

Bolingbroke Castle (EH) Located in the wolds village of Old Bolingbroke are the remains – mainly mounds of earth and stone – of John of Gaunt's castle where his son Henry IV was born (in 1366). The castle was laid waste by the Parliamentarians during the Civil War. Site undergoing conservation – not yet officially open. (D10)

Bolsover Castle (EH) Although its history leads back to Norman times it is Bolsover's 17th-century, slightly fairy-tale keep built on the old foundations, long gallery and ruined terraced buildings that are of special interest. (C2)

Burgh le Marsh Windmill A five-sail tower mill which was built in 1833, ceased operation in 1947 and has recently been restored to working, flour-making order. (D12)

Burntstump Country Park A woodland area within Sherwood Forest laced with footpaths and dotted with areas for informal games. 3 miles (4.8 km) north of Arnold on the A60. See **Sherwood Forest Country Park**. (E3)

Church Farm Museum, Church Road South, Skegness Both a craft centre, with regular demonstrations throughout the summer of spinning, tapestry, butter making, cane seating, peg rug making and other traditional skills, and a museum housing the Bernard Best collection of agricultural, domestic and industrial objects. Reconstructed 19th-century barn complex with exhibition gallery. (D12)

Clumber Park and Chapel (NT) A 3,800 acre (1,538 hectare) expanse of 18th-century landscaped parkland, with farm, lake (with classical bridge) and woodland. Includes the 2 mile (3.2 km) Duke's Drive, the longest double avenue of lime trees in Europe. There are nature trails, fishing and cycle hire. Once the seat of the Duke of Newcastle, the grounds include Clumber Chapel, a good example of Victorian Gothic Revival architecture. To reach Clumber leave the A1 near Worksop and enter the park from the A614. (C3)

Colwick Country Park A grassy 250 acre (101 hectare) area landscaped on old gravel workings beside the Trent, just off the B686 (just beyond the racecourse). Plenty of opportunities for doing nothing or something (walking, sailing, windsurfing, fishing etc.). (G3)

Creswell Crags Limestone gorge and cave scenery with a picnic site and Visitor Centre to put archaeological Stone Age finds into perspective. Access from B6042. (C2/3)

The Dale Abbey Windmill, Cat and Fiddle Lane Built in 1788, the Mill on Cat and Fiddle Lane is a good example of a post mill, one of the earliest designs. Built around a central post, the mill can be rotated to allow the sails to face the wind. 4 miles (6.4 km) north-east Derby on A6096. (F2)

Doddington Hall An Elizabethan brick-and-stone manor house completed in 1600 by Robert Smythson and refurbished in the 18th century. Its delightful grounds include a profusion of spring bulbs, walled rose garden and nature trail; its Georgian interiors are known for their elegant furnishings, textiles, paintings and porcelain. (C6)

Dogdyke Pumping Station A 30 hp beam steam engine used for land drainage (built by Bradley and Craven of Wakefield in 1855) has been restored and reconstructed using all of its original parts. Entry from the A153 via Bridge Farm (signposted when open). (E9)

Eastwood: D.H. Lawrence Birthplace The cottage, 8a Victoria Street, is furnished in the style of the period of Lawrence's birth (1885). Take the A610 from Nottingham and turn right just before the junction with A608. (F2)

Edwinstowe Church (St Mary) Robin Hood married Maid Marian in this 13th-century church, also noted for its 'Pillar Piscina' in the chancel. (C3)

Fossdyke Canal Dates back to the Romans who linked the rivers Trent and Witham with the Fossdyke between Torksey Lock (once the site of a Saxon mint) and Brayford Pool in Lincoln. Most of towpath accessible. (C6)

Gibraltar Point Nature Reserve A nature reserve and Visitor Centre designed to show wildlife lovers the flora and fauna of sand-dunes and saltmarsh scenery. (D12)

Grantham Church (St Wulfram's) An Early English and Decorated structure dating back to the 13th century. Its 282½ ft (86 m) ornate spire is the 6th largest in England. The library contains chained books and there is a 14th-century crypt chapel and fine stained glass windows. Rich and unusual font. Set among Georgian houses in quiet close in town centre. (F6)

Grantham House (NT) The house in Castlegate overlooks the river Witham (the grounds extend to its banks) and dates back to the 14th century. Its most famous guest was Princess Margaret, Henry VII's daughter, who in 1503 stayed there en route to marrying James IV in Scotland. But it has been considerably altered, restored and added to over the years. (F6)

Gunby Hall (NT) Built in 1700 in the style of Wren this red-brick house boasts contemporary wainscoting, portraits by Reynolds and an autographed copy of Boswell's *Life of Johnson*. The walled garden contains roses and a plethora of other blooms. Access from A158. (D11)

Hamlyn Lodge Cottage Industry The showroom on Station Road, Ollerton, displays handmade reproduction furniture, restored antique work and stoneware pottery (the workshop is at Welbeck). (C4)

Hardwick Hall (NT) An excellent example of an Elizabethan house built with a mass of windows by Elizabeth, Countess of Shrewsbury ('Bess of Hardwick'), mother of the 1st Earl of Devonshire. Of particular note is the Great Chamber and the furniture, needlework, tapestries and portraits. The gardens include yew hedges and a herb garden. Approach from M1 (junction 29). (D2)

Harrington Hall Red-brick mansion, altered in 1678, with Elizabethan brickwork and medieval stone foundations (Harrington was mentioned in the Domesday book). The majority of the rooms are panelled and contain paintings, 17th- and 18th-century china and furniture. Tennyson's Maud, of 'come into the garden Maud' fame, lived at Harrington Hall with her guardian. In today's gardens there are many flowering shrubs, roses, lavender, yew hedges and peacocks. (C10)

Hartsholme Country Park, Lincoln Leave Lincoln towards Skellingthorpe to discover a miniature lakeland with grassland and woodland park. There is an on-site Information Centre and a nature trail (guided tours by arrangement). (C6)

of St Mary's has scythe blades above the door said to have been used in the battle. (C9)

Kirkstead Church (St Leonard's) The 13th-century church for lay worshippers stood 'outside the gates' of a Cistercian Abbey. Apart from the church and the transept there are no remains of the original abbey. (D9)

Laxton The village's ancient open field system is not only visible after 1,000 years but still practised by a group of tenants under the eye of the annual Court Leet. (D4)

Longdale Rural Crafts Centre This is the headquarters of the Nottinghamshire Craftsmen's Guild. Hundreds of craftsmen – wood carvers, furniture makers, antique restorers, saddle makers, book binders, toy makers, potters and many others – can be seen at work throughout the year in a recreated old village street. Displays of finished goods, and collection of old tools and equipment in the village craft museum. Situated in the heart of Sherwood Forest at Longdale Lane, Ravenshead, 8 miles (13 km) north of Nottingham off A60. (E3)

Louth Architecturally interesting on account of its blend of 17th-, 18th- and 19th-century buildings and maze of narrow, winding streets, Louth is primarily a Georgian market town situated on the eastern fringe of the Wolds. Its trading prosperity can be traced back to the Danes in the 8th century (*Ludes* was recorded in the Domesday Book). St James's Church (late Gothic Perpendicular) was completed in the mid 15th century and is crowned by the tallest, most beautiful spire in England. Tennyson was educated at the grammar school and was first published in 1827 by a local bookseller. Just over a mile (1.6 km) to the east of the town are the earthwork remains of *Louth Park Cistercian Abbey*, once closely linked to **Fountains** (see Gazetteer 20). (B10)

Mablethorpe Animal and Bird Gardens North of this seaside town lie 2 acres (0.8 hectare) of gardens with mammals and birds (monkeys, seals, llamas, owls, and others). Other features include a walk-in aviary and a children's play area. (B12)

The Lincolnshire Wolds near Louth

Holme Pierrepont Hall The Hall is a brick, crenellated, early Tudor manor and has a historic late 19th-century courtyard garden with a box parterre. The house, which contains 17th-century oak furniture, original fireplaces, Charles II staircase, fine timber framing, is in daily use. Access on minor road off A52. (F3)

Horncastle The Romans built a walled town, Banovallum, at Horncastle on a site of an earlier settlement; part of its original walls can still be seen. Important horse fairs took place in this market town, which is also famous as the place where Cromwell spent the night following the bloody battle at nearby Winceby in 1643. The restored medieval church

Marston Hall A 16th-century manor house with interesting pictures and furniture. It has been owned by the Thorolds since the 14th century. It has an attractive and very ancient garden with notable trees and a Gothic gazebo. Located at Marston on minor road off A1 north of Grantham. (F6)

Melton Carnegie Museum A small museum at Thorpe End, on the Grantham Road (A607), depicting past and present local life and industry including the making of pork pies and Stilton cheese. (H5)

Melton Mowbray Church (St Mary's) Pevsner described it as 'the stateliest and

most impressive of all churches in Leicestershire', no doubt on account of its clerestory of 48 windows, 100 ft (30 m) tower, double aisled transepts and rare medieval glass. (H5)

The Midland Railway Centre The Centre at Butterley Station near Ripley is still developing as a working railway museum illustrating the story of the Midland and LMS Railways. Locomotives, rolling stock and other displays can be seen. 3½ mile (5.6 km) working steam railway. (E1)

National Mining Museum, Haughton All aspects of coal mining are exhibited including machinery, tools, locomotives, lamps and pumping engines, as well as photographs depicting everyday life in the pits. ♿ (C4)

National Water Sports Centre, Holme Pierrepont The Water Sports Centre was created in 1973; facilities open to the public when not in use for events include the angling lagoon, rowing pool, water skiing and the gym. Details of sailing, power-boating, canoeing, waterskiing and courses are obtainable from the Sports Council. Access on minor road off A52. ♿ (F3)

Newark Air Museum, Winthorpe Various aircraft on show (Swift, Vampire, Meteor, Super Sabre, Mystere, Vulcan, Shackleton and others) plus related items. Just off A46 to Lincoln. ♿ (E5)

Newstead Abbey Dissolved by Henry VIII in 1539 Newstead became the ancestral home of the Byrons until Lord Byron, the poet, sold it in 1817 to repay his debts. The house contains several of his manuscripts, books, letters and furniture. The grounds include probably the first example of a Japanese garden in the country, and a walled rose garden with 4,000 blooms. (E3)

North Leverton Windmill A four-sailed tower mill built in 1813 and used to grind grain regularly for local farmers ever since. (B5)

Papplewick Pumping Station Two beam engines built by James Watt & Co in 1884 to provide Nottingham with 1½ million gallons of water a day have been preserved in highly ornate Victorian engine house. Working forge and miniature passenger-carrying railway. (E3)

Ruddington *The Framework Knitters' Museum* is housed in early 19th-century framework knitters' buildings in Chapel Street and includes a restored workshop with hand frames, machinery, samples and photographs. *The Hermitage* (in Wilford Road) is devoted to a miscellany of period costumes, dolls, toys, farm tools, local archaeological finds and other displays. (G3)

Shardlow Canal Exhibition The 'Canal Story' is an exhibition at the Clock Warehouse, London Road, devoted to the history of canals. Housed in a listed and restored 18th-century canal building close to the junction of the Trent and Mersey canal with the river Trent. (G2)

Sherwood Forest Country Park Although the existence of Robin Hood, or rather his significance as a noble outlaw fighting the Norman's forest laws has been widely questioned, the forest itself has long established 'roots'. Today there are a few beautiful glades (though rarely oak-filled) to wander in as well as northern parklands known as the 'Dukeries', named after the local estates that owned large sections of the forest. The Country Park is part of the forest, and contains the Major Oak, many centuries old. The Visitor Centre at Edwinstowe has a permanent Robin Hood exhibition, audio-visual presentations and guided walks, and the 450 acres (180 hectares) of forest surrounding it contain some magnificent oak trees. Nearby the *Rufford Craft Centre and Country Park* has

displays of quality goods, and peaceful lakeside and woodland walks. Also **Creswell Crags**, a narrow limestone gorge with caves once occupied (about 70,000 years ago) by early man and animals now extinct. ♿ (C3)

Skegness Natureland Marine Zoo Located on North Parade (the Promenade) this zoo has an off-beat collection of birds, fishes and animals including sea lions, performing seals, penguins, flamingoes, giant African snails, scorpions, terrapins. ♿ (D12)

Sleaford A delightful market town (Monday is still a busy day) with a 12th-century church of St Denys, noted for its window tracery, and former Bass Maltings, an enormous 4-storey square tower flanked by 8 pavilions. (F8)

Somersby Church (St Margaret's) Best known for its associations with Alfred, Lord Tennyson, who was born in the Old Rectory opposite (his father was Rector of St Margaret's). The church contains several mementoes of the poet and a memorial service to Tennyson is held here or at nearby Bag Enderby in alternate years on the first Sunday in August. (C10)

Southwell Minster The town's Norman minster became a cathedral in 1884. It dates back to the 12th century and has a beautiful chapter house with a door carved with foliage and 13th-century stone carvings. In 1646 Charles I surrendered to the Scottish Commissioners in Southwell's King's Arms (now the Saracen's Head). (E4)

Spilsby A 'border' market town that straddles the upland Wolds scenery to the north and the flat Fenland scenery to the south. Sir John Franklin, discoverer of the North West Passage, was born here and is commemorated by a statue in the market square. (D11)

Stow Church (St Mary's) A Saxon church, one of the largest and oldest in England, and supposedly the mother church to Lincoln cathedral. It has early 11th-century crossing arches and 13th-century murals. (B6)

Stow Church

Sundown Pets Garden and Kiddies Theme Park Created specially for young children, with animated nursery rhymes and toy jungle, pantomime land, Noah's Ark, pets, and many other attractions. At Tresswell Road, Rampton. ♿ (B5)

Tattershall Castle (NT) A square, 100 ft (30 m), 5-storey fortified tower built in the mid 15th century on the site of a

Tattershall Castle

medieval castle by Ralph Cromwell, then Lord High Treasurer to Henry VI. Protected by a moat and 16 ft (5 m) walls, Tattershall Castle is the best example of a brick-built fortified dwelling in the country. There is also a museum containing local archaeological pottery and other finds, as well as a model of the castle as it was in 1693. ♿ Fine collegiate church and 17th-century almshouses nearby. (D9)

Thoresby Hall One of the larger Victorian dwellings in England, built by Salvin between 1864 and 1871. Among its most attractive features are the

library which has a carved fireplace depicting a scene from Robin Hood, the panelled Great Hall and the state apartments. Deer park and lake. Access from A614. (C4)

Woodhall Spa The spring of medicinal (iodine) waters was discovered by accident in the search for coal; a Pump Room and several hotels followed. Although its spa days have passed, the tree-lined town with its pinewoods still retains its former spa gentility. (D9)

Wollaton Hall On the western outskirts of Nottingham, this Elizabethan Hall, built by Sir Francis Willoughby in the 1580s, houses the city's Natural History Museum with a wide variety of exhibits in its galleries. There is a nature trail in the grounds around the lake and fallow and red deer to be spotted. Access from A52. (F3)

Woolsthorpe Manor, Colsterworth (NT) A 17th-century farmhouse, where Sir Isaac Newton was born and returned during the plague years (1665-6) 'in the prime of my age for invention'. 'The' apple is supposed to have dropped in the garden. ♿ (H6)

The Viking Way A long-distance footpath that stretches 150 miles (240 km) from Barton-upon-Humber (Map 18 E8) to Oakham in Leicestershire (Map 11 A12) runs along the western escarpment of the Lincolnshire Wolds and the low-lying lands in the valley of the river Witham, then across heathlands and the limestone edge south of Lincoln. The route has been waymarked with metal plaques featuring the Viking Helmet symbol (especially appropriate since this part of the country came under Norse rule, as the many '-by' ending place names testify). From north to south the route passes through Barnetby le Wold (Map 18 F8), Caistor (Map 18 G9), Normanby le Wold (A8), Tealby (A8), Donnington on Bain (B9), Belchford (C10), Horncastle (C9), Southrey (D8), Waddington (D7), Carlton Scroop (F6), Allington (F6), Woolsthorpe (G6). A single leaflet describing the Humberside section is obtainable (send SAE) from the Director of Technical Services of Humberside County Council, Eastgate, Beverley, North Humberside. Six leaflets on the Lincolnshire section are available from the Head of Secretarial and Legal Services, County Offices, Lincoln. The Woolsthorpe to Oakham section is described in a pamphlet produced by the Planning Department of Leicestershire County Council, County Hall, Glenfield Leicester.

Map 17

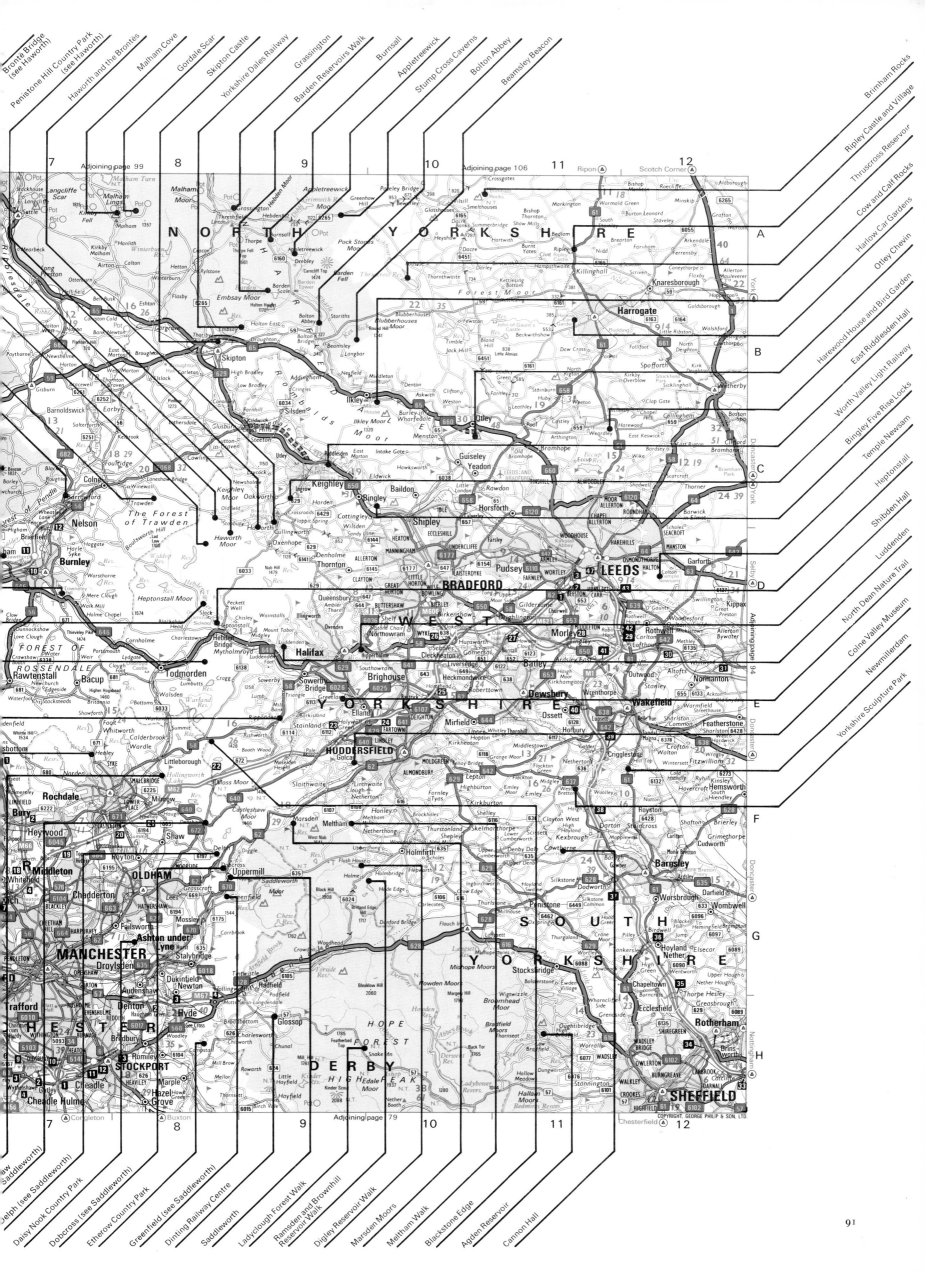

North-West England

Agden Reservoir Cart track along north side of reservoir, westwards from Smallfield Farm, 1 mile (1.6 km) west of Bradfield. Good bird life on easy walk with firm going. Continue to metalled road returning same way (2 miles, 3.2 km). (H11)

Appletreewick Attractive village of limestone houses and cottages, some with interesting associations. Lead-mining centre in Middle Ages, also monastic connections. (A9)

Bailrigg Nature Trail (Lancaster University) A6 south of Lancaster. Trail (often muddy) starts at 'Visitor Parking North', waymarked yellow. Formerly garden and farmland, now campus, landscaped with trees. 1 mile (1.6 km); may be shortened by cutting between buildings. (A4)

Barden Reservoirs Walk Park on level site on upper Barden–Embsay road. Walk northwards down the hill to first acute bend and use former railway track to embankment of upper reservoir and cross. Return by obvious track on north side. 6 miles (9.6 km), easy. (A/B9)

Beacon Fell Country Park 8 miles (13 km) north of Preston. Signposted at Broughton and Brock Bridge (A6) and Longridge (B5269). An extensive area of moorland and conifer forest with walks, picnic areas and spectacular views. (C4)

Beamsley Beacon Sandstone outcrops on moorland, easy ½ mile (.8 km) walk from road, giving splendid views of lower Wharfedale. Unusual 17th-century almshouses in nearby Beamsley village. (B9)

Bingley Five Rise Locks Remarkable staircase of interconnected locks raising Leeds Liverpool Canal by 60 ft (18 m). Built 1774, the earliest staircase in England with more than two chambers. Impressive picture with mills behind, hills beyond. (C10)

Blackstone Edge Claimed as finest paved Roman road in Britain, probably used later as packhorse causeway and turnpike. Pennine Way crosses it near Aiggin Stone, an ancient guidestone ½ mile (.8 km) south of The White Horse pub on A58 (car park, viewpoint). (E8)

Bolton Abbey Picturesque riverside ruins of 12th-century Augustinian Priory, part still used as parish church. Fine woodland and riverside walks nearby, including nature trail in Strid Woods, where Wharfe surges through narrow rocky chasm. (B9)

Bolton by Bowland Rows of white-washed cottages run down from green by 13th-century church. By larger, tree-screened green is old Court House and church school. (B6)

Brimham Rocks (NT) Giant rock towers eroded into fantastic shapes, scattered over a large area of bracken-covered moor and woodland, with fine views especially up Nidderdale. (A10)

Burnsall Stone cottages along a winding main street between river and church, with 17th-century grammar school (now primary school). Broad riverside green by 5-arched stone bridge spanning Wharfe. (A9)

Cannon Hall, Cawthorne 18th-century house by Carr of York containing furniture and glassware. William Harvey Bequest of Dutch and Flemish paintings on permanent display. Also Regimental Museum of 13th/18th Royal Hussars (QMO). Grounds are country park with lake and fishing. (F11)

Chipping Winding lanes converge on this ancient market centre. Traditional stone cottages with porches, mullioned windows; cobbled courtyards, 17th-century grammar school, almshouses and old corn mill (now a restaurant). (C5)

Cockersand Abbey 13th-century octagonal chapter house survives of a Premonstratensian abbey. Around is tumbled masonry, and wall fragments are incorporated into domestic and farm buildings. (B3)

Colne Valley Museum, Cliffe Ash, Golcar Former weavers' cottages house local history museum, with weaving and clog-making workshops. Almost opposite parish church and well-signposted at many points in Golcar. (F9)

Cow and Calf Rocks, Ilkley Famous gritstone outcrops on edge of Ilkley Moor. Scrambling needed to gain crests. Panoramic views. Fine moorland walk 1 mile (1.6 km) west to White Wells. (C10)

Crook O'Lune Picnic Site, Halton Off A683 ½ mile (.8 km) west Caton, over bridge. A picnic area in a favourite spot beside River Lune. (A4)

Cuerden Valley Country Park 700 acres (280 hectares) of farmland, pasture and woodland around Cuerden Hall. Bridleways and waymarked footpaths. Free access area along east bank of stream and by lake. Car parks off A49, B5256, and off A6 near Whittle-le-Woods. (E4)

Daisy Nook Country Park, Newmarket Rd, Ashton under Lyne (NT) A canal and lake in wood and parkland offer fishing, boating, walks and bridleways. (G8)

Digley Reservoir Walk 3 miles (4.8 km) easy walking, but narrow stiles. Park in Holme village; walk through iron gate by children's playground, through fields to Digley Reservoir; left to embankment between Digley and Bilberry Reservoir, cross. Right along north side Digley, circuit reservoir, return by Green lane and tarmac road. (F9)

Dinting Railway Centre, Dinting Lane, Glossop On A57, 10 acre (4 hectare) site. Many steam engines on display, in steam on Sundays and Bank Holidays. 🅰 (H9)

Downham Hillside village of well-kept stone houses, grouped around greens. Stream at bottom; church, Downham Hall and Assheton Arms at top. **Pendle Hill** dominates southward view. (C6)

East Riddlesden Hall (NT) South side A650 east Keighley. Mid 17th-century stone house with contemporary oak panelling, plaster friezes and ceilings, furniture and portraits. Magnificent stone barn with outstanding timberwork in grounds. 🅰 (C9)

Etherow Country Park, Compstall Off A626. Wooded river valley with marshland and ponds and remains of former cotton industry. A 1¾ mile (3 km) nature trail starts at Montagu Street, Compstall. (H8)

Forest of Bowland Extensive moorlands and steep-sided gritstone fells reaching 1,800 ft (550 m), designated an Area of Outstanding Natural Beauty. Mainly devoted to rough grazing, grouse moor and water catchment, with good dairy land in lower valleys. Good riverside walks by Hodder, Ribble and Lune, with attractive woodlands. Crossed by only one east-west road through Trough of Bowland between Dunsop Bridge (B5) and Lee (B4), and one north-south road, High Bentham (Map 19 H9) to Slaidburn (B6).

Formby Point Nature Trail West of Formby village, off A565. 1½ mile (2.4 km) trail through pine woods to beach where dunes have buried former village.

Waders, gulls, red squirrels and natterjack toads may be seen. Trail run by Lancashire Naturalists' Trust. (F2)

Gawthorpe Hall, Burnley Road, Padiham (NT) Unusually compact Jacobean house, 1605, round medieval fortified tower. Additions and alterations c. 1850 by Barry. Rich panelling, stucco ceilings, rare furniture. Kay–Shuttleworth collection of textiles displayed in former Victorian nurseries. 🅰 (D7)

Gawthorpe Hall

Glasson Dock and Lune Estuary Trail Off A588 at Stork Hotel, Conder Green. From picnic area on site of former station, trail follows disused railway to Glasson Dock, returns by Lancaster Canal. 2 miles (3.2 km) easy walking, interesting flora and birds. Railway walk extends further 3 miles (4.8 km) north with excellent views over Lune estuary. (B3)

Gordale Scar 400 ft (122 m) limestone cliffs enclose rocky falls of Gordale Beck at head of green valley. 1¼ miles (2 km) east of Malham (narrow road, no exit; best to walk, preferably by Janet's Foss). (A8)

Grassington Capital of upper Wharfedale. Attractive stone houses around cobbled square and along steep main street. Centre of 18th and 19th-century lead mining – remains on Grassington Moor 2 miles (3.2 km) north. Nearby Grass Wood is a nature reserve. (A8)

Great Harwood Nature Trail From Allsprings Lodge, Great Harwood, off A6064 in centre. Strong shoes advised for 3 mile (4.8 km) walk through woodland, along river gorge with views of **Pendle Hill**. Leaflet at local newsagents. (D6)

Haigh Hall Country Park, Haigh, near Wigan 260 acres (105 hectares) of wood and heathland offering walks, 4 mile (6.4 km) nature trail from main entrance, arboretum and children's playground. Popular golf course, model village and railway, and miniature zoo. 🅰 (F5)

Hall-i'-the-Wood, Crompton Way, Bolton 16th/17th-century half-timbered house, formerly home of Samuel Crompton, inventor of spinning-mule. Furnished as Jacobean manor. (F6)

Hardcastle Crags (NT) Beautiful oak-woods in steep-sided valley, with clear stream from adjoining moors; rocky outcrops; 19th-century industrial remains at Gibson Mill. Slurring Rocks Nature Trail. (D8)

Harewood House and Bird Garden 18th-century house by Carr and Robert Adam containing fine furniture, paintings and porcelain. 'Capability' Brown landscaped grounds contain bird gardens with undercover tropical extension, adventure playground, lakeside walks. 🅰 (C11)

Harlow Car Gardens, Otley Road, Harrogate 60 acres (24 hectares) of ornamental gardens and shrub woodland designed to show appropriate garden plants for the north of England. 🅰 (B11)

Haworth and the Brontës Haworth Parsonage, home of Brontë sisters and their father and brother, now a literary museum, furnished as when they lived there, and displaying many original items associated with the most remarkable family in English literature. Nearby is parish church where all family, except Anne, are buried (C8). Surrounding moors evoke the real spirit of the great Brontë novels, *Wuthering Heights* and *Jane Eyre*. **Top Withins** (D8), which may have inspired the setting of the former, is a 6-mile (10 km) return walk on a well-defined track from the car park on **Penistone Hill** (Country Park) (D9), **Brontë Bridge and Brontë Falls** (D8) about half this on same track (waterfalls disappointing but setting attractive). **Ponden Mill** (C8) (footpath access from Colne road west of Haworth) used to be an old textile factory, but has now been completely renovated throughout. It is known for the wide range of quality linens that it sells, although various other

Haworth Parsonage

Malham village from Malham Cove

craft products are also on sale. Nearby, Ponden Hall (not open to the public) is said to be the original of Thrushcross Grange.

Healey Dell Nature Trail In a wooded, typical South Pennine valley, the trail links a series of small waterfalls, with 100 ft (30 m) high old railway viaduct carrying a footpath across the nature reserve. (E7)

Helmshore Textile Museum, Holcombe Road, Helmshore Two mill museums showing many aspects of the history of Lancashire's textile industry. Working water-wheel and fulling stocks, and major collection of early textile machines, including original from Arkwright's mill at Cromford. Ancillary industries also represented and daily demonstrations of spinning machinery. (E6)

Heptonstall Hilltop village with 18th/19th-century weavers' cottages, ruined medieval church, proud Victorian successor, oldest continually used Methodist Chapel, upland walks along ancient causeways, fine views over adjacent valleys. (D8)

Hoghton Tower 16th-century fortified house, dramatically situated on hilltop. Banqueting Hall was scene of knighting of Loin of Beef by James 1 (1617). Collection of dolls and dolls' houses. Walled and rose gardens. ♿ (E5)

Hollingworth Lake Country Park On B6225. This 117 acre (47 hectare) lake in moorland setting provides motor boating, rowing, sailing and fishing as well as lakeside walks and play areas for children. ♿ (F8)

Hurst Green Attractive village near entrance to Stonyhurst College. 18th-century Shireburn Almshouses re-erected on present site 1948. 3 old inns, neat cottages, stately trees. (C5)

Jumbles Reservoir Country Park, Bradshaw Off A676. Walks in woods and meadowland around reservoir with facilities for coarse fishing. (E6)

Knowsley Safari Park, Prescot Entrance off A58. A 5 mile (8 km) drive through reserves containing lions, tigers, elephants, monkeys and other wild animals and birds. Picnic area and pets corner. ♿ (H3)

Ladyclough Forest Walk From Birchinclough layby on A57 ¼ mile (400 m) north of Snake Inn, a riverside way-marked walk through pine trees up Snake Pass. Strong footwear. 1½ miles (2.4 km) return. (H9/10)

Luddenden Cobbled streets, many-storeyed gritstone houses, church, pub, school cluster compactly at entrance to steep-sided valley, Luddenden Dean, with Victorian mills and older farms on green hillsides. Many field paths. (E9)

Lytham St Anne's Nature Reserve, adjacent to Pontins Camp, Clifton Drive North (A584). Sand dunes and associated flora and fauna. (D2)

Malham Cove Natural amphitheatre of white limestone, 300 ft (90 m) high, 300 yards (270 m) wide. Remarkable pavement on top; River Aire emerges at bottom. Car park and Information Centre in Malham village. (A8)

Marsden Moors Take 'Wessenden' road; park near dam. Easy walk by reservoirs to Wessenden. Fine moorland setting. 4 miles (6.4 km). (F9)

Martin Mere, Burscough Off A59 at Burscough Bridge. Wildfowl Trust provide marshland, wild refuge and landscaped gardens to attract over 100 species of geese, ducks, swans; also flamingos. Hides help visitors to view them and exhibitions to explain them. ♿ (F3)

Meltham Walk Park near centre. Walk along Holmfirth Road, left by stream. Up Knowl Lane, path on left behind works. Through woods, keeping right, then woodland edge to Hassocks Lane, left to bottom of wood, to Wood Bottom Farm and Knowl Lane. Strong shoes, 4 miles (6.4 km). (F9)

Newmillerdam On A61. Reservoir in woodlands offers attractive lakeside walks or picnics. Furniture making and restorations can be seen in nearby craft centre. (F12)

North Dean Nature Trail, West Vale, Greetland From Clay House Park 3 trails of 1, 1½ and 2 miles (1.6, 2.4, 3.2 km) lead through mixed woodlands with varied bird and animal life and interesting geological features. Strong footwear. (E9)

Otley Chevin 900 ft (274 m) wooded hill south of Otley, with magnificent views. Ride of trees planted 1968 commemorates 250th anniversary of birth of Chippendale, great cabinet-maker, in Otley. (C10)

Pendle Heritage Centre, Park Hill, Barrowford Housed in handsome 17th-century farmhouse it shows local social and industrial history. ♿ (C7)

Pendle Hill 1,830 ft (560 m) high outlier of the Pennines, associated with 17th-century Pendle witches. Many hillside walks, especially from Sabden and Barley, where a picnic area has been provided. (C7)

Penistone Hill Country Park 175 acres (70 hectares) of moorland, heath and common land, with stone quarries, 1 mile (1.6 km) west of Haworth. Walks, views, nature trail. (See also **Haworth and the Brontës**.) (D9)

Ramsden and Brownhill Reservoir Walk 2 miles (3.2 km), mainly easy but 2 short climbs. Park in Holme village, walk south opposite Fleece Hotel, signposted path. South-east into Netherley Clough (stream), through woods to Ramsden reservoir; cross dam between it and Brownhill reservoir, contour hillside back to Holme. (G10)

Ribchester Museum and Fort Museum on site of Roman fort includes exposed remains and models in attractive riverside setting. ♿ (D5)

Ripley Castle and Village Planned village with 18th- and 19th-century houses, school, hall, cobbled square, market cross, stocks. Tudor castle with later additions; serpentine lake, beech walk in beautiful grounds by River Nidd. (A11)

Ripponden Attractive conservation area around packhorse bridge, church and old part of village. Local history trail starts at Chapel Fields, near Pennine Farm Museum. (E9)

Rivington Pike High above Rivington reservoir, and reached by a walk and climb, 3 miles (4.8 km) return from car park by Great House Barn, south of Rivington village. Parkland, woods, waterfalls, gardens, grottoes, follies, enliven way to superb viewpoint. (F5)

Roddlesworth Nature Trail, Tockholes Commencing at Royal Arms Hotel, 2½ miles (4 km) walk through Roddlesworth valley. Guide available at Hotel. (E5)

Rufford Old Hall (NT) Off A59. Timbered hall of Tudor house shows richly-detailed exuberance; Carolean wing added 1662. There is magnificent 17th- and 18th-century furniture of the Hesketh family. Houses Ashcroft Museum of Local Life, reflecting life and work in the area since Rufford was first built. ♿ (F3)

Saddleworth and District Cloth manufacture was a common occupation in the central Pennines before the Industrial Revolution, often in association with farming. During the 18th century an increasing number of households concentrated on cloth-making, particularly with weaving the large amounts of yarn made available by mechanised spinning and carding. From 1780 onwards cottages were being built specially for domestic weaving, identified by their upper rooms having a long row of windows separated by stone mullions, illuminating workrooms housing two or three looms.

The area around Saddleworth shows many fine examples of weavers' cottages of the 17th and 18th centuries, and a number of early woollen scribbling or carding mills in small tributary valleys, as well as larger mills of the 19th century. Oldest houses tend to be on hillsides above the valley, by ancient tracks and roads.

Saddleworth Historical Society has produced six Local Interest Trails guiding walkers around the district, each concentrating on a specific area – villages like **Delph, Dobcross** and **Denshaw** (all F8), **Greenfield** and **Saddleworth** (**Uppermill**) (both G8). Uppermill and Greenfield Trails are particularly rewarding, with mixture of road walking and field paths. 2 to 4 hours necessary for each. Good local history museum in Uppermill.

Sawley Abbey (EH) Off A59. Remains of Cistercian abbey founded in 1148, and a more modest church than originally intended due to shortage of funds. ♿ (B6)

Shibden Hall, Halifax On A58. West Yorkshire Folk Museum housed in 15th-century half-timbered hall with 17th and 18th-century furnishings. Agricultural implements, carriages and 18th and 19th-century workshops in adjoining buildings. (E9)

Skipton Castle Some remains of original Norman castle survive, including a gateway. Main entrance by massive 14th-century gatehouse to Lady Anne Clifford's rebuilding of mid 17th century. Some Tudor masonry and windows. (B8)

Slaidburn 17th- and 18th-century houses, cobbled pavements, Grammar School (1717), now primary school, fine church, unusual inn 'Hark to Bounty', and neat stone bridge spanning River Hodder. (B6)

Spring Wood Nature Trail, Whalley At junction of road from Whalley with A671 to east. A ¾-mile (1.2-km) walk through mixed woodlands from a picnic area. (C6)

Stoodley Pike Prominent 120 ft (36 m) monument, 1814, overlooking Calder Valley, superb viewpoint on Pennine Way track. Fairly easy climb (strong footwear) from Hebden Bridge or Mankinholes. (E8)

Stump Cross Caverns On B6265. Electric light enhances the natural beauty of this series of caves. (A9)

Temple Newsam Off A63, 5 miles (8 km) south Leeds. Standing in 900 acres (364 hectares) of parkland landscaped by 'Capability' Brown, this superb Tudor and Jacobean mansion has suite of early Georgian rooms and 16th and 17th-century features. 30 public rooms contain collections of pictures, silver, ceramics and furniture. (D12)

Thruscross Reservoir Ideal spot for fishing and bird watching or just watching the yachts of Leeds Sailing Club. (A10)

Towneley Hall Art Gallery and Museums, Todmorden Road, Burnley 14th-century house with 17th- and 18th-century additions, in extensive parkland. Period furnishings, natural history displays, museum of local crafts and industries. (D7)

Turton Tower, Chapeltown Road, Turton 15th-century pele tower with Tudor additions, partly stone, partly timber-framed, high on edge of Turton Moor. Contains the Ashworth Museum. (F6)

Witton Park, Preston Old Road, Blackburn Nature trails and bridleways over heath and through woodland with a climb to Billinge Hill (800 ft, 244 m) for panoramic views. (D5)

Worth Valley Light Railway A 5 mile (8 km) steam railway operating throughout the year between Keighley and Oxenhope where collection of veteran locomotives is on view. At Haworth other rolling stock may be seen, some awaiting restoration. 'The Railway Children' was filmed at Oakworth station. (C/D9)

Wycoller Country Park 363 acres (147 hectares) of heath, moorland, grassland, with field and valley walks, bridleways. Car park ½ mile (.8 km) from Wycoller village. Packhorse and clapper bridges, 17th-century cottages, ruins of Wycoller Hall ('Ferndean Manor' of *Jane Eyre*). ♿ (C8)

Yorkshire Dales Railway, Embsay Off A65, 1 mile (1.6 km) north Skipton. In steam each Sunday and during holidays for short rides as well as shop, museum and buffet. (B8)

Yorkshire Sculpture Park, Bretton Hall Unique setting for contemporary sculpture in formal or intimate parts of parkland. ♿ (F11)

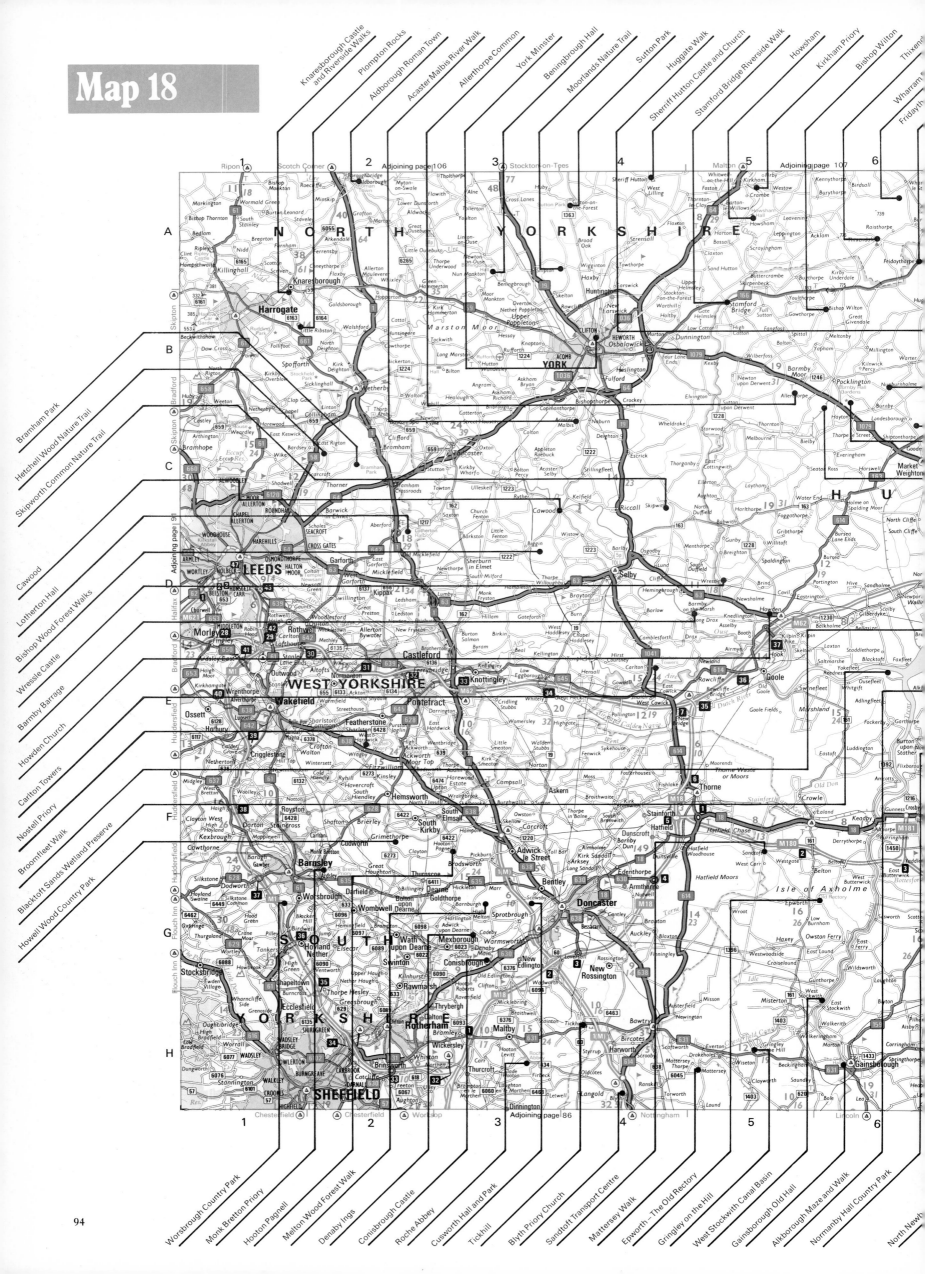

Map 18

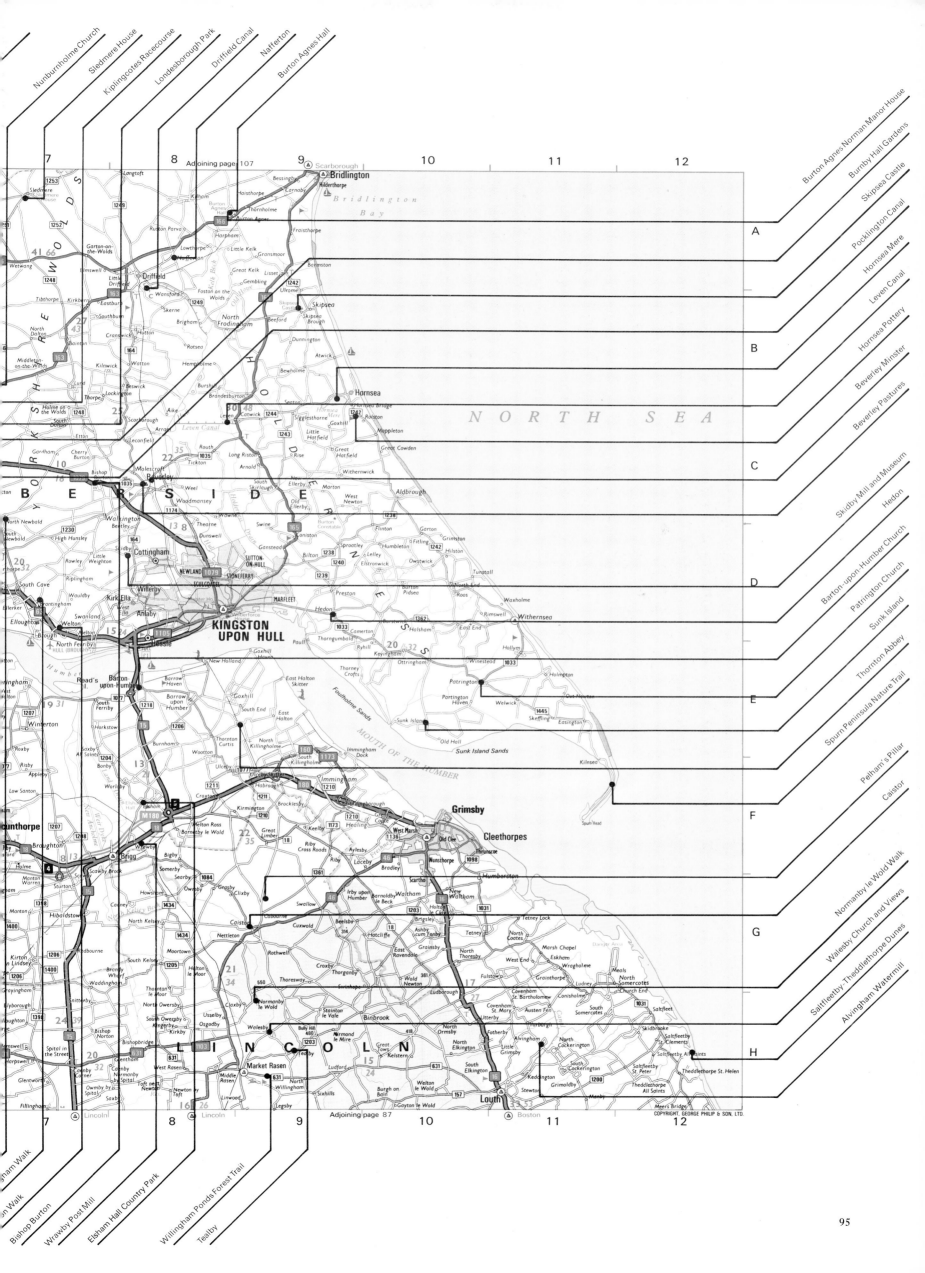

Nunburnholme Church
Sledmere House
Kiplingcotes Racecourse
Londesborough Park
Driffield Canal
Nafferton
Burton Agnes Hall

Burton Agnes Norman Manor House
Burnby Hall Gardens
Skipsea Castle
Pocklington Canal
Hornsea Mere
Leven Canal
Hornsea Pottery
Beverley Minster
Beverley Pastures
Skidby Mill and Museum
Hedon
Barton-upon-Humber Church
Patrington Church
Sunk Island
Thornton Abbey
Spurn Peninsula Nature Trail
Pelham's Pillar
Caistor
Normanby le Wold Walk
Walesby Church and Views
Saltfleetby-Theddlethorpe Dunes
Alvingham Watermill

NORTH SEA

Bridlington Bay

Scarborough
Bridlington
Hilderthorpe

KINGSTON UPON HULL

Grimsby
Cleethorpes

Louth

MOUTH OF THE HUMBER

Bishop Burton Walk
Wrawby Post Mill
Elsham Hall Country Park
Willingham Ponds Forest Trail
Tealby

North-East England

Acaster Malbis River Walk Leaving cars at slipway of former ferry, walk downstream past weir towards Acaster Selby and retrace steps. Some barges, but most activity is from pleasure craft. 2 miles (3.2 km) easy walk (return). (C4)

Aldborough Roman Town (EH) Part of south-west angle of Roman town wall, and two mosaic pavements within the town. Museum of objects found during excavations of this capital of the Brigantes, largest tribe in Roman Britain. Well signposted. ♿ (A2)

Alkborough Maze and Walk South of the church at Julian Bower a maze is cut into the ground; from adjacent ramparts of Countess Close commences a delightful walk through beechwoods overlooking River Trent. (E6)

Allerthorpe Common Distant views of Yorkshire Wolds from secluded picnic place among trees. Forestry Commission plantations. Walks. (B5)

Alvingham Watermill An 18th-century water cornmill now restored as a working museum, its present machinery installed around 1780. The mill has a rare surviving breast wheel still operating. (H11)

Barmby Barrage Tidal barrage where Derwent joins Ouse built to exclude saline water from entering Derwent. Waymarked walks by river. (D5)

Barton-upon-Humber Church (St Peter's) Two churches really – a 10th-century Anglo-Saxon tower-nave, with chancel replaced by 13th-century nave and chancel of later building. (E8)

Beningbrough Hall (NT) Built about 1716 and standing in wooded parkland, it contains superb woodwork, carved friezes, elaborate panelling and a magnificent staircase hall. 100 pictures from the National Portrait Gallery are tastefully displayed, and represent famous personalities 1688–1760. Audio-visual displays describe aspects of the domestic life of the house. Good gardens. ♿ (A3)

Beverley Minster Splendidly isolated on edge of attractive Georgian town. Cathedral-like in white stone, building spans 250 years, from purity of Early English to slender grace of Perpendicular. Furnishings include magnificent misericords, 1520, exquisite Percy tomb, and simple Frid stool. (C8)

Beverley Pastures 2 square miles (500 hectares) of common land on 3 sides of town granted in perpetuity by the Lords of the Manor and ecclesiastical authorities at various times. (C8)

Bishop Burton Particularly attractive village below edge of Wolds. Large greens with mature trees; two ponds, and good groups of whitewashed houses. (C7)

Bishop Wilton Delightful village on western slopes of Wolds. Stream down middle separates greens with flanking cottages set well back. Victorian restored church contains Norman work and unusual tiled floor, 1902, illustrating birds. (B6)

Bishop Wood Forest Walks Picnic areas at Park Nook and Scalm Park in broadleaved and coniferous woodlands. Forest walks and rides link the two places. (D3)

Blacktoft Sands Wetland Preserve (RSPB) Access to car park 1 mile (1.6 km) beyond Ousefleet village. 'Dry' land and reedbed habitat of numerous breeding birds including marsh harrier, bearded tit. Geese on Whitton Sands. Also passage waders. (E6)

Blyth Priory Church Part of former Priory church survives as parish church on edge of green. Rugged early Norman nave, medieval wall paintings. Charming village round triangular green, a conservation area. Earlier market importance. (H4)

Bramham Park Built in Queen Anne style by ancestor of present owner, and standing in magnificently landscaped grounds, Bramham Park contains fine furniture, pictures and porcelain but remains a home. ♿ (C2)

Brantingham Walk Waymarked (red dot on yellow arrow), 3½ miles (5.6 km), starting and finishing in Brantingham village. First follow road up wooded Brantingham Dale and pass church. Climb north-west on to Ellerker Wold, go round Mount Airy Farm, and then circle clockwise to the head of Brantingham Dale. (D7)

Beverley Minster

Broomfleet Walk to Market Weighton canal by taking footpath heading south near pub. In 300 yards (270 m) bear south-west eventually joining embankment of Humber shortly before reaching Weighton Lock. Follow canal towpath northwards for 1 mile (1.6 km) before turning east on unmade road to Broomfleet. (D6)

Burnby Hall Gardens One of the finest collections of water lilies in Europe growing in two lakes. The museum contains variety of trophies and objects collected by Major Stewart on journeys abroad. ♿ (B6)

Burton Agnes Hall Built 1598–1610, filled with treasures including antique furniture, oriental china, French Impressionist and modern paintings – Renoir, Pissaro, Utrillo, Gauguin, Augustus John. Fine Elizabethan carved ceilings, good gardens. (A8)

Burton Agnes Norman Manor House (EH) Rare northern example of Norman stone hall above vaulted undercroft. Encased in brick in early 17th century. In grounds of **Burton Agnes Hall**. ♿ (A8)

Caistor Small town with some Roman walling. Golden sandstone church with Saxon-Norman tower. Easy walking on **Viking Way** (waymarked) north and south (see Gazetteer 16). (G9)

Carlton Towers One of the most elaborate Victorian-Gothic houses still lived in. Staterooms contain pictures from the collection of Prince Benedict, Cardinal York, the last of the Stuarts, and house has a priest's hiding place. (E4)

Cawood Winding streets, brick houses, sugar-beet barges on the Ouse. Early 15th-century castle, former seat of northern Primates (not open). (C4)

Conisbrough Castle (EH) Circular keep of 1185–90 survives almost to its full height. Curtain wall of slightly later date has unusual solid round towers. (G3)

Conisbrough Castle

Cusworth Hall and Park, near Sprotbrough Built in 1740s the Hall is a museum tracing the social history of South Yorkshire. History trail may be followed through attractive parkland. (G3)

Denaby Ings (YNT) Off A6023. Woodland walk along former railway embankment offers splendid views over this 35 acre (14 hectare) reserve which floods most winters, and attracts typical marshland birds and outstanding insect life. (G3)

Driffield Canal The head of the canal is a landscaped waterside open space with former warehouses converted to flats. The canal offers a pleasant walk with plenty of bird life. (A/B8)

Elsham Hall Country Park A recently converted wildlife sanctuary, the park has bird and butterfly gardens, plant centre, arboretum, nature trails and smithy. Giant carp can be hand fed. Children's adventure playground, craftshop and art gallery. Access off A15. (F8)

Epworth – The Old Rectory Built 1709, restored 1957. As the childhood home of John and Charles Wesley this is the oldest Methodist shrine. (G6)

Fridaythorpe Walk Wolds village 500 ft (150 m) high, with ponds and a simple church with Norman door. Pleasant walk in Wolds valley, due south from near Post Office, leads to **Huggate**; return same way. (A6)

Gainsborough Old Hall 15th- and 16th-century manor house retaining a fine medieval kitchen. Contains collections of bygones, furniture, paintings, china, dolls' and period dresses. Was the first meeting-place of early Dissenters – later the Pilgrim Fathers. (H6)

Gringley on the Hill Any hilltop Nottinghamshire village is unusual! Many fine houses, good Perpendicular church, and wide-ranging views from Beacon Hill to east, site of prehistoric fort. (H5)

Hedon Church of cathedral-like proportions dignifies and dominates one of England's oldest boroughs whose street pattern reflects its 12th-century layout. Good houses in Market Hill. (D9)

Hetchell Wood Nature Trail Off A58 on Thorner to East Rigton road. Limestone grassland, woodland and low gritstone cliffs above a beck combine to give a wide variety of flora and fauna over 29 acres (12 hectares). Picnic area near entrance. (C2)

Hooton Pagnell Farming-cum-estate village on limestone ridge. Stone cottages, red pantiles, churchyard with trees and daffodils. 14th-century gatehouse to Hall. Good views to west. (F3)

Hornsea Mere (RSPB) Off B1242. Largest freshwater lake in Yorkshire. Public footpath on south side with easy walking to see birds. Boating and fishing but no access to nature reserve. (B9)

Hornsea Pottery 28 acre (11 hectare) leisure complex: gardens, aviary, butterflies, playground, lake, pottery with tour of factory, model village. (C9)

Howden Church 13th-century collegiate church with proud crossing tower dominating small market town and surrounding countryside. Roofless octagonal chapter-house and ruined 14th-century choir add touches of melancholy. (D5)

Howell Wood Country Park Off B6273. 47 acres (19 hectares) of ornamental and exotic trees with nature trails. (F2)

Howsham From Howsham village – attractive stone cottages on one side of street – walk down to bridge and follow riverside path along west bank of Derwent to Kirkham. 2½ miles (4 km) return; easy, level, pleasant scenery. (A5)

Huggate Walk Follow lane north beyond church, for Northfield House. Continue to lane end, left past wood and earthworks, joining good bridleway from **Fridaythorpe**, returning to Huggate along original route. Easy. 3½ miles (5.6 km). (B6)

Kiplingcotes Racecourse On A163 opposite road to Warter a track leading south is course for Kiplingcotes Derby on third Thursday in March. Other times a gentle 3 mile (4.8 km) return walk. (B7)

Kirkham Priory (EH) Extensive remains of Augustinian priory in beautiful part of Derwent valley. Fine lavatorium and remarkably decorated 13th-century gatehouse. ⓑ (A5)

Knaresborough Castle and Riverside Walks River Nidd curving through limestone gorge provides fine setting for historic small town. Ruined 12th-century castle, 14th-century Court House Museum, attractive Georgian buildings, old shops, Mother Shipton's Well, Dropping Well, rock houses. Boating, swimming, riverside park, zoo. (A2)

Leven Canal Small waterway promoted by an individual to link her estates around Leven to River Hull and the Humber. Towpath to Leven Lock, 2½ miles (4 km) return. Pleasant quiet walk. Fishing. (C8)

Londesborough Park Walk starts from Towthorpe Picnic Site on A163, 2 miles (3.2 km) north Market Weighton. Follow drive and public path northwards through Londesborough Park into village. Return from south end of village through park, cross minor road, follow course of East Beck, passing site of deserted village of Towthorpe, to main road A163 ½ mile (.8 km) west of picnic site. 3 miles (4.8 km). (C6)

Lotherton Hall, near Aberford Off B1217. Edwardian house with fine collection of furniture, oriental ceramics, pictures and silver. Exhibitions of fashion, crafts. (D2)

Mattersey Walk Unsophisticated rural village by River Idle. 1 mile (1.6 km) easy walk to Mattersey Priory – fragments of walls of 12th-century Priory church and parts of later monastery in pleasant setting. (H5)

Melton Wood Forest Walk 3½ miles (5.6 km) west of Doncaster, minor road between Raven Hill and High Melton. A pleasant stroll through mainly broadleaved woodland from picnic site. (G3)

Monk Bretton Priory (EH) Considerable remains of church and claustral buildings of Cluniac priory. Western range partly converted into 17th-century house, gatehouse incorporated into farm buildings. ⓑ (F2)

Moorlands Nature Trail (YNT) Park on verge of A19 and follow path eastwards. Spring bulbs, rhododendrons, azaleas in woodland with two ponds. Avoid approaching hospital. (A3)

Nafferton Large village with interesting 18th- and 19th-century brick houses, a long straggling street, 19th-century maltings and a large pond. (A8)

Normanby Hall Country Park Entrance off Thealby Lane. A Regency mansion with contemporary furniture and decorations, in 350 acres (142 hectares) of wooded parkland including deer park, lido, golf course, riding school, countryside centre and craft pottery. (E6)

Normanby le Wold Walk Lincolnshire's highest village is the starting-point for a pleasant country walk along part of the **Viking Way** (see Gazetteer 16), waymarked to Walesby, from which a return can be made via Lloyd's Farm and the foot of the Wolds. 5 miles (8 km). (H9)

North Newbald Cottages attractively grouped round irregular green north of church, which is built of honey-coloured oolitic limestone. Four Norman doorways with good carving. Open Wold landscapes to east. (D7)

Nostell Priory (NT) Elegant mansion, 1733, by James Paine. Wing added 1766 by Robert Adam, who carried out much of interior decoration. Plasterwork by Joseph Rose, paintings by Zucchi and others, Chippendale furniture. (E2)

Nunburnholme Church Straggling village beside clear chalk stream, with small, white-washed, red-roofed cottages. Church has tiny Norman nave, window, door, and a fine Anglo-Saxon cross-shaft. Rev F.O. Morris wrote 6-volume *History of British Birds* here. (B6)

Patrington Church One of most beautiful English parish churches, cool and unified, *c*. 1300–50. Large, cruciform, with slender spire soaring above shapely coronet. Best view from south, across cricket field. Good 18th-century houses in pleasant village. (E10)

Pelham's Pillar 2 miles (3.2 km) north Caistor off B1361. In a clearing Pelham's Pillar of 1849 commemorates the planting of 12 million trees by first Lord Yarborough. A tall square tower tapering to a square lantern with ogee-capped roof. (G9)

Plompton Rocks 3 miles (4.8 km) from Harrogate along Wetherby road. Huge gritstone rocks near a large lake and pleasant woodlands. Car park, picnic area. (B1)

Pocklington Canal Follows a 9 mile (14 km) course through farmland, with easy walking, and now open for pleasure craft. (C5/6)

Roche Abbey (EH) Extensive monastic remains of 12th-century Cistercian abbey. Walls of church, transepts, and fine gatehouse, all in wild limestone in a beautiful wooded setting. ⓑ (H3)

Saltfleetby-Theddlethorpe Dunes Old and new dunes, freshwater and salt marsh and open shoreline; passage waders, short-eared owls and harriers. Interesting flora including orchids; and habitat of natterjack toad. Access from A1031 at Seaview (farm). (H12)

Sandtoft Transport Centre Off M180/A161 15 miles (24 km) east Doncaster. Working collection of trolley and motorbuses in rural setting. ⓑ (F5)

Sherriff Hutton Castle and Church Gaunt ruins of castle built by Nevilles 1380, and one of Richard III's favourites. Tomb and effigy of Prince Edward, Richard's only son, in church. (A4)

Skidby Mill and Museum A164, 3½ miles (5.6 km) south Beverley. Working windmill with museum relating to milling and corn growing. Built 1821, restored 1968. Four-sailed tower mill, black-tarred, with fantail, dominates adjoining farm buildings. ⓑ (D8)

Skipsea Castle (EH) Little masonry remains, but an impressively massive circular Norman motte separated from bailey by level area formerly covered by Skipsea Mere. Causeway across Mere linked bailey to motte. (B9)

Skipwith Common Nature Trail (YNT) Off A19 at Riccall, along Station Road 1 mile (1.6 km), park on airfield. 1½ mile (2.5 km) walk through heath, woodland, with shallow bogs and ponds. (C4)

Sledmere House Beautiful Georgian house of 1787, home of the Sykes family. Adam ceilings, fine furniture and paintings. Remarkable library 100 ft (30 m) long. Gardens, with park landscaped by 'Capability' Brown. Various interesting memorials in village. ⓑ (A7)

Spurn Peninsula Nature Trail (YNT) Off B1445, 1 mile (1.6 km) south Easington. 3 mile (4.8 km) walk along sand and shingle peninsula only 150 ft (45 m) wide in places. Excellent for bird-watching and seashore life. Limited parking and access. No dogs. (F11)

Stamford Bridge Riverside Walk Pleasant walks beside river Derwent with boating and fishing available. Six-storeyed brick watermill (now restaurant). Site of last Saxon battle on English soil, 1066, just outside to east. (B5)

Wharram Percy Church

Sunk Island Crown estate and parish created 1831, outcome of centuries of reclamation of siltlands from Humber's northern shore. Nowhere more than 15 ft (4.5 m) above sea-level. Now rich farmland. Farms with 'VR' monogram. (E10)

Sutton Park, Sutton-on-Forest An early Georgian house with fine furniture, paintings, porcelain and collection of fans. Beautiful gardens, ice house, woodland walks and nature trail. (A4)

Tealby Houses of limestone and brick, informally terraced on a hillside, are dwarfed by the huge ironstone tower of the church, with wide views to the west. South, in its deerpark, romantically-derelict ruins are all that survive of the Victorian mansion Bayons Manor. (H9)

Thixendale Centred on network of 16 dry valleys, with 6 minor roads converging on it, yet is still one of the Wolds most isolated villages. Occupies valley bottom by chalk stream. Wolds Way path. Splendid scenic variety from intimate to spacious. (A6)

Thornton Abbey, Ulceby (EH) Ruins of octagonal chapter house and south transept of church of Augustinian abbey founded 1139. Late 14th-century gatehouse survives almost complete; one of the most impressive in England. ⓑ (E9)

Tickhill Large village with proud Perpendicular tall-towered church in gleaming stone, remains of 14th-century friary (now two houses), timber-framed St Leonard's Hospital (1470), domed market cross (1777), and extensive millpond south of village, in pleasant surroundings below overgrown castle ruins. (H4)

Walesby Church and Views Square-towered ironstone church on hill above village, now 'Ramblers' Church'. Good furnishings. Pleasant approach through hall gates. Viking Way passes church, fine views from escarpment. (H9)

Welton Walk Attractive village with green, pond, good church and fine houses. Waymarked walk (blue dot on yellow arrow), 4 miles (6.4 km), leaves north end village along Chapel Hill. Then north-east along Welton Wold to Welton Wold Farm, westwards through plantations to Elloughton Dale, eventually back to Welton. (D7)

West Stockwith Canal Basin Trent village of Dutch appearance: winding narrow street, red-brick houses and 1722 church. Terminal basin of Chesterfield canal with keel-lock into Trent. Good surviving canal-side buildings. Boatyard and moorings. (H6)

Wharram Percy Off B1248, ½ mile (.8 km) south Wharram le Street then ½ mile walk. Only the ruined church survives above ground of the vanished village of Wharram Percy. 30 seasons of excavations have revealed traces of other buildings, making this one of the most famous of England's 2,000 medieval deserted villages. Diagram and plans help to re-create the past. (A6)

Willingham Ponds Forest Trail On A631, 2 miles (3.2 km) east Market Rasen. Red walk follows stream through mixed woodlands for 1 mile (1.6 km), easy. Yellow walk through woodlands to viewpoints on slightly steeper ground. 3 miles (4.8 km), easy. (H9)

Worsbrough Country Park and Mill Museum 130 acres (53 hectares) of wood and farmland around a reservoir with 17th-century watermill and 19th-century steam mill both restored to working order. ⓑ (G1)

Wrawby Post Mill Built late 18th century, ceased working 1940. Restored to full working order and incorporates a museum in the roundhouse. Stoneground wholemeal flour obtainable. (F8)

Wressle Castle Only important castle in former East Riding, built 1380 for Sir Thomas Percy. More manorial than military. Two massive towers with south range between, all of very good masonry. Exterior views only, from minor road. (D5)

York Minster The largest English medieval cathedral built 1220–1470 in Early English, Decorated and Perpendicular styles. Has England's greatest concentration of medieval stained glass, principally from the 13th and 14th centuries. The two most famous windows are the Five Sisters and the magnificent 15th-century east window, the largest in the world. The Minster's central tower is the largest lantern tower in Britain. (B4)

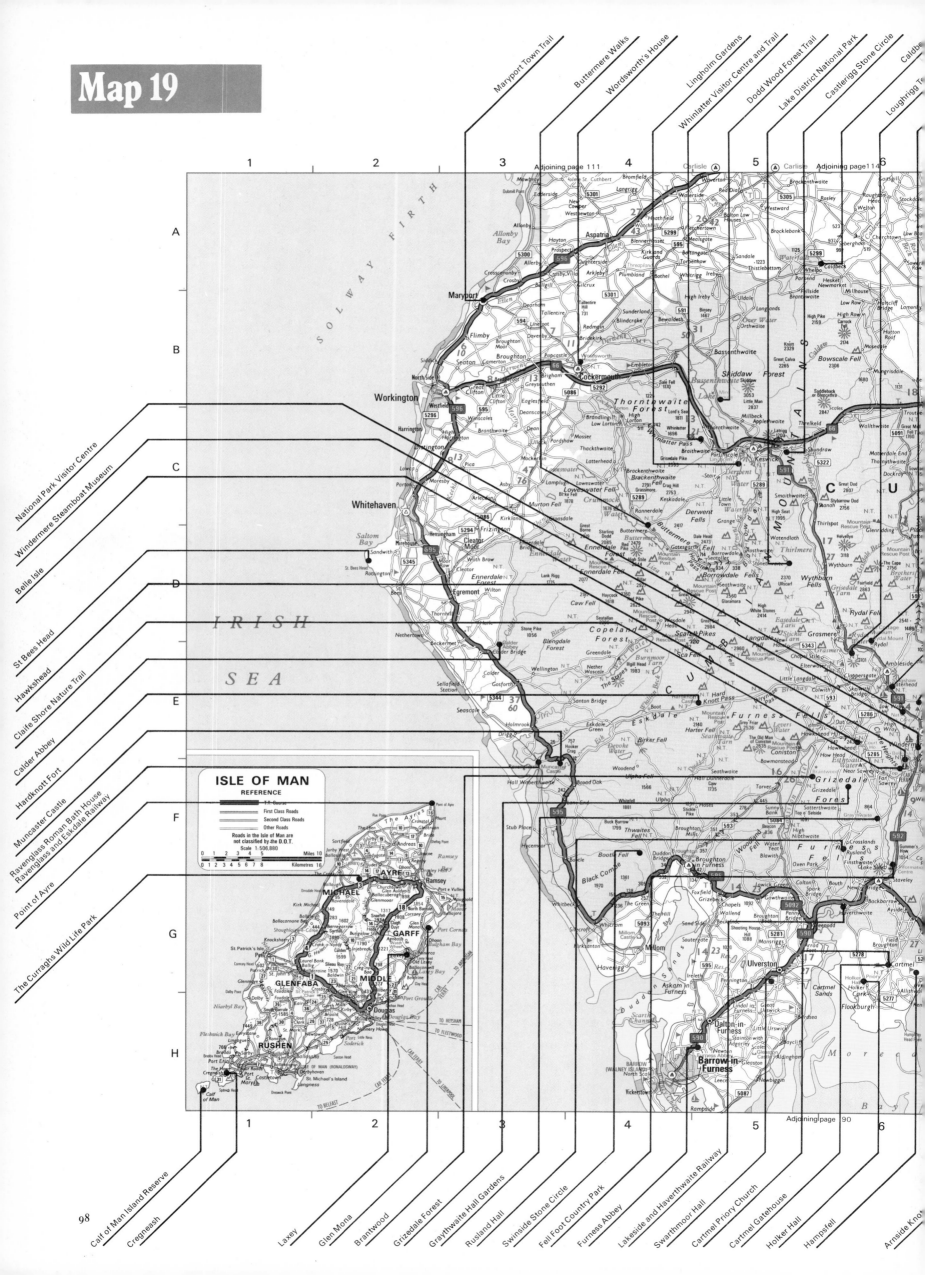

Map 19

North-West England

Abbot Hall Art Gallery and Museum, Kendal Georgian house containing 18th-century furniture, pictures, china, with exhibitions of contemporary work. Stable block houses local trade and industry displays illustrating social, domestic and farming life, traditions and crafts of Lake District. 100 yards (90 m) past church on 'one way' system. & (F7)

Acorn Bank (NT) 18th-century house occupied as a Sue Ryder home (not open). Gardens (open) renowned for spring bulbs, herbaceous border and herbs. & (B8)

Appleby Castle Conservation Centre In Appleby Castle grounds. Several rare breeds of farm animals including White Park cattle, multi-horned Hebridean sheep, and many varied birds. (C9)

Arncliffe Georgian houses, farms and barns around a charming green, with green hills and limestone scars beyond. Nearby, Old Cotes (1650) is best of Littondale's houses. (H11)

Arnside Knott (NT) Winding tracks through bracken, gorse and silver birch give easy access to wooded, 500 ft (150 m) high summit with superb panorama to Lake District hills. (G7)

Arnside Tower Large 15th-century ruined pele tower in beautiful situation. Pleasant woodland walks to Silverdale and Arnside Knott. (G7)

Askham 17th- and 18th-century cottages and farms line both sides of a long green. Colour-washed stone, stately trees, daffodils in spring. (C7)

Aysgarth Falls A series of broad, shallow falls over limestone ledges in wooded gorge of the River Ure. Upper Falls most picturesque, Lower Falls most impressive. (F12)

Bainbridge Stone houses set round a large rectangular green with trees and stocks. River Bain cascades over shallow terraces and separates village from Brough Hill, site of Roman fort. (F11)

Belle Isle A 38-acre (15-hectare) island in Lake Windermere, with unique Georgian round house. Contains portraits by Romney and furniture by Gillow. 'Below stairs' museum. Access by boat from Bowness Bay. (E/F6)

Bowlees Picnic area in wooded valley. Wild flowers and walks here and by River Tees nearby. Visitor centre in converted chapel, with interpretative display. (B11)

Brantwood Ruskin's home for last 28 years of life. Large collection of his paintings and personal possessions. Garden, nature trail. Temporary exhibitions in coach-house gallery. & (F5)

Brigflatts Friends' Meeting House Off A683, 1 mile (1.6 km) south-west Sedbergh. One of the best early Meeting Houses (1675). Cool, dignified simple interior with wooden galleries. (F9)

Brough Castle (EH) Large keep of late Norman castle in prominent position, with ruins of later buildings surrounding a paved courtyard. Repaired 17th century. & (D10)

Brougham Castle (EH) Extensive remains of late Norman keep and other later buildings, by River Eamont. Repaired 17th century. (B8)

Buttermere Walks Separate lakeside walks from Buttermere village along west sides of Buttermere and Crummock Water. Majestic lake and mountain scenery. 2 to 6 miles (3.2 to 9.6 km) return. (C/D4)

Caldbeck Old community by River Caldew which formerly powered a dozen mills. Stone cottages, old village washhouse, brewery, clogger, schoolhouse, and John Peel's grave in churchyard. (A6)

Calder Abbey Off A595 at Calder Bridge. Beautiful, riverside setting for ruins of Cistercian abbey, mainly 12th- and 13th-century church, chapter-house and gatehouse. Part of monastic buildings incorporated into late Georgian mansion c. 1770 (not open). (E3)

Carlin Gill Wild valley on west side Howgill Fells, accessible by minor road from Sedbergh. Black Force, waterfall and ravine, 1¼ miles (2 km) walk from road. Hill scenery and views over Lune valley. (E8)

Cartmel Gatehouse (NT) Early 14th-century building overlooking Market Place, the only surviving structure of Cartmel Priory, apart from church. Now houses a craft and gift shop. (G6)

Cartmel Priory Church Survived Dissolution because of parochial use, much of the building being 1190–1220. 14th- and 15th-century additions included unusual top stage of tower. Magnificent furnishings include fine stalls, misericords and screen. (G6)

Castlerigg Stone Circle (NT) 38 stones form an almost complete Bronze Age circle dramatically situated on a

Castlerigg Stone Circle

grassy plateau in superb amphitheatre of mountains. & (C5)

Cautley Spout Series of tall, slender cascades 1 mile (1.6 km) walk from Cross Keys Inn (NT) on east side of Brant Fell. Dramatic situation, frowning crags, smooth green hillsides. Close approach is steep. (F9)

Claife Shore Nature Trail (NT) Lakeside and woodland walk with information on forestry and freshwater life starts on west shore of Windermere ¼ mile (400 m) north of ferry. 1½ miles (2.4 km) return. (E6)

Cow Green Car park and visitor centre (at reservoir); nature trail in Upper Teesdale Nature Reserve. Easy walk to Cauldron Snout waterfall (1¼ miles, 2 km). Moorland and reservoir bird life. Unique alpine flora; wild, lonely beauty. (B10)

Crosby Ravensworth Delightful village in Lyvennent valley. Clear stream, bridges, splendid church, good 18th-century houses, many field and riverside paths. (D8)

Dalemain Medieval, Tudor and Georgian house occupied by same family for 300 years. Fine furniture, portraits.

Gardens, countryside park, picnic area, agricultural and yeomanry museum. (C7)

Dent Narrow cobbled streets, white-washed cottages, clustered chimneys, Sedgwick (geologist) memorial, large church, walks, hills, views. (F9)

Dodd Wood Forest Trail Waymarked walks for 1½ or 3 miles (2.4 or 4.8 km), through Douglas fir, larch, spruce, mainly forest roads but steep in places. Fine views Bassenthwaite and Derwentwater. Starts from Forestry Commission car park, 3 miles (4.8 km) north Keswick on A591. (B5)

Dufton Colour-washed sandstone cottages and farms along both sides of broad, tree-endowed green, with Pennines beyond. (C9)

Eaves Wood (NT) Walk 2 miles (3.2 km) through mixed deciduous mature woodland including hazel coppice with woodland flowers, limestone pavement, and fine views at top. (G7)

Fell Foot Country Park (NT) 17 acres (7 hectares) of woodland and grassland by east shore of southern end of Windermere. Lake access for swimming, sailing, canoeing. Fine views up lake. & (F6)

Furness Abbey (EH) Extensive remains of church and monastic buildings of Cistercian abbey founded 1127. Red sandstone in a green wooded setting. Infirmary chapel houses early stone effigies of knights in armour. & (H5)

Garrigill Walks Sample Pennine Way (signposted) south-west from village. Walled lane, then well-defined track, to Cross Fell summit, 7 miles (11 km) away. Steady climb, never steep, to 2,930 ft (890 m). (A9)

Graythwaite Hall Gardens Fine displays of flowering shrubs, azaleas, rhododendrons. Small Dutch garden, stream, pond, unusual sundial. (F6)

Grizedale Forest (FC) 7,500 acres (3,035 hectares), mainly coniferous plantations, some broadleaved woodland and farmland. Natural history emphasis. Waymarked forest walks, including Silurian Way illustrating geology, ecology and land use. Treetop observation tower for bird-watching and studying deer. Information room and shop. Wild Life Centre and Deer Museum 3 miles (4.8 km) south Hawkshead on minor road to Satterthwaite. (F6)

Hampsfell Small limestone hill overlooking Kent estuary, with panoramic views north-west to Lake District mountains. 1¼ miles (2 km) easy climb from golf course (Grange-over-Sands to Cartmel road). Rewards far outweigh effort. Limestone pavement and 19th-century hospice on top. (G6)

Hardknott Fort (EH) Impressively situated 800 ft (240 m) above the head of Eskdale. Stone walls and earth embankments, with bath-house and artificially-levelled parade ground to west. (E5)

Hawkshead Narrow streets, small squares, cobbled pavements, stone courtyards, huddled white-washed cottages. Nearby, former Furness Abbey Courthouse (NT) now houses museum of local life. (E6)

Heron Corn Mill, Beetham Restored as a 12th-century working waterwheel-driven corn mill. Educational displays. Stone-ground flour available. (G7)

High Cup Nick 3½ miles (5.6 km) walk and climb from Dufton Town Head, south end of village, on Pennine Way, to cirque of savage cliffs with magnificent views in all directions. (C9)

Holker Hall and Park Former home of Duke of Devonshire. 16th-century with much 19th-century rebuilding, fine craftsmanship and carvings. Extensive gardens, deer-park, displays, motor museum, children's adventure playground. & (G6)

Howtown Walk 6 miles (9.6 km) of quintessence of Lake District. Take Ullswater steamer from Glenridding (car park) to Howtown. Return by delightful undulating path, through rocks, bracken, birches, along eastern side of lake. Magnificent views. (C7)

Hubberholme Church Off B6160. Long, low, with rough-hewn stone walls and rare medieval rood-loft. Fine modern oak furniture by Robert Thompson of Kilburn. Picturesque setting by River Wharfe. (G11)

Hutton-in-the-Forest 14th-century pele tower with important 17th-century additions. Display of pictures, tapestries and furniture spans 450 years of craftsmanship. 17th-century gardens, terraces. Woodland walk and picnic area. & (B7)

Ingleton Glens Paths and bridges in narrow wooded valleys of the Doe and Twiss reveal waterfalls, rocks, and open stretches creating a variety of interest in a 4 mile (6.4 km) round walk, though no need to do whole trip. (H9)

Killhope Interesting picnic area by Killhope Burn, upper Weardale. Killhope Wheel (1870), restored but not working, 33 ft (10 m) diameter, powered lead ore-crushing machinery in mill adjoining. Fell and forest Pennine scenery. (A10)

Kilnsey Crag Spectacular cliff of Great Scar Limestone by roadside in Wharfedale. Famous medieval monastic track, Mastiles Lane, runs westwards to Malham Moor (5 miles, 8 km). (H12)

Kirkoswald Street-village of attractive sandstone houses above River Eden. Camponile on top of hill, church below with well. Nearby ruined tower of 12th-century castle with deep moat. Woodland and riverside walks by Raven Beck. (A8)

Lake District National Park Largest of the 10 National Parks (866 sq miles, 2,240 sq km), the Lake District is unique, a perfect blend of hills, mountains, rivers, valleys and lakes, where nothing is out of scale. Colour, enchantment and beauty exist in full measure, even when it rains. The west is more rugged, the eastern hills more lonely. The heads of Wastwater and Buttermere are grand, of Ullswater glorious. Boats ply on Windermere, Ullswater, Coniston, Derwentwater. Superb walking abounds in level valleys, by lakes and rivers, on low hills like Catbells and Loughrigg, or on challenging fells like Scafell Pike, Great Gable, Bowfell and the Langdales. Roads follow many lake shores, the major valleys, and cross high passes. Every one is a scenic drive, but the best of Lakeland is seen on foot. (B-G3-7)

Lakeside and Haverthwaite Railway
Steam-hauled trains along 3½ miles (5.6 km) of Leven valley in southern Lake District, connecting with Sealink Lake Windermere vessels at Lakeside. Locomotives and rolling stock maintained at Haverthwaite. & (G6)

Langstrothdale Riverside Walk starts and finishes at Hubberholme (1 mile, 1.6 km north-west Buckden off B6160). Climb rough track north-west from church to Scar House at top of wood. Turn left (west), follow orange waymarks to Yockenthwaite, returning by waymarked field path along north side of river (3 miles, 4.8 km). Part rough, but not steep. (G11)

Leighton Hall, Carnforth Off A6 through Yealand Conyers. Beautifully situated Georgian mansion, with delicate neo-Gothic facade, 1810, and later additions, 1860. Home of Gillow family who still live there. Contains much early Gillow furniture. Regular bird of prey displays. & (H7)

Levens Hall Largest Elizabethan house in Cumbria (1580) incorporating medieval pele tower and 17th/18th-century additions. Fine panelling, plasterwork, chimney pieces and furniture. Gardens famous for unique original topiary (1692), yew, box, beech hedge and circle, herbaceous border, parkland. Steam engine collection. & (G7)

Lingholm Gardens Formal and natural gardens on west shore of Derwentwater. Rhododendrons, azaleas, interesting shrubs and trees, glasshouse range. Lake and mountain views. Waymarked tour. & (C5)

Little Salkeld Watermill Off A686 1 mile (1.6 km) north of Langwathby. Water-powered cornmill still producing stoneground flour in traditional manner. Shop and tearoom. & (B8)

Loughrigg Terrace (NT) From White Moss car park on A591, easiest scenic walk in Lake District ½ mile (.8 km) across north slopes of Loughrigg. Superb views over Grasmere Lake and to encircling fells. Little climbing involved. (E6)

Lowther Park Leisure park set in 140 acres (56 hectares) of beautiful parkland with longhorn cattle and deer. Attractions include trains, boats, BMX bikes,

Elter Water and the Langdale Pikes in the heart of the Lake District. (E5)

roller-skating, circus. Many others in preparation. & (C7)

Malham Tarn (NT) 150-acre (60-hectare) natural lake forming part of nature reserve. Tarn House on north let to Field Studies Council. Public access to south shore only. Moorland and water birds, plants, limestone scenery. (H11)

Maryport Town Trail Two walks totalling 3 miles (4.8 km) around town and harbour to show places of historical and industrial interest. Starts Maritime Museum, Senhouse Street, inside harbour. (B3)

Milburn Delightful village at western foot of Pennines, with 18th- and 19th-century houses forming almost continuous frontage round large rectangular green with narrow paths leading to farm buildings behind. Fine views all round. (B9)

Moreland Pleasant village by stream; ducks, watersplash, 18th-century houses, church with Saxon tower. Quiet field paths, views, pastoral and peaceful. (C8)

Muker to Keld Walk A terrace walk along slopes of Kidson to high above River Swale follows the Pennine Way. Return route by riverside path and fine hay-meadows. 6 miles (9.6 km). (E11)

Muncaster Castle Mid-Victorian building, incorporating medieval pele tower, in superb situation above Esk estuary. Outstanding tapestries, china, pictures, with 16th- and 17th-century furniture and a magnificent library. Famous rhododendron gardens, super views. Bird gardens, tree trail, nature trail. & (F3)

National Park Visitor Centre, Brockhole 36 acres (14 hectares) of gardens and grounds. Woodland and lake shore trails. Views across Windermere. Audio-visual presentations tell story of Lake District geography, geology, history, farming. & (E6)

Ravenglass and Eskdale Railway Narrow-gauge railway with mainly steam-hauled passenger trains on 7 mile (11 km) track to Dalegarth, in Eskdale, along line built 1875 to carry iron ore. Restored and working water cornmill at Muncaster. Glorious valley and mountain scenery. & (F3/E4)

Ravenglass Roman Bath House 'Walls Castle', parts of which stand 12 ft (3.6 m) high, is one of the highest Roman structures in the country, the remains of the extensive fort of Clanoventa. ½ mile

(.8 km) walk from road through plantation. (F3)

Ribblehead Focus for Yorkshire's 'Three Peaks' – Ingleborough, Whernside, Pen-y-ghent. Limestone scenery, pavements, scars, caves, potholes. Impressive viaduct on Leeds–Carlisle railway, 1876. (G10)

Rusland Hall 3 miles (4.8 km) north Haverthwaite. Neat early Georgian house with landscaped gardens in quiet setting beneath the hills. Contents include mechanical curios. Signposted from Newby Bridge. & (F6)

Rydal Mount Wordsworth's home 1813–50. Family portraits, furniture, personal possessions of poet, many first editions of works. Interesting small garden designed by Wordsworth. Terraces with rare trees and shrubs. & (E6)

St Bees Head Red sandstone cliffs 300 ft (91 m) high, breeding-place for guillemots, puffins. Views over Solway. Clifftop walk 2 miles (3.2 km) from St Bees village. Lighthouse open. (D2)

Shap Abbey (EH) 13th-century remains of Premonstratensian abbey dominated by a graceful 16th-century tower. Pleasant setting in wooded valley of River Lowther. & (D8)

Sizergh Castle (NT) Off A6 at junction (590). 15th-, 16th- and 18th-century additions to a pele tower of 1340. Fine Elizabethan panelling and chimney pieces. Furniture, paintings, Jacobean and Stuart relics. Home of the Stricklands for 700 years. Rock garden and stately conifers. & (F7)

Stagshaw Garden (NT) Rhododendrons, azaleas, sorbus, magnolia, late-flowering shrubs, daffodils, camellias, moss garden, stream, in 8 acres (3.2 hectares) of woodland, above Windermere's north-east shore. (E6)

Swarthmoor Hall Elizabethan house with mullioned windows, panelled rooms, oak staircase. George Fox's home, and birthplace of Quakerism. (G5)

Swinside Stone Circle Compact Bronze Age circle, 90 ft (27 m) in diameter, on open hill pasture cradled by hills, near Swinside Farm, 1 mile (1.6 km) walk from nearest road at Crag Hall off A595. (F4)

Townend, Troutbeck (NT) 1626 house of a Lakeland 'statesman' family, the Brownes, who occupied it until 1944. Fine woodwork and furniture with books,

papers and family items collected and used through three centuries. (E6)

Upper Dales Folk Museum, Hawes Housed in former railway station buildings, comprehensive collection of bygones; domestic, social, farming, lead-mining and quarrying interest. (F11)

Wetheriggs Pottery 3 miles (4.8 km) south Penrith on unclassified road off A6. A steam-engine drives a potter's wheel at weekends, horses are shod most summer days. Weaving, gallery of local work, museum, playground. & (C8)

Whinlatter Visitor Centre and Trail Illustrates forestry landscaping techniques and man's impact on fells. Waymarked forest trail through spruce, larch, western hemlock, Douglas fir. View Bassenthwaite and Derwentwater. Steep, rugged, but easier options. & in Centre. (C4)

Whitbarrow Abrupt limestone ridge above marshes of Kent estuary. Lower slopes richly wooded. 4 mile (6.4 km) escarpment walk through rocks, bracken and heather. Starts Witherslack. (G7)

Windermere Steamboat Museum Victorian and Edwardian steamboats from 1850–1911; 1780 sailing boat, speedboats and motor-boats, many in undercover wet dock. Shore of Windermere, ½ mile (.8 km) north of Bowness. & (E6)

Wordsworth's House, Cockermouth (NT) Built 1745, retains original staircase, panelling, fireplaces. Wordsworth born here 1770, spent happy childhood in it. Poet's furniture, china, books. (B4)

Yorkshire Dales National Park 680 sq miles (1,760 sq km) of Pennine fells and valleys. Swaledale is narrow and grand; Wensleydale, broad, green, wooded; Wharfedale exquisite, sharing its limestone landscapes with Ribblesdale and Malhamdale. Colours are soft, muted; villages, houses, farms, barns, walls are all of stone. Valley roads are good, those over the tops, narrow and steep. Wild life is abundant. Dales farming concentrates on stock-rearing, and there are miles of fine footpaths. The Pennine Way threads its spiral way by the high fells at the valley-heads. (E-H9-12)

Isle of Man

Calf of Man Island Reserve Breeding-place of Atlantic seals, guillemots, kittiwakes, puffins and razorbills. Boat from Port Erin. (H1)

Cregneash Spectacular coastal scenery around south-west tip of Isle of Man. Dramatic cliffs, impressive tidal races. Attractive village with carefully restored cottages housing *Cregneash Folk Museum* displaying traditional crafts. (H1)

The Curraghs Wild Life Park, Ballaugh Beautiful setting with lakes and woods. Wide variety of animals and birds include Manx cats and the Manx Loaghtan four-horned sheep. & (G2)

Glen Mona Beautiful scenery with wooded glens, paths inland to lower slopes of Snaefell, seawards to cliffs and delightful bays. Neolithic chambered grave nearby at Cashtal-yn-Ard. South of Ramsey. (G2)

Laxey The old harbour town is dominated by world's largest surviving water-wheel built 1854 to pump water from lead mines of Laxey Glen – 'Lady Isabella', 72 ft (22 m) diameter, with 168 buckets, each capable of holding 24 gallons. (G2)

Point of Ayre Miles of good walks on heath-covered shingle ridges of storm beaches behind deserted stretches of sand at northern tip of Isle of Man. Car parks and picnic sites at Ballaghennie and Point of Ayre; old and new lighthouses. (F2)

Piers

The seaside pier, a leisure and amusement platform stretching out for half a mile (0.8 km) or more away from the shore, was one of Victorian Britain's happiest inventions. With its frivolous, light-hearted architecture, its amusements and its splendid opportunities for strolling and enjoying the sea breezes, it was a perfect expression of the holiday mood.

But it was also a remarkable technical achievement, an elaborate assembly of girders and struts and tie-rods, which combined great strength with lightness and more than a little of the feeling of a fairy palace. It was as interesting underneath as on top, an engineering, as well as an architectural triumph.

The pier had two great drawbacks, however. It needed an enormous amount of maintenance and, with its mass of wooden structures, it was terribly vulnerable to fire. While wages were low, the maintenance could be coped with, but in recent years it has, in most cases, fallen sadly behind, and more than one of Britain's finest piers is now in a far from safe condition.

For a Victorian seaside resort a pier was a status symbol, an unmistakable mark of distinction. Brighton (East Sussex) stood out from the rest,

with three piers, but Southend (Essex) made much of the fact that it had the longest. Architecturally, the finest piers are probably those at Weston-super-Mare (Avon) or Lytham St Annes (Lancashire), but Walton and Clacton (Essex) could boast a railway to carry their visitors out to sea. The seaside town without a pier was definitely in the second league.

Piers were a by-product of railways. Until large numbers of people were able to travel cheaply and easily to the seaside, there was no point in having attractions for the masses. The places which built their piers, mostly between 1850 and 1880, were those, like Brighton, Weston, Clacton and Southend, which attracted plenty of day-trippers from nearby big cities, working-class people who intended to enjoy every minute of a long day by the sea. The pier was part of the excitement, and a fine money-making business into the bargain. You paid to go on it – Fleetwood (Lancashire) advertised itself proudly as 'the only free pier in England' – paid to listen to the concert-party and the band, paid for your deckchair, paid for the toys and souvenirs on sale at the kiosks, and paid for the wide range of slot machines which were such a great feature of the Victorian and Edwardian pier.

The 19th-century slot-machines were purely mechanical, made to give pleasure to people who knew nothing about television and the cinema, although some of them were based on techniques which were the predecessors of the movies. 'What

Piers tended to be built in towns that were easily accessible by rail to large numbers of day-trippers. Several towns along the Lancashire coast, for example, built piers to attract workers from the industrial towns of the north, as at Lytham St Annes (below left) and Morecambe (centre right). Blackpool's North Pier (centre and above) is one of three in the town.

the Butler Saw' machines were a special favourite. They consisted of cards fixed to a drum which could be made to revolve by turning a handle. If the drum went round fast enough the pictures appeared to move.

'What the Butler Saw' has long since been replaced by much more elaborate amusement machines, but a few of these old-time favourites can still be seen in museums. Brighton has one or two fine examples in its Seaside Room, together with some of the early electrically operated machines that were popular in the 1920s and 1930s. There is also a fine collection of ancient slot-machines on one of the town's piers, which visitors can operate with old pennies handed to them in exchange for part of their entrance fee.

A pier livened up the appearance of the seafront very considerably. It was the focal point of the promenade, and it added variety to the scene. The kiosks and the pavilions were interesting to look at and the coloured lights strung along the edges of the pier and outlining its buildings looked wonderful after dark. It was no accident that the big seaside towns, like Brighton, were among the first places in the country to have electricity. It provided the extra touch of magic that made all the difference to the holiday atmosphere and no go-ahead Council would refuse to make the investment. Brighton was generating electricity before it was available in Birmingham or Manchester. But the piers and the promenades must have looked good at night-time even in the days of gas.

Piers were built almost to a standard pattern, with pavilions at both the land and the sea end and a deck with glass screens and built-in seats between them. Looked at from above, they are usually dumb-bell shaped, with a bulge at either end and a long narrow section linking the two bulges. There were variations. Some of the very large piers were designed with a third bulge in the centre, to accommodate an extra pavilion.

The most elaborate pier today is the one at Clacton, which has a theatre at the far end and a swimming pool and dance hall at the entrance, together with a remarkable collection of amusement machines. Clacton had its centre section blown up during World War II to prevent the Germans from using the pier for landings. It was restored after the war, but with steel, which will almost certainly not last as long as the wrought-iron used by the original architects. The Victorian piers are, in fact, among the most remarkable monuments to iron, wrought-iron for the structure and cast-iron for the ornamentation above.

Our own century has built no piers. Like parks, they were a Victorian speciality. We continue to enjoy them, and we do our best to keep them going, despite constantly rising costs. Their great days are unfortunately over, but they still offer one of the most pleasant ways of spending an hour or two looking out across the sea, 'ships that don't bob up and down', as one writer put it a hundred years ago.

South coast piers include Eastbourne (below), transformed into a fairy palace after dark, and Brighton (above). Brighton's Palace Pier shown here is one of the town's two surviving piers – the famous Chain Pier was destroyed in a storm in 1896. The pier at Cromer (below centre) was similarly damaged in a storm in 1953 but has since been rebuilt.

Follies

Follies add laughter to the landscape, a smile upon the scenery. Scattered over the country are scores of such structures – sham castles and ruins, towers, pyramids, obelisks, eye-catchers, Gothick remnants, druids' circles, decorative arches or walls, prettified cattlesheds and deer houses. To qualify as a folly a building requires a touch of fantasy, an element of eccentricity. The true folly was created to satisfy and please its builder, and if it also gave 'a livelier consequence to the landscape', so much the better. Follies are often both artistic and whimsical, but only occasionally functional.

Folly-building spans three centuries. Virtually unknown before the Dissolution of the Monasteries, it slowly gathered impetus as men of wealth and leisure, acquiring or developing estates, wanted something individual, perhaps something wilder than pastures or parkland, or a touch of medieval romance. By the 18th century follies were fashionable, a great estate being incomplete without one. Landowners often employed eminent architects – Vanbrugh, Hawksmoor, Miller, Adam included – to design them. Since ideas about buildings and tastes spread downwards through the social scale, lesser gentry followed suit. In the 19th century fewer follies were built, and these by the newly rich rather than the noble.

The most conspicuous follies are those built on commanding sites, either as eye-catchers or as prospect-towers. Unfortunately many have by now become obscured by growth of trees, and can be found only by a diligent search.

Several hundred follies adorn the British landscape, and some even occur in urban surroundings. Generally they are less common in Wales and Scotland. One of the oldest is in Suffolk, where, on the banks of the Orwell near Ipswich, brick-built Freston Tower dates from 1549. Nearly 50 years later came one of the landmarks of folly-building, Rushton Lodge, in Northamptonshire.

Sir Thomas Tresham, an ardent Catholic, whose studies of the occult, theology and mathematics developed in him an obsession about the Trinity, built this with dimensions and details in threes, or products and divisions of three, on a triangular plan.

Other triangular follies, lacking the Trinity motif, usually had turrets or towers at their corners. Horton Tower (Dorset), 1722; Racton Tower (Sussex), 1770; Alfred's Tower, 1772, on the edge of the Stourhead estates (Wiltshire); Midford Castle (near Bath), 1780; Haldon Belvedere (Devon), 1788 and Paxton's Tower (Dyfed), 1811, continued the tradition. Although there are family resemblances, each is highly individual.

There was no logical development of folly design, but certain ideas become fashionable. An arched wall, with pinnacles, makes a splendid eye-catcher on a hilltop. Grange Arch, Creech, in the Purbeck Hills a few miles west of Corfe Castle, Dorset, was built in 1740. It is easily accessible from the nearby road, its arches of Portland stone framing a superb view of Dorset's heathland. About the same time William Kent designed a screen of round-topped arches, crowned with a tiara of pinnacles, to improve a view at Rousham, in the Cherwell valley, Oxfordshire.

West of Leominster (Hereford and Worcester) the unique eye-catcher of Shobdon Arches consists of the chancel arch and two doorways of the Norman church dismantled about 1750 and re-erected on a beautiful hillside above Shobdon Court.

Adding towers or turrets to an arched wall creates a sham castle, one of the commonest types of 18th-century folly. Ralph Allen's Sham Castle on the skyline east of Bath is one of the best-known. It was designed by Sanderson Miller in 1762, a broad Gothick facade of Bath stone. Miller's earlier shams include those at Wimpole Hall (Cambridgeshire), 1750, Hagley (Hereford and Worcester), slightly earlier, and Radway Castle, Edge Hill (Warwickshire), 1747. In Oxfordshire, Shotover's early 18th-century sham castle, with three castellated arches and end towers, is attributed to Hawksmoor.

A single Gothick tower, round or square, with a short curtain wall adjoining, is the simplest type of 18th-century eye-catching folly. Mow Cop, 1750, high on a Cheshire hill, is one of the best-loved of these, with Old John in Bradgate Park (Leicestershire), 1786, running it close. St David's Ruin, above Bingley (West Yorkshire), is a later (1796) but equally worthy example consisting of a tower, curtain wall and arch.

Motives for folly-building are almost as numerous as follies themselves. Mad Jack Fuller built five near Brightling, Sussex – a Needle, Mausoleum, Tower, Rotunda and Observatory – while at Dallington (East Sussex) he added the conical Sugar-loaf to a nearby hilltop, representing the spire of Dallington church, which he swore was visible from his dining-room.

Greystoke Park (Cumbria) has folly-like farm buildings – Bunker's Hill, Fort Putnam and Spire House, all of the 1780s, their names celebrating American victories in the War of Independence. At the beginning of the century, Vanbrugh had built sham fortifications, including farms, on the Earl of Carlisle's Castle Howard estate (North Yorkshire). The eccentric squire of Tattingstone, Suffolk, built in 1760 a folly which is also functional, three brick cottages on the edge of his estate, boxed in on three sides by huge church walls. Equally strange is the Ilton 'Druids' Temple' near Masham (North Yorkshire), a neat little replica of Stonehenge, built in the 1820s by Squire Danby of Swinton Hall to provide employment for workers on his estate. Now a popular picnic-place in a grove of conifers it epitomises the

(Below left) *McCaig's Tower, Oban, built to resemble the Colosseum;* (above left) *Pentlow Tower, Essex;* (above) *Freston Tower, Suffolk, one of the oldest follies;* (above right) *Grange Arch, Dorset, an eye-catcher on the Purbeck Hills;* (centre right) *Rushton Lodge, Northamptonshire, built with dimensions and details in threes;* (right) *Paxton's Tower, Dyfed, also constructed to a triangular design.*

eccentricity, as well as the pleasure-giving qualities, of the true folly. Another, tinier, Stonehenge is one of several delightful follies built for the Earl of Shrewsbury at Alton Towers (Staffordshire) in the 1820s. McCaig's folly, the 'Tower' on the hills behind Oban (Strathclyde), was built by a wealthy, philanthropic banker to provide employment in 1890. It resembles the Colosseum, and demonstrates his love for classical art.

Lord Berners' Folly, near Faringdon (Oxfordshire), completed in 1935, is probably the last true folly to grace the British landscape. Overcoming immense local opposition and planning objections, its 140 ft (42 m) tower on a hilltop site is now largely obscured by trees. Present times and attitudes are scarcely propitious to folly-building, so it behoves us to appreciate these quirky embellishments to the landscape which happily survive.

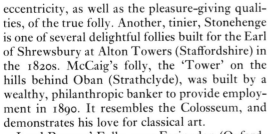

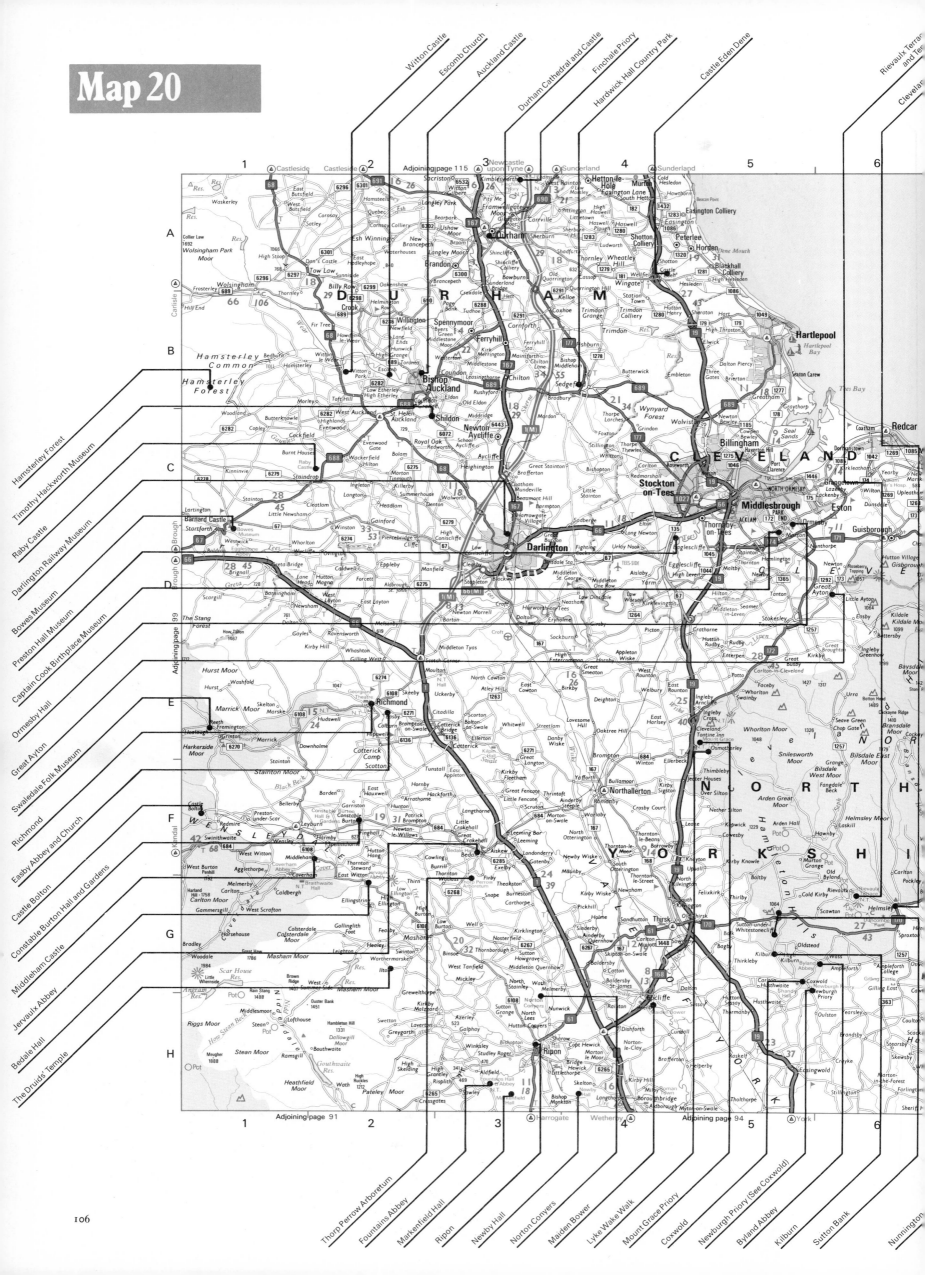

Map 20

Cleveland Way
Danby: The Moors Centre
Boulby Cliff
Staithes
Wheeldale Moor
Kettleness
North Yorkshire Moors Railway
Whitby
Falling Foss
Robin Hood's Bay
Lyke Wake Walk
Ravenscar
May Beck Trail
Goathland
Silpho
Newtondale Halt
n le Hole
e Howard
North Yorkshire Moors National Park
Malton
Flamingo Land
Duggleby
Pickering
Thornton Dale
Ebberston Hall
The Bridestones (see Hole of Horcum)
Hole of Horcum
Wold Newton
Filey Brigg
Cleveland Way
Flamborough Head
Sewerby Hall
NORTH SEA
HUMBERSIDE
Whitby
Scarborough
Filey
Bridlington
Pickering
Malton
Norton
Loftus
Saltburn-by-the-Sea
Robin Hood's Bay
Ravenscar
Goathland
Flamborough Head
Adjoining page 94
Adjoining page 95
COPYRIGHT, GEORGE PHILIP & SON, LTD.

North-East England

Auckland Castle, Bishop Auckland is the official residence of the Bishops of Durham, originally a Norman manor house (open by appointment only). Park (815 acres, 330 hectares) and Deer House (EH). (B2)

Bedale Hall A Georgian mansion, now council offices; has a fine Georgian ballroom and magnificent plasterwork ceiling. Museum exhibits here include local arts and crafts, old clocks and a mid 18th-century man-drawn fire engine. (F3)

Boulby Cliff 666 ft (203 m) high, one of the loftiest cliffs on the English coast. Spectacular views. Access along footpath across two fields by radio mast off A174 opposite Boulby Mine. (C8)

Bowes Museum, Barnard Castle An imposing 19th-century French-style château. Paintings by El Greco, Goya, Boucher, Courbet; period settings of furniture, pottery, porcelain and jewellery, and a fine mechanical silver swan (18th century). Some items were owned by Napoleon. Ruins of 12th-century *Egglestone Abbey* (EH) stand 2 miles (3.2 km) south-east, along B6277. (D1)

Byland Abbey (EH) Impressive Cistercian abbey (12th century). Remains of glazed tiles and round window. (G6)

Captain Cook Birthplace Museum A new museum, in Stewart Park, Marton, describing in lifesize tableaux the life story of the explorer Captain Cook, born locally. Children's pets' corner and aviary in the grounds, with llamas, deer, peacocks, poultry and rabbits. (D5)

Castle Bolton A substantial ruin, the castle has a commanding view of Wensleydale. Built by a former Chancellor of England (14th century). Mary, Queen of Scots imprisoned here. (F1)

Penhill from Preston-under-Scar (F1)

Castle Eden Dene There are picturesque walks along this steep-sided wooded ravine, a 494-acre (200-hectare) nature reserve. High cliffs and rockfalls, notably the 'Devil's Lapstone'. Access 1¼ miles (2 km) along B1281 from A19(T). (A4)

Castle Howard Magnificent 18th-century mansion built by Sir John Vanbrugh and Nicholas Hawksmoor. Paintings by Gainsborough, Holbein, Rubens, Reynolds and Romney; much fine furniture and statuary. Dominant features in the grounds: mausoleum, the fountain, Temple of the Four Winds, and lake. In the stables there is a changing exhibition, drawn from the Howard family's collection of thousands of costumes, dating from the 18th century. (H7)

Cleveland Way Semi-circular path that meanders the 100 miles (160 km) from Helmsley (G6) in the south-east of the North Yorkshire Moors, then northwards to Saltburn (C7), and southwards along the coast to Filey (G11). The Way winds through a variety of beautiful moorland and village scenery, and is waymarked with an acorn symbol. The National Park Department at Bondgate, Helmsley, issues a leaflet about the Way.

Constable Burton Hall and Gardens A fine Palladian villa, *c.* 1760, on a hill with stream nearby. Shrub-lined walks in the beautifully laid-out gardens; and there is a rock garden. (F2)

Coxwold Attractive, partially cobbled village. Laurence Sterne, author of *Tristram Shandy*, lived here in the 1760s in *Shandy Hall* (*c.* 1450), now a museum containing items connected with Sterne and his writings. East of the village is *Newburgh Priory*, formerly an Augustinian foundation, now a variety of buildings developed over centuries. Of note are the Elizabethan porch, and the marble overmantel in the dining-room (1615). Grounds have wide lawns and avenues and a water garden. (G5)

Danby: The Moors Centre Stands in 13 acres (5.3 hectares) of gardens and woodlands and is a visitor centre for the **North Yorkshire Moors National Park.** An exhibition describes moorland life, geology and natural history. Information on local walks and tours. (D7)

Darlington Railway Museum, North Road Station, Darlington Housed in an 1842 building on the pioneer Stockton & Darlington Railway, considered to be the oldest existing railway station in the world. Ancient railway relics and steam locomotives, most famous of which is the original 'Locomotion No. 1' built by railway pioneer George Stephenson in 1825. (D3)

The Druids' Temple, Ilton This convincing folly in Jervaulx Forest was erected *c.* 1820 by Mr William Danby of Swinton Park. Reminiscent of Stonehenge, it has stones 12 ft (3.6 m) high, and is about 75 ft (22.9 m) long. (G2)

Duggleby South-east of the village church is one of the biggest round barrows, or ancient burial mounds, ever discovered in Britain. It is 120 ft (36.6 m) in diameter and 20 ft (6 m) high. (H9)

Durham Cathedral and Castle Landmarks on the banks of the river Wear.

Durham Cathedral above the Wear

The cathedral contains the tombs of the Venerable Bede and St Cuthbert and is one of the most impressive Early Norman buildings in the country. Prince Bishops of Durham once lived in the castle next to it, now part of the University. (A3)

Easby Abbey and Church The abbey (EH) is 1 mile (1.6 km) south-east of **Richmond** – a picturesque 12th-century ruin on the banks of the Swale. Next to it is Easby Church, notable for several fine medieval frescoes in the chancel, representing Biblical scenes and farming activities. (E2)

Ebberston Hall Attractive small house designed in 1718 in the Palladian style by Colen Campbell, Sir John Vanbrugh's draughtsman: a unique example of domestic architecture of the period. Most of the furniture is contemporary with the house. Remains of original water garden in the grounds. (G9)

Escomb Church Claimed to be the best-preserved Saxon church in Britain (*c.* 7th century). Ancient sundial still in place on the wall. Some of the wall stone, as indicated by the inscription 'LEG VI', was taken from the Romans' Sixth Legion camp at Binchester, near Bishop Auckland. (B2)

Falling Foss A pretty 3 mile (4.8 km) beck-side forest trail, past Falling Foss, a 30 ft (9 m) waterfall, impressive in spate after rain. Walk takes in young moorland tree plantations, woodland and valleys (birch, rowan, scrub oak, sitka spruce, larch). Access to Falling Foss and May Beck car parks from A169 and A171. (E9)

Filey Brigg Along this rocky headland is a 1 mile (1.6 km) walk leading along shore and up cliff with much of interest to see – marine creatures and plant life; and fossils may be found. (G11)

Finchale Priory (EH) St Godric, who died at 105, founded this priory in the 12th century; his burial place is marked in the ruin. Attractive riverside setting. Woodland walks nearby. (A3)

Flamborough Head A great rugged, chalky headland, with spectacular views and clifftop walks. Behind the modern lighthouse is one built in 1674 and used until 1806. Bempton Cliffs to the north-west is a huge breeding-ground for seabirds, including Britain's only mainland gannet colony. (H12)

Flamingo Land, Kirby Misperton Zoo with over 1,000 animals, including many exotic varieties. Dolphin, parrot and sea-lion shows. Family funpark with over 30 attractions, railway and large boating lake. Access from A169. (G8)

Fountains Abbey (NT) Founded by the Benedictines in the 12th century, one of the most impressive and best preserved of England's abbeys: an extensive ruin, dominated by a huge 15th-century tower, much of it in excellent condition, such as the long vaulted cellar (300 ft, 91 m). Two approaches: through Studley Royal park (deer, waterfowl), where stands the handsome Jacobean mansion of Fountains Hall, or from B6265, 4 miles (6.4 km) south-west of Ripon. (H3)

Goathland Moorland village on the private **North Yorkshire Moors Railway** (from **Pickering** to Grosmont) with four waterfalls within walking distance: Mallyan Spout, Walker Mill Foss, Water Ark Foss and Nelly Ayre Foss (with a natural swimming pool). 3½-mile (5.6-km) rail trail to Grosmont follows route of George Stephenson's original line from Pickering. (E8)

Great Ayton Explorer Captain James Cook went to school here. His classrooms are now a small museum. Near here are a 51 ft (15.5 m) high sandstone monument to him, erected in 1827 on Easby Moor, and a local high point, Roseberry Topping (1,057 ft, 322 m). (D6)

Hamsterley Forest Covers about 5,000 acres (2,023 hectares) and contains about 60 tree species. Forestry Commission has arranged six waymarked walks of 1½ to 8 miles (2.4 to 12.8 km), three of which are suitable for push-chairs. Walks start at Blackling Hole, The Grove and Low Redford on unclassified road just north of Bedburn joining B6282 west of Woodland. (B1)

Hardwick Hall Country Park Large country park with woodland and lake, information centre, nature trail, arboretum and playground. Ideal picnic spot. Access from A177 about ⅝ mile (1 km) west of Sedgefield. ♿ (B4)

Hole of Horcum A huge natural amphitheatre, about a mile (1.6 km) across, lying just west of A169. Hang-gliding here. Two miles (3.2 km) south-east are the *Bridestones* (NT), a cluster of large mushroom-like rock formations, sculpted by weather, on moorland. Leave main road near Lockton Lane End; access by farm tracks. (F8)

Hutton le Hole In the centre of this, one of Yorkshire's prettiest villages, is *Ryedale Folk Museum*, a rich collection of exhibits illustrating local crafts, pastimes and superstitions. Several reconstructed buildings – including cottages, manor house and glass furnace – in the 2½-acre (1-hectare) grounds. ♿ (F7)

Jervaulx Abbey A Cistercian monastery (12th century) set in an attractive part of Wensleydale and beautiful in its advanced decay. The original design can be clearly discerned. (G2)

Kettleness Headland hamlet with spectacular views of Runswick bay. (D8)

Kilburn Visitors can watch craftsmen in the workshops of the late Robert Thompson, world-famous woodcarver, whose mouse trademark appeared on all his work. His business is continued by his family. Visible from here is the *White Horse of Kilburn*, cut in 1857 in turf on a neighbouring hillside and measuring 228 ft high by 312 ft long (69.5 by 95 m). (G5)

Lyke Wake Walk A 40-mile (64.4 km) route across the North Yorkshire Moors at their widest, from 1½ miles (2.4 km) north of Osmotherley (E5) in the west to Ravenscar (E10) on the east coast. Established in 1955 and should be attempted only by experienced walkers, properly equipped, as some climbing is involved and weather may be poor.

Maiden Bower A wooden motte-and-bailey castle built by a knight of William the Conqueror's on this site. A grass-covered mound marks the spot, on the banks of the Swale. (H4)

Malton Famous for racehorses and Romans. A museum in the market place contains a good collection of local Roman relics, including catapult balls, weapons, coins, jars – and the imprint of a child's foot from Roman villa. (H8)

Markenfield Hall Last of six moated and fortified farmhouses near Ripon. The house was erected in 1310, but has been substantially rebuilt, mainly last century. Set in meadows and cornfields. Access from A61. ♿ (H3)

May Beck Trail A leisurely circular nature trail of about 3 miles (4.8 km), covering moorland, farm and forest, aimed at demonstrating wise use of land for agriculture, forestry, game conservation and recreation. Access from A1416; start at May Beck car park. (E9)

Middleham Castle (EH) Imposing ruins (12th century). Castle is said to have been King Richard III's favourite residence. Original keep, one of the biggest in England, still stands. ♿ 1 mile (1.6 km) south-east is the attractive Ulshaw Bridge, built in 1674. (F2)

Mount Grace Priory (NT, EH) Best-preserved Carthusian monastery in England, 1 mile (1.6 km) north of Osmotherley on the edge of the Cleveland hills. Monks' cells can be seen. ♿ (E5)

Newby Hall Beautiful Adam house in 25 acres (10 hectares) of attractive gardens. Treasures include Adam Gallery of Imperial Roman Sculpture, the Gobelins Tapestries, Chippendale furniture and 18th-century porcelain. Adventure garden for children; miniature riverside railway. ♿ (H4)

Newtondale Halt Small halt on **North Yorkshire Moors Railway** line, starting point for three waymarked Forestry Commission walks, suitable for all abilities, along and up the impressive steep-sided Newtondale valley. (F8)

North Yorkshire Moors National Park The moors comprise a national park covering 553 square miles (1,432 sq km), seen at their best from midsummer to early autumn in their seasonal coat of purple heather. The moors have been protected as a national park since 1952, and are scattered with farms, villages, dales, becks, ruined abbeys, old mine workings and forests that make exploration a delight. Towns are few, and pleasingly small. Roads are winding, narrow and with gradients as steep as 1-in-3. (See separate entries for the **Cleveland Way** and the **Lyke Wake Walk**.) There are information centres at **Danby Lodge** (D7); **Pickering** station (G8), the **North Yorkshire Moors Railway** terminus; and **Sutton Bank**.

North Yorkshire Moors Railway One of the longest private railways in the country (18 miles, 29 km), running from Grosmont (E8) to **Pickering** (G8). Loco shed with viewing gallery and railway displays at Grosmont terminus.

Norton Conyers House began c. 1490, but due to later alterations, is now largely Jacobean. Contains relics of Charlotte Brontë, who is said to have been inspired to use the house as 'Thornfield Hall' in *Jane Eyre*, and collections of toys, Victorian dresses and furniture. 18th-century garden. (G3)

Nunnington Hall (NT) A large, mainly 17th-century manor house by the river Rye, in 8.5 acres (3.4 hectares) of grounds. West wing c. 1580, panelled hall and staircase. Displayed are the Carlisle Collection of Miniature Rooms, furnished in different period styles; tapestries, china. (G7)

Ormesby Hall (NT) 18th-century house, lavishly decorated with contemporary plasterwork showing Adam influence. Fine stable block. ♿ (C5)

Pickering Attractive market town with motte-and-bailey castle (EH), 11th to 14th centuries; once used by royalty as hunting base. *Beck Isle Museum* is a 17-room Regency house, each room having a theme, such as old-world public house or cobbler's shop. Farm implement collection. Pickering church, above main street, contains 15th-century frescoes. (G8)

Preston Hall Museum This museum, in Yarm Road, south Stockton, stands in parkland and contains collections of bygones, pewter, arms and armour, costumes, and reconstructed period rooms. Reconstructed street of 1890s with shops, such as apothecary's, pawn-broker's, and working forge. ♿ (D4)

Raby Castle One of the biggest 14th-century castles in Britain; interior mainly 18th and 19th century; stands in 200 acre (80 hectare) deer park. Medieval kitchen and servants' hall. Pictures of the English, Dutch and Flemish Schools on show, and period furniture. Collection of horse-drawn carriages. ♿ (C2)

Ravenscar Geological trail in **Robin Hood's Bay** (starts from National Trust Shop and Information Centre, Raven Hall Road, Ravenscar); in two sections, 2.5 miles (4 km) of easy walking, and a further 2 miles (3.2 km) involving steep climb. Trail allows study of geological features of rugged coast, including a fault, and takes in a quarry and an old railway line. Booklet available. (E10)

Richmond Norman castle (EH) dominates the town with its 90-ft high (27.4 m) 12th-century keep, with panoramic views. ♿ *Green Howards Regimental Museum* ♿ is in a 12th-century church in the square, and a working *Georgian Theatre*, in its original form, with museum showing playbills and photographs, is in nearby Friars Wynd. (E2)

Rievaulx Abbey

Rievaulx Terrace and Temples (NT) Half-mile (.8 km) long terrace with a classical temple either end, with views of the ruined 13th-century *Rievaulx Abbey* (EH). Ionic temple contains a permanent exhibition of English landscape design in the 18th century. ♿ (G6)

Ripon Historic town with fine buildings and cathedral. *Wakeman's House Museum*, a 13th-century timbered building in market square, commemorates civic customs. *Ripon Prison and Police Museum* in St Marygate houses collection of nasty devices in former gaol. (H3)

Robin Hood's Bay Charming old smugglers' village with network of steep, narrow streets, crowded with houses. St Stephen's church outside the village has box pews. The fine bay curves away 3 miles (4.8 km) to the south. (E9)

Sewerby Hall Beautiful Georgian mansion, standing in 50 acres (20 hectares) of grounds. Fine oak staircase, small art gallery, archaeological remains, and a collection of trophies won by Amy Johnson, the aeronaut. (H12)

Silpho A 2- or 3-mile (3.2- or 4.8-km) Forestry Commission walk waymarked with arrows and starting at Reasty Bank car park, off A171. Short route is flat, easy walking, the long route slightly undulating. Moorland, forest and farmland views. Development of vegetation and afforestation is described. (F9)

Staithes Picturesque fishing village at the foot of a steep road winding down to the harbour. Cottage nearby is identified as being where Captain James Cook lived when working here as a grocer's apprentice in 1745. (C8)

Sutton Bank Beautiful long views, from top of steep escarpment, of the Hambleton Hills. Gliding. Information Centre gives details of nature trails (each 2 miles, 3.2 km) around Sutton Bank and White Horse of Kilburn (see **Kilburn** entry). The former, fairly hard walking, takes in Lake Gormire, the national park's only natural lake; the latter skirts the escarpment to the White Horse, cut in escarpment; possible sightings of birds of prey. (G5)

Swaledale Folk Museum Life as it was in Swaledale is depicted here in Reeth. Farming and lead-mining tools; Dales folk's pastimes, religion and traditions. ♿ (E1)

Thornton Dale One of the area's prettiest villages, with roadside stream, almshouses (1657), an old smithy, two 17th-century inns, and cottages fronting river. Visitors tour the village in pony carts in summer. (G8)

Thorp Perrow Arboretum, Bedale 65 acres (26 hectares) of parkland with 2,000 different species of tree, many of them very rare. Described by one expert as 'the one garden in Yorkshire of world class and importance'. Apart from trees and shrubs, a host of wild flowers and birds can be seen. Access from B6268. ♿ (G3)

Timothy Hackworth Museum, Soho Street, Shildon Exhibition in the home of Timothy Hackworth, George Stephenson's engineer, known as 'father of the railways', illustrates Hackworth's life. First steam locomotive-hauled passenger train began its journey here. There is a 'rail trail'. ♿ (C2)

Wheeldale Moor Two mile (3.2 km) south-west of Goathland is a 1-mile (1.6-km) stretch of original partly-paved and well-preserved Roman road (DoE). Access: walk several hundred yards south from Hunt House, or drive along unfenced road southwards from Egton Bridge. (E8)

Whitby Ruins of *Whitby Abbey* (EH), founded in AD 657, are visible for miles. Caedmon, first English sacred poet, was a monk here, and Captain Cook began his sailing life in Whitby. Town is a mass of narrow streets and cottages round harbour. *Pannett Park Art Gallery and Museum*, in the park between Bagdale, Chubb Hill Road and St Hilda's Terrace, has fine collections of fossils, ship models, Whitby jet and Captain Cook relics. (D9)

Witton Castle Fortified manor house rebuilt with battlements in 15th century, with 16th- to 18th-century additions. In spacious grounds, is now an entertainment and leisure centre for visitors. Swimming, venue for field events, salmon and trout fishing. (B2)

Wold Newton Obelisk between two trees in a field ¾ mile (1.2 km) south-west of the village marks where a 56 lb (25 kg) meteorite fell in December 1795. Erected four years later. (H10)

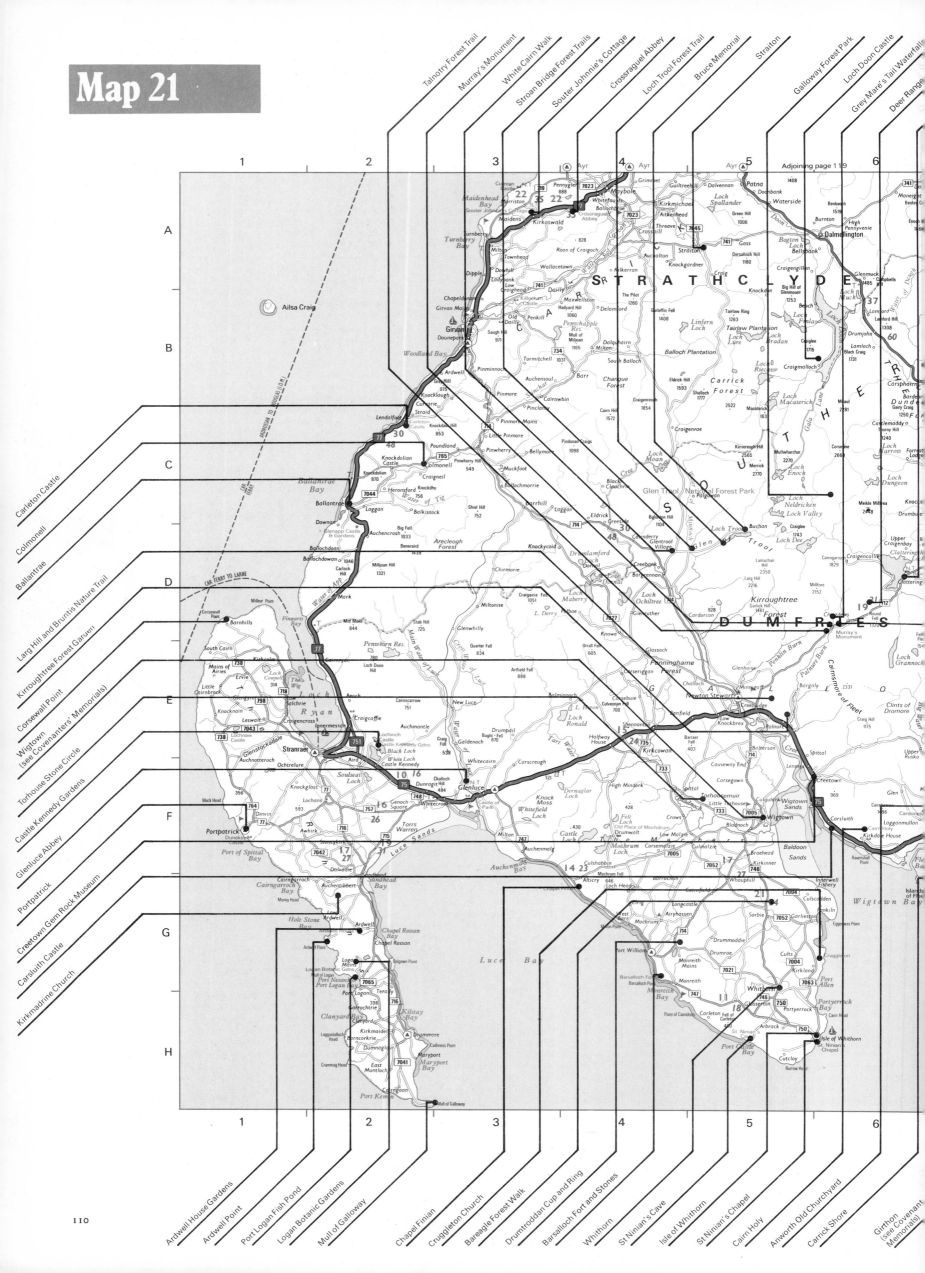

Map 21

Lowland Scotland

Ae Forest Walks From picnic site north of Ae village an easy yellow waymarked walk downstream through spruce, alder and willows (1½ miles, 2.4 km) can be combined with steeper red walk upstream which reaches Craigshiels viewpoint (1½ miles, 2.4 km) to make one continuous walk. (C10)

Anwoth Old Churchyard In beautiful setting, with impressive array of 18th- and 19th-century headstones, elaborately lettered and embellished in local red sandstone. See also **Covenanters' Memorials.** (F7)

Arbigland Gardens Woodlands, formal and water gardens, round a secluded sandy bay. Admiral John Paul Jones's father was gardener here. (F10)

Ardwell House Gardens Daffodils in spring, through rhododendrons, azaleas and roses to the autumn colouring of the trees; a garden for all seasons. (G2)

Ardwell Point Just beyond High Ardwell the unclassified road becomes a track which leads to Doon Castle, the remains of an Iron Age broch. (G2)

Auchencairn Attractive seaside village whose colour-washed houses, gay with flowers, border the steep hill descending to the edge of Auchencairn Bay. (F9)

Balcary Bay At the southern end of Auchencairn Bay, start for coastal path round Balcary Point. Views to Hestan Island which can be reached from the opposite shore at low tide by an ancient mussel-bed causeway. (G9)

Ballantrae At the mouth of the beautiful River Stinchar, its 17th-century ruined castle above trim lawns and hedges looks down on a main street of colourful houses. (C2)

Balmaclellan East of New Galloway, this attractive village on a steep street, close to a small motte-and-bailey castle, was for many years the home of stonemason Robert Paterson, the *Old Mortality* of Scott's novel. See also **Covenanters' Memorials.** (D7)

Bareagle Forest Walk, from Hazelbank, 5 miles (8 km) south Wigtown on A746. A walk through young oaks and mature larches (1 mile, 1.6 km return). (G5)

Barsalloch Fort and Stones Remains of a horseshoe shaped Iron Age fort on edge of raised beach. (G4)

Broughton House, High Street, Kirkcudbright Early 18th-century mansion, once home of artist E.A. Hornel who bequeathed it to the town. It now houses paintings, antiques and a library. (F8)

Bruce Memorial, Loch Trool Commemorates his victory over the English. Its superb viewpoint marks start of a tough waymarked walk to the summit of The Merrick, following the course of Buchan Burn. Very steep in places. 9 miles (14.5 km) return. (D5)

Caerlaverock Castle (SDD) Impressive late 13th-century two-moated castle of unusual triangular shape with two round towers and a gatehouse. Early classical renaissance work of 1634 adds particular distinction. (E11)

Caerlaverock Nature Reserve Six miles (9.6 km) of coastline particularly attractive to winter wildfowl. Easy birdwatching available at Wildfowl Refuge, East Park. (E11)

Cairn Holy (SDD) Two chambered tombs at the end of pleasant, easy stroll off A75. (F6)

Cardoness Castle

Cardoness Castle (SDD) 15th-century four-storeyed tower house retaining original stairway and elaborate fireplaces was the home of the McCullochs of Galloway. (F7)

Carleton Castle 6 miles (9.6 km) south of Girvan off A77, a tall ruined fortalice perched on a high hill. One of a link of Kennedy watchtowers, it was famed in a ballad as the seat of a baron who pushed seven wives over a cliff. (C2)

Carlingwark Loch Boats and canoes available for rowing or sailing and facilities for launching private craft, but no powered boats. (E8)

Carlyle's Birthplace, Ecclefechan (NTS) Thomas Carlyle was born here 1795. Arched house built by his father and uncle, stonemasons, in two wings. (D12)

Carrick Shore Along the eastern edge of Fleet Bay, small rocky headlands separate intimate sandy bays backed by green sward and gorse. Tiny offshore islands; seabirds and sunsets. (F6)

Carsluith Castle (SDD) A roofless 16th-century tower house, unusual because the staircase wing is an addition of 1568. (F6)

Castle Kennedy Gardens Entrance by Castle Kennedy Lodge only. Beautiful gardens containing rhododendrons, azaleas, magnolias and other shrubs, laid out on a peninsula between two lochs. (E2)

Chanlockfoot Waterfalls Adjacent to the road. (B8)

Chapel Finian (SDD) Foundations and lower walls of a small chapel or oratory, probably dating from 10th or 11th centuries, in an enclosure. Beside A747. (G4)

Colmonell A 'dog-leg' street village, now a Conservation Area, in the Stinchar valley, with three ruined castles – Kirkhill, Craigneil, and Knockdolian – below its conical hill. See also **Covenanters' Memorials.** (C2)

Corsewall Point From Barnhills ½ mile (.8 km) walk to lighthouse built by the father of Robert Louis Stevenson with views to Mull of Kintyre. (D1)

Covenanters' Memorials are almost peculiar to Galloway. In quiet kirkyards and on lonely hills neatly-lettered stones commemorate these religious martyrs who died during the 'Killing Time' between 1684 and 1688. 50 years earlier Scottish Presbyterians pledged themselves to uphold their faith and to oppose attempts of Charles I and his Parliament to enforce upon them an English-style episcopacy and a new Service Book. Later Charles II, after initially accepting both Covenants, abjured them in 1660. Episcopacy was restored, and congregations could not elect their own ministers.

Many Presbyterians started to worship at secret assemblies in remote places. In 1670, attendance at these was declared treasonable. The Covenanters rebelled, government persecution began, the struggle grew more bitter. John Graham of Claverhouse led government forces, his vigorous hunting and persecution earning him the name 'Bloody Clavers'. Eventually, the Covenanters' Wars ended with the end of the Stuarts and the 'revolution settlement' of the crown on William and Mary.

A Hawick stonemason, Robert Paterson, left his wife and children in 1758 and spent the next 40 years wandering round Galloway erecting new memorials or re-furbishing old ones to the Covenanters who lost their lives. He died in 1801 at Bankhill and is buried at Caerlaverock, but is immortalised as Scott's character *Old Mortality.*

Monuments: On Dockenkit Moor reached by short moorland walk from minor road leaving A712 2 miles (3.2 km) west of Crocketford (D9). On **Kirkconnell Moor,** accessible by 1 mile (1.6 km) walk from Kirkconnell Farm, 6 miles (9.6 km) north of Kirkcudbright on A762 (F7).

Good kirkyard tombs occur at: **Anwoth** (F7); **Balmaclellan** (D7); **Colmonell** (C2); **Crossmichael** (E8); **Dalry** (C7); **Girthon** (F7); **Kirkcudbright** (F7); **Wigtown** With beautiful lettering covering the whole of its top surface, as well as two adjoining upright stones, these commemorate Margaret Lachlan, 63, and Margaret Wilson, 18, sentenced to death by drowning, and three other martyrs (F5).

Creetown Gem Rock Museum, The Clock Tower A combined museum and walk-round workshop specialising in natural stones. (F6)

Crossraguel Abbey (SDD) Cluniac monastery of 1244 with extensive remains of church, claustral buildings, castellated gatehouse, and abbot's house with strong tower attached. (A4)

Cruggleton Church Small Norman church with 12th-century chancel-arch doors and windows. An arch near the shore is the only remains of a castle. (G6)

Deer Range Red deer can be viewed from vantage point off A712, half way between **Galloway Deer Museum** and **Wild Goat Park.** (D6)

The Doon A picnic site adjacent to B727 from where it is usually possible to watch herons from the heronry on St Mary's Isle (private) in the bay. (G7)

Drumcoltran Tower (SDD) A good example of a mid-16th-century Scottish tower house situated among farm buildings. (E9)

Drumlanrig Castle 17th-century pink sandstone castle containing beautiful paintings, silver and furniture. The surrounding parkland includes an adventure woodland play area. (B9)

Drumtroddan Cup and Ring A group of Bronze Age cup and ring markings on natural rock face. An alignment of three adjacent stones (one fallen) lies 400 yards (360 m) to the south. (G4)

Dundrennan Abbey (SDD) Cistercian foundation 1142, colonised from Rievaulx (North Yorks). Extensive, beautiful ruins, late Norman and Transitional, include parts of church, western claustral range, and rich chapter-house. (G8)

Durisdeer Church and Queensbury Aisle A charming little church of 1699 still retaining its box pews, but famous for the huge black-and-white marble monument by Van Nost in the Queensbury Aisle in memory of the Second Duke and his Duchess. (A9)

Ellesland Farm Robert Burns lived here 1788–91. A display in The Granary shows Burns as a farmer. Some of the poet's most successful works (including *Auld Lang Syne*) were written here before he moved to Dumfries. (C10)

Fleet Forest Trails 3 round walks from Information Office on road to Cally Hotel, all passing through forest nursery. Burn walk (1 mile, 1.6 km), Mote walk to a 12th-century earthwork (1½ miles, 2.4 km) and Coronation walk to an 18th-century folly (3 miles, 4.8 km). (F7)

Galloway Deer Museum Occupies converted farm steading, with features on deer, including display of antlers, and a line trout exhibit, plus other aspects of Galloway wildlife, history and geology. By Clatteringshaws Loch off A712. Hides may be booked for viewing red deer. (D6)

Galloway Forest Park Covering 240 sq miles (622 sq km) of scenic forests and hills, and extending northwards into neighbouring Strathclyde, the Park contains 16 lochs and about a dozen mountains above 2,000 ft (620 m), including Merrick, the highest point in southern Scotland. The boundaries are roughly defined by a line joining Newton Stewart (E5), Loch Ken (E7), New Galloway (D7), Dalmellington (A6) and Barr (B4). Most of the fine range, the Rhinns of Kells, also comes within the forest area. Five separate forests (Bennan, Carrick, Clatteringshaws, Glentrool and Kirroughtree) offer a wealth of walks ranging from a few hundred yards to 20 miles (32 km). With landscapes and habitats including woodland, moorland, bogs, lochs, streams and bare mountain slopes, the range of plant and bird life is very impressive. Buzzards and kestrels are abundant, while peregrines and merlins are not uncommon. This is the only area of southern Scotland where red deer live, and roe deer are very common.

Forest drives, waymarked walks, picnic places, viewpoints and fishing facilities are detailed in leaflets and guidebooks available at Forest Offices. The A712 scenic tourist route between Newton Stewart and New Galloway passes through the heart of the Forest Park.

Gatehouse-of-Fleet Rare and impressive survival of late 18th-century planned village on Murray estates, which became focus of Galloway cotton industry on banks of the Fleet. Other trades developed and declined. Original mills and housing still to be seen in this delightful small town. (F7)

Glenluce Abbey (NTS, SDD) Late 12th-century Cistercian foundation, with extensive ruins in a beautiful setting. South aisle and south transept of church; 15th-century vaulted chapter-house. (F3)

Grey Mare's Tail Waterfalls (NTS) 2 attractive waterfalls within a very short climb from Talnotry picnic site near Talnotry camp site. (D6)

Holme Cultram Abbey At Abbeytown, 12th-century nave of Cistercian monastic church survives as St Mary's Parish church, with fine 16th-century west portal. 17th- and 18th-century restorations and additions. Used also as Arts Centre, with exhibitions, music and drama recitals. (F12)

Isle of Whithorn Not an island but an attractive little harbour, now a dinghy-sailing and sea-angling centre especially for shark and tope. Good cliffs at Burrow Head (2½ miles, 4 km south-west). (H6)

Kirkmadrine Church A short, wooded walk leads from the road to a small isolated church outside which are 3 of the earliest Christian monuments in Britain, showing Chi-Rho symbols and inscriptions from 5th or early 6th centuries. (G2)

Kirroughtree Forest Garden ½ mile (.8 km) north from signpost to Kirroughtree Forest on A75 at Palnure. Waymarked walks wind among 60 different species of both broad-leaved and coniferous trees. (E5)

Larg Hill and Bruntis Nature Trail From Daltamie picnic site (signposted at Palnure on A75) a 4 mile (6.4 km) trail through mature forest with waymarked short cuts to make 1½ and 2½ mile (2.4 and 4 km) walks all leading to Bruntis Lochs. (E5)

Loch Doon Castle (SDD) 14th-century castle constructed to fit island where it was originally built. When hydro-electric scheme raised loch level, castle was dismantled and re-erected on shore. Very thick walls stand over 25 ft (7.5 m) high. (B6)

Loch Ken On the west side of the loch are plenty of places to picnic. Walk through Cairn Edward Forest or watch the sailing and wildfowl on the loch. (D7)

Loch Trool Forest Trail From Caldons camp site at west end a circular waymarked walk through old sessile oak woods, Scots pines and young forest, reaching **Bruce Memorial** (4½ miles, 7.2 km). Shorter circular walk (2½ miles, 4 km) follows Caldons Burn to Jenny's Hill, both walks giving excellent views. (D5)

Loch Whinyeon An anglers' track opposite Laghead on Gatehouse to Laurieston road leads in ½ mile (.8 km) to peaceful shore of loch. This provided water for late 18th-century mills in Gatehouse-of-Fleet 4 miles (6.4 km) away, carried by system of leats. (E7)

Lochmaben Castle Ruined 14th-century castle on promontory in a loch which is a nature reserve. Robert the Bruce is said to have been born here. (C11)

Logan Botanic Gardens, Port Logan A collection of plants from warm temperate regions of the world, flourishing in mildest part of Scotland. Many southern hemisphere species. 🔔 (G2)

Mabie Forest Trails Mabie picnic place, on site of former sawmill, is signposted at lodge 1½ miles (2.4 km) south of Islesteps on A710. From it 4 waymarked walks of 1, 2, 3, and 4 miles (1.6–6.4 km) lead through the forest to various viewpoints. The white (3 mile, 4.8 km) trail has a steep descent back to picnic site. (E10)

Maclellan's Castle, Kirkcudbright (SDD) Reputed to have been built from the stones of the Greyfriars convent after 1577, and ruined since 1752, it remains a handsome castellated mansion overlooking the harbour. 🔔 (F7)

Maxwelton House, Nr. Moniaive The 14th- and 15th-century stronghold of Earls of Glencairn, and later the birthplace of Annie Laurie. Annie Laurie's Boudoir, museum of agriculture and domestic life, tiny private chapel and gardens open. (C9)

Mote of Mark (NTS) An ancient hill fort easily accessible from picnic site at Rockcliffe and giving views to Rough Island (NTS), a 20 acre (8 hectare) bird sanctuary. (F9)

Mote of Urr A good example of a Norman motte-and-bailey fortification; close to the road. (E8)

Mull of Galloway

Mull of Galloway 300 ft (91 m) high cliffs, crowned by an 1828 lighthouse, create Scotland's dramatic southern-most point. Myriads of seabirds wheel above surge and swell of tides, or lashing waves. (H2)

Murray's Monument Built to commemorate Dr Alexander Murray, a shepherd's son who became a Professor of Oriental Languages, the monument marks a viewpoint, and an easy walk of ½ mile (.8 km) reveals his partially restored birthplace at Dunkitterick. (D6)

Orchardton Tower (SDD) A rare circular tower house built by John Cairns in 15th century. The first floor served as hall and chapel. (F9)

Port Logan Fish Pond A tidal pool in the rocks formed in 1788 as a fresh fish larder for Logan House. The fish are so tame they come to be fed by hand. (G2)

Portpatrick From 1650–1850 the main port for Ireland 21½ miles (34 km) away. Now popular, picturesque resort, cliff-sheltered on 3 sides. Sandy harbour, sea-angling and water sports. Tower of ruined church served as beacon. (F1)

Raiders' Road Scenic Drive A 10 mile (16 km) toll drive through Cairn Edward Forest between lochs Ken (off A762 just north Mossdale) and **Clatteringshaws** (southern end) with picnic places beside River Dee and Loch Stroan (from where a waymarked walk to the top of Bennan Hill reveals dramatic views). (D/E6/7)

Rammerscales, Lockerbie Off B7020 2½ miles (4 km) south Lochmaben. Georgian manor house of 1760 with good views over Annandale. Walled garden, picnic area and woodland walks. Collection of modern works of art. (D11)

Rockcliffe–Kippford Walk (NTS) 1¼ mile (2 km) walk above eastern shore of Rough Firth. Birds, views, and ancient hill-fort, and yachts in the bay. (F9)

Ruthwell Cross (SDD) 8th-century preaching cross carved with Runic characters in Ruthwell church. It stands 18 ft (5.5 m) high. Superbly-preserved details make this one of Europe's greatest Dark Age monuments. (E11)

St Ninian's Cave (SDD) From A747 take unclassified road to Kidsdale, then ¾ mile (1.2 km) footpath to coast. A cave on the seashore with early Christian crosses carved on the rock, said to have been a retreat of St Ninian. (H5)

St Ninian's Chapel, Isle of Whithorn (SDD) Ruins of simple 13th-century chapel traditionally associated with St Ninian and evidence of an enclosing wall. Earthworks of an Iron Age fort are visible on the promontory. (H6)

Souter Johnnie's Cottage, Kirkoswald (NTS) This thatched cottage, 1785, was the home of John Davidson, the village cobbler and original Souter Johnnie of *Tam O'Shanter*. Cobbler's tools and Burns relics displayed. (A3)

Straiton High on the east bank of Girvan Water, its main street of neat, colour-washed houses climbs steeply uphill past 18th-century St Cuthbert's church. Good views over Carrick's green hills. (A5)

Stroan Bridge Forest Trails From Stroan Bridge Picnic place ½ mile (.8 km) east of Glentrool village 3 walks through woodlands to viewpoints with the longest walk (3¼ miles, 5.2 km) returning by River Minnoch. (D4)

Sweetheart Abbey (SDD) Founded 1273 by Lady Dervorgilla in memory of her husband John Balliol. Beautiful ruins of red sandstone church, conspicuous tower, within 30 acre (12 hectare) precinct enclosed by remarkable wall. 🔔 (E10)

Sweetheart Abbey

Talnotry Forest Trail At times steep and arduous, this 4 mile (6.4 km) walk over rugged country with panoramic views puts forestry into perspective. Starts from car park at camp site close to **Murray's Monument**. (D6)

Threave Castle (NTS, SDD) 14th-century massive tower of the 'Black Douglases' on lonely island site on River Dee. 4 storeys high, with round towers in outer wall. ¼ mile walk (.4 km), then ring landing-stage bell for ferryman. (E8)

Threave Gardens (NTS) The gardens of the National Trust for Scotland's School of Practical Gardening contain peat, rock and water gardens as well as a fine display of daffodils in spring, and glasshouses. There is also a Visitor Centre. 🔔 (F8)

Torhouse Stone Circle (SDD) A ring of 19 boulders on a low mound. Probably Bronze Age. (F5)

White Cairn Walk From Glentrool Village a circular walk of 1½ miles (2.4 km) through woodland to White Cairn Chambered Tomb. (D4)

Whithorn Pleasant small town with 12th-century priory ruins approached through 17th-century archway called The Pend. *Whithorn Priory and Museum* (SDD), The Pend, contains many fine carved ancient stones. (H5)

Wild Goat Park An area of over 250 acres (100 hectares) in which feral goats can be seen in their natural habitat. (D5)

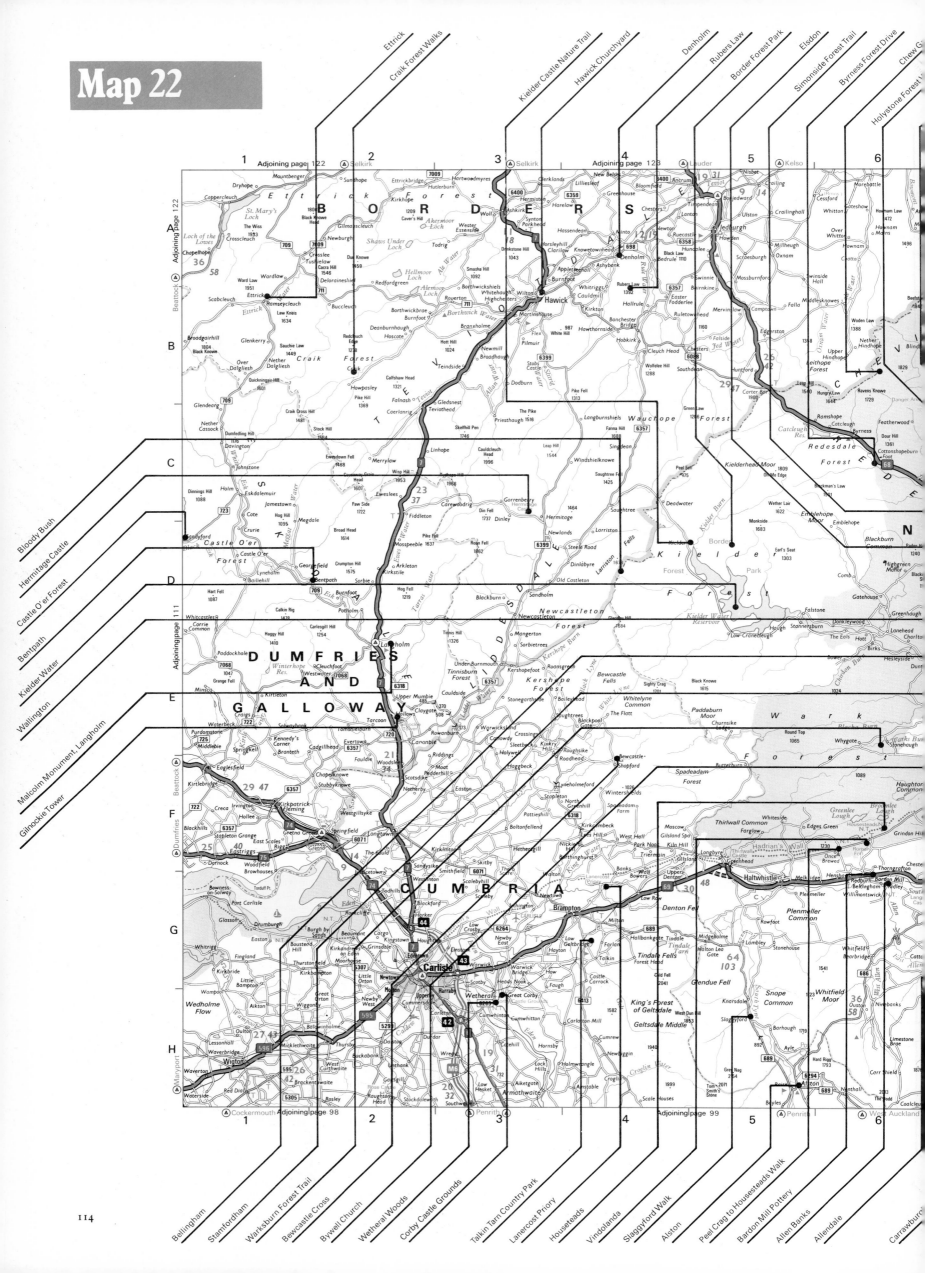

Map 22

Border Country

Allen Banks (NT) ½ mile (.8 km) south A69 3 miles (4.8 km) west Haydon Bridge. Former kitchen garden of Ridley Hall, now picnic site, is start for a wooded riverside walk along steep banks of River Allen. Strong footwear. (G6)

Allendale In valley of West Allen, former lead-mining centre with market function. Large square, inns, shops, houses all stone. Excellent, invigorating riverside and moorland walks, many along old miners' tracks. (G6)

Allensford Park A picnic area and caravan park beside the River Derwent where it flows over a rocky bed. (H9)

Alnwick Castle Early 14th-century fortress of the Percy family, Earls and then Dukes of Northumberland, with 18th- and 19th-century additions by Robert Adam and Salvin providing opulent and Victorian Gothic settings for magnificent decorations, furniture, paintings, books. Still in same family. (B10)

Alston Claims to be England's highest market town. Pleasant walks by South Tyne (Pennine Way) to Garrigill (Map 19 A9), 4 miles (6.4 km), and by River Nent (waterfalls). Moorland walks and 19th-century lead-mining remains. The *South Tynedale Railway*, a narrow-gauge railway running between Alston and Gilderdale Halt, follows the route of the former Alston to Haltwhistle branch, passing along the beautiful South Tyne valley. (H5)

Alwinton Walk 6 miles (9.6 km), part steady climb. Follow Clennell Street

domestic life in the north of England early this century. It includes a 1920s town street, a colliery and 'drift' mine, a farm, railway area and transport collection. ♿ (H10)

Bellingham Walk to Hareshaw Linn, Northumberland's best waterfall, by footpath north from centre of Bellingham which follows wooded glen to beautiful cascade among rocks. Generally easy 3 miles (4.8 km) return, but strong footwear advised. (E7)

Bentpath: Telford associations Small village in valley of the Esk surrounded by green, forest-dappled hills. Telford born nearby, attended village school. Left bequest to found local library. Roadside memorial on B709. (D2)

Bewcastle Cross 8th-century cross in most northerly churchyard in Cumbria, inscribed with Runic letters, scrollwork and carved figures, the most exquisite flowering of Northumbrian art. (F4)

Blanchland Site of 12th-century monastery in Derwent valley developed 1750 as a lead-mining village of remarkable charm. Monastic masonry survives in and near Lord Crewe Arms, gatehouse and church. Splendid scenery. (H8)

Bloody Bush Large pillar on Scottish border, 5 miles (8 km) from Lewisburn in North Tyne valley, 4 miles (6.4 km) from Dinlabyre (B6357) in Liddesdale. Footpath access from either only by forest road, formerly early 19th-century drove road. Forest views. (D4)

Bolam Country Park 2 miles (3.2 km) off A696 north of Belsay. 90 acres (36 hectares) of lake and woodland ideal for birdwatching, fishing and boating. (E9)

Border Forest Park Covers 145,000 acres (59,000 hectares) over western Cheviots and neighbouring hills. Between and beyond the few main roads only forest roads and hill-tracks link

grounds of Hall. Castle with excellently-preserved 15th-century tower-house and gatehouse (not open). (G8)

Cambo (NT) Neat stone village on Wallington estate, its medieval pele tower restored in 19th century now housing village Post Office and shop. (D8)

Carrawburgh (EH) Roman Brocolitia by site of Coventina's Well where hoard of Roman coins was found. Site of Mithraic Temple with 3 altar stones well-displayed. (F7)

Castle O'er Forest At Sandyford on B723. An attractive picnic place besides the Black Esk, with a pleasant walk to the Black Esk Reservoir. (D1)

Causey Arch At the heart of a small country park this single-span arch, built 1726 to carry the Tanfield Colliery Wagonway over a steep-sided dene, is the world's first railway bridge. Off west side A6076 just south of Public House, on unclassified road. (H10)

Chesters (EH) 5 acre (2 hectare) Roman fort which housed one of Hadrian's Wall's few cavalry garrisons. Excellent museum and good remains of Baths complex, all in parkland setting by river, with Roman bridge abutments on opposite bank. ♿ (F7)

Chew Green Remains of complex of Roman marching camps where Dere Street crosses Cheviots. Easiest access (1 mile, 1.6 km walk) from Makendon, at head of Coquet. Pennine Way passes close to camps, 4 miles (6.4 km) north of Byrness, in Redesdale. (B6)

Chillingham Wild White Cattle A Warden guides visitors to this unique herd of wild white cattle descended from herds inhabiting Northumbria in prehistoric times. Apply warden's cottage at entrance. (C12)

Craik Forest Walks 2 waymarked walks from the Borthwick Water picnic place: a 3 mile (4.8 km) winding path through forest to Wolfchleuchhead waterfall and a shorter one joining the first and last parts of long walk. (B2)

Craster Tiny fishing village and harbour. Craster kippers oak-smoked in nearby sheds. 3 acre (1.2 hectare) nature reserve and short woodland walk from main car park. (A10)

Cullernose Point Impressive headland of columnar Whin Sill rock forming a focal point on coastal path south of Craster. (A10)

Denholm Attractive village in Teviot valley associated with stocking-weaving industry. Varied 18th- and 19th-century houses round large English-style green with ornate memorial to poet and oriental scholar, John Leyden. Westgate Hall unusual 17th-century house (not open). (A4)

Derwent Valley Walk A 10-mile (16 km) walkway along former track of Derwent Valley Railway, following the east bank of the river, through wooded and partly industrialised river valley. Many attractive sections easily reached from convenient access points: Ebchester (G9); Rowlands Gill (G10); Shotley Bridge (H9); Swalwell Station (G10), south side Scotswood Bridge; Thornley Wood (G10), 2 miles (3.2 km) south-west Blaydon on A694.

Druridge Bay (NT) A mile (1.6 km) of sands and dunes accessible from unclassified road from Widdrington (on A1068). Shore birds. (D10)

Dunstanburgh Castle (NT, EH) 14th-century gatehouse, curtain walls and towers on a headland above the sea. Accessible only by a mile (1.6 km) walk by the shore from Craster or Embleton. (A10)

Elsdon Attractive stone-built village around a large green with 14th-century church, pele tower, pinfold; formerly the capital of Redesdale, on old drovers' and salters' roads. Impressive early 12th-century motte-and-bailey fort at north end. (D7)

Embleton Dunes (NT) Extensive dunes with fine walking by side of golf-course. Views to **Dunstanburgh Castle**. Shore birds. (A10)

Ettrick Small, lonely village by Ettrick water, below high green hills afforested to south. James Hogg, Ettrick shepherd-poet, and Tibbie Shiel (Elizabeth Richardson), buried in churchyard mile (1.6 km) west of village. Pleasant river scenery. (B1)

Farne Islands (NT) About 30 islands covering 80 acres (32 hectares). Only Inner Farne and Staple Island are accessible, by boat from Seahouses. Breeding-place for 20 species of sea-

Guillemots, kittiwakes and shags on a stack off Inner Farne

Bamburgh Castle

(ancient border track) from north end village to Wholehope. Turn right through forest to Kidlandlee, then south-east into steep-sided Alwin valley. Follow riverside track back to Alwinton. (B7)

Bamburgh Castle Crowning a rocky outcrop above sandy bay, largely Victorian rebuilding but retaining massive Norman keep. Rich in historical associations, a visual crescendo on a superbly scenic coast. (D12)

Bardon Mill Pottery In Bardon Mill (A69). Coal has replaced water but the old wheel may still be seen at the woollen mill turned pottery where traditional methods are still used. (G6)

Beamish, North of England Open-Air Museum England's first open-air museum. Unique displays in 200 acres (80 hectares) of parkland vividly illustrating social, agricultural, industrial and

valleys. Many roadside picnic places, miles of forest walks, many waymarked. Extends to Kershope, Newcastleton, and Wauchope Forests north of border. Northumbrian ones are Kielder, Mounces, Falstone, Wark and Redesdale. (B-F3-6)

Brinkburn Priory (EH) Only the church survives from 12th-century Augustinian priory. Re-roofed and sensitively restored 1858. Cool, calm, Early English purity (1190–1220) in beautiful riverside setting. ½ mile (.8 km) wooded walk from car park. (C9)

Byrness Forest Drive From Blakehopeburnhaugh picnic site on A68 a 12 mile (19 km) drive on forest road, with picnic sites and waymarked walks. Toll. (C6)

Bywell St Andrew's Church has finest Saxon tower in county. St Peter's nearby, good 13th-century church. Most attractive of Tyne villages by landscaped

Corby Castle Grounds Off A69. A woodland walk including rhododendrons. Walks lead to a summerhouse, caves and salmon coops. (H3)

Corstopitum Site of Agricola's first fort guarding Dere Street's crossing of the Tyne and the east-west Stanegate. Supply-base for advance to Scotland, remains include granaries, storehouses, military compounds, houses, shops, and a strong-room. (G8)

Cragside, Rothbury (NT) 900 acre (364 hectare) wooded grounds with lakes, drives, walks and rhododendrons comprise a Country Park with miles of way-marked trails. The house, built by Norman Shaw between 1864 and 1895 for industrialist and inventor Sir William Armstrong, contains original furnishings, some specially designed by Shaw, the rest an intriguing mixture of 18th-century Revival and the Arts and Crafts Movement. ♿ (C9)

birds together with grey seals. Inner Farne has a 14th-century chapel and a pele tower. Saints Aidan and Cuthbert lived here in 7th century. (D12)

Gibside Chapel (NT) Off B6314. Palladian-style chapel by James Paine, 1760, not completed until 1812. Fine tooled masonry outside, superb woodwork and delicate plasterwork within. Faces along avenue of trees to Column of British Liberty. (G10)

Gilnockie Tower, Hollows A 16th-century tower house, once home of Johnny Armstrong, the 16th-century Border freebooter. (E2)

Harbottle Crags From Forestry Commission car park $\frac{1}{2}$ mile (.8 km) north-west of Harbottle village a well-defined path leads through Northumberland Wildlife's Reserve to the Drake Stone, giving excellent views. (C7)

Hawick Churchyard Social history encapsulated. Splendid headstones, with embellishments and epitaphs, illustrative of about 30 different trades carried on in Hawick during 18th and 19th centuries. St Mary's Church, 1763 rebuilding of an older structure, is at heart of Hawick's Anglo-Saxon settlement. (B3)

Hepburn Woods Walks From picnic site above Hepburn green waymarked walk (1 hour) through woodland with optional scramble to crags (orange, $1\frac{1}{2}$ hours) with extension to **Ross Castle** (plus $\frac{1}{2}$ hour). Strong shoes and legs, especially for scramble. (A9)

Hermitage Castle (SDD) Vast, lonely ruin, a Douglas stronghold, 14th and 15th century, restored 19th century. Full of stirring, dour and cruel memories. Here, Queen Mary visited her wounded lover, Bothwell, 1566. ♿ (C3)

Holystone Forest Walks From picnic site $\frac{1}{2}$ mile (.8 km) west of village 3 waymarked walks. Green ($\frac{1}{2}$ hour) through Christmas trees and across a field to Lady's Well (NT). Orange (1 hour) beside coppiced oaks and beech trees with red squirrels. Red ($2\frac{1}{2}$ hours) an extension of Orange to Dove Crag. Strong footwear. (C8)

Housesteads (NT, EH) Best-known, most dramatically-placed of all Roman Wall forts. Impressive remains and layout with civil settlement adjacent. Good museum. $\frac{1}{2}$ mile (.8 km) walk from car park. Site museum. (F6)

Howick Gardens Off B1339. Attractive flower gardens with shrubs and rhododendrons a mile (1.6 km) from the sea. (A10)

Kielder Castle Nature Trail Superb exhibition illustrating growth and use of timber, in Kielder Castle, from where a nature trail of $1\frac{1}{2}$ or $2\frac{1}{2}$ hours follows the Duchess's Drive through woodland by burn, with many viewpoints. ♿ (D4)

Kielder Water Britain's largest man-made lake in Europe's largest man-made forest. Reservoir and surrounds developed for recreation – water-sports, fishing, sailing, nature trails, nature reserves, picnic areas and viewing points along C200 (new road replacing inundated valley road) south of lake. Main information and Visitor Centre at Tower Knowe contains regularly updated models and displays. Large car park. (D5)

Lanercost Priory (EH) Augustinian foundation 1144. Remains of choir, transepts and some claustral buildings, together with gatehouse. Nave of priory church now parish church. (G4)

Lindisfarne Castle (NT) Built about 1550 as a coastal and Border fortress. Transformed 1903 by Sir Edwin Lutyens into a comfortable home for Edward Hudson, with rooms and passages hewn out of the native rock in the lower part of the building. Upstairs a timbered and brick-floored long gallery links a series of bedrooms with beamed ceilings. Good collection of oak furniture. Care needed in access to Holy Island via causeway from mainland, flooded at high tide. (B12)

The kitchen, Lindisfarne Castle

Lindisfarne Priory (EH) Hauntingly beautiful red sandstone ruins of 11th-century priory on site of former priory, the cradle of English Christianity in the north, established by St Aidan, 7th century. Site museum. ♿ Also on Holy Island; see **Lindisfarne Castle.** (B12)

Malcolm Monument, Langholm From riverside car park walk into town, turn by Eskdale Hotel towards golf course. Cross stile behind seat (at end of untarred road) and climb path to monument keeping left of pylon. Enjoy extensive views and retrace steps. (E2)

Marsden Rocks Cliff path near the road gives splendid view of limestone stacks and cliffs housing biggest mainland colony of seabirds, especially kittiwakes, on Northumbrian coast. (G12)

National Park Visitor Centre, Ingram has information and suggestions for enjoyment of the Northumberland Park. Picnic places beside River Breamish, and splendid centre for walking in Cheviots. (A8)

National Tractor and Farm Museum, Hunday Signposted 'Farm Museum' on A69. Shows evolution of farm machinery over last century. 150 tractors and engines displayed; working models; farm and domestic hand tools. Scenic surroundings. Won Museum of Year Award, 1981. ♿ (F8)

Northumberland National Park Nearly 400 sq miles (1,036 sq km) of upland country extending from Hadrian's Wall to the Scottish border by Kirk Yetholm beyond the rounded, green Cheviot Hills. Rocky outcrops and heather moors give the Simonside Hills (C8) their particular character. Old border tracks follow fine river valleys through lonely hills; castles and pele towers speak of a troubled past. Afforestation clothes many hillsides, but sheep outnumber people, and much of the area is still a land of space, solitude and far horizons. (A-F6-8)

Peel Crag to Housesteads Walk Best 3 miles (4.8 km) walk on Hadrian's Wall. Car parks at each end. Includes mile-castles, crags, panoramic views, and Crag Lough's grandeur. Involves some short, steep scrambles. (F6)

Plessey Woods Country Park On A1068. Woodland area beside River Blyth with woodland walks, bridleways, bathing and picnic areas. Visitor Centre. ♿ (E10)

Pow Hill Country Park Off B6306. On south side of Derwent Reservoir, amid undulating moorland, with car parks in a sheltered valley by a stream, or views over reservoir to the dinghy sailing. Bird-watchers' hide available. (H8)

Ross Castle (NT) Hilltop overlooking **Chillingham** Park and Vale of Till with very extensive views. Short steep climb to summit which contains part of an Iron Age fort. (A9)

Rothbury Terraces Series of parallel tracks across the heather and bracken of sandstone fell immediately north of Rothbury Fine views over Coquet valley. Various access points, including narrow passage from Market Street opposite village cross. (C9)

Rubers Law Magnificent views from rocky summit (1,392 ft, 424 m) with Iron Age fort. Old quarries, heather, wild flowers. Access from **Denholm** via Denholmhill Farm. $2\frac{1}{2}$ miles (4 km) to top. (A/B4)

Ryhope Engines Museum By hospitals. 1868 Pumping Station worked continuously until 1967. Now restored to running order, with two huge beam engines all green paint, gleaming brass and steel. Victorian technology in a neat landscape. ♿ (H12)

Simonside Forest Trail Go off the B6342 towards Lordenshaw. Forestry Commission car park in 2 miles (3.2 km). Green trail ($\frac{1}{2}$ hour) visits some plantations; Orange and Red trails ($2\frac{1}{2}$ hours) separate after Little Church Rock, Orange to Raven Heugh Crags, and Red to Simonside summit. Strong footwear. (C8)

Slaggyford Walk Walk south along road to bridge at Williamston, then road on east side river to bend. Leave road for footbridge, through parkland at Barhough, rejoining road. Right at Low Row, descend to river, cross footbridge and railway track to pick up Pennine Way northwards to Slaggyford. 5 miles (8 km), fairly easy. (H5)

Stamfordham 18th-century planned village round enormous green, with 'market cross', lock-up, and neat stone houses. Good 13th-century church, vicarage, and pub with outside stairway. (F9)

Stephenson's Cottage, Wylam-on-Tyne (NT) Built 1750 close to the old Wylam wagonway, now a riverside walk, the cottage was the birthplace in June 1781 of George Stephenson. ♿ (F9)

Talkin Tarn Country Park To east of B6413 south of Brampton. Set in woods and pastureland the tarn is the focal point for quiet watersport and fishing; bridleways around for walking and riding. (G4)

Thrunton Wood Nature Trail From Forestry Commission car park $\frac{1}{2}$ mile (.8 km) west of Thrunton off A697 waymarked walks through mixed woodlands, with deer, to crags and caves. Good views. Strong shoes. (B9)

Tynemouth Castle and Priory (EH) Impressively situated on a promontory north of the river, 12th- and 13th-century ruins of a Benedictine priory are surrounded by curtain-walls, towers and gatehouse-keep of 14th-century castle. ♿ (F12)

Vindolanda (EH) Extensive 4th-century Roman fort with adjoining civilian settlement, the only one along Hadrian's Wall being excavated. Full-size rebuilt section of Roman Wall and turret. Good museum, and impressive Roman milestone *in situ* on Stanegate nearby. ♿ (F6)

Wallington (NT) 1688 house extensively altered 1740s. Fine plasterwork, porcelain, pictures, furniture. Mid-19th-century hall uniquely decorated by William Bell Scott and Ruskin. Walled garden with conservatory. Woods always open. ♿ (E8)

Wansbeck Riverside Park Off A1068. Beside River Wansbeck, 143 acres (58 hectares) of grass and woodland provide picnic sites, woodland walks, boating, sailing and a camping area. (D10)

Warksburn Forest Trail A short forest trail from picnic place opposite Stonehaugh Forestry village. Also waymarked walks: blue $2\frac{1}{2}$ miles (4 km) Crookbank from footbridge; red $2\frac{1}{2}$ miles (4 km) Willowbog from totem poles which extends by $1\frac{3}{4}$ miles (3 km) (green arrows) to Ladyhill. Strong footwear. (E6)

Warkworth Castle (EH) 15th-century keep dominates extensive earlier remains, above attractive village in loop of River Coquet. 14th-century Hermitage in sandstone rock accessible by boat from castle. (B10)

Washington Old Hall (NT) In Washington village. Follow 'District 4'. Built 1613, but incorporating remains of medieval manor house. From 1183–1613 home of Washington family and lineal descendants. Jacobean furniture. Many American items and gifts. ♿ (G11)

Waskerley Way Footpath, bridleway and cycletrack along the former Stanhope and Tyne railway from Consett to Waskerley and over moors towards Stanhope (Map 19 A12). Moorland walking, panoramic views. Access points at Waskerley (H8) and Rowley Station (H9), on A68 south of Castleside.

Wetheral Woods (NT) Woodland walks beside River Eden just south of Wetheral near Priory remains. (H3)

Whittingham Two-part village separated by River Aln. Church has Saxon tower; attractive stone houses include 19th-century court house, and medieval pele tower opposite. Small green, large trees, and Cheviots to the west. (B9)

The Wildfowl Trust: Washington Waterfowl Park Over 1,200 birds representing over 105 different species from every continent. Visitor Centre including bookshop, lecture/observation room, feeding points. Woodland and wetland hides for observing woods, reed-beds and large pools. Off A1231 and A195. ♿ (G11)

Woodhorn Church Restored Saxon church displaying relics of early Christianity, including carved stones and medieval bells. Changing monthly programme of exhibitions. Regular craft demonstrations and local craft centre. On A197. (D11)

World Bird Research Station, Glanton Houses all kinds of birds from hawks to doves, waterfowl to game birds, providing first aid and sanctuary. Native tree arboretum. (B9)

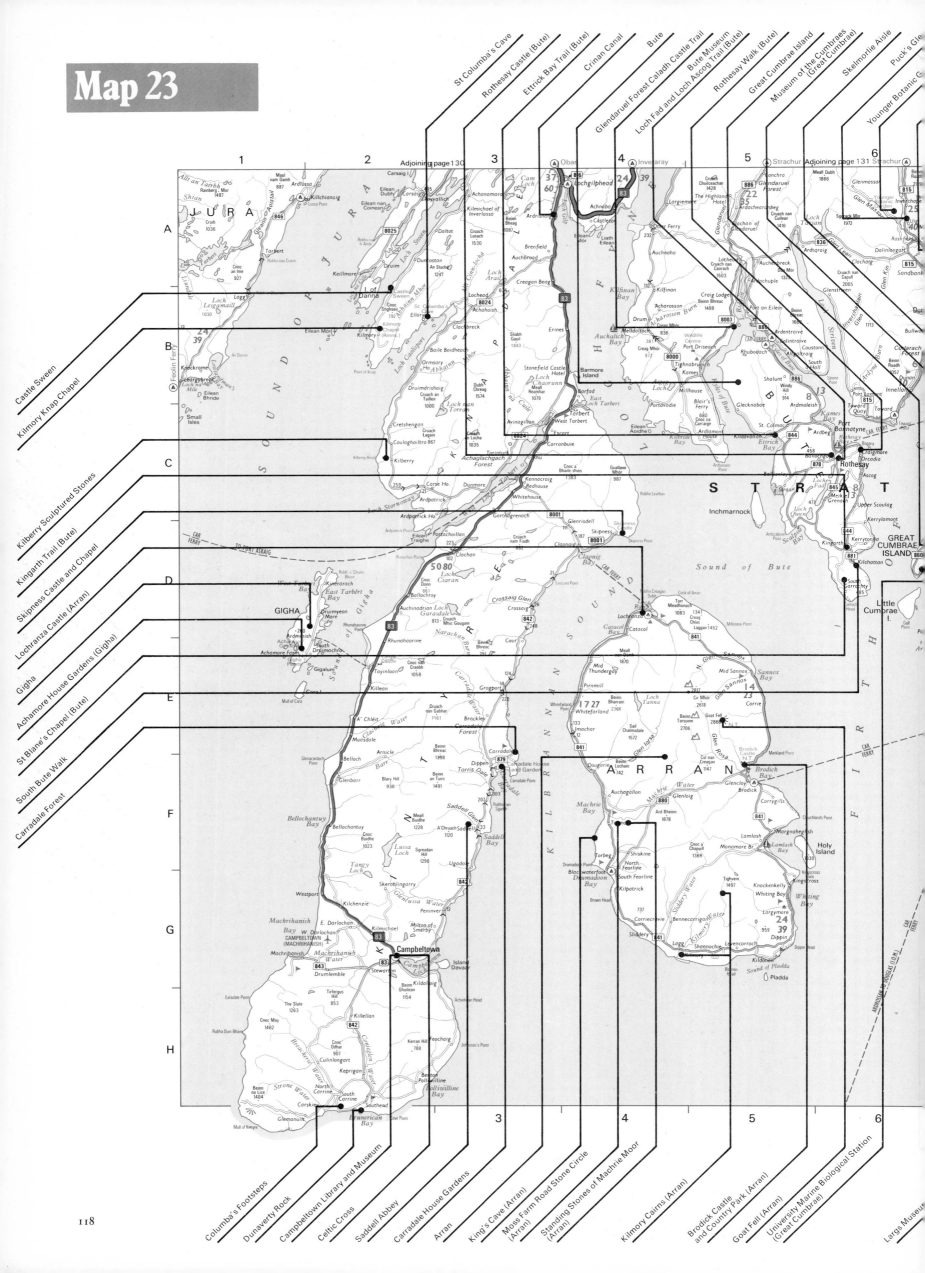

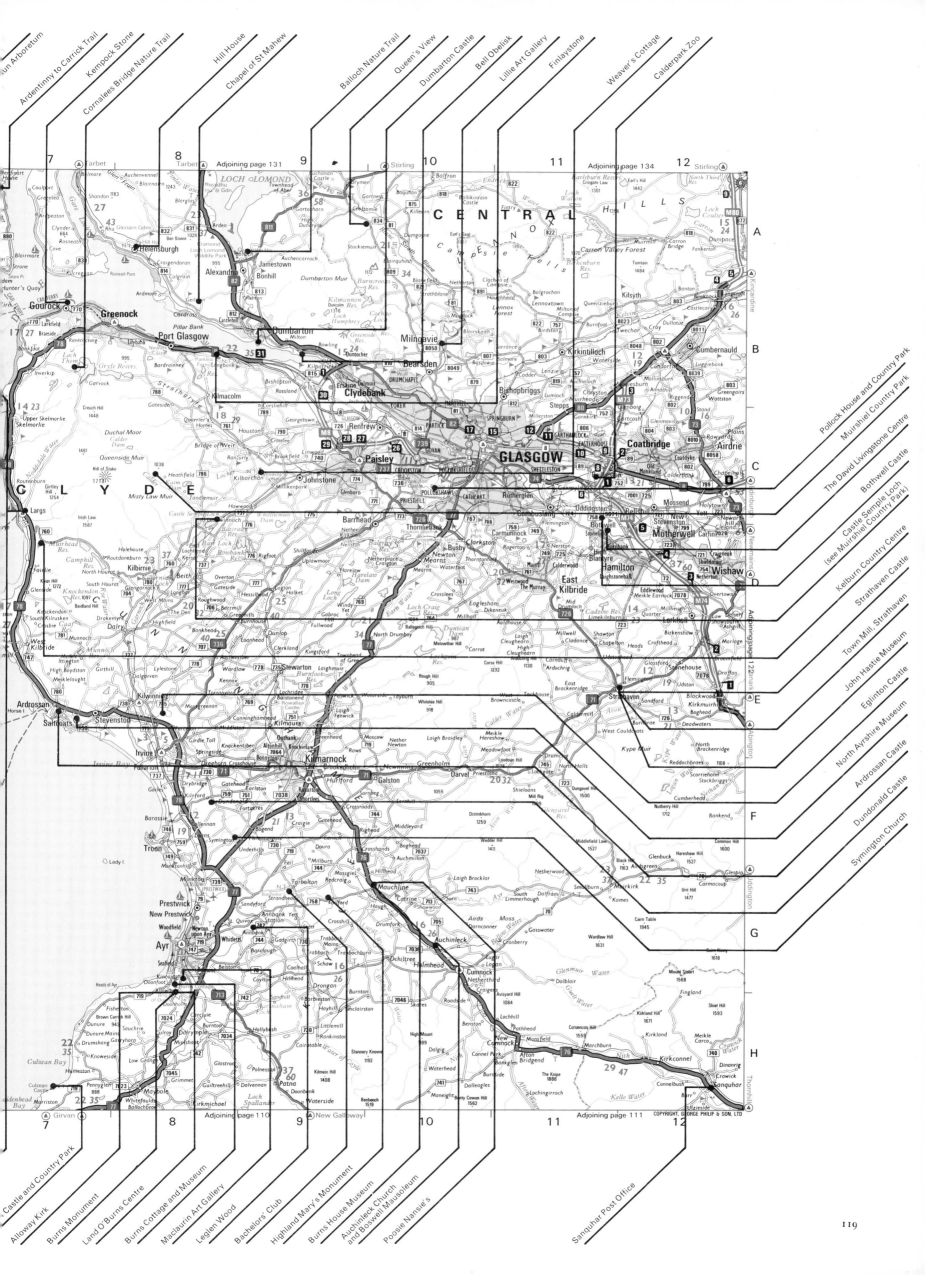

Gazetteer 23

Lowland Scotland

Alloway Kirk William Burnes, father of poet Robert Burns, is buried in this ancient church, now a ruin. (G8)

Ardentinny to Carrick Trail Waymarked woodland walk across rugged terrain. 5 miles (8 km), 3 hours plus return. Tough footwear advisable. Starts ½ mile (0.8 km) north-west Ardentinny village on A880 then further ½ mile (0.8 km) on forest road signposted to beach. (A7 to Map 25 H9)

Ardrossan Castle Ruins of 12th-century castle destroyed by Cromwell. Splendid views of **Arran** and Ailsa Craig. (E7)

Auchinleck Church and Boswell Mausoleum Originally a Celtic cell, church was enlarged in the 12th and 17th centuries. Boswell Mausoleum, attached, is the burial place of James Boswell, Dr Johnson's famous biographer. (G10)

Bachelors' Club, Tarbolton (NTS) The 17th-century house where Robert Burns attended dancing lessons, founded the Bachelors' Club (a debating society) and was later initiated as a Freemason. Period furnishings and memorabilia. (G9)

Balloch Nature Trail, Loch Lomond Park Woodland and grassland by loch and river shore. 1½ miles (2.4 km), 1–2 hours to complete. Picnic areas, car park, guide book. Starts in Balloch at Main gate to Loch Lomond Park. (A8)

Bell Obelisk Commemorates Henry Bell who launched the first Clyde passenger steamer, the *Comet*. At Douglas Point off A82 west of Bowling. (B9)

Bothwell Castle, Uddingston (SDD) In a lovely setting overlooking the Clyde Valley, Bothwell, dating from the 13th century and now ruined, was once the largest stone castle in Scotland. (C11)

Burns Cottage and Museum, Alloway Birthplace of Robert Burns in 1759 and his home until 1766. Museum of Burnsiana adjoins cottage. ♿ (G8)

Burns House Museum, Castle Street, Mauchline 18th-century furnishings in the room which Burns took for Jean Armour in 1788; also other folk objects and Burnsiana, an exhibition of Mauchline boxware and a curling rink. Four of Burns' daughters and friends and contemporaries are buried in nearby Mauchline Kirkyard. (G10)

Burns Monument, Alloway A Grecian-style monument erected in 1823. Nearby is the single arch *Brig o' Doon* (possibly 13th century) made famous by Burns' poem *Tam o'Shanter*. (H8)

Calderpark Zoo, Uddingston A select collection on 45 acres (18 hectares) specialising in cats and reptiles. Also polar bears, rhinos, camels, monkeys, elephants. Picnic sites, children's shows. (C11)

Campbeltown Library and Museum, Hall Street Collections illustrate the natural history, archaeology and geology of Kintyre. ♿ (G2)

Carradale Forest Shore walk through varied forest with extensive views of Arran; 6½ miles (10.4 km), 3½ hours. Picnic places. Sally's Walk through secluded ornamental trees and shrubs; 1 mile (1.6 km), ¾ hour. Both walks start at the Forestry Commission Information Centre at the road junction in Carradale Village. Car park, guide books. (E3)

Carradale House Gardens A delightful walled garden dating from about 1870 containing flowering shrubs, rhododendrons, azaleas. A wild garden has winding paths and an iris pond. Entrance off B842. ♿ (F3)

Castle Sween (SDD) Built in the mid 12th century, this could well be the oldest stone castle on the Scottish mainland. It was destroyed in 1647 by Sir Alexander Macdonald and is now a stark and lonely ruin. On east shore Loch Sween, 15 miles (24 km) south-west Lochgilphead. (B2)

Celtic Cross, Main Street, Campbeltown A cross of uncertain date, possibly *c.* 1500, showing elaborate ornamentation and an inscription in Lombardic letters. (G2)

Chapel of St Mahew The first church was dedicated by St Mahew (*c.* 535), a prophet and disciple of St Patrick, but the present building dates from 1467 and was restored in 1955. ¼ mile (0.4 km) north Cardross. (B8)

Columba's Footsteps The footsteps of St Columba, who is said to have first set foot on Scottish soil near Southend, are imprinted for all to see in a rock near a ruined chapel at Keil, west of Southend. (H2)

Cornalees Bridge Nature Trail Through wooded glen, a site of scientific importance, then out onto open moorland; 1½ miles (2.4 km), 1 hour. Information Centre, car park. Starts 3 miles (4.8 km) above Inverkip on moorland road to Greenock. (B7)

Crinan Canal Running from Ardrishaig to Crinan (Map 25 H5), the canal was constructed at the end of the 18th century to carry ships from Loch Fyne to the Atlantic without rounding Kintyre. Now mainly used for pleasure craft, the canal is 9 miles (14.4 km) long and has 15 locks. (A3)

Culzean Castle and Country Park (NTS) Dating from 1777, Culzean is one of Robert Adam's masterpieces. It has fine plaster ceilings, a magnificent oval staircase and the splendid Round Drawing Room. The Eisenhower Presentation explains the General's association with Culzean. *Culzean Country Park* was the first country park in Scotland, opened in 1970, and includes woodlands, cliff and sea shore. There is a Reception and Interpretation Centre, walled garden, swan pond and camellia house. Guided walks, talks and films in summer. Off A719. ♿ (H7)

The David Livingstone Centre, Blantyre Relics of the Industrial Revolution and of African exploration housed in the 18th-century mill tenement where David Livingstone, the famous missionary/explorer, was born. He also went to school here and worked here while studying medicine. Modern Africa is illustrated in the Africa Pavilion in parkland surrounding the tenements and agriculture, cotton spinning, mining in and around Blantyre are illustrated in a new social history museum. ♿ (D11)

Culzean Castle

Dumbarton Castle (SDD) A dungeon, 12th-century gateway and a sundial, a gift from Mary, Queen of Scots, are preserved in these modern barracks. On Dumbarton Rock, off A814. (B9)

Dunaverty Rock, Southend Known locally as 'Blood Rock' as 300 people were put to death by Covenanters under General Leslie when this was the site of Dunaverty Castle, a Macdonald stronghold in 1647. Dominating the beach and golf course. (H2)

Dundonald Castle (SDD) King Robert II, first Stuart king, died here in 1390. Most of the tower and much of the barmkin wall survive. Seen from outside only. (F8)

Eglinton Castle Ruins of a castle built in 1796 with central tower 100 ft (30.4 m) high. Gardens also open. 2 miles (3.2 km) north Irvine. ♿ (E8)

Finlaystone Victorian relics and an international collection of dolls in the historic house on this family estate. Formal gardens, and garden centre. Estate includes *Finlaystone Woodland Walks*, five walks through 60 acres (24 hectares) of mixed woodland with burn and four waterfalls. Jogging trail. Information Centre, car park. Off A8, west Langbank. (B8)

Glendaruel Forest Caladh Castle Trail Commences at 700 ft (213 m) and drops to sea level. Woodland and shore, views of Kyles of Bute. 1½ miles (2.4 km), 2 hours. Car park, guide book. By A8003 (Glendaruel–Tighnabruaich road) high above Kyles of Bute. (A5)

Highland Mary's Monument, Failford Commemorates the place where, it is said, Robert Burns parted from his 'Highland Mary', Mary Campbell. They exchanged vows, but she died shortly afterwards. (G9)

Hill House, Upper Colquhoun Street, Helensburgh (NTS) Designed and built by Charles Rennie Mackintosh in 1902–4, it contains Mackintosh furniture and other items. (A8)

John Hastie Museum, Strathaven Museum of local history set in Strathaven Park. ♿ (E12)

Kelburn Country Centre, Fairlie Gardens, nature trails, pony trekking, exhibitions and craft shop in converted 18th-century farm buildings. (D7)

Kempock Stone Granny Kempock's, of grey schist, 6 ft (1.8 m) high, was probably of major importance in prehistoric times. It was used by fishermen to ensure fair weather and couples used to encircle the stone to get Granny's blessing on their marriage. Sited on cliff side of Gourock. (B7)

Kilberry Sculptured Stones (SDD) A collection of late medieval sculptured stones. Off B8024, 20 miles (32 km) south-west Lochgilphead. ♿ (C2)

Kilmory Knap Chapel (SDD) A typical small West Highland church with notable sculptured stones. Sited off road along east side of Loch Sween. (B2)

Kilmun Arboretum An unusual and interesting collection of tree species within the **Argyll Forest Park** (see Gazetteer 25). Located by the Forest Office on A880, 1 mile (1.6 km) east junction with A815. (A6)

Land o'Burns Centre, Alloway Visitor centre with landscaped gardens, exhibitions area and audio-visual display on the life and times of Robert Burns. ♿ (G8)

Largs Museum, Manse Court Photographs, local history books and a collection of local items of interest. Mostly Victoriana; also Viking exhibits. ♿ (C7)

Leglen Wood An inscription on a cairn marks the spot frequently visited by Burns in pretty wood overlooking the River Ayr. The wood has associations with Burns' hero, William Wallace. 2 miles (3.2 km) south A758, entrance near Auchinauive House. (G9)

Lillie Art Gallery, Milngavie Modern gallery housing a permanent collection of 20th-century Scottish paintings, sculpture and ceramics and temporary exhibitions of contemporary art. ♿ (B10)

Maclaurin Art Gallery and Rozelle House Museum Fine art, photography, local history displayed in converted stables and servants' quarters belonging to Roselle House. The parkland surrounding the gallery contains a nature trail. 1½ miles (2.4 km) south Ayr. ♿ (G7)

Muirshiel Country Park Walks, picnic sites, information centre in lovely country setting. A 200 acre (81 hectare) water park can be found at Castle Semple loch, 3 miles (4.8 km) south-east. Muirshiel is 9 miles (14.4 km) south-west Paisley. (C8)

North Ayrshire Museum, Saltcoats Interesting old gravestones are among the exhibits of local items in this museum located in a mid-18th-century parish church. (E7)

Pollock House and Country Park, Glasgow A 361 acre (144 hectare) country park, 3½ miles (5.6 km) from city centre at Pollockshaws. Large collection of flowering trees and shrubs, rose garden, nature trails and Highland Cattle. Pollock House, built 1747–52, contains the famous Stirling Maxwell collection of Spanish paintings, European furniture and other decorative arts. Also in the grounds is the Burrell Collection formed by Sir William and Lady Burrell and opened in 1983. Wide-ranging collection includes Chinese ceramics, bronzes and jades, Near Eastern rugs, Turkish pottery and artefacts from the ancient civilizations of Greece, Italy, Iraq and Egypt. It also has one of the most important museum collections of stained glass and tapestries in the world. Paintings range from the 15th to early 20th century and include works by Memling, Bellini, Cranach, Rembrandt, Courbet, Millet, Boudin, Degas, Manet and Cézanne. ♿ (C10)

Poosie Nansie's, Mauchline A pub, still very much in use, which was an alehouse in Burns' era and is said to have inspired his cantata *The Jolly Beggars*. (G10)

Puck's Glen, Benmore Forest Waymarked woodland walks over rugged hillside terrain. Tough footwear and suitable clothing are recommended. Al-

ternative routes taking from 1¼–2¾ hours. Car park. Located by A815, 6 miles (9.6 km) north Dunoon. Access can be made from **Kilmun Arboretum** by leaving via the **Younger Botanic Garden** back gates car park. (A6)

Queen's View, Loch Lomond So named because this was where Queen Victoria had her first view of Loch Lomond in 1879. A path on the west side of A809 12 miles (19.2 km) north-west Glasgow leads to viewpoint. (A9)

Saddell Abbey Sculptured tombstones and the walls still remain of this ancient abbey built in the 12th century by Somerled, Lord of the Isles, or his son Reginald. (F3)

St Columba's Cave In this cave can be found carved crosses above an altar and a large basin which may have been used as a font. The cave was occupied from the Middle Stone Age and is associated, according to tradition, with St Columba's arrival in Scotland. 1 mile (1.6 km) north Ellary. (B2)

Sanquhar Post Office Still in full use, this post office was functioning in 1763, a year before the introduction of the mail coach service. Considered to be Britain's oldest post office. (H12)

Skelmorlie Aisle, Bellman's Close, Largs (SDD) Interesting tombs and monuments and painted roof in splendid mausoleum dating from 1636. ♿ (C7)

Skipness Castle and Chapel (SDD) Remains of enormous 13th-century castle and ancient chapel overlooking bay. Not open; exterior view only. (D4)

Strathaven Castle Ruin of a 15th-century castle sometimes known as Avondale Castle. At junction of Kirk Street and Stonehouse Road. (E12)

Symington Church A beautifully restored church with an ancient roof of open timber and three round-headed Norman windows, dating from the 12th century. (F8)

Town Mill, Strathaven An arts centre situated in a beautifully restored grain mill. (E12)

Weaver's Cottage, Kilbarchan (NTS) Preserved as a typical weaver's home of the 18th century to reflect the era when Kilbarchan was a thriving centre of handloom weaving. Displays looms, weaving equipment and domestic utensils. (C9)

Younger Botanic Garden A splendid avenue of Wellingtonias is a feature of these extensive woodland gardens. Also many shrubs including rhododendrons and azaleas. Access from A815. ♿ (A6)

Arran, Isle of

Often described as 'Scotland in miniature', Arran is filled with mountains and hills, glens and lochs and its coast is indented with delightful rocky coves and sandy beaches. To the north, high granite ridges are dominated by **Goat Fell** and its surrounding area is extremely popular with walkers. To the south the countryside is more gentle, the landscapes pastoral and the shore sandy. Car ferries serve the island from Ardrossan (E7) on the Strathclyde coast (crossing 55 minutes) and Claonaig (D3) on the Kintyre peninsula (crossing 30 minutes).

Brodick Castle and Country Park (NTS) Silver, paintings, porcelain, sporting pictures and trophies housed in castle dating from 13th century and ex-

tended in 1652 and 1844. The country park includes the gardens and grounds of the castle. The woodland garden is one of Britain's finest rhododendron gardens and there is also a walled formal garden. *Brodick Woodland Walk* starts in the grounds of Brodick Castle; 1 mile (1.6 km), ¾ hour to complete. Car park, adventure playground. (F5)

Goat Fell (NTS) The highest peak on Arran (2,866 ft, 874 m) with walking and climbing in Glen Rosa and on Cir Mhor. Hawks and harriers may be seen and possibly the golden eagle. 3½ miles (5.6 km) north-west Brodick. (E5)

Kilmory Cairns Cairn Baan, 3½ miles (5.6 km) north-east Kilmory village, is a notable Neolithic long cairn. The Torrylin Cairn, a Neolithic chambered cairn, is ½ mile (0.8 km) south-west of A841 at the Lagg Hotel. There are many other cairns in the area. (G4)

King's Cave The largest of a series of caves which legend says was occupied by Finn MacCoul and later Robert the Bruce. A possible setting for the famous 'Bruce and the spider' story. Carvings of figures can be seen on the walls. Located on shore, 2 miles (3.2 km) north of Blackwaterfoot golf course. (F4)

Lochranza Castle (SDD) Robert the Bruce is said to have landed here in 1307 on his return from Ireland at the start of his campaign for Scottish independence. The castle, now ruined, was erected in the 13th/14th centuries and enlarged in the 16th. Open on application to keykeeper at Post Office. On north coast of Arran. ♿ (D4)

Moss Farm Road Stone Circle (SDD) Remains of a Bronze Age cairn and stone circle. On south side of Moss Farm Road, 3 miles (4.8 km) north of Blackwaterfoot, east of A841. (F4)

Standing Stones of Machrie Moor (SDD) 15 ft (4.6 m) high standing stones which are the remains of six Bronze Age stone circles. 1½ miles (2.4 km) east of A841, along Moss Farm Road, south of Machrie. (F4)

Bute, Isle of

The famous Kyles of Bute, one of the most beautiful stretches of water in Scotland, separates the island of Bute from the Cowal peninsula. Bute is 15 miles (24 km) long, hilly in the north, flat and more fertile in the south. Its principal town is the resort of Rothesay, an ancient Royal burgh which gives the title of duke to the Prince of Wales. There is a regular car ferry service to Rothesay from Wemyss Bay (C7) (crossing 30 minutes) and to Rhubodach (B5) (crossing 5 minutes).

Bute Museum, Stuart Street, Rothesay Contains exhibits from the island of Bute covering natural history, history (including models of Clyde steamers)

Brodick Castle, Arran

and a prehistoric section with collections from Neolithic burial cairns. (C6)

Ettrick Bay Trail Shore-side trail with two short detours up the hills. Features archaeology. 8 miles (12.8 km). Motorists can drive the first 2¾ miles (4.4 km) from where it takes 3 hours to complete trail. Car park, guide book. Starts Ettrick Bay bus stop. (C5)

Kingarth Trail, Dunagoil and St Blane's By unclassified road to South Garrochty for 1½ miles (2.4 km), then over grassland to St Blane's Chapel and rough grass and shore to Dunagoil Bay. Shore birds, archaeology and geology. 3 miles (4.8 km), return 3½ hours; from St Blane's car park, 2 hours. Start at Cross Roads at Kingarth or at St Blane's car park. (D6)

Loch Fad and Loch Ascog Trail Loch Fad by woodland and farmland road with very little traffic; 4½ miles (7.2 km), 2 hours. Loch Ascog by road, by shore and then quiet road through farmland; 3 miles (4.8 km), 1¼ hours. Contact the Museum, Rothesay, for a guide book. (C6)

Rothesay Castle (SDD) One of Scotland's most important medieval castles, Rothesay was stormed by Norsemen in 1240. Their breach can still be seen. The circular courtyard, which is enclosed by walls heightened in the late 13th century, is unique in Scotland. ♿ (C6)

Rothesay Walk Walk around Rothesay by the shore and round the bay. 1½ miles (2.5 km), 40–60 minutes. Guide book. Starts at Craigmore Old Pier and Museum. (C6)

St Blane's Chapel (SDD) The foundations of a monastery founded by St Blane in the 6th century can be seen near the ruins of a chapel built c. 1700. Exterior view only. 8½ miles (13.6 km) south Rothesay. (D6)

South Bute Walk Path beside shore then by grass, moor, loch side, marsh and over hill. Map has to be followed. Bird life, flowers, geology, archaeology. 3 hours plus. Guide book, car park. Starts Old Pier, Kilchattan Bay. (D6)

Gigha, Isle of

A fertile island off the west coast of Kintyre accessible by ferry (crossing 20 minutes) from West Loch Tarbert (C3) and Tayinloan (E2) (no cars). There is a ruined church at Kilchattan dating back to the 13th century and many seals live on the rocks off Gigha jetty.

Achamore House Gardens Flowering trees and shrubs, azaleas, camellias and rhododendrons. (E1)

Great Cumbrae Island

Slotted in between the busy Strathclyde mainland and the lovely island of Bute, Cumbrae, about 12 miles (19.2 km) around, is a quiet and peaceful retreat with a character markedly different from the busy mainland. Its only town, Millport, is a family resort, set in a bay, with sand, rocks and scattered islets. Regular car ferries from Largs (C7) to Cumbrae Slip (crossing 10 minutes) and seasonal passenger service from Largs to Millport (crossing 30 minutes).

Museum of the Cumbraes, Garrison House, Millport Life on the island from earliest times illustrated with a collection of photographs and objects in a brand new museum. Victorian and Edwardian life is featured particularly and cruising 'Doon the Watter'. ♿ (D6)

University Marine Biological Station, Keppel Pier, near Millport Belonging to the Universities of Glasgow and London, but partially open to the public, this biological station is concerned with marine life in Clyde waters and has an aquarium and museum. (D6)

Map 24

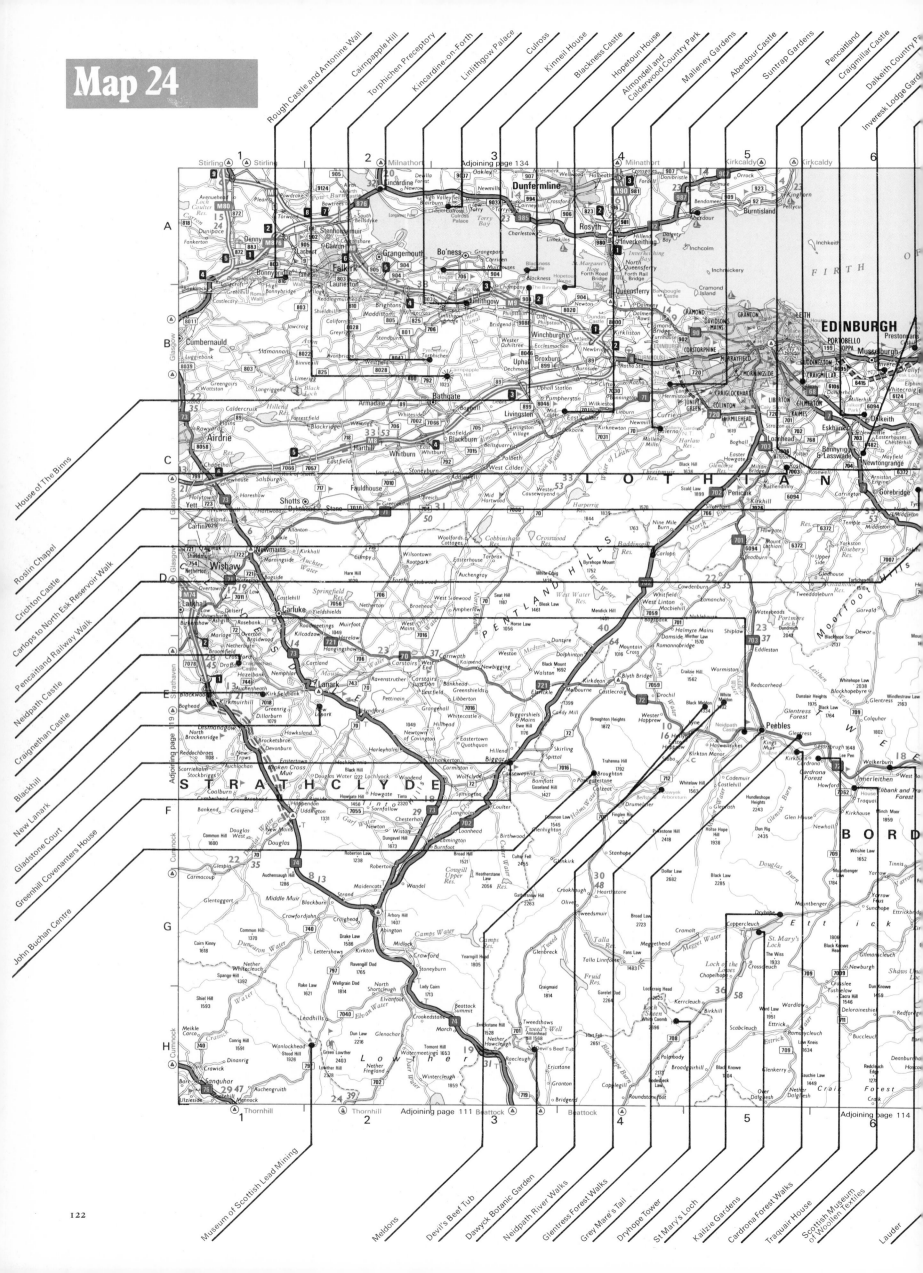

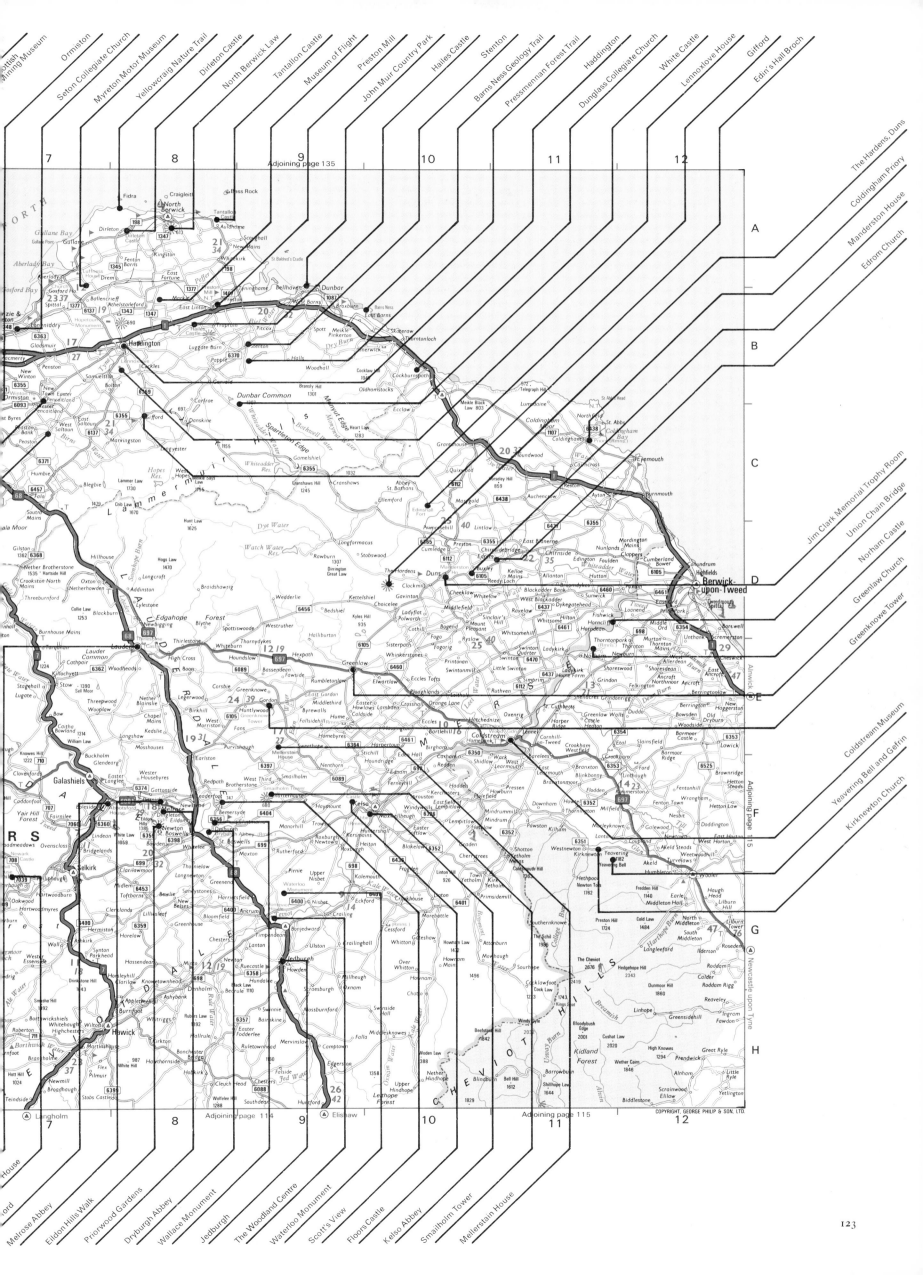

Gazetteer 24

Lowland Scotland

Abbotsford Sir Walter Scott's home from 1811 until his death in 1832. Scott's library, furnishings, and collection of Scottish items add romance and history to this monstrous but lovable mansion. ♿ (F8)

Aberdour Castle (SDD) 14th-century castle with later additions overlooking the harbour of this small Firth of Forth resort. Reconstructed 17th-century terraced gardens. Good circular doocot in grounds, and St Fillans Church, Norman and 16th century, nearby. (A5)

Almondell and Calderwood Country Park In the valley of the River Almond a network of paths and bridges link nature trails with old drovers' roads over the Pentland Hills. (C3)

Barns Ness Geology Trail Starts at White Sands car park off old A1, 2 miles (3.2 km) south of Dunbar, and extends 2½ miles (4 km) to Dry Burn crossing a series of limestone outcrops on the foreshore. It passes a 19th-century limekiln and old quarries; the shore has sandy bays, rock pools and is rich in wild life. (B9)

Blackhill (NTS) At Stonebyres, off B7018 3 miles (4.8 km) west of Lanark. Fine viewpoint on ancient hillfort site above lush landscapes of the middle Clyde valley. (E1)

Blackness Castle (SDD) A well-preserved but modified 15th-century tower used variously as a prison, powder magazine and youth hostel. ♿ (A3)

Bowhill House This 19th-century house contains silverware, porcelain, French furniture and a remarkable collection of paintings. Outside are an adventure playground, gardens and nature trail or pony rides to the remains of Newark Castle. ♿ (G7)

Cairnpapple Hill (SDD) A Neolithic sanctuary remodelled in the Beaker Period as an open air temple and then built over with a Bronze Age cairn. (B3)

Cardrona Forest Walks are all waymarked and start from the picnic site on B7062 near Kirkburn. Red (4½ miles, 7 km) and yellow (3 miles, 4.8 km) pass Cardrona Castle and the Roman fort, whilst Orange (2 miles, 3.2 km) follows the burn before entering woodland. Strong footwear. (F6)

Carlops to North Esk Reservoir Walk From north end of village follow path along east side of Esk, cross footbridge to Fairliehope and track north to reservoir. Cross dam, go east to Spital Farm and then take minor road aligned on Roman road back to Carlops. (D4)

Coldingham Priory Founded 1098 for Durham Benedictine monks. Repeatedly ransacked by English. Partial reconstructions 1662, 1854, but good medieval masonry survives. Now part of parish church. (C11)

Coldstream Museum, Market Square, Coldstream Rebuilt in 1863 in original headquarters of the Coldstream Guards Regiment raised in Newcastle-upon-Tyne in 1650. (E11)

Craigmillar Castle (SDD) On Edinburgh's southern outskirts. Massive 14th-century tower enclosed by 15th-century curtain wall, with increasingly commodious living quarters added 16th and 17th centuries. Interesting outbuildings; melancholy Queen Mary memories. ♿ (B5)

Craignethan Castle (SDD) Off A72. Extensive, well-preserved 16th-century fortress, with unusual, ornate central tower. A Hamilton stronghold during the religious wars, and the 'Tillietudlem' of Scott's *Old Mortality*. (E1)

Crichton Castle (SDD) Splendidly-situated 14th-century tower-house in courtyard surrounded by later additions culminating in spectacular arcaded north range by Earl of Bothwell, 1581–91. (C6)

Culross (NTS, SDD) A unique survival. The centre of this small Royal Burgh, virtually unchanged, is the most complete example of Scottish domestic architecture of the 16th and 17th centuries. Scottish National Trust Town Trail (leaflet). **Culross Palace** (NTS, SDD) Small-scale house, 1597–1611, for wealthy merchant, Sir George Bruce, in mixture of Scottish and Dutch styles, with fine painted timber ceilings and walls. (A3)

Dalkeith Country Park East end Dalkeith High Street. Nature trails, adventure play area and woodland walks in the grounds of Dalkeith Palace which retains an 18th-century park bridge and an orangery. (B6)

Dawyck Botanic Garden provides woodland walks among a fine collection of trees and shrubs. (F4)

Devil's Beef Tub A huge green basin among the hills at the head of Annandale where Border reivers are said to have hidden cattle stolen on their raids. (H3)

Dirleton Castle (NTS, SDD) Beautifully situated in a flower garden in a delightful village. Towers, masonry and doocot spanning 13th–17th centuries, on a rocky outcrop above a 17th-century yew-girt bowling green. ♿ (A8)

Dryburgh Abbey (SDD) Most complete of Border abbeys, exquisitely-situated in a bend of the Tweed. Founded 1150, suffered many English raids. Extensive claustral ruins and church transepts, where Scott and Earl Haig are buried. ♿ (F8)

Dryhope Tower A mile (1.6 km) above the foot of St Mary's Loch, with fine views down Yarrow Water, this 16th-century Scott stronghold, now ruinous, was formerly four storeys high. (G5)

Dunglass Collegiate Church (SDD) On Dunglass estate road, off A1. In attractive setting, founded 1450, church consists of nave, choir, transepts, sacristy, all vaulted, and a central tower. Interior very richly embellished. ♿ (B10)

Edin's Hall Broch (SDD) 1 mile (1.6 km) walk either from A6112 3½ miles (4.6 km) south Grantshouse, or from unclassified road 1 mile (1.6 km) south-east Abbey St Bathans. Iron Age fort and large broch with central paved courtyard surrounded by drystone walls (16 ft (5 m) thick, with narrow chambers set into it. Magnificent views. (C10)

Edrom Church (SDD) Beautifully-carved Norman doorway from ancient, ruined parish church, now standing behind present church. ♿ (D10)

Eildon Hills Walk From Melrose Square, turn left at signpost 200 yards (180 m) on Dingleton road and follow path with stiles to highest hedge line. Turn right at sign for Middle and North Hill, left for easier Wester Hill. From North Hill, skirt plantation and rejoin Wester track back to A6091, turn right, then left to Newstead and return to Melrose by Priors Walk. Superb views. (F8)

Floors Castle Magnificent castle, built 1721 by William Adam, later additions by W.H. Playfair, is still essentially a home containing beautiful tapestries, furniture, paintings and porcelain. Parkland setting by Tweed. (F9)

Gifford Beautiful village, redeveloped in 18th century to attract workers in the agricultural revolution. Now a centre for walking and pony trekking. (C8)

Gladstone Court, Biggar Indoor street museum of bygone shops and workshops, telephone exchange, bank and village library. (F3)

Glentress Forest Walks Four waymarked walks from picnic place on A72. Red (4½ miles, 7 km) on forest roads to viewpoint; blue (4 miles, 6.5 km) on woodland tracks with picnic site; orange (2½ miles, 4 km) links red and blue and passes Roman fort and 2 ponds; yellow, an easy mile (1.6 km). (E5)

Greenhill Covenanters House, Biggar Restored farmhouse, with relics of local Covenanters. 17th-century furnishings, costume dolls, rare animals and poultry. (F3)

Greenknowe Tower (SDD) A turreted tower house of 1581 retaining its iron yett, as well as the armorial bearings of its builder, Seton of Touch. (E9)

Greenlaw Church Rare mixture. Church (1675), separate tower built 1696 as county jail, but to resemble church tower. Church extended 1712 to join it. Grim iron gate and gratings. (E9)

Grey Mare's Tail (NTS) Off A708. A 200 ft (60 m) waterfall in an area renowned for its wild flowers and a herd of wild goats. For safety's sake keep to footpath. (H4)

Haddington Object-lesson in conservation. Haddington preserves complete medieval street-plan. Many fine buildings visited on Town Trail (hour's walk; booklet from local shops or East Lothian Planning Dept, Haddington). Note Town House 1748; 17th-century Nungate Bridge; 14th/15th-century parish church; fine facades in High Street. (B8)

Hailes Castle (SDD) A fortified manor house, later strengthened by a tower and curtain wall. Fine 16th-century chapel. Mary, Queen of Scots stopped here on her flight to Dunbar after Darnley's murder. (B8)

The Hardens, Duns An old hillfort forms a popular viewpoint 3 miles (4.8 km) west of Duns, southern edge of Lammermuirs. (D10)

Hopetoun House Palatial mansion near Forth Bridge, begun 1699 by Sir William Bruce, partly rebuilt and enlarged by William Adam and his sons, John and Robert, 1721–66. Portraits include work by Rubens, Rembrandt, Canaletto. Deer parks with fallow and red deer, St Kilda sheep, exotic birds. Formal rose garden, sea walk, stables, museum. (A4)

House of The Binns (NTS) Off A904. Historic home of the Dalyells is a record of changing architectural fashion. Regency–Gothick facade hides mid 18th-century changes to an early 17th-century fortified stronghold. Splendid plaster ceilings. Forth views, visitor trail. (A3)

Inveresk Lodge Gardens (NTS) On A6124. A new garden of a 17th-century house (not open) with a large selection of plants especially suitable for small gardens. (B6)

Jedburgh Historic Burgh in Jed Water valley. Beautiful red sandstone abbey (SDD), founded 1138, repeatedly sacked and rebuilt. ♿ In town, 16th-century Mary, Queen of Scots' house in Queen Street; 1820 Georgian prison on site of Jedburgh Castle in Castlegate. Attractive town centre. (G9)

Jim Clark Memorial Trophy Room, Newtown Street, Duns A memorial to Jim Clark, world motor racing champion, with many of his trophies. ♿ (D10)

John Buchan Centre, Broughton Memorabilia of the author of *The Thirty-Nine Steps*, who was also a successful lawyer, soldier, politician and historian. On A701 5 miles (8 km) east of Biggar. (F4)

John Muir Country Park, west of Dunbar. This area of coast offers a way-marked clifftop trail with fine seaward views, rich bird and plant life, aspects of geology and history, as well as the wide expanse of Bellhaven Bay ideal for horse riding, sand yachting, surfing and sea fishing. ♿ (B9)

Kailzie Gardens, Peebles Spring bulbs add bright colours to gay herbaceous beds and borders, tinted by trees and shrubs in autumn. Within the grounds are a waterfowl pond, pottery and art gallery. ♿ (E5)

Kelso Abbey (SDD) Impressive fragments, only of the church, remain of David I's great foundation of 12th century. Unique in Scotland with western and eastern transepts, and tower over both crossings. Riverside walks nearby. ♿ (F10)

Kincardine-on-Forth Off A977/985 at roundabout. Small port by the Kincardine Bridge. Notable 17th-century Mercat Cross, many houses with datestones. Ruined Tulliallan Church and Tulliallan Castle nearby, with Devilla Forest (FC) to east. (A2)

Kinneil House, Bo'ness (SDD), south side A904. A 16th/17th-century house containing important murals and decorated ceilings. Nearby 17th-century stables have been converted to house a museum of local industry, including the outhouse where Watt developed his steam engine. (A3)

Kirknewton Church contains unusual survivals of primitive northern architecture – tunnel-vaulted transept and chancel, so low that it has no vertical wall. May have been part of pele tower. 12th-century sculpture shows Three Wise Men apparently wearing kilts. (F11)

Lauder A small Royal Burgh with curious little Tolbooth, and nearby, Parish Church with octagonal steeple. Nice house groups in Conservation Area. ½ mile (.8 km) from Lauder on A68 is 16th- and 19th-century *Thirlestane Castle*. Magnificent ceilings, fine furniture, paintings and china; Border Country Life Museum. ♿ (E8)

Lennoxlove House, Haddington 17th-century mansion with 14th-century parts. Formerly home of William Maitland, secretary to Mary, Queen of Scots, and houses her casket and death mask. Now owned by Duke of Hamilton and contains Hamilton Palace collection of works of art. Off B6137. (B8)

Linlithgow Palace (SDD) Off A803. Mary, Queen of Scots and her father

Jedburgh Abbey

Linlithgow Palace

James V were born in this splendid ruined Palace overlooking its loch. Oldest parts *c*. 1400, but characteristic Gothic and Renaissance detail additions of 16th century. ⬧ (B3)

Malleny Gardens, Balerno (NTS) A garden with many interesting plants and a good collection of shrub roses. ⬧ (C4)

Manderston House A fine Edwardian house in classical style with interesting domestic arrangements. In the grounds an attractive group of farm buildings includes a marble dairy. (D10)

Meldons Ancient forts on either side of an unclassified road with picnic places and inviting footpaths. (E5)

Mellerstain House, Gordon Off A6089. A splendid Adam mansion, begun by William 1725, completed by Robert, 1770–8, containing fine furniture and paintings. Splendid view of Cheviots across the lake from terrace gardens. ⬧ (E9)

Melrose Abbey (SDD) Probably Scotland's most famous Cistercian ruin. Founded 12th century, most of surviving building is 15th century. Finest flowering of Scottish Decorated work, in pink sandstone. Superb figure sculpture. Museum in Commandator's House. (F8)

Museum of Flight, East Fortune Off B1347 by airfield. A collection of aircraft and rockets including Spitfire, an Olympus jet engine and a Blue Streak. ⬧ (A8)

Museum of Scottish Lead Mining, Wanlockhead Pathways lead to features of interest on this former mine site where one can venture underground. A restored water bucket beam engine is particularly striking. (H2)

Myreton Motor Museum, Aberlady A collection of motorised, horsedrawn and historical military vehicles. (A7)

Neidpath Castle, Peebles Restored medieval tower with spectacular views over bend in River Tweed. Pit prison and rock-hewn well. (E5)

Neidpath River Walks At Peebles, follow path west along south bank of Tweed to Artists Rock, 1 mile (1.6 km). Cross by footbridge to **Neidpath Castle**, keep to north bank for a mile (1.6 km), cross Manor Bridge, follow lanes back to Peebles. Alternative riverside path back along north bank from Neidpath. (E5)

New Lanark Scotland's finest industrial community of 18th and early 19th century. Industrial history trail (leaflet available). At south of village, take woodland path to *Falls of Clyde*, in impressive

gorge. Winding track with stairways. Viewing platform. Worth continuing ½ mile (.8 km) to Bonnington Linn and back. (E2)

Norham Castle (EH) Formerly one of the strongest Border castles. Built 1160 by Bishop of Durham. Contains one of the best Norman keeps. (E11)

New Lanark

North Berwick Law Off B1347. A fine viewpoint formed by a volcanic rock crowned by a watch tower and a whalebone archway. (A8)

Ormiston An 18th-century market village which was the centre of John Cockburn's model estates where the first enclosures of the agricultural revolution in Scotland were made. Nearby the former railway station is now a picnic site and access point for **Pencaitland Railway Walk**. (C7)

Pencaitland Twin villages Easter and Wester, divided by the Tyne, united by a bridge. 16th- and 17th-century church, 17th- and 18th-century cottages, mercat cross, doocot and 19th-century school. Attractive groups, colours, character. (C7)

Pencaitland Railway Walk From Saltoun Station (south-west from West Saltoun) a 5 mile (8 km) walk west along former railway to Carberry, through farmland not normally seen by public. (C7)

Pressmennan Forest Trail From car park off unclassified road south of Stenton, a 2 mile (3.2 km) walk through spruce, oak and larch around Pressmennan Lake with views of East Lothian. (B9)

Preston Mill (NTS) Off B1407 at East Linton. A rare 16th-century watermill, extensively renovated 1760, still in working order and in a picturesque setting. Nearby *Phantassie Doocot* is an excellent example of a traditional Scottish dovecote. (B8)

Priorwood Gardens, Melrose (NTS) Beside the abbey, a small garden specialising in flowers suitable for drying, and a visitor centre. (F8)

Roslin Chapel, Roslin Off B7006. 15th-century chapel of an intended collegiate church, with the Prentice Pillar, the exquisite highlight of a richly ornamented interior. (C5)

Rough Castle and Antonine Wall (NTS, SDD) Off B816 6 miles (9.6 km) west of Falkirk. A small but well-preserved fort on the Antonine Wall. The Wall forms its north side and the military road runs through the fort. (A1)

St Mary's Loch A708 runs beside this beautiful loch, now used for sailing and canoeing. Tibbie Shiel's Inn, meeting place of writers in 19th century, is at the south end, and nearer the northern end is a roadside statue of James Hogg, the Ettrick shepherd-poet. (G5)

Scottish Museum of Woollen Textiles, Walkerburn On A72. Interesting exhibits showing growth of Scottish textile trade. ⬧ (F6)

Scottish Mining Museum Two open-air industrial museums converted from former collieries: *The Prestongrange Colliery* at Morrison's Haven on B1348, and the *Lady Victoria Colliery* at Newtongrange on A7. The two are linked by a self-drive Coal Heritage trail. (B6)

Scott's View, Bemersyde One of the great views in Scotland, and the heart of Scott's countryside. The Tweed curves round mature woods and parklands dominated by triple-peaked Eildon Hills. Shapes, proportions, colours blend in landscape perfection. (F8)

Seton Collegiate Church (SDD) Late 14th-century ruined collegiate church with vaulted choir and transepts. ⬧ (B7)

Smailholm Tower (SDD) Off B6404 at Sandyknowe Farm. A 15th-century pele tower on a rocky knoll with commanding views over Border country. ½ mile (.8 km) easy walk, well worthwhile. Dramatic, romantic, magnificent, to be felt as well as seen. Scott knew it as a child. (F9)

Stenton Colour-washed cottages with pantiled roofs. Old chapel is now a doocot in the churchyard and a reconstructed tron for weighing wool makes an unusual feature on one of the greens. (B9)

Suntrap Gardens, Gogarbank This is a Gardening Advice Centre offering courses of instruction and is particularly concerned with small gardens. ⬧ (B4)

Tantallon Castle (SDD) Substantial, exciting ruins of 14th-century castle of the Douglases on the cliffs of the Firth of Forth. Outside the castle is a doocot. Impressive coastal views, and seawards to Bass Rock. ⬧ (A8)

Torphichen Preceptory (SDD) Central tower and transepts of Church of the Knights Hospitallers whose principal Scottish seat this once was. Originally built in 1153 with bell tower dating from 13th century and transepts added in 15th. An exhibition explains the history of the Knights. (B2)

Traquair House, Innerleithen The oldest continually-inhabited house in Scotland rich with patina of centuries of Stuart ownership. Craftsmen can be watched practising their skills, home baking and brewing to be sampled and nature trails and woodland walks to be followed. An experience as well as a building. ⬧ (F6)

Union Chain Bridge First major suspension bridge in Britain. Built by Captain Samuel Brown, 1820, at Horncliffe, to link England and Scotland across the Tweed. Attractive river scenery. (D11)

Wallace Monument A short woodland walk from B6356 or from Dryburgh village (steeper) reveals a huge statue of Sir William Wallace. (F8)

Waterloo Monument Off B6400. A woodland path leads off the unclassified road almost opposite the entrance to Monteviot Park and reaches the column built by Marquess of Lothian and tenants in 1815, on Penielheugh Hill. Views. 2 miles (3.2 km) return. (G9)

White Castle, Garvald One of many Iron Age forts on the Lammermuirs, White Castle is close to the road and gives panoramic views northward over Lothian Plain to the coast. (C9)

The Woodland Centre, Monteviot Park, Jedburgh Woodland walks with an interpretative centre on the theme of woodlands and use of timber. Adventure playground, giant board games. Off B6400. (G9)

Yeavering Bell and Gefrin 13-acre (5 hectare) hill fort on rounded hill on northern edge of Cheviots. By roadside (B6351) below was Gefrin, royal township of 7th-century Anglo-Saxon Northumbrian kings. Commemorative plaque. (F11)

Yellowcraig Nature Trail From car park off B1345 east end Dirleton, 1¼ mile (2 km) trail through woodland and dunes with varied flora and plenty of seabirds. (A8)

Hadrian's Wall

The Romans were in Britain for some three hundred and seventy years (AD 43–AD 410), the most potent reminder of their presence being Hadrian's Wall, which formed the northern frontier of the province. The conquest began in AD 43 under the Emperor Claudius and proceeded slowly; it was not until some forty years later, c. AD 80, that England and Wales were finally subdued. The northern frontier was then established on the Stanegate, a road from Corbridge (Northumberland) to Carlisle (Cumbria), defended by a string of forts. With this frontier as a base the governor of Britain, Agricola, campaigned for several years in Scotland, but was recalled to Rome before any final conquest was completed. Events during the next forty years are obscure but it is known that by about AD 120 the frontier was again back on the Stanegate, all the territory conquered by Agricola having presumably been lost.

By this time the Emperor in Rome was Hadrian (Publius Aelius Hadrianus, AD 117–138). In AD 122 he was in Britain, one of the objectives of his visit almost certainly being the re-organisation of the northern frontier. Building work on the new defence system began in the same year and was substantially finished by AD 128. As finally completed Hadrian's Wall extended for 73 miles (117 km), from Wallsend on Tyne (Tyne and Wear) in the east to Bowness on Solway (Cumbria) in the west. According to section, the stone wall was $7\frac{1}{2}$, $8\frac{1}{2}$ or $9\frac{1}{2}$ ft (2, 2.5 or 3 m) thick, and 16 ft (5 m) high to the wall walk, with another 6 ft (2 m) or so for the breastwork, producing an overall height of c. 22 ft (7 m). In front of (i.e., to the north of) the Wall (except where it ran above high crags) was a wide V-shaped ditch, the material from which was heaped on its outer edge to form a *glacis* or outer obstacle. At intervals of one Roman mile (1,620 yards, 1,480 m) were 80 milecastles, small forts, c. 80 × 90 ft (24 × 27 m) in area, built against the back of the Wall to house the troops on duty in that particular section. Between each milecastle were two towers or turrets, c. 25–30 ft (7.5–9 m) high, at 540 yd (495 m) intervals.

The Wall, milecastles and turrets were further strengthened by fourteen forts, each housing some 500 men. The gaps between the forts vary from 2 to 7 miles (3 to 11 km), the average being about 5 miles (8 km). Some were designed for infantry units and some for cavalry, but all conformed to the standard Roman plan, that of a playing card, a rectangle with rounded corners. Communication along the Wall was provided by the Military Way, a road on the south side linking the forts and the milecastles between. Just beyond the road was the Vallum, an earthwork (two banks with a ditch between) which is generally interpreted as marking off the military zone of the Wall from civilian territory to the south.

Formidable as they were, the Wall, forts, milecastles, and turrets were by no means the end of the story. From the beginning the system extended for 40 miles (64 km) down the vulnerable Cumbrian coast, from Bowness to St Bee's Head, and consisted of four more auxiliary forts, together with milecastles and turrets spaced out in exactly the same way as in the main sector. What was missing here was the linking wall, presumably omitted because the sea was deemed to form the main lengthwise element. There were further auxiliary forts (eight in number) to the north of the Wall, forming a network of outposts designed to give early warning of any movement, hostile or otherwise, among the tribes whose activities the Wall was primarily designed to curtail.

For most of the occupation period we hear very little about the Wall, presumably because nothing much was happening there. The frontier system was doing the job it was designed for and keeping the native tribes quiet. On three occasions, however (AD 197, 296 and 367), there were massive uprisings and the Wall was overwhelmed. Rapacious tribesmen poured into the province wreaking death and destruction wherever they went. When an uprising was put down there was always a great deal of rebuilding to be done before the Wall could be restored to its former state. The evidence for rebuilding has been revealed by excavation in many of the auxiliary forts along the frontier.

As far as visible remains are concerned the Wall can be divided into three sections, east, central and west, with not much now to be seen in the first and last. In the central, 25 mile (40 km) section, however, there is a great deal to be seen, from the remains of the auxiliary fort of Birdoswald (near Greenhead on the A69) to those of another auxiliary fort, Chesters (near Chollerford on the B6318). Between the two, also on the B6318, is perhaps the most famous and best preserved of all the Wall forts, Housesteads. At both Housesteads and Chesters there are excellent site museums. At Vindolanda, about 2 miles (3.2 km) from Housesteads, are the remains of one of the Stanegate forts, and of the recently excavated *vicus* or civilian settlement, together with full-scale replicas of a

section of Hadrian's Wall and a turret. Corbridge, too, was originally a Stanegate fort, although the visible remains are now largely those of a civil settlement with military workshops. There are visible remains of milecastles at Harrow's Scar (No 49) and Poltross Burn (No 48), both near Birdoswald, and on the high crags west of Housesteads (Nos 37 and 39), to mention only the best preserved. Many other remains, of the Wall itself, of other milecastles, of turrets, of the outer ditch, and of the Vallum, can be seen on or close to the B6318 between Chesters and Housesteads. Although much still remains to be discovered there is more than enough of the Wall visible to enable any visitor to appreciate the magnitude of Hadrian's achievement on the most northerly limit of his Empire.

The ruins of Hadrian's Wall are a unique monument of the Roman Empire and they are found in places among some of the most dramatic and beautiful scenery in Britain, as in these sections on Walltown Crags (right) and near Housesteads (below). The Wall was more elaborate than its name suggests and was punctuated at intervals by turrets, milecastles and forts. At Housesteads fort (below left), the best preserved and probably the best known, there is still much to be seen on the ground including the foundations of the headquarters, hospital, barracks, officers' baths and granaries (far left below). Perhaps one of the most striking features of the Roman settlements along the Wall is the evidence they provide of the modern 'conveniences' enjoyed by the Roman forces. The regimental bathhouse at Chesters (far left above), for example, had provision for hot or cold, dry or steam baths.

Crofting

A survival from medieval times or even earlier, crofting is a form of subsistence farming still practised in the Highlands and Islands of Scotland, generally in crofting townships (small farms of a few acres grouped together in an irregular manner). The old pattern of crofting was one of communities practising a kind of co-operative farming, with strips of common land allotted usually to individuals. Examples of the old system survive, but now crofters have their own arable land fenced in while they share the common grazing land. At one time crofting in the Highlands was closely tied in with the clan system and the land was owned by the chief of the clan. Crofters had no security of tenure and paid rent to their chief in warrior service.

Traditionally, crofters grew crops like oats and potatoes, kept a cow and a few sheep, and eked out a living by fishing and weaving. Their home was what is known as a 'black' house, stone walled, thatched with heather and with one door, no chimney and no window. The only fuel for cooking and heating was peat, which had to be dug and dried. Subsistence was never very good and by the mid 18th century most crofters were reduced to a diet of potatoes.

In medieval times the Highland chieftains had the power of life and death over their clansmen, they meted out justice for all their people and were as powerful as the number of fighting men they could muster. With the crushing of the 1745 Jacobite Rebellion fighting became a thing of the past and the power of the clan chief was substantially reduced. Their impoverished vassals, on the other hand, were no longer needed as fighting men and were not able to pay adequate rents for the land that they farmed.

This state of affairs led to the now notorious clearances in the late 18th century, largely carried out on the instructions of the Duke of Sutherland, formerly an Englishman with the name of George Leveson Gower, who owned some 1,700 sq miles (4,400 sq km) in the western Highlands. A desire to benefit from the profits in sheep farming re-resulted in many thousands of crofters being evicted and their land let out to lowland and English sheep farmers. The clearances occurred on a vast scale all over the northern Highlands and the Western Isles and although the Duke of Sutherland was undoubtedly the principal culprit, a number of Highland-born chiefs were also guilty of ill-treating their clansmen.

The many crumbling crofts recall this enforced depopulation, one of the most brutal episodes in Scottish history and one from which many people believe the region has never recovered. The houses

Despite the steady decline in agricultural employment, hill and upland farming and crofting still account for a small but significant percentage of all occupations in the Highlands and Islands. The tenacious crofting population has also done much to prevent the area from becoming nothing more than a beautiful wilderness. The settlement of Scoraig (below left) lies west of Ullapool and the bleak landscape (above) was taken near Lerwick in the Shetlands. In contrast, grouse moors (below right) are a very poor form of land use and only become economic in terms of yield per acre when catering for very rich syndicates.

of those crofters who refused to leave were put to the torch and in many instances ships waited offshore to take the now-homeless families to America. In places whole communities were forcibly uprooted, some landowners even founding settlements in America for the people to go to. The clearances continued from the end of the 18th century to reach a peak around 1830. They were followed by potato blight and famine, forcing many more people from the Highlands to cross the Atlantic. As it turned out, the sheep were poor producers of wool in the face of Australian imports and the sheep were themselves 'cleared' to make way for treeless deer 'forests' offering high rents from ambitious middle-class Victorians seeking the enhanced social status that came from the wholesale slaughter of grouse and deer. Some 2,000,000 acres (809,400 hectares) were enclosed for game, well-to-do sportsmen flocking to these sporting estates on the Glorious Twelfth (of August) when grouse shooting begins.

But the 19th century also saw a series of acts promoted by Gladstone to protect peasants' rights. These culminated in 1886 with the Crofters' Act which gave security of tenure, the right to pass on the tenancy and on giving it up to receive compensation for the value of the buildings on the croft and any improvements to the land. Unfortunately, although this Act was clearly a great advance, it gave full crofters' rights to many holdings so small as to be hopelessly uneconomic. In fact few crofts were ever big enough to provide a family with a living and nowadays a crofter is by definition a man who turns his hand to almost anything, farming, fishing, weaving, tourism and even working for a nearby estate.

Abandoned crofts still litter the empty hills of the Highlands and Islands for emigration has never stopped. As has been written elsewhere, it is ironic that while other Scots were allowing their Highland cousins to be expelled from their homes they were also forming a romantic attachment to the kilt and the tartan.

The inhabitants of the remote island of St Kilda pursued their own unique way of life for centuries. The main settlement was round the small pier at Village Bay on Hirta where the ruined stone houses (above) are now being restored by the National Trust for Scotland. The St Kilda economy was largely bird-based – the inhabitants caught many varieties of sea-birds with nets and (below left) using a long thin pole with a running noose at the end. They also practised an elementary form of crofting. One striking feature of their way of life was the use of cleits (below right), beehive cells of rough stone used as an all-purpose store house. At the end of the seventeenth century there were some 180 inhabitants but by 1929 the economy of the island had virtually collapsed and in the following year the population was evacuated.

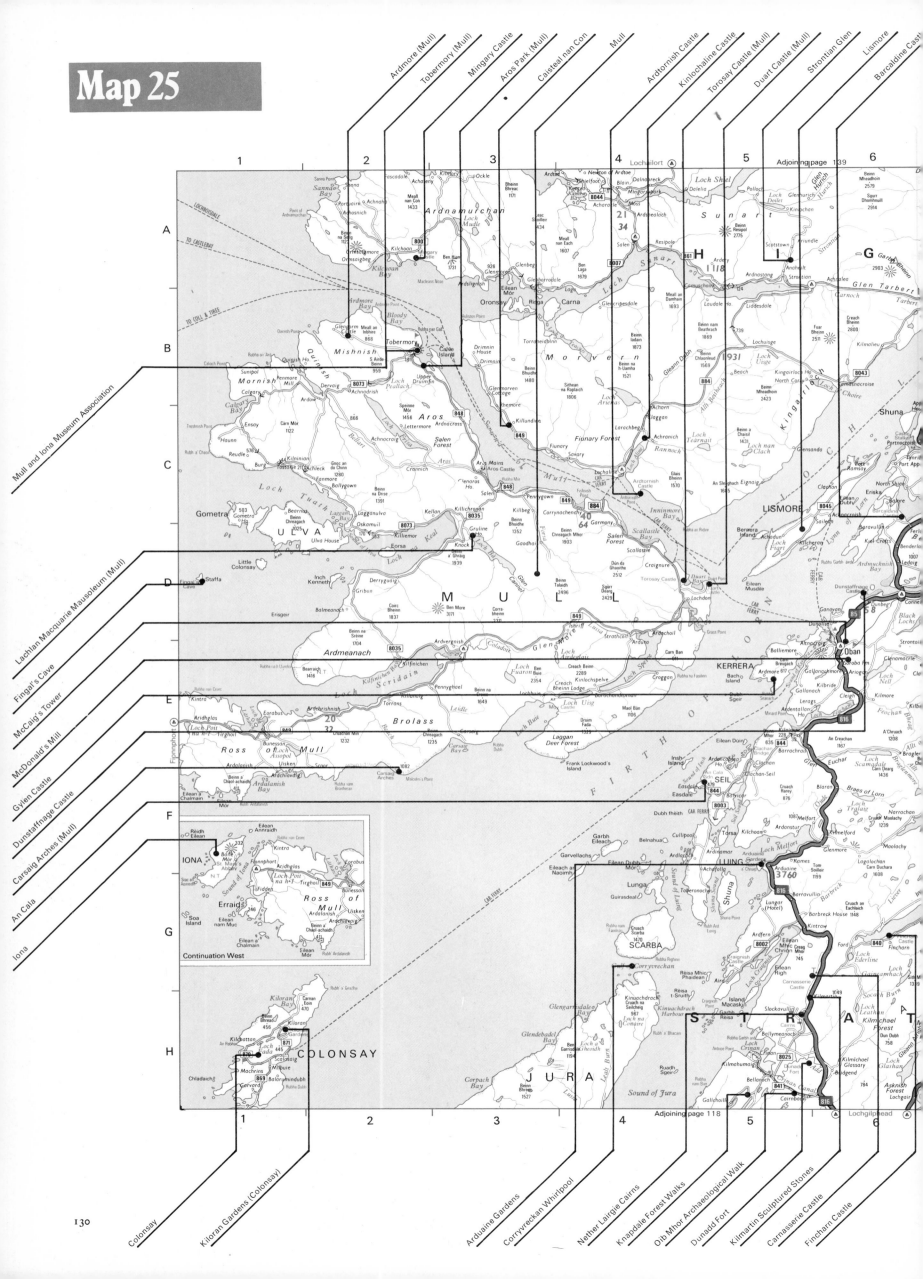

Map 25

Ardmore (Mull)
Tobermory (Mull)
Mingary Castle
Aros Park (Mull)
Caisteal nan Con
Mull
Ardtornish Castle
Kinlochaline Castle
Torosay Castle (Mull)
Duart Castle (Mull)
Strontian Glen
Lismore
Barcaldine Castle

Mull and Iona Museum Association

Lachlan Macquarie Mausoleum (Mull)

Fingal's Cave

McCaig's Tower

McDonald's Mill

Gylen Castle

Dunstaffnage Castle

Carsaig Arches (Mull)

An Cala

Iona

Colonsay
Kiloran Gardens (Colonsay)
Arduaine Gardens
Corryvreckan Whirlpool
Nether Largie Cairns
Knapdale Forest Walks
Oib Mhor Archaeological Walk
Dunadd Fort
Kilmartin Sculptured Stones
Carnasserie Castle
Fincharn Castle

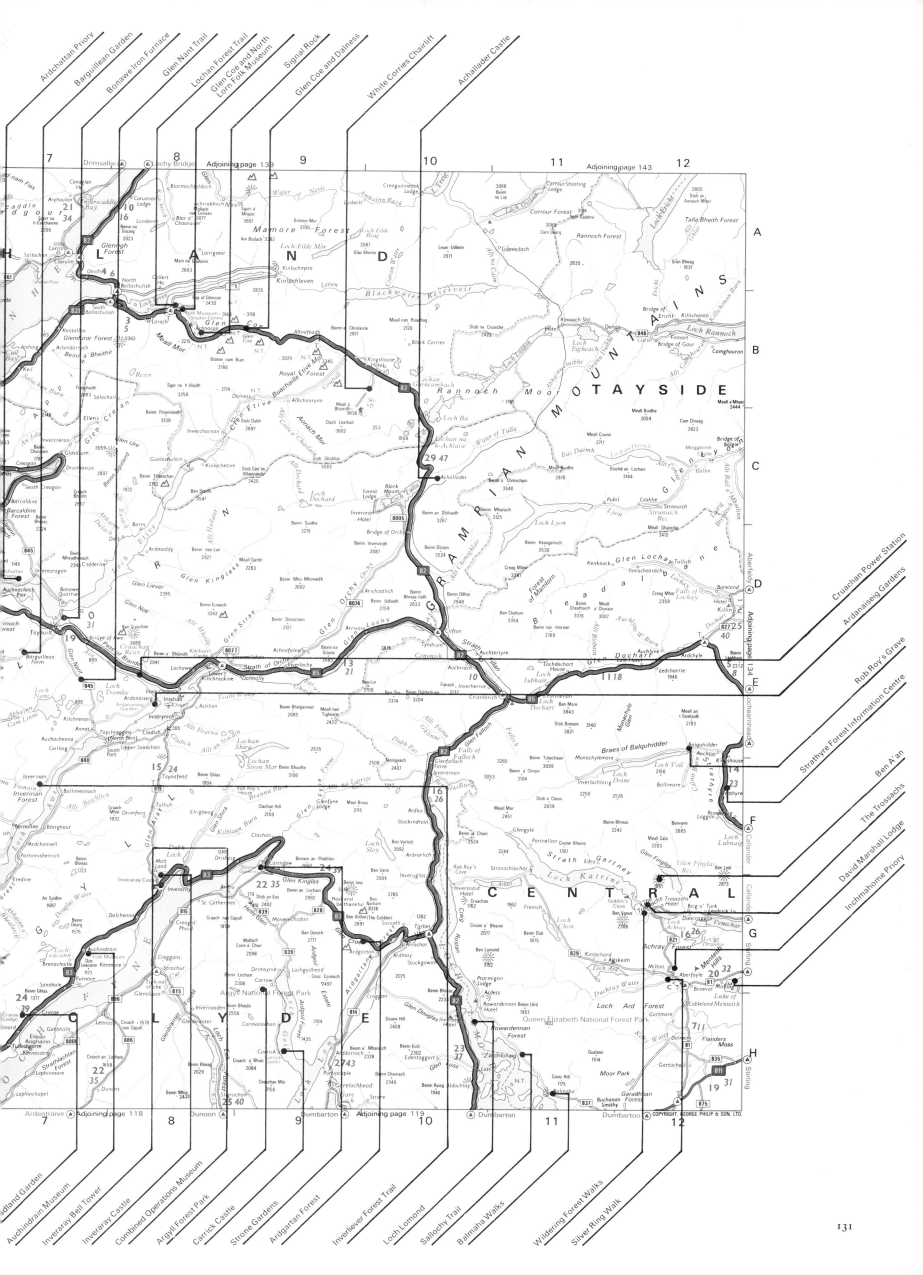

Lowland Scotland

Achallader Castle According to legend, the plot for the massacre of Glen Coe was hatched in this stronghold of the Fletchers and later of the Glenlyon Campbells. The ruins can be seen from a footpath which ascends Glen Tulla from Loch Tulla, off A82 3 miles (4.8 km) north Bridge of Orchy. (C10)

An Cala, Easdale A garden featuring cherry trees, water and rock gardens, roses and azaleas. ♿ (F5)

Ardanaiseig Gardens Wonderful views across Loch Awe from these extensive gardens featuring rhododendrons, rare shrubs and trees. East of B845, 22 miles (35.2 km) east Oban. ♿ (E8)

Ardchattan Priory (SDD) A Valliscaulian house founded in 1230 and used as a meeting place for one of Bruce's Parliaments in 1308. Cromwell's soldiers burned the priory in 1654. The present remains include some carved stones. On north side lower Loch Etive. (D7)

Ardgartan Forest Strenuous but rewarding hill walks to Loch Goil through forest and over high mountainous country. As weather changes can be rapid and extreme, tough footwear and proper clothing must be worn. Car park. Three routes from 5–11 miles (8–17.6 km), 2–6 hours. Start Ardgartan Forest Office, on A83, 3 miles (4.8 km) south-west Arrochar. (G9/10)

Ardtornish Castle Built c. 1340, Ardtornish was the principal stronghold of the Lords of the Isles during the 14th/15th centuries. Ruined square keep and rampart wall remain. Seen from a track on the east side of Loch Aline. (C4)

Arduaine Gardens Beautiful coastal garden noted particularly for rhododendrons, azaleas, magnolias and other rare trees and shrubs. Rock and water gardens. ♿ (F5)

Argyll Forest Park This was Scotland's first Forestry Commission Forest Park, created in 1935, and stretches from Strone Point (Map 23 A7) between Holy Loch and Loch Long, up the shores of Loch Eck and north-east across Loch Goil to Glen Croe and Beinn Ime (G9). Maps, books and advice on the many walks along signposted paths available from Forestry Commission offices at Kilmun (Map 23 A6) and Ardgartan (G10). (G/H8/9)

Auchindrain Museum Traditional dwellings and barns dating from the late 18th and early 19th centuries with furnishings and implements to illustrate a communal-tenancy farm. Land farming is practised using traditional methods. Craft shop, picnic places. (G7)

Balmaha Walks Two walks: one is steep (for the fit and active) through woodland with excellent views of Loch Lomond (1½ miles, 2.4 km); the other is more gentle and on a lower level, through forest with many species of bird to see (1¾ miles, 2.8 km). Guide book, picnic place. Start car park on B837 at Balmaha. (H11)

Barcaldine Castle A fortified keep built by 'Black Duncan' in 1590, it is reputedly haunted. (D6)

Barguillean Garden This garden is particularly attractive in spring as it features daffodils, rhododendrons and azaleas. There are also heathers and other flowering shrubs. (E7)

Ben A'an Short, rough, steep climb through forest to the summit of Ben A'an rewarded by splendid views of Trossachs, Lochs Katrine and Achray. 1 mile (1.6 km), over 2 hours return. Tough footwear and suitable clothing advisable. Starts by A821, 6 miles (9.6 km) from Aberfoyle, just west of Trossachs Hotel. (G12)

Bonawe Iron Furnace (SDD) Furnace and ancillary buildings preserved and restored. The charcoal furnace was used from 1753 until 1874. (D7)

Caisteal nan Con 'Castle of the Dogs', ruins of a castle which is part of a chain of fortresses on Ardnamurchan Peninsula. Just west of Fiunary along B849 on Sound of Mull. (C3)

Carnasserie Castle (SDD) John Carswell, first Protestant Bishop of the Isles, lived here. He translated *Knox's Liturgy* into Gaelic and published it in 1567, the first book to be printed in Gaelic. The castle was captured and partly destroyed during Argyll's rebellion in 1685. Off A816. (G5)

Carrick Castle The walls remain of this large rectangular keep built in the 14th century. It was used as a prison by the Argylls, fortified in 1651 in expectation of a siege, and burned in 1685 by the Earl of Atholl's troops. (H9)

Combined Operations Museum, Cherry Park, Inveraray Inveraray was the first base from which assault landing techniques were developed. This museum, opened in 1984, traces the early training of all three services and shows photographs, cuttings etc of the main Commando raids, culminating in the story of the Normandy landings. Also large scale diorama with models of all landing craft plus supporting aircraft. New exhibits being added. (G8)

Corryvreckan Whirlpool The noise of this incredible and treacherous tide-race can be heard from a considerable distance and be seen from the north end of Jura or from Craignish Point. The whirlpool itself lies between the islands of Jura and Scarba. (G4)

Crarae Glen Garden (Charitable Trust) The gardens of Crarae Lodge are set in a Highland Glen beside Loch Fyne and are one of Scotland's loveliest gardens on view to the public. Of particular significance are the rhododendrons, azaleas, conifers and ornamental shrubs. (H7)

Cruachan Power Station The visitor centre and guides explain the workings of this massive 400,000 kilowatt pumped storage scheme set in a huge cavern inside a mountain (Ben Cruachan). It utilises water pumped from Loch Awe to a reservoir 1,200 ft (365 m) up the mountain. Off A85. (D8)

David Marshall Lodge A picnic pavilion and information centre in the Queen Elizabeth Forest Park. Waterfall trail starts from car park. Scenic *Achray Forest Drive* starts ½ mile (0.8 km) north. On A821, 1 mile (1.6 km) north Aberfoyle. (G12)

Dunadd Fort (SDD) The Celtic Kingdom of Scotland sprang from the ancient capital Dalriada (c. 500–800). Dunadd was the site of this capital and the early kings may well have been invested with their royal power on the highest rock here which is marked with a footprint and the figure of a boar. West of A816, 4 miles (6.4 km) north-west Lochgilphead. (H5)

Dunstaffnage Castle (SDD) This exceptionally fine and well-preserved example of a 13th-century castle still has two round towers and curtain walls, 10 ft (3 m) thick. Off A85. (D6)

Fincharn Castle A Macdonald stronghold, now ruined, perched on a rocky ledge overlooking Loch Awe from the eastern shore. (G6)

Fingal's Cave, Island of Staffa A massive cave has been created in the basaltic rock formations here, 227 ft (69.2 m) long and 66 ft (20.1 m) high above sea level with black-pillared walls and columns. Mendelssohn was inspired by Fingal's Cave to write his *Hebrides* overture. Seen by excursion boat trips from Oban and Mull. (D1)

Glen Coe and Dalness (NTS) The main road (A82) runs right through this, the most famous of all Scottish glens. It still retains a sombre atmosphere that reminds visitors of the massacre of the Macdonald inhabitants in 1692. That apart, the scenery is wild and rugged and there is excellent mountaineering (for the experienced). Wildlife abounds and includes red deer, wild-cat, golden eagle and ptarmigan. There is a ski centre, chair lift and ski tows (for winter weekends) and a Visitor Centre (at Clachaig) giving the history and general information for summer visitors. (B8/9)

Glen Coe and North Lorn Folk Museum, Glencoe Village Collections include relics connected with Prince Charles Edward Stuart, domestic implements, agricultural tools, dairy and slate quarrying equipment, weapons, costumes, dolls and dolls' houses, photographs. The collections are housed in two thatched cottages and their outbuildings. ♿ (B8)

Glen Nant Trail, Fearnoch Forest Through National Forest Reserve – remnant of ancient broadleaved forest. Map board at start. 2½ miles (4 km), 2 hours. Car park. Starts by B845 (Taynuilt–Kilchrenan road) 3 miles (4.8 km) from A85. (E7)

Gylen Castle, Island of Kerrera A ruined MacDougal stronghold which dates from 1587. Passenger ferry from Gallanach, 2 miles (3.2 km) south Oban (crossing time 5 minutes). (E5)

Inchmahome Priory (SDD) On an island in Lake of Menteith. The ruins of an important Augustinian priory, founded in 1238, where the infant Mary, Queen of Scots was sent for refuge in 1547. Ferry from Port of Menteith. (G12)

Inveraray Bell Tower The world's third-heaviest set of ten bells which are chimed daily. They are housed in a 126 ft (38.4 m) high granite tower from which there are excellent views. (G8)

Inveraray Castle An impressive turreted castle, still the seat of the Dukes of Argyll, chiefs of the Clan Campbell. The present castle was started in 1743 and the Adams were involved in its structure. The magnificent interior houses an armoury, state rooms, furniture, tapestries and paintings by Gainsborough, Ramsay and Raeburn. ♿ (G8)

Inverliever Forest Trail Through attractive mature woodland with plenty of wildlife and botanical interest. 2¼ miles (3.5 km), 1½–2 hours. Car park, guide book. Starts at Inverinan car park on west side of Loch Awe, on unclassified road joining B845 from Taynuilt and B840 at Ford, 4 miles (6.4 km) south-west of B845. (F7)

Kilmartin Sculptured Stones (SDD) A number of grave slabs and fragments of at least two crosses are preserved in this West Highland churchyard. One cross, dating back to the 16th century, shows Christ crucified on the front and Christ in Majesty on the back. There are many reminders of prehistoric and Roman times in the area between the Crinan Canal (see Gazetteer 23) and Kilmartin. Bronze Age and earlier remains include *Kilmartin Glebe Cairn*, reached from the north end of the village; *Ri Cruin Cairn*, 1 mile (1.6 km) south on the unclassified road immediately right off the B8025; *Templewood Stone Circle*, c. 2000 BC, on a further turn right, ¾ mile (1.2 km) south-west of Kilmartin. On the A816 1¼ miles (2 km) south of the village is the *Dunchraigaig Burial Cairn*. See also **Nether Lairgie Cairns**. (H5)

Kinlochaline Castle Belonging to the Clan MacInnes, this square turreted tower, built in the 16th century, contains a dungeon with access only through a trap-door in its roof. At tip of Loch Aline north of Lochaline off A884. (C4)

Knapdale Forest Walks Scenic walks (Loch Coille Bhar) by loch and through woodland. Short walk of 1 mile (1.6 km), 1 hour; long walk of 3 miles (4.8 km), 3 hours. Information Centre, car park, guide book. Start is 328 yards (300 m) south of junction B8025 and Achnamara road. Approach from A816 (Oban–Lochgilphead road) at Cairnbaan or just south of Kilmartin. (H5)

Loch Lomond The largest of Scotland's lochs, it is considered by many to be the most beautiful and certainly competes with **Loch Ness** (see Gazetteer 28) for the title of most famous. It is 24 miles (38.4 km) long and varies in width from ¾ to 5 miles (1.2 to 8 km). Follow the twisting road along the east side of the

Glen Coe

loch from Balmaha to Rowardennan which runs through pastoral and wooded scenery with a backdrop of gentle hills rising to the mountain slopes of Ben Lomond (NTS) at its northern end. More than 30 islands add to the beauty of the scenery. There are many parking places and picnic areas along the shores and bays filled with trout and pike. The south-east corner of the loch is a nature reserve. The last paddle steamer to be built in Britain, *Maid of the Loch*, sails from Balloch (Map 23 A8) on cruises around the islands in summer. (F/G/H 11)

Lochan Forest Trail Varied walk through mixed woodland and round lochan with fine views of Loch Leven and Glen Coe. Alternative routes of ½–1½ hours (1–3 miles, 1.6–4.8 km). Information Centre, car park. Starts from entrance to hospital on A82 through Glencoe Village. (B8)

McCaig's Tower, Oban This monument, which dominates the town, was built by McCaig as a memorial for his family to provide employment for local craftsmen from 1897–1900. Its walls are 2 ft (0.6 m) thick and from 30–47 ft (9.1–14.3 m) high. The courtyard within is landscaped and the tower floodlit at night in summer. (E6)

McDonald's Mill Exhibition of the story of spinning and weaving, with demonstrations of hand weaving. Off A816, ½ mile (0.8 km) south Oban. ♿ (E6)

Mingary Castle (SDD) A ruined late 13th-century castle with inner buildings of the 15th century. On B8007, 2 miles (3.2 km) east of Kilchoan on Ardnamurchan peninsula, access by farm road. (A2)

Nether Lairgie Cairns (SDD) Three cairns: north (*c.* 1800–1600 BC), mid (*c.* 1800–1500 BC) and south (*c.* third millennium BC). See also **Kilmartin Sculptured Stones**. (H5)

Oib Mhor Archaeological Walk takes the visitor through forest to various points of archaeological interest. 6 miles (9.6 km), 3 hours. Information Centre, car park, guide book. Starts by B841, ½ mile (0.8 km) north Achnamara junction. Approach from A816 (Oban–Lochgilphead road) at Cairnbaan or just south of Kilmartin. (H5)

Rob Roy's Grave. Balquhidder Churchyard Here lie the graves of Rob Roy, his wife and two of his sons. In the church itself is the 8th-century St Angus' Stone, a 17th-century bell from the former church and old Gaelic Bibles. (E12)

Sallochy Trail, Buchanan Forest Walks, Queen Elizabeth Forest Park Forest trail with named trees and shrubs and fine views over Loch Lomond. 1¼ miles (2 km), 2 hours. Car park, guide book. Starts on unclassified road 3 miles (4.8 km) north Balmaha (on B837). (H11)

Signal Rock, Glencoe Forest Woodland walk (FC) to viewpoints giving excellent views of Glen Coe. Alternative routes possible (1–2 miles, 1.6–3.2 km). Information Centre, car park. Starts on A82, 2 miles (3.2 km) east Glencoe village (other accesses are possible). (B8)

Silver Ring Walk, Loch Ard Forest, Queen Elizabeth Forest Park Nature trail through mixed woodland and by loch, mainly on forest roads. 6 miles (9.6 km), 3 hours. Car park. Walk from public car park in Aberfoyle on A821. Cross bridge over river Forth, trail starts ½ mile (0.8 km) on, at end of south-east branch of unclassified road. (G12)

Strathyre Forest Information Centre An attractive display which illustrates a working forest and also many forms of recreation and leisure to be enjoyed in Scotland's forests. A84 at south end Strathyre Village. (F12)

Strone Gardens The pinetum in these gardens contains what is reputed to be the tallest tree in Great Britain. There are also beautiful displays of daffodils, primulas, rhododendrons and exotic shrubs. (G9)

Strontian Glen Nature Trail Through Ariundle common grazings and oakwood along the Strontian river valley to high moorland above. Plenty of plant and animal life. 4 miles (6.4 km) or 7 miles (11.2 km), 2 hours or 4 hours. Guide book. Turn north off A861 about 1½ miles (2 km) north Strontian. (B5)

The Trossachs This lovely, popular area of rocky outcrops and gentle hills is often called 'the Highlands in miniature'. It extends from the wooded Loch Achray to Loch Katrine between **Ben A'an** to the north and Ben Venue to the south. Sir Walter Scott's novel *Rob Roy* and his poem *The Lady of the Lake* were set in the Trossachs and many of the places mentioned can be identified. Loch Katrine itself is a most attractive and popular tourist centre. (G12)

White Corries Chairlift Chairlift to 2,100 ft (640 m) offers magnificent views of the areas around **Glen Coe** and Rannoch Moor. (C9)

Wildering Forest Walks, Queen Elizabeth Forest Park Explore the foothills of Ben Venue with splendid views of the **Trossachs** and Loch Achray. Alternative routes, all 5 miles (8 km), 3 hours. By A821, 6 miles (9.6 km) north Aberfoyle. (G12)

Colonsay, Isle of

Rocky hills and sandy beaches are the main features of this island which is 8 miles (12.8 km) long and 2 miles (3.2 km) wide. It takes its name from St Columba and its near neighbour Oronsay (not on map) takes its name from Columba's companion, St Oran. The two islands are separated by a narrow sound which is dry and can be crossed by foot for three hours each day. Colonsay is reached by car ferry from Oban which operates three times a week (crossing 2½ hours).

Kiloran Gardens Subtropical gardens noted for their rhododendrons and shrubs including embothriums and magnolias. (H1)

Iona, Isle of (NTS)

St Columba and his followers came to Iona in 563 and founded a monastery. The monks travelled throughout Scotland preaching Christianity to the Picts, thus marking a vital turning point in the history of Scotland. The monastery was rebuilt in 1203 but later fell into decay.

St Mary's Cathedral, Iona

It was restored at the beginning of this century and it is now the home of the Iona Community, founded in 1938, which has lovingly restored the Cathedral. Its beautiful interior and interesting carvings are well worth a visit. In addition visitors can see the restored St Oran's Chapel, built *c.* 1080, the remains of the 13th-century nunnery and, outside the Cathedral, the 10th-century St Martin's Cross, 14 ft (4.3 m) high and elaborately carved. Iona has for centuries been the traditional burial place for kings and chiefs. Reached by ferry from Fionnphort on Mull (no cars, crossing time 5 minutes) or by excursion from Oban (E6). (F/G1)

Lismore, Isle of

Lismore means 'great garden'. Its delightful parish church (1749) contains the surviving parts of a tiny cathedral. The medieval doorways, sedilia and piscina remain. St Moluag founded a monastery here in *c.* 592, and his pastoral staff, the Bachuil Mor, is in the hands of its hereditary keeper, the Baron of Bachuil. Ferry from Port Appin (crossing time 10 minutes). Also car ferry from Oban. (C6)

Mull, Isle of

Mull is a really beautiful island of moorland and mountain offering some wonderful scenic drives. There are little bays of white sand, plenty of wildlife, castles, walks and the lovely little town of **Tobermory**. Car ferries operate from Oban (E6) to Craignure (crossing time

45 minutes); from Lochaline (C4) across Sound of Mull to Fishnish (crossing time 5 minutes); Catamaran passenger services from Oban to Tobermory (no cars) and ferry service (no cars) from Kilchoan (A2) to Tobermory (crossing time 35 minutes).

Tobermory, Mull

Ardmore A walk which encircles the northern point of Mull with magnificent views and seascapes. 4 miles (6.4 km), 1½ hours. Take B8073 from Tobermory and turn right onto unclassified road to Glengorm. Car park 3 miles (4.8 km) on right. (B2)

Aros Park Short footpath around wooded lochan. Also cliff path to Tobermory. Car park, picnic area. Take A848 from Tobermory and turn left into Aros Park gates after 1 mile (1.6 km). (C2)

Carsaig Arches Amazing tunnels formed by the sea in basaltic rock. Reached only at low tide. On the way is the Nun's Cave in which there are curious carvings. It is said that nuns sheltered here when driven out of **Iona** at the time of the Reformation. On shore 3 miles (4.8 km) west Carsaig. (F2)

Duart Castle Home of the Macleans to the present day, the keep was built in the 13th century. The castle was taken and ruined by the Duke of Argyll in 1691. During the 1745 Rising, Sir Hector Maclean of Duart was imprisoned in the Tower of London and his land forfeited. It was only recovered in 1911 when Sir Fitzroy Maclean restored the castle. Off A849 on east point of Mull. (D5)

Lachlan Macquarie Mausoleum On unclassified road off B8035 between Salen and Loch na Keal can be visited the mausoleum of Lachlan Macquarie, the 'Father of Australia', who died in 1824. (D3)

Mull and Iona Museum Association, Tobermory Local folklore museum with island exhibits. (B2)

Tobermory is the 'capital' of Mull, a really lovely town with whitewashed buildings clustered around a wooded bay which provides one of the safest anchorages on the west coast of Scotland. It is popular with yachtsmen, with holidaymakers and for day trips from the mainland. (B2)

Torosay Castle, Craignure A Scottish baronial castle with reception rooms and a variety of exhibition rooms open to the public. The 11 acres (4.4 hectares) of Italian terraced gardens by Lorimer contain a statue walk and a water garden. (D4)

Map 26

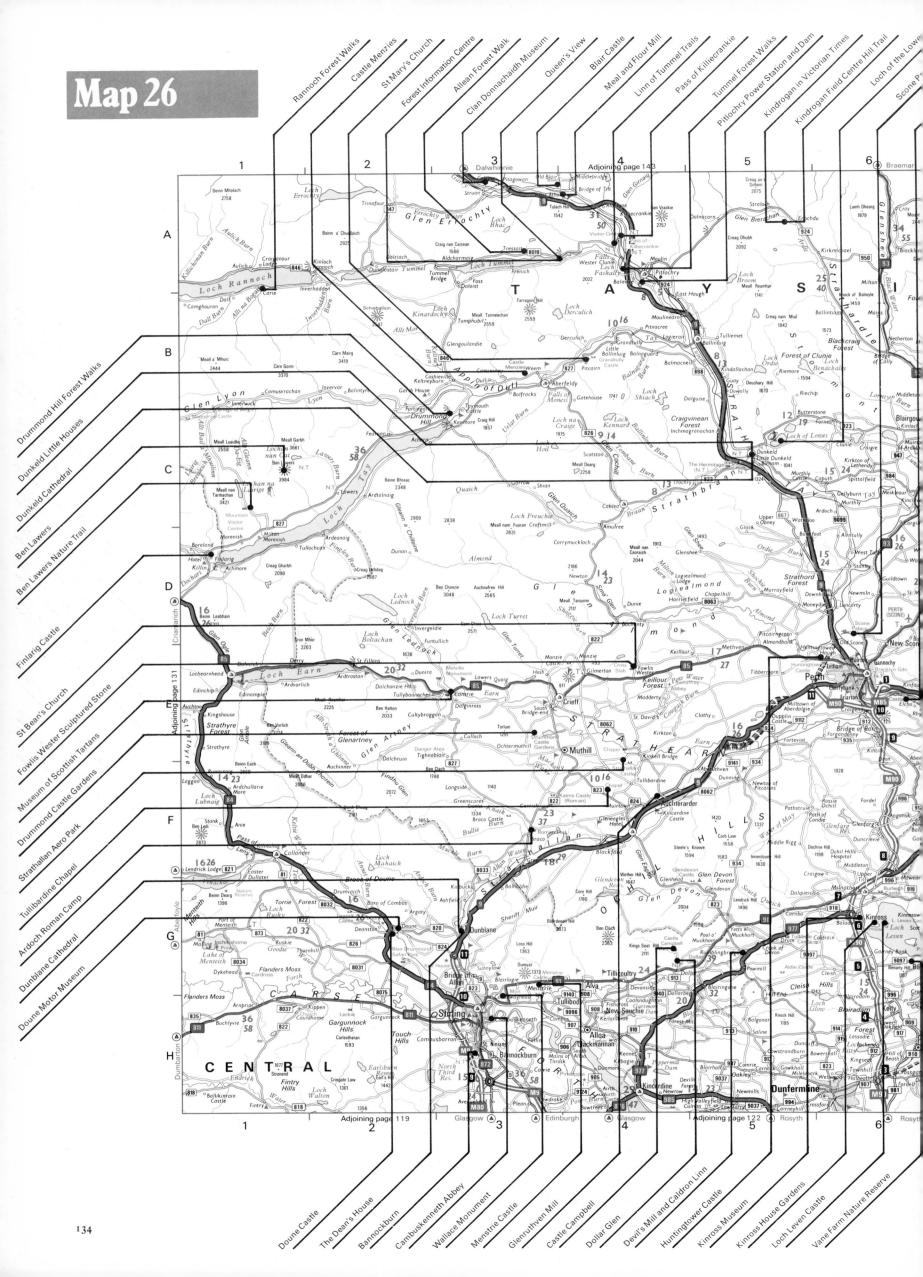

Lowland Scotland

Allean Forest Walks, Tummel Forest Three walks include remains of part-excavated ring fort and reconstructed clachan. Guidebook available from the **Forest Information Centre**. Car park, play areas, ¼ mile (0.4 km) west of **Queen's View** on B8019. (A3)

Alyth Folk Museum A collection of rural agricultural and domestic artefacts. Off A94, 3 miles (4.8 km) north Meigle. (B7)

Angus Folk Museum (NTS) Relics of domestic and agricultural life in the county of Angus, housed in a row of six 19th-century cottages with stone-slabbed roofs. Off A94 at Glamis. (C8)

Arbroath Abbey (SDD) The famous Declaration of Arbroath asserting Robert the Bruce as king was issued from here in 1320. Remains of the cloisters survive from the abbey, founded in 1178, and the abbot's house has been restored as a museum, containing relics, maps, documents etc. ⚅ (C11)

Arbroath Art Gallery, Hill Terrace Subjects of local interest and works by Angus artists are featured in changing exhibitions. (C11)

Arbroath Museum, Signal Tower, Ladyloan Fishing and flax industries, the history of Arbroath and of the Bell Rock Lighthouse (for which the Signal Tower was once the shore base) featured in various collections. (C11)

Ardestie and Carlungie Earth-Houses (SDD) Two large earth-houses attached to surface dwellings, used in the first centuries AD. At Ardestie the gallery is curved and 80 ft (24.4 m) long. The Carlungie earth house is 150 ft (45.6 m) long. Ardestie is about 6 miles (9.6 km) east Dundee at junction of A92 with B962; Carlungie is 1 mile (1.6 km) north on unclassified road to Carlungie. (D10)

Ardoch Roman Camp Dating back to the 2nd century, this is one of the largest Roman stations in Britain. There are a Roman fort and several camps in the surrounding area. A822 at Braco. (F3)

Auchterlonie's Golf Museum, Pilmuir Links, St Andrews Photographs, clubs, balls and other golfing relics illustrating the history of the game. (F9)

Balmerino Abbey (NTS) These ruins of a Cistercian abbey, founded in the 13th century by Alexander 11, can be viewed from the outside. On south shore of river Tay on unclassified road 5 miles (8 km) west Newport. (E8)

Bannockburn (NTS) An audio-visual display, the 'Forging of a Nation', reveals the sequence of events leading up to the victory of the Battle of Bannockburn (1314), a major event in Scottish history. There is also a handsome equestrian statue of Robert the Bruce by Pilkington Jackson. ⚅ (H3)

Ben Lawers (NTS) Perthshire's highest mountain at 3,984 ft (1,214 m), it is important because of its variety of rare alpine flowers and birdlife (buzzard, kestrel, red grouse, curlew). There are a number of guided walks in summer and a Visitor Centre (on unclassified road off A827) with films, audio-visuals, books and leaflets about the flora and fauna of the mountain. **Ben Lawers Nature Trail** starts from the car park next to the Visitor Centre and takes in a variety of upland vegetation (including alpine flowers) and birdlife on lower slopes of Ben Lawers. 2½ miles (4 km), 1½ hours. Guide book, ranger/naturalist service. (C1)

Blair Castle Fine collections of furniture, portraits and Jacobite relics are housed in this white, turreted castle whose oldest part, Cumming's Tower, dates back to 1269. It is the seat of the Duke of Atholl, chief of Clan Murray. The Duke is the only British subject allowed to maintain a private army, the Atholl Highlanders. ⚅ (A3)

Brechin Museum, St Ninian's Square Local history collection of Brechin and its surrounding district. (A10)

Brechin Round Tower (SDD) Dating back to the 10th or 11th century, this is one of only two round towers of this type in Scotland. It is now attached to the cathedral which was restored at the beginning of the century and has some interesting tombstones. ⚅ (A10)

Cambuskenneth Abbey (SDD) Scene of Bruce's Parliament in 1326, the abbey, now ruined, was founded in 1147 as a house of Augustinian Canons. Access over field. ⚅ (H3)

Castle Campbell, Dollar Glen (NTS, SDD) The first Earl of Argyll built this stronghold at the end of the 15th century on its promontory in the **Dollar Glen**. Despite being burned by Cromwell's troops in the 1650s, its courtyard, great hall and the barrel roof of the third floor are worth a visit. (G4)

Castle Menzies, Weem Splendid example of a 16th-century Z-plan transitional fortified tower house with elaborately carved dormers. Houses Clan Menzies museum. (B3)

Church of St Monan, St Monans This attractive church was built c. 1362 by David 11 in gratitude for his recovery, at the tomb of St Moinenn, from a wound. Restored in 1828, the church has a square tower with an octagonal steeple. (G10)

Clan Donnachaidh Museum, Calvine Old and new exhibits housed in this museum include relics associated with the Jacobite Risings of 1715 and 1745. The Clan Donnachaidh comprises Reid, Robertson, MacConnachie, Duncan, MacInroy and others. ⚅ (A3)

Craighall Den Sheltered wooded den along Craighall Burn with botanical and geological interest – extensive bird and plant life, old disused quarries and some waterfalls. 1½ miles (2 km), 1 hour. Car park, guide book. ½ mile (0.8 km) south of Ceres on road to Lower Largo. (F9)

Crail This picturesque fishing village features crow-stepped red-tiled houses, a lovely harbour and the Collegiate Church dating back to the 13th century. *Crail Museum*, Marketgate, houses exhibits of local interest. *Crail Tolbooth, Marketgate*, now the Town Hall, dates from early 16th century and displays a fish weather-vane and a coat-of-arms dated 1602. The bell, dated 1520, was cast in Holland. There have been 18th- and early 19th-century additions. (F10)

The Dean's House, Cathedral Square, Dunblane Dean James Pearson lived in this 17th-century house. Fascinating museum and library. (G3)

Devil's Mill and Caldron Linn Two dramatic waterfalls along the Devon river which runs through some picturesque and spectacular gorges at Rumblingbridge. Access to path by river through hotel grounds. (G5)

Dogton Stone (SDD) An ancient Celtic Cross with traces of animal and figure sculpture. Off B922, 5 miles (8 km) north-west Kirkcaldy. Entry by Dogton Farmhouse. (G7)

Dollar Glen (NTS) 60 acres (24 hectares) of woodland with attractive walks. Steep paths and bridges take the visitor through this romantic wooded glen and lead eventually to **Castle Campbell**. Off A91, above the town. (G4)

Doune Castle (SDD) Ruins are all that remain of this castle, built late 14th or early 15th century, but it is still one of the best-preserved medieval castles in Scotland. It came into the ownership of the Stuarts of Doune, Earls of Moray, in the 16th century. (G2)

Doune Motor Museum The Earl of Moray's collection of vintage and post-vintage cars. ⚅ (G2)

Drummond Castle Gardens The gardens were laid out c. 1630. The parterre was Italianised c. 1830 and embellished with figures and statues from Italy. A sundial in the form of an obelisk tells the time in most of the Capitals of Europe. Castle not open. Off A822. (E3)

Drummond Hill Forest Walks, The Mains Forest walks and viewpoint, ¼ mile (0.4 km) north Kenmore. Car park. (C3)

Dunblane Cathedral (SDD) The existing building dates mainly from the 13th century but was restored 1892–5. ⚅ (G3)

Dunkeld Cathedral (SDD) In a beautiful setting beside the river Tay, the cathedral was founded in the 9th century. The restored choir is in use as the parish church. The nave and the great northwest tower date from the 15th century. ⚅ (C5)

Dunkeld Little Houses (NTS) The Trust owns 20 houses in Cathedral and High Streets (not open). The Visitor Centre tells the story of these 17th-century houses, now restored as private dwellings. (C5)

Eassie Sculptured Stone (SDD) A fine example of an early Christian monument, elaborately carved, in Eassie Old Kirkyard. (C8)

Elcho Castle (SDD) Ancestral seat of the Earls of Wemyss, this preserved,

Eassie Sculptured Stone

fortified mansion (1530) is noted for its tower-like jambs or wings and the wrought-iron grills protecting the windows. On river Tay. ⚅ (E6)

Falkland Palace and Gardens (NTS) A Royal Palace, the favourite seat of James v, who died here in 1542, and of his daughter, Mary, Queen of Scots. The Renaissance-style buildings date from 1501–41. The 16th-century Royal Tennis Court is still in use. (F7)

Fife Folk Museum, Ceres Collections illustrating the domestic and agricultural past of Fife are housed in the 17th-century Weigh House near the bridge in this attractive village. ⚅ (F9)

Finavon Castle A stronghold with foundations dating back to c. 1300 with 16th-century additions, now a ruin. The castle collapsed in the 18th century due to the undermining of the foundations by the Lemno Burn. (B9)

Finavon Doocot The largest two-chamber, lean-to doocot in Scotland containing over 2,000 nesting boxes. Key with Finavon Doocot shop. (B9)

Finlarig Castle A beheading pit, thought to be the only one left in Scotland, is the focal point of this one-time seat of the Breadalbanes, now a ruin. South point of Loch Tay near Killin. (D1)

Forest Information Centre, Queen's View (FC) Displays to illustrate the history of forestry in the area and the methods used today. Nearby are the **Allean Forest Walks** (guide-book

available). Car park, picnic area. On B8019. ⚅ (A3/4)

Fowlis Wester Sculptured Stone (SDD) An 8th-century Pictish stone with remarkably clear carvings. Opposite the church. (E4)

Glamis Castle Fine collections of china, tapestry and furniture can be seen in this famous Scottish castle whose present buildings date from the 17th century, although parts are much older. Glamis is the childhood home of Queen Elizabeth the Queen Mother and birthplace of Princess Margaret. It is also the legendary setting of Shakespeare's play *Macbeth*. (B8)

Glenruthven Mill, Auchterarder Weaving demonstrations. Victorian steam engine on display. Small museum. (F4)

Hill of Tarvit (NTS) Furniture, tapestries, paintings and porcelain housed in a 17th-century mansion, remodelled by Sir Robert Lorimer in 1906. A916, 2 miles (3.2 km) south Cupar. (F8)

Huntingtower Castle (SDD) Once known as Ruthven Castle, this 15th-century castellated mansion was the scene of the Raid of Ruthven in 1582 when James VI was held captive by the Earl of Gowrie and his nobles. The Ruthven Conspirators held power until the Earl was beheaded in 1584. Off A85, 3 miles (4.8 km) north-west Perth. (E5)

Kellie Castle and Gardens, Pittenweem (NTS) The house seen today was completed c. 1606, the last stage in development from a single tower of c. 1360. Professor James Lorimer restored the castle over 100 years ago and it is a fine example of the domestic architecture of Lowland Scotland. The interior is noted for painted panelling, a ceiling painting (c. 1685) and a 16th-century tapestry. 16 acres (6.5 hectares) of gardens. ⚅ (G10)

Kindrogan Field Centre Hill Trail Hill path, steep in places, through forest plantation and heather moorland. Plants, animals, geology of interest and land farms. Extensive views of Strathardle and surrounding Grampian mountains. About 3 miles (4.8 km), 3 hours. Car park, guide book. On A924 10 miles (16 km) north-east Pitlochry. (A5)

Kindrogan in Victorian Times Path through gardens, along riverside and through semi-natural woodland. Illustrates aspects of 19th-century history and their bearing on the present landscape. Views of Strathardle. About 1 mile (1.6 km), 1 hour. Car park, guide book. Directions as above. (A5)

Kinross House Gardens Formal gardens surrounding a 17th-century house. ½ mile (0.8 km) south-east Kinross. ♿ (G6)

Glamis Castle

Kinross Museum, High Street Local military exhibits and other items of local interest include archaeological finds, a display of local linen manufacturing and some examples of peat cutting. (G6)

Leuchars Norman Church The original chapel and apse remain of this superb example of a Norman church, built by the De Quincie family. (E9)

Lindores Abbey Ruins of a Benedictine House founded in the 12th century. Lindores' Abbot Lawrence became Grand Inquisitor in Scotland and he tried many of the men who were burned at the stake as heretics. Off A913, just east of Newburgh. (E7)

Linn of Tummel Trails (NTS) Primarily woodland by the rivers Garry and Tummel. 2½ miles (4 km) or 1¼ miles (2 km). Car park. Information Centre at Killiecrankie 1 mile (1.6 km) north car park with ranger/naturalist services, evening talks or film shows, exhibition. Trail starts from car park, A9/B8019, 3 miles (4.8 km) north Pitlochry. (A4)

Loch Leven Castle (SDD) Mary, Queen of Scots was imprisoned in the tower here in 1567 although she escaped less than a year later. On an island on Loch Leven. Access by ferry from lochside, Kinross. (G6)

Loch of the Lowes (SWT) A Visitor Centre gives details of the area's interesting ecology and there are hides from which the birdlife can be watched, in particular the ospreys which nest in the area. Off A923. ♿ (C5)

Lochty Private Railway Steam-hauled passenger service over 1½ mile (2.4 km) track. Sundays only. On B940. ♿ (F10)

Meal and Flour Mill, Blair Atholl 17th-century watermill making flour and oatmeal. Visitors can go through the mill during working hours and eat food made from mill products in the tea room. (A4)

Megginch Castle Grounds Daffodils, rhododendrons and 1,000-year-old yews are features of these grounds which surround the 15th-century castle home of Captain and the Hon Mrs Drummond of Megginch. A85, 10 miles (16 km) east Perth. (E7)

Meigle Museum (SDD) An amazing collection of 25 sculptured monuments of the Celtic Christian period found either at or near the old churchyard. (C7)

Menstrie Castle Birthplace of Sir William Alexander, James VI's Lieutenant for the Plantation of Nova Scotia, this restored 16th-century castle contains a Nova Scotia Exhibition Room (NTS) displaying the coats of arms of 107 Nova Scotia Baronetcies. (G3)

Museum of Scottish Tartans, Drummond Street, Comrie A library of books, specimens of tartans, pictures, prints, maps, manuscripts and a system that records details of every known tartan make up the largest collection in existence of material relating to tartans and Highland Dress. Custodian is the Scottish Tartans Society. Garden with plants once used for the natural dyeing of cloth. Occasional demonstrations of hand-loom weaving in working weaver's cottage. ♿ (E2)

North Carr Lightship, East Pier, Anstruther A floating museum illustrating the work of, and life on board, a lightship. (G10)

Pass of Killiecrankie (NTS) This wooded gorge is a famous beauty spot. The Visitor Centre provides information about its natural history and offers ranger services. Displays illustrate the history of the battle in 1689 when English troops were routed by Jacobite forces led by 'Bonnie Dundee'. Off A9, 2½ miles (4 km) north Pitlochry. (A4)

Pitlochry Power Station and Dam An exhibition on the workings of a hydro-electric power station is housed inside the power station. Visitors can watch the salmon cleverly scaling the massive dam by means of a fish ladder. (A4)

Queen's View, Loch Tummel Said to be one of Queen Victoria's favourite views, and now a public viewing point. Views along Loch Tummel to the peak of Schiehallion, 3,547 ft (1,080 m). See also **Forest Information Centre**. On B8019. (A3)

Rannoch Forest Walks Three associated walks adjoining Carie Burn and tributaries leading through various types of woodland to higher ground with spectacular views over Loch Rannoch. Up to 6 miles (9.6 km). Car park. Starts at Carie, 3 miles (4.8 km) west Kinloch Rannoch on south lochside road. (A1)

St Andrews Castle (SDD) Founded in 1200 and rebuilt in the late 14th century, this castle, now ruined, overlooks the sea. ♿ (E9)

St Andrews Cathedral (SDD) The east and west gables, south wall of the nave, and portions of the choir and south transept are all that remain of this cathedral, once the largest church in the country. Most of surviving remains belong to the late 12th and 13th centuries. ♿ (E9)

St Andrews Preservation Trust, North Street Small museum and annual exhibition housed in a mid 18th-century cottage in the old quarter of St Andrews. (E9)

St Bean's Church, Fowlis Wester An attractive 13th-century church, restored this century, containing a finely-carved Pictish stone cross (SDD). (E4)

St Fillan's Cave, Cove Wynd, Pittenweem The name Pittenweem is pictish for *The Place of the Cave* and it got its name from St Fillan's. The Priory, Great House and Prior's Lodging above the cave were established by Augustinian monks in the 12th century and restored and rededicated in 1935. (G10)

St Mary's Church, Grandtully (SDD) A 16th-century church, with a remarkable painted wooden ceiling of heraldic and symbolic subjects. Open on application to key-keeper. At Pitcairn Farm, 2 miles (3.2 km) north-east Aberfeldy, off A827. (B3)

St Orland's Stone (SDD) An upstanding sculptured slab of the Early Christian period. 1½ miles (2.4 km) north-east Glamis railway station in a field near the farmhouse of Cossans. (B8)

Scone Palace Splendid collections of porcelain, ivories, furniture, 18th-century clocks and 16th-century needlework are housed in this lovely castellated palace, gothicised in 1803. The palace has extensive grounds and a notable pinetum open to visitors. The famous Stone of Scone was brought here in the 9th century by Kenneth McAlpine, King of Scots. In 1296 the Stone was seized and taken to Westminster Abbey where it can be seen today. (E6)

Scottish Fisheries Museum, Anstruther Harbour The Scottish fisherman's life on land and at sea, both today and in the past, is illustrated by a fascinating collection of items, housed in 16th- to 19th-century buildings, grouped around a cobbled courtyard. Exhibits include old anchors and ship figureheads, personal items taken to sea, displays on sail-making and boat-building, and on different methods of fish-catching. There is also a marine aquarium, a restored sailing boat, *Fifie*, 70 ft (21.3 m) long, two fishing boats and a Zulu type of fishing vessel, 78 ft (23.7 m) long. (G10)

Strathallan Aero Park A small collection of historic aircraft, predominantly from the World War II era and dating back to 1934. Supporting facilities include an audio-visual theatre, shop, picnic area, children's play area etc. The museum is located off the B8062 Crieff to Auchterarder road. Follow the airfield signs from Auchterarder or Muthill. ♿ (F4)

Tealing Earth House and Dovecot (SDD) A well-preserved Iron Age souterrain or earth-house consisting of a passage and long curved gallery with small inner chambers. Nearby is a fine dovecot built in 1595. Off A929, ½ mile (0.8 km) on unclassified road to Tealing and Auchterhouse. (C9)

Tentsmuir Point National Nature Reserve (NCC) Principal interest of reserve is botanical but a large population of migrant birds can be seen on this area of foreshore (Abertay Sands) and inland area of dunes, trees and marsh. South and east of Tayport between estuaries of rivers Tay and Eden. Off B945. (E10)

Tullibardine Chapel (SDD) A Collegiate church remaining much as it was when founded in 1446. Off A823. Open on application to key-keeper. (F4)

Tummel Forest Walks, Faskally Three walks: Red Trail (1 hour), Blue Trail (2 hours) and Yellow Trail (3 hours). Varied ages and species of conifers, variety of flora and fauna. Car park, information centre, guide book. 1 mile (1.6 km) north Pitlochry (A9); follow signs. (A4)

Vane Farm Nature Reserve (RSPB) Visitors can observe wild geese and duck from the end of September to April. A converted farm building houses displays which interpret the surrounding countryside and the loch. On south shore of Loch Leven, on B9097. (G6)

Wallace Monument Commemorates William Wallace, who defeated the English at the Battle of Stirling Bridge in 1297. Officially opened in 1869. 242 steps to the top. There is also an audio-visual display on Wallace's life. Off A907, 1½ miles (2 km) north-east Stirling. (G3)

St Andrews Cathedral

A   B   C   D   E   F

8 7 6 5 4 3 2 1

Corrieshalloch Gorge

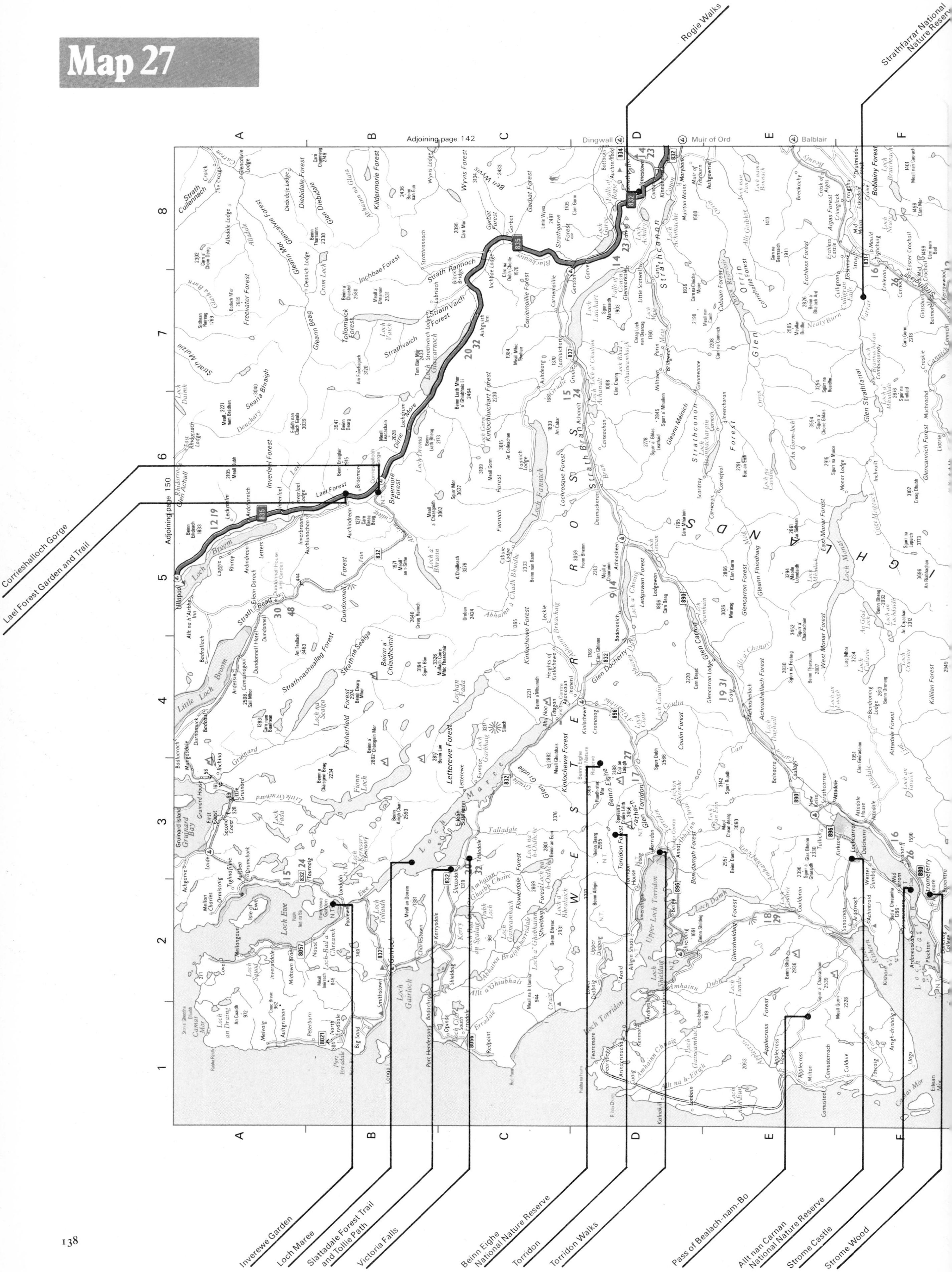

Lael Forest Garden and Trail

Adjoining page 150

Major place and feature labels (selection): Ullapool, Loch Broom, Little Loch Broom, Strath Cuileannach, Strath Mulzie, Freewater Forest, Gleann Mór, Glen Diebidale, Diebidale Forest, Kildermorie Forest, Wyvis Forest, Garbat Forest, Strathvaich Forest, Tollomuick Forest, Inchbae Forest, Strath Rannoch, Strath Vaich, Kinlochluichart Forest, Corriemoillie Forest, Strathconon, Strathconon Forest, Orrin, Glen Strathfarrar, Boblainy Forest, Eccless Forest, Aigas Forest, Inverlael Forest, Braemore Forest, Dundonnell Forest, Strathnasheallag Forest, Fisherfield Forest, Fannich Forest, Letterewe Forest, Kinlochewe Forest, West Monar Forest, Glencannich Forest, Attadale Forest, Killilan Forest, Gruinard Bay, Gruinard Island, Loch Ewe, Loch Maree, Loch Torridon, Upper Loch Torridon, Loch Shieldaig, Torridon Forest, Coulin Forest, Ben Damph Forest, Applecross Forest, Glenshieldaig Forest, Glencarron Forest, East Monar Forest, Achnashellach Forest, Loch Carron, Loch Kishorn, Loch Duich, Benn Eighe National Nature Reserve

Inverewe Garden

Loch Maree

Slattadale Forest Trail and Tollie Path

Victoria Falls

Beinn Eighe National Nature Reserve

Torridon

Torridon Walks

Pass of Bealach-nam-Bo

Allt nan Carnan National Nature Reserve

Strome Castle

Strome Wood

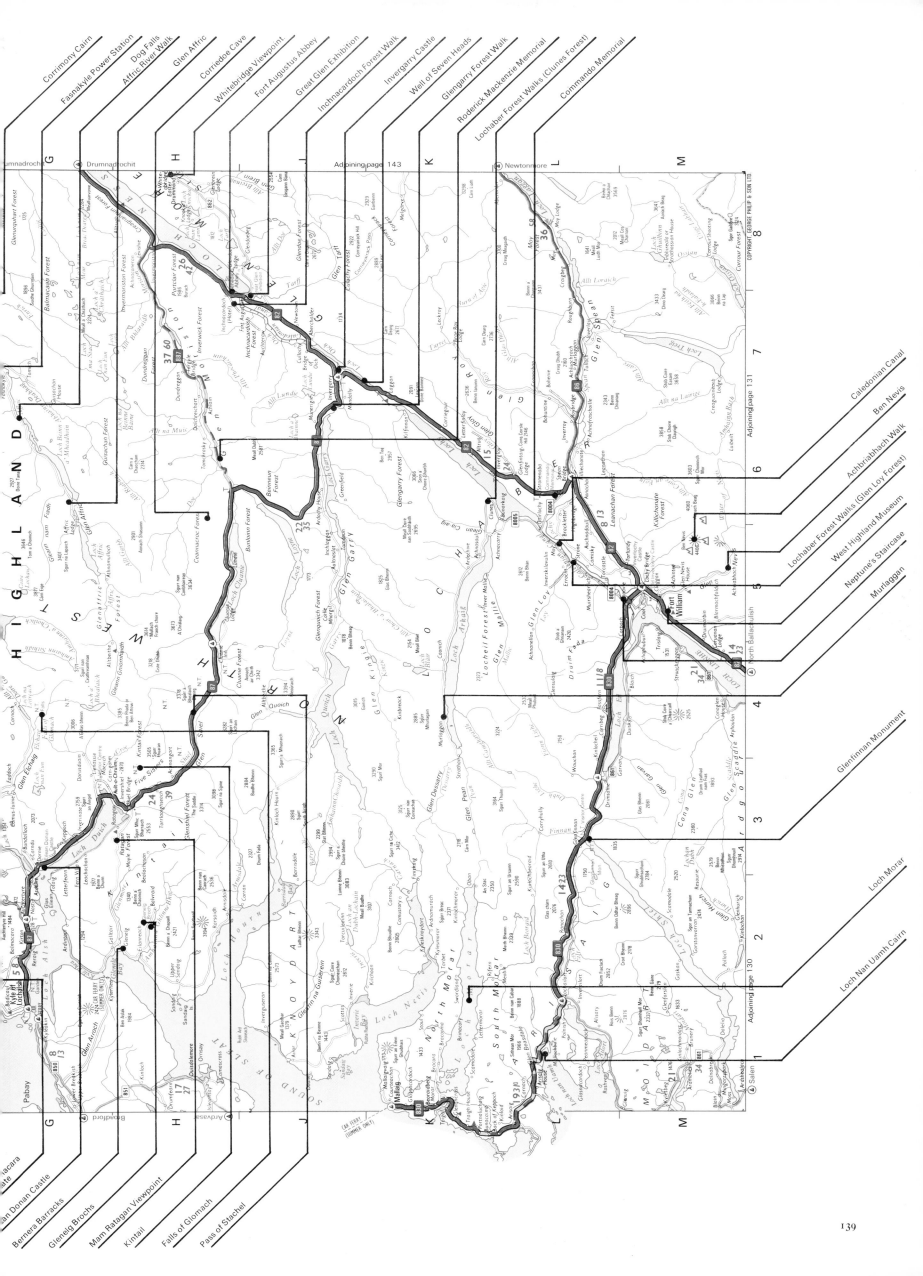

Highland Scotland

Achbriabhach Walk, Lochaber Forest 1 mile (1.6 km) forest road through spruce. On unclassified road up Glen Nevis, 5 miles (8 km) south-east Fort William. (M5)

Affric River Walk Along a classical Highland glen combining all the traditional features – wild rivers, Caledonian Pine, loch and rugged mountains. A shorter walk is also available to a viewpoint. 1 mile (1.6 km), ½ hour to complete walk. Car park, picnic place. See also **Dog Falls**. From Cannich on A831 follow unclassified road to Fasnakyle Power Station and turn right up Glen Affric. Car park 1 mile (1.6 km) beyond end of public road. (G7)

Allt nan Carnan National Nature Reserve An 18 acre (7 hectare) stretch of land with a wooded gorge as deep as it is wide, situated to the north-west of Lochcarron. (E3)

Balmacara Estate (NTS) Most of the Kyle–Plockton peninsula is included in the Balmacara Estate – a truly beautiful region of forest and moorland with breathtaking views over loch and sea. There are woodland walks in the grounds of *Lochalsh House* (not open) with azaleas, rhododendrons and other exotic plants. Also several walks, up to 7 miles (11 km) long, on the Lochalsh peninsula, with wide variety of wild flowers to be seen near Drumbuie. Go to interpretation centre in grounds of Lochalsh House to obtain guidebook and see range of guided walks. Evening lectures in summer. Ranger/naturalist services available. House is south of A87 about 3½ miles (5 km) east of Kyle of Lochalsh. (G2)

Beinn Eighe National Nature Reserve (NCC) Of great geographical and natural history interest, this was the very first National Nature Reserve in Britain. It is the hunting ground of wildcats and pine marten. Visitor Centre at Aultroy Cottage on A832. Nature reserve is west of A896/A832 junction at Kinlochewe. (D3)

Ben Nevis Britain's highest mountain (4,406 ft, 1,343 m) and most popular mountain for both the climber and the hillwalker. From Achintee Farm, 2½ miles (4 km) from Fort William, on the eastern bank of the river Nevis, a stoney 5 mile (8 km) path leads to the summit – but walkers should use extreme care and make sure they are adequately clothed and shod before attempting the walk. For those who don't have a head for heights, the Glen round the mountain's western and southern sides is one of Scotland's most beautiful and amply rewarding. The glen can be ascended by car following the left bank of the Nevis and the road ends in a car park beside a magnificent waterslide. (M5)

Bernera Barracks, Glenelg The remains of Bernera Barracks, erected in *c.* 1722 and used continuously until after 1790. (H2)

Caledonian Canal Constructed in the early 19th century, the Caledonian Canal forges its way across the highest parts of Britain through dramatic scenery from Inverness to Corpach near Fort William. It is 60 miles (96 km) long; 22 miles (35 km) run through man-made cuttings and 38 miles (61 km) through natural lochs. It is possible to hire boats for holidays on the canal and there are pleasure cruises in summer. (M5 to Map 28 E2)

Commando Memorial The Commandos in World War II trained in this area and in 1952 a very distinctive sculp-ture by Scott Sutherland was erected here to commemorate them. There are also splendid views of **Ben Nevis** and Lochaber from this spot. Off A82, 11 miles (17.6 km) from Fort William. (L6)

Corriedoe Cave The Young Pretender lay in this cave from 24–28 August 1746. In Glen Moriston, about 2½ miles (4 km) up river Doe from river Moriston. (H6)

Corrieshalloch Gorge (NTS) The impressive Falls of Measach plunge 150 ft (46 m) into this spectacular gorge which is 200 ft (61 m) deep and one mile (1.6 km) long. A suspension bridge

Corrieshalloch Gorge

crosses the gorge and enables visitors to get a superb view of the water teeming into the depths. A835 at Braemore. (B6)

Corrimony Cairn This Neolithic chambered cairn is surrounded by stone slabs, and by an outer circle of standing stones. (G7)

Dog Falls A walk, part road, part path through open pinewoods, circling a small loch and falling back steeply to the Affric river, crossed by a footbridge. A shorter route is possible. 2½ miles (4 km), 1½ hours to complete. Car park, picnic area. See also **Affric River Walk**. From Cannich, on A831, follow unclassified road to Fasnakyle Power Station and turn right up Glen Affric, car park 2 miles (3.2 km) on left. (G6)

Eilean Donan Castle This famous, much photographed castle, often used to typify Highland scenery, dates back to 1220. Situated on an islet (connected to the mainland by a causeway) in Loch Duich, Eilean Donan was garrisoned by Spanish Jacobite troops in 1719 and blown up by an English man o'war. Now completely restored, it incorporates a war memorial to the Clan MacRae, who held it as hereditary Constables on behalf of the Mackenzies. Off A87, 9 miles (14.4 km) east of Kyle of Lochalsh. (G2)

Falls of Glomach (NTS) One of Britain's highest waterfalls, 370 ft (113 m) above wild Glen Elchaig. A 1½ hour arduous climb from west end of Loch na Leitreach in Glen Elchaig (approach

Eilean Donan Castle

from Ardelve). Or a 7 mile (11.2 km) long-distance walkers' path through the hills via Dorusduain from Croe Bridge on Loch Duich. Stout footwear essential. (G4)

Fasnakyle Power Station Display diagrams explain the hydro-electric scheme. At start of Glen Affric. (G6)

Fort Augustus Abbey Guided tours are conducted by the monks around their Benedictine abbey, started in 1876. The Abbey occupies the much-adapted buildings of the old fort which took its name from William Augustus, Duke of Cumberland, who made it his headquarters after the Battle of Culloden in 1746.   (J7)

Glen Affric The road from Cannich takes the visitor along the Glen for 9 miles (14.5 km), with great reward. Vistas constantly change from loch to mountain and back to island-studded loch with beautiful shades of green from the pine and birch forests. There are plenty of natural parking places and many walks to be enjoyed (see **Affric River Walk, Dog Falls**). (G5/6)

Glenelg Brochs, Glenelg (SDD) Two Iron Age brochs, Dun Telve and Dun Troddan, have walls still over 30 ft (9.1 m) high. 8 miles (19.2 km) west Shiel Bridge. (H2)

Glenfinnan Monument (NTS) A figure of a Highlander stands proudly atop this monument to the raising of Prince Charles Edward Stuart's standard at Glenfinnan on 19 August 1745 as a rallying point for the clans in the 1745 rising. The monument was erected in 1815 by MacDonald of Glenaladale. The story of the Prince's campaign from Glenfinnan to Derby and back to the final defeat at Culloden is told in the Visitor Centre. (L3)

Glengarry Forest Walk By woodland path and forest road to a spectacular waterfall. 1½ and 2¼ miles (2.4 and 3.6 km). Car park, picnic places. Starts by A87, 2 miles (3.2 km) west Invergarry. (J6)

Great Glen Exhibition, Fort Augustus Information about the Clan uprisings is among the items in this open-plan museum. There is also an audio-visual presentation outlining the history of the Great Glen.   (J7)

Inchnacardoch Forest Walk A walk through natural woodland. Car park, guide book. Starts from unclassified road off A82, 2 miles (3.2 km) north-west Fort Augustus. (J7)

Inverewe Garden (NTS) The effect of the Gulf Stream along this north-western coast of Scotland means that many exotic and subtropical plants grow in this garden created over 100 years ago

Five Sisters of Kintail

by Osgood Mackenzie. Vivid colour virtually all year round. Includes plants from Chile and South Africa, Himalayan Lilies and giant forget-me-nots from the South Pacific. The beautiful British rhododendron also plays its part in the springtime display. On A832. ♿ (B2)

Invergarry Castle The ruins of this one-time stronghold of the MacDonells of Glengarry, on the site of two earlier castles, can be seen in the grounds of Glengarry Castle Hotel. (J6)

Kintail (NTS) Stunning Highland scenery between Lochs Cluanie and Duich north of A87. Here the Five Sisters of Kintail, peaks rising to 3,500 ft (1,067 m), tower over the landscape and red deer and wild goats roam freely.

There is a Visitor Centre at Morvich with an audio-visual display. (H3/4)

Lael Forest Garden and Trail A forest garden containing interesting and ornamental trees of native and foreign origin. Car park, guide book. A835. 10½ miles (17 km) south Ullapool. ♿ (B6)

Loch Maree One of Scotland's loveliest lochs with an amazing variety of scenery along its length. Its name probably originated from St Maree or Maelrubha, the monk who traditionally spent his life on an island in the loch and who founded the monastery at Applecross. The loch's shores form part of several estates: the Caledonian pine forest, part of the **Beinn Eighe National Nature Reserve**, and the Slattadale Forestry Commission Estate with its forest trails (west shore) – see **Slattadale Forest Trail**. The group of fir and heather-clad islands form the Loch Maree Islands Nature Reserve, important for the native pinewood and juniper. There is a deer sanctuary at Slioch (east shore). (B/C2/3/4)

Loch Morar 12 miles (19.2 km) long and 1 mile (1.6 km) wide, Loch Morar is remarkable because of its great depth (over 1,000 ft, 304 m). On the largest of the group of islands near the loch's western end Lord Lovat was captured two months after Culloden; an intriguer, he had been playing both sides, but was now taken to London and beheaded. (K1/2)

Loch Nan Uamh Cairn The name, translated, means the Loch of the Caves and it was here that the Young Pretender landed in 1745, the occasion being commemorated by this cairn beside the road. It was from here that he sailed away defeated a year later. (L1)

Lochaber Forest Walks, Clunes Forest Three walks: Ciag, towards Loch Arkaig, 2 miles (3.2 km); Chorrach, through larch and spruce above Loch Lochy, 1½ miles (2.4 km); Glaster, by Loch Lochy, 5½ miles (8.8 km). From Clunes. (K5)

Lochaber Forest Walks, Glen Loy Forest Two walks: Strone, on forest roads with viewpoints, ½ mile (0.8 km); Errocht, on forest road through plantations, 2 miles (3.2 km). Off B8004. (L5)

Mam Ratagan Viewpoint A car park and view indicator in the Pass of Mam Ratagan (1,116 ft, 340 m) approached by a wooded, scenic road. Unclassified road from Shiel Bridge to Glenelg, 8 miles (12.8 km) east Glenelg. (H2)

Murlaggan It is said that at Murlaggan treasure given in support of the Young Pretender by the French was thrown into Loch Arkaig on the occasion of the last Jacobite rally in 1746. At western end of unclassified road along Loch Arkaig. (K4)

Neptune's Staircase A series of 8 locks, built between 1805 and 1822, which raises Telford's Caledonian Canal 64 ft (19.5 m). 3 miles (4.8 km) north-west Fort William off A830 at Banavie. (M5)

Pass of Bealach-nam-Bo Translated this means the 'Pass of the Cattle'. It is one of the highest roads in Britain as it zig-zags across the Applecross mountains in a series of hairpin bends from Applecross to Kishorn. The road reaches a gradient of 1 in 4 as it climbs from sea level to 2,054 ft (626 m) in the Pass itself. It is quite a hair-raising drive as there are sheer drops of hundreds of feet but it is worth it as the views are spectacular. Unclassified road from Applecross to Loch Kishorn. (E/F1)

Pass of Stachel Magnificent jagged mountains cleft with corries overhang the road as it descends through Glen Shiel to the NTS property of **Kintail**. A87 between Loch Cluanie and Shiel Bridge. (H3/4)

Roderick Mackenzie Memorial Mackenzie pretended to be Charles Edward Stuart and was killed by soldiers searching for the Prince after Culloden in 1746. A cairn on the south of the A887 commemorates Mackenzie. (H6)

Rogie Walks A system of walks in broadleaved and conifer woodland to Rogie Falls and beyond. Suspension bridge, salmon leap. Car park, picnic facilities, information boards. On A832, 1 mile (1.6 km) north-west Contin. (D8)

Slattadale Forest Trail and Tollie Path Forest trail and path (the old footpath to Poolewe). Trail of ½ mile (0.8 km); path of 5 miles (8 km). Car park, picnic area, guide book. A832, 7 miles (11.2 km) south-west Gairloch, on Loch Maree. (C2/3)

Strathfarrar National Nature Reserve This is one of the largest surviving areas of native pinewood left in Scotland. It has been virtually unspoilt by felling or conversion to commercial tree crop. The road, for walkers only, runs through Strathfarrar Glen to the end of Loch Monar. Unclassified road up Glen Strathfarrar from B831 at Struy Bridge. (F8)

Strome Castle (NTS) Ruins of ancient castle, destroyed in 1602 after a long siege. Unclassified road off A896, north-west shore of Loch Carron. (F2)

Strome Wood A walk winding through fine scenery in woodland high above Loch Carron. 1 mile (1.6 km), ¾ hour. Car park, picnic facilities. On forest road at junction of old Stromeferry road and A890. (F2)

Torridon (NTS) Some of Scotland's most spectacular mountain scenery with peaks rising to over 3,000 ft (914 m). Of particular interest are Liathach (3,456 ft, 1,053 m) and Beinn Eighe (3,309 ft, 1,008 m) which are of red sandstone, some 750 million years old, topped with white quartzite, some 600 million years old. There is a Visitor Centre with audiovisual displays describing the wildlife of the area at the junction of A896 and Diabaig roads (head of Upper Loch Torridon). At *The Mains* nearby is a static display illustrating the life of the red deer. Off A896, 8 miles (12.8 km) south-west Kinlochewe. (D2/3)

Torridon Walks Six tough walks of interest to geologists and naturalists outlined in guide book. Hillwalking equipment is required. Go first to NTS Visitor Centre at head of Upper Loch Torridon for advice on guided walks and guide book. (D2/3)

Victoria Falls Waterfall named after Queen Victoria who visited Loch Maree and the surrounding area in 1877. Off A832, 12 miles (19.2 km) north-west Kinlochewe, near Slattadale. (C2)

Well of Seven Heads A monument recalls the story of the execution of seven brothers for the murder of the two sons of a 17th-century chief of Keppoch. The monument, surmounted by seven men's heads and inscribed in English, Gaelic, French and Latin stands above a spring. Off A82 on the west shore of Loch Oich. (J7)

West Highland Museum, Cameron Square, Fort William Jacobite relics, which include a secret portrait of Prince Charles Edward Stuart, are housed in this museum together with historical, natural history and folk exhibits, local relics and a tartan section. (M5)

Whitebridge Viewpoint Along the south shore of Loch Ness the B862 climbs through some lovely scenery to 1,162 ft (354 m) and this viewpoint from which there are magnificent views over the loch. On B862 at Whitebridge. (H8)

Map 28

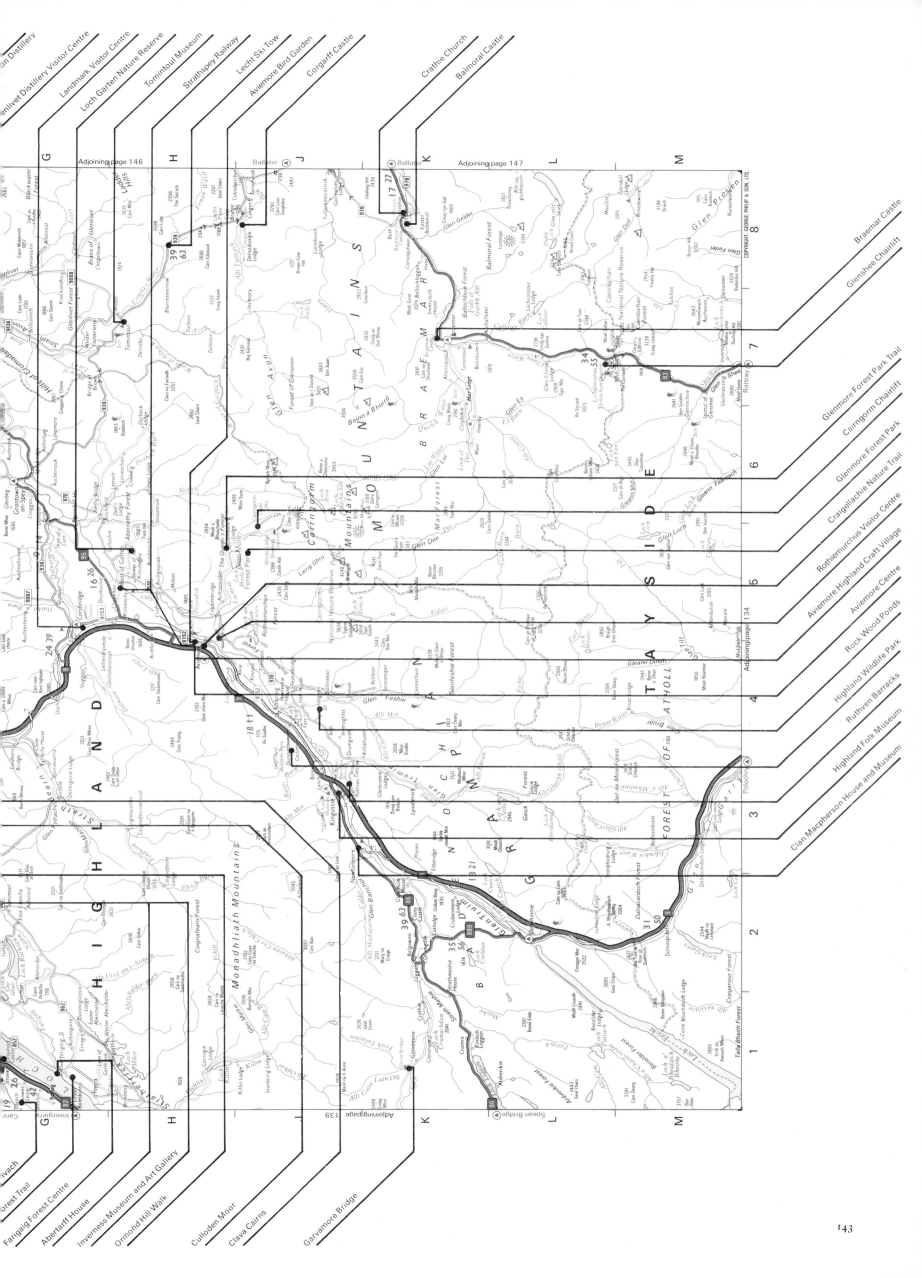

143

Highland Scotland

Abertarff House, Church Street, Inverness (NTS) One of the oldest buildings in Inverness, built 1593, it is a good example of 16th/17th-century domestic architecture, with its crow-stepping and circular stone tower leading to the upper floors. Regional headquarters of the National Trust for Scotland with small shop. (E2)

Ardclach Bell Tower (SDD) A two-storey tower of 1655 whose bell summoned worshippers to the church and warned the neighbourhood in case of alarm. Open on application to Custodian. Off A939, 8½ miles (13.5 km) south-east of Nairn. (E5)

Aviemore Bird Garden Located at Aviemore Centre, breeding work is carried out on many endangered species of birds, including pheasants, owls, waterfowl and others. (H4)

Aviemore Centre Holiday and conference centre with a wide range of sports and entertainment facilities, including cinema, swimming pool, ice rink, saunas, squash, go-karts, artificial ski slope, water sports and skiing according to season. ⅂ (H4)

Aviemore Highland Craft Village Traditional-style village square where craftsmen work on a wide range of arts and crafts. (H4)

Balmoral Castle The family holiday home of the Royal Family for over a century. Prince Albert bought the 11,000-acre (4,452 hectare) estate in 1852; the castle was rebuilt by William Smith of Aberdeen with modifications by Prince Albert, and was first occupied in 1855. Exhibition of pictures, porcelain and works of art in the castle ballroom (remainder not open). Grounds. Not open when any member of the Royal Family is in residence. A93, 8 miles (12.8 km) west of Ballater. ⅂ (K8)

Beauly Priory (SDD) Founded in 1230, one of three houses of the Valliscaulian Order founded in Scotland. Only the church remains, a long narrow building comprising aisleless nave, transepts and chancel. Burial place of the Mackenzies of Kintail. ⅂ (E1)

Birnie Church Small Romanesque church built in the early 12th century on the site of the church (c. 550) of St Brendan the Navigator. It stands on a pre-Christian site (standing stones in churchyard) and is believed to be the oldest parish church in continuous use for worship in Scotland. Unclassified

road off A941, 3 miles (4.8 km) south-east of Elgin. (D8)

Blackstand Walk Easy forest walk with roe deer and capercaillie to be seen. Information Centre, car park, guide book. Starts at Blackstand Forestry Offices, off B9160, 3 miles (4.8 km) north-west of Fortrose. (D3)

Boar Stone (SDD) This roughly-shaped slab, nearly 7 ft (2.1 m) high, has the mirror-case symbol incised at the top; below is the figure of a boar. Also known as Knocknagael Boar Stone. Off B861, 2 miles (3.2 km) south of Inverness. (F2)

Boath Doocot (NTS) A 17th-century dovecote on the site of an ancient castle

Boath Doocot

where Montrose flew the standard of Charles I when he defeated the Covenanters in 1645. The plan of the battle is on display. At Auldearn, 2 miles (3.2 km) east of Nairn. (D5)

Brae Walk Forest track from Brae, passing cairns, including chambered cairn at Woodhead. Fine views. Car park, guide book. Off unclassified road, 9 miles (14.4 km) south-west of Cromarty. (D2)

Braemar Castle Situated near the river Dee, this turreted stronghold, built in 1628 by the Earl of Mar, was attacked and burnt in 1689. It was rebuilt about 1748. Now a fully furnished family home, there is a round central tower, a spiral stair, barrel-vaulted ceilings and an underground pit prison. (K7)

Brodie Castle (NTS) 16th-century castle with 17th- and 19th-century additions, set in Morayshire parkland. Contains fine collections of French furniture, porcelain and major paintings. Also woodland walks, wildlife observation hide, adventure playground. Off A96 25 miles (40 km) east of Inverness. ⅂ (D5)

The Cairngorms

Burghead Museum, 16–18 Grant Street, Burghead Illustrates the archaeology of the Laich of Moray from 2500 BC–AD 1300. ⅂ (C7)

Burghead Well (SDD) This remarkable rock-cut structure within the wall of an Iron Age fort is probably an Early Christian Baptistry. At Burghead. (C7)

Cairngorm Chairlift At the top of the chairlift is the highest restaurant in Britain, the Ptarmigan, with magnificent views over Strathspey to the west, north and east. A951 from A9 at Aviemore. (J5/6)

Caledonian Canal Built between 1803 and 1822, the canal runs across the

Braemar Castle

highest parts of Britain through some of Scotland's most dramatic scenery, in almost a straight line from Inverness to Corpach near Fort William. See also Gazetteer 27. (E2)

Cawdor Castle The old central tower of 1372, fortified in 1454, is surrounded by later additions principally of the 17th century when the gradual conversion of a small defensive fort into a large family mansion was begun. Further work was done in the 18th and 19th centuries. Interesting interior with pictures, tapestries. Notable gardens surround the castle. On B9090. ⅂ (E4)

Clan Macpherson House and Museum, Newtonmore The museum of the clan with relics and memorials including the green banner, swords, decorations and medals. Prince Charles Edward Stuart relics, including letters from the Prince to the Clan Chief (1745) and a letter to the Prince from his father (the Old Pretender). Magnificent silver centrepiece. ⅂ (K2)

Clava Cairns (NTS, SDD) Situated on the south bank of the river Nairn, this group of burial cairns has three concentric rings of great stones. They are of late Neolithic or early Bronze Age date. Near Culloden, off B851, 6½ miles (10.4 km) east of Inverness. (E3)

Corgarff Castle (SDD) A 16th-century tower, which was besieged in 1571. Featured in the campaigns of Montrose

Entrance passage in one of the Clava Cairns

and both the Jacobite Risings. Later a military barracks. Off A939. (J8)

Coulmore Wood Walk Walk through oak trees. Magnificent views up and down the Beauly Firth. Car park, guide book. Starts on B9162, between Kessock and Tore. (E2)

Craigellachie Bridge One of Thomas Telford's most beautiful bridges. Begun in 1812, it carried the main road until 1973 when a new bridge was built alongside. Near A941, just north of Craigellachie. (E8)

Craigellachie Nature Trail, Aviemore Through Nature Reserve past old British Rail reservoir. Possible to see peregrine falcon, roe and red deer. 1 mile (1.6 km) to complete trail. Car park. (H4)

Craig Phadrig Forest Trail On a prominent hill overlooking Inverness, the Beauly Firth and the Moray Firth. 1 mile (1.6 km) long. Car park, guide book. On Leachkin road, off A9, 2 miles (3.2 km) west of Inverness. (E2)

Crathie Church This small church, built in 1895, is attended by the Royal Family when at Balmoral. (K8)

Cromarty Foreshore Walk Rocky path through pebbles, sandstone rock, Scots pine. The cliffs are unstable and

should not be climbed. Car park, guide book. East end of Cromarty. (C4)

Culbokie Loch Walk A trail leading to an artificial loch, with interesting plants. Car park, guide book. From A9169. (D2)

Culloden Moor (NTS) Here Prince Charles Edward's cause was finally crushed at the battle on 16 April 1746. Old Leanach farmhouse has been restored as a battle museum. Information Centre, audio-visual theatre, historical displays. Car park. *Battlefield Trail* starts ¼ mile (0.4 km) west, off B9006, and circles battlefield. Clan and regimental cairns on trail. B9006, 5 miles (8 km) east of Inverness. (E3)

Dingwall Town House Museum of local history in the Town House, which dates from 1730. There is a special exhibit on General Sir Hector MacDonald (1853–1903), born near Dingwall, recalling his distinguished military career. Town centre. (D1)

Duffus Castle (SDD) Massive ruins of a fine motte-and-bailey castle, surrounded by a moat still entire and water-filled. Fine 14th-century tower crowns the Norman motte. Off B9012, 4 miles (6.4 km) north-west of Elgin. (C7)

Elgin Cathedral, North College Street, Elgin (SDD) When entire, this was perhaps the most beautiful of Scottish cathedrals. Much 13th-century work still remains. A 6th-century Pictish slab is in the choir. ♿ (C7)

Elgin Museum, High Street, Elgin Houses a varied collection which includes fossils, notably from Old Red Sandstone, Burghead Bulls (rocks), prehistoric weapons, costumes and local domestic items. (C7)

Falconer Museum, Tolbooth Street, Forres A varied collection which includes shells, fossil fish, birds, weapons, flints and arrowheads from Culbin, local history and the Hugh Falconer exhibit. ♿ (D6)

Falls of Divach A short walk (½ mile, 0.8 km) through oak woods to Divach Falls, impressive in spate. Car park. Go south from Drumnadrochit on A82, turn right in Lewiston and follow signs to Divach. (G1)

Farigaig Forest Centre (FC) Forestry Commission interpretation centre in a converted stone stable, showing the development of the forest environment in the Great Glen. Off B852 in centre of Inverfarigaig. ♿ (G1)

Farigaig Forest Trail Forest trail, car park, guide book. From B852 south Inverfarigaig. (G1)

Fort George (SDD) Begun in 1748 as a result of the Jacobite risings, this is one of the finest late artillery fortifications in Europe. Houses *Queen's Own Highlanders Museum* exhibiting period uniforms, medals etc. ♿ The Georgian garrison church dates from 1767. On B9006. (D3)

Fortrose Cathedral (SDD) The existing portions of this 14th-century cathedral are complete and include vaulting overhead and much fine detail. Open on application to Custodian. At Fortrose. ♿ (D3)

Garvamore Bridge This two-arched bridge at the south end of the Corrieyarrick Pass was built by General Wade in 1735. 6 miles (9.6 km) west of Laggan Bridge, on unclassified road. (K1)

Glenfarclas Distillery Tours of a well-known malt whisky distillery; visual exhibition and museum of old illicit distilling equipment in Reception Centre. Off A95. ♿ (F8)

Glen Grant Distillery, Rothes Established 1840. Traditional methods of distillation of malt whisky are used together with the most modern equipment. Exhibition, shop and Hospitality Bar. (E8)

Glenlivet Distillery Visitor Centre Guided tours of distillery. Exhibition of ancient artefacts connected with the industry and an old whisky still. Off B9008 5 miles (8 km) north of Tomintoul. ♿ (H7)

Glenmore Forest Park (FC) Over 12,000 acres (4,856 hectares) of pine and spruce woods and mountainside on the north-west slopes of the Cairngorms, with Loch Morlich as its centre. Probably the finest area in Britain for wildlife. 7 miles (11.2 km) east of Aviemore, off A951. (J5)

Glenmore Forest Park Trail Three trails in The Queen's Forest, all 1¼ miles (2 km) long. Car park, guide book. By north-east end of Loch Morlich, 6 miles (9.6 km) east of Aviemore. (J5)

Glenshee Chairlift Ascends The Cairnwell, 3,059 ft (932.3 m), from the summit of the highest main road pass in Britain, 2,199 ft (670.2 m). Off A93, 10 miles (16 km) south of Braemar. (L7)

Highland Folk Museum The open-air museum includes an 18th-century shooting lodge, a 'Black House' from Lewis, a Clack Mill, and exhibits of farming equipment. Traditional craft events in season. Off A86 at Kingussie. ♿ (J3)

Highland Wildlife Park This notable park features breeding groups of Highland animals and birds in a beautiful natural setting. Drive-through section has red deer, bison, Highland cattle, etc. 4 miles (6.4 km) off A9 along B9152 from Kingussie. (J3)

Hugh Miller's Cottage, Church Street, Cromarty (NTS) The birthplace of Hugh Miller (1802–56), geologist, naturalist, theologian and writer. Collections of geological specimens, his writings and his personal belongings. (C3)

The 'Indian Temple' Erected by General Sir Hector Munro (1726–1805) as a means of easing local unemployment. The structure is said to represent the gateway to an Indian town Sir Hector captured in 1781. Off A9, above Evanton village on Fynish Hill. (C2)

Inverness Museum and Art Gallery, Castle Wynd, Inverness The museum interprets the social and natural history, archaeology and culture of the Highlands, with fine collection of Highland silver. ♿ (E2)

Kilmuir Walk 1½ hour walk along foreshore; interesting bird life, cave, wild goats. From Kilmuir church, on unclassified road 11 miles (17.6 km) south of Fortrose. (E2)

Landmark Visitor Centre, Carrbridge This Visitor Centre was the first of its kind in Europe. Ten thousand years of Highland history are excitingly shown in the triple-screen audio-visual theatre. Nature trail, woodland walk, sculpture park, adventure playground. ♿ (G4)

Lecht Ski Tow Ski tows operating to slopes on both sides of the Lecht Road, famous for its snowfalls. During skiing season only. Off A939, 7 miles (11.2 km) south-east of Tomintoul. (H8)

Loch Garten Nature Reserve (RSPB) Ospreys, extinct in Scotland for many years, returned here to breed in 1959. Their treetop eyrie may be viewed through fixed binoculars from the observation hut. Off B970, 8 miles (12.8 km) north-east of Aviemore. ♿ (H5)

Loch Ness This striking 24 mile (38.4 km) loch in the Great Glen forms part of the **Caledonian Canal**, which links Inverness with Fort William. Cruisers sail from Inverness, notably to look for the Loch Ness Monster, said to live in the deep waters. (F1/G1)

Loch Ness Centre Situated on A82 at Drumnadrochit, centre houses the Official Loch Ness Monster Exhibition. Varied exhibits relating to the Monster and the natural history of the loch include pictures, film, audio-visual displays, inflatables and a submarine. Also a small loch with a life-size model of 'Nessie'. ♿ (G1)

Lochindorb Castle On an island in a lonely loch stands this 13th-century castle, once a seat of the Comyns. It was occupied by Edward I in 1303 and greatly strengthened. Off A939. (F5)

Mains of Eathie Walk To Eathie foreshore, passing fossil sites and Hugh Miller's fish beds; wild scenery. Car park at farmyard (ask permission), guide book. From Mains of Eathie, unclassified road off A832, 5½ miles (8.8 km) north of Fortrose. (D3)

Morangie Forest Walk Steep hillside paths with views of the Kyle of Sutherland. 1 mile (1.6 km) long. Car park. A9, 4 miles (6.4 km) north-west of Tain. (B3)

Mounthigh to Tore School Walk Mainly through Millbuie Forest, on good paths. About 9 miles (14.4 km) long. Guide book. From Mounthigh, at junction of B9160 and unclassified road, 4½ miles (7.2 km) north-west of Fortrose. (D3)

Muir of Tarradale Walk Starts from old railway track. On road and through croftland, with fine scenery on route. Car park, guide book. From B9169, 1½ miles (2.4 km) east of Muir of Ord. (E1)

Munlochy Bay Walk On quiet road to the north shores of Munlochy Bay, with interesting plants and birds to be seen. Car park, guide book. 1 mile (1.6 km) south of Avoch, off A832. (D3)

Nairn Fishertown Museum, Laing Hall, King Street, Nairn A collection of photographs and articles connected with the Moray Firth and herring fishing industries during the steam drifter era and before. (D4)

Nairn Literary Institute Museum The museum, founded in 1868, is housed in the attics of Viewfield House (early 19th century) and contains displays of local history, archaeology, ethnology and relics of **Culloden**. (D4)

Nelson Tower On Cluny Hill, within Grant Park, overlooking Forres. The tower was erected in 1806 by the survivors of the Battle of Trafalgar and offers magnificent views of Moray Firth, Black Isle and inland mountains. (D6)

Ord Hill Walk Forest trail round Ord Hill, with good views and many wild flowers. Guide book. Just north of North Kessock, opposite Inverness over the Beauly Firth; take B9161 out of Kessock, then right to Drumsmittal School, then right again into the forest. Parking on verges. (E2)

Ormond Hill Walk Sheltered walk along foreshore and round Ormond Hill and Woodhill, passing scant ruins of Ormond Castle. Car park, guide book. 1 mile (1.6 km) south of Avoch, off A832. (D2)

Pluscarden Abbey The original monastery was founded by Alexander II in 1230. Restoration and reconstruction took place in the 14th and 15th century and the Abbey has been re-occupied by the Benedictines since 1948. Abbey church open. From B9010 at Elgin take unclassified road to Pluscarden. ♿ (D7)

Randolph's Leap The river Findhorn winds through a deep gorge in the sandstone, and from a path above are impressive views of the clear brown water swirling over rocks or in still dark pools. Randolph's Leap is the most striking part of the valley. Off B9007. (E5)

Rock Wood Ponds 1 mile (1.6 km) trail circles a group of attractive lochans. Boards give information on bird life. Car park, picnic place. From Aviemore, cross Spey Bridge and turn right at Inverdruie on to the B970 for 7 miles (11.2 km). Turn left on Glen Feshie road from Insh House; site 1 mile (1.6 km) on right. (J4)

Rosemarkie to Fary Glen Walk through gorge, passing earth pillars. Noted for wild flowers. Guide book. Park by A832 on eastern outskirts of Rosemarkie. (D3)

Rosemarkie to Scart Craig Walk Walk along the shore and foreshore, with colourful variety of flowers in season. Take care at the high cliffs at Scart Craig. Guide book. From Rosemarkie promenade, north of Fortrose. (D3)

Rothiemurchus Visitor Centre, Inverdruie Houses displays on forest wildlife and estate management, and is a centre from which to take Ranger-guided walks in Rothiemurchus Forest (half day or whole day), or tractor/trailer tours of the farm and estate (about 2 hours). Visits to the trout farm, red deer herd and Doune House are possible by special arrangement. On junction of B951 and B970 at Inverdruie, near Aviemore. (J4)

Ruthven Barracks (SDD) Considerable ruins of barracks built 1716–18 to keep the Highlanders in check, and added to by General Wade in 1734. On a site once occupied by a fortress of the Wold of Badenoch. On B970, ½ mile (0.8 km) south of Kingussie. (J3)

St Duthus Chapel and Church, Tain Chapel was built between 1065 and 1256. St Duthus died in 1065 and was buried in Ireland, but 200 years later his remains were transferred to Tain. The chapel was destroyed by fire in 1427. Church was built *c.* 1360 by William, Earl and Bishop of Ross. (B3)

St Michael's Chapel Walk To Newhallpoint and Balblair, with many birds to be seen (ducks and waders). Evening cruises in the Firth can be arranged. Guide book. ½ mile (0.8 km) south of Balblair, by the chapel. (C3)

Strathspey Railway The line is part of the former Highland Railway (Aviemore/Forres section), closed in 1965. Since 1972 volunteers have been restoring the line and stations at Boat of Garten and Aviemore, and now offer a limited steam service. Some of the rolling stock is on display, and smaller relics can be seen in the museum at Boat of Garten. Aviemore to Boat of Garten, off A95, 6½ miles (10.4 km) north. (H5)

Sueno's Stone (SDD) One of the most remarkable early sculptured monuments in Scotland, 20 ft (6 m) high with elaborate carving. Beside B9011, 1 mile (1.6 km) north-east of Forres. (D6)

Tamdhu Distillery Guided tour with large graphic display and views of distilling plant from viewing gallery. Off B9102 at Knockando. (E7)

Tomatin Distillery Demonstration of the process of whisky distilling at 3 pm daily. Closed part of July and August. Essential to book. On A9 at Tomatin. (G4)

Tomintoul Museum, The Square, Tomintoul A display relating to local history, including turn-of-the-century photographs, old tools and harness, and a reconstructed farm kitchen. Landscape and wildlife displays. ♿ (H7)

Urquhart Castle (SDD) Historic, mainly 14th-century castle overlooking Loch Ness, destroyed before the 1715 Rising. 2 miles (3.2 km) south-east Drumnadrochit. (G1)

Map 29

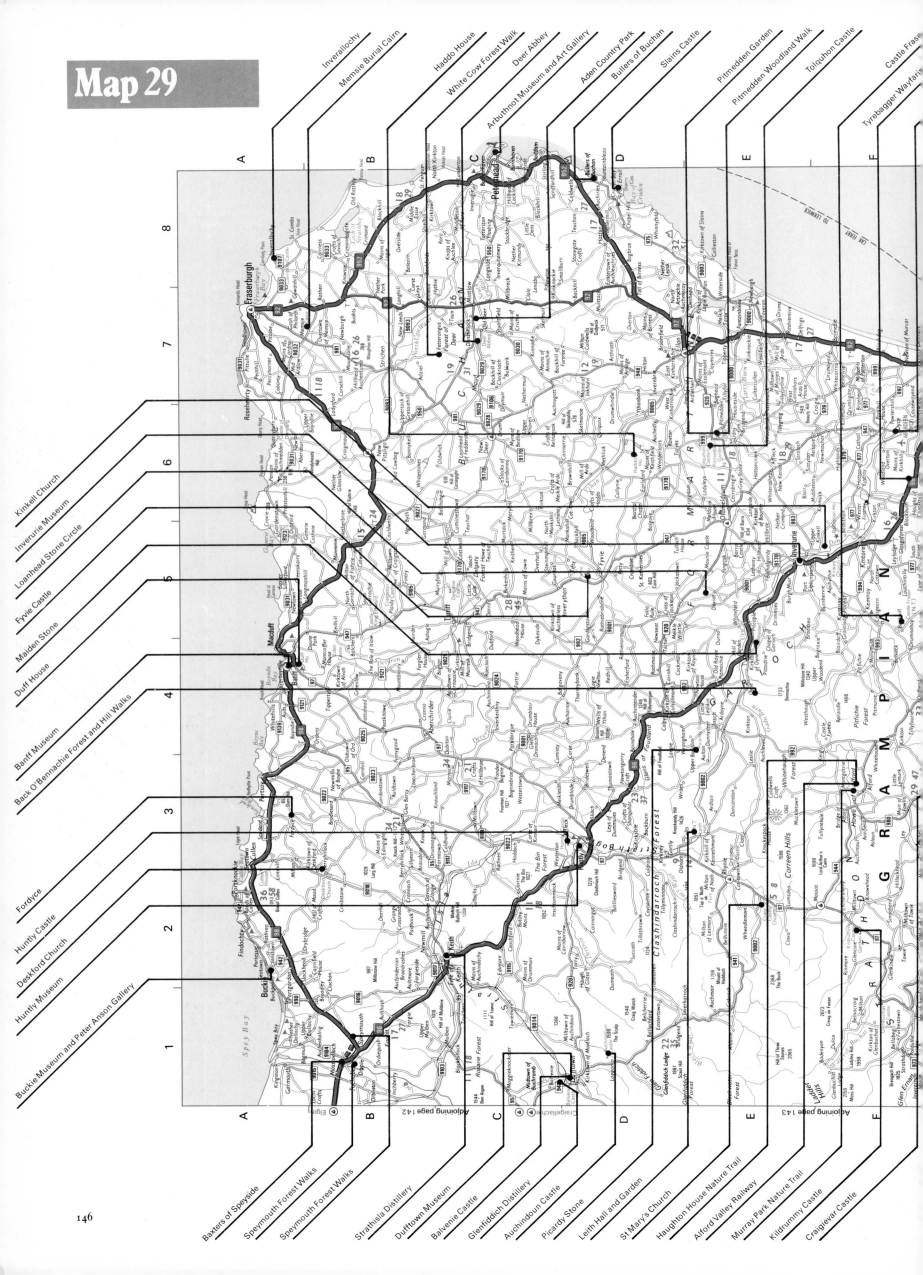

Inverallochy
Memsie Burial Cairn
Haddo House
White Cow Forest Walk
Deer Abbey
Arbuthnot Museum and Art Gallery
Aden Country Park
Bullers of Buchan
Slains Castle
Pitmedden Garden
Pitmedden Woodland Walk
Tolquhon Castle
Castle Fraser
Tyrebagger Wayfaring

Kinkell Church
Inverurie Museum
Loanhead Stone Circle
Fyvie Castle
Maiden Stone
Duff House
Banff Museum
Back O'Bennachie Forest and Hill Walks
Fordyce
Huntly Castle
Deskford Church
Huntly Museum
Buckie Museum and Peter Anson Gallery

Baxters of Speyside
Speymouth Forest Walks
Speymouth Forest Walks
Strathisla Distillery
Dufftown Museum
Balvenie Castle
Glenfiddich Distillery
Auchindoun Castle
Picardy Stone
Leith Hall and Garden
St Mary's Church
Haughton House Nature Trail
Alford Valley Railway
Murray Park Nature Trail
Kildrummy Castle
Craigievar Castle

Adjoining page 142
Adjoining page 143

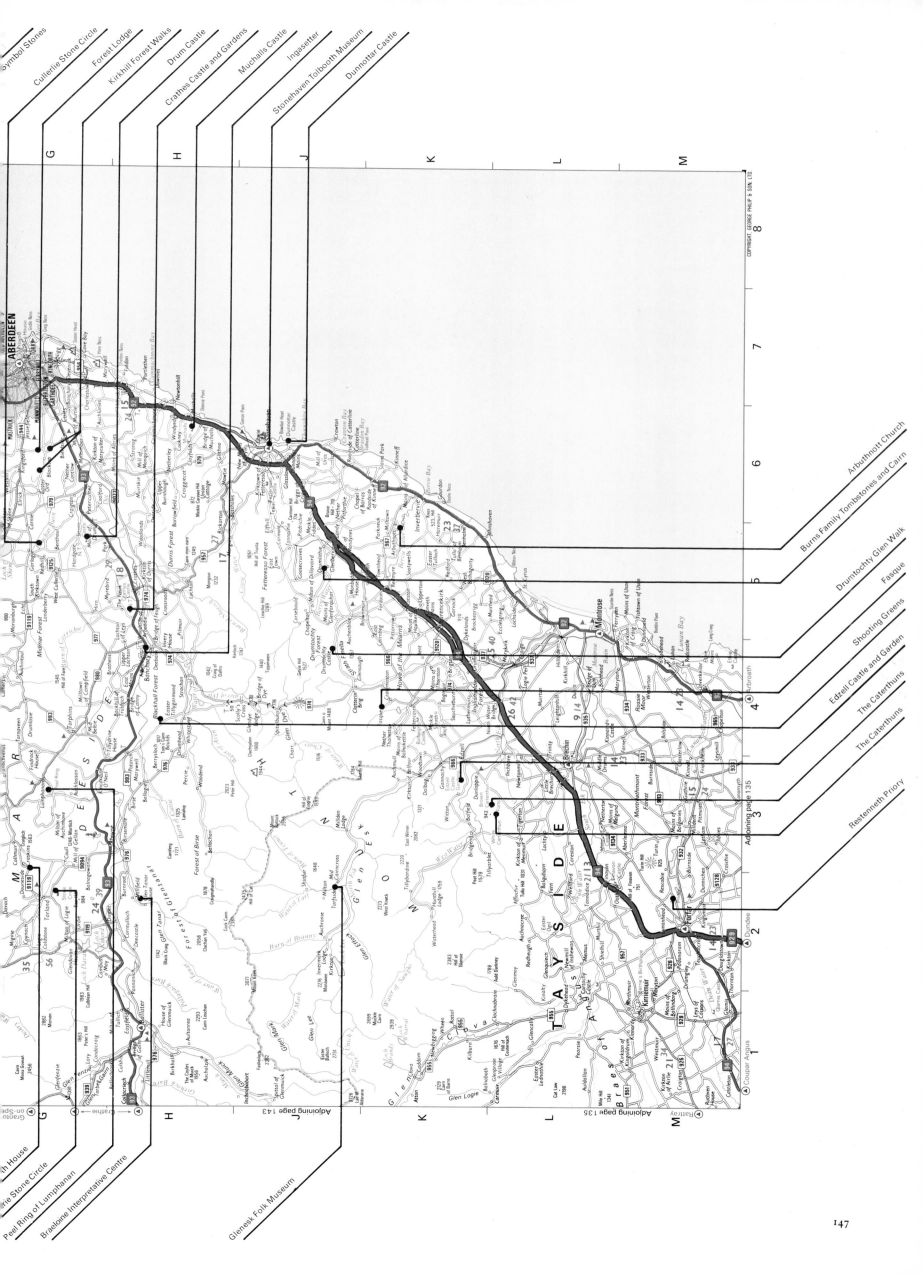

Highland Scotland

Aden Country Park Set in attractive area of mixed woodland, the park offers nature trails, walks and Ranger service. Also Agricultural Heritage Centre with displays of life on former Scottish estates. Fishing, picnicking, children's tree house and play area. 1 mile (1.6 km) west of Mintlaw on A950. ☒ (C7)

Alford Valley Railway, Alford Narrow-gauge passenger railway located in Haughton Park. 1½ miles (2.4 km) of track over nature trails and historic battlefield. Diesel traction with possible addition of steam-hauled trains. (F3)

Arbuthnot Museum and Art Gallery, St Peter Street, Peterhead The development of fishing and whaling, with Arctic exhibits, is featured; also local history. The coin collection can be viewed by appointment. (C8)

Arbuthnott Church This church dates partly from 1242 and has a two-storeyed 16th-century chapel attached. The stained-glass windows depict Faith, Hope and Charity. Off B967. (K5)

Auchindoun Castle (SDD) A massive ruin on the summit of an isolated hill, enclosed by prehistoric earthworks. The corner stones were removed to **Balvenie**. In Queen Mary's wars the castle was the stronghold of the redoubtable 'Edom o' Gordon' who burned Corgarff. Jacobite leaders held a council of war there after Dundee's death at **Killiecrankie** (see Gazetteer 26). View from outside only. In Glen Fiddich, 3 miles (4.8 km) southeast Dufftown. (D1)

Back O'Bennachie Forest and Hill Walks Walks through woodland and on open hill with interesting plant and wild life and magnificent views from hilltops. Short walk ½ mile (0.8 km); long walk 5 miles (8 km), car park, guide book, picnic field. Near B9002, ¾ mile (1.2 km) west of Oyne. (E4)

Balvenie Castle (SDD) Picturesque ruins of a 14th-century moated stronghold originally owned by the Comyns. Visited by Edward I in 1304 and by Mary, Queen of Scots in 1562. Occupied by Cumberland in 1746. The corner stones came from **Auchindoun**. Not open. At Dufftown, A941. (D1)

Banff Museum There is a fine display of birds of Britain in their natural settings and an interesting local history exhibition. On A97 at Banff. (A4)

Baxters of Speyside: Old Baxter Shop and Cellar Fine-foods factory on scenic Speyside with factory tours (except during staff holidays). Visitor Centre, audio-visual presentation of the story of the Baxter family business, Highland cattle, Scottish restaurant. ½ mile (0.8 km) west of Fochabers on A96. (B1)

Braeloine Interpretative Centre There are signposted walks and trails and an exhibition about the wildlife and the history of farming, forestry and land use on this fascinating Highland estate. Glen Tanar, off B976. ☒ (H2)

Buckie Museum and Peter Anson Gallery Maritime museum opened in 1973 containing exhibits relating to the fishing industry in the Moray Firth area from mid 19th century to the present day. Mr Peter Anson donated his collection of 400 pictures of fishing vessels, from the earliest times to modern dual-purpose craft, to the museum. ☒ (A2)

Bullers of Buchan A vast chasm in the cliffs, 200 ft (60.9 m) deep, 'which no man can see with indifference' said Dr Johnson in 1773. A haunt of innumerable seabirds. Off A975. (D8)

Burns Family Tombstones and Cairn The Burnes (Burns) family tombstones in the churchyard were restored in 1968 and a Burns memorial cairn is nearby. Off A94 3 miles (4.8 km) south of Stonehaven, at Glenbervie Church. (J5)

Castle Fraser (NTS) Perhaps the most spectacular of the Castles of Mar. It was begun about 1575, incorporating earlier building, and was completed 1636. Two great families of master masons, Bel and Leiper, took part in the work; the great heraldic panel on the north side is signed 'J Bel'. Off the castle courtyard is an exhibition telling the story of the Castles of Mar. Formal garden. Off unclassified road via Craigearn to Dunecht. (F5)

The Caterthuns (SDD) These remains of Iron Age hill forts stand on hills on either side of the road from Balrownie to Pitmudie, beyond Little Brechin. The Brown Caterthun has four concentric ramparts and ditches; the White Cater-

Craigievar Castle

thun is a well-preserved hill fort with massive stone rampart, defensive ditch and outer earthworks. 5 miles (8 km) north-west Brechin. (L3)

Craigievar Castle (NTS) This lovely castle was completed in 1626 by William Forbes of Aberdeen and has no later additions, its great tower standing alone. Its roof with turrets, crow-stepped gables, conical roofs, balustrading and corbelling contrasts remarkably with the severe lines of the rest of the building. Inside, there are superb, richly-moulded plaster ceilings. (F3)

Crathes Castle and Gardens (NTS) The double square tower of the castle dates from 1553 and the building, an outstanding example of a Scottish tower house, was completed in 1600. The notable interior includes the fascinating painted ceilings, dating from 1599, in the Chamber of the Nine Nobles, the Chamber of the Nine Muses, and the Green Lady's Room. The Queen Anne and Victorian wings, destroyed by fire in 1966, have been rebuilt and house the Visitor Centre. In the gardens there are fine collections of trees and shrubs and yew hedges dating from 1702 enclose a series of small gardens. ☒ *Crathes Castle Woodlands Nature Trails* are four walks in Crathes Castle grounds, up to 3 miles (4.8 km) long: (1) Through mixed woodland, farmland and by pond and quarry; guide book. (2) Through mixed woodland to viewpoints over Deeside. (3) Through mixed woodland along river. (4) Through amenity/plantation woodland. (H5)

Cullerlie Stone Circle (SDD) This stone circle of eight undressed boulders encloses an area on which eight small cairns were later constructed, probably in the late second millennium BC. 1 mile (1.6 km) south Garlogie. ☒ (G5)

Culsh Earth House (SDD) A well-preserved earth house of Iron Age date with roofing slabs intact over a large chamber and entrance. Access by Culsh Farmhouse, near Tarland on B9119. (G2)

Deer Abbey (SDD) The remains of the Cistercian Abbey, founded in 1219, include the southern claustral range, the Abbot's House and the infirmary. The famous Book of Deerk, compiled in the former Celtic monastery on a different site, is now in the University Library at Cambridge. On B9029, off A950. (C7)

The Muses' Ceiling, Crathes Castle

Deskford Church (SDD) This ruined building includes a rich carving which bears an inscription telling that *this present lovable work of sacrament house be* provided by Alexander Ogilvy of Deskford in 1551. Off B9018. ☒ (B3)

Drum Castle (NTS) A massive granite tower built towards the end of the 13th century adjoins a mansion of 1619. The Royal Forest of Drum was conferred in 1323 by Robert the Bruce on his armour-bearer and clerk-register, William de Irwin. The family connection remained unbroken until the death of Mr H.Q. Forbes-Irvine in 1975. The house stands in pleasant grounds with lawns, rare trees and shrubs, and inside are antique furniture and silver, family portraits and relics. *Drum Castle Woodland Walk* is a 1½ mile (2.4 km) walk through Old Forest of Drum – mostly birch, oak and pine with an area of planted exotic shrubs. Car park. (G5)

Drumtochty Glen Walk, Mearns Forest Through mixed woodland rich in plant life with duck pond and stream in woodland setting. Approximately 1 mile (1.6 km) long. Car park, small picnic site. Drumtochty Glen is 5½ miles (8.8 km) north of Laurencekirk to north of the Auchenblae–Clatterin' Brig road. (J4)

Duff House, Banff (SDD) Designed by William Adam for William Duff (later Earl of Fife). The main block was roofed in 1739, but proposed wings were never built. Although incomplete it ranks among the finest works of Georgian Baroque architecture in Britain. An exhibition illustrating the history of the house can also be seen. (A4)

Dufftown Museum, The Tower, The Square, Dufftown Exhibition of local history, including Mortlach Church, Balvenie Castle and Craigellachie Bridge. ☒ (D1)

Dunnottar Castle An impressive ruined fortress on a rocky cliff 160 ft (48.7 m) above the sea, a stronghold of the Earls Marischal of Scotland from the 14th century. Montrose besieged it in 1645. During the Commonwealth wars, the Scottish regalia were hidden here for safety. Cromwell's troops occupied the castle but in 1652 this treasure was smuggled out by the wife of the minister at Kinneff, 7 miles (11.2 km) south, and hidden under the pulpit in his church. Off A92. (J6)

Dyce Symbol Stones (SDD) Two fine examples of Pictish symbol stones. At Dyce Old Church, 5 miles (8 km) north-west of Aberdeen. (F6)

Edzell Castle and Garden (SDD) The beautiful pleasance, a walled garden, was created by Sir David Lindsay in 1604. This outstanding formal garden has heraldic and symbolic sculptures that are

Drum Castle

unique in Scotland, flower-filled recesses in the walls, and a turreted garden house. The castle itself, an impressive ruin, dates from the early 16th century, with a large courtyard mansion of 1580. ♿ (K3)

Fasque Probably the best-preserved occupied house of its age in Britain, with largely original contents. Home of the Gladstone family since 1829, the large mansion reflects the life of the original owner, Sir John Gladstone, and of subsequent generations and their families. Four times Prime Minister, William Gladstone lived at Fasque from 1830 to 1851. Also illustrated is the life and work of the many servants who contributed to the running of the household. Collection of agricultural and other local machinery. Extensive parkland with red deer and Soay sheep. 2 miles (3.2 km) north of Fettercairn on B974. ♿ (K4)

Fordyce A tiny village built round a small 16th-century castle. Adjacent are the remains of the old church with an interesting belfry. Unclassified road off A98. (A3)

Forest Lodge, Countesswells Walks of 1–1½ miles (1.6–2 km) on easy terrain through mixed woodland of varied maturity. Car park. Off Countesswells/Kingswells road, 5 miles (8 km) west of Aberdeen, between A93 and A944. (G6)

Fyvie Castle (NTS) Superb castle with five towers. Dates from 13th century and contains the finest great wheel stair in Scotland. Outstanding portrait collection, with works by Batoni, Raeburn, Ramsay and Gainsborough. Woodland walks. Off A947, 25 miles (40 km) north-west of Aberdeen. (D5)

Glenesk Folk Museum, Tarfside A series of displays show everday life in Glenesk from *c.* 1800 to the present day. ♿ (J2/3)

Glenfiddich Distillery Drawing its water from the 'Robbie Dubh' or 'Black Robert' stream, this distillery was founded in 1887 by Major William Grant in the heart of the Speyside country. A visitor's Reception Centre houses an audio-visual theatre, a malt whisky museum and a gift shop. Just north of Dufftown. (C1)

Haddo House (NTS) A Georgian house designed in 1731 by William Adam as successor to the House of Kellie, the mansion of the Gordons of Methlick until burnt in 1644. Notable portraits and a chapel (1880) with window by Burne-Jones. Gardens and park. Notable opera and concert productions in the Haddo House Theatre. (D6)

Haughton House Nature Trail A woodland walk through the country park, 1 mile (1.6 km) long. Open all year from dawn to dusk. Information and nature trail book, picnic areas, car park, small bird aviary. Guided tours by Ranger for parties by prior arrangement. Unclassified road ¾ mile (1.2 km) north of Alford. See also **Alford Valley Railway.** (F3)

Huntly Castle, Castle Street, Huntly (SDD) An imposing ruin that replaced medieval Strathbogie Castle which, until 1544, was the seat of the Gay Gordons, the Marquesses of Huntly, the most powerful family in the north until the mid 16th century. There are elaborate heraldic adornments on the castle walls. The castle, now in a wooded park, was destroyed by Moray in 1452, rebuilt, then rebuilt again in 1551–4, burned 40 years later and again rebuilt in 1602. (C/D3)

Huntly Museum, Main Square, Huntly Permanent local history exhibitions and temporary thematic exhibitions twice a year. In the Library. (D3)

Ingasetter, North Deeside Road, Banchory Film and tour explaining the growing and distilling of lavender and manufacture of other toilet preparations. (H4)

Inverallochy Small, attractive village with rows of low fishermen's cottages in an area traditionally famous for its fishing. On B9107. (A8)

Inverurie Museum, Town House, Inverurie Permanent display of local archaeology and thematic exhibitions three times a year. Just outside the town, on B993, is a 50 ft (15.2 m) high motte, *The Bass.* (E5)

Kildrummy Castle (SDD) The most extensive example in Scotland of a 13th-century castle. The remains of the four round towers, hall and chapel belong in substance to the original fabric. The great gatehouse and other work is later, of the 16th century. It was the seat of the Earls of Mar, and played an important part in Scottish history until 1715 when it was dismantled. *Kildrummy Castle Gardens* are best-known for the botanically varied alpine garden in the ancient quarry. A burn runs through the Den to the water garden with a shrub bank above it. On A97. (F2)

Kinkell Church (SDD) The ruins of an early 16th-century parish church with some ornate details including a rich sacrament house of unusual design, dated 1524. On the east bank of the Don, off B993. (F5)

Kirkhill Forest Walks: Bloertops, Totten of Gairn and Foggieton Brae Three walks of about 1 mile (1.6 km) in mixed woodland. The Totten of Gairn Walk has some fine views of Deeside. Car parks. Between A93 and A944, west of **Forest Lodge.** (G6)

Leith Hall and Garden (NTS) For three centuries the home of the Leith and Leith-Hay family. The earliest part of the building is incorporated in the north wing and dates from 1650. Additions were made in the 18th and 19th centuries. The family tradition of military service is reflected in the Exhibition Room, which includes a writing case presented by Prince Charles Edward Stuart on the eve of Culloden (1746). A winding path with zig-zag herbaceous border and rock garden is an attractive feature of the gardens. Pond walk with observation hide, picnic area and Soay sheep. ♿ (E3)

Loanhead Stone Circle (SDD) The best known example of a widespread group of recumbent stone circles in east Scotland. ¼ mile (0.4 km) north-west of Daviot, off B9001. (E5)

Maiden Stone (SDD) A notable early Christian monument with a Celtic Cross and Pictish symbols. Off A96, 6 miles (9.6 km) north-west Inverurie. (E4)

Memsie Burial Cairn (SDD) A fine example of a large stone-built cairn

Loanhead Stone Circle

probably dating to *c.* 1500 BC. Near village of Memsie. (B7)

Muchalls Castle Overlooking the sea, this tiny 17th-century castle was built by the Burnetts of Leys in 1619. Ornate plasterwork ceilings and fine fireplaces. Off A92. (H6)

Murray Park Nature Trail A woodland walk, with trees and wild flowers, 1¼ miles (2 km) long. Guide book, picnic areas. Unclassified road ¾ mile (1.2 km) north of Alford, on opposite side to **Haughton House.** (F3)

Peel Ring of Lumphanan (SDD) A major early medieval earthwork 120 ft (36.5 m) in diameter and 18 ft (5.4 m) high. There are links with Shakespeare's *Macbeth.* Off A980. (G3)

Picardy Stone (SDD) A whinstone monolith with ancient Celtic symbols. Other similar stones are in the Insch area. Unclassified road off A96, at Myreton. (E3)

Pitmedden Garden (NTS) The 17th-century Great Garden (recreated by the Trust) was originally laid out by Sir Alexander Seton, with elaborate floral designs, pavilions, fountains and sundials. The 'thunder houses' at either end of the west belvedere are rare in Scotland. A display depicts the evolution of the formal garden. Highland cattle, woodland walk. Outskirts of Pitmedden village, B999 off A920. ♿ (E6)

Pitmedden Woodland Walk (NTS) Follows thin strip of mixed woodland round **Pitmedden Garden** past old limekiln. Good views over surrounding farmland. 1½ miles (2.4 km) long. Commences at car park, Pitmedden Garden, outskirts of Pitmedden village. (E6)

Restenneth Priory (SDD) A house of Augustinian canons, probably founded by David I, in an attractive setting. There are remains of the chapel built in Saxon style by King Nechtan of the Picts in AD 710. A feature of the ruins is the tall square tower, with its shapely broach spire. Access across a field. On B9113, 1½ miles (2.4 km) east Forfar. (M2)

St Mary's Church, Auchindoir (SDD) Ruins of one of the finest medieval parish churches remaining in Scotland; roofless but otherwise entire. ½ mile (0.8 km) west A97 between Lumsden and Rhynie. (E2)

Shooting Greens Pleasant walks through mixed woodland. Fine scenic views of Feughside and Deeside with the Grampian and Cairngorm mountains in the background. The forest incorporates

3 walks: 1 mile (1.6 km); 2 miles (3.2 km); and 3 miles (4.8 km). Car park, picnic site. On unclassified road Feughside/Potarch, 4 miles (6.4 km) west of Banchory. (H3)

Slains Castle Extensive ruins of a castle of 1664 to replace an earlier Slains Castle, 4 miles (6.4 km) south, extended and rebuilt later by the 9th Earl of Errol. Dr Johnson and James Boswell visited here in 1773. Off A975. (D8)

Speymouth Forest Walks Walk starting 1 mile (1.6 km) east of Fochabers on A98 gives fine view of Speyside and Moray Coast from the Peeps Gazebo. Parking, picnic area. Second walk is along valley of Spey south of Fochabers to Allt Dearg, passing unique red 'earth pillars'. Car park. (B1)

Stonehaven Tolbooth Museum This 16th-century former storehouse of the Earls Marischal was later used as a prison. In 1748–9, Episcopal ministers lodged inside and baptised children through the windows. The museum displays local history, archaeology and particularly fishing. At Stonehaven quay. ♿ (J6)

Strathisla Distillery, Keith A typical small old-fashioned distillery, the oldest-established in Scotland, dating from 1786. (C2)

Tolquhon Castle (SDD) Once a seat of the Forbes family, an early 15th-century rectangular tower, with a large quadrangular mansion of 1584–9. Two round towers, a fine carved panel over the door, and the courtyard are features. Off B999. (E6)

Tomnaverie Stone Circle (SDD) The remains of a recumbent stone circle probably dating from 1800–1600 BC. 4 miles (6.4 km) north-west of Aboyne. (G2)

Tyrebagger Wayfaring Trail Woodland wayfaring course, ½ to 1½ miles (0.8 to 2.4 km) long. Car park. On north side of A96. (F6)

White Cow Forest Walk Mainly on forest roads through young and mature woodland. Includes two viewpoints, a stone circle and a badgers' sett marked with coloured waymarker poles. 3 miles (4.8 km) long. There is one short, moderately steep section. Car park, recreation and picnic area. On minor road, 2½ miles (4 km) south of Strichen. (B7)

Map 30

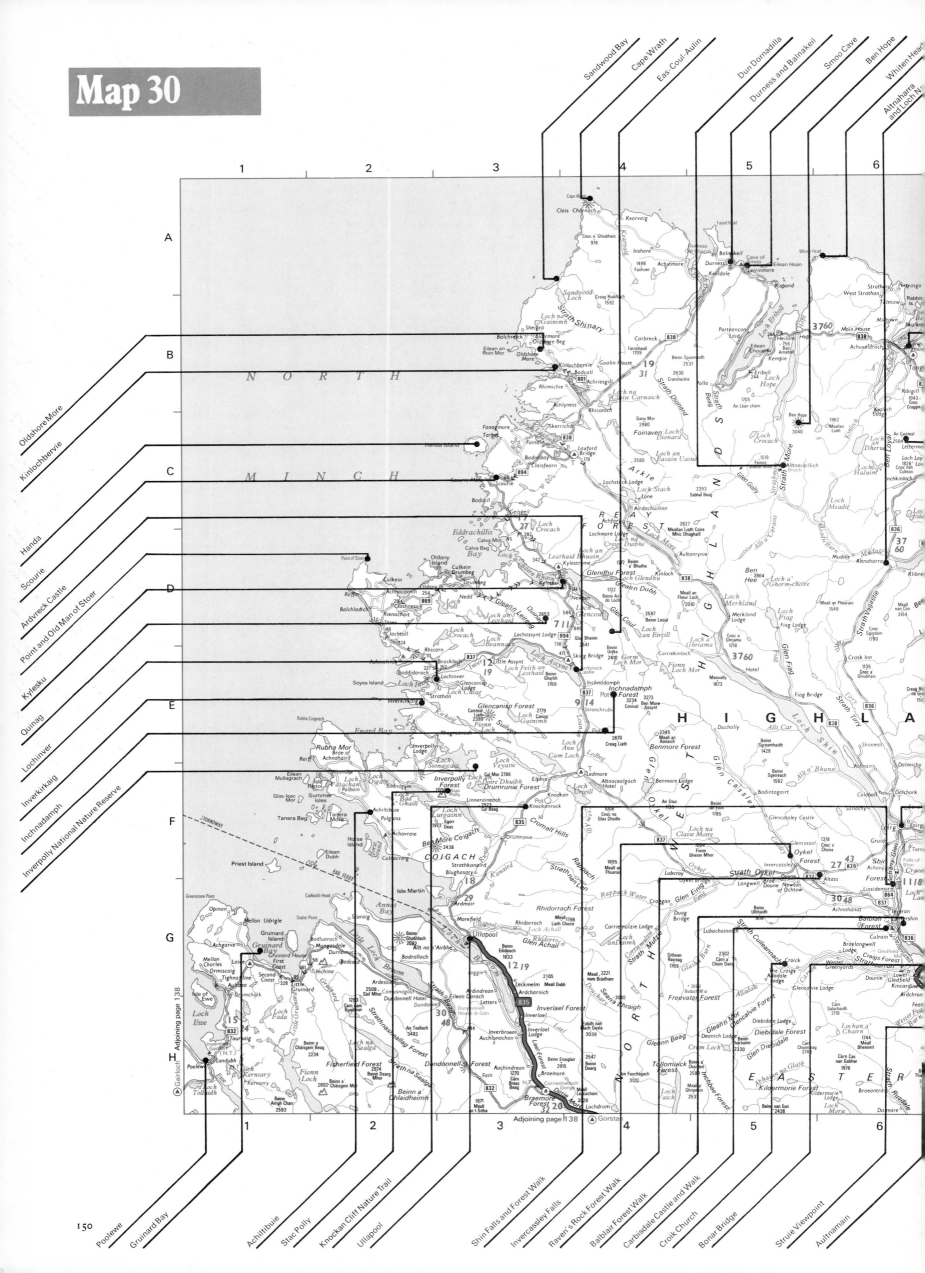

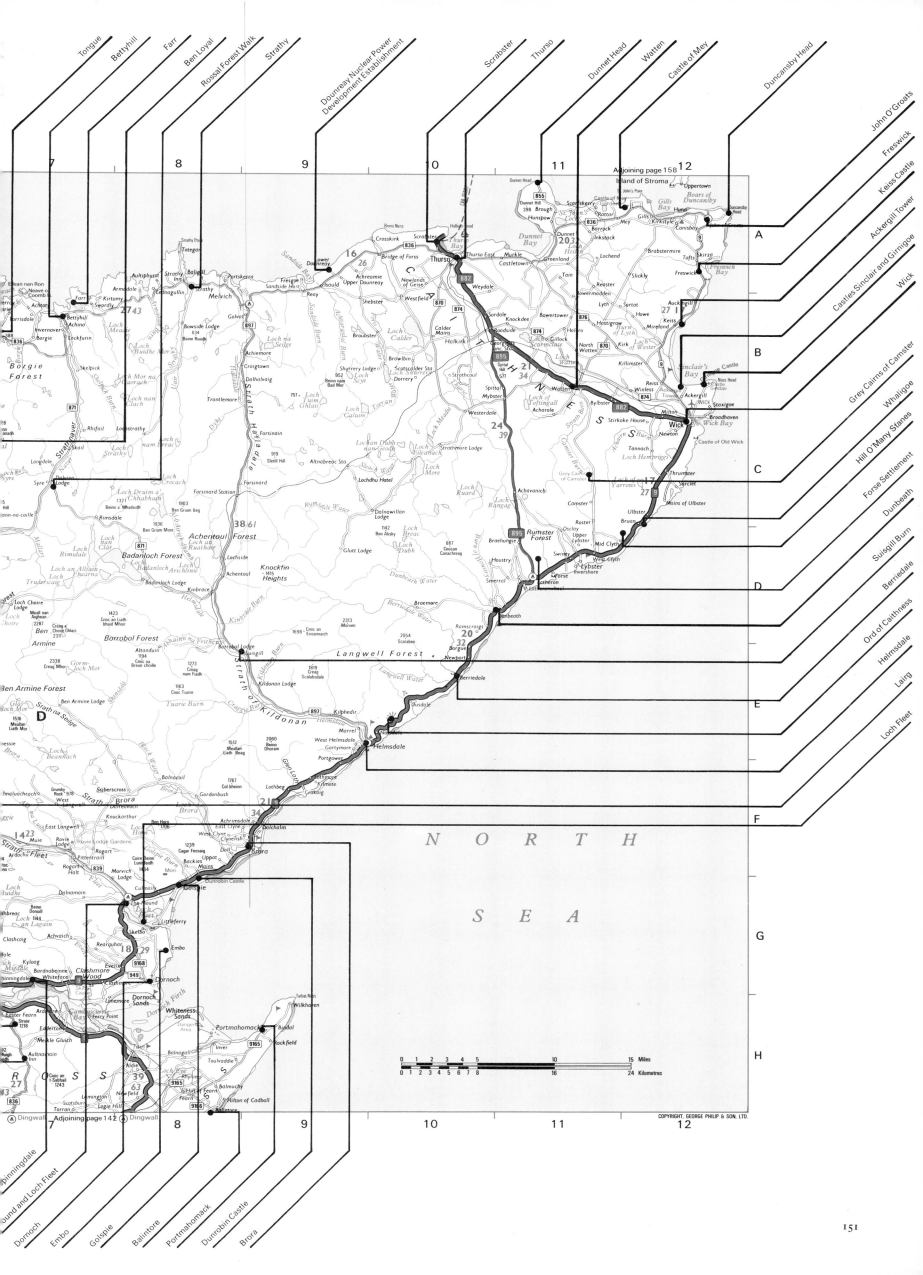

151

Highland Scotland

Achiltibuie A quiet crofting township overlooking the Summer Isles. Boats may be hired to visit them. The whole peninsula out to Rubha Coigeach is of bleak moors and small crofts, and gives superb views to all quarters. (F2)

Ackergill Tower Dating from the 15th century, this is one of the oldest inhabited castles in northern Scotland. Not open. (B12)

Altnaharra and Loch Naver Having crossed miles of treeless country to arrive, the mature trees and rhododendrons at this small crossroads community come as a slight shock. Loch Naver is very beautiful, curled beneath Ben Klibreck. (D6)

Ardvreck Castle 2 ruins beside A837: the gaunt castle ruins on a promontory in Loch Assynt, seat of the Macleods, and the big house, nearer Inchnadamph. (E4)

Aultnamain Old inn on a major one-time drove road. Nearby are commercial peat cuttings, the fuel being used for firing the distillery at Invergordon. (H7)

Balblair Forest Walk 1¾ miles (2.8 km), an easy pleasant walk in mature larch wood, of interest particularly to birdwatchers; here may be seen crossbills, an occasional crested tit, also capercaillie. (G6)

Balintore Between rich farmland and the waters of Moray Firth, this quiet fishing village, with its sandy beach, is a good place to see the salmon catch brought ashore. (H8)

Ben Hope Britain's most northerly mountain over 3,000 ft (3,040 ft, 926 m). Start at **Dun Dornadilla** (*see below*). Follow path on south side of burn ¼ mile (400 m) north; steep for 500 ft (150 m), more gently north-east for 1½ miles (2.4 km); due north up easy ridge to peak. 9 miles (14 km) return, allow 6–7 hours. Do not attempt descent to north or west. (C5)

Ben Loyal 2,504 ft (760 m). Park where convenient about ¾ mile (1.2 km) north of Loch Loyal. 2 miles (3.2 km) moorland walk west, climb eastern flank, then south to summit. A wonderful view from the mountain. 8 miles (13 km) return. (C6)

Berriedale A tiny village and harbour at the foot of fierce hills, typical of many fishing communities along the wild Caithness coast. Langwell House is occasionally open. (E10)

Bettyhill A very attractive crofting and fishing village at the mouth of the Naver. Beautiful sand dunes to the west, semi-precious stones to be found here. (B7)

Bonar Bridge Telford's original bridge having been destroyed by flood and tide, a splendid arch now crosses the kyle, from which the salmon netsmen can be viewed in spring and summer. (G6)

Brora A pleasant 19th-century industrial village, based on the now defunct coal-mine. Brora's main attractions are golf, an excellent beach and the woollen mill which may be visited. (F9)

Cape Wrath Accessible only on foot or by mini-bus from near Durness, a visit to this splendid headland is memorable. The 900 ft (274 m) cliffs of Clo Mor, 3 miles (4.8 km) to the east of the Cape, are a wonderful place for sea-birds in early summer. (A4)

Carbisdale Castle and Walk The dominant castle is a huge Victorian house, now a Youth Hostel, and from its entrance is a forest walk, 2¼ miles (3.6 km) return, which passes Montrose's last, disastrous battlefield. (G6)

Castle of Mey The gardens of this 400-year-old home of Queen Elizabeth, the Queen Mother, are occasionally open in summer. (A11)

Castles Sinclair and Girnigoe Take the road through Wick airport to Noss Head (lighthouse); the two clifftop ruins, built by the Earls of Caithness, are about ½ mile (.8 km) west along the cliffs. Well worth a visit for their dramatic situation on striated sandstone cliffs with the roar of waves echoing through rock-hewn passages. (B12)

Croick Church Well signposted from Ardgay on A9, the church is 9 miles (14.4 km) up quiet Strathcarron; it was a temporary refuge for the dispossessed crofters of the area during the notorious Clearances of the last century; their poignant words are engraved on the east window, a cry from an empty land. (G5)

Dornoch The county town of Sutherland, noted for its 13th-century cathedral, and as the place where Scotland's last witch was burned, in 1722. Ancient golf course, safe clean beaches, local pony-trekking. Recently a craft community has been established. (G8)

Dounreay Nuclear Power Development Establishment High technology in an ancient land, the original Dounreay Reactor was the first to supply nuclear-generated electricity to the public; an exhibition is open throughout the summer, and tours may be arranged at Tourist Information Centre, Thurso. ♿ (A9)

Dun Dornadilla (Dornaig) 4 miles (6.4 km) south of Loch Hope, on the narrow Hope–Altnaharra road, this broch, an Iron Age defensive structure, is one of the best in northern Scotland. The circular walls are hollow, with passages, around a central courtyard. (C5)

Dunbeath Similarly situated to **Berriedale**; ruins of fishermen's cottages lie above the beach; ½ mile (.8 km) north of the village, beside A9, is the *Laidhay Caithness Croft Museum*, traditionally thatched, which gives a fascinating picture of an almost extinct but very old and successful way of life in a harsh land. (D11)

Duncansby Head The north-easterly point of the mainland, a place of high drama. The dangerous waters of the

Duncansby Head

Pentland Firth seethe to the north, and a short clifftop walk south reveals a view of sea-stacks and arches as fine as anywhere in Britain. (A12)

Dunnet Head The northernmost point on the mainland; superb views of the Orkneys, and in good weather, west to **Cape Wrath**. B855 from Dunnet leads straight to the lighthouse which may be visited. (A11)

Dunrobin Castle Beautifully situated, this 19th-century mansion developed from 13th-century keep is the seat of the Countess of Sutherland, whose ancestor, the 1st Duke, is the subject of the monument on Beinn a' Bhragaidh 3 miles (4.8 km) west. (G8)

Dunrobin Castle

Durness and Balnakeil A quiet and beautiful crofting community blessed with good soil derived from an unusual limestone outcrop. Famous craft village west, on road to Balnakeil, where lies Rob Donn, Gaeldom's great poet. Magnificent beaches. (A5)

Eas-Coul-Aulin Highest waterfall in Britain, 658 ft (200 m). Just north of the summit of Inchnadamph–Kylesku road, a well-defined track to east skirts a small loch, then winds over a low ridge into very wild country; descend ¾ mile (1 km), cross first burn, and follow right bank to top of waterfall. Be careful! Strong footwear essential. 7 miles (11 km) return; allow 5 hours. (D4)

Embo Pleasant, clean fishing village, huddled against storm; boats and ponies may be hired, and birdwatchers can have

a field day on the beautiful beach to the north. (G8)

Farr One of the many small coastal settlements which were founded when the crofters were harried from their inland farms during the Clearances; the choices were to scratch a living on a hostile coast, or emigrate. (B7)

Forse Settlement An interesting exercise in deduction can be enjoyed here among the ruins of this old settlement. To reach it turn up a narrow gorsey lane west of A9, ½ mile (.8 km) north-east of Latheron; follow lane to its end. Unsuitable for cars. Leave west to join A895, this gives a 4 mile (6.4 km) circuit walk from Latheron. (D11)

Freswick Attractive old village on Freswick Bay. Starkly situated near Ness Head are ruins of 15th-century Bucholly Castle (visitable). (A12)

Golspie Once an active fishing port. Fine beaches to south, with golf links. Pleasant walks in glen north of village. (G8)

Grey Cairns of Camster (SDD) 110 yards (100 m) west of Watten–Lybster road; in the middle of desolate bogland lie a large round cairn and a large long cairn, both 5,000 or more years old. The burial chamber of the round and both those of the long cairn may be entered, on hands and knees. Notice how the peat-cuttings along the road have the owner's name, necessary in a featureless area. (C11)

Camster Long Cairn

Gruinard Bay Often featured on calendars, the white beaches and rumpled hills of this lovely bay epitomise the beauties of this coast. Gruinard Island is forbidden territory, having been contaminated with anthrax during World War II. (G1)

Handa (RSPB) A wonderful bird-sanctuary, but bird-watcher or not, a boat-ride from Tarbet to see it is a fine experience. Thousands of seabirds nest on the cliffs to the north-west, where stands the precipitous Stack of Handa. The island used to be well populated and there are many ruined crofts. (C3)

Helmsdale Planned village by Duke of Sutherland to house and employ evicted crofters, 1820. At the foot of the lovely Strath Kildonan, Helmsdale is noted for its catch of lobsters, kept alive, claws tied, in a special 'pound' until sufficient are caught to make a load to send south. Visitors are welcome. (E10)

Hill O'Many Stanes A Neolithic site with almost 200 stones set out in 22 parallel rows. 3¼ miles (5.2 km) north-east of Lybster at Mid Clyth off A9. (D11)

Inchnadamph The unusual limestone band parallel to the road has special flora, and caves once used by prehistoric man, in Traligill, off the A837 just north of the Hotel, and at Allt na Uamh, 4 miles (6.4 km) south and 2 miles (3.2 km) into the hills. Much of the area is a nature reserve and reserve notice boards are beside the road. (E4)

Invercassley Falls ¼ mile (400 m) up-river from Rosehall, these delightful falls are an excellent place to watch salmon leaping from May to September. (F5)

Inverkirkaig The river Kirkaig's estuary is a pleasant rocky bay; the walk up the wooded valley, past the weaver's showroom and bookshop, to Falls of Kirkaig is full of charm. Allow 3 hours to savour it. (E2)

Inverpolly National Nature Reserve The hinterland to the 'mad road of Sunderland' is a nature reserve famed for deer, wild cats, pine martens and eagles. (F2)

John O'Groats Here, Jan de Groot began a ferry service to Orkney in 1496. Should the place prove an anti-climax, save the day and visit **Duncansby Head** (2 miles, 3.2 km). (A12)

Keiss House and Castle

Keiss Castle A short walk north along the shore from the small harbour takes you past 2 brochs (see **Dun Dornadilla**) and presently to the ruined castle by the sea. (B12)

Kinlochbervie A wonderfully sheltered fishing port, whose activity is steadily increasing, despite its extreme remoteness. Many boats come in about tea-time. (B3)

Knockan Cliff Nature Trail A small visitor centre and a short walk nearby explain the significance and interest of this extraordinary geological fault. Watch for signs south of the road summit. (F3)

Kylesku Brooded over by the mass of **Quinag**, this hamlet and ferry-crossing (soon to be bridged) is memorable. Inland, three sea-lochs seep into the desolate mountains; boat trips explore these fjords, seals abound, disappointment is rare. (D3)

Lairg At the foot of enormous Loch Shin, Lairg's importance as transport, postal and supply centre for the far north-west is paramount. Tourist information in the village; as you stock up, ponder the logistics of living here! (F6)

Loch Fleet (SWT) Large sandy tidal basin north of Dornoch. Can be viewed from A9 or from a minor road leading to Skelby. An important feeding area for wintering ducks with large numbers of waders. (G8)

Lochinver A busy fishing port, handling a wide range of fish. On the north side of the harbour, near Baddidarach, is an excellent pottery; some way past it there is a surprising view of Lochinver, apparently threatened by the unique bulk of Suilven. (E2)

Mound and Loch Fleet This causeway, designed by Telford, originally carried the Dornoch branch line. The wooded marsh behind the embankment and the shallow waters of Loch Fleet are wonderful places for birds. (G8)

Oldshore More Once the place where a Norse king landed, this small, beautiful bay, with its clean sand and rocks, is simply a very nice place to be. (B3)

Ord of Caithness From this splendid viewpoint can be seen on a fine day, or,

better, at night, the oil-rig working the Beatrice Field some 14 miles (22 km) out to sea. A mile or so (1.6 km) walk from a prominent layby is the ruined village of Badbea. (E10)

Point and Old Man of Stoer A road west of Stoer leads to the lighthouse whence a short clifftop walk leads to the pinnacle called the Old Man; unbelievably, this has been climbed. This is fine scenery, affording views to the Hebrides. (D2)

Poolewe A pleasant village at the mouth of River Ewe; just south is famous Loch Maree. Loch Ewe provides safe swimming and good fishing. (H1)

Portmahomack Another inspiration of Telford, this fishing village is now more orientated to sailors and sea-anglers. Sheltered by Tarbat Ness, where there are good cliff walks, Portmahomack actually faces west. (H9)

Quinag (Spidean Coinich) has the rare virtue of ready access from A894 ¾ mile (1.2 km) north of its junction with A837. Easy, trackless ascent to Spidean Coinich; panorama of a unique landscape, views to Hebrides. Interesting ridge, highest point 2,653 ft (808 m), may be safely followed to its northerly point. Any descent east leads to road; descent west inadvisable. Spidean Coinich and return 3 miles (4.8 km); whole ridge 9 miles (14.4 km). (D3)

Raven's Rock Forest Walk 2 miles (3.2 km) east of Invercassley (Rosehall), signposted from both Lairg and Bonar Bridge roads. A short 1 mile (1.6 km) delightful walk which at one point is on piers over the burn. Craft shop nearby. (F6)

Rossal Forest Walk, Strathnaver From the Kinbrace road east of Syre, this pleasant forest walk leads by the sad ruins of one of the communities so grievously 'cleared' 150 years ago. (C7)

Sandwood Bay 'The most beautiful place on the Scottish mainland'. Glorious sweeps of white sand, with fine cliffs to the south, Cape Wrath to north, big dunes holding back Sandwood Loch. 3½ miles (5.6 km) west of Kinlochbervie, a cart-track (no cars) leads north; allow 1½ hours to loch. Round walk 9 miles (14.4 km). Please control dogs. (A3)

Scourie A remote village of charm and interest to walkers and anglers, surrounded by magnificent wilderness. Narrow roads demand care and nerve. (C3)

Scrabster Ferry-port for the Orkneys, and an increasingly important centre for sea-angling. A few minutes walk past the lighthouse to Holborn Head reveals spectacular cliff scenery. (A10)

Shin Falls and Forest Walk On B864 between Invershin Power Station and Lairg, these falls are famous for the salmon leaping, from late April to autumn. From car park easy 1½ mile (2.4 km) circuit with an excellent viewpoint of this well-wooded glen. (G6)

Smoo Cave 1 mile (1.6 km) east of Durness, this fine cave in a band of limestone may be entered by ordinary mortals to the first chamber only; diving is necessary to go further. (A5)

Spinningdale Reminiscent of south Devon, this village on A9 owes its name to the cotton-mill whose ruins stand near the sea (built in 1790). There are beautiful oakwoods west of Spinningdale. (G7)

Stac Polly The unique pinnacles of this fine mountain suggest a hedgehog. From the big car park by Loch Lurgainn, ascend the direct path to the saddle; very steep but safe. Further directions for this complex ridge would not help; take care, and use your camera. This is special. (F3)

Strathy A beautiful crofting village with a fine beach. Turn off A836 ¾ mile (1.2 km) west, by kirk, to Strathy Point, 3 miles (4.8 km) north; savour the wide clean atmosphere of this north coast. (A8)

Struie viewpoint 650 ft (200 m) above Dornoch Firth, 2 miles (3.2 km) south-east A9/A836 fork. Magnificent panorama of hills and sea; the big mountain north-west is Ben More Assynt. (H7)

Suisgill Burn, Kildonan Here was the focus of the 1869 gold rush; though gold may still be panned from the burn, quantities were never sufficient to rival Klondyke. (E9)

Thurso The northernmost town of mainland Britain still clearly demonstrates its Viking ancestry. Netsmen catch salmon at the river mouth. Interesting ruins of old St Peter's church, mainly 16th and 17th century. (A10)

Tongue Tongue House grounds at east end of new causeway over Kyle of Tongue, where seals and sea-birds abound. Old castle, in woodland, is reached from road south-west of Tongue; follow track on west of river. (B6)

Ullapool The herring fishery was the reason for Ullapool's establishment in 1788; still a substantial fleet based here. Lewis ferry leaves from here, and boats for sea-angling and trips to Summer Isles are ever active. *Loch Broom Highland Museum* in Quay Street; craft shops and pony-trekking. (G3)

Watten Quiet village near the bird- and trout-rich loch. South of the village ¾ mile (1.2 km), then down a lane east, is a fine watermill, unfortunately no longer working. (B11)

Whaligoe 6 miles (9.6 km) north of Lybster; turn right off A9 at telephone kiosk, and park. Path goes past big house, then descends a spectacular flight of over 300 steps to a tiny harbour, dramatically hemmed in by cliffs. Imagine the labour and danger for fishermen and their womenfolk! Whaligoe is unforgettable. (C12)

Whiten Head This is a grand coastal walk, only for the fit, being 15 miles (24 km) over difficult terrain. Start north along east bank of River Hope, and follow the coast. Allow at least 8 hours for return trip. (A6)

Wick Important fishing port; much general cargo also coming in, including road salt and lime. *The Wick Heritage Centre*, Bank Row, is a new museum showing the fishing industry at the turn of the century. At the world-famous Caithness Glassworks, Pulteneytown, visitors may watch almost all the processes leading to production of their famous glass. Visitors also welcome at coastal search-and-rescue headquarters at South Head. Castle of Old Wick (signposted on A9 south) is a ruin surrounded by impressive cliff scenery. (C12)

Map 31

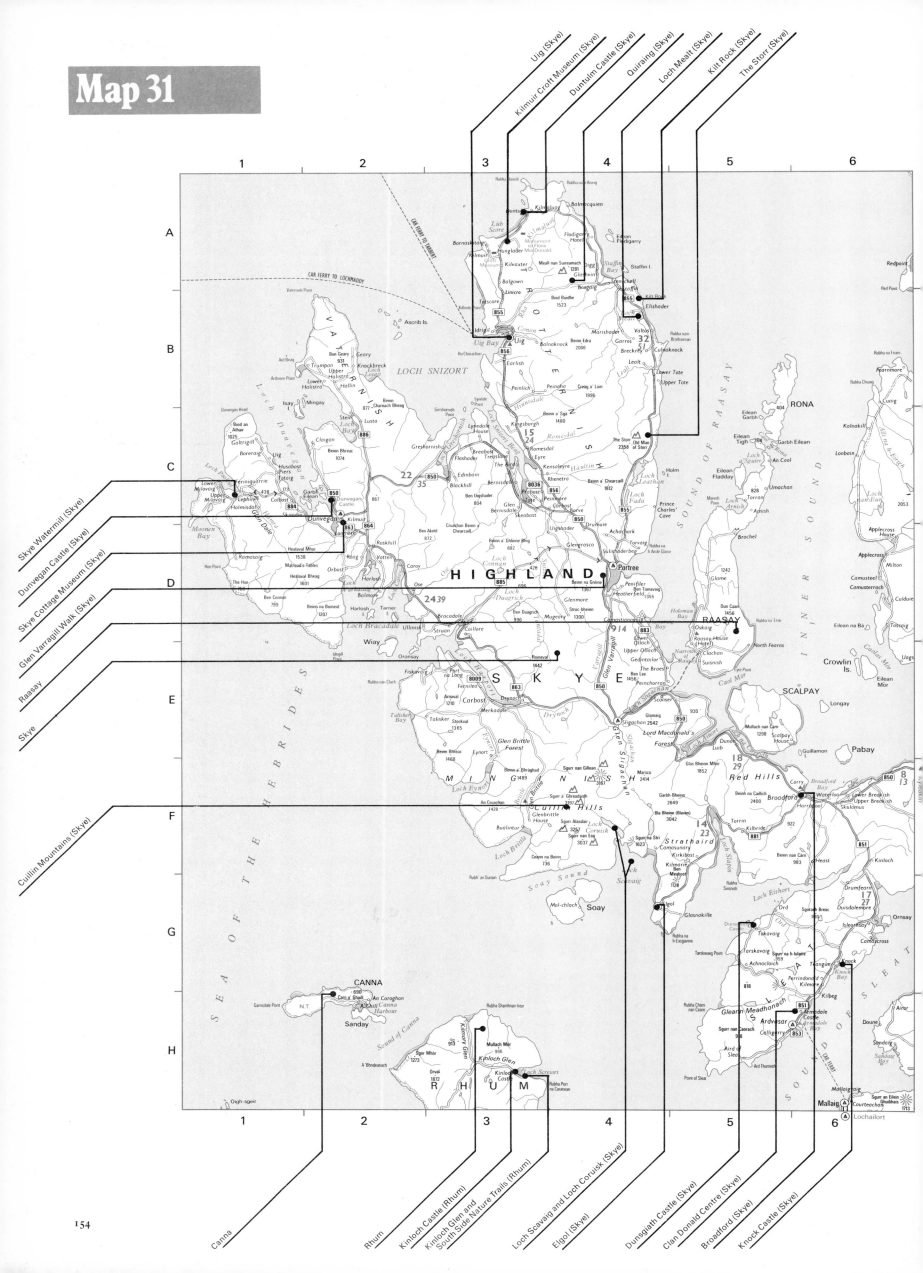

Uig (Skye)
Kilmuir Croft Museum (Skye)
Duntulm Castle (Skye)
Quiraing (Skye)
Loch Mealt (Skye)
Kilt Rock (Skye)
The Storr (Skye)

Skye Watermill (Skye)
Dunvegan Castle (Skye)
Skye Cottage Museum (Skye)
Glen Varragill Walk (Skye)
Raasay
Skye

Cuillin Mountains (Skye)

Canna
Rhum
Kinloch Castle (Rhum)
Kinloch Glen and South Side Nature Trails (Rhum)
Loch Scavaig and Loch Coruisk (Skye)
Elgol (Skye)
Dunsgiath Castle (Skye)
Clan Donald Centre (Skye)
Broadford (Skye)
Knock Castle (Skye)

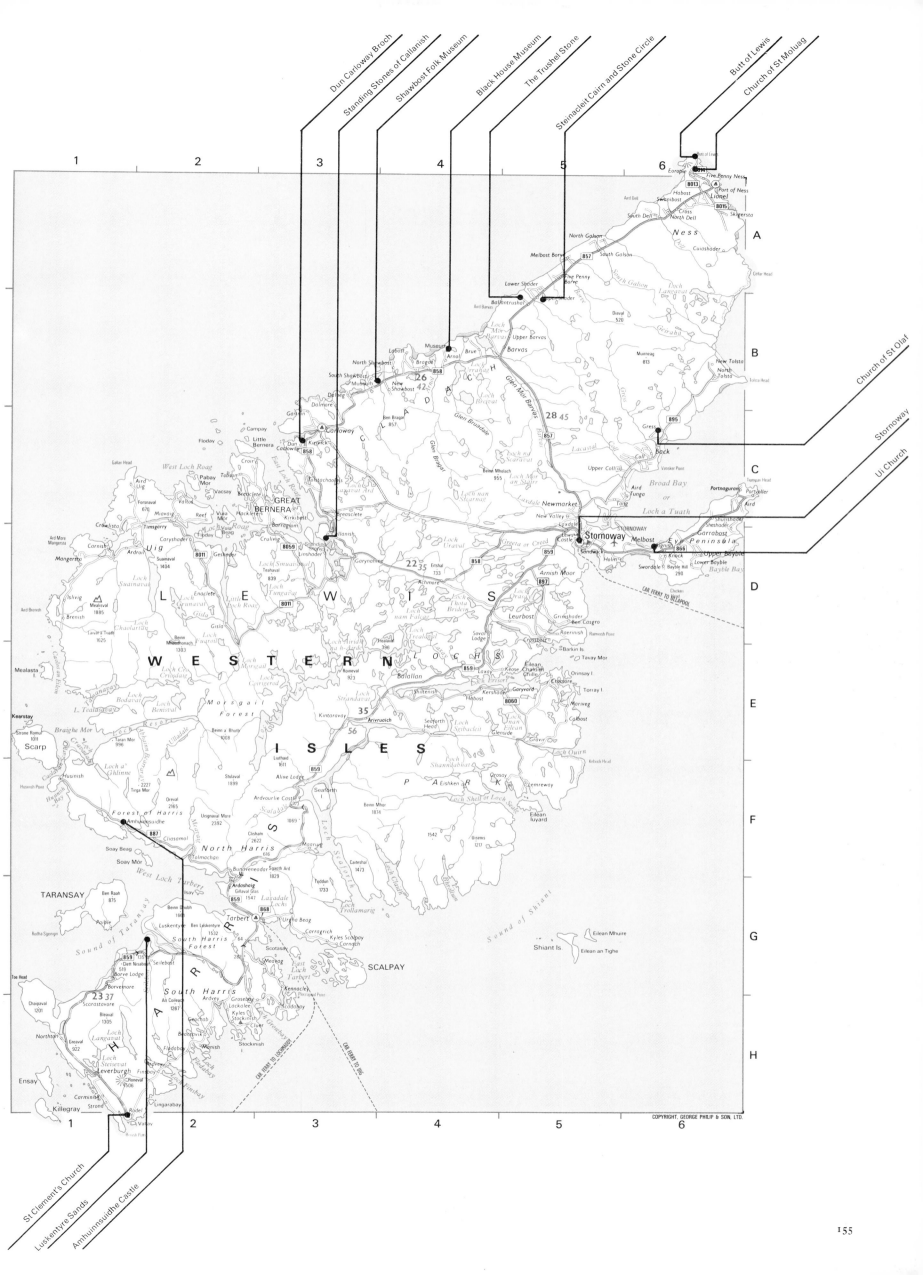

Dun Carloway Broch
Standing Stones of Callanish
Shawbost Folk Museum
Black House Museum
The Trushel Stone
Steinaclett Cairn and Stone Circle
Butt of Lewis
Church of St Moluag

Church of St Olaf

Stornoway

Ui Church

St Clement's Church
Luskentyre Sands
Amhuinnsuidhe Castle

1   2   3   4   5   6

Butt of Lewis
Eoropie
Europie Five Penny Ness
8013 Port of Ness
Habost Lionel
Swainbost
Aird Dell
South Dell North Dell
Cross 8015
North Galson Skigersta

Ness
Cuishader

A

Melbost Borve
857 South Galson

North Galson
Loch
Langavat Cellar Head

Lower Shader
Five Penny
Borve
Shader
Ballantrushal
Aird Barvas

Museum
Lobost Brue Barvas
North Shawbost Brogar Arnol
South Shawbost Upper Barvas
858 North Tolsta
New South Tolsta
Shawbost Loch Mor Barvas
Dalmore Bragar
Garrabost
Dalbeg 26 42 A C Loch
Brevat Muirneag 813 New Tolsta
D Glen Mor Barvas Tolsta Head

B

Glen Bruadale
Campay 28 45
Little Dun
Bernera Carloway
Floday 858 Garynahine 895 Gress
Loch Cruadhail 857
Lacastal Back
Kirkibost
GREAT Aird
BERNERA Upper Coll
Kirkibost Broad Bay Portnaguran
Barraglom Newmarket or Portvoller
Breasclete Loch a Tuath Aird
Cruliviq Callanish New Valley
8059 Standing Stornoway Eye Peninsula
Stones STORNOWAY Shulishader
Linshader Garynahine Melbost Sheshader
8011 Lewis Garrabost
Castle 866 Upper Bayble
Suainaval 22 35 Eitshal Sandwick Swordale Knock Lower Bayble
1404 733 Holm Bayble Hill Bayble Bay
8011 858 290

D

CAR FERRY TO ULLAPOOL

A   C   D

Hebrides

This group of islands off the west coast of Scotland is subdivided into the Inner and Outer Hebrides by the channels called the North Minch and the Little Minch. The Inner Hebrides, an amorphous group just off the Scottish mainland, includes Skye, Mull, Jura, Islay and numerous small islands such as Rhum, Tiree, Iona, Eigg, Coll, Colonsay and Oronsay (not all mapped but see also Maps 23 and 25). The crescent-shaped chain of the Outer Hebrides stretches in a 130 mile (208 km) long line from the Butt of Lewis in the north to Barra Head on the island of Berneray. Lewis is the largest of the islands. The other principal islands are Harris (attached to Lewis), North and South Uist, Benbecula and Barra (only Lewis and Harris are mapped). Long, silvery-white sandy beaches edge these islands and the western shores are continuously pounded by the full force of the Atlantic.

The Hebrides vary scenically from the jagged mountains of Skye to the landscape of North Uist where there are so many lochans that the island seems more water than land. In general the Outer Hebrides are characterised by flat moorland; only Harris has dramatic mountain peaks, soaring from the sea to over 2,500 ft (762 m).

The island communities are remote, their isolation more pronounced in an age when so much of the world is accessible with so little effort. The traditional way of life is still evident, with stacks of peat cut for winter fuel and thatched crofts with their roofs held in place by ropes weighted with rocks as protection against the winter gales. The manufacture of world-famous Harris tweed is still a major industry and a number of fishing vessels operate from island ports. Gaelic is still spoken and place names are sometimes bilingual.

The Hebrides are rich in prehistoric and early Christian remains – chambered cairns, standing stones, brochs, forts and the ruins of small churches. Among the prehistoric remains, the **Standing Stones of Callanish** are outstanding while **Iona** (see Gazetteer 25) is, of course, a cradle of Scottish Christianity.

INNER HEBRIDES

Canna, Isle of (NTS)

To the north is Compass Hill where rich iron deposits in the basalt cliffs are said to affect the magnetic compasses of passing ships. A mutilated sculptured cross stands near Canna Post Office and there are remains of a small Celtic nunnery, where the wall, mill and some cells can still be seen. Accommodation is limited. Ferry from Mallaig (154 H6) and Arisaig (Map 27 L1) (no cars). (154 H2)

Raasay, Isle of

This elongated, 14 mile (22 km) long island is much overshadowed by the **Cuillins**, which lie across the sound to the west.

On the east shore, 10 miles (16 km) north, is *Brochel Castle*, ruined home of the MacLeods of Raasay. A staunch Jacobite, the MacLeod chief joined the Young Pretender with 100 men in 1745, and the next year the MacLeods sheltered the fugitive Prince on Raasay for two nights. Soon after, government troops landed and laid waste the estate. The smaller island of *Rona* (excursions from Portree) lies to the north of Raasay. Car ferry from Sconser (154 E4). (154 D5)

Rhum, Isle of

From 1888 to 1957 Rhum was the private estate of the Bulloughs of Lancashire who in 1901 built **Kinloch Castle**, at a cost of around a quarter of a million pounds. This magnificent residence still contains many of its sumptuous fittings, but is so outrageously out of place in the Scottish countryside it has been likened to 'a vision of St Pancras station in the middle of the Sinai desert'. In 1957 Rhum was acquired by the Nature Conservancy Council, and today the nature reserve is important for geological and botanical research and the study of red deer; research is also carried out into the restoration of woodland. At Kinloch there is a deer park and the **Kinloch Glen and South Side Nature Trails**, the first up Kinloch Glen, the other along the south side of Loch Scresort. The walks start from the Head of the Pier, Kinloch, and a guide book is available. The island rises steeply from the shore to a magnificent group of peaks culminating in Askival, this name and others recalling the period of Norse occupation. Excursions from Mallaig and Arisaig. (154 H3)

Skye, Isle of

The Gaelic description of Skye is *Eilean A'Cheo fo sgail nam beannmor* – 'The Isle of Mist under the shadow of great mountains'. Considered by many to be the loveliest of all Scottish islands, Skye measures some 50 miles (80 km) in length and is the largest of the Inner Hebrides group. It is deeply indented by lochs and rocky headlands which form a series of peninsulas. No part of the island is more than 5 miles (8 km) from the sea.

Most of the islanders still make their living from crofting and fishing and traditions are very strong. There is a rich store of legend bound up with the island's brief encounter with Bonnie Prince Charlie, in particular in connection with Flora Macdonald, whose grave can be seen at *Kilmuir* (154 D2).

The coastline of the island is mainly rocky with a little sand. Some of the finest cliff scenery can be found in the Duirinish district, west of Dunvegan (154 D1), which is only accessible on foot. Among the most notable sights of Skye are the wild and beautiful **Lochs Scavaig and Coruisk**, which lie near Elgol; the fantastic rock formations of the **Quiraing** near Staffin; ancient **Dunvegan Castle**, seat of the chief of the Clan MacLeod; and the magnificent panoramic view of the **Cuillins** rising beyond Loch Scavaig, best seen from above Elgol. The easiest route to Skye is from Mallaig via the car-carrying steamer service. The alternative is the Kyle Akin car ferry from Kyle of Lochalsh (Map 27 G2). Roads on the island have been greatly improved in recent years.

Broadford A meeting point for roads from the ferry ports of Armadale (154 H6), Kylerhea (Map 27 G2) and Kyleakin (Map 27 G1), and a convenient touring centre for Skye. The granite domes of the Red Hills overlook the village. Beinn na Caillich, 2 miles (3.2 km) west, has on its top a large cairn under which lie the remains of a 13th-century Norwegian princess, who said she wanted the winds of Norway to blow over her grave. (154 F5/6)

Clan Donald Centre, Armadale Situated ½ mile (0.8 km) north of the pier at partly ruined Armadale Castle, the centre is a 46 acre (18.5 hectare) country park with gardens, a 200-year old arboretum, scenic views over the Sound of Sleat and nature trails with Ranger service. A restored wing of the castle houses the museum and its audio-visual theatre, which presents dramatic displays of the Clan's history. The stables have been lavishly restored to house a restaurant, gift shop and bookshop. ♿ (154 H6)

Cuillin Mountains These mountains, across the south of Skye, are a tumbled, irregular mass of rough gabbro on basalt, a firm rock affording some of the best rock-climbing in Britain. The mountains are interesting to geologists for the frequent glacial striations and perched boulders. (154 F3/4)

Dunsgiath Castle, Tokavaig Well-preserved ruins of a former Macdonald stronghold. (154 G5)

Duntulm Castle A 17th-century ruin situated above the sea on the site of earlier castles. Was the seat of the Macdonalds *c.* 1616–1732. (154 A3)

Dunvegan Castle Historic stronghold of the Clan Macleod, set on the sea loch of Dunvegan, still the home after 700 years of the Chiefs of Macleod. Possessions on view (books, pictures, arms and treasured relics) trace the history of their Norse ancestry through 30 generations to the present day. Boat trips from the castle jetty to the seal colony. (154 C2)

Elgol This is the village from which Bonnie Prince Charlie left for the mainland. From Elgol boats cross **Loch Scavaig** to **Loch Coruisk** (which was painted by Turner). (154 G4)

Glen Varragill Walk Woodland walk on the steep west side of Glen Varragill with good views over Portree to **Raasay**. 2¼ miles (3.6 km) long. Car park, picnic place. ½ mile (0.8 km) south of Portree on A850. (154 D4)

Kilmuir Croft Museum The museum consists of four thatched cottages giving excellent coverage to the croft house of 100 years ago. It shows a fine selection of implements, tools, etc. used by the men and women of the Highlands and a very interesting collection of old letters, papers and pictures are on display. ♿ (154 A3)

Kilt Rock The top rock is composed of columnar basalt, the lower portion of horizontal beds, giving the impression of the pleats in a kilt. There is also a waterfall nearby. Off A855, 17 miles (27.2 km) north of Portree. Care should be taken not to go too near the edge of the cliff. (154 B4)

Knock Castle A ruined stronghold of the Macdonalds. Off A851. (154 G6)

Loch Mealt Here the remains of a broch can be clearly seen on a small promontory on the north shore. The loch empties as a little stream falling over sheer cliff

The Cuillins, Skye

into the sea, and from here there is a good view of **Kilt Rock**. The river Leat is crossed at a point where the stream drops by waterfall stages into a ravine, and soon the black obelisk of *Old Man of Storr* comes in sight to the south at the foot of **The Storr**. (154 B4)

Loch Scavaig and Loch Coruisk These lochs can be reached by boat hired at **Elgol** (sailings subject to demand from 10.30 am). Loch Scavaig is a broad sea loch, its head overshadowed by bare, jagged peaks. Loch Coruisk, beyond, across a narrow neck, lies at the very foot of the dark, towering **Cuillins** and is considered by many to be Scotland's wildest and grandest loch. The *Isle of Soay* is off the mouth of Loch Scavaig and occasional boat excursions are made from Elgol. The island was the site of an unsuccessful factory for extracting the oil and processing the skins of basking sharks. The inhabitants moved to **Mull** (see Gazetteer 25) in 1953. (154 G4)

Quiraing An extraordinary mass of towers and pinnacles into which cattle were driven during forays. A rough track zigzags up to the 'Needle', an imposing obelisk 120 ft (36.5 m) high, beyond which, in a large amphitheatre, stands the 'Table', a huge grass-covered rockmass. Impressive views. Off A855 just south of Digg. (154 A4)

Skye Watermill, Glendale On the shores of Loch Pooltiel, a 200-year-old grain mill and kiln, recently restored to full working order. (154 C1)

The Storr A steep walk through the young Storr plantations with many steps and broadwalks. One track leads to The Storr, a mass of pinnacles and crags, another circles the forest. Magnificent seascapes and rock scenery. The walk is subject to very high winds. Car park. On A855, 7 miles (11.2 km) north of Portree. (154 C4)

Uig A village on Trotternish, the largest Skye peninsula, and the ferry port for Harris and Uist, in the Outer Hebrides. The ruin of *Monkstadt House*, 1½ miles (2.4 km) north, is where Flora Macdonald brought Bonnie Prince Charlie, disguised as her maid, after their journey 'over the sea to Skye' from the isle of Benbecula. (154 B3)

OUTER HEBRIDES

Lewis

The Lews is another name for Lewis which, together with Harris, forms a land mass some 60 miles (96 km) long and 18 to 28 miles (28.8 to 45 km) wide. **Stornoway** (155 D5), the largest town in the Outer Hebrides and unofficial capital of Lewis, has a 2 mile (3.2 km) long natural harbour which has made it the centre of the Hebridean herring industry. There is also a large lobster pond. Tweed weaving is still a cottage industry here, but Stornoway has five mills for spinning and finishing the cloth. *Lewis Castle* (now a technical college) stands in fine wooded grounds facing the harbour and was given to the town by Lord Leverhulme who bought the island in 1918 with the intention of modernising Lewis' industries. Although he tried to turn the crofters into fish-cannery workers, the project finally failed. *St Peter's Church* has an ancient font and houses Livingstone's Prayer Book. To the south of the town, on Arnish Moor, a cairn and a loch commemorate Prince Charles Edward's visit to a local farm after the Battle of Culloden in 1746.

Stornoway is linked by a narrow strip of land to the Eye Peninsula, at the north-east tip of which is the fine rock scenery and lighthouse of Tiumpan Head. Distant views from here take in the cliffs of Cape Wrath in good weather. A road runs north-east from Stornoway and follows the sandy bays to Gress, where the ruined **Church of St Olaf** (155 C6) is thought to be the only one in the Outer Hebrides dedicated to a Norse saint. Farther northeast, beyond Tolsta, is Tolsta Head, with its magnificent cliffs, fine silver sand, and a lighthouse. The bay of Geiraha is one of the most picturesque on Lewis.

From Stornoway a road runs north-west over moorland dotted with tiny lochans, passing near the 1,000 ft (304.8 m) Barvas Hills (highest point Beinn Mholach). A right turn to Shader leads to Port of Ness and the **Butt of Lewis** (155 A6), with its lighthouse; this is the farthest northern point of the Outer Hebrides. From *Swanibost* (155 A6) there is a fine view of the Eye of the Needle, a rugged cape of rock pinnacles and cliffs near the Butt.

North-west of Garynahine, opposite Callanish (see **Standing Stones of Callanish**), is the island of *Great*

Bernera (155 C3), which can be reached by a road bridge. From Garynahine a narrow road runs south-west into remote country dotted with numerous lochans, beyond which lies the great expanse of Loch Langavat. This road leads to some of the farthest western parts of Lewis, round Little Loch Roag and finishing the lovely Glen Valtos to Uig. Fine cliffs and long stretches of silver sand are to be found here, with the bleak promontory of Gallan Head overlooking island-studded Loch Roag to the north. Views over 20 miles (32 km) of sea encompass the Flannan Isles, or Seven Hunters. A lighthouse was built on these islands in 1900; all three lighthouse keepers on duty vanished soon afterwards during a gale. Ardroil Sands lie 4 miles (6.4 km) south-west of Uig, backed by a range of remote, rocky hills. Beyond the eastern flanks of the latter and the hill of Tarain lies the long, narrow Loch Suainaval, which is over 200 ft (60.9 m) deep in places. This south-west corner of Lewis has no roads, and south of the hills the headland of Braighe Mor (Gearraidh na h-Airde Moire) boasts a collection of beehive houses near the mouth of Loch Resort.

The road to Harris from Stornoway passes near the Parish of the Lochs, so called because the proportion of water to land is even higher here than elsewhere in the islands. Crofters grow potatoes in lazy beds – rows of banked-up soil with their own drainage system. Ballalan lies at the head of lovely Loch Erisort, and from here the road crosses moorland which was once the hunting ground of the Earl of Seaforth, Chief of the Mackenzies. It was he who raised the Seaforth Highlanders regiment.

Small herds of red deer roam wild in these parts, and a road runs down the west side of beautiful Loch Seaforth to Aline, opposite Seaforth Island. This south-east corner of Lewis is known as Park.

Harris

The landscape changes as the road from Lewis runs alongside the shores of Loch Seaforth, and becomes more hilly with lofty, gneiss peaks to the west dominated by 2,622 ft (799 m) Clisham – the highest mountain in the Outer Hebrides. The road from Stornoway climbs the mountain's eastern flanks before descending to

Standing Stones of Callanish, Lewis

Ardhasig Bridge, from where there are fine views of West Loch Tarbert and the lonely hills to the northwest.

Beyond these hills the rocky mountains of the remote Forest of Harris stretch from Loch Resort (155 E2) to West Loch Tarbert (155 F2). One of the finest passes through the hills runs between the peaks of Uisgnaval and Oreval, past the craggy Strone Scourst which rises to over 1,600 ft (491 m) above Loch Scourst. This track ends 4 miles (6.4 km) north of West Loch Tarbert at Loch Voshimid (155 F2). To the east of the road from Stornoway is Outer Loch Seaforth with its fjord-like scenery. *Tarbert* (155 G2), the largest Harris village, stands on a narrow isthmus between East and West Loch Tarbert. Its steamer pier is on the former, and its name means 'a narrow neck of land across which boats may be dragged'.

A scenic road which runs east from Tarbert ends at Kyles Scalpay, over-looking Scalpay Island. To the north of Tarbert, at Ardhasig Bridge, a lovely but narrow road runs west along the shores of West Loch Tarbert to *Amhuinn-suid Castle* (not open), where James Barrie wrote much of *Mary Rose*. The road ends at the enchanting Husinish Bay, overlooking the island of Scarp. The 'main' road from Tarbert runs south into the delightful district of southern Harris and turns west along Glen Laxdale, where cairns mark ancient prehistoric funeral routes. The road then leads to one of Harris' beauty spots – the silver **Luskentyre Sands** (155 G2) lining a deep inlet on the Sound of Taransay, sheltered by the protective bulk of Taransay island. Near Luskentyre village is Loch Fincastle, a salmon loch.

The road continues past sandy bays with views of Toe Head, a peninsula stretching out into the Atlantic. From Chaipaval Hill there are unforgettable views of the **Cuillin** range of **Skye** and the hills of North Uist. Continuing through Glen Coishletter, the road passes near the shores of the Sound of Harris and leads to Leverburgh – or Obbe – where Lord Leverhulme failed in his attempt to create a fishing station. *Rodel* (155 H2), a village on Rodel Bay, is notable for **St Clement's Church** (SDD). Fine views can be enjoyed from 1,506 ft (459 m) Roneval, which rises to the north of Rodel. *Finsbay* (155 H2) lies 4 miles (6.4 km) north-east of Rodel and is a small port on Finsbay Loch, reached by a treacherous little road with acute corners and blind bends.

Black House Museum, Arnol (SDD) A good example of a traditional type of Hebridean dwelling, built without mortar and roofed with thatch on a timber framework and without eaves. Characteristic features are the central peat fire in the kitchen, the absence of any chimney and the byre under the same roof. The house retains many of its original furnishings. ♿ (155 B4)

Church of St Moluag Known in the Gaelic as Teampull mhor (big temple), this chapel was probably built in the 12th century. Now restored; service held every Sunday. (155 A6)

Dun Carloway Broch, Carloway (SDD) One of the best-preserved Iron Age broch towers in the Western Isles. Still standing about 30 ft (9.1 m) high. (155 C3)

Dun Carloway Broch, Lewis

St Clement's Church, Rodel (SDD) A notable cruciform church of *c.* 1500 with rich decoration and sculptured slabs. Open on application to Custodian. (155 H1)

Shawbost Folk Museum Created under the Highland Village Competition 1970, the museum illustrates the old way of life in Lewis. A Norse watermill has been restored; directions at the museum. A858. (155 C3)

Standing Stones of Callanish (SDD) A cruciform setting of megaliths comparable in importance to Stonehenge. It was probably built in a series of additions between 2000 and 1500 BC. An avenue of 19 monoliths leads to a circle of 13 stones, with rows of more stones fanning out. Callanish, off B858. (155 D3)

Steinacleit Cairn and Stone Circle (SDD) The fragmentary remains of a chambered cairn of Neolithic date (*c.* 2000 BC). At the south end of Loch an Duin, Shader, off A857. (155 B5)

The Trushel Stone An impressive monolith 20 ft (6 m) high, probably the tallest in Scotland. Other large stones nearby suggest it was part of a group. ½ mile (0.8 km) north of A857 at Ballantrushal. (155 B5)

Ui Church Ruined church (pronounced 'eye') containing some finely carved ancient tombs of the Macleods of Lewis. At Aignish, off A866. (155 D6)

A traditional Black House

Map 32

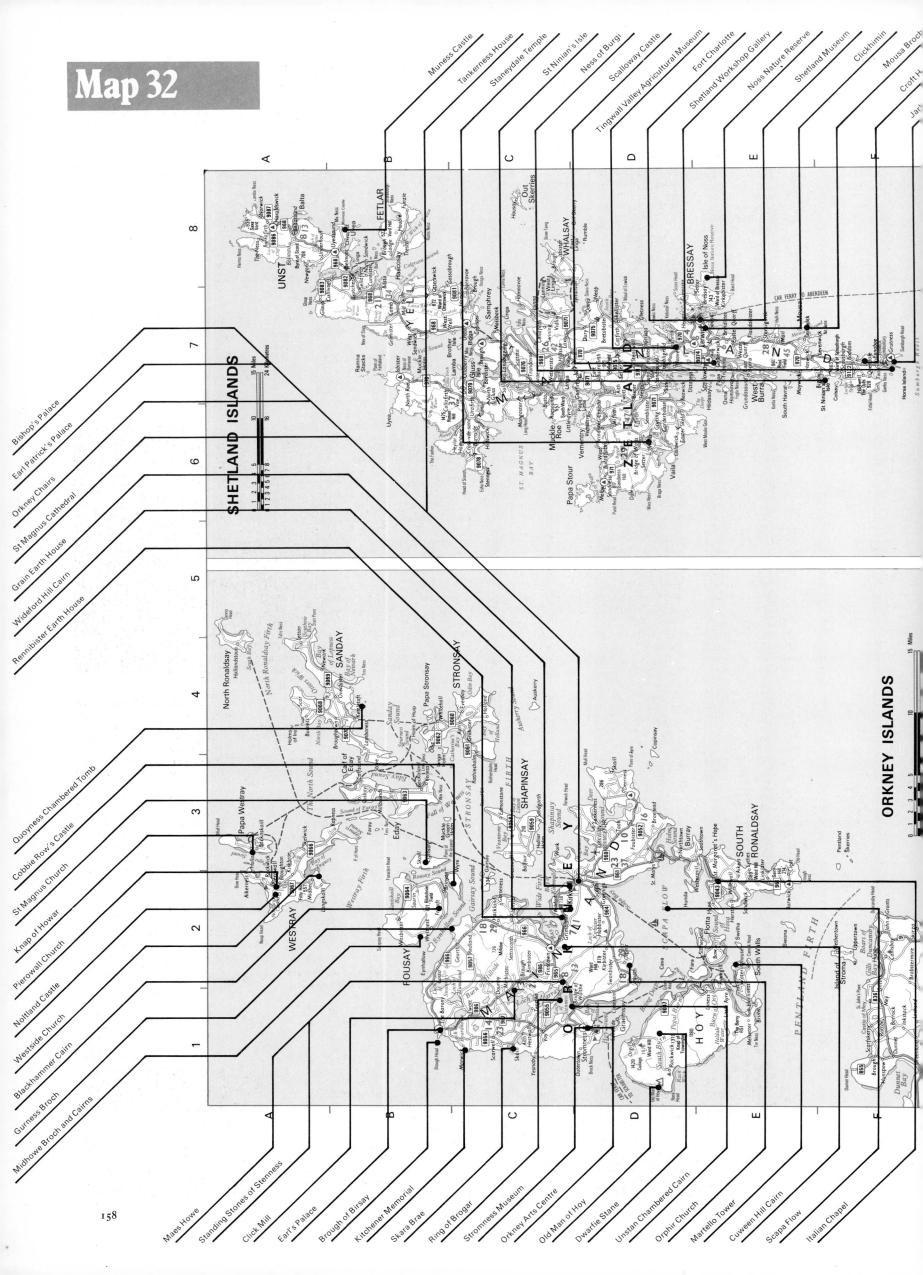

SHETLAND ISLANDS

ORKNEY ISLANDS

Orkneys and Shetlands

Orkney Islands

Of the seventy or so islands which make up the Orkneys only twenty-eight are inhabited. The islands lie about 20 miles (32 km) to the north of the Scottish mainland over the stormy Pentland Firth, and the largest is itself called Mainland. Most of the 18,000 islanders make their living from farming – the soil is surprisingly fertile and the climate mainly mild. Few trees grow on the islands and trout-fishing in the lochs is free. A remarkable feature of both the Orkneys and the Shetlands is that the summer nights are only twilight – or, as Shetlanders call it, 'simmer dim'. There is magnificent cliff scenery in the Orkneys, notably on Hoy, and the islands abound with prehistoric antiquities and rare bird life. The Romans called the islands the Orcades, but it is thought that the Picts were the first colonisers. Norsemen settled here in the 9th century and stayed for 500 years. In 1468–9 the islands passed to Scotland, given by Christian I of Norway as part of his daughter Margaret's dowry when she married James III of Scotland.

Mainland is linked to several of the smaller islands farther south by the Churchill Barriers, remains of World War II naval defences which now serve a more useful purpose. The Orkneys can be reached by steamer from Scrabster near Thurso (to Stromness), and from Aberdeen (to Kirkwall). Other steamer services connect with the Shetlands. Air services operate from the principal Scottish towns to Grimsetter Airport at Kirkwall. Supply bases for North Sea oil have been planned in some parts of the islands.

Stromness, Orkney

Bishop's Palace, Kirkwall (SDD) A ruined palace dating originally from the 12th century. Many subsequent alterations include round tower built by Bishop Reid and later addition of *c.* 1600 by Patrick Stewart, Earl of Orkney. (D2)

Blackhammer Cairn, Rousay (SDD) A long cairn bounded by a well-preserved retaining wall and containing a megalithic burial chamber divided into seven compartments or stalls: probably second millennium BC. North of B9064, on the south coast of the island. (B2)

Brough of Birsay (SDD) The remains of a Romanesque church and a Norse settlement on an island accessible only at low tide. A replica of a Pictish sculptured stone discovered in the ruins is in the grounds; original is in the National Museum of Antiquities in Edinburgh. (B1)

Click Mill (SDD) The only working example of the traditional horizontal water-mill of Orkney. Off A986 south of Dounby. (C2)

Cobbie Row's Castle, Wyre (SDD) Probably the earliest stone castle authenticated in Scotland. In a graveyard near the castle is St Mary's Chapel, a ruin of the late 12th century. (C2)

Cuween Hill Cairn (SDD) A low mound covering a megalithic passage tomb. Contained bones of men, dogs and oxen when discovered. Probably early second millennium BC. Open on application to key-keeper at nearby farmhouse. A965, ½ mile (0.8 km) south of Finstown. (C2)

Dwarfie Stane, Hoy (SDD) A huge block of sandstone in which a burial chamber has been quarried. No other tomb of this type is known in the British Isles. Probably *c.* 2000–1600 BC. Access by boat from Stromness. (D1)

Earl Patrick's Palace, Kirkwall (SDD) Built *c.* 1607 by Patrick Stewart, Earl of Orkney, and considered one of the finest Renaissance buildings in Scotland. Although roofless, much still remains. (D2)

Earl's Palace, Birsay (SDD) The extensive but dilapidated remains of the palace built in the 16th century for Robert Earl of Orkney. (B1)

Grain Earth House, Hatson, Kirkwall (SDD) A bean-shaped Iron Age souterrain with an entrance stair leading to an underground passage and chamber. Open on application to key-keeper. (C2)

Gurness Broch (SDD) An Iron Age broch still over 10 ft (3 m) high, surrounded by stone huts and within a deep ditch. Later inhabited in Dark Age and Viking times. Off A966, 11 miles (17.6 km) north-west of Kirkwall. (C2)

Italian Chapel, St Margaret's Hope Using a Nissen hut, Italian prisoners-of-war in 1943 created this beautiful little chapel out of scrap metal, concrete and other materials. (E2/3)

Kitchener Memorial The cruiser *Hampshire*, taking Lord Kitchener to Russia, was sunk in 1916 off the coast close by this point. At Marwick Head, south-west of Birsay Bay. (C1)

The Kitchener Memorial on Marwick Head, Orkney

Orkney Arts Centre, Stromness The Pier Arts Centre Collection of modern painting and sculpture housed in warehouse building on its own stone pier. Also galleries for visiting exhibitions and children's work. Arts library and reading room in adjacent house. (D1)

Orkney Chairs, 14 Palace Road, Kirkwall One of the few places making traditional Orkney chairs. (D3)

Orphir Church (SDD) The remains of Scotland's only circular medieval church, built in the first half of the 12th century and dedicated to St Nicholas. Its design was greatly influenced by the Crusades. By A964, 6 miles (9.6 km) south-west of Kirkwall. (D2)

Pierowall Church, Westray (SDD) 13th century, with 17th-century alterations, now a ruin consisting of nave and chancel, the latter canted out of alignment. There are some finely-lettered tombstones. (A2)

Knap of Howar, Papa Westray (SDD) Only recently recognised as one of the oldest sites in Europe, these two 5,000-year-old dwellings have also yielded many unusual artefacts – whalebone mallets and a spatula and unique stone borers and grinders. West side of island. (A3)

Maes Howe (SDD) An enormous burial mound, 115 ft (35 m) in diameter, dating back to *c.* 1800 BC, and containing a burial chamber which is unsurpassed in Western Europe. Runic inscriptions upon the walls. Off A965, 10 miles (16 km) west of Kirkwall. (C1/2)

Martello Tower, Hackness, Hoy (SDD) An impressive tower built during the Napoleonic and American wars at the beginning of the 19th century. The tower was renovated in 1866 and used again in World War I. Seen from outside only. (E2)

Midhowe Broch and Cairns, Rousay An Iron Age broch and walled enclosure situated on a promontory cut off by a deep rock-cut ditch. Also on the island is a rich collection of megalithic chambered tombs. On the west coast of the island. (B2)

Noltland Castle, Westray (SDD) This 15th-century ruined castle suffered several sieges and was partly destroyed in 1746. The fine hall, vaulted kitchen, and notable winding staircase are the main features of interest. Open on application to Custodian. (A2)

Old Man of Hoy A 450 ft (137 m) high isolated stack ('pillar') standing off the magnificent cliffs of north-west Hoy. Well seen from the Scrabster–Stromness ferry. (D1)

Quoyness Chambered Tomb, Sanday (SDD) A spectacular tomb with a main chamber standing to a height of about 13 ft (3.9 m). Analysis suggests that the tomb was in use about 2900 BC. Open on application to key-keeper. East side of Els Ness, south coast of island. (B4)

Rennibister Earth House (SDD) An excellent example of the Orkney type of Iron Age souterrain or earth-house, consisting of a passage and underground chamber with supporting roof-pillars. Open on application to key-keeper in farmhouse. About 4½ miles (7.2 km) west of Kirkwall on the Finstown road (A965). (C2)

Ring of Brogar (SDD) Magnificent stone circle of 35 stones (originally 60) surrounded by a deep ditch cut into solid bedrock. Nearby are large mounds and other standing stones, notably the Comet Stone. Between Loch of Harray and Loch of Stenness, 5 miles (8 km) north-east of Stromness. (C2)

Ring of Brogar, Orkney

St Magnus Cathedral, Kirkwall Founded by Earl Rognvald in 1137 and dedicated to his uncle St Magnus. The remains of both men are in the massive central piers. The original building dates

from 1137 to 1200, but additional work went on for a further 300 years. It contains some of the finest examples of Norman architecture in Scotland, with small additions in transitional styles and very early Gothic. (C2)

St Magnus Church, Egilsay (SDD) An impressive church, probably 12th-century, with a round tower somewhat after the manner of the Celtic type, which still stands to a height of nearly 50 ft (15.2 m). Key from nearby farmhouse. (B3)

Scapa Flow A major naval anchorage in both wars and the scene of the surrender of the German Fleet in 1918. Today Scapa Flow is again a centre of marine activity as Flotta has been developed as a pipeline landfall and tanker terminal for North Sea oil. Sea area, enclosed by the mainland of Orkney and the islands of Burray, South Ronaldsay, Flotta and Hoy. (D2)

Skara Brae (SDD) A Neolithic village with about ten one-roomed houses, containing stone beds, fireplaces and cupboards. There are also covered passages from one house to another and a paved open court where communal problems were discussed. The village was probably hastily evacuated in a sandstorm, and it remained under the sand-dunes for many centuries, until uncovered by a storm in 1850. 7½ miles (12 km) north of Stromness. (C1)

Standing Stones of Stenness (SDD) Four large upright stones are the dramatic remains of a stone circle, c. 3000 BC, encircled by a ditch and bank. The area around Stenness is particularly rich in such remains. Between Loch of Harray and Loch of Stenness, 5 miles (8 km) north-east of Stromness. (C1)

Stromness Museum, Alfred Street A fine collection of preserved birds, eggs, and Orkney shells. The maritime collection includes a selection of ship models and a permanent feature on the World War I German Fleet scuttled on **Scapa Flow.** (D1)

Tankerness House, Broad Street, Kirkwall Dating from 1574, this is a fine example of an Orkney merchant-laird's mansion, with courtyard and gardens. Now a museum of life in Orkney through 5,000 years, with additional special exhibitions. ♿ (D2)

Unstan Chambered Cairn (SDD) A cairn containing a chambered tomb (over 6 ft (1.8 m) high) divided by large stone slabs. The type of pottery discovered in the tomb is now known as Unstan Ware. Open on application to key-keeper. 2 miles (3.2 km) north-east of Stromness, by A965. (C/D1)

Westside Church, Westray (SDD) A 12th-century church, with nave and chancel, the former lengthened in the latter Middle Ages. Bay of Tuquoy, south coast of island. (A2/3)

Wideford Hill Cairn (SDD) A conspicuous megalithic chambered cairn with three concentric walls. Open on application to key-keeper. 2½ miles (4 km) west of Kirkwall on west slope of Wideford Hill. (C2)

Shetland Islands

More than a hundred islands make up Shetland, though fewer than twenty of these are inhabited. Muckle Flugga, the north point of Unst, is the most northerly point in Britain – more than 170 miles (272 km) from John O'Groats. However, although the Shetlands are farther north than parts of Alaska, the climate is considerably softened by the benevolent Gulf Stream. Mainland is the largest island, and its capital Lerwick is the only town of importance in Shetland. The islands lie at the centre of rich fishing grounds which support most of the

Lerwick, Shetland

20,000 population. Shetland has more known prehistoric sites than any area of its size in Britain, and splendid cliff and sea loch scenery. The local name for the latter is 'voes'. Apart from fishing, knitting and crofting are the principal industries. Shetland hosiery is famous the world over and Shetland wool and Shetland ponies also have a worldwide reputation. No trees grow on the islands, and the summer is short. During June and part of July, the nights have little or no darkness – the beautiful 'simmer dim' which has to be seen to be fully appreciated. Sea trout abound in the islands' lochs, and in many places fishing is free. Mainland has many excellent roads, but the smaller islands are less well-equipped and motoring is often hazardous.

Clickhimin (SDD) This site was fortified at the beginning of the Iron Age with a stone-built fort. Later a broch, which still stands to a height of over 17 ft (5.1 m), was constructed inside the fort. About ¾ mile (1.2 km) south-west of Lerwick. (E7)

Croft House, Dunrossness This thatched croft complex, comprising mid 19th-century croft house and steading, has been carefully restored and all furnishings are authentic. Watermill nearby. At South Voe on unclassified road east of A970. (F7)

Fort Charlotte, Lerwick (SDD) A roughly pentagonal fort with high walls containing gun ports pointing seawards. Designed by John Mylne and begun in 1665 to protect the Sound of Bressay. ♿ (E7)

Jarlshof (SDD) One of the most remarkable archaeological sites in Britain with the remains of three extensive village settlements occupied from Bronze Age to Viking times, together with a medieval farmstead and the 16th-century house of the Stewart Earls in the islands. Sumburgh Head, 28 miles (45 km) south of Lerwick. (F7)

Jarlshof, Shetland

Lerwick, Shetland

Mousa Broch (SDD) The best-preserved example of the remarkable Iron Age broch towers peculiar to Scotland. The tower stands over 40 ft (12 m) high. On an island off Sandwick, 12 miles (19 km) south of Lerwick. Daily bus service between Lerwick and Sandwick. Boat hire from Sandwick. (E7/8)

Muness Castle, Unst (SDD) A late 16th-century building, rubble-built with fine architectural detail. South-east point of island. Open on application to key-keeper at Castle Cottage. (B8)

Ness of Burgi (SDD) A defensive stone-built structure of Iron Age date, which is related in certain features to the brochs. On the coast at the tip of Scatness, about 1 mile (1.6 km) south-west of **Jarlshof.** (F7)

Noss Nature Reserve (NCC) Spectacular island with 450 ft (137 m) cliffs and vast colonies of breeding auks, gulls and gannets. 5 miles (8 km) east of Lerwick. Access by warden's boat. (E7)

St Ninian's Isle Holy Well, foundations of chapel (c. 12th-century) and pre-Norse church where a hoard of Celtic silver was discovered (now in the National Museum of Antiquities in Edinburgh). By B9122 off west coast of Mainland. (F7)

Scalloway Castle (SDD) Built in 1600 by Earl Patrick Stewart, on the 'two-stepped' plan. When the Earl, a notoriously cruel character, was executed in 1615, the castle fell into disuse. Open on application to Custodian. 6 miles (9.6 km) west of Lerwick. (E7)

Mousa Broch, Shetland

Shetland Museum, Lower Hillhead, Lerwick The collection in this museum is entirely local in character. The theme is the history of man in Shetland from pre-history to the present day. Four galleries are devoted to archaeology, art and textiles, folk life and shipping. Also natural history, maritime archaeology. (E7)

Shetland Workshop Gallery, 4–6 Burns Lane, Lerwick Two old dwelling houses in one of Lerwick's oldest lanes have been combined to provide a gallery for local artists and craftsmen. (E7)

Staneydale Temple (SDD) Second millennium BC structure, heel-shaped externally, and containing a large oval chamber. Access over boggy ground. 2¾ miles (4.4 km) east of Walls. (D6)

Tingwall Valley Agricultural Museum A private collection of tools and equipment used by the Shetland crofter. Housed in a mid 18th-century granary, stables and bothy. At Veensgarth off A971, 5 miles (8 km) north-west of Lerwick. (D7)

Opening Times
Index to Text
Index to Maps

Opening Times

The following list of opening times was correct at the time of going to press. Readers are advised to check that no changes have been made before visiting a property.

Many properties in the care of English Heritage, the Scottish Development Department and Cadw are open during standard hours as set out below. There is open access to many more, particularly in Scotland. Properties in the care of these bodies have only been included in the list if their opening times are *not* standard.

Standard Hours	Weekdays	Sundays
England and Wales		
Mid March to mid October	9.30–6.30	2.00–6.30
Mid October to mid March	9.30–4.00	2.00–4.00
Scotland		
April to September	9.30–7.00	2.00–7.00
October to March	9.30–4.00	2.00–4.00

All monuments in England and Wales are closed on Christmas Eve, Christmas Day, Boxing Day, New Year's Day and those in England also on May Day Bank Holiday; those in Scotland on Christmas Day, Boxing Day, New Year's Day and 2 January. Some of the smaller monuments may close for the lunch hour (normally 1–2). Where readers are advised to 'apply to the key keeper' for access there will be a notice giving directions at the site concerned.

Most properties not in the care of the State are also closed over Christmas (some for a fortnight) and on New Year's Day and May Day Bank Holiday. Where the closing time is given as, for example, 6 (or dusk) this means the property will close at 6 unless dusk is earlier.

The following properties in the care of The National Trust may be visited by uncomfortably large numbers on Bank Holidays and Sundays in summer. 'Full House' notices may be posted at these properties and tickets issued for timed entry only: Ascott (Bucks), Belton House (Lincs), Chartwell (Kent), Farne Islands (Northumberland), Hidcote Manor Garden (Glos), Housesteads (Northumberland), Oxburgh Hall (Norfolk), Polesden Lacey (Surrey), Sheffield Park Garden (East Sussex), Sissinghurst (Kent), Snowshill Manor (Glos), Speke Hall (Merseyside), Stourhead (Wilts), Waddesdon (Bucks).

GAZETTEER 1

Antony House April to end Oct: Tues, Wed, Thurs and Bank Holiday Mon 2–6. **Barbara Hepworth Museum** July and Aug: Mon–Sat 10–6.30, Sun 2–6; April to June, Sept: Mon–Sat 10–5.30; Oct to March: Mon–Sat 10–4.30. **Bodmin Park Farm** Late May to late Sept: Sun–Fri 10–6. **Boscastle Museum of Witchcraft** Easter to mid Oct: daily 10–dusk. **Camborne School of Mines** All year: Mon–Fri 9.30–4.30. Closed Bank Holidays. **Carnglaze Slate Caverns** Easter to end Sept: daily 10.30–5. **Cornish Engines** April to end Oct: daily 11–6 (or sunset). Last admission ½ hour before closing. **Cornish Seal Sanctuary** All year: daily 9.30–6. **Cornucopia** Good Fri to end Oct: daily 10–5 (high season 10–10). **Cornwall Aero Park** Easter to end Oct: daily 10–5. **Cotehele** End March to end Oct: daily 11–5.30 (*house* closed Fri, except Good Fri); Nov to late Dec: *hall and kitchen* open daily 11–4; Nov to end March: *gardens* open daily during daylight. **County Demonstration Garden** All year: Mon–Fri 10–5; May to Sept: Sun and Bank Holidays 2–6. **Dairyland and Cornish Country Life Museum** April, early May, Oct: daily 1.30–5.30; Easter, late May to Sept: daily 10–6. Last admission 1 hour before closing. **Delabole Slate Quarry** All year: Mon–Fri 8–4.30. **Forest Railroad Park** Wed before Good Fri to end Sept: daily 10–6. Last admission 5. Reduced opening times in Oct. **Glendurgan Garden** March to end Oct: Mon, Wed, Fri 10.30–4.30. Closed Good Fri. **Godolphin House** May, June: Thurs 2–5; July, Sept: Tues, Thurs 2–5; Aug: Tues 2–5, Thurs 10–1, 2–5. Also open Bank Holidays but closed Good Fri. **Helston Folk Museum** All year: daily 10.30–1, 2–4.30 (except Wed 10.30–1). Closed Sun, Bank Holidays. **Lanhydrock House** April to end Oct: daily 11–6 (last admission 5.30); Nov to end March: *garden only* open daily during daylight. **Lappa Valley Railway** Easter to end Sept: daily 10.30–5.30. **Megavissey Folk Museum** Easter to end Sept: Mon–Fri 11–6, Sat, Sun 2–4. **Monkey Sanctuary** Fortnight over Easter, 1st Sun in May to end Sept: daily 10.30–6. **North Cornwall Museum** April to end Sept: Mon–Sat 10.30–5. **Padstow Tropical Bird Garden** All year: daily 10.30–7. **Paradise Park** All year: daily 10–1 hour before dusk. **Paul Corin Musical Collection** Easter week from Good Fri, May to end Sept: daily 11–1, 2.30–5. **Pencarrow House** Easter to end Sept: daily (except Fri, Sat) 1.30–5 (11–5 on Bank Holiday Mon, and from June to early Sept). **Penjerrick Gardens** End March to end Sept: Wed, Sun 1.30–4.30 (advisable to check). **Poldark Mine** Early April to end Oct: daily 10–5.15. **St Michael's Mount** Nov to end March: Mon, Wed, Fri (guided tours only); April to end May: Mon–Fri (except Thurs) 10.30–5.45; June to end Oct: Mon–Fri 10.30–5.45. Last admission 4.45. **Tintagel Castle** Standard hours and Sunday mornings in summer. **Tintagel Old Post Office** April to end Oct: daily 11–6 (or sunset). Last admission ½ hour before closing. **Trelissick Garden** March to end Oct: Mon–Sat 11–6, Sun 1–6 (or sunset). **Trengwainton Garden** March to end Oct: Wed–Sat and Bank Holiday Mon 11–6. **Trerice** April to end Oct: daily 11–6. Last admission 5.30. **Tresco Abbey Gardens** All year: daily 10–4. **Trewithen Garden** March to end Sept: Mon–Sat 2–4.30. **Wheal Martyn Museum** April to end Oct: daily 10–5.

GAZETTEER 2

Alscott Farm Museum Easter to end Sept: daily 12–dusk. **Arlington Court** April to end Oct: daily (except Sat, but open Bank Holiday Sat) 11–6 (last admission 5.30). *Garden and park* all year daily during daylight. **Ashley Countryside Collection** Easter to 1st Sun in Oct: Sun, Mon, Wed 10–6; Aug: daily (except Thurs) 10–6. Open Bank Holidays. **Bradley Manor** Early April to end Sept: Wed (also some Thurs in season) 2–5. Last admission 4.45. **Brixham Marine Aquaria** Easter to end Oct: daily 10–10. **Buckfast Abbey** *Abbey church* open daily. **Buckland Abbey** Good Fri to end Sept: Mon–Sat and Bank Holidays 11–6, Sun 2–6; Oct to Easter: Wed, Sat, Sun 2–5. Last admission ½ hour before closing. **Buzzacott Manor Gardens** Easter to Oct: daily 10.30–6. **Castle Drogo** Good Fri to end Oct: daily 11–6. Last admission 5.30. **Chambercombe Manor** Good Fri to end Sept: Mon–Fri 10.30–12.30, 2–4.30, Sun 2–4.30. **Compton Castle** April to end Oct: Mon, Wed, Thurs 10–12.15, 2–5. Last admission 4.30. **Croyde Gem, Rock and Shell Museum** All year: daily 9.30–5 (10 in summer). **Dartington Hall** No opening times as such. *Great Hall* can be visited when not in use. **Dartmoor Wildlife Park** All year: daily 10–dusk. **Dart Valley Steam Railway** Easter week, Spring Bank Holiday, Sun to mid June, then daily to early Sept. **Ebbingford Manor** Temporarily closed for restoration. **Garden House** April to Sept: daily 2–5. Closed Bank Holidays. **Hele Mill** Easter to end Oct: Mon–Fri 10–5, Sun 2–5. **Kingsbridge Miniature Railway** Easter week, mid May to mid Sept: daily 11–5. **Lydford Gorge** April to end Oct: daily 10.30–6; Nov to end March: daily from waterfall entrance as far as waterfall only. **Marwood Hill Gardens** All year: daily dawn to dusk. **Morwellham Quay** All year: daily 10–6 (or dusk). Last admission 4.30 (winter 2.30). **Mount Edgcumbe** *House* May to Sept: Mon, Tues afternoons. *Park* open throughout the year. **National Shire Horse Farm Centre** All year: daily 10–5; *parades* 11.30, 2.30, 4.15. **North Devon Maritime Museum** Easter to end Sept: daily 2–5.30 (also 11–1 Tues–Fri). **Okehampton Castle** Standard hours and Sun morning in summer. **Overbecks Museum and Garden** *Garden* always open. *Museum* April to end Oct: daily 11–1, 2–6. Last admission 12.45 and 5.30. **River Dart Country Park** April to end Sept. **Rosemoor Garden Trust** April to end Oct: daily dawn to dusk. *Nursery* open all year. **Saltram** April to end Oct: Sun–Thurs, Good Fri, Bank Holiday Fri and Sat *house* 12.30–6, *kitchen, art gallery and garden* 11–6. Last admission 5.30. *Garden only* open daily Nov to April. **Shaldon Wildlife Trust** Summer: daily 10–7; winter: daily 11–4. **Sticklepath Museum of Rural Industry** April to end Oct: daily 10.30–5.30; Nov to end March: daily 10.30–dusk. **Stover Park** All year daily. **Tapeley Park** Good Fri to Oct: daily (except Mon, but open Bank Holiday Mon) 10–6. Conducted tours only. *Gardens* open in winter during daylight. **Ugbrooke Park** May Bank Holiday to early Sept: daily *grounds* 12.30–5.30, *house* 2–5.

GAZETTEER 3

Abbotsbury Sub Tropical Gardens Mid March to mid Oct: daily 10–6. **Abbotsbury Swannery** 2nd week in May to mid Sept: daily 9.30–4.30. **A la Ronde** April to end Oct: Mon–Sat 10–6, Sun 2–7. **Ambleside Water Gardens** Easter to Oct: daily (except Mon, but open Bank Holiday Mon) 10.30–5.30. **Athelhampton** Summer: Wed, Thurs, Sun and Bank Holidays 2–6; also Mon and Tues in Aug. **Barford Park** May to Sept: Wed, Thurs and Bank Holiday weekends 2–6. **Barrington Court** *Garden* Easter to late Sept: Sun, Wed 2–5.30. *Court* Easter week to end Sept: Wed 2–5 (last tour 4). **Bickleigh Castle** Easter week to Spring Bank Holiday: Wed, Sun and Bank Holiday Mon 2–5; end May to early Oct: daily (except Sat) 2–5. **Bickleigh Mill and Craft Centre and Farm** Jan to March: Sat, Sun 10–5; April to early Dec: daily 10–6 (closed 5 Nov). **Bicton Park** April to Oct: daily 10–6; winter: telephone Colaton Raleigh 68495. **Brympton d'Evercy** May to Sept: Sat–Wed 2–6. **Clapton Court Gardens** All year: Mon–Fri 10–5, Sun 2–5. **Clouds Hill** April to end Sept: Wed, Thurs, Fri, Sun and Bank Holiday Mon 2–5; Oct to end March: Sun 1–4. **Coleridge Cottage** Easter to end Sept: Tues–Thurs, Sun 2–5. **Cricket St Thomas Wildlife Park** April to end Oct: daily 10–6; Nov to March: daily 10–5. **Dunster Castle** Easter Sat to end Sept: *castle* Sat–Wed, *grounds* daily 11–5; Oct: same days 2–4. Last admission ½ hour before closing. **East Somerset Railway** April to Oct: daily 9–5.30; Nov to March: Sat, Sun 9–4. Steam-hauled passenger services Sun and Bank Holidays April to Oct (also Wed and Sat in July and Aug). **Fleet Air Arm Museum** March to Oct: daily 10–5.30; Nov to Feb: daily 10–4.30. **Forde Abbey** Easter Sun, May to Sept: Sun, Wed and Bank Holidays 2–6; March, April, Oct: *garden only* Sun 2–4.30. **Fyne Court** All year: daily 9–6 (or sunset). **Gaulden Manor** Easter Sun and Mon, 1st Sun in May to end June: Sun, Thurs 2–5.30; July to 2nd Sun in Sept: Sun, Wed, Thurs 2–5.30. **Hadspen House** All year (except Jan): Tues–Sat 10–5; April to Oct: Sun and Bank Holidays 2–5. **Hardy's Cottage** *Garden only* April to end Oct: daily (except Tues morning) 11–6 (or dusk). *House* by written appointment. **Hatch Court** July to mid Sept: Thurs 2.30–5.30. **Isle of Portland: Portland Castle** Standard hours April to Sept only. **Killerton** April to end Oct: daily 11–6 (last admission 5.30). *Garden and park* all year daily. **King John's Hunting Lodge** April to end Sept: daily 2–5. **Knightshayes Court** April to end Oct: daily *garden* 11–6, *house* 1.30–6. Last admission 5.30. **Longleat** Easter to end Sept: daily 10–6; Oct to Easter: daily 10–4. **Lytes Cary** April to end Oct: Wed, Sat 2–6 (or dusk). **Mapperton Gardens** Early March to early Oct: Mon–Fri 2–6. **Midelney Manor** June to mid Sept: Wed and Bank Holidays 2–5.30. **Milton Abbey House** Easter period, mid July to end Aug: daily 10–dusk. *Church* always open. **Minterne** April to end of autumn colouring: daily 10–7. **Montacute** April to end Oct: daily (except Tues) 12.30–6. Last admission 5.30. **Oakhill Manor** Good Fri to end Sept: daily 11–5; Oct: weekends only. **Otterton Mill** All year: daily 10.30–5.30; winter: weekends 2–5. **Parnham House** April to end Oct: Sun, Wed, and Bank Holidays 10–5. **Pilton Manor Vineyard** June to Sept: Wed, Thurs, Fri 12–2.30; also Sun and Bank Holiday Mon 12–6 from late Aug to late Sept. **Powderham Castle** May Bank Holiday Sun to early Sept: daily (except Fri, Sat) 2–5.30. Last admission 5. **Somerset and Dorset Railway Trust** Easter to Sept: Sun and Bank Holidays; also Wed in Aug. **Stourhead** *Garden* all year: daily 8–7 (or sunset). *House* April, Oct: Sat–Wed 2–6 (or dusk); May to Sept: daily (except Fri) 2–6. Last admission ½ hour before closing. **Tintinhull House** April to end Sept: Wed, Thurs, Sat and Bank Holiday Mon 2–6. Last admission 5.30. **Tiverton Castle** Easter to late Sept: Sun–Thurs 2.30–5.30. **Tropical Bird Gardens** Summer: daily 10.30–7 (last admission 6); winter: daily 10.30–sunset. **Wolfeton House** May to Sept: Sun, Tues, Fri 2–6; Aug: daily (except Sat) 2–6. **Wookey Hole** Winter: daily 10.30–4.30; summer: daily 9.30–5.30. **Worldwide Butterflies** April to Oct: daily 10–5.

GAZETTEER 4

Amberley: Chalk Pits Museum April to end Oct: Wed–Sun and Bank Holiday Mon 10–5. **Arundel Castle** April to end Oct: Sun–Fri 1–5 (June, July, Aug and all Bank Holidays 12–5). **Avington Park** May to Sept: Sat, Sun and Bank Holiday Mon 2.30–5.30. **Basing House** April (from Easter), May, Sept: Sat, Sun 2–6; June, July, Aug: daily (except Thurs) 2–6. Open all Bank Holidays. **Beaulieu Abbey** May to Sept: daily 10–6; Oct to May: daily 10–5. **Bignor Roman Villa** April, May: daily (except Mon, but open Bank Holiday Mon) 10–6; June to Sept: daily 10–6; March, Oct: daily (except Mon) 10–5. **Bohunt Manor Gardens** All year: Mon–Fri 10–5. **Breamore House** April to end Sept: daily (except Mon and Fri, but open Bank Holidays) 2–5.30. **Broadlands** April to end Sept: daily (except Mon) 10–5 (open Mon in Aug, Sept, and all Bank Holidays). **Buckler's Hard: Maritime Museum** Easter to Spring Bank Holiday: daily 10–6; Spring Bank Holiday to Sept: daily 10–9; Oct to Easter: daily 10–4.30. **Clandon Park** April to mid Oct: daily (except Mon and Fri, but open Bank Holiday Mon) 2–6. Last admission 5.30. **Corfe Castle** March to end Oct: daily 10–6 (or sunset); Nov to end Feb: Sat, Sun 12–4. **Cranborne Manor Gardens** April to Oct: 1st weekend in every month, Sat 9–5, Sun 2–5. **Denmans Garden** End March to Oct: daily (except Mon and Tues, but open Bank Holiday Mon) 1–6. **Exbury Gardens** March: daily 1–5.30; April to mid July: daily 9–5.30. **Fishbourne Roman Palace** March, April, Oct: daily 10–5; May to Sept: daily 10–6; Nov: daily 10–4; Dec to Feb: Sun 2–4. Last admission 20 minutes before closing. **Furzey Gardens** All year: daily 10–5. **Goodwood** May to mid Oct: Sun, Mon 2–5 (also Tues–Thurs in Aug). **Hatchlands** April to mid Oct: Wed, Thurs, Sun, Bank Holiday Mon 2–5. Last admission ½ hour before closing. **The Hawk Conservancy** Easter to Oct: daily 10.30–4 (5 in high season). **Heale House Garden** *Nursery* open all year. *Garden and nursery* Easter to end Sept: Mon–Sat, Bank Holidays and 1st Sun in month 10–5. **Highdown Garden** All year: Mon–Fri 10–4.30; April to end Sept: Sat, Sun and Bank Holidays 10–8. **Hillier Arboretum** All year: Mon–Fri 10–5; March to early Nov: Sat, Sun and Bank Holidays 1–6. **Jane Austen's House** April to end Oct: daily 11–4.30; Nov, Dec, March: Wed–Sun 11–4.30; Jan, Feb: Sat, Sun 11–4.30. **Loseley House** End May to end Sept: Wed–Sat (also Spring and Aug Bank Holiday Mon) 2–5. Last admission 4.30. **Marwell Zoological Park** Summer: daily 10–6 (last admission 5); winter: daily 10–1 hour before dusk. **Mid Hants Railway** Early March to late Oct: weekends and Bank Holidays; end May to end July: also midweek; end July to end Aug: daily. **Mottisfont Abbey** April to end Sept: *grounds* daily (except Fri, Sat) 2–6, *house* Wed, Sun 2–6 (last admission 5). **National Motor Museum** May to Sept: daily 10–6; Oct to May: daily 10–5. **Newhouse** June, July, Aug: Sat, Sun 2–6 (also all Bank Holiday Mon). **Oates Memorial Museum and Gilbert White Museum** March to Oct: daily (except Mon, but open Bank Holiday Mon) 12–5.30. Last admission 5. **Palace House, Beaulieu** May to Sept: daily 10–6; Oct to May: daily 10–5. **Parham** Easter to 1st Sun in Oct: Wed, Thurs, Sun and Bank Holidays *house* 2–6, *gardens* 1–6. **Petworth** *House and pleasure gardens* April to end Oct: daily (except Mon and Fri, but open Bank Holiday Mon and closed Tues following) 2–6. Last admission 5.30. *Park* open all year daily 9–sunset. **Polesden Lacey** March, Nov: Sat, Sun 2–5; April to Oct: Wed–Sun 2–6, Good Fri, Bank Holiday Sun and Mon 11–6. Last admission ½ hour before closing. **Portchester Castle** Standard hours and Sun morning in summer. **Shipley Windmill** Easter Mon, 1st weekend in month from May to Oct and Aug Bank Holiday: 2.30–5.30. **Smedmore** June, July, Aug: Wed 2.15–5.30 (also 1st two Wed in Sept and last Sun in Aug). **Stonehenge**

Standard hours and Sun morning all year. **Uppark** April to end Sept: Wed, Thurs, Sun and Bank Holiday Mon 2–6. Last admission 5.30. **The Vyne** April to mid Oct: daily (except Mon and Fri) 2–6, Bank Holiday Mon (but closed Tues following) 11–6. Last admission 5.30. **Wardour Castle** *Old Castle* Standard hours in summer and Sun morning April to Sept only; weekends in winter: Sat 9.30–4, Sun 2–4. *New Castle* end July to early Sept: Mon, Wed, Fri, Sat 2.30–6. **Watts Gallery** April to end Sept: Mon, Tues, Fri, Sun 2–6, Wed, Sat 11–1, 2–6; Oct to end March: Mon, Tues, Fri, Sun 2–4, Wed, Sat 11–1, 2–4. Closed Thurs. **Weald and Downland Open Air Museum** April to Oct: daily 11 5; Nov to March: Wed, Sun 11–4. **West Dean Gardens** April to end Sept: daily 11–6. Last admission 5. **Wilton House** Early April to early Oct: Tues–Sat and Bank Holidays 11–6, Sun 1–6. **Winkworth Arboretum** All year. **Isle of Wight: Arreton Manor** One week before Easter to end Oct: Mon–Fri 10–6, Sun 12–6. **Blackgang Chine** All year: daily 10–5; end May to end Sept: daily 10–10. **Brading Roman Villa** April to end Sept: Mon–Sat 10–5.30, Sun 10.30–5.30. **Godshill Model Village** Easter to end Sept: daily 10–5.30 (or dusk). **Isle of Wight Steam Railway** Easter Sun and Mon; April to Sept: Sun and Bank Holiday Mon; July, Aug: Thurs (also daily 1st week in Aug). Three-day 'Island Steam Extravaganza' end Aug. **Osborne House** End March to early Oct: daily 10–5.

GAZETTEER 5

Alfriston Clergy House April to end Oct: daily 11–6 (or sunset). Last admission ½ hour before closing. **Bateman's** April to end Oct: daily (except Thurs and Fri, but open Good Fri) 11–6. Last admission 5.30. **Bedgebury National Pinetum** All year: daily 10–dusk. **Bodiam Castle** April to end Oct: daily 10–7 (or sunset); Nov to March: Sat 10–sunset. Open Good Fri. **Borde Hill Gardens** March, Oct: Sat, Sun; April to Sept: Tues, Wed, Thurs, Sat, Sun; all Bank Holidays including Good Fri: 10–6. **Boughton Monchelsea Place** Good Fri to early Oct: Sat, Sun and Bank Holidays (also Wed in July and Aug) 2.15–6. **Bramber: House of Pipes** All year: daily 9–7.30. **Bridge Cottage** Sat 10–4 (until completion of restoration May 1986). **Chartwell** March, Nov: Sat, Sun, Wed 11–4; April to Oct: Tues, Wed, Thurs 12–5, Sat, Sun, Bank Holiday Mon 11–5. **Chiddingstone Castle** April to end Sept: Wed–Sat 2–5.30 (also Tues mid June to mid Sept), Sun and Bank Holidays 11.30–5.30; Oct: weekends only. **Chilham Castle** *Gardens* mid March to end Oct: daily 11–6. Last admission 5. **De Tillens** May, June: Sat 2–5; July to Sept: Wed, Sat 2–5. Open all Bank Holidays May to Sept. **Dover Castle** Standard hours and Sun morning in summer. **Drusillas** April to end Oct: daily 10.30–5.30. **Emmetts Garden** April to end Oct: Tues–Fri, Sun, Bank Holiday Mon 2–6. Last admission 5. **Grange Museum and Art Gallery** All year: Mon, Thurs, Sat 10–5, Tues, Fri 10–1, 2–5, Sun 2–5. Closed Wed. **Great Dixter** Easter, April to mid Oct: Tues–Sun and Bank Holiday Mon 2–5; also last two weekends in Oct. **Herstmonceux Castle and Greenwich Observatory** Good Fri to end Sept: daily 10.30–5.30. Last admission 4.30. **Hever Castle** Good Fri to early Nov: daily *garden* 11–6 (last admission 5), *castle* 12–6 (last admission 5.15). **Horsham Museum** All year: Tues–Fri 1–5, Sat 10–5. **Howletts Zoo Park** All year: daily 10–5 (or dusk). **Hythe: Romney, Hythe and Dymchurch Light Railway** Easter to Sept: daily; March to early Nov: weekends. **Lamb House** April to end Oct: Wed, Sat 2–6. Last admission 5.30. **Lewes Castle and Museum of Sussex Archaeology** All year: Mon–Fri 10–5; April to Oct: Sun 11–5. **Marlipins Museum** May to Sept: Mon–Sat 10–1, 2–5, Sun 2–5. **Michelham Priory, Forge and Wheelwrights Museum** Good Fri to mid Oct: daily 11–5.30 **Museum of Local History** Mid Feb to Nov: Mon–Fri 10–5.30; April to Oct: Sun 2–5.30. Last admission 5. **Newtimber Place** May to Aug: Thurs 2–5. **Nymans Garden** April to end Oct: daily (except Mon and Fri, but open Bank Holiday Mon) 11–7 (or sunset). Last admission 1 hour before closing. **The Old Mill** Easter Sun to end Oct: Sun 2–6. **Penshurst Place** April (or Good Fri if earlier) to 1st Sun in Oct: daily (except Mon) *grounds* 12.30–6, *house* 1.30–5.30 (last admission 5). **Polegate Windmill and Milling Museum** Easter to Sept: Sun 2.30–5.30; also Easter Mon, Bank Holiday Mon in May and Aug, and Wed in Aug. **Post Mill** Easter to Sept: last Sun of each month and Bank Holiday Sun and Mon 2.30–5.30. **Quebec House** March: Sun 2–6; April to end Oct: daily (except Thurs and Sat) 2–6. Last admission 5.30. **Scotney Castle Garden** *Garden only* April to mid Nov: Wed–Fri 11–6, Sat, Sun, Bank Holiday Mon 2–6 (or sunset). Last admission 5.30. *Old castle* open May to late Aug same times as garden. **Sheffield Park Garden** April to early Nov: Tues–Sat 11–6, Sun, Bank Holiday Mon 2–6 (1–sunset on Sun in Oct and Nov). Last admission 1 hour before closing. **Sissinghurst Castle Garden** April to mid Oct: Tues–Fri 1–6.30, Sat, Sun 10–6.30. Last admission 6. Closed Mon including Bank Holidays. **Springhill Wildfowl Park** All year: daily 10–6 (or dusk). **Standen** April to end Oct: Wed, Thurs, Sat, Sun 2–6. Last admission 5.30. Closed Good Fri and Bank Holidays. **Swanton Mill** April to end Sept: Sat, Sun 3–6, and by appointment. **Union Mill** Easter to end Sept: Sat, Aug Bank Holiday Mon 2.30–5. **Wakehurst Place Garden** Jan, Nov, Dec: daily 10–4; Feb, Oct: daily 10–5; March: daily 10–6; April to end Sept: daily 10–7. Last admission ½ hour before closing. **Watermill Museum** Easter to end Sept: weekends and Bank Holidays 11–6; July to end Sept: Mon–Thurs 2–6. **Woods Mill** Easter to late Sept: Tues, Wed, Thurs, Sat 2–6, Sun and Bank Holidays 11–6.

GAZETTEER 6

Afan Argoed Country park *Park* daily during daylight. *Countryside Centre* April to Oct: daily 10.30–6.30; Nov to March: Sat, Sun 10.30–5.30. **Caldey Island Monastery** Island is open to the public from end May (Whitsun) to end Sept. A fleet of boats runs from Tenby Harbour. **Cardigan Wildlife Park** All year: daily 10–5.30. **Carmarthen Museum** All year: Mon–Sat 10–4.30. **Carreg Cennen Castle** Standard hours and Sun morning in summer. **Cefn Coed Museum** March to Oct: daily 11–6. Last admission 5.15. **Dan-yr-Ogof Caves** Easter to end Oct: daily 10–5. **Felin Geri Flour Mill** Easter to end Sept: Mon–Fri 10–5.30, Sat, Sun 11–5. **Fishing Museum and Salmon Leap Gallery** Easter to Oct: daily 10–6. **Graham Sutherland Gallery** April to Sept: daily (except Mon) 10.30–5. **Gwili Railway** Good Fri to Easter Tues, May Day Sun and Mon, Spring Bank Holiday Sat–Tues, Sun June to Sept, Sat–Wed mid July to end Aug. **Kidwelly Castle** Standard hours and Sun morning in summer. **Lampeter: St David's College** *College* open all year. *Library* in term: Mon–Fri 9–9.45, Sat 9–4.45, Sun 2–5.15; out of term: Mon–Fri 9–4. **Manorbier Castle** Easter week, Whitsun to Sept: daily 10.30–5.30. **Manor House Wildlife and Leisure Park** Easter to end Sept: daily 10–6. **Margam Park** April to Oct: daily 10.30–8; Nov to March: Wed–Sun 10.30–1 hour before dusk. **Margam Stones Museum** Easter Mon to end Sept: Mon–Sat 10.30–4.30. **Museum of the Welsh Woollen Industry** April to Sept: Mon–Sat 10–5.30; Oct to March: Mon–Fri 10–5.30. **Nant y Coy Museum and Mill** Easter to Oct: daily 10.30–5.30. **Oystermouth Castle** April to end Sept: Mon–Fri 10.30–6, Sat, Sun 10–6.15; end Sept to end March: Mon–Fri 11–3.30. **Pembrey Country Park** Daily during daylight. *Visitor Centre* Easter to end Sept: daily 10–6; Oct to Easter: daily 10–4. **Pembroke Castle** Easter to end Sept: daily 10–6 (last admission 5.30); Oct to Easter: Mon–Sat 10–4 (last admission 3.30). **Penscynor Wildlife Park** Summer: daily 10–6; winter: daily 10–5 (or dusk). **St David's: Bishop's Palace** Standard hours and Sun morning in summer. **Scolton Manor Museum and Country Park** *Park* Easter to end Sept: daily (except Mon, but open Bank Holiday Mon) 10.30–7; Oct to Easter: daily (except Mon) 10.30–4.30. *Museum* June to Sept: daily (except Mon, but open Bank Holiday Mon) 10.30–6. **Tregwynt Woollen Mill** All year: Mon–Sat 9–5 (operates Mon–Fri only). **Tudor Merchant's House** Easter Sun to end Sept: Mon–Fri 10–1, 2.30–6, Sun 2.30–6. Last admission 5.45. **Wallis Woollen Mill** All year: Mon–Fri 10–6. **Welsh Miner's Museum** April to Oct: daily 10.30–6; Nov to March: Sat, Sun 10.30–5. **Weobley Castle** April to Sept: Mon–Sat 10–7, Sun 2–7; Oct to March: Mon–Sat 10–dusk, Sun 2–dusk.

GAZETTEER 7

Abbey Dore Court March to end Oct: daily 10.30–6.30. **American Museum** Late March to end Oct: daily (except Mon) 2–5. **Ashleworth Tithe Barn** All year: daily 9–6 (or sunset). **Barton Farm Country Park** Open all reasonable hours. **Berkeley Castle** April: Tues–Sun 2–5; May to Aug: Tues–Sat 11–5, Sun 2–5; Sept: Tues–Sun 2–5; Oct: Sun 2–4.30. Open Bank Holiday Mon in period 11–5. **Blaise Castle House** All year: Sat–Wed 10–1, 2–5. **Caerleon Legionary Museum** Standard Hours and Sun morning in summer. **Caerphilly Castle** Standard hours and Sun morning in summer. **Caldicot Castle** March to Oct: Mon–Fri 11–12.30, 1.30–5, Sat 10–1, 1.30–5, Sun 1.30–5. **Castell Coch** Standard hours and Sun morning in summer. **Chavenage House** Easter Sun, May to Sept: Thurs, Sun and Bank Holidays 2–5. **Chepstow Castle** Standard hours and Sun morning in summer. **Clevedon Court** April to Sept: Wed, Thurs, Sun and Bank Holiday Mon 2.30–5.30. Last admission 5. **Corsham Court** Mid Jan to mid Dec: Tues–Sun and Bank Holiday Mon 2–4 (2–6 during June to Sept and all Bank Holidays). **The Courts** April to end Oct: daily (except Sat and Sun) 2–6. **Cyfartha Castle** April to Sept: Mon–Sat 10–1, 2–6 (5 on Fri), Sun 2–5; Oct to March: Mon–Sat 10–1, 2–5 (4 on Fri), Sun 2–5. **Dyffryn House Gardens** April to Sept: daily 10–7. **Dyrham Park** *Park* all year: daily 12–6 (or sunset). *House and garden* April, May, Oct: daily (except Thurs, Fri) 2–6; June to end Sept: daily (except Fri) 2–6. Last admission 5.30. **Eastnor Castle** May to end Sept: Sun and Bank Holiday Mon 2.15–6; July, Aug: Wed, Thurs 2.15–6. **Elmore Court** May to Aug: 1st Sun in month 2–6. **Falconry Centre** March to Oct: daily (except Tues) 10.30–5.30 (or dusk). **Frocester Tithe Barn** Open all reasonable hours on request. **Great Chalfield Manor** April to end Sept: Tues–Thurs 12–1, 2–5. **Hellens** Good Fri to end Sept: Wed, Sat, Sun and Bank Holidays 2–6. **Horton Court** April to end Oct: Wed, Sat 2–6 (or sunset). **Lacock Abbey** *House and grounds* April to end Oct: daily (except Tues and Good Fri) 2–6. *Fox Talbot Museum* March to end Oct: daily (except Good Fri) 11–6. Last admission 5.30. **Llanfihangel Court** Easter, Sun in July and Aug, Bank Holidays: 2.30–6. **Luckington Court** *Garden* all year: Wed 2–6. *House* by appointment. **Lydney Park Gardens** End April to mid June: Sun, Wed, Bank Holidays 11–6; also daily for one week after late Spring Bank Holiday. **Model Farm Folk Collection** Easter to end June: Sat, Sun, Mon 11–6; July to Sept: daily 11–6; Oct, Nov: Sun 2–5.30. **Monmouth Castle** Exterior only at any reasonable time. **Norchard Steam Centre** All year daily for static display. Rides on Bank Holiday Sun and Mon, Sun from June to Sept, and Wed afternoons in Aug. **North Gloucestershire Railway** Easter to end Aug: Sun, Bank Holidays 1–5. **Odda's Chapel** Any reasonable time. **Painswick House** Daily in Aug. **Pembridge Castle** May to Sept: Thurs 10–7. **Penhow Castle** Easter to Sept: Wed–Sun and Bank Holidays 10–6. **Raglan Castle** Standard hours and Sun morning in summer. **Sheldon Manor** April to end Sept: Sun, Thurs and Bank Holidays 2–6, *garden* 12.30–6. **Skenfrith Castle** All year at any reasonable time. **Slimbridge: The Wildfowl Trust** All year: daily 9.30–5 (or dusk). **Sufton Court** Last two weeks in May and Aug: daily 2–5.30. **Tintern Abbey** Standard hours and Sun morning in summer. **Tredegar House and Country Park** *House* Good Fri to end Sept: Wed–Sun and Bank Holidays 12.30–4.30. *Park* all year 6.15 to sunset. **Welsh Folk Museum** All year: Mon–Sat 10–5, Sun 2.30–5. Closed Good Fri, May 1. **Westbury Court Garden** April to end Oct: Wed–Sun, Bank Holiday Mon 11–6. **Westonbirt Arboretum** All year: daily 10–8 (or sunset). *Visitor Centre* summer: daily 10–5 (closed mid Nov to Easter). **Westwood Manor** April to Sept: Sun, Mon 2–5.

GAZETTEER 8

Arlington Mill March to Oct: daily 10.30–7; winter: weekends 10.30–dusk. **Ascott** *House and garden* late July to mid Sept: Tues–Sun 2–6 (and late Bank Holiday Mon). *Garden only* April to mid July and last Sun in Sept: Thurs, and every last Sun in month 2–6. Last admission 5.30. **Ashdown House** April to end Oct: Wed, Sat 2–6. **Avebury** *Stone circle* daily. *Museum* late March and early Oct: Mon–Sat 9.30–6.30, Sun 2–6.30; April to end Sept: daily 9.30–6.30; mid Oct to mid March: Mon–Sat 9.30–4, Sun 2–4. *Great Barn* April to end Oct: daily 10–5.30; Nov to Mid March: Sat, Sun 2–4.30. **Aynhoe Park** May to Sept: Wed, Thurs 2–4.30. **Barnsley House Garden** Wed throughout year 10–6; May to Aug: Mon–Fri 10–6, 1st Sun in month 2–6. **Basildon Park** April to end Oct: Wed–Sat 2–6, Sun and Bank Holiday Mon 12–6. Last admission 5.30. Closed Good Fri. **Batsford Park Arboretum** April to Oct: daily 10–5. **Bekonscot Model Village** April to Oct: daily 10–5. **Birdland Zoo Garden** March to Nov: daily 10–6; Dec to Feb: daily 10.30–4. **Blenheim Palace** *Park* daily throughout year. *Palace* mid March to end Oct: daily 11–6. *Plant and Butterfly Centre* mid March to Dec 23: daily 10–6 (*Butterfly House* April to Oct only). Last admission 5. **Boarstall Duck Decoy** Good Fri to Aug Bank Holiday Mon: Wed 2–5, Sat, Sun, Bank Holiday Mon 10–5. **Bowood House and Gardens** April to Sept: daily 11–6. *Rhododendron walks* mid May to mid June: daily 11–6. **Brill Post Mill** April to end Sept: Sun 2.30–5.30. **Buckinghamshire Railway Centre** Easter to end Oct: Sun, Bank Holiday Mon. **Buscot Park** April to end Sept: Wed, Thurs, Fri 2–6; also 2nd and 4th Sat and immediately following Sun in each month 2–6. **Chastleton House** Good Fri to end Sept: Fri, Sat, Sun and Bank Holidays 2–5. Last admission 5.30. **Cliveden** *House* April to end Oct: Thurs, Oct: Tues–Sun and Bank Holiday Mon 11–6; Nov to early Dec, Feb: Wed–Sun 11–4. **Chenies Manor** Early April to end Oct: Wed, Thurs 2–5; also late May and late Aug Bank Holiday Mon 2–6. **Child Beale Wildlife Trust** End March to end Sept: daily (except Fri) 10–6. **Claydon House** April to end Oct: Sat–Wed 2–6, Bank Holiday Mon 1–6. Last admission 5.30. **Cliveden** *House* April to ehd Oct: Thurs, Sun 3–6 (last admission 5.30). *Grounds* March to Dec: daily (including Good Fri) 11–6 (or sunset). **Cogges Farm Museum** May to Oct: daily 10.30–5.30 (4.30 in Oct). **Cotswold Countryside Collection** April to Oct: Mon–Fri 10–5.30, Sun 2–5.30. **Courage Shire Horse Centre** March to end Oct: daily (except Mon, but open Bank Holiday Mon) 11–4. **Denfurlong Farm** Open at any reasonable time. **Didcot Railway Centre** March to Oct: Sat, Sun, Bank Holidays 11–5; end July to early Sept: Mon–Fri 11–4.30. 'Steaming days' 1st and last Sun of month, Bank Holidays, and Sun and Wed in Aug. **Ditchley Park** Twelve days in late July 2–5. **Donnington Castle** Any reasonable time. **Great Coxwell Great Barn** All year daily at reasonable hours. **Greys Court** April to end Sept: *house* Mon, Wed, Fri (closed Good Fri) 2–6, *garden* Mon–Sat 2–6. Last admission 5.30. **Hughenden Manor** March: Sat, Sun 2–6; April to end Oct: Wed–Sat 2–6, Sun and Bank Holiday Mon 12–6. Last admission 5.30. **Kingston House** April, May, June: Sat, Sun, Bank Holiday Mon 2.30–5.30. **Long Crendon Courthouse** April to end Sept: Wed 2–6, Sat, Sun and Bank Holiday Mon 11–6. **Mapledurham House** Easter Sun to last Sun in Sept: Sat, Sun and Bank Holidays 2.30–5.30. *Watermill and Country Park picnic area* 12–5.30. **Mentmore** All year: Sun, Bank Holidays 1–4; early April to late Oct: daily 1–5. Last admission 4. **Milton Manor** Easter weekend to late Oct: Sat, Sun and Bank Holidays 2–5.30. **Milton's Cottage** Feb to end Oct: Tues–Sat 10–1, 2–6; also Spring and Summer Bank Holidays. **Nether Winchendon House** May to Aug: Thurs 2.30–5.30; also Bank Holiday weekends, 1st weekend in June, 2nd weekend in Aug. **Pendon Museum** Sat and Sun afternoons throughout year, and Summer Bank Holidays 11–6 **Pitstone Windmill** May to end Sept: Sun and Bank Holiday Mon 2.30–6. Last admission 5.30. **Pusey House Gardens** April to mid Oct: daily (except Mon and Fri, but open Bank Holidays) 2–6. **Rousham House** *Gardens* all year: daily 10–6. *House* April to Sept: Wed, Sun and Bank Holidays 2–5.30. **Savill Garden** All year: daily 10–6 (or sunset). **Sezincote Garden** Jan to Nov: Thurs, Fri and Bank Holiday Mon 2–6. *House* May, June, July, Sept: Thurs, Fri 2.30–6. **Snowshill Manor** April and Oct: Sat, Sun and Bank Holiday Mon 11–1, 2–6 (or sunset); May to end Sept: Wed–Sun and Bank Holiday Mon 11–1, 2–6. Closed Good Fri. **Stockgrove Park** Open all year. **Stonor** Easter to end Sept: Wed, Thurs, Sun 2–5.30, Bank Holiday Mon 11–5.30. **Stratfield Saye** Easter Sat, Sun and Mon, weekends in April, and daily (except Fri) May to Sept: 11.30–5. **Sudeley Castle** April to Oct: daily 12–5, *grounds* from 11. **Waddesdon Manor** *House* March, April, Oct: Wed–Fri 2–5, Sat, Sun 2–6; May to end Sept: Wed–Sun 2–6. *Grounds* March to Oct: Wed–Sat 1–6, Sun 11–6. Good Fri and Bank Holiday Mon *house and grounds* open 11–6 but closed following Wed. **Wellplace Zoo** April to Sept: Mon–Fri 10–5.30, Sun 10–6. Open winter weekends if weather suitable. **West Wycombe Park** *Grounds only* Easter and Spring Bank Holiday Sun and Mon 2–6. *House and grounds* June: Mon–Fri 2–6; July and Aug: daily (except Sat) 2–6. Last admission 5.30. **Whipsnade** All year: daily 10–sunset. **Windsor Safari Park** Daily throughout year from 10. **Winslow Hall** July to mid Sept: daily (except Mon) 2.30–5.30. *Gardens only* May, June: Sun 2–5. **Woburn Abbey** Early Jan to end March: Sat, Sun *park* 10.30–3.45, *abbey* 11–4; end March to end Oct: Mon–Fri *park* 10–4.45, *abbey* 11–5, Sun and Bank Holidays *park* 10–5.15, *abbey* 11–5.30. **Wild Animal Kingdom** Mid March to Oct: daily 10–5, **Wotton House** Aug to end Sept: Wed 2–4. Last admission 3.

GAZETTEER 9

Allington Castle All year: daily 2–4. **Aylesford Friary** All year: daily 9–dusk. **Benington Lordship Garden** Easter Mon and every Sun and Wed in May, June, July: 2–6; also Bank Holidays in May and Aug. **Beth Chatto Gardens** March to end Oct: Mon–Sat 9–5; Nov to end Feb: Mon–Fri 9–4. Closed Sun and Bank Holidays. **Bourne Mill** April to mid Oct: Bank Holidays and weekends 2–6; July to Sept: Tues 2–6. **Chart Gunpowder Mills** All year: Sun and Bank Holidays 2.30–4.30. **Cheslyn Gardens** April to Sept: daily (except Thurs) 10–8; Oct to March: daily (except Thurs) 10–4. **Chessington Zoo** Winter: daily 10–4; summer: daily 10–5. **Claremont Landscape Garden** April to end Oct: daily 9–7 (or sunset); Nov to end March: daily 9–4. Last admission ½ hour before closing. **Cobham Hall** Easter, end July to early Sept: Wed (usually), Thurs and Sun 2–5; also late Summer Bank Holiday Mon. **Dedham: Castle House** Early May to early Oct: Wed, Sun and Bank Holidays, also Thurs and Sat in Aug 2–5. **Fingringhoe Wick Nature Reserve** All year: daily (except Mon, but open Bank Holiday Mon) 9–4.30. **Gorhambury House** May to Sept: Thurs 2–5. **Ham House** All year: daily (except Mon, but open Bank Holiday Mon) 11–5. Last admission 4.30. Closed Good Fri, 1st Bank Holiday Mon in May. **Hampton Court** *Palace* May to Sept: Mon–Sat 9.30–6, Sun 11–6; March, April, Oct: Mon–Sat 9.30–5; Nov to Feb: Mon–Sat 9.30–4, Sun 2–4. Last admission 1 hour before closing. *Gardens* daily until dusk. *Palace* closed Good Fri, 1st Mon in May. **Hatfield House** Late March to 2nd Sun in Oct: Tues–Sat 12–5, Sun 2–5.30. Open Bank Holiday Mon but closed Good Fri. **Hollytrees** All year: Mon–Sat 10–1, 2–5 (4 on Sat from Oct to March). **John Webb's Windmill** May to Sept: Sat, Sun and Bank Holidays 2–6. **Knebworth House** April, May: Sun, Bank Holidays and School Holidays; June to Sept: daily (except Mon, but open Bank Holidays) *park* 11–5.30, *house and gardens* 12–5. **Knole** April to end Oct: Wed–Sat and Bank Holiday Mon 11–5, Sun 2–5. Last admission 4. **Lullingston Roman Villa** Standard hours and Sun morning in summer. **Luton Hoo** April to early Oct: Mon, Wed, Thurs, Sat and Good Fri 11–5.45, Sun 2–5.45. **Marsh Farm Country Park** All year: daily 10–12.30, 1.30–5. **Minster Abbey** All year: daily 11–12 (except Sun); May to Oct: Mon–Fri 2–4.30, Sat 3.30–5. Closed last three days in Lent. **Mole Hall Wildlife Park** All year: daily 10.30–6. **Parndon Wood Nature Reserve** Sun throughout year 9–1, 2–6; April to Oct: Tues 7–9. **Paradise Park** Summer: daily 10–6 (last admission 5); winter: daily 11–1 hour before dusk. **Paycocke's** April to mid Oct: Wed, Thurs, Sun and Bank Holiday Mon 2–5.30. **Powell-Cotton Museum** *Museum only* Oct to April: Sun 2.15–6; April to Sept: Wed, Thurs, Fri (in Aug), Sun 2.15–6. Open Bank Holidays. **Rayleigh Windmill** April to end Sept: Sat 10–12.30. **Roman Theatre of Verulamium** All year: daily 10–5 (or dusk). **St John's Jerusalem Garden** April to end Oct: Wed 2–6. Last admission 5.30. **Saling Hall** Mid May to end July, Sept to mid Oct: Wed, Thurs, Fri 2–5. **Shaw's Corner** April to end Oct: Mon–Thurs 2–6, Sun and Bank Holiday Mon 12–6; March to end Nov: Sun–Thurs 11–6. Last admission 5.30. **Spains Hall** *House* by appointment. *Garden* May, June, July: Sun and Bank Holidays 2–5. **Stansted Mountfitchet Windmill** April to Oct: 1st Sun in month, Bank Holiday Sun and Mon, and every Sun in Aug: 2.30–7. **Stour Valley Railway Centre** All year: daily 11–5.30. Steam days 1st Sun in month and Bank Holidays April to Oct. **Thaxted Guildhall** Easter to end Sept: Sun and Bank Holidays 2–6. **Twyritt Drake Museum of Carriages** All year: Mon–Sat 10–1, 2–5; April to Sept: Sun and Bank Holidays 2–5. **Upminster Mill** April to Sept: 3rd weekend of each month, afternoons only. **Wisley Gardens** All year: daily 10–dusk, except Sun which is members only until 2.

GAZETTEER 10

Abergynolwyn Museum Opening uncertain; enquire at village Post Office. **Acton Round Hall** May to Sept: Thurs 2.30–5.30. **Acton Scott Working Farm Museum** Early April to end Oct: Mon–Sat 10–5, Bank Holidays and Sun 10–6. **Attingham Park** April to end Sept: Sat–Wed 2–5.30, Bank Holiday Mon 11.30–5.30; Oct: Sat, Sun 2–5.30. Last admission 5. **Benthall Hall** Easter Sat to end Sept: Tues, Wed, Sat and Bank Holiday Mon 2–6. Last admission 5.30. **Berrington Hall** April, Oct: Sat, Sun and Easter Mon 2–5; May to end Sept: Wed–Sun and Bank Holiday Mon 2–6. **Bridgnorth North Gate Museum** April to Sept: Sat and Bank Holidays 2–4; also Mon, Tues, Wed from mid July to early Sept. **Burford House Gardens** April to Oct: Mon–Sat 11–5, Sun 2–5. *Nursery* all year: Mon–Fri 9–5, Sun 2–5 (or dusk). **Burton Court** Spring Bank Holiday to mid Sept: Wed, Thurs, Sat, Sun and Bank Holiday Mon 2.30–6.30. **Centre for Alternative Technology** All year: daily 10–5.30 (or 1 hour before dusk). **Clee Hill Bird Garden** All year: daily 10–5.30. **Clun: Town Hall Museum** Easter to Nov: Tues, Sat 2–5, all Bank Holiday weekends Sat–Tues 11–1, 2–5. **Corris Railway Museum** Easter weekend, Bank Holiday weekends, and weekdays mid July to early Sept: 10.30–5; week after Easter, June to mid July, 2nd week in Sept: weekdays 12–5. **Croft Castle** April, Oct: Sat, Sun and Easter Mon 2–5; May to end Sept: Wed–Sun and Bank Holiday Mon 2–6. **Cwmmau Farmhouse** Easter, Spring and late Summer Bank Holidays: Sat, Sun, Mon 2–6. **Fairbourne Railway** Good Fri to end Sept: daily. **Hergest Croft Gardens** Late April to mid Sept: daily 11–7; Oct: Sun 11–7. **Ironbridge Gorge Museum** April to Oct: daily 10–6; Nov to March: daily 10–5. **Lilleshall Abbey** Standard hours April to Sept only. **Llandrindod Wells Museum** All year: Mon–Sat 10–12.30, 2–5 (closed Bank Holidays, and Sat afternoons from Oct to end April). **Llanidloes Museum** Easter to end Sept: Mon–Sat 11–1, 2–5. **Llywernog Silver-Lead Mine** Easter to end Aug: daily 10–6; Sept: daily 10–5; Oct: daily 11–4. **Lower Brockhampton** April to end Oct: Wed–Sat and Bank Holiday Mon (closed Good Fri) 10–1, 2–6, Sun 10–1. **Ludlow Castle** Feb to April and Oct to Nov: daily 10.30–4; May to Sept: daily 10–6.30. Closed Dec, Jan. **Moccas Court** April to Sept: Thurs 2–6. **Mortimer's Cross Water Mill** April to Sept: Thurs 12–5. **Much Wenlock Museum** Early April to late Sept: Mon–Sat (and Sun in June to Aug only) 10.30–1, 2–5. **Nanteos Welsh Stately Home** All year: daily 10.30–5.30. **Newtown Textile Museum** April to Oct: weekdays (except Mon) 2–4.30. **Powis Castle** *Castle and garden* daily fortnight from Easter Sat; May, June, Sept: Wed–Sun 1–6, Bank Holiday Mon 11.30–6; July, Aug: *castle* Tues–Sun 1–6, *garden* daily 12–6. Last admission 5.30. **Shipton Hall** May to Sept: Thurs, Bank Holidays 2.30–5.30; July, Aug: Sun 2.30–5.30. **Strata Florida** Standard hours Easter to end Sept only. **Stokesay Castle** 1st Wed in March to end March: daily (except Tues) 10–5; April to Sept: daily (except Tues) 10–6; Oct: daily (except Tues) 10–5; Nov: weekends 10–dusk. **Talyllyn Railway** Early April to end Oct daily. **Upton Cressett Hall** May to Oct: Thurs 2.30–5. **The Weir** April to early May: daily (except Sat) 2–6; early May to end Oct: Wed and Bank Holiday Mon 2–6.

GAZETTEER 11

Althorp All year: daily 1.30–5.30 (11–6 July, Aug, Sept and Bank Holidays). Connoisseurs' days on Wed (longer tours). **Anne Hathaway's Cottage** April to Oct: weekdays 9–6, Sun 10–6 (Oct closes 5); Nov to March: weekdays 9–4.30, Sun 1.30–4.30. **Arbury Hall** Easter to end Sept: Sun, Bank Holiday Mon *hall* 2–5.30 (last admission 5), *gardens* 1–6; also Tues and Wed in July and Aug. **Avoncroft Museum of Buildings** June, July, Aug: daily 11–5.30; April, May, Sept, Oct: daily (except Mon) 11–5.30; March, Nov: daily (except Mon and Fri) 11–4.30. Open Bank Holidays. **Baddesley Clinton** Sat before Easter to end Sept: Wed–Sun and Bank Holiday Mon (closed Good Fri) 2–6; Oct: Sat, Sun 2–5. **Battlefield of Bosworth** *Battle Trail* open all year. *Visitor Centre* Wed before Easter to last Sun in Oct: Mon–Sat 2–5.30, Sun 1–6. **Bewdley Folk Museum** March to Nov: Mon–Sat 10–5.30, Sun 2–5.30. **Billing Aquadrome and Milling Museum** Late March to mid Oct daily. **Boscobel House** Standard hours and Sun morning in summer. **Boughton House** Aug: daily *grounds* from 12, *house* 2–5. **Broughton Castle** Mid May to mid Sept: Wed, Sun, Bank Holiday Sun and Mon 2–5; also Thurs in July and Aug. **Castle Ashby** July to end Aug: daily 2–5. **Charlecote Park** April, Oct: Sat, Sun and daily in week following Easter 11–5 (closed Good Fri); May to end Sept: daily (except Mon and Thurs, but open Bank Holiday Mon) 11–6. **Chicheley Hall** Good Fri to end Sept: Bank Holidays and Sun 2.30–6. **Chillington Hall** Early May to mid Sept: Thurs, all Sun in Aug, Easter Sun and Sun before Spring and Summer Bank Holidays 2.30–5.30. **Coombe Abbey** All year: daily 7.30–dusk. No access to interior. **Coton Manor Gardens** April to end Sept: Thurs, Sun, Bank Holiday Mon and Tues, and Wed in July and Aug 2–6; Oct: Sun 2–6. **Coughton Court** Easter week (except Fri): daily 2–5; April, Oct: Sat, Sun, Bank Holiday Mon 2–5; May to end Sept: daily (except Mon and Fri, but open Bank Holiday Mon) 2–6. Closed Good Fri. **Deene Park** Sun June to end Aug, and all Bank Holidays: *park* 1.15–5.30, *house* 2–5.30. **Donington le Heath Manor House** Easter to late Sept: Wed, Sun 2–6, and Bank Holiday Mon and Tues in summer. **Dorsington Manor Gardens** April to Oct: daily 11.30–6. **Drayton Manor Park and Zoo** Easter to Oct: daily 10.30–6. **Dudmaston** April to end Sept: Wed, Sun 2.30–6. Last admission 5.30. **Eastnor Castle** Mid May to end Sept: Sun, Bank Holiday Mon 2.15–6; July, Aug: Wed, Thurs 2.15–6. **Elgar's Birthplace Museum** May to end Sept: daily (except Wed) 10.30–6; Oct to mid Jan, mid Feb to April: daily (except Wed) 1.30–4.30. **Farnborough Hall** April to end Sept: Wed, Sat, May Day Bank Holiday Sun and Mon 2–6, *terrace walk only* Thurs, Fri, Sun 2–6. **Fleece Inn** Open daily during licensed hours. **Guilsborough Grange Wildlife Park** All year: daily 10–7 (or dusk). **Hagley Hall** Easter to July: Bank Holiday Sun and Mon 2–5; July, Aug: daily (except Sat) 2–5. **Hanbury Hall** April and Oct: Sat, Sun, Easter Mon 2–5; May to end Sept: Wed–Sun, Bank Holiday Mon 2–6. **Hanch Hall** Easter Sun to end Sept: Sun, Bank Holiday Mon and Tues 2–6; June to Sept: Tues, Wed, Thurs and Sat 2–6. **Hartlebury Castle Museum** *State Rooms* Easter to Sept: 1st Sun in month and Bank Holiday Sun, Mon and Tues 2–5. *Country Museum* March to Oct: Mon–Fri 2–5, Sun 2–6, Bank Holidays 11–5 (closed Good Fri). **Harvington Hall** Feb to Nov: daily (except Mon, but open Bank Holiday Mon and closed Fri following) 2–6 (or dusk); also open 11.30–1 Easter to Sept. Closed Good Fri. **Hidcote Manor Garden** April to end Oct: daily (except Tues and Fri) 11–8. **Kenilworth Castle** Standard hours and Sun morning in summer. **Kinwarton Dovecote** All year: daily 9–6 (or sunset). **Lamport Hall** Easter to end Sept: Sun and Bank Holiday Mon 2.15–5.15; also Thurs in July and Aug. **Lord Leycester Hospital** Summer: daily (except Sun) 10–5.30; winter: daily (except Sun) 10–4. Last admission 15 minutes before closing. **Lyddington Bede House** Standard hours April to Sept only. **Mary Arden's Home** April to Oct: weekdays 9–6, Sun 10–6 (Oct closes 5); Nov to March: weekdays 9–4.30, closed Sun. **Moseley Old Hall** March and Nov: Sun, Easter Mon and Tues 2–6 (or sunset); April to end Oct: Wed, Thurs, Sat, Sun, Bank Holiday Mon and Tues 2–6 (or sunset). Last admission 5.30. **Naseby Battle and Farm Museum** Early April to end Sept: Sun and Bank Holidays 2–6. **Oakham Castle** April to Oct: Tues–Sat and Bank Holiday Mon 10–1, 2–5.30; Nov to March: same times but closes 4. Closed Good Fri. **Packwood House** April to end Sept: Wed–Sun and Bank Holiday Mon 2–6; Oct: Sat, Sun 2–5. **Ragley Hall** April to Sept: daily (except Mon and Fri) 1.30–5.30. **Rockingham Castle** Easter Sun to end Sept: Thurs, Sun, Bank Holiday Mon and Tues 2–6; also Tues in Aug. **Rutland County Museum** All year: Tues–Sat 10–1, 2–5; April to Oct: Sun 2–5, Bank Holiday Mon 10–1, 2–5. Closed Good Fri. **Southam Zoo** All year: daily 10–7 (or dusk). **Spetchley Park** April to end Sept: Mon–Fri 11–5, Sun 2–5.30, Bank Holiday Mon 11–5.30. **Stanford Hall** Easter to end Sept: Thurs, Sat, Sun, Bank Holiday Mon and Tues 2.30–6. *Grounds and museum* open from 12 on Bank Holidays. **Stoke Park Pavilions** June: Sun 2–6; July, Aug: Sat, Sun 2–6. **Stowe Gardens** Easter weekend, mid July to early Sept: Fri, Sat, Sun 11–4. **Sulgrave Manor** April to Sept: daily (except Wed) 10.30–1, 2–5.30; Oct to March: daily (except Wed) 10.30–1, 2–4. Closed Jan. **Twycross Zoo** All year: daily from 10. **Upton House** April to end Sept: Mon–Thurs, Bank Holiday Monand some summer weekends 2–6. Last admission 5.30. **Warwick Castle** March to end Oct: daily 10–5.30; Nov to end Feb: daily 10–4.30. **Waterways Museum** Easter to Oct: daily 10–6; Oct to Easter: daily (except Mon) 10–4. **West Midland Safari and Leisure Park** Mid March to end Oct: daily 10–5. **Weston Park** All school holidays: daily; April to Sept: weekends; June, July: daily (except Mon and Fri); Aug: daily. *House* 1–5, *park* 11–7. **Wightwick Manor** All year (except Feb): Thurs, Sat, Bank Holiday Mon and some summer weekends 2–6. Last Wed 2.30–5.30.

GAZETTEER 12

Anglesey Abbey *House* April: Sat, Sun and Easter Mon; May to mid Oct: Wed–Sun and Bank Holiday Mon. *Garden* April to end June: Wed–Sun; July to mid Oct: daily. *Lode Mill* April to mid Oct: Sat, Sun and Bank Holiday Mon. All open 1.30–5.30. **Ashwell Village Museum** All year: Sun and Bank Holidays 2.30–5. **Audley End** April to Sept: daily (except Mon, but open Bank Holiday Mon) 1–5.30, *grounds* from 12. Closed May Day. **Ayscoughfee Hall Museum** April to Sept: afternoons. **Buckden Palace** Aug, Sept: Tues 2–6. **Burghley House** April to 1st Sun in Oct: daily 11–5, Good Fri 2–5. **Cromwell Museum** April to Oct: Tues–Fri 11–1, 2–5, Sat, Sun 11–1, 2–4; Nov to March: Tues–Fri 2–5, Sat 11–1, 2–4, Sun 2–4. Closed Bank Holidays except Good Fri. **Duxford Airfield** Mid March to end Oct: daily 10.30–5.30. Closed Good Fri and May Day Bank Holiday. **Elstow Moot Hall** All year: Tues–Sat 2–5, Sun 2–5.30 (or dusk). Open Bank Holidays. **Heckington Mill** All year: Sun 2–4.30; April to Sept: Sat, Bank Holidays 2–4.30. **Hinchingbrooke House** April to Aug: Sun, Bank Holidays 2–5. **Kimbolton Castle** Easter, Spring Bank Holiday Sun and Mon, Aug Bank Holiday Mon, and Sun in late July to late Aug: 2–6. **King's Lynn: St George's Guildhall** All year (when not in use): Mon–Fri 10–1, 2–5, Sat 10–12.30. **Lynn Museum of Local History** All year: Mon–Sat 10–5. Closed Bank Holidays. **Museum of Social History** All year: Tues–Sat 10–5. Closed Bank Holidays. **Lilford Bird Park** Easter to Oct: daily 10–6. **Linton Zoo** Summer: daily 10–7; winter: daily 10–dusk. **Lyveden New Bield** All year daily. **Oxburgh Hall** *Hall and garden* April, early to mid Oct: Sat, Sun 1.30–5.30, Easter Mon 11.30–5.30; May to Sept: daily (except Thurs and Fri) 1.30–5.30, Bank Holiday Mon 11–5.30. **Peakirk Waterfowl Gardens** April to Sept: daily 9.30–5.30; Oct to March: daily 9.30–4.30. **Peterborough Museum and Art Gallery** Oct to end April: Tues–Sat 12–5; May to end Sept: Tues–Sat 10–5. **Ramsey Abbey Gatehouse** April to end Oct: daily 10–5. **Royston Museum** All year: Wed, Sat 10–5. **Sandringham** Easter Sun to late Sept: Sun–Thurs *grounds* 10.30–5, *house* 11–4.45 (opens 1 hour later on Sun). Closed last week July, 1st week Aug. **Shuttleworth Collection** All year: daily 10.30–5.30 (or dusk in winter). **Springfields Gardens** Early April to mid May, mid June to Oct: daily 10–6. **Trinity Hospital** All year: Tues, Thurs, Sat 10–12, 2–6 (2–4 Nov to March). **Welney Wildfowl Trust** All year: daily 10–5. **Wimpole Hall** *House and garden* April to end Oct: daily (except Mon and Fri) 1.30–5.30. *Park* open all year. **Wisbech: Peckover House** April, 1st fortnight in Oct: Sat, Sun, Bank Holiday Mon 2–5.30; May to end Sept: Sat–Wed 2–5.30. **Wisbech and Fenland Museum** All year: Tues–Sat 10–1, 2–5 (4 in winter). **Wolferton Station** April to end Sept: Mon–Fri 11–1, 2–6, Sun 2–6. **Wrest House and Gardens** April to Sept: Sat, Sun and Bank Holidays (except May Day) 9.30–6.30.

GAZETTEER 13

Aldeburgh Moot Hall Easter and Spring Bank Holidays, weekends in May, daily June to Sept: Mon–Sat 10–5, Sun 2–5 (10–5 in Aug). **Banham Classic Collection** April to Sept: daily 11–6. **Banham Zoo** All year: daily 10–6 (or dusk). **Berney Arms Windmill** April to end Sept: daily 9.30–6.30. **Blickling Hall** April to late Oct: daily (except Mon and Thurs, but open Bank Holiday Mon) 1–5, *garden* 12–5. **Bungay Castle** All year: daily. **Bury St Edmunds: Angel Corner** All year: daily (except Sun) 10–1, 2–5 (Nov to March 2–4). Closed Good Fri, Easter Sat, May Day. **Moyses Hall** March to Oct: Mon–Sat 10–1, 2–5 (Nov to Feb 2–4). Closed winter Bank Holidays. **Suffolk Regiment Museum** All year: Mon–Fri 10–12, 2–4. Closed Good Fri, Bank Holidays and when in use. **Theatre Royal** All year: daily (except Sun) 10–6. Closed Good Fri, Bank Holidays and when in use. **Caister Castle** Mid May to end Sept: daily (except Sat) 10.30–5. **Castle Hedingham** Easter weekend, May to end Oct: daily 10–5. **Cockley Cley Folk Museum** Easter to end Sept: Sun and Bank Holiday Mon 1.30–5.30. **East Anglia Transport Museum** May: Sun 11–5; June to Sept: Sat 2–4, Sun 11–5; Aug: Mon–Sat 2–4, Sun 11–5. **East Dereham: Bishop Bonner's Cottage** May to end Sept: Tues–Fri 2.30–5, Sat 3–5.30. **Euston Hall** June to Sept: Thurs 2.30–5.30. **Fairhaven Garden Trust** Easter to mid May: Sun, Bank Holidays 2–6; mid May to early Sept: Wed–Sun, Bank Holidays 2–6; also last two Sun in Sept. **Felbrigg Hall** April to late Oct: Mon, Wed, Thurs, Sat, Sun *house* 1.30–5.30, *garden* 11–5.30. **Framlingham Castle** Standard hours and Sun morning in summer. **Fritton Lake Country Park** April to Sept: daily 9–7. **Glemham Hall** Easter Mon to last Sun in Sept: Sun, Wed, Bank Holidays 2.30–5.30. **Helmingham Hall** May to Sept: Sun 2–6. **Holkham Hall** End May to end Sept: Sun, Mon, Wed (in July and Aug), Thurs 1.30–5, Spring and Summer Bank Holiday Mon 11.30–5. **Houghton Hall** Easter Sun to end Sept: Thurs, Bank Holidays 12–5.30, Sun 1.30–5.30. Last admission 5. **Ickworth** April, Oct: Sat, Sun and Easter Mon 1.30–5.30;

May to end Sept: daily (except Mon and Thurs, but open Bank Holiday Mon) 1.30–5.30. *Park* open all year. **Ixworth** All year by prior appointment. **Kilverstone Wildlife Park** March to Oct: daily 10–6.30; Oct to March: daily 10–dusk. **Lavenham Guildhall** April to late Oct: daily 11–1, 2–5.30; Nov to late Dec: Wed–Sun 11–4. **Lavenham: Little Hall** Easter to mid Oct: Sat, Sun and Bank Holidays 2.30–6. **Laxfield and District Museum** June to Oct: Wed, Sat, Sun and Bank Holidays 2–5. **Long Melford: Melford Hall** April to end Sept: Wed, Thurs, Sun and Bank Holiday Mon 2–6. **Kentwell Hall** Easter to end Sept: Wed, Thurs, Sun and Bank Holidays 2–6; also Fri and Sat mid July to end Sept. Annual recreation of Tudor life three weeks ending mid July. **Museum of East Anglian Life** Easter to end Oct: Mon–Sat 11–5, Sun 12–5 (June to Aug 12–6). **Norfolk Wildlife Park** All year: daily 10–6 (or sunset). **North Norfolk Railway** *Sheringham Station* Easter to mid Oct: daily 10–5. **Otter Trust** April to Oct: daily 10.30–6 (or dusk). **Pettitts** Easter to end Oct: Mon–Fri 10–6, Sun 1–5.30. **Saxtead Green Windmill** Standard hours April to Sept only. Closed Sun. **Shell Museum** All year: Mon–Thurs 10–12.30, 2–4, Fri, Sat 2–4.30. Closed Sun. **Sheringham Hall** May, June: Mon–Sat 10–1, 2–6, four middle Suns 2–6. **Somerleyton Hall** Easter Sun to end Sept: Thurs, Sun, Bank Holidays 2–5.30; also Tues, Wed in July and Aug. *Gardens only* all other days except Sat 2–5.30. **Sudbury: Gainsborough's House Museum** All year: Tues–Sat 10–5, Sun and Bank Holiday Mon 2–5 (closes 4 Oct to Maundy Thurs). Closed Good Fri. **Suffolk Wildlife Park** April to Oct: daily 10–6 (or dusk). **Thetford: Ancient House Museum** All year: Mon–Sat 10–5; Spring Bank Holiday to late Summer Bank Holiday: Sun 2–5. **Thursford Collection** Good Fri to end Oct: daily 2–5.30; Nov, March, April: Sun 2–5. **Walsingham Abbey Grounds** April: Wed; May, June, July, Sept: Wed, Sat, Sun; Aug: Mon, Wed, Fri, Sat, Sun; Bank Holidays Easter to Sept. Open 2–5. **Walsingham: Shirehall Museum** Maundy Thurs to end Sept: daily 11–1, 2–4; Oct: weekends only 11–1, 2–4.

GAZETTEER 14

Aberconwy House April to end Sept: daily (except Tues) 11–5; Oct: Sat, Sun 11–5. Last admission 4.45. **Barclodiad y Gawres** June to Sept: daily 2–5. **Basingwerk Abbey** March to Sept: any reasonable time. **Beaumaris Castle** Standard hours and Sun morning in summer. **Bodnant Garden** Mid March to end Oct: daily 10–5. **Bodrhyddan Hall** June to Sept: Tues, Thurs 2–5.30. **Bryn Bras Castle** Spring Bank Holiday Sun to mid July, and Sept: daily (except Sat) 1–5; mid July to end Aug: daily (except Sat) 10.30–5. **Caernarfon Castle** Standard hours and Sun morning in summer. **Castell Dinas Bran** Open access. **Conwy Castle** Standard hours and Sun morning in summer. **Denbigh Castle** Standard hours and Sun morning in summer. **Dolwyddelan Castle** Standard hours except Sun 9.30–4. **Ffestiniog Railway** End March to end Oct: daily; also over Christmas, and weekends in Feb and March. **Gloddfa Ganol Slate Mine** Easter to Oct: daily 10–5.30. **Gwydir Castle** Easter to end Sept: daily (except Sat) 10–5. **Harlech Castle** Standard hours and Sun morning in summer. **Llanberis Lake Railway** April, May: Mon–Thurs, Bank Holiday Sun; June to Oct: Mon–Fri and Sun afternoons. **Llechwedd Slate Caverns** April to end Oct: daily 10–5.15. **Lleyn Peninsula: Criccieth Castle** Standard hours and Sun morning in summer. **Lloyd George Memorial Museum** Easter weekend; Spring Bank Holiday to Sept: weekdays 10–5; July, Aug: Sun 2–4. **Moel Fammau Country Park** Open access. **Padarn Country Park** *Park* open daily. *Information Centre* Spring Bank Holiday to end Sept: daily 10–5. *Welsh Slate Museum* Easter to Sept: daily 9.30–6.30. *Quarry Hospital Visitor Centre* Spring Bank Holiday to end Sept: daily 10–5. *Lake Railway* Easter to early Oct. **Penrhyn Castle** April to end Oct: daily (except Tues) 12–5. Last admission 4.30. **Plas Newydd** (NT) April to end Sept: daily (except Sat) 12–5; Oct: Fri, Sun 12–5. Last admission 4.30. **Plas Newydd, Llangollen** May to Sept: weekdays 10–7, Sun 11–4. **Rhuddlan Castle** Standard hours and Sun morning in summer. **Valle Crucis Abbey** Standard hours and Sun morning in summer. **Welsh Mountain Zoo** Easter to end Sept: daily 9.30–8; Oct to Easter: daily 10–4. **Welsh Slate Museum** Standard hours and Sun morning in summer.

GAZETTEER 15

Adlington Hall Good Fri to end Sept: Sun 2.30–5.30; also Wed and Sat in Aug, and Bank Holidays. **Alton Towers** Easter to end Oct: daily 10–5/6/7 (as indicated on gate). **Arbor Low** Although EH, owner retains right to decide how and whether public admitted. **Bridgemere Wildlife Park** March to Dec: daily 10.30–6. **Buxton Country Park and Poole's Cavern** Good Fri to early Nov: daily (closed Wed except in high season) 10–5. **Capesthorne Hall** April to Sept: Sun; May to Sept: Wed, Sat; July to Sept: Tues, Thurs; also Good Fri and Bank Holidays. Open *gardens* 12–6, *hall* 2–5. **Castleton Caves: Blue John** Winter: daily 9.30–dusk; summer 9.30–5.30. **Peak Cavern** April to late Sept: daily 10–5. **Speedwell** All year: daily 9.45–6 (5 in winter). **Treak Cliff** Summer: daily 9.30–6 (later weekends and Bank Holidays); winter: daily 9.30–4. **Cavendish House Museum** All year: daily 9.30–6 (dusk in winter). **Chatsworth** End March to end Oct: daily 11.30–4.30. **Cheddleton Flint Mill** All year: Sat and Sun afternoons. **Chirk Castle** Easter to end Sept: Sun, Tues, Wed, Thurs, Bank Holiday Mon 12–5; Oct: Sat, Sun 12–5. Last admission 4.15. **Cholmondeley Castle Gardens** Easter to end Sept: Sun and Bank Holidays 12–6. **Crich Tramway Museum** End March to end Oct: Sat, Sun and Bank Holidays 1.30–6.30; early May to late Sept: Mon–Thurs 10–4.30; also Fri in Aug. **Cromford Steam Museum** April to Sept for public and private steamings. **Arkwright's Cromford Mill** Nov to March: Wed–Fri 10–4.30, Sun 11–5; April to Nov: Wed–Fri 10–4.30, weekends 11–5. **Delamere Forest Information Centre** All year: Mon–Fri 8–4. **Dorfold Hall** April to Oct: Tues, Bank Holiday Mon 2–5. **Dunham Massey** April to end Oct: *house* Mon–Thurs 1–5, *garden* 12–5.30, Sat, Sun and Bank Holiday Mon *house* 12–5, *gardens* 11–5.30. Last admission 4.30. **Ednaston Manor Gardens** Easter to last Sun in Sept: Mon–Fri 1–4.30, Sun 2–6. **Elvaston Castle Country Park** *Park* open daily until dusk. *Museum* Easter to Oct: weekdays (except Mon, Tues) 1–5, Sun and Bank Holidays 10–5. **Erddig** April to mid Oct: daily (except Fri, but open Good Fri) 12–5.30. Last admission 4.30. **Gawsworth Hall** April to Oct: daily 2–6. **Haddon Hall** April to end Oct: daily (except Mon, and also closed Sun in July and Aug) 11–6. Open Easter and Bank Holidays. **Hoar Cross Hall** Variable opening times. **Hodnet Hall Gardens** 1st Sun in April (or Good Fri if earlier) to last Sun in Sept: weekdays 2–5, Sun and Bank Holidays 12–6. **Jodrell Bank Radio Telescope** End March to end Oct: daily 10.30–5.30; winter: weekends 2–5. **Kedleston Hall** Easter Sun, Mon, Tues; end April to end Aug: Sun, Bank Holiday Mon and Tues (except Spring Bank Holiday) *house* 1–5.30, *gardens* 12–6. **Little Moreton Hall** March, Oct: Sat, Sun 2–6 (or sunset); April to end Sept: Wed–Mon 2–6. Last admission 5.30. **Lyme Park** April to end Sept: Tues–Sat 2–5, Sun and Bank Holiday Mon 1–6 (last admission 4.30 and 5.30); Oct: Sat, Sun 2–4. *Park* open all year 8–dusk. **Melbourne Hall** *House* June to Oct: Wed 2–6. *Gardens* April to Sept: Wed, Sat, Sun and Bank Holiday Mon 2–6. **Ness Gardens** All year: daily 9–sunset. **Nether Alderley Mill** April, May, June, Oct: Wed, Sun and Bank Holiday Mon 2–5.30 (or sunset); July, Aug, Sept: daily (except Mon, but open Bank Holiday Mon) 2–5.30. **Peak District Mining Museum** Mid Feb to mid Nov: daily 11–4 (longer in season); winter: weekends 11–4. **Peover Hall** June to Sept: Mon (including Bank Holidays) 2.30–4.30. **Riber Castle Wildlife Park** All year: daily from 10. **Shugborough Hall** Mid March to end Oct: Tues–Fri (including Good Fri), Bank Holiday Mon 10.30–5.30, Sat, Sun 2–5.30; Nov to mid March: *museum and farm only* Tues–Fri 10.30–4.30, Sun 2–4.30. **Speke Hall** April to end Sept: Mon–Sat 10–5, Sun 2–7, Bank Holidays 10–7; Oct to end March: Mon–Sat 10–5, Sun 2–5. Closed Good Fri. **Stapeley Water Gardens** Easter to end Aug: Mon–Fri 9–6, Sat, Sun 10–7; Sept to Easter: Mon–Fri 9–5, Sat, Sun 10–5. Bank Holidays as weekends. **Staunton Harold Church** April to end Oct: Wed–Sun 11–1, 2–6 (or sunset). **Styal** April, May: Tues–Sun and Bank Holiday Mon 11–5; June to end Sept: daily 11–5; Oct to end March: Tues–Sun 11–4. *Country park* daily during daylight. **Sudbury Hall** April to end Oct: Wed–Sun and Bank Holiday Mon 1–5.30 (or sunset). Closed Good Fri. **Tatton Park** Daily all year. Easter to mid May, Sept to end Oct: *house* 1–4 (Sun and Bank Holiday Mon 1–5); *garden* 11.30–5 (Sun and Bank Holiday Mon 10.30–5.30); *park* pedestrians 9–6, others 11–6 (Sun and Bank Holiday Mon 10–6). Mid May to end Aug: *house* 12.30–5 (Sun and Bank Holiday Mon 12–5); *garden* 11–5.30 (Sun and Bank Holiday Mon 10.30–6); *park* pedestrians 9–8, others 10.30–7 (Sun and Bank Holiday Mon 10–7). Nov to Easter: *house* closed (but open Sun in Nov and March); *garden* 1–4 (Sun and Bank Holidays 12–4); *park* pedestrians 9–sunset; others 11–sunset. **Tutbury Castle** April to Oct: daily 10–6.

GAZETTEER 16

Alford: Manor House Folk Museum May to Sept: Mon–Fri 10.30–1, 2–4.30. **Belton House** End March to end Oct: Wed–Sun and Bank Holiday Mon 1–5.30 (last admission 5). *Gardens* open 12. Closed Good Fri. **Belvoir Castle** April to early Oct: Tues, Wed, Thurs, Sat 12–6, Sun 12–7, Bank Holiday Mon 11–7, Bank Holiday Tues 12–6; Oct: Sun 2–6. **Burgh le Marsh Windmill** All year daily during daylight. **Church Farm Museum** April to Oct: daily 10.30–5.30. **Clumber Park and Chapel** *Park* always open. *Chapel* closed for repairs 1986. **Dale Abbey Windmill** All year by appointment with Mrs Richardson, Ilkeston 301585. **Doddington Hall** May to Sept: Wed, Sun and Bank Holiday Mon (including Easter) 2–6. **Dogdyke Pumping Station** Easter Sun and 1st Sun in month from May to end Oct: 2–5. **Eastwood: D. H. Lawrence Birthplace** All year: Mon–Sat 10–5. Closed Bank Holidays. **Grantham House** April to end Sept: Wed, Thurs 2–5. **Gunby Hall** *House and garden* April to end Sept: Thurs 2–6. Last admission 5.30. **Hamlyn Lodge Cottage Industry** All year: Tues–Sat 10–5, Sun 12–5 (12–4 Oct to March). **Hardwick Hall** April to end Oct: *hall* Wed, Thurs, Sat, Sun and Bank Holiday Mon 1–5.30 (or sunset), *garden* daily 12–5.30. *Park* open daily throughout year. **Harrington Hall** *House* Easter to end Sept: Thurs 2–5; also some Suns for charity. *Gardens and garden centre* April to end Oct: Wed, Thurs, Charity Suns, and some other days in May, June, July. **Hartsholme Country Park** *Information Centre*: March to end Oct: daily (except Wed, Thurs) 11–5. **Holme Pierrepont Hall** Easter Sun, Mon and Tues, Spring Bank Holiday weekend 2–6; June to Aug: Sun, Tues, Thurs, Fri 2–6; Sept: Sun 2–6. **Longdale Rural Crafts Centre** All year: daily 9–6. **Mablethorpe Animal and Bird Gardens** March to Oct: daily 10–7.30 (or dusk). **Marston Hall** By appointment and some Charity Suns. **Melton Carnegie Museum** Easter to Sept: Mon–Sat 10–5, Sun 2–5; Oct to Easter: Mon–Fri 10–4.30, Sat 10.30–4. **Midland Railway Centre** Weekends all year. Trains operate weekends and Bank Holidays April to Oct. **National Mining Museum** All year: Tues–Sat 10–5.30, Sun 2–5.30. **Newark Air Museum** April to Oct: Mon–Fri 10–5, Sat 1–5, Sun 10–6; Nov to March: Sun 10–dusk. **Newstead Abbey** *Grounds* all year: daily 10–dusk. *House* Good Fri to end Sept: daily 2–6. **North Leverton Windmill** Open when working, and Sat 10–5, Sun 2–5. **Papplewick Pumping Station** April to Oct: Sun 11–5. 'Steaming weekends' most Bank Holiday weekends and others advertised in local press: Sat 2–5, Sun 11–5. **Ruddington: Framework Knitter's Museum** April to Oct: Wed 7–9. **Shardlow Canal Exhibition** April to Oct: daily 9–5.30; Nov to March: weekends 10–4. **Sherwood Forest Visitor Centre** March to Sept: daily 10.30–5; Oct to Feb: daily 10.30–4.30. *Country Park* open all year dawn to dusk. **Rufford Country Park** Jan, Feb: weekends 11–4.30; March to Dec: daily 11–5. **Cresswell Crags Visitor Centre** Feb to April, Oct: Tues–Sun 10.30–4.30; May to Sept: Tues–Sat 10.30–5, Sun 10.30–4.30; Nov to Jan: Sun 10.30–4.30. **Skegness Natureland Marine Zoo** All year: daily from 10. **Sundown Pets Garden and Kiddies Theme Park** All year: daily 10–7 (or dusk). **Tattershall Castle** April to Oct: Mon–Sat 11–6.30, Sun 1–6.30 (or sunset); Nov to March: Mon–Sat 12–6, Sun 1–6.30 (or sunset). Last admission ½ hour before closing. **Thoresby Hall** Easter Sun, Mon, Bank Holidays, and Sun from May to Aug: 1–5, *park* 11–6.30. **Wollaton Hall** April to Sept: Mon–Sat 10–7, Sun 2–5; Oct, March: Mon–Sat 10–5.30, Sun 1.30–4.30; Nov to Feb: Mon–Sat 10–4.30, Sun 1.30–4.30. **Woolsthorpe Manor** April to end Oct: Sun–Thurs 1.30–6. Last admission 5.30.

GAZETTEER 17

Cannon Hall All year: weekdays 10.30–5, Sun 2.30–5. Closed Good Fri. **Cockersand Abbey** View from outside only. **Colne Valley Museum** All year: Sat, Sun and Bank Holidays 2–5. **Cuerden Valley Country Park** Open access. **Dinting Railway Centre** All year: daily 11–4.30. Engines 'in steam' every Sun late March to end Oct. **East Riddlesden Hall** April to end Oct: Wed–Sun and Bank Holiday Mon 2–6 (11–6 in June, July, Aug). Last admission 5.30. **Gawthorpe Hall** *House* closed 1986 for repairs. Mid March to late Dec: daily *craft gallery* 10–5, *garden* 10–6. **Haigh Hall Country Park** *Park* open all year. *Zoo* April to Oct: daily 9–5. **Hall-i'the-Wood** April to end Sept: Mon–Sat (except Thurs) 10–6, Sun 2–6; Oct to March: Mon–Sat (except Thurs) 10–5. **Harewood House and Bird Garden** April to end Oct: daily from 10 (*house* from 11); Feb, March and Nov: same times on Sun only. **Harlow Car Gardens** All year: daily 9–9 (or dusk). **Haworth: The Brontë Parsonage** All year: daily 11–5.30 (4.30 Oct to March). Closed 1st three weeks in Feb. **Ponden Mill** All year: daily 9–5.30. **Helmshore Textile Museum** March: Mon–Fri 2–5; April to June, Oct: daily (except Sat) 2–5; July, Aug: Mon–Fri 10–5, Sat, Sun 2–5; Sept: Mon–Fri 10–5, Sun 2–5; Bank Holiday weekends 2–5. **Hoghton Tower** Easter to Oct: Sun 2–5; also Sat in July and Aug. **Hollingworth Lake Country Park Information Centre** Easter to end Oct: daily 10.30–5.30; Nov to Easter: weekends 10.30–dusk. **Knowsley Safari Park** Easter to end Sept: daily 10–4. **Martin Mere** All year: daily from 9.30. **Pendle Heritage Centre** Easter to Nov: daily (except Mon and Fri) 2–4.30. **Ribchester Museum** March to June, Sept to Nov: daily 2–5; June to Aug: daily 11.30–5.30; Dec to Feb: Sun 2–5. **Ripley Castle** April, May: Sat, Sun 11.30–4.30; June to 2nd Sun in Oct: Sat, Sun, Tues, Wed, Thurs 11.30–4.30; Bank Holidays in season 11–4.30. *Gardens* April to Oct: daily 11–5.30. **Rufford Old Hall** April to end Oct: daily (except Fri) 2–6. Last admission 5.30. **Shibden Hall** Feb: Sun 2–5; March, Oct, Nov: Mon–Fri 10–5, Sun 2–5; April to Sept: Mon–Sat 2–6, Sun 2–5. **Skipton Castle** All year: Mon–Sat 10–7, Sun 2–7 (or sunset). Closed Good Fri. **Stump Cross Caverns** Easter to Oct: daily 10–5.30; Nov to Easter: weekends 11–4. **Temple Newsam** All year: Tues–Sun 10.30–6.15; May to Sept: Wed 10.30–8.30, Bank Holiday Mon 10.30–6.15. **Towneley Hall** All year: Mon–Fri 10–5.30 (5.15 in winter), Sun 12–5. **Turton Tower** All year: Sat–Wed 12–6. **Worth Valley Light Railway** Main season March to Oct but open daily even when trains not running. **Yorkshire Dales Railway** Easter to mid Oct: *Trains run* Sun 11–4.30; July and Aug: Tues 11–4.30; Aug: Sat 1.30–3.45; Bank Holidays 11–4.30. *Site* open weekends all year and daily in summer. **Yorkshire Sculpture Park** All year: daily 10–6.

GAZETTEER 18

Alvingham Watermill Bank Holiday Sun and Mon 11–5.30; July, Aug: Mon, Thurs and 2nd and 4th Suns 2–5.30. **Beningbrough Hall** April to end Oct: Tues, Wed, Thurs, Sat, Sun 12–6. Last admission 5.30. **Blacktoft Sands Wetland Preserve** Open all year. **Bramham Park** June to Aug: Tues–Thurs, Sun and Bank Holiday Mon 1.15–5.30. *Gardens only* Easter weekend and Spring Bank Holiday weekend. **Burnby Hall Gardens** Easter to end Sept: daily 10–7. **Burton Agnes Hall** End March to end Oct: daily 11–5. **Conisbrough Castle** Standard hours and Sun morning in summer. **Cusworth Hall and Park** All year: Mon–Sat (except Fri) 11–5, Sun 1–5 (4 from Nov to Feb). **Elsham Hall Country Park** Easter to Sept: weekdays 11–5.30, Sun and Bank Holidays 11–6.30; Oct to Easter: Sun 11–4. **Epworth: The Old Rectory** March to Oct: weekdays 10–12, 2–4, Sun 2–4. **Gainsborough Old Hall** All year: weekdays 10–5, Sun (Easter to Oct) 2–5. **Hornsea Pottery** All year: daily from 10. **Knaresborough Castle** Easter and Spring Bank Holiday to end Sept: weekdays 10–5, weekends and Bank Holiday Mon 10–7. **Knaresborough: Court House Museum** Oct to March: Sun 1.30–4.30; April to Sept: Mon–Sat 10–5, Sun 11–5. **Lotherton Hall** May to Sept: daily (except Mon) 10.30–6.15; Oct to April: daily (except Mon) 10.30–dusk. **Normanby Hall** Nov to March: weekdays 10–12.30, 2–5, Sun 2–5; April to Oct: Mon, Wed, Thurs, Fri, Sat 10–12.30, 2–5.30, Sun 2–5.30 (Sat opening liable to fluctuation). **Nostell Priory** April, May, June, Sept, Oct: Sat 12–5, Sun 11–5; July, Aug: daily (except Fri) Mon–Sat 12–5, Sun 11–5; also open all Bank Holiday Mon and Tues, including Easter Mon and Tues. **Sandtoft Transport Centre** April to Sept: Sun 12–6. Trolley days selected weekends April to Sept. **Sherriff Hutton Castle** Open all year by appointment. **Skidby Mill and Museum** May to Sept: Tues–Sat 10.30–4, Sun 1.30–4.30. **Sledmere House** Easter weekend, Sun in April, daily (except Mon and Fri) from early May to end Sept: 1.30–5.30. **Sutton Park** Easter weekend (Fri–Mon), Sun in April, and Sun and Tues May to early Oct: 1.30–5.30. **Thornton Abbey** Standard hours and Sun morning in summer. **Worsbrough Country Park** Open all time. *Mill Museum* all year: Wed–Sun 10–6 (or dusk). **Wrawby Post Mill** Easter Mon, Summer Bank Holiday Mon, last Sun in June and July: 1–5.

GAZETTEER 19

Abbot Hall Art Gallery and Museum All year: Mon–Fri 10.30–5.30 (*museum to* 5), Sat, Sun 2–5. Closed for two weeks over Christmas and New Year, and Good Fri. **Acorn Bank** *Garden only* March to end Oct: daily 10–5.30. **Appleby Castle Conservation Centre** Easter week and May to Sept: daily 10.30–5. **Belle Isle** May to Sept: daily (except Fri, Sat). Boats every ½ hour from 10.15. **Brantwood** Mid March to mid Nov: daily 11–5.30; mid Nov to mid March: Wed–Sun 11–4. **Brougham Castle** Standard hours and Sun morning in summer. **Cartmel Gatehouse** April to end Oct: key from the Manager, The Priory Hotel, Cartmel. **Dalemain** Easter Sun to 2nd Sun in Oct: Sun–Thurs 11.15–5. **Graythwaite Hall Gardens** April to end June: daily 10–6. **Grizedale Forest Wildlife Centre and Deer Museum** Easter to Oct: daily 10–5; Nov to Easter: Mon–Fri 10–4. **Hawkshead Courthouse** May to end Sept: daily (except Mon and Sat, but open Bank Holiday Mon) 2–5. **Heron Corn Mill** April to Sept: Tues–Sun 11–12.15, 2–5. **Holker Hall and Park** Easter Sun to last Sun in Oct: daily (except Sat) 10.30–6. Last admission 4.30. **Lakeside and Haverthwaite Railway** Easter, Sun in April (from Easter) and Oct, daily from early May to end Sept. **Leighton Hall** May to Sept: daily 2–5. Last admission 4.30. **Levens Hall** Easter Sun to end Sept: Sun–Thurs 11–5, *steam collection* 2–5. **Lingholm Gardens** April to end Oct: daily 10–5. **Little Salkeld Windmill** By appointment only (except for selected open days). *Mill shop* all year: Mon–Fri 9.30–12.30. Closed Bank Holidays. **Lowther Park** Fortnight from Mon before Easter, early May to mid Sept: daily 10–5; last three weekends in Sept: 10–5. **Muncaster Castle** Good Fri to end Sept: daily (except Mon) *gardens* 12–5, *castle* 1.30–4.30. **National Park Visitor Centre** Late March to early Nov: daily from 10. **Ravenglass and Eskdale Railway** All year except Dec 22–25 and limited, weekday only service in winter (Nov to March). **Ravenglass Roman Bath House** Open access. **Rusland Hall** April to Sept: daily 11–6. **Rydal Mount** March to Oct: daily 10–5.30; Nov to end Feb: daily (except Tues) 10–12.30, 2–4. **Sizergh Castle** April to end Oct: Mon, Wed, Thurs, Sun 2–5.45. Last admission 5.15. **Stagshaw Garden** April to end June: daily 10–6.30; July, Aug: by appointment. **Swarthmoor Hall** Mid March to mid Oct: Mon, Tues, Wed, Sat 10–12, 2–5. Thurs and Sun by appointment. **Townend** April to end Oct: daily (except Mon and Sat, but open Bank Holiday Mon) 2–6 (or dusk). Last admission 5.30. **Upper Dales Folk Museum** April to Sept: Mon–Sat 11–5, Sun 2–5; Oct: Tues–Sat 11–5, Sun 2–5. **Wetheriggs Pottery** All year: daily 10–5. **Windermere Steamboat Museum** Easter to Oct: daily 10–5. **Wordsworth's House** April to end Oct: Mon–Sat (except Thurs) 11–5, Sun 2–5. Last admission 4.30. **Isle of Man: Cregneash Folk Museum** All year: Mon–Sat 10–1, 2–5, Sun 2–5. **Curraghs Wildlife Park** Good Fri to Easter Mon, mid May to end Sept: Mon–Sat 9–5, Sun 10–6. **Laxey Waterwheel** Easter to end Sept: daily 10.15–5.15.

GAZETTEER 20

Auckland Castle *Park* open all year during daylight. **Bedale Hall** Easter, May to Sept: Sat, Sun, Tues and Bank Holidays. **Bowes Museum** May to Sept: Mon–Sat 10–5.30, Sun 2–5; March, April, Oct: Mon–Sat 10–5, Sun 2–5; Nov to Feb: Mon–Sat 10–4, Sun 2–4. **Captain Cook Birthplace Museum** Summer: daily 10–6; winter: daily 9–4. Last admission 45 minutes before closing. **Castle Bolton** Easter to end Sept: daily (except Mon, but open Bank Holiday Mon) 10–5; Oct to Easter: daily (except Mon) 10–4. **Castle Howard** End March to end Oct: daily 11–5, *grounds* from 10. Last admission 4.30. **Constable Burton Hall** *Gardens only* April to Aug daily. *House* limited times: ring Bedale 50428. **Coxwold: Shandy Hall** June to Sept: Wed 2–4.30, Sun 2.30–4.30. **Newburgh Priory** Mid May to end Aug: Wed 2–6. **Danby: The Moors Centre** Easter to end Oct: daily 10–5; Nov to March: Sun 12–4. **Darlington Railway Museum** All year: Mon–Sat 10–4, Sun 2–4. **Durham Castle** Easter and Spring Bank Holidays 2–4.30; July to Sept: weekdays 10–12, 2–4.30; Oct to June: Mon, Wed, Sat 2–4.30. **Ebberston Hall** Good Fri to end Oct: daily 10–6. **Finchale Priory** Standard hours and Sun morning in summer. **Flamingo Land** April to end Sept: daily from 10. **Great Ayton: Captain Cook Museum** End March to end Sept: daily 2–4.30; Oct: weekends 2–4.30. **Hardwick Hall Country Park** Open all year. **Hutton le Hole: Ryedale Folk Museum** End March to end Oct: daily 11–6. Last admission 5.15. **Jervaulx Abbey** All year daily. **Malton Museum** May to Sept: Mon–Sat 10–4, Sun 2–4; Oct to April: Sat 1–3. Closed in Dec. **Markenfield Hall** May to Sept: Mon 10–12, 2–4. **Newby Hall** Easter, April to Sept: daily (except Mon, but open Bank Holiday Mon) *gardens* 11–5.30, *house and miniature train* 1–5. **North Yorkshire Moors Railway** Easter to late Oct. Daily service May to Sept. **Norton Conyers** June to early Sept: Bank Holiday Sun and Mon 2–5.30. **Nunnington Hall** April to end Oct: Tues, Wed, Thurs, Sat, Sun 2–6 (12–6 July and Aug), Bank Holiday Mon 11–6. Last admission 5.30. **Ormesby Hall** April to end Oct: Wed, Sat, Sun and Bank Holiday Mon 2–6. Last admission 5.30. **Pickering: Beck Isle Museum** Easter to end Oct: daily 10.30–12.30, 2–5 (10.30–7 in Aug). **Preston Hall Museum** All year: Mon–Sat 9.30–5, Sun 2–5. **Raby Castle** Easter to end June: Wed and Sun; July to Sept: daily (except Sat); also Bank Holiday Sat–Tues in period. *Park and gardens* open 1–5.30, *castle* 2–5. **Richmond Castle** Standard hours and Sun morning in summer. **Richmond: Green Howards Regimental Museum** Feb: Mon–Fri 10–4.30; March, Nov: Mon–Sat 10–4.30; April to Oct: Mon–Sat 9.30–4.30, Sun 2–4.30. Closed Dec to Feb. **Rievaulx Terrace and Temples** April to end Oct: daily 10.30–6 (*Ionic temple* closed 1–2). Last admission 5.30. **Rievaulx Abbey** Standard hours and Sun morning in summer. **Ripon: Wakeman's House Museum** Easter to Sept: Mon–Sat 10–5, Sun 1–5. **Prison and Police Museum** May to Sept: Tues–Sun 1.30–4.30. **Sewerby Hall** Easter to end Sept: Sun–Fri 10–12.30, 1.30–6, Sat 1.30–6. **Swaledale Folk Museum** Good Fri to end Sept: daily 10.30–6. **Thorp Perrow Arboretum** Last weekend in March to 2nd weekend in Nov: daily during daylight. **Timothy Hackworth Museum** April to end Sept: Wed–Sun 10–6. **Whitby Abbey** Standard hours and Sun morning in summer. **Whitby: Pannett Park Art Gallery and Museum** May to Sept: Mon–Sat 9.30–5.30, Sun 2–5; Oct to April: Mon, Tues, Thurs, Fri 10.30–1, Wed, Sat 10.30–4, Sun 2–4. **Witton Castle** All year daily.

GAZETTEER 21

Arbigland Gardens May to Sept: Tues, Thurs, Sun 2–6; daily last week in May and Aug. **Ardwell House Gardens** All year: daily 10–6. **Broughton House** April to Oct: daily (except Sun) 11–1, 2–5. **Carleton Castle** Open at any reasonable time. **Carlyle's Birthplace** Easter to end Oct: Mon–Sat 10–6. **Carsluith Castle** Standard hours: apply key keeper. **Castle Kennedy Gardens** April to Sept: daily 10–5. **Creetown Gem Rock Museum** All year: daily 9.30–5 (6 in summer). **Crossraguel Abbey** Standard hours but closed Thurs afternoon and Fri. **Drumlanrig Castle** May, June: Mon–Sat (except Fri) 1.30–5, Sun 2–6; July, Aug: Mon–Sat (except Fri) 11–5, Sun 2–6. **Ellesland Farm** Open daily. **Galloway Deer Museum** April to Oct: daily 10–5. **Glenluce Abbey** Standard hours but closed Mon and Fri in winter. **Kirroughtree Forest Garden** Open at all times. **Lochmaben Castle** Open at all reasonable times. **Logan Botanic Gardens** April to Sept daily. **Maxwelton House** April to Sept: *gardens and hot houses* Mon–Thurs 2–5, *chapel* daily 10–6; July and Aug: *Annie Laurie Boudoir and Museum* Mon–Thurs 2–5. **Orchardton Tower** Standard hours; apply key keeper. **Rammerscales** 1st Sun to last Thurs in May: Sun, Tues, Thurs 2–5; 1st Sun in Aug to 2nd Sun in Sept: Wed, Thurs and alternate Sun/Tues 2–5. **Ruthwell Cross** Any reasonable time; apply key keeper. **Souter Johnnie's Cottage** April to end Sept: daily 12–5. **Threave Gardens** All year: daily 9–sunset, *walled garden and glasshouses* 9–5. *Visitor Centre* open end March to end Oct.

GAZETTEER 22

Alnwick Castle Early May to early Oct: daily (except Sat, but open Sat on Bank Holiday weekends) 1–5. Last admission 4.30. **Alston: South Tynedale Railway** Easter weekend, weekends in May, daily end May to Sept: Mon–Sat 10.15–5.15, Sun 11.15–5.15. **Bamburgh Castle** April to Oct: daily 1–4.30. **Bardon Mill Pottery** All year: weekdays 9–5; Easter to Sept: weekends 9–5. **Beamish, North of England Open Air Museum** April to mid Sept: daily 10–6; mid Sept to Easter: daily (except Mon) 10–5. Last admission always 4. **Chesters** Standard hours and Sun morning in summer. **Corby Castle Grounds** April to Sept: daily 2–5. **Cragside** *Country park* April to end Sept: daily 10.30–6; Oct: daily 10.30–5; Nov to end March: Sat and Sun 10.30–4. *House* April: Wed, Sat, Sun 2–6; May to end Sept: daily (except Mon, but open Bank Holiday Mon) 2–6; Oct: Wed, Sat, Sun 2–5. Last admission ½ hour before closing. **Dunstanburgh Castle** Standard hours and Sun morning in summer. **Farne Islands** Only Inner Farne and Staple Islands open: April to end Sept daily. **Gibside Chapel** April to end Sept: Wed, Sat, Sun, Good Fri and Bank Holiday Mon 2–6; Oct: same times 2–5. **Gilnockie Tower** Open all reasonable times. **Holystone Forest Walks: Lady's Well** All year during daylight. **Housesteads** Standard hours and Sun morning in summer. **Howick Gardens** April to Sept: daily 2–7. **Kielder Castle Visitor Centre** Easter to end Sept: daily 10–5 (10–6 in Aug). **Lanercost Priory** Standard hours April to Sept only. **Lindisfarne Castle** Easter week from Good Fri: daily 11–5; April: Wed, Sat, Sun 11–5; May to end Sept: daily (except Fri) 11–5; Oct: Sat, Sun 11–5. **Lindisfarne Priory** Standard hours and Sun morning in summer. **National Tractor and Farm Museum** Easter to Sept: daily 10–6; Oct to Easter: daily (except Sat) 10–5. **Ryhope Engines Museum** Easter to end Dec: weekends 2–5; 'in steam' Bank Holiday weekends 11–5. **Stephenson's Cottage** April to end Oct: Wed, Thurs, Sat and Sun 2–5. **Tynemouth Castle and Priory** Standard hours and Sun morning in summer. **Vindolanda** Jan, Feb, Nov, Dec: daily 10–4; March, April, Sept, Oct: daily 10–5; May, June: daily 10–6; July, Aug: daily 10–6.30. **Wallington** *House* Easter week from Good Fri: daily 2–6; April: Wed, Sat, Sun 2–6; May to end Sept: daily (except Tues) 2–6; Oct: Wed, Sat, Sun 2–5. Last admission ½ hour before closing. *Walled garden* April to end Sept: daily 10–7; Oct: daily 10–6; Nov to March: daily 10–4. *Grounds* all year daily. **Warkworth Castle** *Castle* standard hours and Sun morning in summer. *Hermitage* standard hours April to Sept only. **Washington Old Hall** Easter week from Good Fri: daily 11–5; April, Oct: Wed, Sat, Sun 11–5; May to end Sept: daily (except Fri) 11–5. Last admission 20 minutes before closing. **The Wildfowl Trust: Washington Waterfowl Park** All year: daily 9.30–5.30 (or dusk). **Woodhorn Church** All year: Wed–Sun 10–12.30, 1–4; also most Bank Holidays. **World Bird Research Station** July, Aug: daily with guide 2.45 and 3.45.

GAZETTEER 23

Ardrossan Castle All year any reasonable time. **Bachelors' Club** Easter to end Oct: daily 10–6. **Bothwell Castle** Standard hours but closed Thurs afternoon and Fri in winter. **Burns Cottage and Museum** June, July, Aug: Mon–Sat 9–7, Sun 10–7; April, May: Mon–Sat 10–5, Sun 2–5; Nov to end March: Mon–Sat 10–4. **Burns House Museum** Easter to end Sept: Mon–Sat 11–5, Sun 2–5; Oct to Easter: weekends by arrangement. **Calderpark Zoo** All year: weekdays 9.30–5, weekends 10–5. **Campbeltown Library and Museum** All year: Mon–Fri (except Wed) 10–1, 2–5, 6–8, Wed, Sat 10–1, 2–5. Closed Sun and Bank Holidays. **Carradale House Gardens** March to Sept: daily 10–5. **Culzean Castle and Country Park** *Castle* Easter to end Sept: daily 10–6; Oct: daily 12–5. *Country park* all year. **David Livingstone Centre** All year: Mon–Sat 10–6, Sun 2–6. **Eglinton Castle** *Gardens* open at all times. **Finlaystone** *Woods and gardens* all year: Mon–Sat 9–5, Sun 2–5. *House* April to Aug: Sun 2.30–4.30. **Hill House** All year: daily 1–5. **John Hastie Museum** April to Sept: Mon–Fri 2–5 (Thurs 4.30), Sat 2–7. **Kelburn Country Centre** Easter to mid Oct: daily 10–6; winter: Sun 10–5. **Kilmun Arboretum** All year dawn to sunset. **Land o' Burns Centre** Oct to May: daily 10–5; June, Sept: daily 10–6; July, Aug: Mon–Fri 10–9, Sat, Sun 10–6. **Largs Museum** June to Sept: Mon–Sat 2–5. **Lillie Art Gallery** All year: Tues–Fri 11–5, 7–9, Sat, Sun 2–5. **Maclaurin Art Gallery and Rozelle House Museum** April to Oct: Mon–Sat 11–5, Sun 2–5; Nov to March: (*Rozelle House* closed) Mon–Sat 11–5. **North Ayrshire Museum** School summer holidays: Mon–Sat 10–4; rest of year: Thurs–Sat 10–4. **Pollock House and Country Park** *Country park* all year: daily 7–dusk. *Pollock House* and *Burrell Collection* all year: Mon–Sat 10–5, Sun 2–5. **Skelmorlie Aisle** Standard hours April to Sept; apply key keeper in winter. **Weaver's Cottage** Easter, May, Sept, Oct: Tues, Thurs, Sat, Sun 2–5; June, July, Aug: daily 2–5. **Younger Botanic Garden** April to Oct: daily 10–6. **Isle of Arran: Brodick Castle and Country Park** *Castle* April (from Easter): Mon, Wed, Sat 1–5; May to end Sept: daily 1–5. *Country park and gardens* all year: daily 10–5. **Isle of Bute: Bute Museum** April to Sept: Mon–Sat 10.30–12.30, 2.30–4.30; mid June to Sept: Sun 2.30–4.30; Oct to March: Tues–Sat 2.30–4.30. **Rothesay Castle** Standard hours but closed Thurs and Fri morning in winter. **St Blane's Chapel** Exterior view only. **Isle of Gigha: Achamore House Garden** All year: daily 10–dusk. **Great Cumbrae Island: Museum of the Cumbraes** June to Sept: Tues–Sat 10.30–4.30. **University Marine Biological Station** All year: daily 9.30–12.30, 2–5.

GAZETTEER 24

Abbotsford Late March to end Oct: daily 10–5, Sun 2–5. **Blackness Castle** Standard hours but closed Mon afternoon and Tues in winter. **Bowhill House** *House* early July to mid Aug: weekdays 11.30–4.30, Sun 2–6. *Grounds and adventure woodland* May to end Aug: weekdays (except Fri) 11.30–4.30, Sun 2–6. Last admission 45 minutes before closing. **Cairnpapple Hill** April to Sept only: standard hours but closed Mon morning and Fri. **Coldstream Museum** Whitsun to Sept: Sun, Tues–Fri 2–5, Sat 10–1. **Craigmillar Castle** Standard hours but closed Thurs afternoon and Fri. **Culross Palace** Under guardianship of SDD; open standard hours. **Dawyck Botanic Garden** April to Sept: daily 10–5. **Floors Castle** End April to end Sept: Sun–Thurs (Fri in July and Aug) 11–4.45. *Garden centre* all year: daily 9.30–5. **Gladstone Court** Easter to Oct: weekdays 10–12.30, 2–5, Sun 2–5. **Greenhill Covenanters House** Easter to Oct: daily 2–5. **Greenknowe Tower** Standard hours; apply key keeper. **Hopetoun House** Easter weekend, May to late Sept: daily 11–5.30. **House of the Binns** Easter Sat and Sun, May to Sept: daily (except Fri) 2–5, *parkland* 10–7. Last admission 4.30. **Inveresk Lodge Garden** All year: Mon, Wed, Fri 10–4.30 (also Sun 2–5 when house occupied). **Jim Clark Memorial Trophy Room** Easter to end Sept: Mon–Sat 10–1, 2–6, Sun 2–6. **John Buchan Centre** Easter to mid Oct: daily 2–5. **Kailzie Gardens** Mid March to end Oct: daily 11–5.30. **Kinneil House** Standard hours but closed Tues afternoon and Fri. **Lauder: Thirlestane Castle** (and *Border Country Life Museum*) Mid to end May, June, Sept: Sun, Wed 2–5; July, Aug: daily (except Fri) 2–5. **Lennoxlove house** April to Sept: Wed, Sat, Sun 2–5. **Malleny Garden** May to end Sept: daily 10–dusk. **Manderston House** Mid May to end Sept: Thurs, Sun 2–5.30; also Bank Holiday Mon. **Mellerstain House** May to Sept: daily (except Sat) 12.30–5. **Museum of Flight** July, Aug: daily 10–4. **Museum of Scottish Lead Mining** Easter to Sept: daily *museum* 11–4, *Loch Nell Mine* 11–3.30. **Myreton Motor Museum** Easter to Oct: daily 10–6; Oct to Easter: daily 10–5. **Neidpath Castle** Thurs before Easter to mid Oct: Mon–Sat 10–1, 2–6, Sun 1–6. **Preston Mill** Easter to Oct: Mon–Sat 10–12.30, 2–5.30, Sun 2–5.30 (closes 4.30 in Oct); Nov to Easter: Sat 10.30–12.30, 2–4.30, Sun 2–4.30. **Priorwood Gardens** April, Nov to Christmas Eve: Mon–Sat 10–1, 2–5.30; May, June, Oct: Mon–Sat 10–5.30, Sun 1.30–5.30; July to Sept: Mon–Sat 10–6, Sun 1.30–5.30. **Scottish Mining Museum** *Prestongrange* summer: Tues–Fri 10–4, Sat, Sun 12–5; winter: Tues–Fri 10–3, Sat, Sun 12–3. *Lady Victoria* times not yet finalised. **Scottish Museum of Woollen Textiles** All year: Mon–Sat 9.30–5; Easter to Oct: Sun 12–4.30. **Smailholm Tower** Standard hours April to Sept only. **Suntrap** All year: daily 9–dusk. *Advice Centre* all year: Mon–Fri 9.30–12.30, 2–5; April to end Sept: Sat, Sun 2.30–5. **Traquair House** Easter to mid Oct: daily 1.30–5.30 (10.30–5.30 in July and Aug). **The Woodland Centre** Easter to Oct: Sun, Wed 1–5.30; July, Aug: daily (except Fri, Sat) 1–5.30.

GAZETTEER 25

Ardanaiseig Gardens April to end Oct: daily during daylight. **Arduaine Gardens** April to Oct: daily (except Thurs and Fri) 10–6. **Auchindrain Museum** April, May, Sept: daily (except Sat) 11–4; June to Aug: daily 10–4. **Barguillean Garden** April to Oct: daily during daylight. **Bonawe Iron Furnace** April to Sept: weekdays 9.30–7 (closed Fri, and Thurs afternoon), Sun 2–7. **Combined Operations Museum** April to June, Sept, Oct: Mon–Sat (except Fri) 10–1, 2–6, Sun 1–6; July, Aug: daily 10–6. **Crarae Glen Garden** All year: daily 9–6. **Cruachan Power Station** Easter to Oct: daily 9–5. **David Marshall Lodge** Easter to Sept: daily 10–6. **Dunstaffnage Castle** Standard hours but closed Thurs afternoon and Fri. **Glen Coe and North Lorn Folk Museum** Mid May to end Sept: Mon–Sat 10–5.30. **Glen Coe Visitor Centre** Easter to end May, Sept to late Oct: daily 9.30–5.30; June to Aug: daily 9–6. **Inchmahome Priory** Standard hours but closed Thurs and Fri in winter. **Inveraray Bell Tower** Late May to late Sept: Mon–Sat 10–1, 2–5, Sun 3–6. **Inveraray Castle** April, May, June, Sept, Oct: Mon–Sat (except Fri) 10–1, 2–6, Sun 1–6;

July, Aug: Mon–Sat 10–6, Sun 1–6. **Kinlochaline Castle** Open any reasonable time. Keys available from cottage on Loch Aline below castle. **McCaig's Tower** Always open. **McDonald's Mill** All year: Mon–Fri 9–7.30, Sat 9–5. Demonstration weekdays only. **Strathyre Forest Information Centre** May to end Sept: daily 8–6. **Strone Gardens** April to end Sept: daily 9–9. **White Corries Chairlift** June to mid Sept: daily 10–5; weekends in Jan, Sat, Sun and Mon in Feb and March, Easter and weekends in April: 9–5.30. **Colonsay: Kiloran Gardens** All year: daily at any reasonable time. **Mull: Duart Castle** May to Sept: daily 10.30–6. **Mull and Iona Museum Association** Late May to late Sept: daily (except Sun) 11–5. **Torosay Castle** Easter, early May to early Oct: daily 11–5. *Gardens* all year dawn to dusk.

GAZETTEER 26

Alyth Folk Museum May to Sept: Tues–Sat 1–5. **Angus Folk Museum** May to Sept: daily 12–5. **Arbroath Art Gallery** All year: Mon–Fri 9.30–6, Sat 9.30–5. **Arbroath Museum** April to Oct: Mon–Sat 10.30–1, 2–5, Sun 2–5 (in July and Aug); Nov to March: Mon–Fri 2–5, Sat 10.30–1, 2–5. **Auchterlonie's Golf Museum** All year: Mon–Sat 9–5. **Bannockburn** *Site* open all year. *Exhibition* March to Oct: daily 10–6. **Ben Lawers: Visitor Centre** Easter to end May, and Sept: daily 11–4; June to end Aug: daily 10–5. **Blair Castle** A week over Easter, Sun and Mon in April, daily from May to early Oct: Mon–Sat 10–6, Sun 2–6. Last admission 5. **Brechin Museum** All year: Mon–Fri 9.30–6 (Wed 9.30–7), Sat 9.30–5. **Brechin Round Tower** Exterior view only from churchyard. **Cambuskenneth Abbey** Standard hours in summer only. **Castle Campbell** Standard hours but closed Thurs afternoon and Fri in winter. **Castle Menzies** April to Sept: Mon–Sat 10.30–5, Sun 2–5. **Clan Donnachaidh Museum** Easter to Oct. **Crail Museum** Easter, June to Sept: Mon–Sat 10–12.30, 2–5, Sun 2–5. **The Dean's House** June to Sept: Mon–Sat 10.30–12.30, 2.30–4.30. **Doune Motor Museum** April to Oct: daily 10–5 (10–5.30 June to Aug). **Drummond Castle Gardens** April, Sept: Wed, Sun 2–6; May to Aug: daily 2–6. **Dunkeld Visitor Centre** Easter to end May, Sept to 23 Dec: Mon–Sat 10–1, 2–4.30; June to Aug: Mon–Sat 10–6, 2–5. **Falkland Palace** Easter to Sept: Mon–Sat 10–6, Sun 2–6; Oct: Sat 10–6, Sun 2–6. Last admission 5.15. **Fife Folk Museum** April to Oct: Mon–Sat (except Tues) 2–5, Sun 2.30–5.30. **Forest Information Centre, Queen's View** Easter to mid Oct: daily 10–5.15. **Glamis Castle** Easter weekend, May to Sept: daily (except Sat) 1–5. **Glenruthven Mill** All year: Mon–Fri 9–5; also Sat in summer. **Hill of Tarvit** Easter, April, Oct: Sat, Sun 2–6; May to Sept: daily 2–6. Last admission 5.30. *Gardens and grounds* all year 10–dusk. **Kellie Castle** *Castle* Easter, April, Oct: Sat, Sun 2–6; May to Sept: daily 2–6. Last admission 5.30. *Gardens and grounds* all year 10–dusk. **Kinross House Gardens** May to Sept: daily 2–7. **Kinross Museum** May to Sept: Tues–Sat 1–5. **Loch of the Lowes Visitor Centre** April, Sept: daily 10–5; May, Aug: daily 10–7; June, July: daily 10–8. **Lochty Private Railway** Late June to early Sept: Sun 2–5. **Meal and Flour Mill, Blair Atholl** All year: weekdays 10–6, Sun 12–6. **Megginch Castle Grounds** Wed throughout year 2–5; daily in Aug 2–5. **Meigle Museum** Standard hours but closed Sun. **Menstrie Castle** *Nova Scotia Room* May to end Sept: Mon 2.30–4.30, Wed 9.30–12, Thurs 6–8. **Museum of Scottish Tartans** Easter to Sept: Mon–Sat 10–5, Sun 2–4; Oct to Easter: Tues–Fri 2–4, Sat 10–1. **North Carr Lightship** April (from Easter), May, June: daily 10–5; July, Aug, Sept: daily 10–6. **Pass of Killiecrankie Visitor Centre** Easter to end June, Sept to late Oct: daily 10–6; July, Aug: daily 9.30–6. **St Andrews Preservation Trust** March to June, Sept to Nov: Tues–Fri 2–5; July, Aug: Tues–Sun 2–5. **Scone Palace** Good Fri to early Oct: Mon–Sat 10–5.30, Sun 2–5.30 (11–5.30 July and Aug). **Scottish Fisheries Museum** April to Oct: weekdays 10–5.30, Sun 2–5; Nov to March: daily (except Tues) 2–5. **Strathallan Aero Park** April to Oct: daily 10–5. **Vane Farm Nature Reserve** Jan to March: Sat, Sun 10–4; April to Dec: daily 10–5. **Wallace Monument** Feb, March, Oct: daily (except Wed, Thurs) 10–4.30; April, Sept: daily 10–5.30; May to Aug: daily 10–6.30.

GAZETTEER 27

Balmacara: Lochalsh House Woodland Garden All year daily. *Coach House* Easter to end Oct: daily 10–6. *Kiosk* June to Sept: Mon–Sat 10–1, 2–6. **Eilean Donan Castle** Easter to end Sept: daily 10–12.30, 2–6. **Fort Augustus Abbey** April to end Oct: guided tours daily at 11 and 4.30. **Glenfinnan Monument** Easter to end June, Sept to late Oct: daily 9.30–6; July, Aug: daily 9–6.30. **Great Glen Exhibition** Easter to Oct: daily 9.30–5.30. **Inverewe Garden** All year: daily 9.30–dusk. *Visitor Centre* end March to early May, early Sept to late Oct: Mon–Sat 10–5, Sun 12.30–5; early May to early Sept: Mon–Sat 10–6.30, Sun 12–6.30. **Kintail: Morvich Information Centre** June to end Sept: Mon–Sat 9–6, Sun 1–6. **Lael Forest Garden** Open at all times. **Strome Castle** Open at all reasonable times. **Torridon: Deer Museum and Visitor Centre Display** June to end Sept: Mon–Sat 10–6, Sun 2–6. **West Highland Museum** All year daily except Sun. June, Sept: 9.30–5.30; July, Aug: 9.30–9; rest of year: 10–1, 2–5.

GAZETTEER 28

Abertarff House All year: office hours. *Shop* Easter, June to mid Oct: Mon–Fri 10–4. **Aviemore Bird Garden** All year: daily 10–dusk. **Aviemore Centre** Open all year daily. **Balmoral Castle** May to July: daily (except Sun) 10–5. May not be open when any member of the Royal Family is in residence. **Beauly Priory** Standard hours but closed Mon and Tues morning in winter. **Boath Doocot** *Dovecot* seen from outside only. **Braemar Castle** May to early Oct: daily 10–6. **Brodie Castle** Easter weekend, May to Oct: Mon–Sat 11–6, Sun 2–6. Last admission 5.15. **Burghead Museum** All year: Tues 1.30–5, Thurs 5–8.30, Sat 10–12. **Cawdor Castle** May to Sept: daily 10–5. **Clan Macpherson Museum** May to Sept: Mon–Sat 10–5.30, Sun 2.30–5.30. **Corgarff Castle** Standard hours; apply key keeper in winter. **Culloden Moor** *Site* open all year. *Visitor Centre* Easter to end May, Oct: daily 9.30–5.30; June to Sept: daily 9–7.30. **Dingwall Town House** April to Sept: Mon–Sat 10–12, 2–4. **Elgin Museum** April to mid Sept: Mon–Fri 10–4, Sat 10–12; rest of year: Sat 10–12. **Falconer Museum** May, June, Sept: Mon–Sat 9.30–5.30; July, Aug: Mon–Sat 9.30–6.30, Sun 2–6.30; Oct to April: Mon–Fri 10–4.30. **Farigaig Forest Centre** April to Oct: daily 9.30–6. **Glenfarclas Distillery** All year: Mon–Fri 9–4.30; also Sat from July to Sept. **Glen Grant Distillery** Easter to early Oct: Mon–Fri 10–4. **Glenlivet Distillery** Easter to mid Oct: Mon–Sat 10–4. **Highland Folk Museum** April to Oct: Mon–Sat 10–6, Sun 2–6; Nov to March: Mon–Fri 10–3. **Highland Wildlife Park** Mid March to early Nov: daily from 10. **Hugh Miller's Cottage** Easter to end Sept: Mon–Sat 10–12, 1–5; also Sun 2–5 from June to Sept. **Inverness Museum and Art Gallery** All year: Mon–Sat 9–5. **Landmark Visitor Centre** April, May, Sept, Oct: daily 9.30–6; June, July, Aug: daily 9.30–9.30; Nov to March: daily 9.30–5. **Loch Garten Nature Reserve** May: daily 10–6.30; June to Aug: daily 10–8.30. **Loch Ness Centre** *Exhibition* all year daily: May to June 9–8; July to Sept 9–9.30; Oct to Nov 9–5; Dec to March 10–4; March to May 9–5. **Nairn Fishertown Museum** All year: Mon, Wed, Fri 6.30–8.30, Tues, Thurs, Sat 2.30–4.30. **Nairn Literary Institute** June to Sept: Mon–Sat 2.30–4.30. **Pluscarden Abbey** *Church* all year daily from 5 a.m. to 8.30 p.m. **Rothiemurchus Visitor Centre** All year: daily 9–6. **Strathspey Railway** Easter to May: weekends; May, Sept: also Mon; June to Aug: daily. **Tamdhu Distillery** May to Sept: Mon–Fri 10–4. **Tomatin Distillery** All year: Mon–Fri at 3. Essential to book in advance. **Tomintoul Museum** April, May, Oct: Mon–Sat 9–5.30; June, Sept: Mon–Sat 9–6, Sun 2–6; July, Aug: Mon–Sat 9–7, Sun 11–7.

GAZETTEER 29

Aden Country Park *Park* all year. *Agricultural Heritage Centre* May to Sept: daily 12–6. **Alford Valley Railway** April, May, Sept: weekends 11–5.30; June to Aug: daily 11–5.30. **Arbuthnott Museum and Art Gallery** All year: Mon–Sat 10–12, 2–5. **Banff Museum** All year: daily (except Thurs and Sun) 2–5. **Baxters of Speyside** April to Oct: Mon–Fri 10–4. **Braeloine Interpretative Centre** April to Sept: daily 10–5. **Buckie Museum and Peter Anson Gallery** All year: Mon–Fri 10–8, Sat 10–12. **Castle Fraser** May to end Sept: daily 2–6. Last admission 5.15. *Garden and grounds* all year 9.30–sunset. **Craigievar Castle** May to end Sept: daily 2–6. Last admission 5.15. *Grounds* all year 9.30–sunset. **Crathes Castle and Gardens** *Castle* Easter weekend and May to end Sept: Mon–Sat 11–6, Sun 2–6. Last admission 5.15. *Gardens and grounds* all year 9.30–sunset **Deer Abbey** Standard hours in summer only; also closed Mon–Wed. **Drum Castle** May to end Sept: daily 2–6. Last admission 5.15. *Grounds* all year 9.30–sunset. **Duff House** Standard hours in summer; apply key keeper in winter. **Dufftown Museum** May, June, Sept: Mon–Sat 9.30–5.30; July, Aug: Mon–Sat 9.30–6.30, Sun 2–6.30. **Edzell Castle and Garden** Standard hours but closed Tues and Thurs afternoon. **Fasque** May to Sept: daily (except Fri) 1.30–5.30. **Fyvie Castle** May to Sept: daily 2–6. Last admission 5.15. *Grounds* all year 9.30–sunset. **Glenesk Folk Museum** Easter weekend to May: Sun 2–6; June to Sept: daily 2–6. **Glenfiddich Distillery** All year: Mon–Fri 9.30–4.30; mid May to mid Oct: Sat 9.30–4.30, Sun 12–4.30. **Haddo House** May to end Sept: daily 2–6. (*Visitor Centre* 11–6), Sun 2–6. Last admission 5.15. *Garden and country park* all year 9.30–sunset. **Huntly Museum** All year: Tues–Sat 10–12, 2–4. **Inverurie Museum** All year Mon–Fri 2–5, Sat 10–12. **Leith Hall and Garden** *Hall* May to end Sept: daily 2–6. Last admission 5.15. *Gardens and grounds* all year 9.30–sunset. **Muchalls Castle** May to Sept: Sun, Tues 3–5. **Pitmedden Garden** *Museum and exhibition* May to end Sept: daily 11–6. Last admission 5.15. *Garden and grounds* all year 9.30–sunset. **Slains Castle** Open at all times. **Stonehaven Tolbooth Museum** June to Sept: Mon, Thurs, Fri, Sat 10–12, 2–5, Wed, Sun 2–5. Closed Tues. **Strathisla Distillery** Mid June to end Aug: Mon–Fri 9–4.30.

GAZETTEER 30

Dunbeath: Laidhay Caithness Croft Museum Easter to Sept: daily 10–6. **Dunrobin Castle** June to mid Sept: Mon–Sat 10.30–5.30, Sun 1–5.30. **Ullapool: Loch Broom Highland Museum** April to Sept: daily 9–6 (9–10 in July and Aug). **Wick: Wick Heritage Centre** June to Sept: Mon–Sat 10.30–12, 2–4.30; July, Aug: Sun 2–5. **Caithness Glassworks** All year: Sat 9–12 (4.30 in summer).

GAZETTEER 31

Rhum: Kinloch Castle Easter weekend to end Sept: open most days – conducted tours to fit in with limited scheduled crossings from Mallaig, Skye. **Clan Donald Centre** Easter to Oct: Mon–Sat 10–5.30; June to Sept: Sun 1–5.30. **Dunsgiath Castle** All reasonable times. **Dunvegan Castle** Easter to mid Oct: daily (except Sun) 2–5 (10.30–5 June to Sept). **Kilmuir Croft Museum** April to Oct: Mon–Sat 9–6. **Skye Watermill** All year: Mon–Sat 10–6. **Lewis: Black House Museum** Standard hours but closed Sun. **Shawbost Folk Museum** April to Nov: Mon–Sat 9–6.

GAZETTEER 32

Orkneys

Bishop's Palace, Kirkwall Standard hours but closed Fri afternoon and Sat in winter. **Earl Patrick's Palace, Kirkwall** Standard hours but closed Fri afternoon and Sat in winter. **Gurness Broch** Standard hours but closed Sat in winter. **Orkney Arts Centre** All year: Tues–Sat 10.30–12.30, 1.30–5; July, Aug: Sun, Mon 2–5. **Orkney Chairs** All year: Mon–Fri 8.30–5. **Stromness Museum** All year: Mon–Sat 11–12.30, 1.30–5 (Thurs 11–1); July, Aug: Mon–Sat 10.30–12.30, 1.30–5. **Tankerness House** All year: Mon–Sat 10.30–12.30, 1.30–5; May to Sept: Sun 2–5.

Shetlands

Croft House May to Sept: Tues–Sun 10–1, 2–5. **Jarlshof** Standard hours but closed Tues and Wed afternoon. **Shetland Museum** All year: Mon, Wed, Fri 10–1, 2.30–5, 6–8, Tues, Sat 10–1, 2.30–5, Thurs 10–1. **Shetland Workshop Gallery** All year: daily (except Wed, Sun) 9.30–1, 2.15–5. **Tingwall Valley Agricultural Museum** All year: Tues, Thurs, Sat 10–1, 2–5.

Index to Text

Principal entries are indicated in bold; map references in italic.

Index to Maps

ABBREVIATIONS

Beds. – Bedfordshire
Berks. – Berkshire
Bucks. – Buckinghamshire
Cambs. – Cambridgeshire
Cas. – Castle

Ches. – Cheshire
Co. – County
Com. – Common
Corn. – Cornwall
Cumb. – Cumbria
Derby. – Derbyshire

Dumf. & Gall. – Dumfries & Galloway
Dur. – Durham
E. – East
E. Sussex – East Sussex
Glos. – Gloucestershire
Gt. – Great
Grn. – Green
Hants. – Hampshire
Heref. & Worcs. – Hereford & Worcester
Hth. – Heath
Herts. – Hertfordshire

Ho. – House
Humber. – Humberside
I.o.M. – Isle of Man
I.o.W. – Isle of Wight
Junc. – Junction
Lancs. – Lancashire
Leics. – Leicestershire
Lincs. – Lincolnshire
Lo. – Lodge
London – Greater London
Manchester – Greater Manchester
Mid Glam. – Mid Glamorgan

Norf. – Norfolk
N. – North
N. Yorks. – North Yorkshire
Northants. – Northamptonshire
Northumb. – Northumberland
Notts. – Nottinghamshire
Oxon. – Oxfordshire
Salop. – Shropshire
Som. – Somerset
S. – South
S. Glam. – South Glamorgan
S. Yorks. – South Yorkshire
Staffs. – Staffordshire

Sta. – Station
Suff. – Suffolk
War. – Warwickshire
W. – West
W. Glam – West Glamorgan
W. Mid. – West Midlands
W. Sussex – West Sussex
W. Yorks. – West Yorkshire
W. Isles – Western Isles
Wilts. – Wiltshire

A

47 Amersham Com. D 10
115 Amersidelaw C 12
26 Amesbury B 3
155 Amhuinnsuidhe F 2
62 Amington B 6
111 Amisfield Town C 11
74 Amlwch Port A 4
74 Amlwch A 4
35 Ammanford F 9
107 Amotherby H 7
26 Ampfield D 5
122 Ampherlaw D 3
106 Ampleforth Coll. G 6
106 Ampleforth G 6
46 Ampney Crucis D 2
46 Ampney St. Mary D 2
46 Ampney St. Peter D 2
26 Amport B 4
67 Ampthill L 1
71 Ampton H 2
34 Amroth F 5
134 Amulree C 4
154 An Caol C 5
154 An Coroghon H 2
130 Anaheilt A 5
138 Anancaun C 4
87 Ancaster F 7
55 Anchor D 7
123 Ancroft Northmoor E 12
123 Ancroft E 12
123 Ancrum G 9
87 Anderby C 12
19 Anderson F 12
78 Anderton C 5
26 Andover Down B 5
26 Andover B 5
46 Andoversford B 1
98 Andreas F 2
134 Angansk F 6
10 Angarrak F 3
114 Angerton G 1
34 Angle G 2
98 Anglers' Hotel D 3
74 Anglesey C 4
27 Angmering F 12
27 Angmering-on-Sea F 12
94 Angram, N. Yorks. B 3
99 Angram, N. Yorks. E 11
134 Anie F 1
142 Ankerville B 4
95 Anlaby D 8
66 Anmer C 8
26 Anna Valley B 5
111 Annan E 12
138 Annat, Highland D 3
131 Annat, Strathclyde E 7
119 Annathill B 12
119 Annbank Station G 9
119 Annbank G 9
86 Annesley Woodhouse E 2
115 Annfield Plain H 10
146 Annfield F 3
115 Annitsford F 11
55 Annscroft B 10
115 Annstead D 12
19 Ansford C 10
62 Ansley C 6
79 Anslow Gate H 10
79 Anslow H 10
27 Anstey, Hants. B 8
67 Anstey, Herts. M 5
63 Anstey, Leics. A 9
135 Anstruther Easter G 10
135 Anstruther Wester G 10
63 Ansty, War. D 7
26 Ansty, Wilts. C 1
30 Ansty, W. Sussex F 2
27 Anthill Common E 8
111 Anthorn F 12
70 Antingham B 6
11 Antony D 11
14 Anvil Corner E 2
87 Anwick E 8
110 Anwoth F 6
66 Apes Hall F 6
66 Apethorpe F 1
87 Apley C 8
86 Apperknowle B 1
39 Apperley B 11
99 Appersett F 10
130 Appin House C 6
99 Appleby, Cumbria C 9
95 Appleby, Humber. F 7
62 Appleby Magna A 6
62 Appleby Parva A 6
138 Applecross House E 1
138 Applecross E 1
14 Appledore, Devon C 3
18 Appledore, Devon E 4
31 Appledore Heath E 8
31 Appledore, Kent E 8
46 Appleford E 6
26 Appleshaw A 4
98 Applethwaite C 5
106 Appleton, N. Yorks. E 4
46 Appleton, Oxon. D 5
94 Appleton Roebuck C 3
78 Appleton Thorn B 5
107 Appleton-le-Moors F 7
107 Appleton-le-Street H 7
123 Appletreehall H 8
91 Appletreewick A 9
90 Appley Bridge F 4
18 Appley D 4
27 Apse Heath H 7
50 Apsley End A 1
27 Apuldram F 9
146 Aquhythie F 5
142 Arabella B 4
138 Araid D 2
138 Aranarff F 3
147 Arbeadie H 4
135 Arbirlot C 10
47 Arborfield Cross G 8
47 Arborfield G 8
110 Arbrack H 5
135 Arbroath C 11
147 Arbuthnott K 5
142 Archiestown E 8
78 Arclid Green D 6
118 Ardachearanbeg A 5
130 Ardachoil D 4
118 Ardachuple A 5
139 Ardachvie K 5
131 Ardanaiseig E 8
138 Ardaneaskan F 2
130 Ardanstur F 5
138 Ardarroch F 2
118 Ardbeg C 6
150 Ardcharnich G 3
130 Ardchiavaig F 1
131 Ardchonnell F 7
130 Ardchrishnish E 2
134 Ardchullarie More F 1
131 Ardchyle E 12
135 Ardcross G 10
131 Arddarroch H 9
55 Arddleen A 8
130 Ardelanish F 1
50 Ardeley A 3
139 Ardelve G 2
106 Arden Hall F 5
119 Arden A 8
130 Ardencaple Ho. F 5
62 Ardens Grafton G 5
130 Ardentallan Ho. E 5
118 Ardentraive B 5
134 Ardeonaig D 2
130 Ardery A 5
131 Ardess H 10
150 Ardessie G 2
130 Ardfern G 5
131 Ardgartan G 10
150 Ardgay G 6
155 Ardhasig G 2
138 Ardheslaig D 2
130 Ardinamar F 5
150 Ardindrean G 3
30 Ardingly E 2
46 Ardington E 5
139 Ardintoul G 2
146 Ardlair E 3
118 Ardlamont House C 5
130 Ardlarach F 5
71 Ardleigh M 3
135 Ardler C 7
46 Ardley A 6
131 Ardlui F 10
118 Ardlussa A 2
131 Ardmaddy D 8
150 Ardmair G 3
118 Ardmaleish C 6
131 Ardmay G 10
118 Ardminish E 2
139 Ardmolich M 1
151 Ardmore, Highland H 7
119 Ardmore, Strathclyde B 8
130 Ardmore, Strathclyde E 5
130 Ardnacross C 3
119 Ardnadam A 7
142 Ardnagrask E 1
139 Ardnamurach K 2
130 Ardnastang A 5
119 Ardneil D 7
131 Ardno G 8
146 Ardo House E 7
134 Ardoch C 6
119 Ardochrig E 11
151 Ardochu F 7
139 Ardochy House J 6
130 Ardow B 2
146 Ardoyne E 4
118 Ardpatrick House C 3
118 Ardpatrick C 3
119 Ardpeaton A 7
118 Ardrishaig A 3
155 Ardroil D 1
142 Ardross Castle B 2
119 Ardrossan E 7
130 Ardshealach A 4
91 Ardsley East E 11
91 Ardsley G 12
130 Ardslignish A 3
134 Ardtalnaig C 2
118 Ardtaraig A 5
130 Ardtoe A 4
134 Ardtrostan E 2
130 Arduaine F 5
142 Ardullie C 1
130 Ardura E 4
154 Ardvasar H 5
130 Ardvergnish E 3
143 Ardverikie L 1
155 Ardvey, Loch Finsbay H 2
155 Ardvey, Loch Stockinish H 2
131 Ardvorlich, Strathclyde F 10
134 Ardvorlich, Tayside E 1
155 Ardvourlie Castle F 3
134 Ardwell, Dumf. & Gall. G 2
110 Ardwell, Strathclyde B 3
62 Areley Kings E 2
27 Arford B 9
134 Argaty G 2
54 Argoed Mill F 5
38 Argoed D 5
131 Arichastlich D 10
130 Aridhglas F 1
138 Arinacrinachd D 1
130 Ariogan E 6
139 Arisaig House L 1
139 Arisaig L 1
130 Ariundle A 5
94 Arkendale A 2
67 Arkesden M 6
99 Arkholme H 8
99 Arkle Town E 12
111 Arkleby H 12
114 Arkleton D 2
50 Arkley D 2
94 Arksey F 4
86 Arkwright Town C 2
39 Arle B 12
98 Arlecdon C 3
67 Arlesey L 3
55 Arleston A 12
78 Arley, Cheshire B 5
62 Arley, War. C 6
39 Arlingham C 10
14 Arlington Beccott B 5
14 Arlington, Devon B 5
30 Arlington, E. Sussex G 4
46 Arlington, Glos. C 2
154 Armadale Castle H 6
151 Armadale, Highland B 8
122 Armadale, Lothian C 2
99 Armathwaite A 7
70 Arminghall E 5
62 Armitage A 4
91 Armley D 11
62 Armscote H 6
87 Armston G 2
94 Armthorpe G 4
99 Arncliffe Cote H 11
99 Arncliffe H 11
135 Arncroach G 10
26 Arne G 1
63 Arnesby C 9
118 Arnicle F 2
139 Arnisdale H 2
154 Arnish C 5
122 Arniston Engine C 6
155 Arnol B 4
95 Arnold, Humber. C 9
86 Arnold, Notts. F 3
134 Arnprior H 1
99 Arnside G 7
130 Aros Mains C 3
98 Arrad Foot G 5
95 Arram C 8
106 Arrathorne F 2
27 Arreton G 7
67 Arrington K 4
131 Arrivain D 10
131 Arrochar G 10
62 Arrow F 4
142 Artafallie E 2
91 Arthington C 11
63 Arthingworth D 11
54 Arthog A 2
146 Arthrath D 7
27 Arundel E 11
131 Aryhoulan A 7
95 Asby cum Fenby G 10
98 Asby C 3
118 Ascog C 6
47 Ascot G 10
46 Ascott-under-Wychwood B 4
106 Asenby H 4
86 Asfordby Hill H 4
86 Asfordby H 4
66 Asgarby, Lincs. A 2
87 Asgarby, Lincs. D 10
14 Ash Bullayne E 6
63 Ash Green D 7
14 Ash Hill D 6
31 Ash, Kent B 11
30 Ash, Kent B 5
78 Ash Magna F 4
63 Ash Priors C 5
19 Ash, Somerset D 8
27 Ash, Surrey A 10
38 Ash Thomas E 3
27 Ash Vale A 10
46 Ashampstead F 6
71 Ashbacking K 5
79 Ashbourne F 10
18 Ashbrittle D 4
15 Ashburton J 6
14 Ashbury, Devon F 4
46 Ashbury, Oxon. F 4
87 Ashby by Partney D 11
87 Ashby de la Launde E 7
79 Ashby de la Zouch H 12
70 Ashby Dell E 8
63 Ashby Folville A 10
63 Ashby Magna C 9
63 Ashby Parva C 8
87 Ashby Puerorum C 10
63 Ashby St. Ledgers E 9
70 Ashby St. Mary E 6
95 Ashby F 7
39 Ashchurch A 12
38 Ashcombe, Avon H 6
18 Ashcombe, Devon H 3
19 Ashcott C 8
47 Ashcroft F 8
67 Ashdon L 7
27 Ashe A 7
51 Asheldham D 9
47 Ashendon C 8
67 Ashen L 8
134 Ashfield, Central G 3
35 Ashfield, Dyfed D 10
71 Ashfield Green H 6
71 Ashfield, Suffolk J 5
55 Ashford Bowdler E 10
55 Ashford Carbonel E 10
79 Ashford, Derby C 10
14 Ashford, Devon C 4
26 Ashford, Hants. E 3
46 Ashford Hill H 6
31 Ashford, Kent D 9
47 Ashford, Surrey G 11
79 Ashford-in-the-Water C 10
119 Ashgill D 12
99 Ashgillside A 10
18 Ashill, Devon E 4
70 Ashill, Norfolk E 2
18 Ashill, Somerset D 6
51 Ashington, Essex E 8
115 Ashington, Northumb. D 10
19 Ashington, Som. D 9
27 Ashington, W. Sussex E 12
123 Ashkirk G 7
26 Ashlett F 6
39 Ashleworth B 11
67 Ashley, Cambs. J 8
78 Ashley, Cheshire B 6
14 Ashley, Devon E 5
39 Ashley, Glos. E 12
47 Ashley Green D 10
26 Ashley, Hants C 5
26 Ashley, Hants G 4
26 Ashley Heath F 3
31 Ashley, Kent C 12
63 Ashley, Northants. C 11
78 Ashley, Staffs. F 6
46 Ashmansworth H 5
14 Ashmansworthy D 2
46 Ashmore Green G 6
19 Ashmore D 12
62 Ashorne F 6
86 Ashover D 1
62 Ashow E 6
55 Ashperton H 11
15 Ashprington K 7
14 Ashreigney E 5
30 Ashtead B 1
78 Ashton, Cheshire C 4
39 Ashton Common H 12
10 Ashton, Cornwall G 3
46 Ashton Keynes E 2
63 Ashton, Northants. G 11
67 Ashton, Northants. G 2
62 Ashton under Hill H 3
91 Ashton under Lyne G 8
39 Ashton Watering G 8
55 Ashton, Heref. & Worcs. F 10
90 Ashton-in-Makerfield G 5
90 Ashton-upon-Mersey H 6
26 Ashurst, Hants. E 5
30 Ashurst, Kent D 4
30 Ashurst, W. Sussex F 1
30 Ashurstwood D 3
14 Ashwater F 3
67 Ashwell, Herts. L 4
63 Ashwell, Leics. A 12
70 Ashwellthorpe F 4
19 Ashwick A 9
66 Ashwicken D 8
123 Ashybank H 8
98 Askam in Furness G 4
94 Askern F 3
19 Askerswell G 9
94 Askham Bryan B 3
94 Askham Richard B 3
99 Askham C 7
130 Asknish H 6
99 Askrigg F 11
91 Askwith B 10
66 Aslackby C 2
70 Aslacton F 4
86 Aslockton F 5
146 Asloun F 3
111 Aspatria G 12
50 Aspenden A 4
63 Aspley Guise H 12
47 Aspley Heath A 10
90 Aspull F 5
94 Asselby D 5
87 Asserby B 12
71 Assington L 2
142 Assynt House C 2
79 Astbury D 7
63 Astcote G 10
55 Asterley B 9
55 Asterton C 9
46 Asthall Leigh C 4
46 Asthall C 4
55 Astley Abbots C 12
90 Astley Bridge F 6
62 Astley Cross E 2
90 Astley Green G 6
62 Astley, Heref. & Worcs. E 1
78 Astley, Salop. H 4
62 Astley, War. C 6
47 Aston Abbotts B 9
47 Aston, Berks. F 9
55 Aston Botterell D 11
62 Aston Cantlow F 5
78 Aston, Cheshire B 4
78 Aston, Cheshire E 5
47 Aston Clinton C 9
75 Aston, Clwyd C 12
39 Aston Crews B 10
39 Aston Cross A 12
79 Aston, Derby B 10
50 Aston End B 3
55 Aston Eyre C 12
62 Aston Fields E 3
63 Aston Flamville C 8
55 Aston, Heref. & Worcs. E 10
55 Aston, Heref. & Worcs. F 10
50 Aston, Herts. B 3
39 Aston Ingham B 10
78 Aston juxta Mondrum D 5
63 Aston le Walls G 8
46 Aston Magna A 3
55 Aston on Clun D 9
79 Aston on Trent G 12
46 Aston, Oxon. D 4
55 Aston Pigott B 9
55 Aston Rogers B 9
47 Aston Rowant D 8
55 Aston, Salop A 11
78 Aston, Salop. G 4
47 Aston Sandford C 8
62 Aston Somerville H 4
78 Aston, Staffs. F 6
79 Aston, Staffs. G 7
62 Aston Subedge H 5
86 Aston, S. Yorks. B 2
46 Aston Tirrold F 6
46 Aston Upthorpe E 6
62 Aston, W. Midlands C 4
67 Astwick L 3
62 Astwood Bank F 4
67 Astwood K 1
66 Aswarby B 2
87 Aswardby C 10
55 Atcham B 11
71 Athelington H 5
19 Athelney C 7
123 Athelstaneford B 8
14 Atherington, Devon D 5
27 Atherington, W. Sussex F 11
62 Atherstone on Stour G 5
62 Atherstone B6
90 Atherton G 5
139 Athnamulloch G 5
106 Atley Hill E 3
79 Atlow E 10
138 Attadale F 3
70 Attleborough, Norfolk F 3
63 Attleborough, War. C 7
70 Attlebridge D 4
123 Attonburn G 10
147 Atton K 1
95 Atwick B 9
39 Atworth H 11
86 Aubourn D 6
131 Auchachenna E 7
118 Auchagallon F 4
143 Auchallater K 7
110 Auchalton A 4
143 Auchavan M 7
118 Auchbroad A 3
146 Aucheldy D 6
111 Auchenbainzie B 9
147 Auchenblae J 5
111 Auchenbrack B 8
118 Auchenbreck A 5
111 Auchencairn, Dumf. & Gall. C 10
111 Auchencairn, Dumf. & Gall. F 9
119 Auchencarroch A 9
110 Auchencrosh D 2
123 Auchencrow C 11
122 Auchendinny C 5
111 Auchengibbert D 9
122 Auchengray D 3
111 Auchengruith A 9
146 Auchenhairig B 1
122 Auchenheath E 1
110 Auchenmalg F 3
110 Auchensoul B 3
110 Auchentibbert G 2
119 Auchentiber E 8
119 Auchenvennel A 8
111 Auchenvey D 8
143 Auchernack G 6
143 Auchgourish H 5
118 Auchinadrian D 2
146 Auchinderran B 2
131 Auchindrain G 6
138 Auchindrean B 6
146 Auchinhove B 2
146 Auchininna C 4
119 Auchinleck G 10
119 Auchinloch B 11
134 Auchinner F 2
146 Auchintender D 4
146 Auchintoul, Grampian F 3
147 Auchintoul, Grampian G 4
146 Auchiries D 8
146 Auchleven E 4
122 Auchlochan F 1
147 Auchlossan G 3
150 Auchlunachan H 3
147 Auchlunies G 6
131 Auchlyne E 12
146 Auchmacoy D 7
110 Auchmantle E 2
119 Auchmillan F 10
135 Auchmithie C 11
135 Auchmuirbridge G 7
147 Auchmull K 3
131 Auchnacloich Pier D 7
130 Auchnacraig D 4
139 Auchnadaull L 5
134 Auchnafree D 3
142 Auchnagallin F 6
146 Auchnagatt C 7
118 Auchnaha A 4
143 Auchnahannet G 5
142 Auchnahillin F 3
110 Auchnotteroch F 1
147 Aucholzie H 1
131 Auchrioch E 10
143 Auchroisk G 6
147 Auchronie J 2
134 Auchterarder F 4
139 Auchteraw J 7
135 Auchterderran H 7
135 Auchterhouse C 8
135 Auchtermuchty F 7
138 Auchterneed D 8
143 Auchterteang G 5
135 Auchtertool H 7
142 Auchtertyre, Grampian D 7
131 Auchtertyre, Central E 10
139 Auchtertyre, Highland G 2
134 Auchtoo E 1
151 Auckingill B 12
94 Auckley G 4
146 Auckmair E 1
91 Audenshaw G 8
78 Audlem F 5
67 Audley End L 6
78 Audley E 6
146 Auds A 4
94 Aughton, Humber. C 5
90 Aughton, Lancs. G 3
99 Aughton, Lancs. H 8
86 Aughton, S. Yorks. B 2
46 Aughton, Wilts. H 3
135 Auldallan A 8
142 Auldearn D 5
55 Aulden G 10
111 Auldgirth C 10
123 Auldhame A 8
119 Auldhouse D 11
146 Auldtown of Carnousie C 4
146 Auldtown B 3
134 Aulich A 1
86 Ault Hucknall D 2
139 Ault-a-chruinn H 3
150 Aultanrynie D 4
150 Aultbea G 1
138 Aultdearg C 7
142 Aultfearn E 1
138 Aultgowrie E 8
138 Aultgrishan A 1
138 Aultguish Inn C 7
146 Aulthash B 1
151 Aultiphurst A 8
146 Aultmore B 1
143 Aultnagoire G 1
142 Aultnamain Inn B 2
143 Aultnancaber H 5
139 Aultnaslat J 5
146 Aulton E 3
147 Aultonrea H 1
143 Aundorach H 5
18 Aunk F 4
66 Aunsby B 1
39 Aust E 9
47 Austenwood E 10
94 Austerfield H 4
62 Austrey B 6
99 Austwick H 10
87 Authorpe Row C 12
87 Authorpe B 11
46 Avebury G 2
50 Aveley F 6
39 Avening E 12
86 Averham E 5
15 Aveton Gifford L 6
143 Avielochan H 5
143 Aviemore H 4
118 Avinagillan C 3
46 Avington, Berks. G 5
27 Avington, Hants. C 7
142 Avoch D 3
39 Avon, Co. F 9
63 Avon Dassett G 7
122 Avonbridge B 2
46 Avon F 1
39 Avonmouth F 8
15 Avonwick K 6
26 Awbridge D 5
110 Awhirk F 2
39 Awkley F 9
18 Awliscombe F 5
39 Awre D 10
86 Awsworth F 2
19 Axbridge A 8
27 Axford, Hants. B 7
46 Axford, Wilts. G 3
18 Axminster F 6
18 Axmouth G 6
106 Aycliffe C 3
115 Aydon F 8
39 Aylburton D 9
114 Ayle H 5
18 Aylesbeare G 4
47 Aylesbury C 9
95 Aylesby F 9
14 Aylescott D 5
30 Aylesford B 6
63 Aylestone B 9
70 Aylmerton B 5
31 Aylsham C 11
70 Aylsham C 5
39 Aylton A 9
55 Aymestrey F 9
46 Aynho A 6
50 Ayot St. Lawrence B 2
50 Ayot St. Peter B 2
119 Ayr G 8
99 Aysgarth F 12
18 Ayshford E 4
98 Ayside G 6
63 Ayston B 12

35 Burry Port G 8
35 Burrygreen H 8
90 Burscough F 3
90 Burscough Bridge F 3
94 Bursea D 6
94 Bursea Lane Ends D 6
95 Burshill B 8
26 Bursledon E 6
79 Burslem E 7
71 Burstall L 4
19 Burstock F 7
71 Burston, Norfolk G 4
79 Burston, Staffs. G 8
30 Burstow D 2
95 Burstwick D 10
99 Burtersett F 11
78 Burton, Cheshire D 4
99 Burton, Cumbria G 8
19 Burton, Dorest G 10
26 Burton, Dorset G 3
34 Burton, Dyfed F 3
87 Burton, Lincs. C 7
78 Burton, Merseyside C 2
115 Burton, Northumb. D 12
18 Burton, Somerset B 5
39 Burton, Wilts. F 11
95 Burton Agnes A 9
19 Burton Bradstock G 8
87 Burton Coggles H 7
95 Burton Contable C 9
63 Burton Dassett G 7
107 Burton Fleming H 11
78 Burton Green, Clwyd D 2
62 Burton Green, W. Midlands E 6
63 Burton Hastings C 7
99 Burton in Lonsdale H 9
86 Burton Joyce F 4
63 Burton Latimer E 12
86 Burton Lazars H 5
91 Burton Leonard A 12
86 Burton on the Wolds H 3
79 Burton-on-Trent H 10
63 Burton Overy B 10
66 Burton Pedwardine A 2
95 Burton Pidsea D 10
94 Burton Salmon D 3
94 Burton upon Stather E 6
90 Burtonwood H 4
78 Burwardsley D 4
55 Burwarton D 11
30 Burwash F 5
30 Burwash Common F 5
30 Burwash Weald F 5
67 Burwell, Cambs. J 7
87 Burwell, Lincs. B 10
74 Burwen A 4
158 Burwick E 2
67 Bury, Cambs. G 4
91 Bury, Manchester F 7
18 Bury, Somerset C 3
27 Bury, W. Sussex E 11
50 Bury Green B 4
71 Bury St Edmunds J 2
94 Burythorpe A 6
119 Busby D 10
107 Buscel G 9
46 Buscot D 3
147 Bush L 5
55 Bush Bank G 10
71 Bush Green G 5
62 Bushbury B 3
50 Bushey D 1
50 Bushey Heath E 2
39 Bushley A 11
46 Bushton F 2
158 Busta C 7
115 Buston Barns B 10
50 Butcher's Pasture B 6
39 Butcombe H 8
115 Buteland E 7
19 Butleigh C 8
19 Butleigh Wootton C 8
47 Butler's Cross C 9
62 Butlers Marston G 6
71 Butley K 7
78 Butt Green E 5
114 Butterburn F 5
94 Buttercrambe A 5
106 Butterknowle C 1
18 Butterleigh E 3
98 Buttermere, Cumb. D 4
46 Buttermere, Wilts. H 4
78 Butters Green E 6
91 Buttershaw D 10
134 Butterstone C 5
79 Butterton E 9
106 Butterwick, Dur. B 4
66 Butterwick, Lincs. A 5
107 Butterwick, N. Yorks. H 10
107 Butterwick, N. Yorks. G 7
55 Buttington B 8
63 Buttock's Booth F 11
62 Buttonoak D 1
26 Butt's Green C 4
26 Buttsash E 6
71 Buxhall J 3
123 Buxley D 10
30 Buxted F 4
79 Buxton, Derby C 9
70 Buxton, Norfolk C 5
70 Buxton Heath C 5
38 Bwlch B 5
75 Bwlchgwyn E 11
54 Bwlchllan F 1
74 Bwlchtocyn H 3
75 Bwlch-y-cibau H 11
75 Bwlch-y-ddâr H 11
35 Bwlchyfadfa B 8
54 Bwlch-y-ffridd C 6
34 Bwlch-y-groes C 6
54 Bwlch-y-sarnau E 6
111 Byeloch D 11
106 Byers Green B 2
63 Byfield B 8
47 Byfleet H 11
55 Byford H 9
67 Bygrave L 4
151 Bylbster B 11
75 Bylchau D 9
78 Byley C 6
94 Byram E 3
35 Bynea G 9
123 Byrewalls E 9
114 Byrness C 6
67 Bythorn H 2
55 Byton F 9
115 Bywell G 8
27 Byworth D 11

C

134 Cablea C 4
95 Cabourne G 9
146 Cabrach E 1
138 Cabule Lodge C 5
18 Cadbury F 3
14 Cadbury Barton D 6
147 Caddam K 1
119 Cadder B 11
131 Cadderlie D 7
47 Caddington B 11
123 Caddonfoot F 7
30 Cade Street F 5
63 Cadeby, Leics. B 7
94 Cadeby, S. Yorks. G 3
18 Cadeleigh E 3
122 Cademuir F 5
114 Cadgillhead E 2
10 Cadgwith H 4
135 Cadham G 7
90 Cadishead H 6
35 Cadle G 9
46 Cadley, Wilts. G 3
26 Cadley, Wilts. A 4
47 Cadmore End E 8
26 Cadnam E 4
95 Cadney G 8
75 Cadole D 11
35 Cadoxton-Juxta-Neath G 11
150 Cadubh G 3
38 Caehopkin C 2
74 Caeathraw D 4
87 Caenby A 7
87 Caenby Corner A 7
35 Caeo C 10
34 Caer Farchell D 1
38 Caerau E 2
35 Cae'r-bryn F 9
74 Caerdeon H 6
74 Cae'r-geiliog B 3
75 Caergwrle D 12
75 Caerhun C 7
114 Caerlanrig C 2
38 Caerleon E 6
34 Caerlleon E 6
74 Caernarvon D 4
38 Caerphilly F 5
54 Caersws C 6
35 Caerwedros A 7
39 Caerwent E 8
75 Caerwys C 10
111 Cairn C 10
146 Cairnargat D 2
130 Cairnbaan H 5
146 Carinbrogie E 6
123 Carincross C 11
110 Cairnderry D 4
131 Carndow E 9
146 Cairness B 8
122 Cairneyhill A 3
110 Cairnfield G 5
146 Cairnfield House B 2
110 Cairngaan H 2
110 Cairngarroch G 1
111 Cairnhall C 10
146 Cairnhill D 4
146 Cairnie, Grampian C 2
147 Cairnie, Grampian G 5
146 Cairnorrie D 6
110 Cairnryan E 2
110 Cairnsmore E 5
119 Cairntable H 9
110 Cairnwhin B 3
138 Caiseachan D 6
70 Caister-on-Sea D 8
95 Caistor G 9
70 Caistor St. Edmund E 5
115 Caistron C 8
123 Caitha Bowland E 7
155 Calbost E 5
26 Calbourne G 6
87 Calceby C 11
62 Calchems Corner E 6
39 Calcot Farm E 11
47 Calcot Row G 7
142 Calcots Station C 8
31 Calcott B 10
98 Caldbeck A 6
106 Caldbergh G 1
67 Caldecote, Beds. L 3
67 Caldecote, Cambs. K 4
67 Caldecote, Cambs. G 2
63 Caldecott, Leics. C 12
67 Caldecott, Northants H 1
98 Calder, Cumb. E 3
123 Calder, Northumb. G 12
98 Calder Bridge E 3
91 Calder Grove E 11
151 Calder Mains B 10
90 Calder Vale C 4
119 Calderbank C 12
91 Calderbrook E 8
122 Caldercruix C 1
119 Caldermill E 11
119 Calderwood D 11
39 Caldicot E 8
123 Caldside E 9
106 Caldwell D 2
78 Caldy B 1
35 Caledfwlch D 10
35 Caledrhydiau B 8
158 Calfsound B 3
130 Calgary B 1
142 Califer D 6
122 California, Central B 2
70 California, Norf. D 8
71 California, Suff. L 5
15 California Cross K 6
79 Calke H 12
115 Callaly B 9
134 Callander F 1
155 Callanish D 3
55 Callaughton C 11
131 Callert House A 8
10 Callestick E 5
154 Callgarry H 5
11 Callington C 10
39 Callow A 8
62 Callow End G 2
62 Callow Hill, Heref. & Worcs. E 1
62 Callow Hill, Heref. & Worcs. F 4
46 Callow Hill, Wilts. F 1
47 Callowhill G 11
55 Callows Grave F 11
26 Calmore E 5
46 Calmsden C 1
46 Calne G 1
86 Calow C 1
26 Calshot F 6
11 Calstock C 11
46 Calstone Wellington G 1
70 Calthorpe B 5
99 Calthwaite A 7
91 Calton, N. Yorks. A 8
79 Calton, Staffs. E 9
78 Calveley D 4
79 Calver C 11
55 Calver Hill G 9
78 Calverhall F 5
18 Calverleigh E 3
91 Calverley C 10
63 Calverton, Bucks. H 11
86 Calverton, Notts. E 3
134 Calvine A 3
111 Calvo F 12
39 Cam D 10
154 Camascross G 6
130 Camasnacroise B 6
138 Camasterach E 1
154 Camastianavaig D 4
35 Camasunary F 4
142 Camault Muir F 1
158 Camb B 7
31 Camber F 8
47 Camberley H 9
50 Camberwell F 3
94 Camblesforth D 4
135 Cambo, Fife F 10
115 Cambo, Northumb. D 8
115 Cambois E 11
10 Camborne F 4
67 Cambridge, Cambs. J 5
39 Cambridge, Glos. D 10
67 Cambridgeshire Co. K 5
134 Cambus H 3
147 Cambus o'May G 2
134 Cambusbarron H 3
134 Cambuskenneth H 3
119 Cambuslang C 11
138 Cambussorray F 7
50 Camden E 3
50 Cameley H 9
11 Camelford A 8
122 Camelon A 2
27 Camelsdale C 10
142 Camerory F 6
19 Camerton, Avon A 10
98 Camerton, Cumb. B 3
134 Camghouran B 1
139 Camisky L 5
147 Cammachmore H 6
86 Cammeringham B 6
118 Campbeltown G 2
115 Camperdown F 11
135 Campmuir C 7
67 Camps Green L 7
94 Campsall F 3
71 Campsea Ashe K 6
67 Campton L 2
114 Camptown B 5
34 Camrose E 3
134 Camserney B 3
151 Camster C 11
139 Camus-luinie G 3
130 Camuschoirk A 5
150 Camusnagoul G 2
138 Camusteel E 1
134 Camusvrachan B 1
26 Canada D 4
147 Candacraig G 1
146 Candacraig House F 1
87 Candlesby C 11
147 Candy J 5
122 Candy Mill E 3
47 Cane End F 8
51 Canewdon D 9
50 Canfield End B 6
26 Canford Bottom F 2
26 Canford Magna F 2
151 Canisbay A 12
19 Cann D 12
19 Cann Common D 12
11 Cannaframe B 9
19 Cannards Grave B 9
138 Canncih F 7
18 Cannington B 6
62 Cannock A 3
62 Cannock Wood A 4
39 Cannop C 9
55 Canon Bridge H 10
55 Canon Pyon G 10
114 Canonbie E 2
63 Canons Ashby G 9
10 Canonstown F 2
31 Canterbury B 10
70 Cantley, Norfolk E 7
94 Cantley, S. Yorks. G 4
38 Canton G 5
142 Cantraybruich E 3
142 Cantraydoune E 3
142 Cantraywood E 3
99 Cantsfield H 8
51 Canvey F 8
87 Canwick C 7
10 Canworthy Water B 2
139 Caol M 5
139 Caonich K 4
30 Capel D 1
54 Capel-Bangor D 2
54 Capel Betws Lleucu G 2
74 Capel Carmel G 1
74 Capel Curig D 6
74 Capel Cynon B 7
35 Capel Dewi, Dyfed E 8
54 Capel Dewi, Dyfed D 2
35 Capel Dewi, Dyfed C 8
75 Capel Garmon E 7
35 Capel Gwyn E 8
35 Capel Gwynfe E 10
35 Capel Hendre F 9
35 Capel Isaac D 9
34 Capel Iwan C 6
31 Capel le Ferne D 11
38 Capel Llanilterne F 4
71 Capel St. Andrew K 7
71 Capel St. Mary L 4
54 Capel Seion D 2
54 Capel Trisant E 3
34 Capel Tygwydd C 6
74 Capel-côch B 4
74 Capel-gwyn C 3
35 Capel-lago C 9
74 Capel-uchaf E 4
75 Capelulo C 7
38 Capel-y-ffin A 6
78 Capenhurst C 2
99 Capenwray H 8
115 Capheaton E 8
122 Cappercleuch G 5
122 Capplegill H 4
15 Capton, Devon K 7
18 Capton, Somerset B 4
134 Caputh C 6
86 Car Colston F 4
10 Carbis Bay F 2
154 Carbost, Skye E 3
154 Carbost, Skye C 4
150 Carbreck B 4
86 Carbrook A 1
70 Carbrooke E 3
86 Carburton C 3
11 Carclaze D 7
119 Carcluie H 8
94 Carcroft F 3
135 Cardenden H 7
55 Cardeston A 9
38 Cardiff G 5
34 Cardigan B 5
67 Cardington, Bedfordshire K 2
55 Cardington, Salop. C 10
11 Cardinham C 8
110 Cardorcan D 5
142 Cardow E 7
122 Cardrona F 6
119 Cardross B 8
111 Cardurnock F 12
66 Careby D 1
147 Careston L 3
34 Carew G 4
34 Carew Cheriton G 4
34 Carew Newton F 4
114 Carewoodrig C 3
39 Carey A 9
119 Carfin D 12
123 Carfrae B 8
111 Cargenbridge D 10
134 Cargill C 6
114 Cargo G 2
11 Cargreen C 11
123 Carham F 10
18 Carhampton B 3
10 Carharrack F 4
134 Carie A 1
26 Carisbrooke G 6
98 Cark G 6
11 Carkeel D 11
10 Carland Cross D 5
114 Carlatton Mill H 4
66 Carlby D 2
91 Carlecotes G 10
10 Carleen G 3
114 Carleton, Cumb. H 3
110 Carleton, Dumf. & Gall. H 5
91 Carleton, N. Yorks. B 8
70 Carleton Forehoe E 4
70 Carleton Rode F 4
10 Carlidnack G 5
107 Carlin How C 7
39 Carlingcott H 10
114 Carlisle G 2
122 Carlops D 4
155 Carloway C 3
67 Carlton, Beds. K 1
67 Carlton, Cambs. K 7
106 Carlton, Cleveland C 4
63 Carlton, Leics. B 7
106 Carlton, N. Yorks. F 6
106 Carlton, N. Yorks. G 1
94 Carlton, N. Yorks. E 4
86 Carlton, Notts. F 3
91 Carlton, S. Yorks. F 12
71 Carlton, Suffolk J 7
94 Carlton, W. Yorks. D 1
70 Carlton, Colville F 8
63 Carlton Curlieu B 10
106 Carlton Husthwaite G 5
106 Carlton in Cleveland E 5
86 Carlton in Lindrick B 3
106 Carlton Miniott G 4
86 Carlton Scroop F 6
86 Carlton-le-Moorland D 6
86 Carlton-on-Trent D 5
122 Carluke D 1
11 Carlyon Bay D 7
122 Carmacoup G 1
35 Carmarthen E 7
75 Carmel, Clwyd C 11
35 Carmel, Dyfed E 9
74 Carmel, Gwynedd E 4
74 Carmel, Gwynedd B 3
35 Carmel Chapel D 10
98 Carmel Fell F 6
155 Carminish H 1
147 Carmont J 5
119 Carmunnock D 11
119 Carmyle C 11
135 Carmyllie C 10
95 Carnaby A 9
139 Carnach, Highland L 1
139 Carnach, Highland G 4
155 Carnach, W. Isles G 3
151 Carnachy C 7
143 Carnachuin K 4
143 Carnaquheen K 8
135 Carnbee F 10
134 Carnbo G 5
139 Carndu G 3
119 Carnduff E 11
10 Carne F 6
119 Carnell F 9
38 Carnetown E 4
99 Carnforth H 7
139 Carn-gorm G 3
34 Carnhedryn Uchaf D 2
10 Carnhell Green F 3
155 Carnish D 1
10 Carnkie F 4
54 Carno C 5
139 Carnoch, Highland K 2
138 Carnoch, Highland F 7
138 Carnoch, Highland E 6
134 Carnock H 5
10 Carnon Downs F 5
135 Carnoustie D 10
122 Carnwath E 3
75 Carog E 7
154 Caroy D 2
99 Carperby F 12
86 Carr A 2
90 Carr Cross F 3
114 Carr Shield H 6
86 Carr Vale C 2
118 Carradale E 3
155 Carragrich G 3
143 Carrbridge G 5
91 Carrbrook G 8
74 Carreglefn A 3
34 Carregwen C 6
135 Carrick, Fife E 9
131 Carrick, Strathclyde H 9
122 Carriden A 3
90 Carrington, Manchester H 6
87 Carrington, Lincs. E 10
122 Carrington, Lothian C 6
75 Carrog F 10
122 Carron, Central A 2
142 Carron, Grampian E 8
119 Carron Bridge A 12
111 Carronbridge B 9
122 Carronshore A 2
119 Carrot E 10
39 Carrow Hill E 7
111 Carrutherstown D 11
106 Carrville A 3
118 Carsaig, Strathclyde A 2
130 Carsaig, Strathclyde E 3
110 Carscreugh F 3
118 Carse House C 2
110 Carsebuie E 4
110 Carsegown F 5
110 Carseriggan E 4
111 Carsethorn F 10
50 Carshalton G 3
79 Carsington E 11
118 Carskiey H 2
110 Carsluith F 6
110 Carsphairn B 6
122 Carstairs E 2
122 Carstairs Junction E 2
114 Carter Bar B 5
123 Carterhaugh G 7
26 Carter's Clay D 4
46 Carterton C 4
115 Carterway Heads H 8
11 Carthew D 7
106 Carthorpe G 3
115 Cartington C 8
122 Cartland E 1
98 Cartmel G 6
35 Carway F 8
19 Cary Fitzpaine D 9
155 Caryshader D 2
111 Carzield C 10
55 Cascob F 8
131 Cashlie C 12
26 Cashmoor E 1
46 Cassey Compton C 1
46 Cassington, Oxon C 5
19 Cassington, Som. B 7
106 Cassop A 4
66 Casswell's Bridge C 3
38 Castell-y-bwch E 6
99 Casterton G 8
70 Castle Acre D 1
63 Castle Ashby F 11
79 Castle Bank H 7
99 Castle Bolton F 12
62 Castle Bromwich C 5
66 Castle Bytham D 1
55 Castle Caereinion B 7
67 Castle Camps L 7
114 Castle Carrock G 4
19 Castle Cary C 10
39 Castle Combe F 11
86 Castle Donnington G 2
111 Castle Douglas E 8
46 Castle Eaton E 2
106 Castle Eden A 4
146 Castle Forbes F 4
55 Castle Frome H 12
47 Castle Green H 10
79 Castle Gresley H 11
123 Castle Heaton E 11
71 Castle Hedingham L 1
30 Castle Hill D 6
107 Castle Howard H 7
135 Castle Huntly D 8
114 Castle Kennedy F 2
34 Castle Morris D 3
114 Castle O'er D 1
55 Castle Pulverbatch B 9
66 Castle Rising C 8
142 Castle Stuart E 3
34 Castlebythe D 4
119 Castlecary B 12
122 Castlecraig, Borders E 4
142 Castlecraig, Highland C 4
111 Castlefairn C 8
94 Castleford E 2
122 Castlehill, Borders F 5
146 Castlehill, Grampian C 5
119 Castlehill, Strathclyde B 9
122 Castlehill, Strathclyde D 1
110 Castlemaddy C 6
34 Castlemartin G 3
111 Castlemilk D 12
39 Castlemorton A 11
115 Castleside H 9
63 Castlethorpe H 11
114 Castleton, Borders D 3
79 Castleton, Derby B 10
91 Castleton, Manchester F 7
38 Castleton, Gwent F 6
107 Castleton, N. Yorks D 7
118 Castleton, Strathclyde A 4
135 Castleton, Tayside C 8
19 Casteltown, Dorset H 7
151 Castletown, Highland A 11
142 Castletown, Highland E 3
98 Castletown, I.o.M. H 1
115 Castletown, Tyne & Wear G 11
91 Castley C 11
70 Caston F 2
66 Castor F 2
35 Caswell H 9
79 Cat and Fiddle Inn C 8
118 Catacol D 4
39 Catbrain F 9
39 Catbrook D 8
10 Catchall G 2
114 Catcleugh C 6
86 Catcliffe A 2
19 Catcott B 7
19 Catcott Burtle B 7
30 Caterham C 2
70 Catfield C 7
158 Catfirth D 7
50 Catford G 4
90 Catforth D 4
38 Cathays F 5
119 Cathcart C 10
38 Cathedine B 5
27 Catherington E 8
19 Catherston Leweston G 7
55 Catherton E 12
123 Cathpair E 7
111 Catlins C 12
143 Catlodge K 2
114 Catlowdy E 3
46 Catmore F 5
90 Caton A 4

K

119 Lenzie B 11
146 Leochel-Cushnie F 3
55 Leominster F 10
39 Leonard Stanley D 11
26 Lepe F 6
154 Lephin C 1
131 Lephinchapel H 7
131 Lephinmore H 7
94 Leppington A 5
91 Lepton F 10
130 Lerags E 6
11 Lerryn D 8
158 Lerwick E 7
115 Lesbury B 10
135 Leslie, Fife G 7
146 Leslie, Grampian E 3
122 Lesmahagow E 1
10 Lesnewth B 2
70 Lessingham C 7
114 Lessonhall H 1
110 Leswalt E 1
50 Letchmore Heath D 2
67 Letchworth M 3
46 Letcombe Bassett F 5
46 Letcombe Regis E 5
135 Letham, Fife F 8
135 Letham, Tayside B 10
134 Letham, Tayside E 6
135 Letham Grange C 11
142 Lethen House D 5
143 Lethendryveole H 5
146 Lethenty D 5
71 Letheringham J 6
70 Letheringsett B 4
15 Lettaford G 6
158 Lettan A 4
138 Letterewe C 3
139 Letterfearn G 3
139 Letterfinlay K 6
139 Lettermorar K 1
130 Lettermore C 2
150 Letters H 3
122 Lettershaws G 2
34 Letterston D 3
143 Lettoch, Highland H 6
142 Lettoch, Highland F 6
55 Letton, Heref. & Worc. E 9
55 Letton, Heref. & Worc. H 9
50 Letty Green C 3
86 Letwell B 3
135 Leuchars E 9
142 Leuchars House C 8
155 Leurbost D 5
62 Levedale A 3
95 Leven, Humberside C 8
135 Leven, Fife G 8
118 Levencorroch G 5
99 Levens G 7
91 Levenshulme H 7
158 Levenwick F 7
155 Leverburgh H 1
66 Leverington D 5
66 Leverton, Berks. G 4
87 Leverton, Lincs. E 11
87 Leverton Outgate E 11
71 Levington L 5
107 Levisham F 8
139 Levishie H 8
46 Lew D 4
11 Lewannick B 9
15 Lewdown G 3
30 Lewes G 3
34 Leweston E 3
50 Lewisham G 3
143 Lewiston G 1
38 Lewistown E 3
47 Lewknor D 8
14 Leworthy B 5
155 Lews Castle D 5
31 Lewson Street B 8
15 Lewtrenchard G 3
11 Ley, Cornwall C 9
146 Ley, Grampian F 3
30 Leybourne B 5
106 Leyburn F 1
78 Leycett E 6
50 Leygreen B 2
47 Leyhill D 10
90 Leyland E 4
146 Leylodge F 5
146 Leys B 7
142 Leys Castle F 2
135 Leys of Cossans B 8
146 Leys of Dummuies D 3
31 Leysdown-on-Sea A 9
135 Leysmill B 10
50 Leyton E 4
50 Leytonstone E 4
11 Lezant B 10
138 Liatrie F 6
38 Libanus B 3
122 Liberton, Lothian B 5
122 Libberton, Strathclyde E 3
62 Lichfield A 5
62 Lickey E 3
62 Lickey End E 3
27 Lickfold D 10
130 Liddesdale B 5
46 Liddington F 3
67 Lidgate J 8
67 Lidlington L 1
46 Lidstone B 4
139 Lienassie G 3
135 Liff D 8
15 Lifton G 3
15 Liftondown G 2
63 Lighthorne G 7
47 Lightwater H 10
79 Lightwood F 7
63 Lilbourne D 9
123 Lilburn Hill G 12
115 Lilburn Tower A 8
62 Lilleshall A 1
46 Lilley, Berks. F 5
50 Lilley, Herts. A 1
123 Lilliesleaf G 8
63 Lillingstone Dayrell H 10
63 Lillingstone Lovell H 10
19 Lillington, Dorest E 9
63 Lillington, War. E 7
26 Lilliput G 2
18 Lilstock B 5
119 Lilybank B 8
90 Limbrick F 5
91 Limefield F 7
119 Limekilnburn D 12
122 Limekilns A 3
122 Limerigg B 1
26 Limestone H 6
114 Limestone Brae H 6
19 Limington D 8
70 Limpenhoe E 7
39 Limpley Stoke H 11
30 Limpsfield C 3
122 Linburn C 4
86 Linby E 3
27 Linchmere C 10
111 Lincluden D 10
87 Lincoln C 7
87 Lincolnshire, Co. D 8
62 Lincomb E 2
98 Lindal in Furness H 5
98 Lindale G 6
123 Lindean F 7
30 Lindfield E 2
27 Lindford C 9
135 Lindifferon E 8
91 Lindley E 10
91 Lindley Green B 11
135 Lindores E 7
55 Lindridge E 12
50 Lindsell A 6
71 Lindsey L 3
98 Linefoot B 3
51 Linford, Essex F 7
26 Linford, Hants. E 3
98 Lingague H 1
107 Lingdale D 7
55 Lingen F 9
30 Lingfield D 3
30 Lingfield Com. D 3
78 Lingley Green A 4
70 Lingwood E 7
114 Linhope, Borders C 2
115 Linhope, N'thumb. A 8
46 Linkenholt H 5
11 Linkinhorne B 10
158 Linklater E 2
135 Linktown H 7
55 Linley Green G 12
122 Linlithgow B 3
122 Linlithgow Bridge B 3
150 Linneraineach F 3
34 Linney G 2
111 Linns D 11
155 Linshader D 3
115 Linshiels B 7
150 Linsidemore G 6
47 Linslade B 10
71 Linstead Parva G 6
114 Linstock G 3
123 Linthaugh F 12
91 Linthwaite F 9
123 Lintlaw D 11
146 Lintmill A 3
123 Linton, Borders G 10
67 Linton, Cambs. K 7
62 Linton, Derby A 6
39 Linton, Heref. & Worc. B 9
30 Linton, Kent C 6
91 Linton, N. Yorks. A 8
91 Linton, W. Yorks. B 12
94 Linton-on-Ouse A 3
26 Linwood, Hants. E 3
87 Linwood, Lincs. B 8
119 Linwood, Strathclyde C 9
75 Lioc C 10
155 Lionel A 6
27 Liphook C 9
18 Liscombe C 2
11 Liskeard C 9
27 Liss C 9
27 Liss Forest C 9
95 Lisset A 9
87 Lissington B 8
38 Lisvane F 5
39 Liswerry F 7
70 Litcham D 2
63 Litchborough G 9
26 Litchfield A 6
90 Litherland G 2
67 Litlington, Camb. L 4
30 Litlington, E. Sussex H 4
67 Little Abington K 6
67 Little Addington H 1
62 Little Alne F 5
150 Little Assynt E 3
62 Little Aston B 4
26 Little Atherfield H 6
158 Little Ayre E 1
106 Little Ayton D 6
51 Little Baddow C 7
39 Little Badminton F 11
134 Little Ballinluig B 4
114 Little Bampton G 1
67 Little Bardfield M 8
67 Little Barford J 3
70 Little Barningham B 4
46 Little Barrington C 3
78 Little Barrow C 3
107 Little Barugh G 8
115 Little Bavington E 8
71 Little Bealings K 5
46 Little Bedwyn G 4
51 Little Bentley A 11
50 Little Berkhampsted C 3
63 Little Billing F 11
39 Little Birch A 8
71 Little Blakenham K 4
99 Little Blencow B 7
27 Little Bookham A 12
63 Little Bowden C 11
67 Little Bradley K 8
55 Little Brampton D 9
51 Little Braxted B 8
147 Little Brechin L 3
47 Little Brickhill A 10
63 Little Brington F 10
51 Little Bromley A 10
78 Little Budworth D 5
50 Little Burstead E 6
66 Little Bytham D 1
110 Little Cairnbrock E 1
87 Little Carlton, Lincs. B 11
86 Little Carlton, Notts. D 5
66 Little Casterton E 1
87 Little Cawthorpe B 10
47 Little Chalfont D 11
31 Little Chart D 8
19 Little Cheney G 9
67 Little Chesterford L 6
26 Little Cheverell A 2
67 Little Chishill L 5
51 Little Clacton B 11
98 Little Clifton B 3
146 Little Colp C 5
62 Little Comberton H 3
46 Little Compton A 4
71 Little Cornard L 2
55 Little Cowarne G 11
46 Little Coxwell E 4
106 Little Crakehall F 3
70 Little Cressingham E 2
90 Little Crosby G 2
63 Little Dalby A 11
55 Little Dawley B 12
146 Little Dens C 8
39 Little Dewchurch A 8
95 Little Driffield A 8
70 Little Dunham D 2
134 Little Dunkeld C 5
50 Little Dunmow B 6
50 Little Easton B 6
79 Little Eaton F 12
70 Little Ellingham E 3
19 Little Elm B 10
50 Little End D 5
67 Little Eversden K 5
71 Little Fakenham H 2
46 Little Faringdon D 3
106 Little Fencote F 3
94 Little Fenton D 3
70 Little Fransham D 2
47 Little Gaddesden C 11
39 Little Garway B 8
67 Little Gidding G 2
71 Little Glemham J 6
67 Little Gransden K 4
19 Little Green A 10
87 Little Grimsby A 10
150 Little Gruinard G 1
50 Little Hadham B 4
66 Little Hale B 2
50 Little Hallingbury B 5
47 Little Hampden D 9
63 Little Harrowden E 12
47 Little Haseley D 7
95 Little Hatfield C 9
34 Little Haven F 2
62 Little Hay B 5
79 Little Hayfield A 9
79 Little Haywood H 8
55 Little Hereford F 11
71 Little Horkesley M 2
50 Little Hormead A 4
30 Little Horsted F 3
91 Little Horton D 10
47 Little Horwood A 9
63 Little Houghton F 11
79 Little Hucklow B 10
90 Little Hulton G 6
63 Little Irchester E 12
95 Little Kelk A 8
47 Little Kimble C 9
47 Little Kingshill D 10
98 Little Langdale E 5
26 Little Langford C 2
146 Little Ledikin E 4
78 Little Leigh C 5
51 Little Leighs B 7
90 Little Lever F 6
63 Little Linford H 11
30 Little Londond, E. Sussex F 4
26 Little London, Hants. A 5
47 Little London, Hants. H 7
66 Little London, Lincs. C 5
91 Little London, W. Yorks. C 10
79 Little Longstone C 10
146 Little Lynturk F 3
62 Little Malvern H 1
71 Little Maplestead M 1
39 Little Marcle A 10
47 Little Marlow E 9
70 Little Massingham C 1
70 Little Melton E 5
34 Little Milford F 3
38 Little Mill D 6
47 Little Milton D 7
47 Little Missenden D 10
78 Little Ness H 3
78 Little Neston C 2
34 Little Newcastle D 3
106 Little Newsham C 1
51 Little Oakley, Essex A 12
63 Little Oakley, Northants. D 12
114 Little Orton G 2
94 Little Ouseburn A 2
67 Little Paxton J 3
10 Little Petherick B 6
110 Little Pinmore C 3
70 Little Plumstead D 6
86 Little Ponton G 6
14 Little Potheridge E 4
67 Little Raveley G 4
91 Little Ribson B 12
46 Little Rissington B 3
70 Little Ryburgh C 3
115 Little Ryle B 8
99 Little Salkeld B 8
26 Little Samborne C 5
67 Little Sampford M 7
47 Little Sandhurst H 9
71 Little Saxham J 1
138 Little Scatwell D 7
67 Little Shelford K 5
14 Little Silver, Devon F 7
18 Little Silver, Devon E 3
90 Little Singleton C 3
94 Little Smeaton E 3
70 Little Snoring B 2
39 Little Sodbury F 10
46 Little Somerford F 1
106 Little Stainton C 4
78 Little Stanney C 3
67 Little Staughton J 2
87 Little Steeping D 11
71 Little Stonham J 4
63 Little Stretton, Leics. B 10
55 Little Stretton, Shropshire C 10
99 Little Strickland C 8
67 Little Stukeley H 3
115 Little Swinburne E 8
123 Little Swinton E 11
46 Little Tew A 5
67 Little Thetford H 6
67 Little Thurlow K 8
50 Little Thurrock F 6
110 Little Torhouse F 5
14 Little Torrington D 4
115 Little Tosson C 8
51 Little Totham C 9
98 Little Town C 5
142 Little Urchany E 4
98 Little Urswick H 5
51 Little Wakering E 9
71 Little Waldingfield L 2
70 Little Walsingham B 2
51 Little Waltham C 7
50 Little Warley E 6
95 Little Weighton D 7
71 Little Welnetham J 2
55 Little Wenlock B 12
71 Little Whittingham Green H 6
115 Little Whittington F 8
67 Little Wilbraham J 6
26 Little Wishford B 2
62 Little Witley F 1
46 Little Wittenham E 6
46 Little Wolford A 3
63 Little Woolstone H 12
67 Little Wymington J 1
50 Little Wymondley A 2
62 Little Wyrley B 4
71 Little Yeldam L 1
158 Little-ayre C 6
107 Littlebeck E 9
91 Littleborough, Manchester F 8
86 Littleborough, Notts. B 5
31 Littlebourne B 10
19 Littlebredy G 9
67 Littlebury L 6
90 Littledale A 4
39 Littledean C 10
151 Littleferry G 8
14 Littleham, Devon D 3
18 Littleham, Devon H 4
27 Littlehampton F 11
15 Littlehempston J 7
115 Littlehoughton A 10
147 Littlemill, Grampian H 1
142 Littlemill, Highland E 5
115 Littlemill, Northumb. A 10
119 Littlemill, Strathclyde H 9
46 Littlemore D 6
79 Littleover G 11
67 Littleport G 7
67 Littleport Bridge G 7
31 Littlestone-on-Sea F 9
106 Littlethorpe H 3
78 Littleton, Ches. D 3
111 Littleton, Dumf. & Gall. F 7
26 Littleton, Hants. C 6
19 Littleton, Som. C 8
27 Littleton, Surrey A 11
47 Littleton, Surrey G 11
135 Littleton, Tayside D 7
39 Littleton Drew F 11
26 Littleton Panell A 2
39 Littleton upon Severn E 9
106 Littletown A 4
47 Littlewick Green F 9
39 Littleworth, Glos. D 11
46 Littleworth, Oxon D 4
62 Littleworth, Heref. & Worc. G 2
62 Littleworth, Staffs. A 4
79 Littleworth, Staffs. H 8
30 Littleworth, W. Sussex F 1
79 Litton, Derby C 10
99 Litton, N. Yorks. H 11
19 Litton, Som. A 9
78 Liverpool A 2
91 Liversedge E 10
107 Liverton, Cleveland D 7
15 Liverton, Devon H 7
122 Livingston C 3
75 Lixwm C 11
10 Lizard H 4
74 Llaingoch B 2
54 Llaithddu D 6
54 Llan B 4
38 Llan-Rumney F 5
74 Llanaber H 5
74 Llanaelhaearn F 3
35 Llanaeron A 8
54 Llanafan E 2
54 Llanafan-fawr G 5
54 Llanafan-fechan G 5
74 Llanallgo B 4
74 Llanarmon F 4
75 Llanarmon Dyffryn Ceiriog G 10
75 Llanarmon-yn-Ial E 11
35 Llanarth, Dyfed A 7
39 Llanarth, Gwent C 7
35 Llanarthney E 8
75 Llanasa B 10
74 Llanbabo B 3
54 Llanbadarn Fawr D 2
54 Llanbadarn Fynydd E 6
55 Llanbadarn-y- garreg G 7
39 Llanbadoc D 7
74 Llanbadrig A 3
39 Llanbeder E 7
74 Llanbedr, Gwynedd H 5
38 Llanbedr, Powys B 6
55 Llanbedr, Powys H 7
75 Llanbedr-Dyffryn-Clwyd D 10
74 Llanbedr-goch B 4
74 Llanbedrog G 3
75 Llanbedr C 7
74 Llanberis D 5
38 Llanbethery G 4
54 Llanbister E 6
38 Llanblethian G 3
34 Llanboidy E 5
38 Llanbradach E 5
142 Llanbryde D 8
54 Llanbrynmair B 5
38 Llancadle G 4
38 Llancarfan G 4
39 Llancayo D 7
39 Llancloudy B 8
55 Llancoch E 7
38 Llandaff F 5
74 Llandanwg G 5
35 Llandarcy G 10
34 Llandawke F 6
74 Llanddaniel Fab C 4
35 Llanddarog E 8
54 Llanddeiniol E 1
74 Llanddeiniolen D 5
75 Llandderfel F 9
35 Llanddeusant, Dyfed E 11
74 Llanddeusant, Gwynedd B 3
38 Llanddew A 4
35 Llanddewi H 8
54 Llanddewi-Brefi G 2
39 Llanddewi Rhydderch C 7
34 Llanddewi Velfrey E 5
54 Llanddewi'r Cwm G 6
75 Llanddoget D 7
74 Llanddona B 5
34 Llanddowror F 6
75 Llanddulas B 8
74 Llanddyfnan B 4
38 Llandefaelog Fach A 4
38 Llandefaelog ter-graig A 4
38 Llandefalle A 4
74 Llandegai C 5
74 Llandegfan C 5
39 Llandegfedd E 7
75 Llandegla E 11
55 Llandegley F 7
35 Llandeilo E 9
54 Llandeilo Graban H 6
38 Llandeilo'r Fan A 2
74 Llandeloy D 2
39 Llandenny D 7
39 Llandevenny F 7
34 Llandewi Velfrey E 5
54 Llandewi Ystradenny E 6
34 Llandilo D 4
39 Llandinabo A 8
54 Llandinam D 6
34 Llandissilio E 5
39 Llandogo D 8
38 Llandough, S. Glam. G 5
38 Llandough, S. Glam. G 3
35 Llandovery D 11
38 Llandow G 3
54 Llandre, Dyfed D 2
35 Llandre, Dyfed C 10
75 Llandrillo F 9
75 Llandrillo-yn-Rhos. B 7
54 Llandrindod Wells F 6
55 Llandrinio A 8
75 Llandudno B 7
75 Llandudno Junc. B 7
74 Llandwrog E 4
35 Llandybie E 9
35 Llandyfaelog F 7
35 Llandyfan E 9
35 Llandyfriog C 7
74 Llandyfrydog B 4
34 Llandygwydd C 6
75 Llandyrnog D 10
75 Llandysilio H 12
55 Llandyssil C 7
35 Llandyssul C 7
38 Llanedeyrn F 5
54 Llaneglwys H 6
54 Llanegryn B 2
35 Llanegwad E 8
74 Llaneilian A 4
75 Llanelian-y-Rhos C 8
75 Llanelidan E 10
38 Llanelieu A 5
38 Llanellen C 6
35 Llanelli, Dyfed G 8
38 Llanelli, Gwent C 5
74 Llanelltyd H 6
54 Llanelwedd G 6
74 Llanenddwyn H 5
74 Llanengan G 2
74 Llanerchymedd B 4
54 Llanerfyl A 6
74 Llanfachraeth B 3
75 Llanfachreth H 7
74 Llanfaelog C 3
74 Llanfaelrhys G 2
39 Llanfaenor C 7
74 Llanfaes, Gwynedd C 5
38 Llanfaes, Powys B 4
74 Llanfaethlu B 3
74 Llanfalgan D 4
74 Llanfair G 5
54 Llanfair-Caereinion B 6
54 Llanfair-Clydogau G 2
75 Llanfair Dyffryn Clwyd E 10
34 Llanfair Nant-Gwyn C 5
75 Llanfair Talhaiarn C 8
55 Llandfair Waterdine E 8
74 Llanfairfechan C 6
74 Llanfair-P.G. C 5
74 Llanfairpwllgwngyll C 5
74 Llanfairynghornwy A 3
74 Llanfair-yn-Neubwll C 2
34 Llanfallteg E 5
34 Llanfallteg West E 5
54 Llanfaredd G 6
54 Llanfarian E 2
75 Llanfechain H 11
74 Llanfechell A 3
54 Llanfendigaid B 1
75 Llanferres D 11
74 Llanfflewyn A 3
74 Llanfigael B 3
54 Llanfihangel A 6
38 Llanfihangel Crucorney B 6
75 Llanfihangel Glyn Myfyr E 9
38 Llanfihangel Nant Bran A 3
55 Llanfihangel Rhydithon F 7
39 Llanfihangel Rogiet F 8
38 Llanfihangel Tal-y-llyn A 4
35 Llanfihangel ar-arth C 8
55 Llanfihangel-nant-Melan G 7
35 Llanfihangel-uwch-Gwili E 8
54 Llanfihangel-y-Creuddyn E 2
74 Llanfihangel yn Nhowyn C 3
54 Llanfihangel-y-Pennant B 2
74 Llanfihangel-y-Pennant F 5
74 Llanfihangel-y-Traethau G 5
38 Llanfilo A 4
38 Llanfoist C 6
35 Llanfor G 8
38 Llanfrechfa E 6
74 Llanfrothen F 5
38 Llanfrynach B 4
75 Llanfwrog, Clwyd D 10
74 Llanfwrog, Gwynedd B 2
75 Llanfyllin H 10
75 Llanfynydd, Clwyd E 12
35 Llanfynydd, Dyfed D 9
34 Llanfyrnach D 6
54 Llangadfan A 6
35 Llangadog, Dyfed D 10
35 Llangadog, Dyfed F 7
75 Llangadwaladr, Clwyd G 11
74 Llangadwaladr, Gwynedd C 3
74 Llangaffo C 4
35 Llangain E 7
54 Llangammarch Wells H 5
38 Llangan G 3
39 Llangarron B 8
38 Llangasty-Tal-y-llyn B 5
35 Llangathen E 9
38 Llangattock C 5
39 Llangattock Lingoed B 7
38 Llangattock nigh Usk C 6
39 Llangattock Vibon-Avel C 8
75 Llangedwyn H 11
74 Llangefni C 4
38 Llangeinor F 2
74 Llangeinwen D 4
54 Llangeitho F 2

31 Old Romney E 9
134 Old Scone D 6
94 Old Snydale E 2
39 Old Sodbury F 10
87 Old Somerby G 7
63 Old Stratford H 11
78 Old Swan A 3
99 Old Tebay E 8
106 Old Thirsk G 4
99 Old Town, Cumb. A 7
99 Old Town, Cumbria G 8
10 Old Town, Is. of Scilly D 2
115 Old Town, Northumb. D 7
86 Old Tupton D 1
67 Old Warden L 2
67 Old Weston H 2
47 Old Windsor G 10
31 Old Wives Lees C 9
47 Old Woking H 11
150 Oldany D 3
62 Oldberrow F 5
14 Oldborough E 6
55 Oldbury, Salop C 12
62 Oldbury, War. C 6
62 Oldbury, W. Midlands C 3
39 Oldbury on the Hill E 11
39 Oldbury-upon-Severn E 9
38 Oldcastle, Gwent B 6
38 Oldbury, Mid Glam. F 2
86 Oldcotes A 3
62 Oldfield, Heref. & Worc. F 2
91 Oldfield, W. Yorks. C 8
19 Oldford A 11
91 Oldham G 8
123 Oldhamstocks B 10
39 Oldland G 10
146 Oldmeldrum E 6
146 Oldnoth D 3
55 Oldpark A 12
150 Oldshore Beg B 3
150 Oldshore More B 3
106 Oldstead G 5
146 Oldtown of Ord B 4
38 Oldway H 9
14 Oldways End D 7
146 Oldwhat C 6
122 Oliver G 4
26 Oliver's Battery C 6
158 Ollaberry C 7
78 Ollerton, Ches. C 6
86 Ollerton, Notts. C 4
78 Ollerton, Salop H 5
54 Olmarch G 2
63 Olney G 12
62 Olton D 5
39 Olveston F 9
62 Ombersley F 2
86 Ompton D 4
114 Once Brewed F 6
98 Onchan H 2
79 Onecote E 9
39 Onen C 7
55 Ongar D 5
66 Onger Hill C 7
55 Onibury D 10
131 Onich A 7
38 Onllwyn C 2
55 Ongar Street F 9
78 Onneley F 6
27 Onslow Village A 11
119 Onthank E 9
91 Openshaw G 7
86 Openwoodgate E 1
138 Opinan, Highland C 1
150 Opinan, Highland G 1
123 Orange Lane E 10
114 Orbost D 2
87 Orby C 12
118 Orcadia C 6
14 Orchard Hill C 3
18 Orchard Portman D 6
26 Orcheston B 2
39 Orcop B 8
39 Orcop Hill A 8
154 Ord G 5
158 Ordale A 8
146 Ordens B 4
146 Ordhead F 4
147 Ordie G 2
146 Ordiequish B 1
86 Ordsall B 4
31 Ore G 7
78 Orford, Cheshire A 5
55 Oreton, Salop D 12
71 Orford, Suffolk K 7
26 Organford G 1
158 Orgill D 1
62 Orgreave A 5
158 Orkney, Co. C 2
31 Orlestone E 8
55 Orleton, Heref. & Worc. F 10
55 Orleton, Heref. & Worc. F 12
63 Orlingbury E 12
106 Ormesby C 5
70 Ormesby St. Margaret D 8
70 Ormesby St. Michael D 8
150 Ormiscaig G 1
123 Ormiston B 7
98 Ormely Hall F 2
130 Ormsaigbeg A 2
130 Ormsaigmore A 2
118 Ormsary House B 2
90 Ormskirk F 3
155 Orosay F 5
158 Orphir D 2
50 Orpington G 5
90 Orrell, Merseyside G 2
90 Orrell, Manchester G 4
90 Orrell Post G 4
135 Orrock H 7
50 Orsett F 6
50 Orsett Heath F 6
62 Orslow A 2
86 Orston F 5
98 Orthwaite B 5
99 Orton, Cumbria D 8
63 Orton, Northants. D 11
66 Orton Longueville F 3
62 Orton on the Hill B 6
146 Orton Station B 1
66 Orton Waterville F 3
67 Orwell K 5
90 Osbaldeston D 5
94 Osbaldwick B 4
63 Osbaston B 7
66 Osbournby B 2
151 Osclay D 11
78 Oscroft D 4
154 Ose D 2
86 Osgathorpe H 2
87 Osgodby, Lincs. A 8
94 Osgodby, N. Yorks. D 4
107 Osgodby, N. Yorks. G 10
154 Oskaig D 5
130 Oskamuil D 2
79 Osmaston F 10
19 Osmington H 10
19 Osmington Mills H 10
91 Osmondthorpe D 12
106 Osmotherley E 5
31 Ospringe B 8
91 Ossett E 11
86 Ossington D 5
51 Ostend D 9
106 Oswaldkirk G 6
90 Oswaldtwistle D 6
78 Oswestry G 2
30 Otford B 4
31 Otham C 7
19 Othery C 7
71 Otley, Suffolk K 5
91 Otley, W. Yorks. C 10
118 Otter Ferry A 4
26 Otterbourne D 6
115 Otterburn, Northumb. D 7
91 Otterburn, N. Yorks. A 7
115 Otterburn Camp C 7
10 Otterham B 2
18 Otterhampton B 6
47 Ottershaw H 11
158 Otterswick B 7
18 Otterton H 4
18 Ottery St. Mary G 5
31 Ottinge D 10
95 Ottingham E 10
99 Oughtershaw G 11
111 Oughterside H 12
91 Oughtibridge H 11
106 Oulston H 6
114 Oulton, Cumb. H 1
70 Oulton, Norfolk C 4
79 Oulton, Staffs. G 7
70 Oulton, Suffolk F 8
91 Oulton, W. Yorks. D 12
70 Oulton Broad F 8
70 Oulton Street C 5
67 Oundle G 1
99 Ousby B 8
151 Ousdale E 10
67 Ousden J 8
94 Ousefleet E 6
115 Ouston, Dur. H 10
115 Ouston, Northumb. F 9
114 Ouston, Northumb. H 6
98 Out Gate E 6
95 Out Newton E 11
90 Out Rawcliffe C 3
115 Outchester C 12
158 Outertown D 1
99 Outhgill E 10
91 Outlane E 9
66 Outwell E 6
50 Outwick D 3
30 Outwood, Surrey D 2
91 Outwood, W. Yorks. E 12
91 Ovenden D 9
123 Ovenscloss F 7
67 Over, Cambs. H 5
78 Over, Cheshire D 5
39 Over, Glos. F 9
19 Over Compton E 9
122 Over Dalgleish H 5
79 Over Haddon D 10
111 Over Hazlefield G 8
99 Over Kellet H 7
99 Over Kiddlington B 5
46 Over Norton A 4
106 Over Silton F 5
18 Over Stowey B 5
19 Over Stratton E 8
78 Over Tabley B 6
26 Over Wallop B 4
62 Over Whitacre C 6
123 Over Whitton G 10
86 Over Woodhouse C 2
158 Overbister B 4
62 Overbury H 3
146 Overhall C 5
19 Overleigh C 8
62 Oversley Green F 4
78 Overpool C 3
62 Overseal A 6
146 Overside B 8
31 Oversland B 9
63 Overstone E 11
70 Overstrand B 5
63 Overthorpe H 8
78 Overton, Ches. C 4
78 Overton, Clwyd F 2
111 Overton, Dumf. & Gall. E 10
146 Overton, Grampian F 6
146 Overton, Grampian D 7
26 Overton, Hants. A 6
90 Overton, Lancs. A 3
94 Overton, N. Yorks. B 3
55 Overton, Salop E 10
119 Overton, Strathclyde D 8
35 Overton, W. Glam. H 8
75 Overton Bridge F 12
78 Overton Green D 6
122 Overtown, Strathclyde D 1
99 Overtown, Lancs. H 8
46 Overtown, Wilts. F 3
146 Overtown of Memsie B 7
70 Overy Staithe A 1
47 Oving, Bucks. B 8
27 Oving, W. Sussex F 10
30 Ovingdean H 2
115 Ovingham G 9
106 Ovington, Durham D 2
71 Ovington, Essex L 1
27 Ovington, Hants. C 7
70 Ovington, Norfolk E 2
115 Ovington, Northumb. G 9
26 Ower D 5
19 Owermoigne H 11
79 Owler Bar B 11
86 Owlerton A 1
47 Owlswick C 8
87 Owmby-by-Spital B 7
26 Owslebury D 6
63 Owston, Leics. A 11
94 Owston, S. Yorks. F 3
94 Owston Ferry G 6
95 Owstwick D 10
86 Owthorpe G 4
66 Oxborough E 8
87 Oxcombe C 10
98 Oxen Park F 5
99 Oxenholme F 8
91 Oxenhope D 9
123 Oxenrig E 11
46 Oxenton A 1
46 Oxenwood H 4
46 Oxford D 6
14 Oxford Cross B 3
46 Oxfordshire, Co. C 5
50 Oxhey D 1
62 Oxhill G 6
62 Oxley B 2
51 Oxley Green C 9
123 Oxnam G 9
47 Oxshott H 12
91 Oxspring G 11
30 Oxted C 3
123 Oxton, Borders D 7
86 Oxton, Notts. E 3
94 Oxton, N. Yorks. C 3
35 Oxwich H 8
35 Oxwich Green H 8
150 Oykel Bridge G 5
146 Oyne E 4
35 Oystermouth H 9

P

19 Packers Hill E 10
63 Packington A 7
62 Packington Park D 5
135 Padanaram B 9
47 Padbury A 8
50 Paddington F 3
31 Paddlesworth D 10
30 Paddock Wood D 5
142 Paddockhaugh D 8
114 Paddockhole E 1
78 Paddolgreen G 4
91 Padfield G 9
78 Padgate A 5
91 Padiham D 7
75 Padog E 8
91 Padside A 10
10 Padstow B 6
47 Padworth G 7
106 Page Bank B 3
27 Pagham F 10
51 Paglesham E 9
155 Paible G 1
15 Paignton K 8
63 Pailton D 8
55 Painscastle H 7
115 Painshawfield G 9
39 Painswick C 12
31 Painter's Forstal B 8
119 Paisley C 9
146 Paithnick B 2
70 Pakefield F 8
71 Pakenham J 2
75 Pale G 9
30 Palehouse Com. F 4
26 Palestine B 4
47 Paley Street G 9
110 Palgowan C 5
71 Palgrave G 4
31 Palmarsh E 10
50 Palmers Green E 3
111 Palnackie F 9
110 Palnure E 5
86 Palterton C 2
47 Pamber End H 7
47 Pamber Green H 7
47 Pamber Heath H 7
26 Pamphill F 1
67 Pampisford K 6
19 Panborough B 8
135 Panbride D 10
14 Pancrasweek E 2
75 Pandy, Clwyd G 11
39 Pandy, Gwent B 7
54 Pandy, Gwynedd B 2
54 Pandy, Powys B 5
75 Pandy Tudor D 8
51 Panfield A 7
47 Pangbourne F 7
111 Panlands C 11
91 Pannal B 11
147 Pannancih H 1
78 Pant H 1
54 Pant Mawr D 4
74 Pant-glas, Gwynedd E 4
55 Pantglas, Salop C 8
35 Pantgwyn, Dyfed D 9
34 Pantgwyn, Dyfed B 6
35 Pant-lasau G 10
87 Panton B 9
54 Pant-perthog B 3
54 Pant-y-dwr E 5
55 Pant-y-ffrid B 7
35 Pantyffynnon F 9
38 Pantygasseg D 5
39 Pant y Goitre C 7
34 Pantymenyn D 5
75 Pantymwyn D 11
38 Pant-yr-awel E 3
70 Panxworth D 6
98 Papcastle B 3
123 Papple B 8
86 Papplewick E 3
67 Papworth Everard J 4
67 Papworth St. Agnes J 4
11 Par D 8
90 Parbold F 4
18 Parbrook C 9
75 Parc G 8
34 Parcllyn B 6
98 Pardshaw C 3
71 Parham J 6
111 Park, Dumf. & Gall. B 10
147 Park, Grampian G 5
130 Park, Strathclyde C 6
47 Park Corner, Berks. F 9
30 Park Corner, E. Sussex D 4
106 Park End, Cleveland C 5
115 Park End, Northumb. E 7
27 Park Gate E 7
114 Park Nook F 4
146 Parkdargue C 4
98 Parkend, Cumb. A 5
39 Parkend, Glos. D 9
71 Parkeston M 5
78 Parkgate, Ches. B 1
111 Parkgate, Dumf. & Gall. C 11
30 Parkgate, Surrey D 1
122 Parkgatestone F 4
14 Parkham D 3
14 Parkham Ash D 2
142 Parkhead F 8
146 Parkhill House F 6
39 Parkhouse D 8
26 Parkhurst G 6
35 Parkmill H 9
147 Parkneuk K 5
78 Parkside E 3
26 Parkstone G 2
26 Parley Cross F 2
14 Parracombe B 5
78 Parrah Green F 6
79 Parsley Hay D 10
66 Parson Drove E 5
51 Parson's Heath A 10
119 Partick C 10
90 Partington H 6
87 Partney C 11
98 Parton, Cumb. C 2
111 Parton, Dumf. & Gall. E 8
39 Parton, Glos. B 12
30 Partridge Green F 1
79 Parwich E 10
63 Passenham H 11
27 Passfield C 9
70 Paston B 6
14 Patchacott F 3
30 Patcham G 2
27 Patching E 12
14 Patchole B 5
39 Pathway F 9
91 Pateley Bridge A 10
51 Paternoster Heath B 9
134 Path of Condie F 5
19 Pathe C 7
135 Pathead, Fife H 8
122 Pathead, Lothian C 6
119 Pathhead H 11
134 Pathstruie F 5
119 Patna H 9
46 Patney H 2
98 Patrick G 1
106 Patrick Brompton F 2
90 Patricroft G 6
95 Patrington E 10
31 Patrixbourne C 10
98 Patterdale D 6
114 Pattieshill F 3
62 Pattingham B 2
63 Pattishall G 10
51 Pattiswick Green B 8
10 Paul G 2
63 Paulerspury G 10
95 Paull E 9
19 Paulton A 10
115 Pauperhaugh C 9
67 Pavenham K 1
18 Pawlett B 6
123 Pawston F 11
62 Paxford H 5
123 Paxton D 12
18 Payhembury F 4
91 Paythorne B 7
30 Peacehaven H 3
79 Peak Dale C 9
79 Peak Forest B 9
146 Peaknowe B 4
139 Peanmeanach L 1
147 Pearsie L 1
30 Pearsons Green D 6
30 Pease Pottage E 1
19 Peasedown St. John A 10
46 Peasemore F 5
71 Peasenhall H 7
27 Peaslake B 12
31 Peasmarsh F 7
123 Peaston Bank C 7
135 Peat Inn F 9
146 Peathill A 7
63 Peatling Magna C 9
63 Peatling Parva C 9
55 Peaton D 10
71 Pebmarsh M 2
62 Pebworth G 5
91 Peckett Well D 8
78 Peckforton E 4
50 Peckham F 3
63 Peckleton B 8
114 Pedderhill F 3
31 Pedlinge E 10
62 Pedmore D 3
19 Pedwell C 8
122 Peebles E 5
98 Peel G 1
27 Peel Common F 7
31 Peening Quarter E 7
67 Pegsdon M 2
115 Pegswood D 10
154 Peinaha B 4
154 Peinchorran E 4
154 Peinlich B 3
154 Peinmore C 4
34 Pelcomb Cross E 3
51 Peldon B 9
62 Pelsall B 4
115 Pelton H 10
115 Pelton Fell H 10
111 Pelutho G 12
11 Pelynt D 9
35 Pemberton, Dyfed G 8
90 Pemberton, Manchester G 4
35 Pembrey G 7
55 Pembridge G 9
34 Pembroke G 3
34 Pembroke Dock G 3
30 Pembury D 5
35 Pen Rhiwfawr F 10
19 Pen Selwood C 11
35 Pen-Sarn E 7
39 Penalt C 8
34 Penally G 5
39 Penalt A 9
11 Penare F 7
38 Penarth G 5
54 Pen-bont-rhyd-y-beddau D 2
34 Penbryn B 6
35 Pencader C 8
35 Pen-cae A 7
74 Pencaenewydd F 3
74 Pencarnisiog C 3
35 Pencarreg C 8
38 Pencelli E 3
35 Penclawdd G 9
38 Pencoed F 3
39 Pencoid B 8
55 Pencombe G 11
39 Pencraig, Heref. & Worc. B 9
75 Pencraig, Powys G 9
10 Pendeen F 1
38 Penderyn C 3
34 Pendine F 6
90 Pendlebury G 6
90 Pendleton, Lancs. C 6
91 Pendleton, Manchester G 7
39 Pendock A 11
11 Pendoggett B 7
19 Pendomer E 8
38 Pendoylan G 4
38 Pendre F 2
54 Penegoes B 3
34 Penfeidir D 2
35 Pen-ffordd, Dyfed C 8
34 Pen-ffordd, Dyfed E 4
38 Pengam D 5
50 Penge G 3
11 Pengelly A 8
38 Pengenffordd A 5
11 Pengover Green C 10
38 Pen-groes oped D 6
10 Penhale H 4
10 Penhalurick F 4
46 Penhill E 2
39 Penhow E 7
30 Penhurst F 6
54 Peniarth B 2
122 Penicuik C 5
35 Peniel E 8
154 Penifiler D 4
118 Peninver G 4
74 Penisar-waum D 5
91 Penistone G 11
78 Penketh A 4
110 Penkill B 3
110 Penkiln G 6
62 Penkridge A 3
78 Penley F 3
35 Penllergaer G 9
74 Pen-llyn, Gwynedd B 3
38 Penllyn, S. Glam. G 3
75 Penmachno E 7
35 Penmaen H 8
74 Penmaenen C 6
74 Penmaenmawr C 6
74 Penmaenpool H 6
75 Penmaenrhos B 8
38 Penmark G 4
74 Penmon B 6
130 Penmore Mill B 1
74 Penmorfa F 5
74 Penmynydd C 4
47 Penn E 10
47 Penn Street E 10
54 Pennal B 3
146 Pennan A 6
75 Pennant, Clwyd G 9
35 Pennant, Dyfed A 8
75 Pennant, Gwynedd D 7
54 Pennant, Powys C 4
75 Pennarft-Melangell H 9
35 Pennard H 9
55 Pennerley C 9
98 Pennington, Cumb. G 5
26 Pennington, Hants. G 4
38 Pennorth B 4
98 Penny Bridge G 5
66 Penny Hill C 5
130 Pennyghael E 3
119 Pennyglen H 7
130 Pennygown C 3
14 Pennymoor E 7
115 Pennywell G 11
34 Penparc, Dyfed B 5
34 Penparc, Dyfed D 2
54 Penparcau D 2
38 Penpelleni D 6
11 Penpillick D 8
11 Penpoint B 8
10 Penpol F 5
111 Penpont, Dumf. & Gall. B 9
38 Penpont, Powys A 3
34 Penrherber C 6
35 Penrhiw C 6
38 Penrhiwceiber E 4
35 Penrhiw-goch E 9
35 Penrhiwllan C 7
35 Penrhiwpal B 7
39 Penrhos, Gwent C 7
74 Penrhos, Gwynedd G 3
38 Penrhos, Powys C 1
74 Penrhos,garnedd C 5
74 Penrhyn A 3
75 Penrhyn Bay B 7
54 Penrhyn-coch D 2
74 Penrhyndeudraeth F 5
75 Penrhynside B 7
35 Penrice H 8
34 Penrieth C 6
99 Penrith B 7
10 Penrose C 6
98 Penruddock B 6
10 Penryn F 5
75 Pensarn B 9
62 Pensax E 1
78 Pensby B 1
39 Pensford H 9
115 Penshaw H 11
30 Penshurst D 4
11 Pensilva C 10
123 Penston B 7
11 Pentewan E 7
74 Pentir D 5
10 Pentire D 5
10 Pentireg B 6
34 Pentlepoir F 5
71 Pentlow L 1
66 Pentney D 8
26 Penton Mewsey A 5
74 Pentraeth B 5
75 Pentre, Clwyd D 10
75 Pentre, Clwyd F 12
38 Pentre, Mid Glam. E 3
55 Pentre, Powys B 8
55 Pentre, Powys C 8
54 Pentre, Powys D 6
55 Pentre, Salop A 9
75 Pentre Bagillt C 11
74 Pentre Berw C 4
54 Pentre Dolau-Honddu H 5
35 Pentre Gwenlais E 9
74 Pentre Gwynfffryn G 5
75 Pentre Halkyn C 11
75 Pentre-Isaf C 8
38 Pentre Meyrick G 3
35 Pentrebach, Dyfed B 9
38 Pentrebâch, Mid Glam. D 4
38 Pentre-bach, Powys A 2
35 Pentrebach, W. Glam. F 9
55 Pentrebeirdd A 7
75 Pentre-bont E 7
35 Pentre-cagal C 7
75 Pentre-celyn E 10
75 Pentre-cwrt C 7
75 Pentre-dwfr F 11
35 Pentre-dwr G 10
35 Pentrefelin, Dyfed E 9
74 Pentrefelin, Gwynedd A 4
75 Pentrefoelas E 8
34 Pentre-galar D 5

S

39 Turnastone A 7
110 Turnberry A 3
79 Turnditch F 11
30 Turner's Hill E 2
19 Turners Puddle G 11
122 Turnhouse B 4
19 Turnworth E 11
146 Turriff C 5
90 Turton Bottoms F 6
123 Turvelaws F 12
63 Turvey G 12
47 Turville E 8
47 Turville Heath E 8
63 Turweston H 9
122 Tushielaw G 6
79 Tutbury G 10
62 Tutnall E 3
39 Tutshill E 8
70 Tuttington C 5
47 Tutts Clump G 7
11 Tutwell B 11
86 Tuxford C 4
158 Twatt, Orkney Is. C 1
158 Twatt, Shetland Is. D 7
119 Twechar B 11
122 Tweeddaleburn D 5
123 Tweedmouth D 12
122 Tweedshaws H 3
122 Tweedsmuir G 4
10 Twelveheads E 5
78 Twemlow Green C 6
66 Twenty C 3
39 Twerton H 10
50 Twickenham G 2
39 Twigworth B 11
30 Twineham F 1
39 Twinhoe H 10
71 Twinstead L 2
71 Twinstead Green L 2
14 Twitchen, Devon B 4
14 Twitchen, Devon C 7
55 Twitchen, Salop D 9
15 Two Bridges H 5
79 Two Dales D 11
62 Two Gates B 5
14 Two Pots B 4
63 Twycross B 7
47 Twyford, Berks G 9
47 Twyford, Bucks B 7
79 Twyford, Derby G 11
26 Twyford, Hants D 6
63 Twyford, Leics. A 10
70 Twyford, Norf. C 3
39 Twyford Com A 8
35 Twyn Llanan E 11
38 Twyncarno C 4
111 Twynholm F 7
39 Twyning A 12
62 Twyning Green H 3
35 Twyn-mynydd F 10
39 Twyn-y-Sheriff D 7
63 Twywell D 12
74 Ty-Hen G 1
55 Tyberton H 9
35 Tycroes, Dyfed F 9
74 Ty-croes, Gwynedd C 3
75 Tycrwyn H 10
66 Tydd Gote D 5
66 Tydd St. Giles D 5
66 Tydd St. Mary D 5
75 Tyddyninco G 9
51 Tye Green, Essex B 7
67 Tye Green, Essex L 7
34 Ty-hen E 6
90 Tyldesley G 6
31 Tyler Hill B 10
47 Tylers Green, Bucks. E 10
30 Tyler's Grn., Surrey C 2
38 Tylorstown E 3
54 Tylwch D 5
75 Ty-nant, Clwyd F 9
75 Ty-nant, Gwynedd H 8
54 Tyncwm D 4
131 Tyndrum E 10
19 Tyneham H 12
115 Tyne & Wear, Co. F 10
122 Tynehead C 6
115 Tynemouth F 11
38 Tynewydd D 3
123 Tyninghame B 8
130 Tynribbie C 6
111 Tynron B 9
54 Tynswydd F 2
75 Ty'n-y-ffridd G 10
74 Ty'n-y-gongl B 4
75 Ty'n-y-groes C 7
74 Tyn-y-pwll B 4
75 Tyn-y-Wern G 10
63 Tyringham G 12
14 Tythecott D 3
38 Tythegston F 2
39 Tytherington, Avon E 10
79 Tytherington, Ches C 7
26 Tytherington, Wilts. B 1
19 Tytherington, Wilts. B 11
19 Tytherleigh F 7
11 Tywardreath D 8
11 Tywardreath Highway D 8
75 Tywyn B 7
54 Tywyn Mer B 2

U

138 Uags F 1
71 Ubbeston Green H 6
39 Ubley H 8
106 Uckerby E 3
30 Uckfield F 4
39 Uckington B 12
119 Uddingston C 11
122 Uddington F 1
31 Udimore F 7
146 Udny Green E 6
119 Udston E 12
119 Udstonhead E 12
46 Uffcott F 2
18 Uffculme E 4
66 Uffington, Lincs. E 2
46 Uffington, Oxon E 4
55 Uffington, Salop A 10
66 Ufford, Cambs. E 2
71 Ufford, Suffolk K 6
63 Ufton F 7
47 Ufton Green G 7
47 Ufton Nervet G 7
118 Ugadale F 3
15 Ugborough K 5
71 Uggeshall G 7
107 Ugglebarnby D 9
50 Ugley A 5
107 Ugthorpe D 8
154 Uig, Skye C 1
154 Uig, Skye B 3
118 Uig, Strathclyde A 6
154 Uigshader D 4
130 Uisken F 1
151 Ulbster C 12
87 Ulceby, Humberside F 8
87 Ulceby, Lincs. C 11
87 Ulceby Cross C 11
95 Ulceby Skitter F 9
31 Ulcombe C 7
98 Uldale B 5
39 Uley D 11
115 Ulgham D 10
150 Ullapool G 3
62 Ullenhall E 5
39 Ullenwood C 12
94 Ulleskelf C 3
63 Ullesthorpe C 8
86 Ulley B 2
55 Ullingswick G 11
154 Ullinish D 2
98 Ullock C 3
26 Ullwell H 2
98 Ulpha F 4
95 Ulrome B 9
158 Ulsta C 7
123 Ulsoon G 9
130 Ulva House D 2
98 Ulverston G 5
111 Ulzieside A 8
154 Umachan C 5
14 Umberleigh D 5
150 Unapool D 4
94 Uncleby A 6
114 Under Burnmouth E 3
30 Under River C 4
99 Underbarrow F 7
94 Undercliffe D 10
119 Underhills F 9
158 Underhoull A 8
86 Underwood E 2
39 Undy F 7
158 Unifirth D 6
147 Union Croft H 6
98 Union Mills H 2
86 Unstone C 1
86 Unstone Green C 1
114 Unthank, Cumb. H 2
99 Unthank, Cumb. A 8
99 Unthank, Cumb. B 7
123 Unthank, Northumb. E 12
99 Unthank End B 7
19 Up Cerne F 10
18 Up Exe F 3
39 Up Hatherley B 12
90 Up Holland G 4
27 Up Marden E 9
27 Up Nately A 8
26 Up Somborne C 5
19 Up Sydling F 9
26 Upavon A 3
31 Upchurch A 7
14 Upcott, Devon E 4
55 Upcott, Heref. & Worc. G 8
18 Upcott, Somerset D 3
122 Uphall B 3
122 Uphall Station B 3
14 Upham, Devon E 7
27 Upham, Hants D 7
55 Uphampton,
Heref. & Worc. F 9
62 Uphampton,
Heref. & Worc. F 2
38 Uphill H 6
119 Uplawmoor D 9
39 Upleadon B 10
106 Upleatham C 6
31 Uplees B 8
19 Uploders G 8
18 Uplowman E 4
18 Uplyme G 6
50 Upminster E 6
18 Upottery E 5
??? Uppat F 8
55 Upper Affcott D 10
150 Upper Ardchronie G 6
62 Upper Arley D 1
47 Upper Arncott B 7
63 Upper Astrop H 8
150 Upper Badcall C 3
155 Upper Barvas B 5
47 Upper Basildon F 7
155 Upper Bayble D 6
30 Upper Beeding G 1
66 Upper Benefield F 1
62 Upper Bentley E 3
146 Upper Boddam E 4
63 Upper Boddington G 8
54 Upper Borth D 2
27 Upper Bourne B 9
146 Upper Boyndie A 6
62 Upper Brailes H 6
154 Upper Breakish F 6
55 Upper Breinton H 10
86 Upper Broughton H 4
46 Upper Bucklebury G 6
26 Upper Burgate D 3
147 Upper Burnhaugh H 6
67 Upper Caldecote L 3
26 Upper Canterton E 4
63 Upper Catesby F 8
54 Upper Chapel H 6
18 Upper Cheddon C 6
26 Upper Chicksgrove C 1
38 Upper Church Village F 4
26 Upper Chute A 4
26 Upper Clatford B 5
111 Upper Clifton F 10
74 Upper Clynnog F 4
155 Upper Coll C 5
110 Upper Craigenbay D 6
91 Upper Cumberworth F 10
38 Upper Cwmbran E 6
146 Upper Dallachy A 1
111 Upper Dalveen A 9
67 Upper Dean H 1
91 Upper Denby F 11
114 Upper Denton G 4
142 Upper Derraid F 6
138 Upper Diabaig D 2
30 Upper Dicker G 4
151 Upper Dournreay A 9
130 Upper Druimfin B 2
79 Upper Elkstone D 9
79 Upper End C 9
142 Upper Ethie C 3
39 Upper Framilode C 10
62 Upper Gornal C 3
67 Upper Gravenhurst L 2
46 Upper Green H 5
39 Upper Grove Com B 9
27 Upper Hale A 10
154 Upper Halistra B 2
47 Upper Halliford G 11
30 Upper Halling B 6
63 Upper Hambleton A 12
31 Upper Hardress Court C 10
30 Upper Hartfield E 3
94 Upper Haugh G 2
55 Upper Heath D 11
70 Upper Hellesdon D 5
94 Upper Helmsley A 5
55 Upper Hergest G 8
63 Upper Heyford,
Northants F 10
46 Upper Heyford, Oxon B 6
55 Upper Hill G 10
114 Upper Hindhope B 6
91 Upper Hopton E 10
30 Upper Horsebridge G 5
79 Upper Hulme D 8
46 Upper Inglesham D 3
143 Upper Inverbrough G 4
135 Upper Kenley F 10
35 Upper Killay H 9
146 Upper Kinkell E 5
146 Upper Knaven C 6
142 Upper Knockando E 7
46 Upper Lambourn F 4
39 Upper Langford H 8
79 Upper Leigh F 8
147 Upper Lochton H 4
62 Upper Longdon A 4
151 Upper Lybster D 11
39 Upper Lydbrook C 9
55 Upper Lye F 9
154 Upper Milovaig C 1
46 Upper Minety E 1
91 Upper Moor Side D 11
39 Upper Morton E 9
146 Upper Mulben B 1
114 Upper Mumble E 2
123 Upper Nisbet G 9
47 Upper North Dean D 9
134 Upper Obney C 5
154 Upper Ollach E 4
62 Upper Penn C 3
94 Upper Poppleton B 3
143 Upper Port G 6
62 Upper Quinton G 5
26 Upper Ratley D 5
55 Upper Rochford F 11
110 Upper Rusko E 6
139 Upper Sandaig H 2
55 Upper Sapey F 12
118 Upper Scoulag C 6
46 Upper Seagry F 1
155 Upper Shader B 5
67 Upper Shelton L 1
70 Upper Sheringham A 4
122 Upper Side D 6
119 Upper Skelmorlie C 7
46 Upper Slaughter B 3
131 Upper Sonachan E 8
39 Upper Soudley C 10
39 Upper Stanton Drew H 9
67 Upper Stondon M 3
63 Upper Stowe F 10
26 Upper Street, Hants. D 3
70 Upper Street, Norf. D 7
62 Upper Strensham H 3
47 Upper Sundon A 11
46 Upper Swell B 3
70 Upper Tasburgh F 5
79 Upper Tean F 8
134 Upper Tillyrie F 6
154 Upper Tote B 4
39 Upper Town, Avon H 8
55 Upper Town,
Heref. & Worc. G 11
63 Upper Tysoe H 7
46 Upper Upham F 3
30 Upper Upnor A 6
63 Upper Wardington G 8
63 Upper Weald H 11
63 Upper Weedon F 9
27 Upper Wield B 7
47 Upper Winchendon C 8
26 Upper Woodford B 3
146 Upper Woodhead F 4
27 Upper Wootton A 7
62 Upper Wyche H 1
114 Upperby H 2
91 Uppermill G 8
146 Uppertack of Gressiehill B 6
91 Upperthong F 10
147 Upperton, Grampian K 5
27 Upperton, W. Sussex D 11
158 Uppertown F 2
55 Uppington A 11
106 Upsall F 5
50 Upshire D 4
31 Upstreet B 11
47 Upton, Berks F 10
66 Upton, Cambs. E 2
67 Upton, Cambs. G 3
78 Upton, Cheshire C 3
14 Upton, Cornwall E 1
18 Upton, Devon F 4
26 Upton, Dorset G 1
19 Upton, Dorset H 11
26 Upton, Hants. D 5
86 Upton, Lincs. B 6
78 Upton, Merseyside A 1
70 Upton, Norfolk D 7
63 Upton, Northants F 10
86 Upton, Notts. C 5
86 Upton, Notts. E 4
26 Upton, Notts. A 5
46 Upton, Oxon E 6
18 Upton, Somerset C 3
19 Upton, Somerset D 8
62 Upton, War. F 5
94 Upton, W. Yorks. F 3
39 Upton Bishop B 9
39 Upton Cheyney G 10
55 Upton Cressett C 12
27 Upton Grey A 8
14 Upton Hellions F 7
26 Upton Lovel B 1
55 Upton Magna A 11
19 Upton Noble B 10
18 Upton Pyne F 3
39 Upton St. Leonards C 11
19 Upton Scudamore A 12
62 Upton Snodsbury G 3
62 Upton upon Severn H 2
62 Upton Warren E 3
27 Upwaltham E 10
67 Upware H 6
66 Upwell E 6
19 Upwey H10
67 Upwood G 4
158 Urafirth C 6
142 Urchal E 3
46 Urchfont H 2
158 Ure C 6
155 Urgha Beag G 3
106 Urlay Nook D 4
90 Urmston H 6
142 Urquhart, Grampian C 8
142 Urquhart, Highland D 1
106 Urra E 6
142 Urray D 1
106 Ushaw Moor A 3
39 Usk D 7
95 Usselby H 8
142 Ussie D 1
158 Ustaness D 7
115 Usworth G 11
91 Utley C 9
14 Uton F 7
95 Utterby H 10
79 Uttoxeter G 9
74 Uwchmynydd H 1
50 Uxbridge F 1
158 Uyeasound B 8
34 Uzmaston F 3

V

34 Vachelich D 1
74 Valley B 2
11 Valley Truckle A 8
154 Valtos, Skye B 4
155 Valtos, W. Isles C 2
54 Van D 5
51 Vange E 7
38 Varteg Hill D 6
154 Vatten D 2
38 Vaynor C 4
35 Velindre, Dyfed C 7
34 Velindre, Dyfed C 4
38 Velindre, Powys A 5
18 Vellow B 4
158 Vementry D 6
158 Veness B 3
18 Venn Ottery G 4
55 Vennington A 9
14 Venny Tedburn F 7
27 Ventnor H 7
46 Vernham Dean H 4
46 Vernham Street H 4
34 Verwig B 5
26 Verwood E 2
10 Veryan F 6
18 Vicarage G 5
98 Vickerstown H 4
11 Victoria, Corn. D 7
38 Victoria, Gwent D 5
158 Vidlin C 7
30 Vinehall Street F 6
30 Vine's Cross F 5
39 Viney Hill D 9
47 Virginia Water G 10
15 Virginstow G 3
19 Vobster A 10
158 Voe C 7
39 Vowchurch A 7
158 Voy C 1

W

106 Wackerfield C 2
70 Wacton F 5
62 Wadborough G 3
47 Waddesdon B 8
95 Waddingham G 7
90 Waddington Lancs. C 6
87 Waddington, Lincs. D 7
11 Wadebridge B 7
18 Wadeford E 6
67 Wadenhoe G 1
50 Wadesmill B 4
30 Wadhurst E 5
79 Wadshelf C 11
79 Wadsley A 11
86 Wadsley Bridge A 1
39 Wadswick G 11
94 Wadworth G 3
75 Waen D 10
75 Waen Fach H 11
87 Wainfleet All Saints D 12
87 Wainfleet Bank D 11
115 Wainfordrigg C 7
86 Waingroves E 1
10 Wainhouse Corner B 2
30 Wainscott A 6
91 Wainstalls D 9
99 Waitby D 10
91 Wakefield E 12
66 Wakerley F 1
51 Wakes Colne A 9
71 Walberswick H 8
27 Walberton E 11
115 Walbottle F 10
114 Walby G 3
66 Walcot, Lincs. B 2
87 Walcot, Lincs. E 8
55 Walcot, Salop A 11
55 Walcot, Salop D 9
62 Walcot, War. F 5
46 Walcot, Wilts. F 3
63 Walcote D 9
70 Walcott B 7
99 Walden Head G 12
94 Walden Stubbs E 3
30 Walderslade B 6
27 Walderton E 9
19 Walditch G 8
79 Waldley F 9
115 Waldridge H 10
71 Waldringfield L 6
30 Waldron F 4
86 Wales B 2
87 Walesby, Lincs. A 8
86 Walesby, Notts. C 4
39 Walford, Heref. & Worc. B 9
55 Walford, Heref. & Worc. E 9
78 Walford, Salop H 3
78 Walford Heath H 3
78 Walgherton E 5
63 Walgrave E 11
26 Walhampton F 5
91 Walk Mill D 7
90 Walkden G 6
115 Walker G 11
90 Walker Fold C 5
122 Walkerburn F 6
86 Walkeringham A 5
86 Walkerith A 5
50 Walkern A 3
55 Walker's Green H 10
135 Walkerton G 7
26 Walkford G 4
15 Walkhampton J 4
95 Walkington C 8
86 Walkley A 1
115 Wall, Northumb. F 7
62 Wall, Staffs. B 4
114 Wall Bowers G 4
55 Wall under Heywood C 10
111 Wallaceton C 9
110 Wallacetown A 4
78 Wallasey A 2
98 Wallend, Cumbria G 5
51 Wallend, Kent F 8
47 Wallingford E 7
27 Wallington, Hants. E 7
67 Wallington, Herts M 4
50 Wallington, London H 3
27 Walliswood B 12
158 Walls D 6
115 Wallsend F 11
98 Wallthwaite C 6
122 Wallyford B 6
31 Walmer C 12
90 Walmer Bridge E 3
91 Walmersley F 7
62 Walmley C 5
71 Walpole H 7
66 Walpole Crosskeys D 6
66 Walpole Highway D 6
66 Walpole Island D 6
66 Walpole St. Andrew D 6
66 Walpole St. Peter D 6
62 Walsall B 4
62 Walsall Wood B 4
91 Walsden E 8
63 Walsgrave on Sowe D 7
71 Walsham le Willows H 3
90 Walshaw F 6
91 Walshford B 12
66 Walsoken D 6
122 Walston E 3
50 Walsworth A 2
47 Walter's Ash D 9
38 Walterston G 4
39 Walterstone B 7
31 Waltham, Kent C 9
95 Waltham, Humber. G 10
50 Waltham Abbey D 4
27 Waltham Chase E 7
50 Waltham Cross D 4
50 Waltham Forest E 4
86 Waltham on the Wolds H 2
47 Waltham St. Lawrence F 9
50 Walthamstow E 3
63 Walton, Bucks. H 12
66 Walton, Cambs E 3
114 Walton, Cumb. G 3
86 Walton, Derby C 1
63 Walton, Leics C 9
55 Walton, Powys F 8
78 Walton, Salop H 4
19 Walton, Som. C 8
71 Walton, Suffolk L 6
62 Walton, War. G 6
94 Walton, W. Yorks. B 2
91 Walton, W. Yorks. E 12
39 Walton Cardiff A 12
19 Walton Elm D 11
34 Walton East E 4
39 Walton-in-Gordano G 7
90 Walton-Le-Dale D 4
47 Walton-on-Thames G 12
90 Walton on the Hill,
Merseyside H 3
79 Walton-on-the-Hill,
Staffordshire H 8
30 Walton on the Hill,
Surrey C 1
51 Walton on the Naze B 12
86 Walton on the Wolds H 3
39 Walton Park G 7
79 Walton upon Trent H 10
34 Walton West F 2
75 Walwen C 11
115 Walwick F 7
115 Walwick Grange F 7
106 Walworth C 3
34 Walwyn's Castle F 2
18 Wambrook E 6
111 Wamphraygate B 12
114 Wampool H 1
27 Wanborough, Surrey A 10
46 Wanborough, Wilts F 3
122 Wandel G 2
115 Wandon C 11
50 Wandsworth F 3
115 Wandylaw A 9
71 Wangford G 8
63 Wanlip A 9
122 Wanlockhead H 2
30 Wannock H 4
66 Wansford, Cambs. F 2
95 Wansford, Humber. B 8
50 Wanstead E 4
19 Wanstrow B 10
39 Wanswell D 10
46 Wantage E 5
39 Wapley F 10
63 Wappenbury E 7
63 Wappenham H 9
94 Warcop D 9
30 Warbleton F 5
27 Warblington F 8
47 Warborough E 7
67 Warboys G 4
90 Warbreck C 2
10 Warbstow B 2
78 Warburton A 5
71 Ward Green J 4
31 Warden A 9
63 Wardington G 8
122 Wardlaw, Borders H 5
119 Wardlaw, Strathclyde E 8
78 Wardle, Ches. E 5
91 Wardle, Lancs. E 8
63 Wardley B 11
79 Wardlow C 10
115 Wardon F 7
67 Wardy Hill G 6
50 Ware, Herts. C 4
31 Ware, Kent B 11
26 Wareham G 1
31 Warehorne E 8
115 Waren Mill C 12
115 Warenford C 12
115 Warenton C 12

50 Wareside B 4
67 Waresley, Cambs. K 3
62 Waresley, Heref. & Worc. E 2
47 Warfield G 9
15 Warfleet L 7
66 Wargate C 3
47 Wargrave F 9
70 Warham All Saints A 3
70 Warham St. Mary A 2
115 Wark, Northumb E 7
123 Wark, Northumb. E 11
14 Warkleigh D 5
63 Warkton D 12
63 Warkwork H 8
115 Warkworth B 10
106 Warlaby F 4
91 Warland E 8
11 Warleggan C 8
62 Warley C 3
30 Warlingham B 2
91 Warmfield E 12
78 Warmingham D 5
27 Warminghurst D 12
66 Warmington, Cambs. F 2
63 Warmington, War. G 7
19 Warminster B 11
31 Warmlake C 7
39 Warmley G 10
39 Warmley Tower G 10
94 Warmsworth G 3
19 Warmwell H 11
62 Warndon F 2
27 Warnford D 8
30 Warnham E 1
27 Warningcamp E 11
30 Warninglid E 1
79 Warren, Ches. C 7
34 Warren, Dyfed G 3
15 Warren House Inn H 5
47 Warren Row F 9
31 Warren Street C 8
63 Warrington, Bucks. G 12
78 Warrington, Ches. A 5
26 Warsash E 6
79 Warslow D 9
86 Warsop C 3
86 Warsop Vale C 3
94 Warter B 6
106 Warthermarske G 2
94 Warthill B 4
30 Wartling G 5
86 Wartnaby H 4
90 Warton, Lancs. D 3
99 Warton, Lancs. H 7
115 Warton, Northumb. C 8
62 Warton, War. B 6
114 Warwick, Cumb. G 3
62 Warwick, War. F 6
114 Warwick Bridge G 3
62 Warwickshire, Co. F 6
114 Warwicksland E 3
158 Wasbister B 2
98 Wasdale Head D 4
46 Wash Common H 5
11 Washaway C 7
15 Washbourne K 7
79 Washerwall E 8
18 Washfield E 3
106 Washfold E 1
18 Washford B 4
14 Washford Pyne E 7
87 Washingborough C 7
115 Washington, Tyne & Wear G 11
27 Washington, W. Sussex E 12
47 Wasing H 7
106 Waskerley A 1
62 Wasperton F 6
106 Wass G 6
18 Watchet B 4
46 Watchfield, Oxon E 3
19 Watchfield, Som. B 7
99 Watchgate E 8
111 Watchhill G 12
98 Watendlath D 5
15 Water, Devon H 6
91 Water, Lancs. E 7
50 Water End, Herts. C 2
94 Water End, Humber. C 6
66 Water Newton F 2
62 Water Orton C 5
47 Water Stratford A 7
38 Water Street F 1
98 Water Yeat F 5
67 Waterbeach J 6
114 Waterbeck E 1
70 Waterden B 2
47 Waterend C 11
79 Waterfall E 9
91 Waterfoot, Lancs. E 7
119 Waterfoot, Strathclyde D 10
26 Waterford, Hants. G 5
50 Waterford, Herts. B 3
98 Waterhead, Cumb. E 6
111 Waterhead, Dumf. & Gall. B 12
111 Waterhead, Dumf. & Gall. C 8
119 Waterford, Strathclyde H 10
147 Waterhead, Tayside K 2
122 Waterheads D 5
106 Waterhouses, Dur A 5
79 Waterhouses, Staffs. E 9
87 Watering Dyke Houses B 7
30 Wateringbury C 6
158 Wateringhouse E 2
39 Waterlane D 12
86 Waterloo, Derby D 1
26 Waterloo, Dorset G 2
34 Waterloo, Dyfed G 3
90 Waterloo, Merseyside G 2
70 Waterloo, Norf. D 5
154 Waterloo, Skye F 6
122 Waterloo, Strathclyde D 1
134 Waterloo, Tayside C 5
18 Waterloo Cross E 4
27 Waterlooville E 8
122 Watermeetings H 2
47 Waterperry C 7
18 Waterrow D 4
78 Waters Upton H 5
27 Watersfield E 11
114 Waterside, Cumb. H 1
146 Waterside Grampian E 7
110 Waterside, Strathclyde A 5
119 Waterside Strathclyde E 9
119 Waterside, Strathclyde B 11
47 Waterstock D 7
34 Waterston F 3
50 Watford, Herts. D 1
63 Watford, Northants. E 9
106 Wath, N. Yorks. G 3
106 Wath, N. Yorks. H 2
98 Wath Brow D 3
94 Wath upon Dearne G 2
39 Watley's End F 9
66 Watlington, Norf. D 7
47 Watlington, Oxon E 8
86 Watnall Chaworth F 2
151 Watten B 11
71 Wattisfield H 3
71 Wattisham K 3
55 Wattlesborough Heath A 9
95 Watton, Humberside B 8
70 Watton, Norf. E 2
50 Watton-at-Stone B 3
119 Wattston B 12
38 Wattstown E 3
139 Wauchan L 3
54 Waun Fawr D 2
35 Waunarlwydd G 9
87 Waunfawr D 5
38 Waunlwyd D 5
63 Wavendon H 12
114 Waverbridge H 1
78 Waverton, Ches. D 3
114 Waverton, Cumb. H 1
95 Wawne C 8
70 Waxham C 7
95 Waxholme D 11
18 Way Village E 3
30 Wayfield B 6
19 Wayford F 7
19 Waytown F 8
18 Weacombe B 5
46 Weald D 4
50 Wealdstone E 2
91 Weardley C 11
19 Weare A 7
14 Weare Giffard D 3
79 Wearhead A 11
99 Weasdale E 9
70 Weasenham All Saints C 1
70 Weasenham St. Peter C 1
78 Weaverham C 5
107 Weaverthorpe H 9
62 Webheath E 4
39 Webton A 7
146 Wedderlairs D 6
123 Wedderlie D 9
63 Weddington C 7
46 Wedhampton H 2
19 Wedmore A 8
62 Wednesbury C 3
62 Wednesfield B 3
47 Weedon B 9
63 Weedon Bec F 9
63 Weedon Lois G 9
62 Weeford B 5
14 Week, Devon C 4
14 Week, Devon D 6
14 Week St. Mary F 1
26 Weeke C 6
63 Weekely D 12
95 Weel C 8
51 Weeley B 11
51 Weeley Heath B 11
134 Weem B 3
55 Weeping Cross, Shropshire A 10
79 Weeping Cross, Staffordshire H 8
71 Weeting G 1
90 Weeton, Lancs. D 3
91 Weeton, N. Yorks. B 11
123 Weetwoodhill F 12
91 Weir E 7
39 Weirend B 9
86 Welbeck Abbey C 3
70 Welborne E 4
87 Welbourn E 7
107 Welburn, N. Yorks. G 7
107 Welburn, N. Yorks H 7
106 Welbury E 4
87 Welby F 7
67 Welches Dam G 6
14 Welcombe D 1
63 Weldon C 12
46 Welford, Berks. G 5
63 Welford, Northants. D 9
62 Welford-on-Avon G 5
63 Welham C 11
50 Welham Green C 2
27 Well, Hants. A 9
87 Well, Lincs. C 11
106 Well, N. Yorks. G 3
19 Well Bottom E 12
47 Well End E 9
30 Well Hill B 4
18 Well Town E 3
62 Welland H 2
135 Wellbank C 9
111 Welldale E 12
62 Wellesbourne G 6
106 Wellfields A 4
147 Wellford L 2
50 Welling F 5
63 Wellingborough E 12
70 Wellingham C 2
87 Wellingore E 7
98 Wellington, Cumb. E 3
55 Wellington, Heref. & Worc. H 10
55 Wellington, Salop A 12
18 Wellington, Som. D 5
55 Wellington Heath H 12
55 Wellington Marsh H 10
39 Wellow, Avon H 10
26 Wellow, I.o.W. G 5
86 Wellow, Notts. D 4
19 Wells B 9
70 Wells-next-the-Sea A 2
146 Wells of Ytham D 4
63 Wellsborough B 7
15 Wellswood J 8
134 Wellwood H 6
66 Welney F 6
14 Welsford D 1
39 Welsh Bicknor C 9
78 Welsh Frankton G 2
34 Welsh Hook D 3
39 Welsh Newton B 8
38 Welsh St. Donats G 4
78 Welshampton G 3
55 Welshpool B 8
19 Welton, Avon A 10
98 Welton, VB. A 6
95 Welton, Humberside D 7
87 Welton, Lincs. B 7
63 Welton, Northants E 9
87 Welton le Marsh C 11
87 Welton le Wold B 10
95 Welwick E 11
50 Welwyn B 2
50 Welwyn Garden City C 2
78 Wem G 4
18 Wembdon C 6
50 Wembley E 2
15 Wembury L 4
14 Wembworthy E 5
119 Wemyss Bay B 7
67 Wendens Ambo L 6
46 Wendlebury B 6
70 Wendling D 2
47 Wendover C 9
10 Wendron G 4
67 Wendy K 4
71 Wenhaston H 7
67 Wennington, Cambs. G 3
99 Wennington, Lancs. H 8
50 Wennington, London F 5
79 Wensley, Derby. D 11
106 Wensley, N. Yorks. F 1
94 Wentbridge E 3
55 Wentor C 9
67 Wentworth, Cambs. G 6
91 Wentworth, S. Yorks G 12
38 Wenvoe G 4
55 Weobley G 9
55 Weobley Marsh G 9
66 Wareham E 8
62 Wergs B 2
38 Wern C 4
35 Wernffrwd H 8
39 Wernyrheolydd C 7
66 Werrington, Cambs. E 3
11 Werrington, Corn. A 10
79 Werrington, Suffolk E 8
78 Wervin C 3
90 Wesham D 3
86 Wessington D 1
143 West Aberchalder G 1
70 West Acre D 1
46 West Adderbury A 5
18 West Adsborough C 6
123 West Allerdean E 12
115 West Allotment F 11
15 West Alvington L 6
26 West Amesbury B 3
14 West Anstey C 7
14 West Ash D 2
87 West Ashby C 9
27 West Ashling E 9
19 West Ashton A 12
106 West Auckland C 2
107 West Ayton G 10
147 West Balhagarty K 5
18 West Bagborough C 5
87 West Barkwith B 8
107 West Barnby D 8
123 West Barns B 9
110 West Barr G 4
70 West Barsham B 2
19 West Bay G 8
70 West Beckham B 4
47 West Bedfont G 11
115 West Benridge D 10
51 West Bergholt A 9
19 West Bexington H 9
66 West Bilney D 8
123 West Blackadder D 11
30 West Blatchington G 2
122 West Bold F 6
115 West Boldon G 11
111 West Bowhill D 12
91 West Bowling D 10
70 West Bradenham E 2
90 West Bradford C 6
19 West Bradley C 9
91 West Bretton F 11
86 West Bridgford G 3
62 West Bromwich C 4
119 West Browncastle E 11
14 West Buckland, Devon C 5
18 West Buckland, Som. D 5
158 West Burrafirth D 6
27 West Burton, W. Sussex E 11
99 West Burton, N. Yorks F 12
106 West Butsfield A 1
94 West Butterwick G 6
47 West Byfleet H 11
123 West Byres C 7
70 West Caister D 8
122 West Calder C 3
19 West Camel D 9
146 West Cannahars E 7
94 West Carr F 5
119 West Cauldcoats E 11
19 West Chaldon H 11
46 West Challow E 4
19 West Chelborough F 9
115 West Chevington C 10
27 West Chiltington D 12
27 West Chiltington Common D 12
19 West Chinnock E 8
26 West Chisenbury A 3
27 West Clandon A 11
31 West Cliffe D 12
151 West Clyne F 9
151 West Clyth D 11
19 West Coker E 8
19 West Compton, Dorset G 9
19 West Compton, Som. B 9
94 West Cowick E 4
19 West Cranmore B 10
71 West Creeting Grn. J 4
143 West Croftmore H 5
35 West Cross H 9
147 West Cullerley G 5
114 West Curthwaite H 2
118 West Darlochan G 2
26 West Dean, Hants. C 4
27 West Dean, Sus. E 10
66 West Deeping E 2
78 West Derby A 3
66 West Dereham E 7
115 West Ditchburn A 9
14 West Down B 4
50 West Drayton, London F 1
86 West Drayton, Notts. C 4
115 West Edington E 9
95 West Ella D 8
39 West End, Avon G 8
47 West End, Berks. G 9
74 West End, Gwynedd G 3
26 West End, Hants. E 6
50 West End, Herts C 3
95 West End, Humber. D 7
95 West End, Lincs. G 11
70 West End, Norf. D 8
122 West End, Strathclyde E 2
47 West End, Surrey H 10
26 West End, Wilts. D 1
115 West Fallodon A 10
30 West Farleigh C 6
78 West Felton H 2
30 West Firle G 3
46 West Ginge E 5
35 West Glamorgan, Co. G 10
46 West Grafton H 3
47 West Green H 8
26 West Grimstead D 4
30 West Grinstead F 1
94 West Haddlesey D 3
63 West Haddon E 9
46 West Hagbourne E 6
62 West Hagley D 3
114 West Hall F 4
86 West Hallam F 2
95 West Halton E 7
50 West Ham F 4
46 West Hanney E 5
51 West Hanningfield D 7
94 West Hardwick E 2
26 West Harnham C 3
19 West Harptree A 9
115 West Harrington H 11
106 West Hartlepool B 5
18 West Hatch D 6
39 West Hay H 8
66 West Head E 7
151 West Helmsdale E 9
46 West Hendred E 5
107 West Heslerton H 9
39 West Hill, Avon G 8
18 West Hill, Devon. G 4
30 West Hoathly E 3
19 West Holme H 12
123 West Hopes C 8
50 West Horndon E 6
19 West Horrington A 9
27 West Horsley A 12
115 West Horton C 11
31 West Hougham D 11
18 West Huntspill B 6
47 West Hyde E 11
31 West Hythe E 10
46 West Ilsley F 6
27 West Itchenor F 9
87 West Keal D 10
46 West Kennett G 2
119 West Kilbride E 7
30 West Kingsdown B 5
39 West Kington F 11
146 West Kinharrachie D 7
146 West Kinnernie F 5
78 West Kirby B 1
107 West Knapton H 9
19 West Knighton G 10
19 West Knoyle C 11
115 West Kyloe B 11
19 West Lambrook D 7
31 West Langdon C 11
151 West Langwell F 7
27 West Lavington, W. Sussex D 10
26 West Lavington, Wiltshire A 2
106 West Layton D 2
86 West Leake G 3
123 West Learmouth F 11
70 West Lexham D 1
94 West Lilling A 4
115 West Linkhall A 10
122 West Linton D 4
27 West Liss C 9
39 West Littleton G 11
11 West Looe D 9
18 West Luccombe B 2
19 West Lulworth H 11
107 West Lutton H 9
19 West Lydford C 9
115 West Lyham C 12
19 West Lyng C 7
66 West Lynn D 7
115 West Mains, Northumb. B 12
119 West Mains, Strathclyde D 8
122 West Mains, Strathclyde D 2
30 West Malling B 5
62 West Malvern G 1
27 West Marden E 9
86 West Markham C 4
95 West Marsh F 10
91 West Marton B 8
27 West Meon D 8
51 West Mersea C 10
62 West Midlands, Co. C 4
19 West Milton G 8
31 West Minster A 8
47 West Molesey G 12
26 West Moors F 2
19 West Morden G 12
123 West Morrison F 8
107 West Ness G 7
95 West Newton, Humberside C 9
66 West Newton, Norfolk C 8
15 West Ogwell J 7
19 West Orchard E 11
46 West Overton G 2
26 West Parley F 2
15 West Panson G 2
30 West Peckham C 5
115 West Pelton H 10
19 West Pennard B 9
10 West Pentire D 5
18 West Porlock B 2
14 West Putford D 2
18 West Quantoxhead B 5
115 West Rainton H 11
87 West Rasen A 8
70 West Raynham C 2
106 West Rounton E 4
67 West Row H 8
70 West Rudham C 1
70 West Runton A 5
123 West Saltoun C 7
14 West Sandford F 7
158 West Sandwick B 7
106 West Scrafton G 1
122 West Sidewood D 3
111 West Skelston C 9
115 West Sleekburn E 11
70 West Somerton D 7
19 West Stafford G 10
94 West Stockwith H 6
27 West Stoke E 9
99 West Stonesdale E 11
19 West Stoughton A 7
19 West Stour D 11
31 West Stourmouth B 11
71 West Stow H 1
46 West Stowell H 2
150 West Strathan B 6
26 West Stratton B 6
31 West Street C 8
106 West Summer Side G 2
30 West Sussex, Co. E 1
106 West Tanfield G 3
11 West Taphouse C 8
118 West Tarbert C 3
123 West Third F 9
115 West Thirston C 10
27 West Thorney F 9
50 West Thurrock F 6
27 West Tisted C 8
134 West Tofts D 6
87 West Torrington B 8
39 West Town, Avon G 8
39 West Town, Avon H 8
27 West Town, Hants F 8
55 West Town, Heref. & Worc. F 10
26 West Tytherley C 4
46 West Tytherton G 1
66 West Walton D 6
66 West Walton Highway D 6
14 West Warlington E 6
135 West Wemyss H 8
39 West Wick H 7
67 West Wickham, Cambs. K 7
50 West Wickham, London G 4
34 West Williamston F 4
26 West Willow D 4
66 West Winch D 7
26 West Winterslow C 4
27 West Wittering F 9
106 West Witton F 1
115 West Woodburn D 7
46 West Woodhay H 5
19 West Woodlands B 11
27 West Worldham B 9
67 West Wratting K 7
47 West Wycombe E 9
158 West Yell C 7
91 West Yorkshire, Co. D 10
14 Westacott C 5
31 Westbere B 10
86 Westborough F 6
26 Westbourne, Dorset G 2
27 Westbourne, W. Sussex E 9
46 Westbrook G 5
47 Westbury, Bucks. A 7
55 Westbury, Salop A 9
19 Westbury, Wilts. A 12
19 Westbury Leigh A 12
39 Westbury on Trym G 9
39 Westbury-on-Severn C 10
19 Westbury-sub-Mendip A 8
90 Westby D 3
27 Westcatt A 12
51 Westcliff on Sea E 8
19 Westcombe B 10
46 Westcote B 3
47 Westcott, Bucks B 8
18 Westcott, Devon F 4
46 Westcott Barton B 5
30 Westdean H 4
143 Wester Aberchalder G 1
134 Wester Balgedie G 6
122 Wester Causewayend C 3
134 Wester Clunie A 4
123 Wester Essenside G 7
146 Wester Fintray F 6
150 Wester Greenyards G 6
122 Wester Happrew E 4
123 Wester Housebryres F 8
142 Wester Milton D 5
135 Wester Newburn G 9
122 Wester Ochiltree B 3
123 Wester Pencaitland C 7
158 Wester Quarff E 7
142 Wester Rarichie B 4
158 Wester Skeld D 6
138 Wester Slumbay F 3
151 Westerdale, Highland C 10
107 Westerdale, N. Yorks E 7
71 Westerfield K 5
27 Westergate F 10
30 Westerham C 3
115 Westerhope F 10
39 Westerleigh F 10
158 Westermill E 3
106 Westerton, Dur. B 3
146 Westerton, Grampian C 3
135 Westerton, Tayside B 11
27 Westerton, W. Sussex E 10
146 Westertown C 3
98 Westfield, Cumb. B 2
31 Westfield, E. Sussex F 7
146 Westfield, Grampian E 7
62 Westfield, Heref. & Worc. G 1
151 Westfield, Highland B 10
70 Westfield, Norf. D 3
115 Westfield, Northumb. D 12
19 Westfields F 10
134 Westfields of Rattray C 6
99 Westgate, Dur. A 11
94 Westgate, Lincs. F 5
70 Westgate, Norf. B 3
31 Westgate on Sea A 11
114 Westgillsyke F 2
71 Westhall G 7
19 Westham, Dorset H10
30 Westham, E. Sussex H 5
19 Westham, Som. B 7
27 Westhampnett E 10
146 Westhaugh E 4
19 Westhay B 8
90 Westhead F 3
47 Westheath H 9
55 Westhide H 11
147 Westhill G 6
55 Westhope, Heref. & Worc. G 10
55 Westhope, Salop D 10
66 Westhorpe, Lincs. B 3
71 Westhorpe, Suff. H 3
90 Westhoughton G 5
99 Westhouse H 9
86 Westhouses D 2
30 Westhumble C 1
14 Westleigh, Devon C 3
18 Westleigh, Devon D 4
90 Westleigh, Gtr. Manchester G 5
71 Westleton H 7
55 Westley, Salop B 9
71 Westley, Suffolk J 1
67 Westley Waterless K 7
47 Westlington C 8
114 Westlinton G 2